True incidence, 126
True schizophrenia, 176
Tumors, cranial, 427, 440
Twin Oaks, Virginia, 647
Twin studies, 144, 147
    of schizophrenia, 175, 176

Ulcer (*see* Gastric ulcer)
Ulcerative colitis, 287
Unconditional positive regard, 565
Unconditioned response, 93
Unconditioned stimulus, 93
Unconscious:
    definition, 76
    iceberg model, 75
University of Cincinnati, 511
University of Florida, 528

Vaginismus, 355
Vagus nerve, 287
Validity, 33
Valium, 269, 340 (*see also* Diazepam)
Vampirism, 55
Verbal disturbances (*see* Speech problems)
Verbigeration, 161

Viruses, in schizophrenia, 179
Voyeurism, 362

Wastebasketing syndrome, 541
Waxy flexibility, 161
Wechsler Adult Intelligence Scale (WAIS), 47
    subtests (table), 48
Wechsler Intelligence Scale for Children–
    Revised (WISC-R), 47
Wechsler Preschool and Primary Scale of Intel-
    ligence (WPPSI), 47
"Wild beast" rule, 15
Withdrawal:
    from alcohol, 324
    from barbiturates, 340
    definition, 318
Women's Christian Temperance Union, 320
Woodworth Personality Inventory, 32
World Health Organization (WHO):
    statistics on murder, 400
    statistics on suicide, 385, 388

YAVIS pattern, 558
Youth, characteristics of, 521–522

ABNORMAL PSYCHOLOGY

PERSPECTIVES ON BEING DIFFERENT

MARSHALL DUKE AND STEPHEN NOWICKI, JR.

Emory University

BROOKS/COLE PUBLISHING COMPANY
MONTEREY, CALIFORNIA
A Division of Wadsworth Publishing Company, Inc.

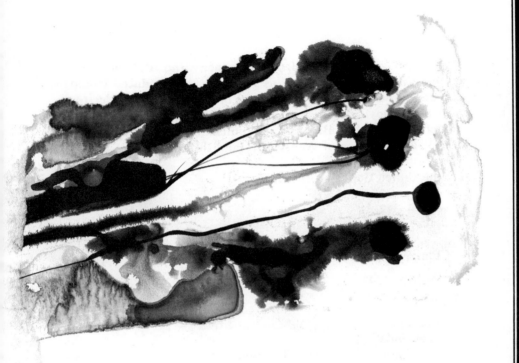

ABNORMAL PSYCHOLOGY

PERSPECTIVES ON BEING DIFFERENT

Consulting Editor: Lawrence S. Wrightsman

Printed in the United States of America

10 9 8 7 6 5 4 3 2 1

Library of Congress Cataloging in Publication Data

Duke, Marshall P   1942–
    Abnormal psychology.

    Bibliography: p. 669
    Includes index.
    1. Psychology, Pathological. I. Nowicki, Stephen, joint author. II. Title. [DNLM: 1. Psychopathology. WM100.3 D877a]
RC454.D84   616.8'9   78–7584
ISBN 0–8185–0274–6

Acquisition Editor: *William H. Hicks*
Project Development Editor: *Claire Verduin*
Manuscript Editor: *Beth Luey*
Production Editor: *John Bergez*
Interior and Cover Design: *Linda Marcetti*
Photo Research: *Belinda Raven Dumont*
Illustrations: *Robert Carlson*
Typesetting: *Holmes Composition Service*

To our children, Sharon, Noah, Jon, and Andy:
    Remember us? We're your fathers!
To our parents:
    We hope you're proud of this (even though you
    often said people can't learn everything from
    books).
And to our wives, Sara and Kaaren:
    No one could have helped us the way
    you two did.

PREFACE

From a broad point of view, abnormal psychology may be seen as the study of people who, by their behavior or feelings, are set apart in some way. In this book we have chosen to view these people as "different" rather than simply "abnormal." We've chosen this language in part because, as a concept, abnormality is, in many ways, in the eye of the observer. More importantly, being or feeling different can be *experienced* as well as observed, and we believe that this experiential perspective is one essential part of a comprehensive view of abnormal psychology. We have therefore included in the text numerous "personal experiences"—first-person accounts—as well as the more traditional case histories. These accounts and descriptions should enable our readers to learn a bit of what it has been like for some people to be abnormal.

In addition to the experiential perspective, we have used the descriptive, experimental, theoretical, and therapeutic perspectives in our approach to abnormal psychology. Together, these multiple perspectives provide a clear and complete introduction to the study of abnormal behavior. From the descriptive perspective, we present word-pictures of the varieties of behavior patterns widely considered to be abnormal. The experimental perspective allows us to describe relevant scientific investigations that have shed some light on abnormal behavior, including its development, diagnosis, and treatment. The theoretical perspective provides insight into the ways in which people have tried to understand and explain abnormality. The therapeutic perspective, for which abnormal behavior is a target for alteration, involves a discussion of a variety of therapies, some specific to particular disorders, others of a more generally applicable nature.

Although we have endeavored to make our text comprehensive, we have emphasized the traditional topics of the schizophrenias, the psychoneuroses, and the psychotherapies. In addition, special features of the book include chapters on calamitous death (suicide and murder) and on the disorders of different age groups, including college students. The comprehensive coverage may make this book useful in courses in the psychology of adjustment, as well as in the abnormal-psychology courses for which it is primarily intended.

The book is written and organized in such a way that each of the eight major sections may be used as a self-contained unit. An advantage of this organization is that sections may be covered in a number of different orders, depending upon the needs and wishes of the instructor.

In Section I, we present the basic foundations for the study of abnormal psychology. These foundations include the basis of diagnosis and methods of assessment, as well as a historical perspective on the underpinnings of modern lay and professional attitudes toward those who are different.

Section II includes coverage of three major approaches to the explanation of behavior. We discuss selected psychological, sociological, and biological conceptualizations of the acquisition and maintenance of behavior.

In Section III, we begin to look specifically at the varieties of being different. Our descriptions of the schizophrenias and the affective psychoses place special emphasis on recent biological research. We also discuss a group of rare psychiatric conditions often not covered in abnormal-psychology texts.

Section IV examines the disorders primarily associated with anxiety. These disorders include the psychoneuroses and the psychophysiological disturbances.

In Section V, we discuss disorders of behavioral self-control. Here we describe personality disorders, sexual disturbances, disorders associated with abuse of drugs, and the behavior patterns of suicide and murder.

In Section VI, we describe the disorders associated primarily with damage to the brain or diseases of the nervous system. The section includes chapters dealing with brain syndromes and mental retardation.

Section VII consists of a set of chapters unique to this text. In four chapters on disorders of special age groups, we discuss problems specific to children, adolescents, college students, and the elderly. The chapter on problems among college students draws heavily on our own research in the area of college-student counseling and student maladjustment.

The final set of chapters in the text, Section VIII, gives general descriptions of the types of therapeutic approaches used to help those who are different. Here, our coverage touches upon individual psychotherapies, group psychotherapies, the biological therapies, and various community-psychology approaches.

Throughout the book we have tried to present material in a person-to-person style that we believe will result in improved communication between us and our readers. We hope our readers enjoy reading the book as much as we've enjoyed writing it.

We wish to express our appreciation to the many people who have been so helpful to us during the preparation of this text. Among the colleagues who helped us by their ideas, suggestions, and comments were David Edwards, David Freides, Don Gordon, John Hollender, Donald Kiesler, Anna Nemec, Michael Nichols, and Bonnie Strickland. We also want to thank several students who gave generously of their time and energy, often well beyond our expectations. They include Marcia Ladd, Gayle Lewis, Ellen Chamow Martin, Mark McLeod, Carolyn Oxenford, Ken Perlmutter, David Schwartz, and Karen Schwartz. The manuscript would never have been completed if it had not been for the constant "emergency" typing of Betsy Baker, Jean Fletcher, Mary Ann Gurnee, Rosemary Richter, Rita Thomas, and Lila Trout; a more tolerant group of people does not exist.

We also wish to express our gratitude to the folks at Brooks/Cole who were so supportive of us during the development of the manuscript; these special people include Claire Verduin, J. Richard Verduin, Larry Wrightsman, Bill Hicks, Terry Hendrix, John Bergez, Beth Luey, and Jamie Brooks. Thanks are also due to the book's reviewers for their help at various points in the preparation of the manuscript. They include: James Anker, University of South Florida; Hal Arkowitz, University of Arizona; James Butcher, University of Minnesota; Thomas Coleman, Essex County College; Douglas Denney, University of Kansas; George Domino, University of Arizona; Jerry Higgins, University of California, Santa Barbara; T. Mark Morey, State University of New York at Oswego; A. A. Sappington, University of Alabama; Robert Titley, Colorado State University; and Leon Vande Creek, Indiana University.

However, final appreciation must be given to our families, especially our wives, Sara and Kaaren, for their own unique and, at times, incomprehensible ways of supporting our endeavor.

Marshall Duke
Stephen Nowicki, Jr.

CONTENTS

SECTION I   **BASIC FOUNDATIONS FOR THE STUDY OF PEOPLE WHO ARE DIFFERENT** 2

Chapter 1   **Conceptual and Diagnostic Approaches to the Experience of Being Different** 5

Our Conceptualization of Abnormal Psychology   7
How Does a Person Come to Be Called "Different"?   11
Systems for Classifying People Who Are Different   19
Concluding Comments   28
Chapter Summary Chart   29

Chapter 2   **Assessment of People Who Are Different** 30

Assessment of Personality   31
Assessment of Intelligence   47
Assessment of Brain Damage   47
Concluding Comments   49
Chapter Summary Chart   50

Chapter 3   **Historical Perspectives on Being Different** 51

History: An Interpretation   51
Social Responses to Those Who Are Different: The Mental Hospitals   64
Concluding Comments   68
Chapter Summary Chart   69

SECTION II   **EXPLANATIONS OF HUMAN BEHAVIOR** *70*

Chapter 4   **Psychological Explanations** *73*

The Psychological Theory of Sigmund Freud   *74*
Neo-Freudian Developmental Theories   *85*
Humanistic and Existential Theories of
     Behavior   *88*
Learning Theories of Human Behavior   *92*
Concluding Comments   *101*
Chapter Summary Chart   *102*

Chapter 5   **Sociological Explanations** *104*

Sociological and Sociopsychological Explanations of
     Abnormal Behavior   *106*
Sociological Correlates of Being Different   *118*
Concluding Comments   *128*
Chapter Summary Chart   *128*

Chapter 6   **Biological Explanations** *130*

The Nervous System and Behavior   *131*
The Endocrine System and Behavior   *136*
Biological Factors in Being Different   *139*
Concluding Comments   *148*
Chapter Summary Chart   *148*

SECTION III   **THE PSYCHOSES** *150*

Chapter 7   **Schizophrenia** *153*

Descriptions   *154*
Diagnostic Subtypes   *161*
Alternative Classifications   *164*
Explanations   *169*
Treatment   *184*
Concluding Comments   *188*
Chapter Summary Chart   *188*

Chapter 8   **Affective Disorders** *190*

Descriptions   *191*
Alternative Classifications   *204*

Explanations   206
Treatment   213
Concluding Comments   217
Chapter Summary Chart   218

Chapter 9   **Paranoid Conditions and the Rare Psychological Disturbances** 220

The Paranoid Conditions   220
Rare, Unusual, and Exotic Disorders   229
Concluding Comments   233
Chapter Summary Chart   234

SECTION IV   **DISORDERS RELATED TO ANXIETY AND STRESS** 236

Chapter 10   **Psychoneuroses** 239

Descriptions   240
Explanations   260
Treatment   266
Concluding Comments   269
Chapter Summary Chart   270

Chapter 11   **Psychophysiological Disorders** 272

Cardiovascular Disorders   277
Gastrointestinal Disorders   284
Respiratory Disorders   288
Headaches   291
Concluding Comments   294
Chapter Summary Chart   295

SECTION V   **DISORDERS OF BEHAVIORAL SELF-CONTROL** 296

Chapter 12   **Personality-Development Disturbances** 299

Personality Disorders   300
Socialization Disturbances   306
Concluding Comments   314
Chapter Summary Chart   315

Chapter 13   **Drug and Alcohol Addiction and Dependence** *316*

*The Definitions and Classifications of Drug
     Use   317*
Alcohol   320
Other Drugs of Dependence   332
Concluding Comments   346
Chapter Summary Chart   347

Chapter 14   **Disorders of Sexual Behavior** *349*

Sexual Dysfunctions   350
Sexual Deviations   355
Sexual-Orientation Disturbances   367
Concluding Comments   376
Chapter Summary Chart   377

Chapter 15   **Calamitous Death: Suicide and Murder** *379*

Suicide   382
Murder   399
Murder Followed by Suicide   406
Concluding Comments   410
Chapter Summary Chart   410

SECTION VI   **DISORDERS PRIMARILY ASSOCIATED WITH
BRAIN AND NERVOUS-SYSTEM
DISTURBANCES** *414*

Chapter 16   **The Brain Syndromes** *417*

Descriptions   418
Etiologies   422
Treatment   427
Concluding Comments   430
Chapter Summary Chart   430

Chapter 17   **Mental Retardation** *432*

Description   433
Etiologies   435
Treatments   442
Concluding Comments   449
Chapter Summary Chart   450

SECTION VII **DISORDERS OF SPECIAL AGE GROUPS** 452

Chapter 18 **Children** 455

Psychosis in Children 456
Developmental Deviations 466
Treatments 478
Concluding Comments 486
Chapter Summary Chart 486

Chapter 19 **Adolescents** 488

Descriptions 488
Explanations 492
Treatments 497
Concluding Comments 500
Chapter Summary Chart 501

Chapter 20 **College Students** 502

Descriptions 504
Explanations 519
Treatments 522
Concluding Comments 529
Chapter Summary Chart 530

Chapter 21 **The Elderly** 531

Descriptions 532
Explanations 536
Treatments 540
Concluding Comments 546
Chapter Summary Chart 547

SECTION VIII **TREATMENTS FOR THOSE WHO ARE DIFFERENT** 548

Chapter 22 **The Individual Psychotherapies** 551

General Overview 552
Psychoanalytic Therapies 560
Humanistic and Existential Therapies 564
Behavioral Therapies 569
Other Individual Therapies 577

Concluding Comments   582
Chapter Summary Chart   583

Chapter 23   **Group and Family Therapy** 585

General Overview   585
Early Group Therapies   588
Later Innovations in Group Techniques   591
Peer Self-Help Groups   600
Family Therapies   603
Concluding Comments   610
Chapter Summary Chart   611

Chapter 24   **The Physical Therapies** 613

Chemical Therapy   613
Electroconvulsive Therapy (ECT)   622
Psychosurgery   625
Biofeedback   626
Concluding Comments   627
Chapter Summary Chart   628

Chapter 25   **Community Approaches** 630

Historical Perspective   631
Motivating Forces   633
Inhibiting Forces   636
*A Theory of Prevention and Community
    Intervention*   638
Problems and Solutions   640
Concluding Comments   650
Chapter Summary Chart   651

Glossary 653

References 669

Index 699

PERSONAL EXPERIENCES

On a Ward in a Mental Hospital   *27*

A Hebephrenic Speaks in Clang   *162*
The Fears of a Paranoid Schizophrenic   *162*

What Is It Like to Be Severely Depressed or Manic?   *193*
Mania   *195*
Manic-Depressive Psychosis, Circular Type   *198*
Involutional Melancholia   *200*
Postpartum Depression   *202*

Paranoia   *222*
A Paranoid State   *224*

Anxiety   *239*
Anxiety Neurosis   *242*
Fear of Flying   *243*
Fear of Moths   *244*
Hyperesthesia   *251*
Pseudocyesis   *253*
Obsessive Neurosis   *255*
A Compulsive Reaction   *256*

Heart Attack   *277*
Ulcers   *284*
Asthma   *288*
Migraine Headaches   *292*

Paranoid Personality   *300*
Alternating Affective Personality   *301*

PERSONAL
EXPERIENCES

Schizoid Personality   *302*
Hysterical Personality   *302*
Asthenic Personality   *303*
Explosive Personality   *304*
Psychopathic Personality   *309*

Alcoholism   *324*
Heroin Addiction   *333*
Cocaine Use   *339*

Impotence   *352*
Fetishism   *356*
Frottage   *360*
The Victim of an Exhibitionist   *361*
Voyeurism   *362*
Sadism   *364*

Excerpt from the Diary of a Suicide Victim   *382*
Suicide Prevention   *396*
Murder   *404*

Brain Damage   *418*
Epilepsy   *425*
Post-Trauma Family Counseling   *429*

The Father of a Severely Retarded Child   *448*

Living with an Autistic Child   *461*
How Does It Feel to Have a Child with Specific Learning
    Disabilities?   *477*

Adolescent Withdrawal   *489*
Unsocialized Aggressive Reaction   *490*

Suicide   *510*
Test Anxiety   *515*
Freshman Adjustment Reaction   *517*

Forced Disengagement   *538*

Being in Psychotherapy   *553*
Being a Therapist   *556*

Prescribing Drugs for People Who Are Different   *621*

A College-Student Companion   *643*

ABNORMAL PSYCHOLOGY

PERSPECTIVES ON BEING DIFFERENT

SECTION I
BASIC FOUNDATIONS FOR THE STUDY OF PEOPLE WHO ARE DIFFERENT

Chapter 1
Conceptual and Diagnostic Approaches to the Experience of Being Different

Chapter 2
Assessment of People Who Are Different

Chapter 3
Historical Perspectives on Being Different

Having opened this book in anticipation of learning about abnormal behavior, many of you may be disappointed to see that we won't begin to describe in detail the patterns of abnormal behavior until Section III, six chapters into the text. Although we are keenly aware of most students' desire to "get to the real stuff" as soon as possible, we are also aware that without a basic understanding of the foundations of abnormal psychology, you may not benefit optimally from your study of people who are different. With this in mind we will begin our text with some basic (and limited, we assure you) preparatory information. In Section I we will present the basic foundations for the study of abnormal psychology. The foundations in Chapter 1 include knowledge about conceptualizations and classifications or diagnoses of abnormality. In Chapter 2, we will discuss methods by which diagnoses are derived; specifically, we will look at psychological testing and interviewing as they may be applied by professional diagnosticians. Reflecting the fact that we have not always been as "sophisticated" as we are now, Chapter 3 will provide a historical overview of beliefs about people who are different and some of the treatments used by our ancestors.

These archaic "theories" represent a basic foundation for the introduction of the modern psychological, sociological, and biological theories that Section II will embody. With the basic foundations from Section I and the theoretical knowledge from Section II, we believe that your enjoyment of the rest of the text will be enhanced.

CHAPTER 1
CONCEPTUAL AND DIAGNOSTIC APPROACHES TO THE EXPERIENCE OF BEING DIFFERENT

Ralph R. was born March 24, 1944, in a small town near Chicago. He progressed normally through his first five years of life, though when he was 3 he smeared his feces all over the walls of his baby sister's bedroom. His parents and pediatrician chalked up that incident to development and "sibling rivalry," and little more was ever said about it. Ralph had a more difficult time in elementary school. He seemed to get into a great deal of trouble with his teachers and inevitably ended up crying and saying that they were picking on him. A lonely child, Ralph was rarely asked to birthday parties or to sleep over at friends' houses. He admits now that he had few friends and that he spent most of his out-of-school time in solitary activities like burning ants and shooting at flies with rubber bands. His parents remember him as "nice, quiet, and no big problem." However, at the age of 17 Ralph began to experience a strange mixture of feelings. On many days he woke up and for no apparent reason would begin crying. In addition, Ralph, who had never been really comfortable with people, began to feel more and more uneasy around others. Often he found himself tongue-tied and feeling foolish when talking to classmates during the school day.

After he graduated from high school, Ralph's symptoms continued to worsen. More and more of his day was spent in feeling sad or sorry for himself. In addition, however, Ralph began to feel like hurting either himself or others. At the age of 23, Ralph experienced a depression severe enough to require hospitalization. During this time, Ralph would sit weeping quietly, speaking little, and relating to no one, not even his parents. After intensive treatment efforts such as psychotherapy and electroconvulsive therapy, Ralph's depression lifted, and he was able to return to his previous life-style. Unfortunately, Ralph was hospitalized again at the age of 25, this time for climbing to the 14th floor of a building and threatening to "show the world that he was immortal and could fly to the ground." Again, treatment efforts relieved the symptoms of his disordered behavior, and Ralph once more returned to his everyday life. He has experienced no severe depressions for the past five years.

Ralph R. is abnormal. His behavior and feelings have made him miserable, worried those close to him, and required the intervention of professional helpers. Ralph's story is not unique; there are large numbers of people throughout the world who may be considered abnormal and who, owing to their abnormality, may be treated in special ways. The focus of this text is on people who are abnormal or different, on those who are set apart from the majority by their modes of behaving or feeling.

Statistics suggest that about 15 of the people pictured here will experience severe mental disturbance during their lifetimes. (Photo by David Powers.)

Abnormal psychology is one of the most popular academic courses in America. Upwards of half a million students formally enroll to study this subject annually, reflecting the widespread desire of people to understand the variety of human experience. Perhaps this interest is so great because we are living in unusually difficult times. Statistics regarding the incidence of behaviors considered unusual, incapacitating, or uncomfortable can give us a good idea of the extent of the difficulties. Half of the hospital beds in the United States are filled by mental patients; three out of every four persons going to physicians with physical symptoms are found to have an emotional basis for their complaints. In 1977, the U.S. National Institute of Mental Health estimated that there were over 10 million neurotic persons, 2 million psychotic persons, 9 million alcoholics, 5.5 million emotionally disturbed children, and 4 million antisocial personalities in the United States—and the list goes on. No group of physical disorders even comes near these rates of occurrence. In fact, "mental illness is America's costliest health problem" (Ramsey, 1974, p. 168). Although government experts estimate that psychological problems cost Americans nearly $21 billion a year, this estimate does not include losses that cannot be quantified, such as misery, anguish, and the lowering of the quality of life.

No wonder there is so much interest in abnormal psychology. Abnormal behavior surrounds and touches us frequently. Since abnormal behavior occurs so often yet is so aversive, many of us seek to find out as much as we can about it. Some of our most important goals in this text are to describe for you the wide range of human behavior disorders, to acquaint you with explanations of these behaviors and treatments for them, and to provide you with a sense of what it is like to experience the feeling of being abnormal. While facts are important, if they are all you take from your study of abnormal psychology, then, in our opinion, you have missed much. Just as important as scientific knowledge is the human understanding of what is going on inside the heads and hearts of those whom society considers "different." We hope that through this text you will develop a scientific *and experiential* appreciation for the forms and sources of abnormal behavior.

OUR CONCEPTUALIZATION OF ABNORMAL PSYCHOLOGY

Before plunging into the study of abnormal behavior such as that experienced by Ralph R. and others, we would like to describe for you the particular perspective on abnormal psychology that influenced the organization and contents of this text. From our perspective, the study of abnormal behavior involves four major components. As represented in Figure 1-1, the first of these is *description.* Description, including diagnosis and classification, is generally believed to be an integral part of any approach to

7

CHAPTER 1:
CONCEPTUAL AND
DIAGNOSTIC
APPROACHES TO THE
EXPERIENCE OF
BEING DIFFERENT

Description

Ralph R. is a 25-year-old Caucasian male with a history of depression and self-destructive acting-out. He describes a history of alienation, loneliness, and discomfort in the presence of others. Current episode involved his climbing to the 14th floor of a building and threatening to jump. Previous episodes occurred when he was 23 years old. Symptoms include weeping, withdrawal, and mutism along with suicidal ideation. Diagnostic impression: manic-depressive psychosis-depressive type, DSM-II code 296.20.

Explanation

Depression may reflect a neurobiological reaction to extended experiences of loneliness and alienation. Neurotransmitter substances are depleted and neurocommunication is hampered. Fear of aggression toward parents may have resulted in anger turning inward in the form of depression and suicidal behavior.

Treatment

Ralph R. will be placed on Elavil, 25 mg, three times per day. Since his suicidal thoughts may be dangerous, suggest course of electroconvulsive therapy to reduce depression rapidly. Individual and group psychotherapy should be instituted shortly. Group treatment should focus on increasing Ralph's comfort in interactions with peers. Prognosis is guarded. Chemical therapy will be altered as required.

Experience

"I'm scared . . . petrified . . . so alone. My insides feel like they're being torn apart. I feel sick, nauseous—I can't eat. Please help me . . . please! I'm so scared to be alone . . . I think about killing myself all the time, but I'm too weak to even do that. I've been this way too long . . . nothing helps . . . I've tried drugs . . . nothing helps. No one can help me . . . no one . . . I'm worthless."

Figure 1-1. *A four-component model of abnormal psychology*

9

CHAPTER 1:
CONCEPTUAL AND
DIAGNOSTIC
APPROACHES TO THE
EXPERIENCE OF
BEING DIFFERENT

abnormal psychology. In addition to describing symptoms and other inordinate behaviors, abnormal psychology has a scientific commitment to attempt to explain the causes and correlates of such behaviors. Thus, *explanation* is at least as important as description of behavior. Once behavior is described and explained, *treatment* can be developed.

Most textbooks in abnormal psychology have primarily emphasized these three components—description, explanation, and treatment. But to us and to many of our students, a fourth component is essential to the study of abnormal psychology: the *experience* of being different. The experiential component reflects the fact that there are, after all, *people* associated with abnormal behavior patterns and that, with few exceptions, these people *feel* their difficulties. In this text we have tried to bring into equal partnership with description, explanation, and treatment this fourth component in our perspective on abnormal psychology—the *experience* of being different.

A few words must be said here about our use of the word *different* to describe those who are portrayed by many other texts as "abnormal," "mentally disturbed," "disorganized," "deviant," or "disordered." It is our opinion that, although all of these words do communicate certain aspects of abnormal behavior (indeed, we shall use many of them interchangeably in the text), none of them can effectively express the four-component approach to abnormal psychology as well as the word *different*. Any of the words mentioned above could be associated with descriptions, explanations, or treatments of abnormal behavior. We can *describe* a "disorganized" person; we can theoretically *explain* the behavior of a "deviant" individual; we can discuss the *treatment* of a "disturbed" man or woman. No word but *different*, however, can so accurately express the experiential component of abnormal behavior. Although a few people suffering from behavior disorders may say "I feel disorganized," "I feel mentally disturbed," or "I feel deviant," most are likely to say "I feel different; I am, in some way, set apart from the others around me; there are differences between those I know and myself—and I suffer because of those differences."

We are aware that the concept of "being different" is not limited to abnormal behavior and thus may be subject to misinterpretation. For example, extremely intelligent, good-looking people are "different." But being different for these people is usually a positive, pleasurable experience. For those with psychological difficulties, the experience of being different means that *negative* differences are observed or felt. We believe that most of you will agree with our choice of the somewhat controversial term *being different* to describe the inner experience of those with psychological problems.

The specific manner in which we present information in this text reflects the four-component model depicted in Figure 1-1. Generally each variety of being different categorized by the American Psychiatric Association will be *described* through statistics, data, and case histories. In addition, for each variety of being different we describe, we will provide several possible *explanations*. After presenting descriptions and explanations, we'll

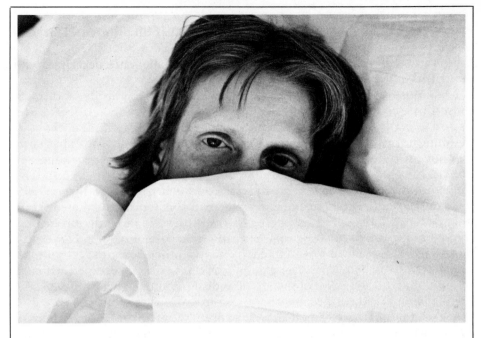

As well as having its statistical, cultural, and legal aspects, abnormality is also a personal experience. (Photo by Mary Ellen Mark, Magnum Photos, Inc.)

discuss types of *treatment* available for those who are different. When unique therapeutic approaches exist for given behavior patterns, we will present them in association with the particular pattern. General treatment approaches will be covered in the final section of the text. As suggested by our four-component model, we will present the *experiential* component of abnormal psychology in equal partnership with description, explanation, and treatment. To accomplish this objective, we will present throughout the text *Personal Experiences*—first-person accounts of what it is like to experience the psychological difficulties we describe. By including these descriptions we believe that we can present a more complete picture of abnormal behavior.[1]

In the remainder of this first chapter, we will lay some of the groundwork for your later study of specific disorders. This background material includes how a person comes to be called different and an evaluation of the variety of labels that may be applied to people who are different.

---

[1]Although each Personal Experience is based on real life, we have altered some details to protect the identities of the individuals involved. In all cases, the individuals have granted us permission to use the material included in this book.

HOW DOES A PERSON COME TO BE CALLED "DIFFERENT"?

CHAPTER 1:
CONCEPTUAL AND
DIAGNOSTIC
APPROACHES TO THE
EXPERIENCE OF
BEING DIFFERENT

Our four-component model depends on adequate description for a foundation. However, the basis upon which a person is classified as different or abnormal sometimes isn't clear. For example, it seems obvious that Ralph R. was in psychological pain; but is that a sufficient basis for the label "abnormal"? Further, Ralph created a public disturbance when he climbed up to the 14th floor of a building and threatened to fly. Is creating a scene of this magnitude enough to warrant such a label? Even without this spectacular act of bizarre behavior, Ralph generally showed *unusual* behavior: he just wasn't like most of us. Is that enough for the label "different"? The answer to these and sundry other questions lies in the definition of abnormality that we choose. Although there is support for each of a variety of ways of defining abnormality, no one definition may be considered the best. In truth, each definition probably works better than others at certain times. The differences among the views or models of abnormal behavior can be shown most clearly by presenting how each would deal with Ralph R. First, though, a few comments about what a *model* is.

A model is a framework or way of thinking about observed behavior. Several models have been used over the years. Some are *descriptive:* they represent ways of conceptualizing what is or is not abnormal. Some are *explanatory:* they attempt to explain the manner in which abnormal behavior develops.

Descriptive Models of Abnormality

Descriptive models of abnormality represent ways of conceptualizing the people who exhibit a certain set of behaviors. Probably four of the most popular descriptive models are those based upon infrequency of occurrence, social unacceptability, violation of the law, and personal discomfort.

Infrequency as Abnormality: The Statistical Model.   In the statistical descriptive model, abnormality is basically equated with infrequency of behavior in a population. The frequency of any particular characteristic can be determined numerically and represented by means of a graph such as Figure 1-2, which is a hypothetical representation of the heights of adult males in the United States. In such a curve we find heights greater or less than the "average" height of 5 feet, 8 inches. The greater the difference from the average, the more infrequent the occurrence of that deviant height. Thus, for example, heights of 6 feet, 8 inches, are rare, as are those of 4 feet, 8 inches. Heights that occur with such low frequency may be classified as abnormal (away from the norm) and may be given special labels differentiating them from the majority of heights encompassed by the normal

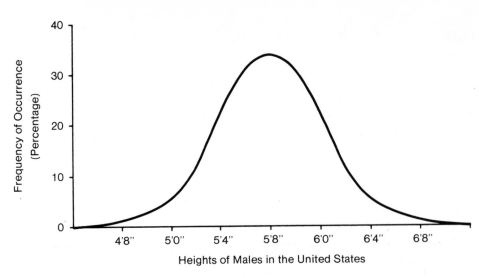

Figure 1-2. *A normal curve*

curve. For example, very tall people may be called giants; very short people are termed midgets.

Extending the statistical model of abnormality in height to the example of Ralph R. may help you to see how the statistical model can be applied to determine who should be labeled different or disordered. Ralph R.'s behavior may be considered abnormal from the statistical perspective because it does not occur with great frequency in our society. It is unusual for a person not to talk to other people at all; the vast majority will speak if spoken to. Ralph did not, so he stood out as an oddity, as "different." Further, Ralph was unusual because he wept frequently at the age of 23. Most 23-year-old males do not cry for the greater part of the day. Ralph was exhibiting some infrequent behaviors and therefore might be considered abnormal on that basis.

Using statistical infrequency as a basis to classify Ralph's behavior as abnormal does have some difficulties. Some behaviors exhibit a frequency that does not follow the normal curve; masturbation as a function of age is one such behavior. Some people may consider masturbation abnormal at any age, irrespective of the frequency of its occurrence; others may consider its frequency as a function of age to be normal, even though it does not describe a normal curve.

Besides not being able to describe effectively some frequency distributions of behavior, the statistical model fails to discriminate between "good" and "bad" behavior. For example, a common normal curve is that describing the frequency of intelligence-test scores. Here, those who fall very far below the average may be considered mentally inferior and may be labeled "mentally retarded." As rare as retardates are those at the other

13

CHAPTER 1:
CONCEPTUAL AND
DIAGNOSTIC
APPROACHES TO THE
EXPERIENCE OF
BEING DIFFERENT

extreme, people with very high IQs, who may be called "geniuses" and usually are positively valued. For reasons such as these, the statistical model seems insufficient to describe abnormal behavior accurately.

Socially Unacceptable Behavior as Abnormality: The Cultural-Situational Model. According to the cultural-situational model, it is not statistical infrequency but society that defines abnormality. Specific behaviors may not in themselves be considered abnormal, but they are judged so on the basis of where and under what social circumstances they occur. For example, eating a hot dog or wearing a fur coat may not be abnormal in themselves, yet a person wearing a fur coat and eating a hot dog in St. Patrick's Cathedral during a high mass in July would most likely be considered different! This example illustrates how behavior abnormality may be defined by the acceptable behavioral norms of a group (be it a culture, a social club, a political organization, or some other group) and the circumstances under which the behavior is emitted. To take a more realistic example, the behavior known as "speaking in tongues" may be seen by most people as undesirable and abnormal, but within certain religious groups it is highly valued as a sign of great faith.

According to the cultural-situational model of abnormality, Ralph R. is considered abnormal because his society considers it inappropriate for males to cry in public except in appropriate circumstances. If Ralph were weeping at his mother's grave, few would categorize his behavior as abnormal. Likewise, were Ralph to climb to the 14th floor of a building as part of a widely advertised publicity stunt, few would consider him to be in need of hospitalization or treatment. The point is that if Ralph's behavior were emitted in a cultural setting where it was acceptable or appropriate, he would not be considered abnormal. However, Ralph had no obvious culturally appropriate reason for climbing the building or for his crying and sadness, so he was deemed abnormal from the cultural-situational perspective.

The cultural-situational model appears to avoid several of the difficulties associated with the statistical description of abnormality. First, frequent behavior such as incapacitating fear of snakes might not be clearly identified as abnormal in the statistical model, but from the cultural-situational perspective the fear can be defined societally as often inappropriate to the danger involved, and therefore deviant. Second, the cultural-situational model allows for differences among social groups, whereas the statistical model typically does not. For example, obesity is statistically infrequent and may be considered "different" within our culture, yet there are other cultures where obesity occurs with approximately equal infrequency yet is considered a very positive attribute.

In spite of the fact that the cultural model includes the necessary effect of social values on the definition of abnormality, it still is not a sufficient basis for explaining what makes a particular pattern of behavior abnormal. Although the social context is important, the fact is that infrequency and other descriptive aspects of abnormality also seem necessary for accurate categorization of some people as different.

Breaking the Law as Abnormality: <u>The Legal Model</u>. Along with statisticians, sociologists, and anthropologists, legal theorists have struggled to arrive at a satisfactory descriptive model for abnormality. After all, insanity is a legal term, and for over 200 years lawyers and courts have attempted to arrive at the proper criteria for making this judgment. Such judgments are important in deciding whether to commit to mental hospitals those not in conflict with the law and to determine responsibility in certain criminal proceedings. A plea frequently offered as a defense in trials for major crimes in the United States is "not guilty by reason of insanity."

Sirhan Sirhan, convicted assassin of Robert F. Kennedy, pleaded innocent by reason of insanity. (Photo by Wide World Photos.)

Sirhan Sirhan, the convicted murderer of Robert Kennedy, and Arthur Bremer, the assailant of George Wallace, are recent examples of defendants who attempted to use this plea. In these cases, a great deal of time in court was devoted to assessing the mental state of the defendants. Psychiatrists and psychologists were called in on both sides, some testifying that the criminal acts were a result of mental disturbance, others claiming that they were not. Although some vague guidelines are provided by decisions in previous cases, each plea of insanity usually brings with it a unique set of complexities that must be judged anew.

CHAPTER 1:
CONCEPTUAL AND
DIAGNOSTIC
APPROACHES TO THE
EXPERIENCE OF
BEING DIFFERENT

From the legal perspective, Ralph R. might have been considered abnormal because his behavior suggested he was not legally responsible for his actions. The police were involved in getting him down from the 14th floor, and previously he had been arrested on charges of trespassing and disturbing the peace. However, once his history of mental disturbance and hospitalization was made known, the charges were dropped and he was sent for treatment at a mental hospital. In essence, Ralph's violations of the law were excused because they were due to "insanity."

A major question faced by legal theorists is how defective a person must be to be considered not responsible for his or her actions. Over time, the stated standard has changed from the "wild beast" criterion to the M'Naughton and Durham rules. In probably the earliest application of legal criteria (1724), the "wild beast" rule stated that "an accused could escape punishment if he doth not know what he is doing no more than . . . a wild beast" (Kittrie, 1971, p. 42). Similar to the "wild beast" criterion in that they emphasized knowing right from wrong, the M'Naughton rules were derived from an 1843 English murder case in which the defendant, a man named M'Naughton, was acquitted on the basis that he was adjudged to be insane. These rules state basically that to be considered legally insane a person must have some defect in reason or some mental disease at the time of a crime. Further, this mental defect or disease must have rendered the defendant incapable of knowing what he or she was doing at the time of the crime; or, if the defendant was aware of these actions, the defect must have prevented him or her from knowing that the actions were wrong.

Though frequently difficult to apply effectively, the M'Naughton rules were used with only slight modification for over 100 years. However, beginning in 1954 with the *Durham* decision there was an attempt to liberalize the process of judging a criminal insane and to base this process on the philosophy that it is the responsibility of society to require an offender to undergo therapeutic rather than penal treatment. The Durham rule states simply that a defendant is not considered criminally responsible if his unlawful act was the product of mental disease or defect. Heralded as a means of clarifying who should be classified as insane and protecting those who should be treated rather than punished, in practice the ruling has sometimes led to more confusion. For example, on whose testimony should the judge and jury rely? An expert witness's? A psychiatrist's? A psychologist's? Can experts agree? Some of the dangers of a blind application of the

Durham rule are exemplified by the case of Frederick Lynch, who was convicted of passing bad checks. Although he asserted he was mentally responsible for his actions, the court found him not guilty by reason of insanity and sent him to a mental hospital for an indeterminate amount of time. Whereas he could have received a maximum of 12 months in prison, his stay at the mental institution had no such limitation. "Harassed, branded, and tired, Lynch committed suicide" (Kittrie, 1971, p. 22).

A recent attempt to provide clearer guidelines for the legal determination of insanity was made by the District of Columbia Court of Appeals in 1972. Based upon the Model Penal Code of the American Law Institute, the Brawner rule (named for the defendant in the case) states: "A person is not responsible for criminal conduct if at the time of such conduct, as a result of mental disease or defect, he lacks the *substantial capacity* to appreciate the wrongfulness of his conduct or to conform his conduct to the requirements of the law" (Gerard, 1973, pp. 39–40). In practice, the Brawner rule reduces the power of expert witnesses (psychiatrists and psychologists), in as much as they may be cross-examined and asked to provide support other than their own opinion for their contentions. The Brawner rule seems superior to the Durham rule in that more usable evidence must be presented to a jury in insanity decisions. The word of one expert will not be enough to label a person abnormal, nor should unsupported opinion be so potent in the courtroom as it once was.

The problems of interface between psychiatry and the law have given rise to a new field of psychiatric-legal endeavor, *forensic psychiatry.* People within this discipline are trained in both psychiatry and law and address themselves in part to the difficult problems associated with the legal definition of insanity.

The complexities of the legal model make it difficult to apply to many cases of abnormal behavior. For example, what about the person who is constantly miserable but doesn't do anything illegal, or the person whose behavior bothers other people but isn't criminal? Such people may be seen as different but probably would not be adjudged insane and committed to a mental hospital as a result of the legal definition of abnormality.

Feeling Bad as Abnormality: The Experiential Model. A major shortcoming of the legal model—its inability to include personal misery as a criterion of disordered behavior—is focused on by the *experiential model.* Rather than a court decision, the experiential model requires that abnormality be defined primarily by a person's subjective experience of emotional and psychological discomfort. Proponents of this model believe that simple statistical infrequency or cultural unacceptability may not be the prime criterion for judging whether a person is different. Rather, on the experiential model, a person must *feel* abnormal to be abnormal. As in the case of some physical illnesses, the experiential model proposes that some "pain" must be present for there to be a disorder. Thus, anxiety, depression, difficulty in sleeping, fear of tall buildings, and the like are true signs of abnormality.

CHAPTER 1:
CONCEPTUAL AND
DIAGNOSTIC
APPROACHES TO THE
EXPERIENCE OF
BEING DIFFERENT

Some people, pushed out of the mainstream of society, may feel unhappy, frightened, miserable, and alone. (Photo by Joseph Czarnecki.)

Abnormality evidenced by statistical or social criteria, but not *felt* by the individual, may not be true abnormality.

From the perspective of the experiential model, Ralph R. probably would be considered abnormal because he *feels* bad. He feels frightened, unhappy, miserable, and alone. He is not content, nor does he have the minor ups and downs that most people feel. Experientially he is miserable; therefore he is considered disturbed. If Ralph exhibited the same symptoms but was not deeply upset by them, the pure experiential model might not classify him as abnormal.

In our opinion, the experiential model is probably a necessary component in any definition of abnormality, but it is not sufficient as a descriptive model of all disordered behavior. Certain patterns of deviance are not accompanied by discomfort. For example, in the disorders known as neurotic conversion reactions, paralyses may occur about which the affected individual is relatively unconcerned. Somewhat different are those varieties of disorders that may not be stressful in any way to the individual but probably are disturbing to other family members, friends, and society as a whole. Examples of such patterns are psychopathy, antisocial personality, severe mental retardation, and the like. Though the experiential model taps an important dimension of abnormality, it does not include the significant criteria of cultural importance, frequency of occurrence, and legal considerations.

Explanatory Models of Abnormality

While the descriptive models help us to conceptualize which current characteristics of behavior may be used to label people as abnormal, the explanatory models focus upon the processes by which abnormal behaviors come about. To reflect the dominant issues prevalent in current explanatory models, we have chosen to present two contrasting explanatory models of being different. The first conceptualizes abnormal behavior as deriving from an underlying psychological dysfunction; the second views abnormal behavior as a result of faulty learning.

Abnormality as Underlying Dysfunction: The "Disease" Model. In the "disease" model, abnormal behavior is seen as a manifestation of some underlying malfunctioning psychological process. Note that we are not talking about physical illness here; psychological malfunction can be caused by a number of determinants such as social factors, faulty upbringing, weak ego, and the like. The idea is that something psychologically harmful has produced the symptoms. The disease model parallels the classic relationship in medicine between physical symptoms and physical disease. In physical disease, if you experience a soreness in your throat, difficulty in swallowing, and a fever, your physician may decide that you suffer from tonsillitis and prescribe antibiotics to attack the *source* of the symptom, the bacterial infection. When the underlying source of the infection abates, the symptoms usually disappear as well, *whether they have been treated directly or not.* According to the disease model, should the underlying cause not be treated, the disease might become worse.

When a similar disease-model approach is applied to abnormal behavior, mental symptoms may be seen as *signs* of an underlying psychological dysfunction. In fact, the disease model dictates that the *source* of symptoms be found and treated, instead of merely the symptoms themselves. If the underlying cause is not found and treated, the model suggests, the disease will spread to other aspects of the patient's mental functioning.

In the case of Ralph R. the disease model would indicate that some underlying psychological defect has produced symptoms such as depression, weeping, and difficulties in relating to other people. In his history, there are hints that Ralph R. did not relate well to others while growing up and that he engaged in the somewhat unusual practices of burning ants and killing flies. Disease modelers may interpret these behaviors as symptoms of some problem in his early development, a problem that also has resulted in his present depression and other disturbed behavior. To help Ralph, the disease model would suggest going back into his past and exploring his

19

CHAPTER 1:
CONCEPTUAL AND
DIAGNOSTIC
APPROACHES TO THE
EXPERIENCE OF
BEING DIFFERENT

current fantasies to find out what traumas or errors in psychological development may lie at the source of his present problems.

Sigmund Freud, whose theories will be more thoroughly discussed in Chapter 4, adopted the disease model as his main perspective to explain disordered behavior. As you will read, his theoretical framework rests primarily on perceiving disordered behavior as symptomatic expressions of an underlying psychological defect. Perhaps as a result of Freud's influence there seems to be a strong tendency in our society to describe unusual, deviant, and negative behavior in disease-model terms. A person who has committed some terrible crime, such as rape or murder, is often described as "sick"; we frequently hear comments about a "sick society." Many students and professionals seem to have accepted the disease model as the only accurate representation of mental "illness."

Abnormality as Faulty Learning: The Behavioral Model. Whereas the disease model holds that psychological symptoms reflect underlying dysfunction, the *behavioral model* concludes that maladjustive behavior is not a special result of "disease" but most probably is learned and maintained in the same manner as any other behavior. Ullmann and Krasner (1965, 1969, 1975; Krasner & Ullmann, 1965) have offered one behavioristic position on maladaptive behavior. They believe that since maladaptive behavior is learned according to the same basic principles that govern all learning, the changing of such behavior should be governed by those same factors. Further, since behaviorists believe that the symptom *is* the disease, changing the behavior is all that is necessary; in the behavioral model there is typically little concern about underlying disease processes.

If we apply the behavioral model to Ralph R., we can view his abnormal behavior as the result of faulty learning. Because of his inability to learn how to relate to others, he now finds himself quite alone. He probably wished to get along better with other kids when he was younger, but he *never learned how.* Now, as an adult who sees many people relating effectively to one another, he may feel his loneliness even more intensely. Some results of Ralph's faulty learning are feelings of helplessness, severe depression, and a desire to end his life. From the perspective of the behavioral model, Ralph probably needs to learn new interpersonal skills that would make it possible for him to establish deep interpersonal relationships. What has gone wrong previously probably can be corrected by new learning.

SYSTEMS FOR CLASSIFYING PEOPLE WHO ARE DIFFERENT

The descriptive and explanatory models are ways of trying to understand and diagnose the varieties of disordered behavior. Diagnosis usually helps direct physicians to the proper sorts of treatment for physical ailments. Over the years, many mental-health professionals have also tried to develop classification systems that would facilitate diagnosis and, therefore, correct treatment. Although most mental-health workers favor the diagnostic process, others feel that diagnosis may be unnecessary, and perhaps even harmful.

The Current System

The present official classification system for psychological disturbances is the *Diagnostic and Statistical Manual of Mental Disorders*, 2nd edition (known as DSM-II). Published by the American Psychiatric Association (1968), DSM-II is based primarily on symptoms as the key factors in determining diagnosis. DSM-II replaced DSM-I, which was published in 1952. The main differences between DSM-I and DSM-II lie in the latter's emphasis on psychological disturbances as "reactions" to psychological stresses and the former's emphasis on disturbances as identifiable "syndromes" or patterns of symptoms. As an example, DSM-II describes "schizophrenic reaction," while DSM-I describes "schizophrenia." DSM-III, a revision of DSM-II, is currently being prepared by the American Psychiatric Association. Although DSM-III has not yet been officially adopted, we will briefly describe some of its probable emphases and differences from DSM-II later in this chapter.

In view of the fact that DSM-II is the dominant classification system at present, this text will deal primarily with disorders described within it. (One exception will be the discussion of problems of children, in which we use an alternative system proposed by the Group for the Advancement of Psychiatry [1966].) In Table 1-1 we have outlined the major categories of disorders included in DSM-II; each of these categories will be described in more detail later in the book. For now, we would like you merely to be aware of the wide variety of patterns of "being different" and of the way in which the major categories of psychosis (severe disturbances), neurosis (anxiety-based disturbances), and other disturbances are generally described.

While we will discuss the various types of diagnoses later, it must be noted that having an official diagnostic system does not necessarily mean that everyone is pleased with that system or that all the parts of the system are equally useful. In fact, there is some evidence that diagnosticians have trouble agreeing with one another in using the present system. A major share of the problems relating to unreliable and inaccurate diagnosis stems from the fact that classification systems usually are based upon human judgment. In a recent review of research regarding the unreliability of diagnosis, Spitzer and Wilson (1975) found a very low level of agreement among psychiatric diagnosticians. Basically, the more general the diagnosis, the better the experts seem to agree. For example, it was usually easier for experts to agree on whether a person was psychotic than to agree on whether a person fit a subcategory of psychosis like simple schizophrenia. Many believe that unreliable diagnosis stems from the fact that DSM-II

Table 1-1. *A brief outline of DSM-II*

CHAPTER 1:
CONCEPTUAL AND
DIAGNOSTIC
APPROACHES TO THE
EXPERIENCE OF
BEING DIFFERENT

   I. *Mental retardation.* Borderline, mild, severe, and profound retardation.
  II. *Organic brain syndromes.* Disorders associated with or caused by impairment of brain tissue and its functions.
 III. *Psychosis not attributed to physical conditions listed previously.* Severe disorders for which there seems to be no definite organic basis.
  IV. *Neuroses.* Milder than the psychoses, neuroses typically have *anxiety* as a basic causative factor.
   V. *Personality disorders and certain other nonpsychotic disorders.* A wide variety of behavior patterns, including sexual deviations and drug use.
  VI. *Psychophysiological disorders.* Physical symptoms deemed to be psychogenic (psychologically caused).
 VII. *Special symptoms.* Many disorders such as bed-wetting, speech disorder, and the like are so specific and so different from those above that they are placed in this special grouping.
VIII. *Transient situational disturbances.* Temporary syndromes for which there is usually a clear-cut external stress.
  IX. *Behavior disorders of childhood and adolescence.* Certain specific types of childhood behaviors are seen as stable, common patterns of symptoms.
   X. *Conditions without manifest psychiatric disorder and nonspecific conditions.* Supposedly not including any forms of true mental disease, this group is composed of marital problems and several forms of social maladjustment.

is based primarily upon symptoms and behavioral description and not upon etiology or cause.

As we mentioned earlier, accurate diagnosis in physical medicine usually is closely related to treatment. For example, the symptoms of "sore throat and difficulty in swallowing" could be caused by tonsillitis, cancer, presence of some foreign object, and so on. Unless the cause is known, the disease is not actually diagnosed, and treatment cannot be confidently administered. To determine the cause, the physician may use various diagnostic tests and indicators. However, consider the current classification of mental disorders. A person may manifest hallucinations, anxiety, delusions, or the like. These are *symptoms,* and as such may parallel the symptom of sore throat in our example of physical disease. The family physician most likely would not start treatment with his sore-throat patient without tests to determine cause; yet psychiatric diagnosticians frequently *must* classify behavior disorders on the basis of symptoms only and decide upon treatment without really knowing about etiology. The psychiatrist may be forced to begin to treat the psychological symptom before being sure of what caused it. Given this state of affairs, it is no wonder that some see diagnosis as an academic exercise. To be sure, a few psychological disorders can be diagnosed on the basis of etiology. Examples of these *organic disorders* (those caused by known physical damage) are alcohol-induced psychosis, mental retardation associated with head injury, and general paresis, a disorder caused by syphilis and characterized by a variety of motor and behavioral difficulties. However, the number of patterns in this organic category is quite small compared to that of *functional disorders* (those which are psychologically caused).

The problems inherent in DSM-II suggest to some professionals that classification may not be necessary or desirable in many cases of abnormal behavior. Often diagnosis does not direct our treatment efforts and tells us little or nothing about etiology. Some therapists may not diagnose at all, on the theory that diagnosis may mask their clients' individual characteristics and make it harder to help them. On the other hand, proponents of diagnosis note that we must be able to group disorders to determine similarities among people with the same problems as a first step toward isolating some causative factors. Further, accurate diagnosis can be an assurance that thorough understanding of the disordered person has been sought before treatment is begun. Finally, proponents of classification see diagnosis as a kind of shorthand; for example, one professional can tell another that a client is "compulsive" and give a *basically* sound idea about the *general* characteristics of the client in question without going into many details of his or her specific behaviors.

A Future Alternative to DSM-II

The third revision of the diagnostic and statistical manual represents an extension and attempted refinement of the symptom-based DSM-II. DSM-III is now described as a *multiaxial classification system* that provides for classification on as many as five distinct axes or dimensions, as shown in Table 1-2. The multiaxial approach of DSM-III probably will allow diagnosticians simultaneously to communicate details of existent ad-

Table 1-2. *DSM-III: A proposed multiaxial classification system*

Axis I: *Clinical psychiatric syndromes and other conditions,* such as depressive disorder.
Axis II: *Personality disorders in adults and specific developmental disorders in children,* such as compulsive personality disorder.
Axis III: *Nonmental medical disorders that are potentially relevant,* such as diabetes in a child with a specific developmental disorder such as bed-wetting.
Axis IV: *Severity of psychosocial stressors.* Permits diagnostician to judge severity of stress that has contributed to an episode of a disorder. Can range from code 1 (none), through code 5 (severe, such as marital separation), and code 7 (catastrophe—multiple family deaths and the like).
Axis V: *Highest level of adaptive functioning.* Axis V allows diagnosticians to record the degree of adjustment or impairment during the year prior to the diagnosis. Prognosis (chance of recovery) can be based on such information. Can range from code 1 (superior), through code 4 (fair adjustment—generally functioning adequately, but some impairment in at least one area), and code 7 (grossly impaired).

This and all other quotations from this source from *Diagnostic and Statistical Manual of Mental Disorders* (2nd and 3rd eds.). Copyright 1968 and 1977 by the American Psychiatric Association. Reprinted by permission.

23

CHAPTER 1:
CONCEPTUAL AND
DIAGNOSTIC
APPROACHES TO THE
EXPERIENCE OF
BEING DIFFERENT

justment and personality disorders (axes I and II), relevant physical information (axis III), information about environmental stresses on the person (axis IV), and indications from predisorder adjustment (axis V) that may be used in assessing the individual's chances of recovery (*prognosis*).

Besides being multiaxial, DSM-III differs from DSM-II in its primary use of the term *disorder* to describe patterns of abnormality as opposed to terms like *reaction, illness,* or *disease.* The use of the term *disorder* reflects the continuing acceptance of the medical or disease model of mental disturbance. As you have read, in the disease model psychological difficulties may be described as dysfunctions due to biological, social, psychological, and/or environmental factors.

Perhaps one of the most exciting innovations in DSM-III will be the addition of *operational criteria* for the diagnosis of specific disorders. The use of clearly observable criteria should increase the agreement among diagnosticians in identifying particular disorders. In Table 1-3 we present the diagnostic description of psychotic depression from DSM-II and the set of operational criteria for what most likely will be called "depressive disorder" in DSM-III. It may be apparent to you that the operational criteria of DSM-III could help reduce some of the confusion and problems in diagnosis.

Prior to its final adoption, DSM-III is undergoing extensive field-testing in hospitals and clinics. At the time of this writing, at least three more revisions of the original proposal are planned prior to its final adoption. To many, DSM-III holds exciting prospects, but to some its promise is diminished by the fact that the manual is still symptom-based and thus will share many of the problems of its predecessors (Schacht & Nathan, 1977). However, the primary developers of DSM-III (Spitzer, Sheehy, & Endicott, 1977) believe the new system will have many advantages over DSM-II:

> DSM-III is the first national classification system in psychiatry to utilize operational criteria, explicit principles of classification, a multi-axial approach to diagnosis, and extensive field testing prior to adoption. . . . We believe that the principles that are guiding the development of DSM-III will prove fruitful for both the scientific and clinical development of psychiatry [p. 12].

"Diagnosis May Be Hazardous to Your Mental Health"

While newer systems of diagnosis may hold promise for clearer and more reliable classification of disordered behavior, some professionals believe that diagnosis of any sort may be unnecessary, or even harmful. One such professional, Thomas Szasz (1961), believes that behavioral disturbances do not belong within the domain of the healing arts because they are not real "illnesses" requiring medical "treatment." He describes the concept of "mental illness" as a myth perpetuated by mental-health professionals.

Table 1-3. *A comparison of diagnostic guidelines in DSM-II and DSM-III*

DSM-II

Manic-depressive illness, depressed type
(Manic-depressive psychosis, depressed type)

This disorder consists exclusively of depressive episodes. These episodes are characterized by severely depressed mood and by mental and motor retardation progressing occasionally to stupor. Uneasiness, apprehension, perplexity and agitation may also be present. When illusions, hallucinations, and delusions (usually of guilt or of hypochondriacal or paranoid ideas) occur, they are attributable to the dominant mood disorder. Because it is a primary mood disorder, this psychosis differs from the Psychotic Depressive Reaction, which is more easily attributable to precipitating stress. Cases incompletely labeled as "psychotic depression" should be classified here rather than under Psychotic Depressive Reaction.

DSM-III

Operational criteria (tentative and subject to revision) for an episode of Depressive Disorder

A. Dysphoric mood or pervasive loss of interest or pleasure. The disturbance is characterized by symptoms such as the following: depressed, sad, blue, hopeless, low, down in the dumps, "don't care anymore," irritable, worried. The disturbance must be prominent and relatively persistent but not necessarily the most dominant symptom. It does not include momentary shifts from one dysphoric mood to another dysphoric mood, e.g., anxiety to depression to anger, such as are seen in states of acute psychotic turmoil.

B. At least four of the following symptoms:
   1. Poor appetite or weight loss or increased appetite or weight gain (change of one lb. a week or ten lbs. a year when not dieting).
   2. Sleep difficulty or sleeping too much.
   3. Loss of energy, fatigability, or tiredness.
   4. Psychomotor agitation or retardation (but not mere subjective feelings of restlessness or being slowed down).
   5. Loss of interest or pleasure in usual activities, or decrease in sexual drive (do not include if limited to a period when delusional or hallucinating).
   6. Feelings of self-reproach or excessive or inappropriate guilt (either may be delusional).
   7. Complaints or evidence of diminished ability to think or concentrate such as slow thinking, or indecisiveness (do not include if associated with obvious formal thought disorder).
   8. Recurrent thoughts of death or suicide, or any suicidal behavior, including thoughts of wishing to be dead.

C. The period of illness has had a duration of at least 1 week from the time of the first noticeable change in the patient's usual condition.

D. None of the following which suggests Schizophrenia is present.
   1. Delusions of being controlled or thought broadcasting, insertion, or withdrawal.
   2. Hallucinations of any type throughout the day for several days or intermittently throughout a one week period unless all of the content is clearly related to depression or elation.
   3. Auditory hallucinations in which either a voice keeps up a running commentary on the patient's behaviors or thoughts as they occur, or two or more voices converse with each other.

25

CHAPTER 1:
CONCEPTUAL AND
DIAGNOSTIC
APPROACHES TO THE
EXPERIENCE OF
BEING DIFFERENT

4. At some time during the period of illness had delusions or hallucinations for more than one month in the absence of prominent affective (manic or depressive) symptoms (although typical depressive delusions, such as delusions of guilt, sin, poverty, nihilism, or self-deprecation, or hallucinations of similar content are permitted).
5. Preoccupation with a delusion or hallucination to the relative exclusion of other symptoms or concerns (other than delusions of guilt, sin, poverty, nihilism, or self-deprecation, or hallucinations with similar content).
6. Marked formal thought disorder if accompanied by either blunted or inappropriate affect, delusions or hallucinations of any type, or grossly disorganized behavior.

According to Szasz, only those mental deviations whose source is clearly defined physically or neurologically (such as head injuries) should be seen as legitimately within the purview of the disease model. The so-called functional disorders (those having no clear biological basis, such as schizophrenia and neurosis) may be better understood as problems in living. Szasz conceptualizes these problems in living as being caused by people's awareness of themselves and their world and the unreasonable demands a complex society makes on people. He believes that people must be required to be responsible for themselves. Szasz argues that by diagnosing problems in living as "disease," mental-health professionals may have foisted upon a naïve society the idea that mental problems are a sickness. As a result, people with psychological problems often are relieved of their responsibilities. According to Szasz, it isn't right to place these individuals in safe environments where they can avoid dealing with the complexities faced by most productive members of society. While Szasz's point of view has caused significant negative reaction from many areas of psychology and psychiatry, his anti-disease model stance has received some acceptance among behaviorists and others.

Whereas Szasz has presented a primarily philosophical-conceptual argument that diagnosis may mislead people, David Rosenhan has provided some research evidence that suggests the controversial conclusion that diagnosis actually may be harmful in some cases. In one of Rosenhan's studies (1973), eight normal people gained admission to a number of mental hospitals with bogus complaints of disordered behavior such as hearing voices, being unable to think clearly, and the like. Immediately after being admitted, these pseudo-patients ceased simulating symptoms of mental disorder and informed staff members that they felt fine and were ready to go home. Not one of the pseudo-patients was ever detected as a simulator by staff members, and upon discharge each was diagnosed as "schizophrenic, in remission." In other words, once applied, the label of schizophrenic was not removed but only modified. No pseudo-patient was ever reclassified as normal; if they hadn't taken the precaution of using pseudonyms, they would have left the hospital with records of mental disorder that could have remained with them for the rest of their lives.

In describing the possible dangers of diagnosis, Rosenhan noted that "a psychiatric label has a life and an influence of its own" (1973, p. 252). Hospital staff members may interpret behaviors they observe in a patient through that patient's diagnosis. For example, most people would probably respond with help or support to an unlabeled individual who was crying or weeping (as we observed in Ralph R. earlier in the chapter). However, were the crying person labeled "psychotic depressive," the behavior might be ignored as "part of the syndrome" or "just symptomatic." In addition to influencing staff, Rosenhan notes, diagnosis frequently affects patients' self-perceptions. Some patients may come to see themselves as being like their labels and act accordingly. One of us remembers a patient in a hospital who described himself as "Gerard W., the catatonic schizophrenic," and then would demonstrate the characteristics of "his disorder" by assuming stereotyped poses and becoming mute and withdrawn for a few minutes.

That patients may have the capacity to "act their parts" once these parts have been assigned (via diagnosis) was demonstrated in a study by

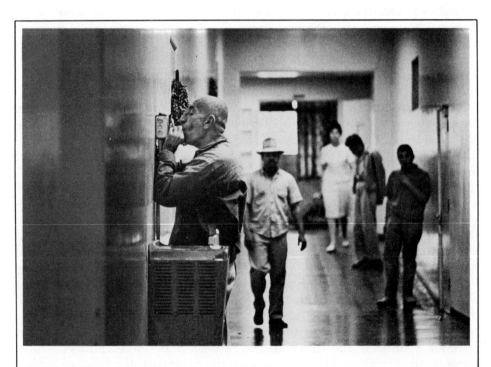

The atmosphere of some mental hospitals may not be conducive to improved functioning. (Photo by Robert Foothorap.)

27

CHAPTER 1:
CONCEPTUAL AND
DIAGNOSTIC
APPROACHES TO THE
EXPERIENCE OF
BEING DIFFERENT

Braginsky and Braginsky (1967). Based upon the premise that many hospitalized patients with diagnoses of psychosis can actually "role-play" their diagnosis when necessary, these researchers interviewed two groups of hospitalized patients. These patients, who had been hospitalized for several years, were assumed to have a strong desire to remain in the security of the hospital. One group of patients was told that the interview would determine whether they were ready to be released from the hospital. The other group was told that the interview was to determine whether they could be moved to an open ward with more privileges. Rapidly, and often dramatically, subjects in the first group began to exhibit symptoms of their psychoses that were severe enough to "convince" staff personnel that they should remain in the hospital. In the second group, the patients showed little new evidence of psychological disturbances.

Braginsky and Braginsky do not contend that the patients they studied were faking their symptoms, but rather that the symptoms may have served as an allowable mode of communication within a limited range of behavior possibly forced upon them by their diagnoses. Some support for this interpretation comes from a first-person account of the modes of communication used by some patients in a mental hospital, written by a newspaper reporter who had gained admission.

PERSONAL EXPERIENCE: *On a Ward in a Mental Hospital*

The noise was ceaseless. When all the sounds—the moaning, the babbling, the shouting, the crying, and the singing—got going at once, sleeping, or reading, or doing anything normal was impossible . . . my frustration caused me to dub [the racket] the "chorus of the crazies."

This chorus included a man who often lapsed into the role of a preacher, giving sermons to himself and lecturing others in a . . . booming voice. There was a woman who walked stiff-leggedly and determinedly around the room, striking up conversations with the more regressed patients who never answered . . . this woman would sit and sing the same off-key verses over and over again, sometimes for 15 minutes.

A 70 year old woman, with hand held to lowered head, moaned and groaned continuously as though in severe pain. She could be quieted only when given tobacco to chew.

Another woman, when forced to sit down or refused a cigarette, raged obscenities at anyone who tried to calm her.

Added to the uproar was the constant, discordant sound of rock music [at] full volume . . . and the blare of soap opera dialogue. . . .

The effect was painful to my ears and shattering to my nerves.

There was one patient who really frightened me. He was a man in his mid-twenties who got a kick out of tormenting the other patients when the nurses weren't watching. He often went up behind an old man, for example, and pulled his hair. Or he approached the women patients, particularly those who were most regressed and lifeless, and tried to kiss or fondle them.

From "Impressions of a 'Normal' News Reporter Who Gained Admission to a Mental Hospital for Five Days," by M. Barker, *Washington Post*, July 16, 1972. Copyright © by The Washington Post. Reprinted by permission.

The studies by Rosenhan and the Braginskys are but two of a larger number suggesting that diagnosis may not always be in the best interest of people who are different. Although most professionals will continue to use diagnosis, studies such as these remind us that the classification process is subject to error and abuses if not used carefully.

CONCLUDING COMMENTS

The difficulties as well as the excitement of dealing with disordered behavior are highlighted in our first chapter. Professionals from many disciplines have grappled with how to differentiate what is normal from what is not. You probably are aware of the unresolved complexities in such an endeavor. Evaluating behavior as good or bad, acceptable or not, is a value-laden task; we all have our own ideas about how people should behave. However, setting criteria for acceptable behavior is usually a more scientific undertaking than personal opinion. While not perfect, attempts by various professionals to come up with practical and scientific criteria for what is normal behavior have clarified matters considerably. In like manner, DSM-III appears to promise a much clearer statement about diagnosable mental disorders. The sharp criticism of classification systems helps to prevent a lazy approach to the crucial problems of diagnosis. You will read next about the methods used by professionals in their attempts to arrive at accurate diagnosis of those who are different. The tasks of diagnosis and classification seemingly are never completed, but they do become clearer because of the patient work of dedicated professionals.

CHAPTER SUMMARY CHART

CHAPTER 1:
CONCEPTUAL AND
DIAGNOSTIC
APPROACHES TO THE
EXPERIENCE OF
BEING DIFFERENT

In Chapter 1, we first described for you our conceptualization of abnormal psychology:

Description	*Treatment*
"What do abnormal people do?"	"How can we help abnormal people?"
Explanation	*Experience*
"Why do abnormal people do what they do?"	"How does it feel to be different?"

Next, we considered a selection of models for thinking about people who are different:

Descriptive models	*Explanatory models*
Abnormality as:	Abnormality as:
Infrequency	Underlying "disease" or dysfunction
Socially unacceptable behavior	Faulty learning
Breaking the law	
Feeling bad	

Finally, we discussed diagnosis and some of the problems associated with the process of labeling those who are different:

DSM-II	*DSM-III*
Our current system	The future system
Symptom-based	Multiaxial classification
Often applied inaccurately	Operational criteria

Hazards of diagnosis

Szasz—problems in living and the "myth" of mental illness
Rosenhan—pseudo-patients and the adverse effects of labeling
Braginsky and Braginsky—role-playing among the hospitalized

CHAPTER 2
ASSESSMENT OF PEOPLE WHO ARE DIFFERENT

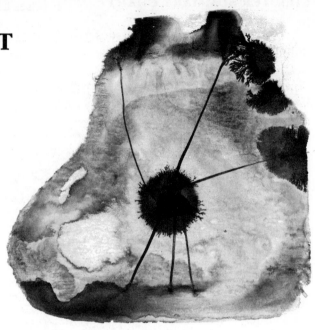

Imagine that you are observing a man. He is sitting in a chair with his legs crossed, and he is leafing through a magazine. He has on khaki slacks, a sport shirt, brown socks, and a pair of brown loafers. His hair is fairly long and neatly combed. Although his nose is slightly too large and his ears are a bit too small, there is little unusual about his face.

Imagine further that shortly you will have to meet this man and come to some judgments about his psychological state. All you know is that he was referred to you by the college dean because he was having "difficulties." Your job is to find out how severe these difficulties are and, if possible, what caused them. You look at this young man and he looks like any of the thousand young men you see any day at any university. What do you do?

This is the problem faced by those who have the responsibility for assessing disordered behavior. In Chapter 1 we pointed out some of the deficiencies that characterize the current diagnostic system. In spite of these shortcomings, the job of diagnosing and classifying disordered behavior remains a most important task that requires skill and information. Skill requires training, and information requires the use of a number of procedures to be described in this chapter. Basically, diagnostic information may be gathered via psychological tests of personality, intelligence,

30

and organic functioning, and through interviewing and observation. The various kinds of information and the procedures used to gather it are shown in Table 2-1. Except for the use of intelligence tests in assessing mental retardation and tests for organic impairment needed to diagnose brain damage, the diagnostic process may be seen as assessing an individual's personality. For this reason most of the chapter will emphasize the procedures for the assessment of personality; the remainder will describe the basic procedures for assessing intelligence and organic functioning.

ASSESSMENT OF PERSONALITY

Allport (1937) pointed out that there are at least 50 definitions of personality. However, the following definition appears sufficient for our

Table 2-1. *Sources of information in psychological assessment*

Source	Variants	Information Yield
Observation	1. Direct observation (natural setting)	1. Reactions to everyday situations. Scars. Tattoos. Expressive behaviors. Characteristic modes of responding to specific persons. Ratings of any of these.
	2. Direct observation (laboratory)	2. Reactions to "rigged" stimuli. Information about specific behaviors under controlled conditions. Ratings of any of these.
	3. Indirect observation	3. Reports or ratings by others who remember (or do not) the subject.
Interview	1. Employment or personnel interview	1. Information for and about job candidate. Generally, the interview yields data about content of individual's thinking.
	2. Diagnostic interview	2. In medicine, the past history of the patient. In psychological assessment, the mental status of the respondent.
	3. Stress interview	3. Reactions of persons under unusual or stressful conditions.
Psychological tests	1. Self-report inventories	1. Responses about personal habits, attitudes, beliefs, or fantasies.
	2. Projective tests	2. Responses to ambiguous or unstructured situations. These responses are assumed to reflect inner states of the person.

From *Personality Measurement: An Introduction*, by B. Kleinmuntz. Copyright © 1967 by The Dorsey Press, Homewood, Illinois. Reprinted by permission of the publisher and The Psychological Corporation.

purposes: "The term personality refers to the unique organization of factors which characterizes an individual and determines his pattern of interaction with the environment" (Kleinmuntz, 1967, p. 9).

Aspects of personality may be assessed in a variety of ways. We will consider three major approaches to this assessment effort: psychological tests, interviewing, and observation.

Psychological Tests

From the first commercially produced personality test, the Wood-worth Personality Inventory (1920), the testing industry has grown to a $100 million per year business. In this section we will consider the variety of measures designed to evaluate the presence and degree of psychological characteristics that make people different. We will first discuss the characteristics of psychological tests generally and then specifically describe self-report tests and projective tests of personality.

Basic Characteristics. A test may be defined as "a standardized instrument or systematic procedure designed to obtain an objective measure of a sample of behavior" (Kleinmuntz, 1967, p. 28). By *standardized* we

Each individual presents unique problems for the psychological assessor. (Photo by Michael P. Dumont.)

mean that all materials and instructions to the subjects are identical so that administrations of the test are the same for all people.

As well as being standardized, a test must possess several other important characteristics. To help make these characteristics clear we return for a moment to the man you have the responsibility for assessing. You would want your assessment of his personality to be consistent over time *(reliability)*. Besides being standardized and reliable, the assessment should be relevant, that is, it should measure the important aspects of his personality *(validity)*. Last, you would probably want to know how this young man compared with his peers on the relevant personality variables *(norms)*. The test characteristics of reliability, validity, and availability of norms are essential to accurate measurement of the important aspects of a person's behavior.

Reliability requires that a test measure a particular characteristic of personality accurately and consistently. One basic assumption about personality is that it is relatively stable and enduring. Thus it is important that measured aspects of personality also be relatively stable and enduring. However, a person's test score might be influenced by a number of chance factors. For example, the young man waiting for you might be feeling physically ill today, or he might be bothered by noise from repairmen fixing something near the testing area. The tester must be aware of these possible confounding effects and try to minimize them so that, whatever is measured, it is measured accurately. One of several ways to assess whether a test is measuring a characteristic consistently is to administer the test two or more times to the same person over a period of days and compare the test scores. If the scores are similar, then it is assumed that the test is measuring something reliably. (For other means of assessing reliability, see Anastasi, 1976.)

Measuring a personality characteristic reliably is a necessary component of a good test, but it is not enough to make a test useful. The test also should be valid; that is, it should measure the *relevant* aspects of personality. Validity of a test is usually defined by how well the test predicts certain other important behaviors called *criteria*. Let's take the measurement of anxiety. Patients in a state mental hospital have psychological problems and should have more anxiety than people who aren't in such a facility. If a test of anxiety can discriminate between groups in and out of a hospital, then it has shown some validity.

Besides being standardized, reliable, and valid, a subject's personality-test score should be comparable with the scores of his or her peers. Let us return again to the man whom you are going to be evaluating. His scores would be compared to those obtained by others on the same test to ascertain whether he seems similar to or different from his peers. His score would be meaningless unless it could be compared to the scores of others. For example, suppose the man you are evaluating receives a score of 22 on a test for anxiety. The score means nothing until you obtain the additional information that the average score on the test among college students is 12

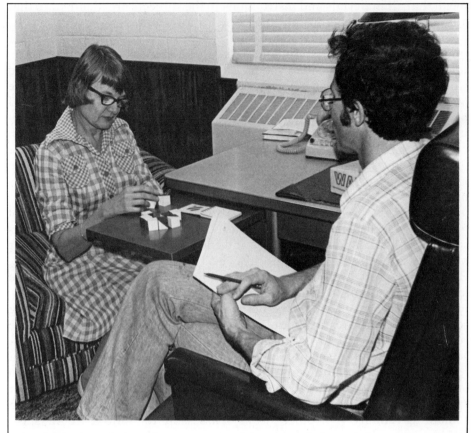

Standardized psychological testing is one of the assessor's basic tools.

and that only 3% of students obtain a score above 22. With this information you can conclude that your subject is manifesting more anxiety than most of his peers.

To be useful in diagnosing people, then, psychological tests should be standardized, reliable, valid, and have norms appropriate for the subject to be evaluated. If these requirements are met, then psychological tests can be useful in assessing the psychological state of people who are different.

Self-Report Inventories. An often used type of psychological test, the self-report inventory, usually consists of a list of standardized verbal statements to which a person may respond by answering yes or no, true or false. The questions are the same sort you might ask in an interview, but instead of responding freely, in the inventory the subjects must answer in a fixed manner.

Probably the most widely used self-report inventory is the Minnesota Multiphasic Personality Inventory (MMPI), constructed by Hathaway and McKinley (1942). The MMPI has been the source of at least 3500 referenced studies (Anastasi, 1976). It consists of 566 items to which the subject responds "true," "false," or "cannot say." These 566 items were selected from a pool of over 1000 items gathered from textbooks, psychiatric-examination forms, and other tests. The items retained for the final inventory were those endorsed more frequently by psychiatric-patient groups than by normal groups. The psychiatric patients were divided into groups on the basis of diagnosis, and the frequency of the endorsement of items determined whether those items were retained in the test. For example, a possible item such as "I feel tight about the forehead" might be given to a group of people diagnosed as depressed and a group of normal subjects. If a greater number of depressed people answered yes to that item than did normal subjects, then the item would be retained and placed on the depression scale. This is how items were found for most of the scales that make up the MMPI.

Although the MMPI scales originally were designed to differentiate between diagnostic groups and normal people, the scales are now used to indicate certain personality characteristics. For example, high scores on a scale that originally indicated the presence of "psychasthenia" now have come to indicate feelings of worry and guilt. Most practitioners who use the MMPI to assess personality employ a *pattern-analysis approach*; that is, certain patterns of scores seem to be related to certain behaviors.

The use of the MMPI as an assessment tool has entered the computer age. It is now possible to have an individual complete the MMPI and send the score sheet into a central computer service that will return a complete written interpretation in less than a week.

The MMPI is one of the many hundreds of self-report inventories used extensively and effectively in schools, counseling centers, and hospitals. However, such wide use may be ill advised, because self-report inventories have several shortcomings. First of all, the language of self-report inventories can be misinterpreted. For example, the word *nervous* may mean "panic-stricken" to one person, and just "slightly tense" to another. Second, people differ in their degree of self-knowledge and therefore may not be able to answer all questions with equal ease. Perhaps more important than problems arising from language and self-knowledge are difficulties that result from different test-taking attitudes. For example, some people tend to answer yes (yeasayers) or no (naysayers) to self-report questions, regardless of content. Others may try to answer in a way that presents an unrealistically good picture of themselves. Such people are said to be responding on the basis of the social desirability of responses rather than on the basis of their true feelings. These shortcomings make the use of self-report inventories risky. Because of this risk, tests such as projectives may be used along with the self-report inventory.

Projective Techniques. While the self-report tests of personality generally consist of straightforward verbal statements that have to be answered in a fixed-response format, projective techniques consist of ambiguous stimuli to which a person can reply in limitless ways. Most projective techniques incorporate a few brief, perhaps ambiguous, instructions into their administration. The ambiguous instructions may aid in the process of "projection" that is the basis for these tests. The projective approach is based on the belief that, if people are given amorphous stimuli such as inkblots or vague pictures to look at, they will tend to project onto these amorphous stimuli their inner feelings, drives, and needs. Projective techniques seem more deceptive in their approach than do self-report inventories. That is, subjects taking a projective test usually do not know how their responses will be used or scored. Because of this, projectives often can be used to get around some of the problems of the self-report tests, such as response bias and language difficulty. Anastasi (1976) stated: "Projective techniques present a curious discrepancy between research and practice. When evaluated as psychometric instruments the large majority make a poor showing. Yet their popularity in clinical use continues unabated" (p. 558). This suggests that such tests, while useful in generating information about an individual, may not be very helpful for research studies in which the comparability and standardization of results are important. We will describe two of the most popular projective techniques, the Rorschach inkblot test and the Thematic Apperception Test (TAT).

Rorschach Inkblots. Leonardo da Vinci reportedly used images seen in clouds and fireplace ashes to test the creativity of his students and to gain some insight into their personalities. However, it remained for Hermann Rorschach, a Swiss psychiatrist, to create a standardized set of ten inkblots and use them to diagnose his patients (Rorschach, 1942). Legend has it that Rorschach discovered the utility of using nebulous stimuli to study personality while riding in the country with his two children. During this ride, Rorschach's children were arguing about what the clouds looked like. Rorschach supposedly was impressed by the fact that the differences in his children's personalities were reflected in what they saw in the clouds. From his observation, Rorschach began to experiment with inkblots. The result is now the most frequently used projective test (Sundberg, 1961). The ability of the inkblot stimuli to elicit a wide variety of responses is shown in Table 2-2, which presents the responses of a group of 100 college students to a single inkblot.

In the formal administration of the Rorschach, the subject is handed ten cards with inkblots on them, one at a time, and is instructed to tell the examiner what the blot "could be, might be, or looks like." The subject is free to give as many responses as he or she wishes, using all or part of the inkblot. After all ten cards have been responded to in this manner, the examiner goes back over the responses given by the examinee to ascertain where the person saw what he or she saw and what made it look that way. There are a number of complex scoring techniques available to deal with Rorschach responses (Beck, Beck, Levitt, & Molish, 1961; Klopfer,

Table 2-2. *Responses of college students to an inkblot stimulus*

Inkblot Responses	Percentage of Students Giving the Response
Bats	18
Wolf, werewolf, coyote	15
Bird	7
Fox, fox face	7
Two animals back to back	5
Birds, dogs, wolves	5
Emblem, AMA symbol	5
Monster, devil, evil face	5
Halloween mask, pumpkin	4
Pelvis, hip bones	3
Owl	2
An inkblot	2
Valley with mountains	2
Angry animal (cat)	2
Two witches	1
Two horseheads	1
Animal skull	1
Vertebra of human spine	1
Two bears dancing	1
Shadow of a bear	1
Rabbit	1
Animal configuration (birds, wolf)	1
Two baby elephants kissing	1
Siamese twins	1
Two people protecting a child	1
Dance formation, woman in middle	1
Two cherubs and a drinking fountain	1
Angel with spread wings	1
Trees reflecting on a lake	1
Pagoda	1
Cover of "Yes" album	1
Boat with oarsmen splashing	1
Motorcycle with two girls in burlesque costumes	1

Ainsworth, Klopfer, & Holt, 1954). Although scoreable and interpretable, the Rorschach fares poorly on reliability and validity. Kleinmuntz (1967) concluded that "studies of projectives have rarely met with any noteworthy success" (p. 283).

In spite of the Rorschach's reliability and validity shortcomings, many clinicians use it because of its potential as a "hypothesis generator" in assessing personality. That is, the manner and contents of the client's responses to the inkblots may give the clinician some insights into the client's personality and behavior that might not be obtained from formal interviews or objective tests. One of the authors, when a graduate student, participated unknowingly in a simple experiment that showed how the

Rorschach can at times be more useful in assessing personality than more structured techniques. Through a one-way mirror, our graduate class watched the assessment of a man, supposedly from the state mental hospital. On the basis of our observation of his interview and test responses, our task was to decide whether he was retarded or dangerous. As the man completed the interview and then the intelligence tests, we were almost all certain that he was dangerous and probably retarded. Then came the Rorschach, and as the man gave his responses to the inkblots, it appeared to us that his responses were not consistent with the test behaviors we had previously observed. After the testing session was completed and we discussed the test results, everyone seemed to share the same uneasy feeling that this man was not what he had first seemed. Our uneasiness stemmed, for the most part, from the manner in which he had responded to the Rorschach. Our professor then let us know what he had done. The man interviewed was actually a professional actor who had spent the better part of two years playing the role of Lenny, the retarded, well-meaning but potentially violent character in John Steinbeck's play *Of Mice and Men.* Our instructor asked him to play Lenny during the testing session. He played the role most convincingly, except for the way in which he responded to the Rorschach. In discussing his experience afterwards, the actor confessed that the Rorschach made it very difficult for him to stay in his role; he did not know how Lenny would perceive these nebulous blots.

This anecdote may help to explain why the Rorschach is still used by so many clinicians in spite of the lack of substantial validity support. However, because of its psychometric shortcomings, the Rorschach is most often employed with other types of tests.

Thematic Apperception Test. Because they are pictures and not inkblots, the Thematic Apperception Test (TAT) stimuli are more structured than those of the Rorschach. The TAT was introduced by Murray (1938) primarily as a research tool to study personality. However, in spite of its original purpose, the main impact of the TAT seems to have been as a clinical-assessment instrument. Like the Rorschach, the TAT was devised to expose unconscious needs and conflicts, but unlike the Rorschach, which presents a series of nebulous inkblots, the TAT presents a series of pictures of real-life situations for subjects to project upon. The constructors of the TAT assumed that subjects would draw on their own feelings, motives, and needs to produce stories in response to a given picture. Typically subjects are asked to create stories with a beginning, middle, and end, and to tell how the characters in the story are feeling. Although more structured than the Rorschach, TAT stimuli often elicit a great number of responses that theoretically reflect differences in personality needs. The TAT is a popular assessment instrument for clinicians, ranking behind only the Rorschach in usage (Zubin, Eron, & Schumer, 1965). Table 2-3 is a selection of TAT stories told by a group of college students in response to a card depicting a boy staring at what appears to be a violin.

Table 2-3. *Responses of college students to a TAT picture*

1. What we have here is a frustrated little boy who has had his parents pushing him to learn to build things, eat properly, and play the violin. Their intentions are good because they want him to be a success and an object they can display and be proud of. At the present moment, he is too young to appreciate and desire these admirable talents and lacks inner motivation. The end result may be that he rebels against those pressures and heads in other directions when he may have enjoyed acquiring talents had he not been forced at such a young age. A common problem of today's youth.

2. The child has just recently started to take violin lessons. His parents wanted him to take the lessons so now he is satisfying their wishes. The child must practice quite a bit but he really doesn't want to. He would rather be outside playing with his friends. He doesn't even like the violin. Well, he is debating when to start. As we all know, he will start in a few minutes and then run outside to play.

3. A child is being punished for not practicing his violin. He is very sad. He is commanded to play but he will not. He is waiting in the corner for his father to get home.

4. This little guy (Billy) is angry at his dog because he just gathered up all kinds of odds and ends (sitting on table) and he was going to make his dog a birthday present. But before he could begin construction of the not-yet-decided-upon-present, his dog came up to little Billy and bit him on the leg. Billy became angry and strangled his little Pekingese. This picture doesn't show the dog lying at his feet—dead.

5. Within the damp setting of the little wooden house, Ray sat at his little desk composing his assignment for school. His mind keeps drifting off the subject, because he is faced with a problem which is worrying him more. Ray finally decides that he will talk to his father the next day after school about his misfortune. Then he closes his books, and retires for the night.

6. Little Tommy Scott was looking in his attic one day when he came upon a strange kind of instrument. What the heck is this, he is saying to himself. As he sat staring in amazement at the strange instrument, it leaped up into his hands and started ringing out a slow ballad. He ran outside and told all his friends about the strange happening but everyone laughed.

7. Joey wanted to be a famous musician but he also wanted to be a baseball star and see his picture on bubble gum cards. He had started his violin lessons and was exceptionally good. His teacher said that he had a fine potential. Joey was very happy. Just yesterday he came home from school, bubbling with excitement. "Mom, guess what, they're starting a baseball league at school next week." His mother was also excited but it soon became apparent that his lessons for violin and softball practice were on the same day. He now had a tough decision. What should he do? He is very depressed because he doesn't know what to do.

8. A small boy sitting by himself drowning in his sorrows. His mother has punished him for a reason he doesn't understand very well. All he can do now is moan since his favorite possession and pastime was taken away and he knows he has to just sit and wait until next week when he can once again play his violin with joy and happiness.

9. Sitting alone in a classroom after class, waiting for the teacher to yell at you for not finishing your work can be very lonesome. Outside all the other little boys

Table 2-3. *(continued)*

are playing. The boy, patiently awaiting his teacher, is left with nothing to do but think of his misfortune in being caught or perhaps just ponder over his guilt.

10. The little boy has been practicing his violin for hours. The musical score is very difficult and he is very tired of playing. At the moment, he is contemplating going to sleep or at least giving up on the instrument. I suspect he is trying to think of some way to get out of practicing. In any event, at least he doesn't have to play while he's thinking.

11. This little boy plays the violin in the elementary school symphony. He would like to play well, and has dreams of being a great musician. But at this time in his life, it is coming very hard for him. There are times that he would rather be outside playing with his friends, rather than being inside practicing. Particularly when the results are poor and slow in coming. This is one such time. And yet, he doesn't really have a choice, for the concert is Saturday and today is Thursday and he still doesn't know the music.

In comparison to the objective personality tests, projective personality tests are somewhat more difficult to fake, mainly because the subject cannot as easily guess the "socially desirable" response. The results gathered from projective personality tests are often useful in generating hypotheses concerning the subject's psychological state. These hypotheses can give assessors an idea of which direction additional assessment should take.

Although projective personality tests are difficult to fake, may allow for the assessment of unique characteristics, and can be used to generate hypotheses, they have failed at times to be related to important criteria such as diagnosis. Also, the very richness of responses that the projectives produce frequently makes them difficult to score accurately. Even those aspects of projective-test results that can be reliably scored and remain consistent over time often have turned out to be unrelated to disordered behavior. All of these restrictions suggest that the results of projective tests should be used carefully.

Interviewing

The standardized tests, both objective and projective, involve a subject's responding to some type of stimulus. In contrast, the "interview is a face-to-face verbal communication between two people, initiated for the specific purpose of allowing the interviewer to learn about the respondent's personality characteristics" (Kleinmuntz, 1967, p. 143). Interviewing was used by Hippocrates and other early Greek physicians. Catholic priests have long used the confession to conduct what may be seen in essence as an interview to find out the psychological as well as the spiritual state of a person. Kleinmuntz makes the point that interviewing is closely related to the procedure of psychotherapy (verbal interaction between a client and therapist to deal with psychological problems; see Chapters 22–25). Interviewing differs from everyday conversation because its purpose is to gain as much information as possible about the interviewee. In many ways interviewing appears to be the most logical procedure for finding out information from another person.

Before we describe and evaluate interviews, we want to comment on the important effects of the situation on what transpires in the interview. Chances are that an interviewee has had little experience in being interviewed and may have a number of erroneous expectations about what is going to take place. Take the case of the man who still is waiting to be assessed by you. How would he react if you were 60 years old, with gray hair and spectacles, and spoke with a Viennese accent? Would he have the same reaction if you were a 30-year-old, curly-haired man wearing jeans and a flowered shirt? Or how about a 30-year-old, curly-haired woman wearing jeans and a flowered shirt? The point, of course, is that an interviewer must be aware of his or her own impact on interviewees. The interviewer must process the various situational demands, put the client at ease, build a feeling of trust, and obtain information relevant to the interviewee's problem—no easy task.

Unstructured Interviewing.   In an unstructured verbal interaction, the interviewer usually is free to cover as wide a range of topics as she or he desires. The interviewer has only a few constraints on what may be asked of the interviewee or how particular topics may be discussed. The key word for an unstructured interview is *flexibility*. Part of the price for the freedom to roam from topic to topic, though, is the consequent difficulty in comparing one interview with another. For this reason, the unstructured interview is rarely used in research. However, like the Rorschach inkblots, the unstructured interview is sometimes used as a hypothesis generator.

One of the more unstructured of the unstructured interviews is the "nondirective" interview popularized by Carl Rogers, a renowned clinical therapist and practitioner (see Chapters 4 and 22). Typically, in the nondirective interview the client is encouraged to talk about whatever he or she may feel is of interest and concern, while the interviewer's job is usually to help and encourage the client by clarifying feelings. Generally, the nondirective interviewer asks few questions and talks very little.

The following example shows you a bit of how this kind of interview would go:

> *Interviewer:*   I'd like to talk with you awhile so that I might be able to get a better understanding of the things that have been troubling you.
> *Client:*   That's fine.
> *I:*   Begin by telling me what made you come in for help at this time.
> *C:*   Well, I think that it's mainly because of the troubles I've been having since I left college.

I: Go on.

C: Well, I was asked to leave college because I was having a lot of trouble in my coursework. I failed several courses and the dean told me I would have to leave.

I: And how did that affect you?

C: I felt pretty bad about it. I had always wanted to finish college and get a good job, but there I was out on my ear with no place to go and no skill.

I: No skill?

C: I was trained for nothing. I couldn't hold my head up and feel that I was as good as anyone else. All the people from my high school had pretty good jobs or were doing well in college and me . . . I was just fooling around wasting my time and feeling lousy.

I: Not being in school made you feel lousy?

C: Not just that. I had no friends, nobody wanted to go out with me.

Based on the authors' experience, it would be safe to say that most unstructured interviews have more structure than this. More common is an unstructured interview with a general outline of questions that the interviewer wants to cover, but not in any special order. For example, in what is referred to as a *mental-status examination* (usually done with a person who has a psychological problem), a number of specific topic areas have to be covered. Some of the areas may be general appearance, emotional state, intelligence, insight into problems, and the like. However, the interviewer usually has the freedom to choose the order and depth of coverage of the topic areas.

Structured Interviewing. While the unstructured interviewer usually is free to cover as wide a range of topics as she or he desires, and in any order, the structured interviewer most often must ask the same questions in the same way to all interviewees. The structured interview is more often used in research projects when the data from interviews need to be compared. In clinical settings probably the most common use of the highly structured interview is to elicit life-history data.

The major advantages of the structured interview are that it "guarantees that important information is obtained concerning various aspects of the person . . . provides standardization . . . and requires less psychological acumen and experience than the unstructured one" (Kleinmuntz, 1967, p. 148). However, it is also clear that these advantages may come at the cost of a more rigid and artificial communication process. A structured interview is definitely not just two people conversing about some topic or other.

The following is an example of a structured-interview interaction:

Interviewer: I'd like to ask you a few questions if you don't mind. The kind of information we obtain will help us to get a better understanding of the problems you've been having.

Client: I'll help any way I can.

I: Where were you born and what is your birthdate?

C: July 8, 1942; Jersey City, New Jersey.

I: What do you remember about your life as a young child?

C: It was generally happy, but I fought with my sister a lot.

I: Did you have difficulties with other members of your family?

C: No, not really, just my sister.

I: What was your elementary-school experience like?

C: I did well in elementary school. Got pretty good grades and was pretty happy.

I: How about high school?

C: In high school I had some problems, especially in getting dates or in socializing with boys.

I: What were the problems in specific?

C: No one seemed to want to date me. I spent many a Saturday night at home alone, crying.

I: Did the same things continue into college?

C: Yes. But I also had academic difficulties in college.

I: What kind of difficulties?

C: I failed many courses and eventually was asked to leave by the college dean.

I: What did you do after college?

C: I began looking for work.

The value of the interview as an assessment tool probably varies according to its degree of structure (Anastasi, 1976). If the interview is structured, it is usually easier to establish reliability. However, the unstructured interview often is similar to normal conversation and thus can facilitate freer expression of feeling. Research suggests that interview procedures do not seem to add much to the accurate assessment of personality (Berg, 1966). Nevertheless, the interview remains a popular tool for clinicians to assess those who are different. As with the Rorschach, one of the major uses of the interview is as a hypothesis generator. Data provided by the interviewee give the interviewer some ideas about the interviewee's personality that can be investigated further by different means.

Observation

Testing and interviewing as methods of gathering information about personality are largely indirect in that they *predict* a person's behavior on the basis of a sample of test or interview data. In *direct observation* the person's behavior is *seen* firsthand. Let us return once more to the man waiting outside your office to be evaluated. You might already have begun to observe him as he waits. Is he smoking? Is he cracking his knuckles? Is he talking to the receptionist? And if he is or is not exhibiting these or other behaviors, what does it all mean?

As a trained observer, you probably would be more systematic and deliberate in your observations of behavior than would the layperson. Many laypeople come to quick conclusions about others based on a small amount of interaction, while investigators of human behavior tend to be more cautious about concluding what directly observed behavior means. In any case, the real advantage of observing behavior directly is that "it permits the noting of behavior simultaneously with its spontaneous occurrence" (Kleinmuntz, 1967, p. 83). Behavior can be observed either in its natural setting or under more controlled conditions.

When an observer wishes to ascertain how a person behaves in familiar territory, the observer should move out of the office and go to where the person lives and works. Without being too obtrusive, the observer may be able to see how the client behaves in more natural surroundings. Firsthand, the observer can see how the client behaves and does not have to rely solely on more removed test data or interview-derived inferences about what occurred. However, being passive in these naturalistic settings will probably force the observer to wait for behavior to unfold. We will see later that the observer who chooses controlled instead of naturalistic observation does not necessarily adopt such a passive stance.

An example of naturalistic observation in assessment is the home visit often made by those evaluating child and family problems. Essentially, the diagnosticians invite themselves to the family's home. The assessment team usually asks the family to interact as normally as possible, and they observe such things as parent-child interactions, sibling conflicts, and marital discord. By observing the natural functioning of the family, evaluators are released from depending only on the information given by family members during office interviews, which is often biased either intentionally or unintentionally.

The home visit is a type of unstructured naturalistic observation that provides general information about human functioning. However, it is often necessary to have more control over observations so that the effects of various treatments can be assessed adequately. To obtain such control, samples of behavior may be taken either in the natural setting or in a laboratory situation.

In one such type of sampling, called *time sampling*, a specific behavior is observed and the observers note whether it occurs within certain designated time periods. For example, if you are observing a child who has the habit of pulling out his hair, you could break your observation time into 10-second periods and count the number of periods in which hair-pulling occurred. In that way you could record the occurrence of the behavior over a long period of time.

Incidence sampling focuses on the occurrence of certain behaviors regardless of the time period employed. In terms of hair-pulling, for exam-

Observing where people live can give the psychological assessor added insights. (Photo by David Powers.)

ple, incidence sampling would be concerned with the total number of times the child pulled at his hair. You would record whether he pulled his hair 3 times or 50 times in a 5-minute period. Incidence sampling is more often used when an observer wishes to assess different rates of behavior under different conditions. For example, using the same case, you might ask the mother to play with her son while you count the number of times the boy pulls his hair. You would then compare how often the child exhibits this behavior in his mother's presence with his behavior in his mother's absence.

An Application

We have given you a selective overview of the broad range of techniques available to those who wish to assess personality. It is now up to you to choose among these techniques to assess the man outside your office, who by now has put down his magazine and is waiting expectantly for you to see him. You know that the self-report approaches allow you to obtain information about how the person views his situation, as well as his stated beliefs, attitudes, and feelings. They also allow you to compare him with other pertinent groups such as college students or diagnosed patients. These self-report inventories are easy to administer and score. So perhaps you should use these. . . . But wait! You also know that these self-report inventories can be faked and that the person may give you erroneous information about himself. Further, not all of the inventories have acceptable reliability, validity, and normative information. And, finally, many of these inventories provide data that divide up the person into a number of traits rather than viewing the individual as a whole. Perhaps you believe the man outside your office may be more than a bundle of five, six, or ten traits.

These shortcomings of self-report tests may help you to decide that the projective approaches are also part of the answer to your assessment problems. After all, in some ways they are more difficult to fake and they do seek to measure the "whole" person. They might allow you to get under the person's façade and find out more of what really is going on under his skin. Yes, you decide you will use the projective tests. However, you now remember that there is very little available research support indicating that the projective tests do what they set out to do. You remember the conclusions of reviewers who stated that the projectives have little reliability or validity support and that the normative groups are far smaller and less representative than those available for most of the self-report approaches.

The receptionist has told your client that you are ready to see him, and he is coming back to your office. But you are still in a quandary. Perhaps the interview is a way of assessing your client. Yes, that's it! You'll just sit and talk with this young man in an unstructured way and find out what's bothering him. But this approach also has its risks. Perhaps you won't cover the areas you need to in order to obtain an accurate picture of this man's problem. It may be better to be more structured in interviewing so that all the important areas are covered and the proper information is available for you to make your assessment. So you reach in your desk and bring forth an outline of questions and areas to be covered. And now it strikes you that this may be a very artificial way of interacting with another human being. In fact, you become afraid that you might sound like the district attorney and offend this man deeply.

More pondering brings you to the conclusion that maybe you'll have to observe this man in his own element. Perhaps you can set up something with the dorm counselors so that you or they could observe him in interaction with his peers. Then you think about the difficulties in getting this stranger and others in the dorm to agree to be observed. In addition, you realize that you will be very obtrusive, and perhaps this will make it difficult for your client to act naturally. Also he may not want the entire dorm to know he's having psychological troubles.

Well, you had better make up your mind soon because he's at your door. Our guess is that if you are like most people who find themselves in similar situations, you probably will choose a combination of these procedures with the hope that you will obtain converging evidence from all the approaches. This convergence can help you to make a more accurate and realistic appraisal of this man's personality. There is little room for sloppy or lazy assessment, because inaccurate assessment and diagnosis can have devastating effects on people who are different.

ASSESSMENT OF INTELLIGENCE

More structured than the personality tests, intelligence tests provide important information in the clinician's attempts to diagnose mental retardation, as well as in the assessment of intellectual strengths and weaknesses of those disordered people who may not be retarded. The earliest scientifically developed individual intelligence test was devised by Binet (1905), who was attempting to differentiate in a group of low-achieving children those who probably could benefit from public-school education from those who probably could not. Binet believed that intelligence was best viewed as one global ability similar to practical judgment. Although the Binet test, (Binet & Simon, 1905) and its revisions (Terman, 1916; Terman & Merrill, 1937, 1960; Thorndike, 1973) were translated into many languages and were the most widely used measure of intelligence for 50 years, presently the most popular individual intelligence tests are those constructed by David Wechsler, a psychologist at Bellevue Hospital in New York City.

Sharing only partially Binet's global view of intelligence, Wechsler believed intelligence to be made up of several separate abilities. Wechsler further believed that different patterns of intellectual abilities might be associated with different psychiatric disorders. To examine this and other possibilities, he constructed his intelligence test as a series of subtests to reflect these separate abilities. However, little evidence was found for the hypothesis that psychiatric disorders would show different patterns of intellectual ability (Matarazzo, 1972). In spite of this shortcoming, the Wechsler intelligence tests have proved to be the most popular measure of intelligence for a wide age range of subjects. Included in this series of tests are the Wechsler Preschool and Primary Scale of Intelligence (WPPSI) (Wechsler, 1967), the Wechsler Intelligence Scale for Children, Revised (WISC-R) (Wechsler, 1974), and the Wechsler Adult Intelligence Scale (WAIS) (Wechsler, 1955). Each test includes a number of subtests whose procedure may vary from having the subject answer questions of general information (for example, What is the population of Canada?) to having the subject place blocks together to correspond to presented designs. Table 2-4 (see following page) contains a description of the subtests and what they are supposed to measure.

ASSESSMENT OF BRAIN DAMAGE

Besides personality and intelligence, psychologists may be concerned with the assessment of brain damage. Brain damage (see Chapters 16 and 17) usually is assumed to be reflected in differential deficits in such areas as memory, spatial perception, abstraction, or concept formation (Anastasi, 1976). Tests that assess brain damage are often directed at identifying such deficits. One widely accepted test, the Bender Visual Motor Gestalt Test

Table 2-4. *A description of the subtests of the Wechsler Adult Intelligence Scale*

1. Information	29 questions to test the subject's range of general information.
	Example: What is the population of Canada?
2. Comprehension	12 items that measure the subject's practical judgment ability.
	Example: Why are banking laws needed?
3. Arithmetic	A timed subtest made up of 11 items that measure arithmetic ability.
	Example: How much is $7 and $4?
4. Similarities	13 items that ask the subject to state how things are the same. It measures the ability to abstract verbally.
	Example: In what way are trees and bushes alike?
5. Memory for digits	Measures the ability to concentrate and repeat numbers verbally administered.
	Example: Repeat these numbers: 8—4—6—2.
6. Vocabulary	40 words that the subject is to define.
	Example: What is a scissors?
7. Digit symbol	A timed subtest in which the subject copies symbols below appropriate numbers.
8. Picture completion	21 items in which the subject is to point out what is wrong with a picture. Measures ability to note small detail.
9. Block design	A timed task in which the subject must put blocks together to correspond to a design picture.
10. Picture arrangement	A timed task in which the subject is asked to put in correct order cards that are in the wrong order. This measures logical reasoning and attention to detail.
11. Object assembly	A timed task in which the subject is to put together four puzzles to make a picture of a real-life item.

Adapted from *Manual for the Wechsler Adult Intelligence Scale*, by D. Wechsler. Copyright © 1955, The Psychological Corporation.

Bender, 1938) is used frequently by clinicians to detect signs of brain damage. The test consists of nine designs that the subject is to look at and copy one at a time onto a sheet of paper. Scoring systems are available for children (Koppitz, 1975) and adults (Pascal & Suttell, 1951). Both scoring systems have had some success in discriminating those who have an organic brain disorder from those who do not. These systems generally are based upon how well the person reproduces the designs. If there are significant distortions in designs, such as in Figure 2-1, the likelihood of diagnosing brain damage is increased. Distortions in designs may be the result of deficits in visual memory, which are known to be related to brain injury.

A second test for organic brain damage is the Benton Visual Retention Test (Benton, 1974). Similar to the Bender in that it requires subjects to reproduce designs, the Benton differs from the Bender in its inclusion of designs composed of several separate figures and in the availability of several parallel forms. The advantage of having more complex figures is that deficits can be more easily identified; the advantage of having parallel forms is that a person who is recovering from temporary brain damage (as in the case of alcohol

Original   Drawing by Brain-Damaged Person

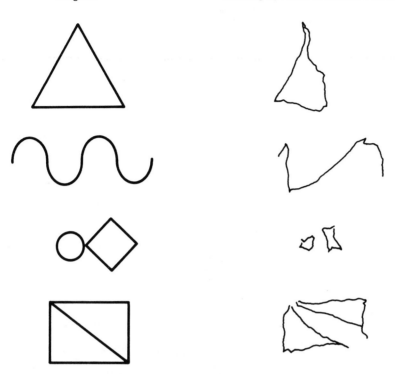

Figure 2-1. *Distortion of drawings by brain-damaged persons such as might be seen with the Bender Gestalt or Benton Visual Retention Tests (diagrams are similar to those included in these tests)*

withdrawal) may be given similar tests from time to time to assess progress yet not be given the exact same figures that he might remember from previous evaluations.

CONCLUDING COMMENTS

The assessment of human behavior is a complex and important task. We could present hundreds of pages of data on the more than 10,000 published tests, but there is some danger that you would be overwhelmed. Excellent texts on psychological tests already exist (Anastasi, 1976; Cronbach, 1976), and the more popular tests are reviewed constantly elsewhere (see Buros, 1972, 1974). Nevertheless, we believe that you need some knowledge of psychological-assessment procedures to see more clearly their role in dealing with important aspects of disordered behavior. For example, the somewhat complicated and relatively unreliable diagnosis and classification of disordered behavior highlighted in Chapter 1 can be improved by the proper use of tests. Further, as you will see in the next chapter, on the history of disordered behavior, the use of modern-day standardized assessment techniques is quite an improvement over procedures used by past assessors of human behavior. Today most people stand a better chance of being helped than their predecessors because of the time, effort, and skill of those who assess human behavior. However, mistakes still may be made, and we intend to highlight special assessment difficulties and discuss them extensively whenever they are involved in the disorders being described. One example is the role of intelligence scores in diagnosing mental retardation. In any case, we want to remind you that although we may take a critical attitude toward assessment procedures, we believe that most present procedures are a vast improvement over those of the past and allow us to deal more effectively with people who need our help.

CHAPTER SUMMARY CHART

In this chapter we described ways in which people assess those who are different. We first considered the assessment of personality:

Psychological tests	*Interviewing*	*Observation*

Basics: standardization, reliability, validity, norms
Self-report inventories: MMPI
Projective tests
    Rorschach inkblots
    TAT
	Unstructured
	Structured
		Direct observation
		Naturalistic observation
		Controlled sampling

We then discussed the assessment of intelligence and brain damage:

Intelligence	*Brain damage*
Binet Wechsler	Bender Gestalt Test Benton Visual Retention Test

CHAPTER 3
HISTORICAL
PERSPECTIVES
ON BEING
DIFFERENT

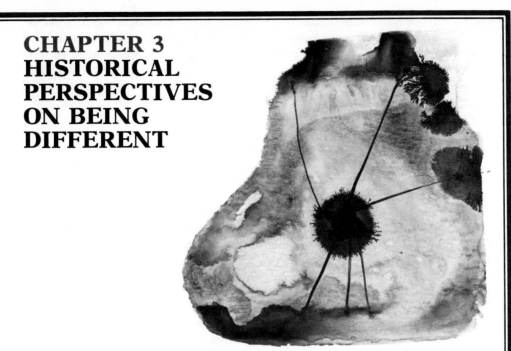

The conceptualizations of being different and the methods for assessing those who are different described in Chapters 1 and 2 represent modern perspectives on abnormal behavior. However, such enlightened points of view have not always been dominant. In this chapter we will discuss the development of our varied present-day views of disordered behavior. We will present the wide, rich history of disordered behavior from prehistoric to present times. Lengthy books have been written about historical antecedents to our modern approaches to disordered behavior (see Zilboorg & Henry, 1941), so we won't give you a mass of details here. Rather, we seek to present an overview of the highlights of this history. Other relevant historical information will be presented in appropriate places throughout the book.

HISTORY: AN INTERPRETATION

The intriguing thing about history is that it gives us a chance to second-guess and reinterpret past events. Although new information may come to light, what generally changes over time is our interpretation of consistent facts. In essence, any presentation of historical facts must be biased. We are no different from other historians; we are going to tell it as we see it. And, as we see it, the history of disordered behavior can be viewed as the interplay among three general explanations of its causes: spirit possession, physiological causes, and psychological causes. From the beginning these three theories seem to have battled for ascendancy in people's attempts to make sense of behavior that seemingly made no sense.

Belief in Possession by Demons and Spirits

The oldest explanation of disordered behavior, possession by spirits, has its roots in prehistoric societies. Those who study primitive people by examining their paintings and artifacts have generally concluded that early humans believed spirits originating in nature were responsible for causing such irrational behavior as nightmares and hallucinations. Some anthropologists believe that prehistoric people may have attempted to cure these kinds of disordered behavior by boring a hole into the heads of those afflicted to allow the bad spirits to escape. Skulls with such holes, or *trephines*, have been found at many archaeological sites.

Spirit possession seems also to have been accepted as a major cause of disordered behavior by the great cultures of Egypt, Israel, Greece, and Rome, as well as by Europeans during the Middle Ages. In some instances the theory of spirit possession was expanded to include the existence of both good and bad spirits. In a belief system based on spirit possession, the major assessors and treaters of disordered behavior were most often members of religious professions. Although there were great medical men, such as Hippocrates, Cicero, and Galen, who espoused somewhat different theories of disordered behavior, spirit possession generally remained the major explanation for disordered behavior throughout ancient times.

The popularity of the spirit-possession theory probably reached its peak in the Middle Ages. During these dark days in the history of attitudes toward abnormal behavior, the belief in spirits flourished. The world seemed to abound in weird and deviant behavior. People showing such behavior were usually assumed to be possessed by spirits and devils, so responsibility for dealing with those unfortunate individuals most often fell to the clergy. At first most clergymen, guided by pronouncements from the papacy, perceived the disordered as innocent victims of the devil and dealt kindly with them. For example, the possessed person might first be prayed over or sprinkled with holy water. If these measures failed, more severe procedures were sometimes used. These sterner measures, which included *exorcism* for eradicating the spirits, ranged from having the person drink a mixture made of blood and sheep dung to physically beating the disordered individual. Though severe, these distasteful procedures were the same ones practiced by the priests and monks among themselves to deal with the devil. At this point, then, exorcism may have been the most appropriate and humane treatment the times could offer.

During the 15th century, priests routinely performed rites of exorcism on the mentally ill. (Courtesy of the Bancroft Rare Books Library, University of California, Berkeley.)

One common "cure" for demon possession was burning. (Courtesy of the Bancroft Rare Books Library, University of California, Berkeley.)

However, afflicted people were not to receive such favored treatment for long. The clergy, who at first usually differentiated between those who were innocent victims of the devil and those who were in league with Satan, apparently abandoned this distinction in the 14th century. Just about all disordered people came to be thought of as possessed by spirits and in league with the devil, and they were punished accordingly. Interestingly enough, the devil saw fit to possess many more women than men; at least this was the judgment of those whose responsibility it was to evaluate such things. These judges (most of whom were men) suggested, among other things, that more women than men were possessed because women were lustful creatures who were more evil than men, as they believed the story of Adam and Eve had shown.

In 1487, clergy and government leaders organized in their attempt to deal with the disordered behavior that some thought was running rampant. Two monks, under a directive from Pope Innocent VIII, wrote a manual entitled *Malleus Maleficarum*, or *Hammer of Witches*, a how-to book for the detection and treatment of witches. From the vantage point of the pres-

---

An Example of Exorcism

The following excerpt is an example of the primary method used in the Middle Ages to deal with hysteria (a disorder usually accompanied by such difficulties as tremors, paralysis, and tics). Because hysteria was then believed to result from the wandering of the uterus in search of a child, this incantation was recited or shouted by a priest until the uterus quieted down and returned to its original and natural place.

In the name of God the Father, God the Son and God the Holy Spirit. O Lord of Hosts surrounded by the archangels who in trembling awe say; Holy, holy, holy. O Lord Zebaoth, look at our infirmity, at our weakness, direct Thy attention toward the form of our nature and do not despise us, the work of Thy hands! For Thou hast made us and not we ourselves. Stop the womb of Thy maid . . . and heal its affliction, for it is moving violently. . . .

I conjure thee, O womb, by our Lord Jesus Christ . . . not to harm that maid of God, not to occupy her head, throat, neck, chest, ears, teeth, eyes, nostrils, shoulderblades, arms, hands, heart, stomach, spleen, kidneys, back, sides, joints, navel, intestines, bladder, thighs, shins, heels, nails, but to lie down quietly in the place which God chose for thee.

Source: G. Zilboorg and G. Henry, *A History of Medical Psychology* (New York: Norton, 1941), pp. 131–132.

ent, we can see that this manual and the motivation for its publication came from a society that was frightened by the occurrence of disordered behavior and wanted to find convenient scapegoats. The writers of this era generally give the impression that there were more than enough guilt-ridden and strange people to keep witch hunters busy for well over 250 years. The part played by colonial Americans in this sad story is represented by the famous Salem witch trials of the 1700s. Generally witch-hunting continued in Europe until the end of the 18th century and was largely a sexist event. *Fifty* female witches were burned, hanged, pressed between stones, drowned, or flogged to death for every male witch similarly treated.

Spirits seem to have been held accountable for a wide range of bizarre activity during the Middle Ages. Many people believed in *lycanthropy* (evil spirits changing a man into a wolf at the time of the full moon), *vampirism* (evil spirits causing people to suck the blood from their victims), and *tarantism* (in which people bitten by a spider would dance out of control). Tarantism is graphically described in the following excerpt from Sigerist (1943):

> The disease occurred at the height of the summer heat. ... People, asleep or awake, would suddenly jump up, feeling an acute pain like the sting of a bee. Some saw the spider, others did not, but they knew that it must be the tarantula. They ran out of the house into the street, to the market place, dancing in great excitement. Soon they were joined by others who like them had been bitten or by people who had been stung in previous years. ...
>
> Thus groups of patients would gather, dancing wildly in the queerest attire. ... Others would tear their clothes and show their nakedness, losing all sense of modesty. ... Some called for swords and acted like fencers, others for whips and beat each other. ... Some of them had still stranger fancies, liked to be tossed in the air, dug holes in the ground, and rolled themselves into the dirt like swine. They all drank wine plentifully and sang and talked like drunken people [pp. 103, 106–107].[1]

Like the medieval belief in tarantism, the belief in demonic possession and evil spirits as a cause for disordered behavior remains with us today, although in a minor way. Some churches still teach the doctrine of Satan as an entity in the world, and several cults of devil worship are flourishing. However, as a major theory for explaining disordered behavior, demonic possession no longer seems viable.

[1]From *Civilization and Disease*, by H. E. Sigerist. Copyright 1943 by Cornell University Press.

Belief in Physiological Explanations

Although spirit possession has passed its peak as an explanation of disordered behavior, the belief in an underlying *physiological* cause still flourishes. We will now return to ancient times and trace the growth of this explanation.

We must look to early Greece and to Hippocrates for the primary origins of the physiological explanation of disordered behavior. Although most other Greeks of his time espoused either a philosophical or a spiritual theory, Hippocrates believed that actual brain pathology or body-fluid imbalance was primarily responsible for the appearance of disordered behavior. Hippocrates saw three major kinds of behavior disorder: *melancholia, mania,* and *phrenitis.* Melancholia was probably similar to what we currently call depression; mania may have been like manic states; and phrenitis, a disorder of thought, seems similar to schizophrenia. Hippocrates prescribed treatment for each of these disturbances. For example, for melancholia he prescribed quiet, a good diet, and abstinence from sex to make the person strong of body and brain (Zilboorg & Henry, 1941).

When spirit-possession theories were dominant, the logical people to deal with the afflicted were experts in spiritual problems, the religious leaders. However, if disordered behavior were caused by some underlying *physical* condition, then the most appropriate person to deal with it was the physician. Indeed, in Greece and Rome in the first few centuries after Christ, it was the physician, following the beliefs of Hippocrates, who was primarily responsible for treating disordered behavior. Unfortunately, many physicians also accepted some of the erroneous particulars of Hippocrates' theory. For example, Hippocrates assumed that good health depended on the balance among "four

---

Hippocrates (c. 460–c. 370 B.C.) on Disordered Behavior

And by this [the brain] . . . we acquire wisdom and knowledge, and see and hear, and know what are foul and what are fair, what are bad and what are good, what are sweet and what unsavoury; some we discriminate by habit, and some we perceive by their utility. By this we distinguish objects of relish and disrelish, according to the seasons; and the same things do not always please us. And by the same organ we become mad and delirious, and fears and terrors assail us, some by night and some by day, and dreams and untimely wanderings, and cares that are not suitable, and ignorance of present circumstances, desuetude, and unskilfulness. All these things we endure from the brain when it is not healthy, but is more hot, more cold, more moist, or more dry than natural, or when it suffers any other preternatural and unusual affection.

Source: The Genuine Works of Hippocrates, Volume II (F. Adams, trans.). London: Sydenham Society, 1848.

humors" of the body: blood, black bile, yellow bile, and phlegm. In melancholia, thought to be caused by the overbalance of black bile, the main course of action was to drain the patient's black bile. This unfortunately also involved the removal of large quantities of blood. Thus, the depressed patient was left in a weaker physiological state. Although the acceptance of the Hippocratic view of disordered behavior sometimes led to mistakes in the treatment of both mental and physical problems, the basic belief that such behavior was governed by the effects of certain body structures and substances foreshadowed the more modern organic views of the causes of disordered behavior.

As the Greek-influenced Roman civilization began its decline in the third and fourth centuries after Christ, so did the physiological explanation of disordered behavior. Its place was taken again by the belief in spirit possession. Galen, who lived in the third century, is seen by historians as one of the last physicians of note for centuries; both his work and that of others in categorizing and assessing the physical aspects of disordered behavior were generally forgotten for the next 1500 years. In fact, it was not until the 19th century that Griesinger in Germany and Morel in France revived the explanation that mental disorders were probably related to nervous-system dysfunction.

In the 19th century the progress of and support for a physiological basis of disordered behavior went hand in hand with increasing knowledge of the central nervous system. The early Greeks had believed that it was a sacrilege to operate on the human body, and the Romans and Christians had also been loath to do so. As a result, only in the 19th century did dissection and experimentation lead to increased knowledge of the functioning of the brain and its role in behavior.

The success of this approach was exemplified by the study of the disorder called general paresis (Zilboorg & Henry, 1941). General paresis is a mental disorder now known to be caused by the progressive infiltration and subsequent destruction of brain tissue by spirochetes of syphilis. It is characterized by a wide variety of behavioral and physical abnormalities. Physical and personality disintegration go hand in hand and the person may "hear voices," forget recent happenings, and show wide swings in moods.

The finding of the cause and cure for general paresis reads like a well written textbook in support of the scientific method. The following is a brief chronology of how the successful investigation proceeded.

1. In 1798, Haslam described the symptom complex of general paresis consisting of delusions of grandeur, dementia, and progressive paralysis. He also described patients as having defective speech and memory as well as showing a progressive loss of control over voluntary muscle movements.

2. In 1805, Esquirol, a French physician, pointed out that those patients who had this symptom complex never recovered from the disorder. They deteriorated and died. With this information, investigators now had described a symptom complex with a typical progress and predictable outcome.

3. Further investigation using hospital records and observations revealed that the disorder appeared three times as often in men as in women,

with the time of onset somewhere between 30 and 50 years of age. However, investigators were unsure as to how one got the disease. Early guesses implicated tobacco or alcohol. In fact, since the disease seemed so prevalent among the elite of the community, such as government officials, doctors, writers, and the like, it led some investigators to conclude that high intelligence must be a primary cause.

4. Post-mortem examination of the brains and nervous systems of general paretics revealed damaged tissue. Improved microscopes helped investigators to see that the damaged tissue was accompanied by a growth of foreign-appearing connective tissue. Thus, by 1860, researchers were sure of the involvement of the brain in this psychological disorder.

5. In 1894, Fournier, studying the case histories of paretic patients, concluded that a syphilitic infection was involved in a significant number of paretic patients (65%) as compared to other mental disorders (10%). This led him to conclude that general paresis originated from a syphilitic infection.

6. In 1897, Krafft-Ebing ran an experiment that confirmed the relationship between general paresis and syphilis. In the examination of case histories of paretics, he noted that there were some instances in which histories of syphilis were not obtained. It was Krafft-Ebing's belief that there was necessarily a syphilitic infection first that led to general paresis. He reasoned that the lack of a one-to-one relationship in the case studies resulted because some patients did not want to admit to the indiscretions that led them to contract syphilis. To test this assumption, Krafft-Ebing took nine paretic patients who had denied any previous syphilitic infection and inoculated them with fluid drawn from a syphilitic patient. None of them developed signs of syphilis. While it is doubtful that any present-day committee on human rights in experiments would allow such a procedure, this was 1897, and it did prove beyond a doubt that those nine individuals had previously contracted syphilis and that Krafft-Ebing's assumption that there had to be a syphilitic infection prior to general paresis was supported.

7. Further studies showed that the blood and cerebrospinal fluid of both syphilitics and paretics shared common characteristics. This linked the two disorders even more closely.

8. In 1905, the syphilitic infectious agent, *Treponema pallidum*, was identified.

9. In 1913, Noguchi and Moore found this agent in the brain tissue of general paretics. The cause of general paresis was now directly identified; syphilis, if not treated in its early stages, caused this dread disorder.

In the study of general paresis, the scientifically tested assumption that a disordered behavior had a physical cause had borne fruit; the etiology of a dread disorder was exposed and its agents of destruction identified. The hope for biological explanations of *all* mental disorders emerged here and still continues in the minds of many people.

Buoyed by the successful application of the physiological explanation of disordered behavior, physicians and others grew optimistic about the possibility of "curing" other forms of disordered behavior. Many psychiatrists endorsed the assumption that brain or nervous-system damage underlay all types of psychological disorders. Emil Kraepelin (1896), a German psychiatrist whose writing most influenced the thinking of psychiatrists from 1900 to the mid-1920s, used hospital records to classify behavior disorders in the same manner as physical disorders. By organizing these data in such a manner, Kraepelin reasoned, he could identify typical symptom complexes and describe typical patterns of onset, course, and outcome. The descriptions would prepare the way for finding the causal agents and eventually the "cure" for disorders. Kraepelin concluded from his work that there were two major groups of symptom complexes: *manic-depressive psychosis*, characterized by swings in mood states but with no deterioration in speech or memory, and *dementia praecox* (now primarily known as schizophrenia), characterized by an early onset and progressive deterioration in thought processes. Since these two groups of symptoms afflicted two-thirds of mental-hospital patients, it seemed that their elimination would do much to solve the problem of disordered behavior. Kraepelin's own guesses differentiated the underlying causes of the two disorders. He believed the cause of manic depression to be an irregularity in metabolism, whereas he believed the basis of schizophrenia to be a malfunctioning of the sex glands that resulted in chemical imbalances. Kraepelin and other investigators attempted to apply the methodologies that had uncovered the origin of general paresis to finding the cause and cure of these two major "diseases." However, the actual causes of these disorders have resisted clarification. Kraepelin's attempt to classify disordered behavior was laudable, but he never found physiological causes (Zilboorg & Henry, 1941). (We will describe modern opinions about physical bases for abnormal behavior in Chapter 6.)

Besides spurring Kraepelin and others to classify disordered behavior, the success of the physiological approach had other profound effects, not the least of which was the creation of a climate favorable for attempting a variety of physical treatments. We will discuss and evaluate these specific physical-treatment approaches in Chapter 24; for now, suffice it to say that many people were convulsed, shocked, and operated on, often with procedures lacking both scientific and medical justification. These procedures were used because of an almost religious belief that disordered behavior had a physical cause and could be treated by physical methods. This kind of fallacious reasoning led to some dark moments in the history of disordered behavior, especially in the use of psychosurgery, in which parts of many patients' brains were destroyed permanently.

It was also within the atmosphere favoring the physiological approach that Dorothea Dix began her work to get every person who seemed in need of help for "mental disease" into hospitals for treatment. Because of the prevailing belief in the physiological explanation of disordered behavior, these patients were generally treated as medical patients. However, there were few proven, effective treatments available. Mental patients and the mental hospitals in which they were housed waited for the "cures" for the "diseases" to appear. We know now that they had a long, long wait.

Belief in Psychogenic or Psychological Explanations

We have now traced the explanations that implicated either spirits or an underlying physical defect as the cause of disordered behavior. A final explanation suggests that such behavior has psychological causes. It was through the study of *hysteria*, a disorder thought in the past to occur only in women,[2] that the psychogenic approach gained importance. Known to the ancient Greeks and Romans, hysteria may be manifested by physical symptoms such as blindness, paralyses of body parts, and even convulsive attacks and memory dysfunctions—all without apparent physical cause. In some cases the paralyses may be anatomically nonsensical, while in others the paralyses may shift unpredictably from one part of the body to another. These characteristics puzzled investigators of the 18th and 19th centuries who no longer wished to assume that such symptoms were due to the person's being possessed or in league with the devil. As with general paresis, there was an orderly progression of events leading to the psychological solution to the riddles of hysteria.

Mesmer and Hysteria. Among the earliest people to develop a theory and subsequent "cure" for hysterical disorders was Anton Mesmer, an Austrian physician. In the course of his university studies, he hit upon the theory of *universal magnetism* to explain human behavior. To Mesmer, the universe was made up of magnetic fluid; when it became imbalanced, people experienced behavioral difficulties. At first Mesmer used a specially prepared metal rod to touch others in his attempts to correct imbalances in their fluid. However, Mesmer later came to believe that he himself was a source of "animal magnetism" and used his own hands or objects he touched to "cure" others. His techniques for correcting imbalances in fluid via animal magnetism became known as "Mesmerism," which has been likened to hypnotism, a word introduced by Braid (1795–1860). Mesmer's spectacular and theatrical manner of practice earned him the animosity of many members of the professional community wherever he practiced, and eventually led to his ruin. However, his ability to influence the behavior of people and to "cure" a wide variety of symptoms is unquestioned.

It was in Paris that Mesmer seemed to have his greatest success and, as a result, his greatest difficulty. A Parisian commission investigated his activities and concluded that while Mesmer assumed the changes he wrought to be due to physical processes, the panel believed that the changes were due instead to "the excitement of the imagination." In essence, this panel of esteemed scientists (which included Ben Franklin) was saying that Mesmer could bring about these dramatic changes in behavior merely by manipulating the expectancies of his patients. Although damning to Mesmer, the commission's conclusion that expectancies significantly determined behavior sounds very modern. These critics seemed to be helping

---

[2]It was thought by the practitioners in ancient Greece and during the Middle Ages to be caused by the wandering of the woman's uterus, in search of children.

At the height of Mesmer's success, great numbers of the fashionable elite of Paris came to his drawing room for treatment. (Courtesy of the National Library of Medicine.)

Charcot sketched some of his hysterical patients, including a woman whose legs could not be uncrossed without danger of breaking them. (Courtesy of the Bancroft Rare Books Library, University of California, Berkeley.)

The Methods of Anton Mesmer

The central feature of Mesmer's treatment room was the *baquet*. Considered to be the focal point for the magnetic fluid (a physical force Mesmer claimed to be able to manipulate), this contraption consisted of a large oaken tub filled with iron filings, water, and powdered glass. Its lid was pierced with holes through which jointed iron rods protruded. The baquet was said by Mesmer to have been magnetized. It was able to transmit this magnetic force through the rods to the patients. Patients sat around the baquet, linked hands, touched the rods and waited for Mesmer, the great magnetizer, to appear, wearing a fantastic lilac-colored silk robe and carrying a wand. He passed among the patients, touching some, making passes at others with his wand, and occasionally fixing patients with a stare and ordering them to sleep. Gradually the individual patients became agitated and restless until a "crisis" occurred. One patient would scream, break into a sweat, and convulse. Others soon followed suit, until hysterical convulsions had seized most of those present. After these violent episodes, tension subsided, patients felt calm and relaxed, and many experienced remission of their symptoms.

From *Catharsis in Psychotherapy*, by M. Nichols and M. Zax. Copyright 1977 by Gardner Press, Inc. Reprinted by permission.

to define a psychological theory for the determination of disordered behavior. Perhaps the only involved party to realize this was a pupil of Mesmer's who asked: "If Mesmer had no other secret than that he was able to make the imagination exert an effective influence upon health, would he not still be a wonder worker?" (Janet, 1925, p. 161).

Charcot and Hysteria. From our present vantage point, we can conclude that Mesmer was probably most successful in dealing with hysterical disorders. Mesmer himself commented that his "animal magnetism" appeared to work best on certain kinds of people who are descriptively similar to those classified today as hysteric. After the furor over Mesmer died down, the next significant person to become involved in the complexities of hysteria was the eminent neurologist Jean Charcot. Once again, it was hypnosis that brought the disorder to the attention of the scientific community. Unknown to Charcot, some of his students, by means of hypnotism, prepared a physically healthy woman to show all the behavioral signs of hysteria. They then asked Charcot to diagnose her without telling him what they had done. When he had concluded after his examination that she was hysteric, they showed Charcot how these "hysterical" symptoms could be removed by waking her from her hypnotic state. In our opinion, these students took quite a chance, for making a fool of your professor can be dangerous, especially around exam time. Fortunately, however, Charcot was more interested than angered by what had happened. The idea that the whole complex of hysterical symptoms could be brought into existence and then made to disappear via hypnosis was intriguing to him. Charcot soon changed his theoretical position that hysterical symptoms were the result of a defect in or injury to the nervous system and instead launched studies to find the nonphysical antecedents for the disorder.

Janet and Hysteria. Although Charcot made great strides, it was left to Pierre Janet, his student, to continue the work on hysteria. Consistent with Charcot's approach, Janet also looked for nonphysical causes, but he was more impressed by the memory difficulties found in some hysterical patients. Cases of amnesia (loss of memory) and sleepwalking showed that many hysterics had a propensity to adopt styles of thinking that departed from normal processes. His observations of other patients allowed Janet to describe not only the symptom complex known as hysteria, but also one he called *psychasthenia*, characterized by ruminations, doubts, and obsessions. Thus, by the beginning of the 1900s, there was a rudimentary classification of neurotic as well as psychotic disorders and some evidence, at least in the case of neurotic disorders, that there was a significant psychological component in their etiology.

Breuer and Hysteria. At the same time that Charcot and Janet were studying the causes of hysteria, Joseph Breuer was involved in what would turn out to be a new treatment for this disorder. Breuer called on a young colleague from Vienna, Sigmund Freud, to help in the treatment of a woman called, for purposes of confidentiality, Anna O. Anna O. presented a number of symptoms varying from leg paralysis to dreamy states of consciousness during which she would mumble to herself as she walked around. Breuer hypnotized her and repeated to her what she had mumbled about in her dreamy states. This feedback apparently caused her to express her fantasies and in special instances to reexperience intense emotions felt during certain past interactions. As a result of these procedures, she would wake up from her hypnotic state refreshed and symptom-free. The release of feeling, or *abreaction*, appeared to Breuer and Freud to be a key factor in successfully treating hysterical disorders. This conclusion laid the groundwork for a psychological theory of the etiology and treatment of an entire class of disordered behavior. It took Freud years to expand and illuminate the implications of such an approach (see Chapter 4), but by 1900 the theoretical situation was similar to what we have today: somatic and psychological theories of disordered behavior paired off against each other, with spirit-possession explanations of behavior of only minor importance.

SOCIAL RESPONSES TO THOSE WHO ARE DIFFERENT: THE MENTAL HOSPITALS

The manner in which Western societies instituted "treatment" for those who need psychiatric help is one part of our historical review that cuts across all three explanations of disordered behavior. Historically reflecting prevailing views of disordered behavior, mental hospitals seem to have their origins in the shrines of ancient Greece. These shrines existed for about 1500 years and at the height of their popularity numbered well over 700. People with problems often went to these shrines to be subjected to a wide variety of treatment, from drugs to physical beating.

In the Middle Ages, the institutions that cared for "insane" people were the monasteries and churches, and the caretakers were the clergy. As time passed and the prevailing view of disordered behavior changed from a religious to a physical one, the caretakers changed from clergymen to physicians. Unfortunately, regardless of who the caretakers were, with few exceptions the care of deranged people remained poor until more humane treatments began to appear toward the end of the Middle Ages.

Asylums in the Middle Ages

The Middle Ages were chaotic, and terrible things were frequently done to people to "help" them. Nevertheless, some voices of caution and reason were heard. One such voice belonged to Joseph Weyer, a physician who reasoned that many people described as witches were merely physically and spiritually ill and could benefit from kindly treatment. Although Weyer had some impact on the thinking of his day, in reality his was a very small voice in a very large wilderness.

Later in the Middle Ages, some physicians did influence the thinking of society and, as a result, asylums were constructed, first in Spain (1409) and later in England and France, in hopes of giving better care to those less fortunate. Unhappily, better care did not always follow. Instead, many of these asylums served as dumping grounds for political and social misfits. St. Mary of Bethlehem in England ("Bedlam" to its inmates) and the Tower of Vienna in Austria (where prisoners were placed between the inner and outer walls for better viewing by the public) were notorious for the cruelties often inflicted on patients. The situation was no better anywhere else. In the United States, the major institutional treatment facility available for disordered persons in the late 1700s consisted of three rooms in the basement of a hospital in Pennsylvania. It was not until 1798 that the first U.S. mental hospital was constructed in Williamsburg, Virginia.

The Rise of Humane Treatment: Philippe Pinel

About 1800, mental-health treatment took one of its rare turns for the better, mainly because of the work of Philippe Pinel. As superintendent

Before Pinel's reforms, many institutionalized people were kept like animals and thought to be dangerous, as shown in this illustration from a book published in 1806. (Courtesy of the National Library of Medicine.)

of La Bicetre, a large mental hospital in Paris, Pinel risked his job by suggesting that all means of unreasonable restraint be abolished and replaced by a treatment program including fresh air and activities. Thought by many to be mad himself, Pinel won a trial experiment for his "heretical" ideas and was soon vindicated by the spectacular improvement of many of the supposedly incurably insane. These reforms led to more humane treatment in other French asylums, and parallel progress was made in treatment facilities in England and later in the United States. Pinel also introduced clear and consistent record-keeping on the progress of patients and insisted that the effectiveness of any treatment for a disorder be evaluated by comparison to gains made simply by waiting for the disorder to run its course. He was truly a significant force in obtaining reforms in institutional treatment for those suffering from mental disorders.

In 18th- and 19th-century Europe, a diverting outing might include a visit to an asylum to gape at and mock the inmates. (Courtesy of the National Library of Medicine.)

In the United States, some hospitals began programs in the spirit of Pinel's reforms. Patients were treated with respect and instilled with the expectation that they would get better. These "moral-treatment" programs were very successful, with 60 or 70% of the patients being discharged as improved and adjudged as maintaining their progress years after release.

The Fall of Humane Treatment: Dorothea Dix

Discouragingly, the successes of the moral-treatment hospitals did not lead to their growth; instead, they actually diminished in number. This retreat may have been due in large part to the crowding of hospitals owing to the efforts of a self-styled mental-health evangelist, Dorothea Dix. From 1841 until her death, Dix made it her personal goal to get every disordered person who needed mental-hospital care into a mental institution. Though suffering from tuberculosis, she was unrelenting in her task and, largely through her efforts, the number of patients in mental hospitals grew from 2561 in 1840 to 74,028 in 1890 (Deutsch, 1937). Hospitals were not always prepared to deal with these large numbers of new patients. Beds had to be placed in halls previously used for recreation, and qualified help was often unavailable to take care of this torrent of patients. As a result, many mental hospitals gave up their moral-treatment programs and became largely custodial.

Modern Approaches

The kinds of treatment that people received during the fall of humane treatment were best publicized by Clifford Beers (1931), who suffered from a psychosis; he was hospitalized for three years but recovered from the psychotic episode to write about his experiences as a patient in a mental hospital. In his book, *A Mind That Found Itself*, Beers wrote about his perceptions of the cold, unfeeling, uneducated attendants whose main job seemed to be to maintain order and who were usually hired on the basis of physical strength. He wrote about the crowded, dirty, and dehumanizing conditions in his mental hospital and the manner in which the staff reinforced patient passivity and meekness. He described the physical punishments and "treatments" prescribed by medical doctors who sometimes were untrained and unprepared to deal with mental patients. As one result of Beer's writings, the National Committee for Mental Hygiene was formed

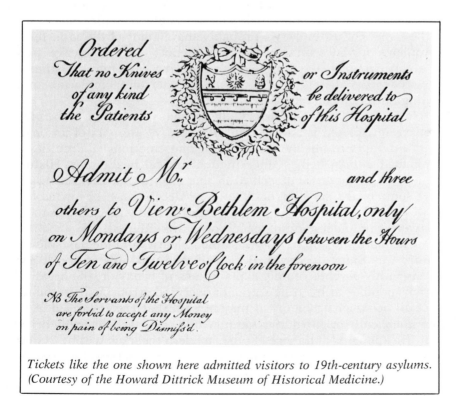

Tickets like the one shown here admitted visitors to 19th-century asylums. (Courtesy of the Howard Dittrick Museum of Historical Medicine.)

to lobby for remediation of these conditions. However, relatively few professionals joined Beers's crusade, and when the Joint Commission on Mental Illness and Health (1961) examined the state of care provided by mental hospitals, they found conditions distressingly similar to those of Beers's time: largely custodial care and dehumanizing attitudes and procedures still seemed to prevail. The report of the 1961 commission set the stage for the first real reform of the hospital system in the United States and the growth of the community psychology and psychiatry movements. As opposed to institutionalization, the community movement emphasizes prevention and nonhospitalization, sending the professional to the people rather than vice-versa. We will describe community psychology and psychiatry more fully in Chapter 25.

CONCLUDING COMMENTS

One of the lessons a history of disordered behavior can teach us is that there probably is no single explanation for the wide-ranging psychological problems shown by people throughout the ages. In fact, it seems that the greatest abuses usually have occurred when one explanation was heavily relied on as a basis for dealing with abnormality. Another lesson of history seems to be that abnormal behavior is always different yet somewhat the same. For example, we probably share many of the same feelings and problems our ancestors experienced; anxiety felt by the cave dweller when a saber-toothed tiger prowled outside the cave may be similar in many ways to the anxiety felt by the businessperson facing a tax auditor "prowling" through the records.

In part, the lessons of history suggest that we who live in the present are not on an isolated island of time. Rather, we are part of an ongoing series of attempts to alleviate behavioral and emotional difficulties that have plagued human beings since their historical beginnings. Historical accounts such as those we described in this chapter may help us to avoid making some of the same errors as our predecessors. Perhaps, as others have, we can glean from our history information that will enable us to make new advances in understanding people who are different.

One man who apparently was able to learn from the past and affect the future was Sigmund Freud. Because Freud was able to create a new emphasis in his psychodynamic explanations of behavior, the organic explanations popular at his time were not overused erroneously in the treatment of all behavior problems. It may be said that Freud carried us from the physiologically oriented 19th century into the psychologically oriented present. His thoughts and those of other modern theorists will be examined in Section II, where we consider the variety of explanations for human behavior.

CHAPTER SUMMARY CHART

In this chapter we looked at three basic historical trends in thinking about the causes of abnormal behavior:

Possession by demons	*Physiological explanations*	*Psychological explanations*
Trephinization	Hippocrates:	Hysteria as the key to the
Exorcism	Melancholia, mania,	psychological ap-
Pope Innocent VIII	and phrenitis	proach
and the *Malleus*	Imbalance of body	Mesmer:
Maleficarum	humors	Animal magnetism
Witch hunts	Greek progressiveness	Suggestion
Lycanthropy, vam-	The cause of general	Mesmerism
pirism, and	paresis	Charcot:
tarantism	Kraepelin:	His students tricked
Satan cults	Classification of	him
Clergy as treaters	mental "diseases"	Janet:
	Physicians as treaters	Rudimentary classifi-
		cation of neuroses
		Breuer and Freud:
		The case of Anna O.
		Psychological cause
		and psychological
		treatment
		Psychiatric specialists
		as treaters

We then described the history of mental hospitals:

Asylums	*Humane treatment rises*	*Reforms*
Bedlam	Pinel at La Bicetre	Beers:
Vienna Tower		*A Mind That Found*
"See the animals"	*Humane treatment falls*	*Itself*
	Dix overloads the mental	Joint Commission of
	hospitals	1961
		Community psychology
		movement

SECTION II
EXPLANATIONS
OF HUMAN BEHAVIOR

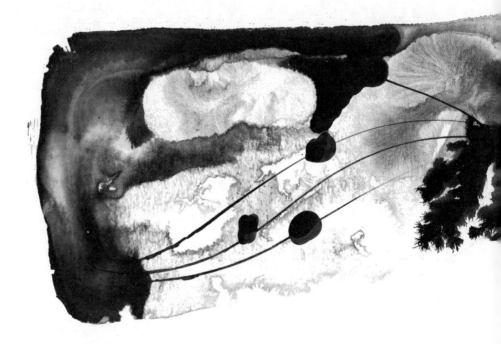

Chapter 4
Psychological Explanations

Chapter 5
Sociological Explanations

Chapter 6
Biological Explanations

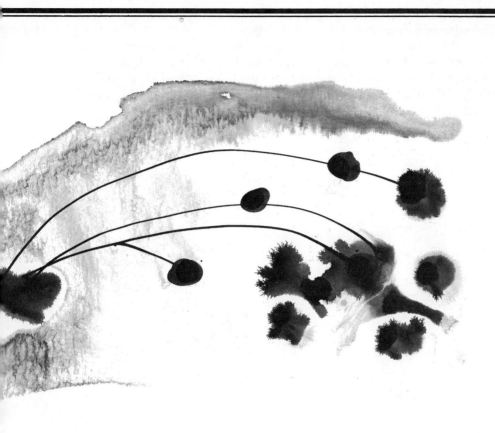

The four-component model of abnormal psychology dictates that explanations of behavior be included in our discussion of the varieties of being different. However, specific explanations of abnormal behavior usually are derived from larger bodies of explanation of human behavior in general. The specific explanations we include later in the text will be more meaningful if you have a basic grounding in the general theories from which they emerge.

Abnormal behavior may be seen as a subset of general behavior, so we must first present conceptions of what is normal to understand and explain what is abnormal. In this section we will describe the general explanations of human behavior from three major perspectives. Each theoretical perspective differs from the others in its emphasis on a certain basis for the development of normal and abnormal behavior. The psychological explanations, our first perspective, are based primarily upon the belief that an individual's psychological composition and interactions with important others are crucial to human development and personality. The sociological explanations, in contrast, emphasize social and cultural factors as being responsible for the significant shaping of both normal and abnormal behavior patterns. The biological explanations, our final perspective, are

71

based upon the assertion that there is a neurological, genetic, or biochemical basis for behavior.

We will present the major theoretical explanations within all three perspectives, and they will form the broad base for your understanding of normal behavior. Application of these explanations to abnormal behavior will be included in the chapters dealing with the specific categories of disordered behavior.

CHAPTER 4
PSYCHOLOGICAL
EXPLANATIONS

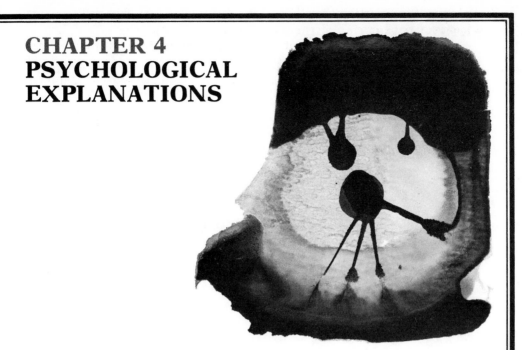

Within general psychology—and consequently in abnormal psychology—there is wide disagreement in regard to the roles played by internal psychological functioning versus external stimuli and reinforcement in the determination of behavior. We have found that the variety of psychological explanations for behavior are applicable differentially to aspects of abnormality. In other words, although one theory may explain one type of disorder best, some alternative explanation may do better for another behavior pattern. To reflect the emphasis on either internal or external causation that differentiates these theories, we will discuss the various explanations, beginning with the psychoanalytic approach, which relies primarily on personal-internal processes. We then will consider the neoanalytic and humanistic approaches, which focus more upon the individual as a member of society. Finally, we will describe the behavioral approach, which focuses upon external stimuli and reinforcement as the primary determinants of behavior.

THE PSYCHOLOGICAL THEORY OF SIGMUND FREUD

Psychoanalytic theory, as developed by Sigmund Freud in the late 19th and early 20th centuries, holds a place in psychology and psychiatry unequaled by that of any other school of thought. Freud gave us a language with which to think about the mind and brought emotional disorders within the realm of medicine and the helping arts. Although there are many critics of his theory, its social and professional impact cannot be denied.

A Historical Perspective

In Chapter 3, we discussed the historical precursors of Sigmund Freud. As is true of most important ideas, some of the concepts that eventually emerged from Freud's work were not new. They can be found in the writings of such men as Mesmer, Braid, Charcot, and Janet. However, it was Freud whose intellectual tenacity brought seemingly disparate ideas together into a cohesive and intelligible theory.

Trained as a neurologist, Freud became interested in the *psychogenic* (psychologically caused) aspects of disease through his ten-year association with Joseph Breuer (ca. 1885–1895). In a now classic work, *Studies of Hysteria*, published in 1895, Freud and Breuer asserted that in certain emotionally labile people (hysterics), emotional conflicts were not dealt with directly, but instead were made *unconscious* only to be expressed later, symbolically, as symptoms. Breuer and Freud first attempted to "cure" a hysterical patient through hypnosis. They reasoned that in this way they could induce in patients emotional reactions (*abreactions*) to past events so that unconscious tensions could be released and symptoms reduced.

Freud soon concluded that hypnosis was not the best treatment for neuroses such as hysteria. The curative effects obtained through posthypnotic suggestions were often temporary, with the symptoms returning after treatment ceased. This lack of permanent effects in those who could be hypnotized, plus the fact that some patients couldn't be hypnotized at all, led Freud to consider other approaches. He still believed that abreaction or catharsis of emotion was necessary for successful treatment. His search for new methods eventually led Freud to develop *free association*, the cornerstone therapeutic technique of psychoanalysis. In free association, patients were asked to imagine that they were sitting in a moving railroad car observing the countryside. They were further instructed to imagine that all things going through their minds were much like the passing countryside; they were to make no effort to censor, vary, or alter their thoughts, and they were to express these thoughts to the therapist. Most of Freud's hysterical patients eventually responded to the free association with catharsis, followed by a sustained abatement of symptoms.

Freud began to observe certain common phenomena among his patients. He noticed that many dealt with stress in somewhat similar ways, and that their dreams often reflected the manner in which they handled emotional conflict. Moreover, he also began to notice the importance of sex in psychological difficulties. Freudian theory would be easier to present if it were static and unchanging, but Freud continued to alter his explanations of human behavior on the basis of his experiences until his death in 1936. In the following section, we will present those ideas of personality development which were among the most stable.

Basic Concepts of Behavior

It is difficult to cover all of the intricacies of Freudian theory briefly, but we can concentrate on three major concepts. The first of these, the *unconscious*, is basic to understanding behavior. Another concept involves the *psychic triumvirate,* or three-part system, composed of the id, ego, and superego, that determines behavior. Finally, we will turn to *psychosexual development*, Freud's hypothesized normal course of psychological growth. Deviation from such normal development is associated with abnormality.

The Unconscious. Freud (1953) theorized that thinking was composed of three levels of mental activity—conscious, preconscious, and unconscious (see Figure 4-1). The highest level includes *conscious* mental activities—those events of which a person may be aware at a given moment. For example, you are aware of this book in front of you as you read this chapter; perhaps you are conscious of your surroundings as well. *Precon-*

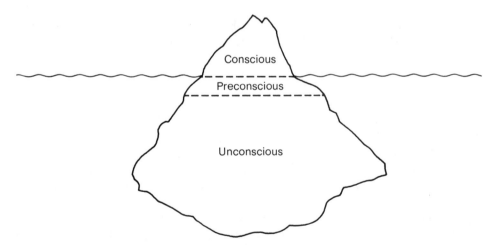

Figure 4-1. *The iceberg model of the unconscious. Only a relatively small portion of one's psychological store is conscious; the vast majority, like the subsurface portion of an iceberg, is hidden from one's awareness.*

scious thoughts differ from conscious mental activities in that they are ideas, feelings, or events which, though retrievable, are not in awareness at the given moment. Thus, if we ask you to become aware of your clothing as it rests upon your skin, you find that this is relatively easy to do, although you had not been thinking of it until then. The last level, the *unconscious*, differs from both the conscious and preconscious in that it represents a collection of psychological events (feelings, ideas, and so on) that can be brought into awareness only with great difficulty. One of Freud's most controversial examples of unconscious thought was that all of us had incestuous feelings about our opposite-sexed parent.

Freud hypothesized that thoughts entered the unconscious level through a process or structure he termed an *intrapsychic censor*. That is, threatening ideas and feelings may be *repressed* (unconsciously forgotten) and pushed down into the unconscious. Rarely if ever will these ideas and feelings be allowed to surface at the preconscious or conscious level. Because Freud believed that the roots of mental disorder lay in the unconscious mind, he directed his therapeutic energies toward uncovering unconscious thoughts. Freud believed these thoughts were the source of psychological symptomatology (that is, the underlying "disease"). Indeed, a main goal of free association was to release unconscious repressed material.

The Psychic Triumvirate. The levels of consciousness also may be reflected in the concept of the three-part governing system that describes the nature of normal personality functioning. As a physician, Freud (1953) believed that an understanding of normal functioning was necessary before abnormality could be defined. To this end, he conceived three major normal processes operating within the psyche: the id, ego, and superego.

The first component of the psychic triumvirate, the *id*, may be thought of as a system composed of inborn instincts present from the beginning of life. The id is a bubbling cauldron of demands, needs, and wishes such as hunger, thirst, and the need for comfort, security, and love. According to Freud, *any* physiological or psychological imbalance may produce tension and thus immediately call into play the process of *homeostasis*, or a return to a balanced, tensionless state. The id requires tension reduction regardless of whether the tension is biological (such as hunger) or psychological (such as fear).

From the id processes also emerge the energizing forces for the mental apparatus or *psyche*. These psychic forces include the life instinct, *eros*, and the death instinct, *thanatos*. *Libido*, the energy of the life instinct, drives that part of the system which involves hunger, thirst, sex, and other needs maintaining survival. Sex was a very broad concept for Freud and generally was equated with pleasure. Indeed, the id operates on what Freud called the *pleasure principle*. According to Freud, pleasure is constantly sought and may be defined as any reduction of psychological or physical tension. Freud developed the concept of thanatos later in his life and generally saw it as a process competing with the life force and seeking to direct the psyche toward its own destruction, and hence quiescence. While it isn't completely clear from his writing, Freud seemed to believe that life itself was an unstable state that sought to return to the homeostatic state of death. It is not a happy thought that we may possess a drive toward self-destruction, but such a drive might explain such behaviors as cigarette-smoking in the face of the surgeon general's warnings or motorcycle-racing in spite of the dangers involved.

Besides being the source of both life and death forces, the id is characterized by its own particular mode of thought, called *primary-process thought*. According to Freud, the id cannot differentiate between what is real and what is imagined. Thus, thinking of a pastrami sandwich on rye may be the id's way of trying to satisfy the instinctual need of hunger. However, in reality, nothing satisfies hunger but real food. To deal with "reality," the *ego* develops, energized by the id for its own purposes.

Although the id can't differentiate reality from unreality, the ego can. The ego has the task of satisfying id demands in light of the exigencies of the world. For example, the infant's budding ego "knows" that a loud cry will bring mother to change a diaper or provide food. A problem solver and mediator between the id and reality, the ego usually operates on the *reality principle* as opposed to the id's pleasure principle. The ego acts primarily on the basis of what is real; it "knows" the only way to satisfy hunger is with real food. Further, unlike the id's primary-process thought, the ego is characterized by *secondary-process thought*, which develops between the first and second years of life. The ego's thinking deals with reality by means of logic and rational problem-solving.

The *superego* develops after the id and ego and out of the rules and regulations of parents and society. For example, in the real world the ego "sees" food and logically considers taking it and eating it. But the child learns soon that taking food from the plate of one's younger sibling can meet with stern disapproval from parents. Between the ages of 2 and 5 the child learns that some behaviors are "wrong" and some "right." Id needs usually cannot be met simply by considering reality, and the psyche requires a process to "watch over it" to ensure that it does not violate moral or societal codes. The overseer is the superego, composed of the *ego ideal* (a listing of "do's") and the *conscience* (a catalog of "don't's").

The ego ideal represents a person's image of his perfect self. In a boy, this might be a pro football star; in the boy's father, it also might be a pro football star! Failing to live up to the ego ideal can result in feelings of *shame* or lack of self-worth. Most contemplated behaviors are compared with the ideal behavior as represented in the ego ideal, and if the behavior doesn't measure up to ideals, feelings of worthlessness may ensue. Similarly, violating the precepts of the conscience (being a "bad" person) evokes feelings of *guilt*. Shame and guilt are usual emotional consequences that the superego may employ to control a person's behavior.

The conscience and ego ideal are *introjected* (taken in) from important people in the child's outside world, such as parents. According to Freud, rigidity or laxity of the superego may play a major role in the type of personality that evolves. For example, a rigid superego may produce a frightened person who feels guilty about "bad" thoughts or deeds such as masturbating. A lax or absent superego would be evident in those who show little or no regard for social and moral codes and who have low impulse control.

With the development of the superego, the components of the psychic triumvirate interact. Ideally, needs are mediated by the ego in balance with the id and superego; input is obtained from each of these systems prior to any behavior's being emitted. As an example, consider a situation in which a boy is pushed aside by another. The pushee's id might in essence say, "That makes me mad! Push that guy! Hit him! Break him to pieces!" The ego adds its voice of moderation and reality: "Listen, this guy is bigger than I am, his friends are with him, and I'm alone. If I cross him he'll beat me to a pulp!" The superego then might add its restrictive opinion: "Besides, hitting isn't nice! Remember what Mom and Dad always said. You'll feel very bad if you do this mean thing." Given all these inputs, the ego must decide what to do; in this instance, we hope it will choose not to fight. But these decisions often are compromises, and compromises usually don't work well with unreasonable instinctual demands. The ego must still fulfill the requirement of maintaining balance in the system.

Consider the plight of the ego, a sort of psychic traffic cop charged with the responsibility of meeting the needs of the organism and keeping things flowing smoothly, emotionally and physically, without severe congestion or traffic jams. Id demands and superego restrictions both must be dealt with. Reality contact must be upheld and *most* needs fulfilled. In order to protect the individual's psychological organization, the ego evolves a set of *defense mechanisms* to maintain its own stability. These defense mechanisms are considered the normal result of development. However, when used to excess they can lead to abnormal behavior. The basic defenses outlined by Freud are presented in Table 4-1. Defenses can soften disappointment and help a person adjust to everyday stresses.

We can give you an example of how defenses work by returning to the child in the fight. When we left him, we hoped his ego had chosen not to engage in battle, but that left his id still seething with aggression. The ego now has the problem of placating the id. One possible choice would be to aid the instinct release by fighting with a safer foe, such as a baby sister. However, the superego probably will not allow hitting a baby sister without ample justification, so the child may go home and wait for his sister to do something "wrong" so he can justifiably strike her. The id and superego are then basically satisfied, and the pressure on the ego is reduced. This particular defense mechanism is called *displacement* and is among the cognitive maneuvers available to the ego (see Table 4-1). Generally, defense mechanisms function so that the ego can maintain its integrity as well as its touch with reality.

In another defense mechanism, *reaction formation*, a person acts on and believes the opposite of his or her actual desires. Take a middle-aged woman whose id suddenly states, "I want to look at dirty pictures—lewd,

Table 4-1. *The ego defense mechanisms*

1. Rationalization	Sour grapes: "I didn't want to win the game; games aren't important." Sweet lemons: "I really wanted a harder exam, because it challenged me and made me aware of my weaknesses."
2. Repression	Unconscious forgetting of painful or dangerous thoughts: "How can you remember something you never knew you forgot?"
3. Projection	Placing blame for one's problems on other people or on things: After a bad shot in a tennis match, a player looks at his or her partner or racquet.
4. Regression	Going back to an earlier developmental level with lesser requirements and lower levels of aspiration: acting like a baby under pressure.
5. Introjection	Incorporating values or characteristics of feared others so that threat from these others is reduced: POWs are often reported to act like their captors or to beat fellow prisoners in hopes that their guards won't hurt them.
6. Denial	Refusal to accept existence of a threat so that fear of it is never really felt or justified: "What are you doing about Rocky's challenge to fight you in the schoolyard?" "What challenge?"
7. Displacement	Discharging feelings on persons or things that are less threatening than the actual feared object or person: A man is angry at his boss, so he gestures at other drivers all the way home.
8. Intellectualization	Dealing with problems only with the intellect, cutting off all feeling components: "Actually I'm not deeply concerned about my current state of affairs; in a classic treatise, Plato once said that one could rise above such things."
9. Reaction formation	Avoiding dangerous thoughts by acting as if the exact opposite thoughts existed: A woman who has had a terrible time on a date says over and over what a wonderful time she had, to convince herself as well as others.

lascivious, filthy porno!" Her ego might say, "You are a fine, warm person; people respect you. You'll lose face and dignity if you do this." Her superego might chime in, "You're a religious, good woman. You must never do this—that's bad!" Under stress, the ego may decide to deceive the superego and society by having the woman become a crusader *against* pornography. The woman may get herself appointed to a censorship board to "protect our youth," where she can view pornography, yet receive respect from the community, accolades from her superego, and a highly satisfied id!

Psychosexual Development. Freud (1953) proposed a series of five stages of development through which all people must pass on their way from birth to adulthood. At each stage, sexual instincts are gratified in a different way. Given the proper conditions, the development from one phase to the next can progress normally. However, if conditions aren't right, psychological difficulties may result. In fact, Freud goes so far as to say that all adult psychological problems may have their source in the failure to deal properly with the development stages before the age of 6. Sources of these problems were called *fixations* by Freud. In fixation, an individual fails to pass successfully through (*resolve*) a particular psychosexual phase or subphase. Progress through the psychosexual stages requires great amounts of the limited supply of psychic energy. If difficulties develop at a particular stage and some of the energy is committed to dealing with an early problem, a person may be left with less energy to deal with problems later, in the other stages of development. The particular point of fixation plays some part in determining adult personality types.

At birth, the infant emerges at the lowest developmental level, called the *oral stage*, where sexual gratification is focused primarily on the mouth. *Oral dependence*, the first substage, exists during the time the child is suckled and survives by receiving nourishment passively by mouth. However, the mouth can give as well as take, and with the appearance of teeth (at about 6 to 8 months of age) the child enters the *oral-aggressive* phase. Now the infant can affect the environment orally—by biting the nipple. Freud theorized that the person fixated at this level would be verbally aggressive—sarcastic and fond of making "biting" comments.

At approximately 1 year of age, the focus of sexual gratification changes from the mouth to the anus. Due to maturation and external pressures from parents to toilet train, the child enters the *anal phase*. Obviously, the time at which toilet training becomes most important usually depends upon parental decision. In recent years, the onset of training typically has come later; when the child is 2 to 3 years of age. Of course, there may be competitive parents who begin this phase earlier. For example, Felix Unger, the compulsive fellow in the Neil Simon comedy *The Odd Couple*, claims to have been trained by the age of 4 months! Regardless of when toilet training actually begins, it is seen to represent a crucial step in personality development. Freud believed that two different extreme personality types could result from difficulties at this stage: the *anal retentive* individual (exemplified by Felix Unger) and the *anal expulsive* individual (represented by Oscar Madison, Felix's sloppy other half in the play).

As the child's pants become clean and dry and the bed no longer needs airing, the focus of gratification shifts once again—to the *genitals*. The so-called *phallic stage*, so named in spite of the fact that girls also go through it, occurs somewhere around ages 4 to 6. The phallic stage determines the child's sexual identity and lays the foundation for adult sexual behavior. The developmental task of the child at the phallic stage varies according to gender. Freud theorized primarily about the development of the male, considering the female only in passing.

Theoretically, at the onset of the phallic stage, a boy changes his sexual focus from eliminative functions to people. The energizing force of the id leads him to have sexual thoughts about his mother. At this point the boy is in the *Oedipal phase*. Because of the father, the Oedipal phase soon becomes the Oedipal crisis. Let us explain: As the attraction to his mother arises, the boy's

According to Freud, how children deal with toilet training may significantly affect their later personalities. (Photo by Joseph Czarnecki.)

ego fears that if the father finds out about his sexual motives he will cut off his young penis. This *castration anxiety* drives the child to resolve his forbidden sexual feelings. Freud chose the term *Oedipal* because of the similarity between his theoretical notions and the mythical story of Oedipus Rex, who unknowingly killed his father and married his own mother. Most 5-year-olds would find this a difficult method for resolving their conflicts. Normally, the child instead represses and pushes even deeper into the unconscious the threatening sexual thoughts. According to Freud, the child forgets the sexual thoughts even though he never was aware of them. In spite of the repression, the sexual impulses may continue to seek expression. To guard against the possibility that these impulses may be observed by the father, the child begins to act like his father. Through this ego process of identification he can safely protect himself from his father's wrath.

Freud's theorizing about females at this stage is more sketchy and confusing. He introduces the *Electra phase,* in which there is a shift from initial attachment to the mother to sexual love for the father, and then back again to identification with the mother. The male fear of castration also occurs in females, but earlier. Freud hypothesized that females feel they have been cheated by not having a penis. The girl supposedly blames her mother for the loss because she observes that her mother "lost" her penis too. This *penis envy* leads to resentment toward the mother and a closer relationship with the father in hope of regaining a penis. This relationship with her father is called the Electra relationship. The Electra complex is resolved by the girl's identifying with her mother so as not to lose her love. Fearing the loss of love in the case of the girl is admittedly less horrible than fearing the loss of love plus one's penis in the case of the boy. According to Freud, this difference leads to a less complete resolution of the Electra conflict in females than of the Oedipal conflict in males. As a result, females may never be as strongly identified with their mothers as boys are with their fathers. Further, girls usually remain closer to their fathers than boys do to their mothers.

Following the phallic period, and reflecting the successful operation of repressed sexuality, the child enters the *latency* or *homoerotic phase*, which lasts to the onset of puberty. During this time, boys and girls usually don't play with one another. There is marked animosity between the sexes, and interactions are likely to be characterized by teasing and fighting. The signs that all sexual impulses have not been completely repressed may be observed in the child's telling of simple "dirty jokes," playing games of doctor where one child "examines" the other, and sensitivity to parental sexual behavior.

Following the latency period, which is predominantly sexually dormant, comes the sexually active phase, the *genital period*. Beginning at puberty, energized by physiological-hormonal changes, the repressed phallic-stage sexuality typically reappears. The fear also reappears that if sexuality is directed at the opposite-sexed parent, guilt or castration may result. To prevent possible harm, the ego usually implements the defense of *displacement*, in which the repressed sexual instincts may be expressed, but are redirected toward peers of the opposite sex. If successful, displacement allows the child more successfully to complete his or her psychosexual development. The chain of life can continue toward courting, marriage, and procreation.

Concept of Being Different

With the last stage of psychosexual development, there should be a smooth interaction among the id, ego, and superego; needs and wishes will generally be fulfilled directly or indirectly through defensive manipulations. However, when things go wrong inside the psychic system, abnormal behavior may develop. To Freud (1953), mental symptoms were merely "signs" that something was wrong with the "inside" workings of the id, ego, and superego.

For example, Freud thought that a psychotic symptom pattern was usually an indication that unconscious impulses were so strong that the ego was overwhelmed and could not maintain its touch with reality. Severe emotional breakdowns typically were seen as the result of "weak ego" or "ego disintegration." In other words, the id impulses come to control the psychic system, and primary-process thought in the form of hallucinations

During the genital phase of healthy psychosexual development, sexual attraction (once focused on opposite-sex parents) is redirected toward opposite-sex peers. (Photo by David Powers.)

and delusions replaces the rational thought of the secondary process. Under such pressure, people can no longer function at their high level of psychosexual development, but must regress to an earlier, simpler stage. Freud perceived severely disturbed people as regressed to infantile levels. In his terms, they are attempting to satisfy their own needs through fantasy

The Hydraulic Model of Symptom Development in Freudian Theory

The following diagram may be thought of as representing the psychic system. Internal and external demands are represented by the downward-moving piston. The tank, filled with water that cannot be compressed indefinitely, portrays the source of behaviors. Normal channels of behavior are represented by the faucets, which are socially and personally acceptable outlets for pressure. If demands on the system are great and do not have acceptable outlets, the system, requiring tension release, breaks open and allows abnormal release of pressure in the form of a symptom. The goal of the Freudian psychotherapist is not simply to patch the hole, but to reduce the pressure on the system. Reducing the pressure would allow the break to "heal" and thus restore normal avenues of release. Pressure is relieved by the therapist via his or her attempts to determine the cause of the increased stress upon the system.

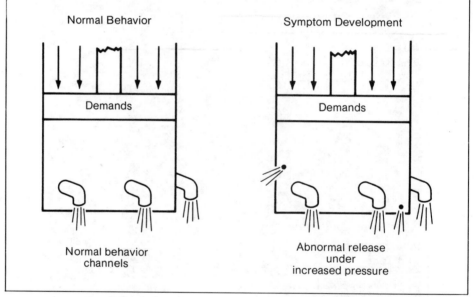

Normal Behavior

Demands

Normal behavior
channels

Symptom Development

Demands

Abnormal release
under
increased pressure

and are not facing reality. Because the ego can't deal with reality demands, these people will frequently exhibit sexual behavior characteristic of earlier stages of development; they may masturbate in public or smear feces on walls, for example.

In neurosis, the ego doesn't disintegrate; rather, sets of rigid behaviors develop which are designed to protect the ego from further harm. In a sense, defense mechanisms are overused, so that threatening impulses usually are not consciously experienced and thus not dealt with. Since the ego ties up so much psychic energy in controlling id impulses, there is less available for dealing effectively with new conflicts, and the general level of functioning falls. For Freud, neurotic symptoms reflect ways of trying to cope with anxiety generated in the internal psychic system. Symptoms also may serve as signals that something is wrong with that system.

Psychoanalytic theory has been used in the explanation and treatment of a majority of behavior disorders. Reflecting its importance, we have included psychoanalytic explanations in most of the descriptive and treatment chapters of this text.

NEO-FREUDIAN DEVELOPMENTAL THEORIES

Also called ego psychologists, neo-Freudians are credited with changing the primary emphasis of psychoanalytic theory from the id to the ego. Although they maintain their affiliation with most of the assumptions of psychoanalysis, their theoretical differences with Freud led them to develop alternative explanations for human behavior. For example, early neo-Freudians such as Carl Jung, Alfred Adler, and Karen Horney generally moved away from the emphasis on sex as a motivator of behavior, which characterized Freud's thinking, and focused more on personal and interpersonal aspects of behavior. Later neoanalysts considered social as well as personal components of life to be important in the development of behavior patterns. We will describe more fully two neoanalysts' theories that are applicable to the explanation of abnormal behavior. First, we will describe the social-interpersonal perspective of Harry Stack Sullivan; second, we will discuss the theory of psychosocial development of Erik Erikson. These explanations will be important in later discussions of the psychoses and disorders of special age groups.

The Social and Interpersonal Theory of
Harry Stack Sullivan

Harry Stack Sullivan emphasized interpersonal relationships as the single most important factor in normal personality development. Sullivan (1953) proposed six stages of development, each representing increasing degrees of awareness of self and others and of integration into society. Unlike psychosexual developmental stages, indices of successful completion of Sullivan's stages are *interpersonal* and *behavioral* rather than intrapsychic and instinctual (Levy, 1970).

Infancy (birth to language acquisition), the first of the six stages, is characterized by autistic communication—communication that is idiosyncratic, illogical, or individualized. With the onset of speech the individual enters the stage called *childhood*, where socialization is rapid (eating and toilet habits are taught). Self-generated anxiety first appears here and functions, as it did for Freud, as a warning that the person is being exposed to experiences that are inconsistent with his or her current concept of self. The need for what Sullivan calls *compeers* signals the beginning of stage three, the *juvenile era* (at about 8 or 9 years of age). Compeers are people on the same age level who have extremely similar attitudes. Through interactions with compeers, infantile autistic thinking and acting usually fade into the background. Fourth is the *preadolescent* stage, which generally lasts until around age 12. It is in preadolescence that the capacity to love typically develops and children find others meaning as much to them as their own selves. They share thoughts and feelings with others (usually one best friend or "chum" of the same sex). In this stage, the child also experiences *consensual validation*, learning about others and their effects upon him or her, and about his or her effects upon others. The physiological onset of puberty signals entrance into stage five, early *adolescence*, where sexual impulses appear. In the face of cultural taboos against sex and early marriage, if the individual can establish a stable pattern of sexual behavior, he can then enter the final stage of *mature adulthood*.

Although their theoretical stages of development differ, Sullivan seemed to agree with Freud in focusing on anxiety as the core of maladjustment. Sullivan saw the security of the self as very important and to be maintained at all costs. To ensure this, Sullivan postulated, people develop *security operations* (similar to defense mechanisms) which aid in avoiding

Sullivan believed that normal development included the formation of intimate relationships with same-sex peers between the ages of 9 and 12. (Photo by David Powers.)

experiences leading to anxiety and threat to the self. Neurosis develops when security operations are imperfect and anxiety is not avoided, or when rigid dependence on unsuccessful security operations occurs. Schizophrenia is seen as extensive distortion in which reality-oriented functioning is so severely repressed that for most purposes patients are no longer in contact with the outside world. Disordered behavior is usually brought about by *interpersonal* frustrations and conflicts. Psychotic behavior represents the final phase in a series of attempts to avoid or establish effective interpersonal relationships.

The Psychosocial Perspective of Erik Erikson

Erik Erikson also proposes a normal personality-development sequence. In his *Childhood and Society* (1963), Erikson presents eight *psychosocial stages* of development, each of which includes a *basic developmental conflict* that must be successfully resolved if the person is to become normally adjusted. Table 4-2 presents Erikson's stages and their associated goals and conflicts. Among the most crucial stages is that of puberty and adolescence, in which the *identity crisis* (Who am I? Why do I exist?) occurs and a person moves closer to psychological and social well-being. Like Sullivan, Erikson strongly emphasizes adolescence as a crucial period in the developing personality. Erikson's conflicts do not simply come and go, but are always present; certain ones emerge as more salient at different times of life. However, resolution of earlier conflicts can affect resolution of later ones. For example, failure to resolve the identity-crisis conflict can be a source of maladaptive behavior and may prevent an individual from successfully meeting the demands of later stages. Such a person couldn't establish intimate long-term relationships, might stagnate and cease to grow emotionally, or might experience despair and hopelessness in later life. On the other hand, the person who successfully

Table 4-2. *Erikson's psychosocial stages of development and their associated nuclear conflicts*

Psychosocial Stage	Conflict
1. Oral-sensory	Basic trust versus mistrust
2. Muscular-anal	Autonomy versus shame and doubt
3. Locomotor-genital	Initiative versus guilt
4. Latency	Industry versus inferiority
5. Puberty and adolescence	Identity versus role confusion
6. Young adulthood	Intimacy versus isolation
7. Adulthood	Generativity versus stagnation
8. Maturity	Ego integrity versus despair

Based on Erikson, 1963.

emerges from the ego-identity stage feels unified and can enter into deep relationships with others.

HUMANISTIC AND EXISTENTIAL THEORIES OF BEHAVIOR

Unlike Freud, who perceived people as instinct-driven beings in need of control, the humanistic and existential theorists typically perceive people as social beings who are inherently good, have a drive toward maximizing their capabilities, and possess free will. The various humanistic theorists emphasize slightly different aspects of behavioral development, but they are all generally optimistic about people's basic potential for positive growth. The humanistic-existential theories are important in the text in that they form the foundation for many of the individual and group psychotherapies we will discuss in Section VIII.

Carl Rogers and Self-Actualization

In addition to the primary humanistic concept of people as basically good, Carl Rogers considered the most important characteristic of the psychological structure to be an *actualizing tendency* acting as the initiator and motivator of behavior. The actualizing tendency may be thought of as a driving force that directs a person toward maintaining or enhancing the self. The primary motivation of each person is not merely to survive, but to grow, to develop his or her full potential, and to experience *pleasurable tension*. For Rogers, behavior seems to serve the purpose of achieving or maintaining actualization.

Normal behavior usually involves a certain sequence of events, beginning with the innate drives of actualization and concluding with the conscious evaluation of actions, as shown in Figure 4-2. In general, a person avoids

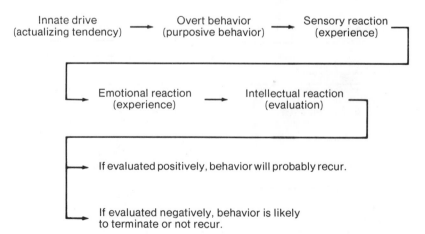

Figure 4-2. *A summary of innate self-evaluative sequences as conceptualized by Carl Rogers*

negatively valued experiences and pursues those that are positively valued. If experiences result in maintenance or enhancement of self, they are repeated; if not, they tend to disappear from the behavioral repertoire. For example, a person who experiences success and pleasure on dates is likely to continue dating; one who fails may seek other social outlets. Rogers believes that people go through this evaluative sequence almost continuously. Behavior disorder is thought to occur if and when evaluative behavior patterns (self-evaluation) are distorted by inappropriate learning. In the healthy individual, learned self-

According to Rogers, the experience of unconditional positive regard in the family encourages self-actualization. (Photo by Sherry Suris.)

evaluative responses and the seeking of approval from others agree with one's own "organismic evaluation." A child who receives *unconditional positive regard* (an atmosphere necessary for normal growth and crucial to psychotherapy) doesn't have to fight an uphill battle for acceptance and can effect innate and learned self-evaluative sequences unhampered. In simpler words, a child who feels totally accepted as a person by his or her parents is free to develop in other areas and need not worry about being secure at home. If this unhampered condition is reached, the person moves toward positive self-regard and self-actualization.

In an adjusted person, Rogers believes, the same behaviors usually end up satisfying both self and others. Abnormal behavior can result from a conflict between one's own self-evaluation and the evaluations that one accepts from others. Thus, a child who learns from parents to believe that she or he is bad may experience conflict between this evaluation and the self-actualizing tendency that says she or he is good. The result is anxiety.

Anxiety may occur when a person becomes aware of behavior that contradicts his or her usual self-evaluations; this anxiety can be handled with one of two defenses. A person may stop experiencing anxiety either by *denial to awareness* of the anxiety-producing event (such as not paying attention to the fact that a bully is making threats of bodily harm) or by *distortion in awareness* (seeing the bully's threats as really being friendly advice). Neurotic and psychotic symptoms, respectively, can be understood as one of these two basic faulty habit patterns. For Rogers, other people are extremely important in whether personality development is normal, and the atmosphere in which a child is reared can have dramatic effects on his or her later functioning.

Abraham Maslow's Emphasis on a Need Hierarchy

Similar to Rogers in his humanistic emphasis on inherent goodness and potential for growth and actualization, Abraham Maslow has focused on human needs and their effects upon behavior (Maslow, 1968, 1971). Theorizing that unless basic needs are met, higher ones cannot be satisfied, Maslow proposed the hierarchy of needs depicted in Figure 4-3. People are motivated to reach the top of the hierarchy, but some may stop for fear of losing what they have, while others may be blocked by external social forces. Those who can't continue may experience deep feelings of nonfulfillment, move toward a feeling of nonbeing, and exhibit disordered behavior.

Phenomenological-Existential Analysis

Different from Rogers and Maslow in their greater emphasis on conscious choice and awareness, the phenomenologist-existentialists believe that behavior is determined by the manner in which a person *perceives* life's events. People are typically seen as logical, feeling beings whose fate is not under the control of base forces within them but, rather, is rationally directed. Among the most forceful of the existential analysts is Binswanger (1963). He theorizes

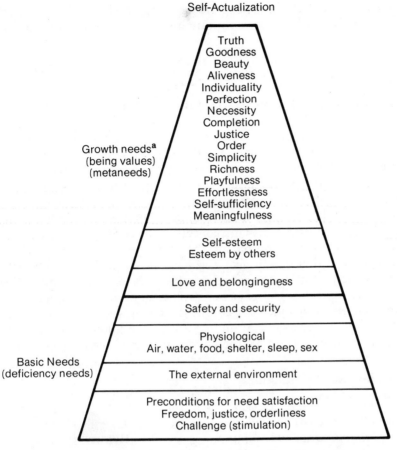

Self-Actualization

Truth
Goodness
Beauty
Aliveness
Individuality
Perfection
Necessity
Completion
Justice
Order
Simplicity
Richness
Playfulness
Effortlessness
Self-sufficiency
Meaningfulness

Growth needs[a]
(being values)
(metaneeds)

Self-esteem
Esteem by others

Love and belongingness

Safety and security

Physiological
Air, water, food, shelter, sleep, sex

Basic Needs
(deficiency needs)

The external environment

Preconditions for need satisfaction
Freedom, justice, orderliness
Challenge (stimulation)

[a]Growth needs are all of equal importance (not hierarchical).

Figure 4-3. *Maslow's hierarchy of human needs. Based on* Motivation and Personality, *2nd Edition, by A. H. Maslow. Copyright © 1970 by Abraham H. Maslow. Reprinted by permission of Harper & Row, Publishers, Inc.*

that the healthy individual enjoys a balance of three experiential modes: the *Umwelt* (the realm of biological drives and physical limitations); the *Mitwelt* (the world of other people); and the *Eigenwelt* (one's own collection of phenomenological experiences). The normal person functions well in all three; the abnormal person usually does not. Anxiety and disordered behavior can occur when an individual's perception of what is good for him disagrees with values and attitudes imposed on him by powerful others.

The philosopher Søren Kierkegaard (1946) differs from Binswanger in his greater emphasis on the idea that people are what they make themselves. Through free choice, a person can adopt an authentic versus a nonauthentic mode of being. In the latter, the person depends on and is shaped by others; in the former, he takes full responsibility for himself and what happens to him.

Existential anxiety, a universal experience, occurs when each person faces the responsibilities for his or her own fate and rejects a nonauthentic mode of living.

LEARNING THEORIES OF HUMAN BEHAVIOR

Having traced the theoretical movement away from Freud's emphasis on intrapsychic control of behavior to the existentialists' focus on free will, we arrive now at the learning-theory approaches to normal and abnormal behavior. The learning explanations are based upon a belief that rather than being motivated by internal, instinctual forces or being consciously and freely chosen, behavior is instilled and maintained by events and forces outside individuals. Learning theorists usually conceive of abnormal behavior as simply a subset of all behavior, acquired by the same rules of learning as so-called normal behavior. Abnormality is viewed as faulty learning, or nonlearning, of appropriate actions and thoughts. Since these theorists believe that learning processes are at the core of behavior problems, an understanding of normal learning processes is a logical requirement. Among the theories based on learning, those underlying classical and operant conditioning and imitation are among the most important for the understanding of behavior.

Classical Conditioning

The most important early work on classical conditioning was performed by the Russian physiologist Ivan Pavlov (1927). Also known as *respondent conditioning*, classical conditioning is considered by many psychologists to be a basic form of learning. The learning process diagrammed in Figure 4-4 emerged from Pavlov's study of learning in dogs. Pavlov placed a dog in which he had implanted a salivary fistula (a tube through the side of the cheek ending

Before conditioning (innate reflexes):

UCS   ⟶   UCR
(food powder)   (salivation)

During conditioning:

CS   +   UCS ⟶ UCR
(bell)   (food powder)   (salivation)

After conditioning:

CS   ⟶   CR
(bell)   (salivation)

Figure 4-4. *Classical conditioning*

in the salivary gland) in a restraining apparatus. When food powder was blown into the animal's mouth, the dog responded by salivating and the saliva flowed through the tube for collection and measurement. The food powder was called the *unconditioned stimulus* or UCS. Without any previous learning, the UCS led to the response of salivation, which was the *unconditioned response* or UCR. Pavlov then associated the UCS with a previously *neutral stimulus* such as the ringing of a bell. Time after time the bell was sounded just before the food powder was presented. After many trials, Pavlov found that when the bell was sounded *alone*—without the food powder—the animal salivated. The previously neutral stimulus was now a *conditioned stimulus* (CS) and resulted in a *conditioned response* (CR). Although the CR was of lesser magnitude than the UCR, it was still salivation and it was elicited by a previously neutral stimulus. This, then, is an example of a simple form of learning: by contiguous (in time) association with a UCS, a once neutral event takes on the ability to produce new behavior, whereas prior to conditioning it had little real effect.

An example of classical conditioning in humans to which you may be able to relate is the following. Suppose a piece of sour pickle were placed in your mouth. You would no doubt salivate heavily. Were a buzzer to be sounded just prior to this pickle placement, after a short time you would salivate at the sound of the buzzer. In this example, the pickle in the mouth is the UCS; the once neutral buzzer, the CS; the salivation in response to the pickle, the UCR; the *learned* salivation in response to the buzzer, the CR.

Basic Phenomena in Classical Conditioning. To understand fully the way in which classical conditioning can be used to explain human behavior, it is necessary to understand the phenomena common to this form of acquiring behaviors. The development of a classically conditioned response and the procedure for varying the strength of such a response are depicted in Figure 4-5. In the first phase of response development, called *acquisition*, the association between CS and UCS is built. Usually the more repetitions (trials) of the pairing of CS and UCS and the stronger the UCS, the stronger the association. A second stage is *extinction*. Here the CS is presented repeatedly *without* the UCS; soon the CS no longer elicits the CR—the conditioned response is extinguished. A last phase, *spontaneous recovery*, represents an increase in the strength of the CR after extinction is complete and time has passed. Thus, in our pickle example, if you had stopped salivating to the CS (buzzer) following extinction, were we to bring you back in a week and sound the buzzer again, you would salivate. However, without presentation of the UCS (pickle) once again, extinction would usually recur, this time more rapidly.

In a demonstration of a phenomenon termed *higher-order conditioning*, Pavlov later showed that another neutral stimulus such as a light could be paired with an original CS such as a bell (see Figure 4-6). Without ever having been associated with the *original* UCS (food powder), the light could yield salivation (CR) on its own. To complicate matters further, CRs occurred not only to the original CS but to *similar* stimuli, such as bells of different tones. This phenomenon is called *stimulus generalization* and is a

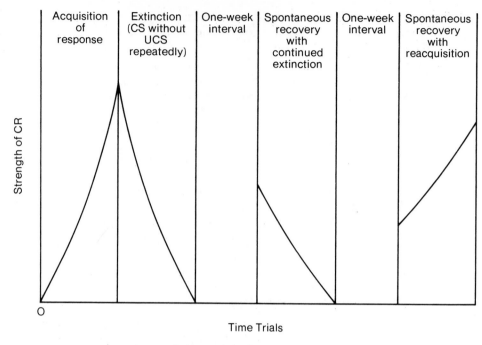

Figure 4-5. *Phases of classical conditioning*

very important concept in the behavioral analysis of abnormality, as we will see in later chapters on anxiety and schizophrenia. Figure 4-7 provides an example of stimulus generalization. Essentially the opposite of generalization is *discrimination learning,* in which an organism learns to respond only to certain specific situations. An example is a child's learning that red means stop and green means go on traffic lights.

Classical Conditioning and Behavior That Is Different. The concepts of conditioning, generalization, and discrimination can be helpful in understanding normal and abnormal behavior. A clear application of these Pavlovian concepts to the development of an abnormal fear came from the noted behaviorist John B. Watson. Watson and Rayner (1920) performed an

During conditioning:

$$CS \quad + \quad CS \longrightarrow CR$$
$$(light) \qquad (bell) \qquad (salivation)$$

After higher-order conditioning:

$$CS \longrightarrow CR$$
$$(light) \qquad (salivation)$$

Figure 4-6. *Higher-order conditioning*

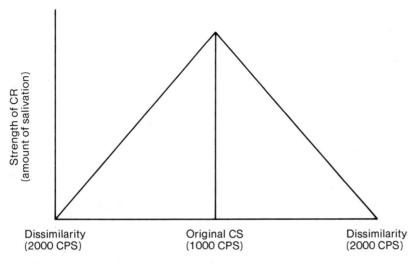

Figure 4-7. *Stimulus generalization of a conditioned response of salivation to a 1000 CPS tone*

experiment of dubious ethicality in classically conditioning fear in an 11-month-old infant named Albert. In their classical conditioning of Albert, the UCS was the noise from a hammer striking a steel bar behind the child's head when he wasn't expecting it. The UCR was the infant's startle reaction to the loud noise (screaming, trembling, and shrieking). The CS was a white rat that was shown immediately before the presentation of the unexpected loud noise. After a few trials, Albert responded to the furry rat (not Watson) alone in the same way he did to the loud noise—he began to cry violently. The white rat was now a CS and Albert's startle reaction to the CS was a CR. Later theorists have termed his reaction a *conditioned emotional response*, or learned fear.

Stimulus generalization from the original CS soon occurred, and Albert reportedly became afraid of a host of other white, furry things, such as stuffed animals, his grandfather's white beard, and Santa Claus. In this experiment, Watson and Rayner demonstrated that a phobialike irrational fear could be created simply by classical conditioning.

Pavlov also had observed seemingly learned abnormal behavior developing in animals in his laboratory. While studying dogs' abilities to handle increasingly difficult discriminations, Pavlov required his animals to differentiate between a circle and an ellipse. Initially, he made the discrimination quite easy, but as trials progressed the ellipse was made more and more circular and thus harder to distinguish from a circle. When the discrimination became extremely difficult, some of his dogs began to whine, squeal, and thrash about in the apparatus. Several normally docile animals became wild. Pavlov, thinking that perhaps this "abnormal" behavior was due to their being overworked and fatigued, removed them from the apparatus and gave them a rest. However, later, when he tried to put them back into their harnesses, the dogs again became upset. Pavlov termed their behavior *experimental neurosis*. He found that an effective treatment was several nights on a farm in the country away from the lab *and from Pavlov*. Later analysts realized the dogs' problems probably stemmed from an insoluble discrimination task that resulted in an anxiety-producing conflict. To the learning theorist, the important implication of experimental neurosis is that response patterns similar to abnormal behavior in humans can be produced by simple classical conditioning.

Operant Conditioning

Unlike classical conditioning, in which a response is elicited by an outside stimulus, in *operant learning* a response typically is emitted by an organism prior to some reward or punishment. Classical learning is thought to be limited in humans to the involuntary musculature and operant learning is seen as primarily involving voluntary movement. While we will maintain this distinction throughout the text, there is recent evidence (Hearst, 1975) that in actuality there may be no real difference between these two types of learning.

Basic Phenomena in Operant Conditioning. The basic phenomena of reinforcement, extinction, and punishment are common to both classical and operant conditioning, so they won't be redescribed here. We will begin the discussion of operant conditioning with a description of its basic methodology, which diverges considerably from that of classical conditioning. The classic apparatus for studying operant conditioning is the Skinner Box, named for its inventor, B. F. Skinner (1938). A brief discussion of this apparatus will allow us to present the concepts relevant to understanding operant conditioning. Consider a rat, deprived of water for 24 hours and placed in the strange surroundings of a Skinner Box. It experiences thirst which can be satisfied by drinking water available from a water dipper in the box. When this dipper enters the box through a small opening it makes a clearly audible click. The rat, which tends to orient to the sound, usually explores the area around the click and finds the water. The rat responds as though it "knows" where water is in the box. The experimenter now can begin a shaping procedure in which movements toward the goal of pressing a metal bar (usually near the dipper) for water are *selectively reinforced* by the appearance of water. In this method, called *successive approximation*, the rat at first need only face the bar to receive water; later, it may have to press the bar, and so forth. We should note here that this operant training contains a classical-conditioning component, because each time the click is sounded it is associated with water. The click becomes a CS and after training can be used to reinforce future learning. Through its association with water, the *primary* reinforcer, the click, becomes a *secondary* reinforcer.

Once the bar-press response is acquired through shaping and approximation, the experimenter may alter the rat's behavior by manipulating various factors such as the amount of water given, the time the animal goes without water, and, most important for us, the schedules of reinforcement. Until now we have discussed continuous or 100% reinforcement. Although usually a requirement for successful classical conditioning, continuous reinforcement may be neither necessary nor optimal in operant learning.

As an alternative to continuous reinforcement, partial or intermittent reinforcement was originally used by Skinner because he was tired of using up his rewards of food pellets so quickly (Skinner, 1959). Since he had to make them by hand—a tedious task—he decided to give the reward every few responses rather than every time. Serendipitously he discovered the *partial-reinforcement effect:* strength and resistance to extinction of acquired responses vary under different reinforcement schedules. Specifically, extinction of responses doesn't occur as readily when reinforcement during learning is administered intermittently rather than continuously. Partial reinforcement is a better approximation of the real world, where it is rare for any response to be followed *always* by reinforcement. Behavioral stability seems to depend on partial reinforcement. A stapler is a good example of a machine that usually provides us with continuous reinforcement. In using a stapler we usually extinguish after one or at most two nonreinforcement trials; that is, if no staple comes out, we will stop to check whether another response is needed, such as reloading. However, if our stapler sometimes sticks and we are used to receiving a staple anywhere from every one to ten presses, when the stapler is empty (that is, extinction has begun), we may go on pressing a large number of times before we check for reloading. We continue to press the stapler long into extinction because of the partial-reinforcement effect. Partial reinforcement can be given in various ways and according to a variety of schedules. As seen in Table 4-3, many real-life behaviors can be seen as maintained by partial-reinforcement schedules.

Having now looked at schedules of reinforcement, we are ready to look at reinforcements per se. A reinforcer is any event that, when presented after a given behavior, tends to increase the probability that the behavior will occur again. E. L. Thorndike (1913) presented the *law of effect,* one of the earliest conceptualizations of reinforcement. He proposed that behaviors resulting in a satisfying state of affairs tend to occur more often; those resulting in annoyance lead to a reduction in frequency. Defining his concepts of *satisfaction* and *annoyance,* Thorndike stated:

> By a satisfying state of affairs is meant one which an animal does nothing to avoid, often doing such things as to attain and preserve it. By a discomforting or annoying state of affairs is meant one which the animal commonly avoids and abandons [p. 245].

Besides being conceptualized as a satisfying event, a reward can also be seen as a *drive-reducing* event: the satisfaction of a biological or psychological drive is

Table 4-3. *Variations in partial reinforcement*

Reinforcement Schedule	Reward Method	Example
Fixed-ratio	Reward given after a *specific* number of responses	A child receives a gold star for every ten math problems done correctly. Work on the nine nonrewarded problems is maintained by a fixed-ratio schedule.
Variable-ratio	Reward given *on the average* after some number of responses	A person playing a slot machine wins *on the average* after every ten plays —sometimes after five plays, other times after fifteen, and so on. Continuous play on nonreinforced trials is maintained by a variable-ratio schedule.
Fixed-interval	Reward given after a *specific* amount of time has passed and responding has continued.	A worker is paid once a week for working an entire week without receiving pay each day. Working on days other than payday is maintained by a fixed-interval schedule.
Variable-interval	Reward given after a variable period of time but *on the average* occurs after some identifiable interval.	A salesman's rewards come irregularly in the form of commissions. If sales occur intermittently, rewards occur intermittently. Selling between commissions is maintained by a variable-interval schedule.

seen as reinforcing to an individual and will produce an increase in frequency of behavior. For example, a hungry child is reinforced by food because food reduces the hunger drive. A description of how behavior frequency can be varied using reinforcement is found in Figure 4-8. Note that positive and negative experiences can be manipulated to maintain or alter behavior.

The principles demonstrated in Figure 4-8 can be applied to what Becker (1964) has called *grandma's rule.* This simply states, "You can do something you want to do a lot, if you first do something you don't want to do as much." Grandma's rule is also known as *the principle of prepotency* as a determiner of what is reinforcing (Premack, 1959, 1965). According to Premack, *any* behavior can be reinforcing if the circumstances are such that an organism would prefer performing it more than some other behavior. Utilizing this principle, Premack (1965) has demonstrated that a child can be placed in a situation where she or he will eat candy (traditionally *the* reinforcer) in order to be allowed to play a pinball machine (a response that at the time was

	Positive Reward	Punishment
Present	Increased frequency	Decreased frequency
Withdraw	Decreased frequency	Increased frequency

Figure 4-8. *Differential effects upon frequency of behavior of presenting or withholding reinforcers. Positive rewards include such things as money, privileges, or verbal praise. Punishments might include having to rewrite a term paper or pay a fine.*

prepotent to candy-eating). The exact nature of reinforcement is unclear, but one thing is certain: there are *no* universal reinforcers that can alter all behaviors.

Operant Conditioning and Behavior That Is Different. Simple positive reinforcement of any behavior usually will result in its increase, and different behavioral strengths usually will be achieved, depending upon the schedule of reward. By rewarding a child for withdrawal from others and by punishing the child's approach to parents, a caretaker can shape him or her to be a loner. By responding to a child only when he or she breaks something or is noisy, parents may unwittingly be reinforcing aggressive behavior. By listening only to sadness, weeping, and self-pity, parents may increase the frequency of depressive behavior. From the operant perspective, most behaviors can be altered in strength and frequency by presenting or withdrawing positive and negative stimuli.

Operant conditioning alone can be used to explain acquisition of certain abnormal behavior, but the combination of operant learning with classical conditioning affords a more realistic view of the relationship between anxiety and symptom development. A combination of these two types of conditioning, *dual-process theory*, was applied to the production of abnormal behavior in animals by Solomon and Wynne (1954). These experimenters trained dogs to jump across a barrier between two sides of a box in order to escape from a strong shock. After the dogs learned how to escape the shock, they were kept in a limited area of the box and given a number of "unavoidable" shocks (UCS) that were paired with a buzzer. The buzzer then became a CS and was reacted to as if it were as aversive as the shock. Finally, when escape once again was made possible, the buzzer was sounded to determine whether the dogs would jump the hurdle to escape from it. Over 80% of the dogs responded to the buzzer by leaping the barrier, manifesting what could best be described as "irrational fear" of the buzzer (irrational to those not knowing what the animal had experienced previously). This experimental procedure is called *avoidance learning* and involves an organism's acquisition of an avoidance response that works so well that the actual aversive stimulation (shock) rarely is experienced. However, the animal never seems to find out whether the shock is present or not. It always behaves as if it were there.

Solomon and Wynne later removed the shock apparatus from the jumping box and attempted without much success to extinguish the fear response to the buzzer. Trial after trial, they found that the dogs would continue to jump at the sound of the buzzer. The reason for the continuous jumping probably lay in the establishment of a fear-reducing response system that produced reinforcement for the jumping behavior. In this system, the presentation of the buzzer elicited fear (process 1—classical conditioning); fear is a negative, aversive state for an organism, and the animal tries to reduce it. Jumping out of the situation after the buzzer comes on helps the animal escape the box before it can learn that the shock is not forthcoming. Reduction of fear is assumed to be reinforcing, and since this reinforcement follows jumping out of the area of the box where the shock had been produced, jumping is strengthened every time the animal is placed in the box (process 2—operant conditioning). Thus, even though the experimenters were trying to extinguish the fear response, they couldn't easily overcome the "neuroticlike avoidant behavior" of their animals.

Dual-process development and maintenance of a fear response can be helpful in understanding a simple phobia in humans. Consider the person who possesses an irrational fear of tall buildings. Imagine that the fear originated when as a child he was lost by his mother at the top of a 30-story skyscraper. The fear of being lost may have become associated with the tall building via classical conditioning. Later, when approaching other tall buildings, the CR of anxiety appears. Because anxiety is aversive, the person attempts to reduce it by turning and walking away from the building, thereby dissipating the anxiety. The reduction of an aversive stimulus is a reward, so walking away from tall buildings is strengthened as a response. However, the avoidance of tall buildings prevents a person from ever facing the fear and finding out that the buildings are harmless. Like the jumping of Solomon and Wynne's dogs, the phobic behavior probably will be maintained and never extinguish without corrective learning (treatment).

Dual-process theory will be relevant to our later description of neurotic symptom development and behavioral therapies. Although not adequate in all instances (Bolles, 1975), the theory is still accepted as an explanation for certain types of abnormal behavior in which anxiety is a primary factor (Bandura, 1977).

Observational Learning

Although classical conditioning and operant learning can account for a wide range of behaviors, people don't learn everything they know by actually experiencing stimulation, response, and reinforcement. In fact, as Bandura (1977) has pointed out:

Most human behavior is learned observationally through modelling; from observing others one forms an idea of how new behaviors
are performed, and on later occasions this coded information serves
as a guide for action [p. 22].

An example of Bandura's point is that as a result of watching numerous
Western movies, if we were ever lost in the desert, most of us would probably know how to get water from a cactus.

Bandura has noted that four processes are necessary for the successful acquisition of specific behaviors via this type of modeling. First, *attentional processes* are necessary: people can't learn by observation if they
don't perceive accurately the significant components of observed behavior.
Besides attention, a modeling theory requires *retention processes;* that is,
people must be able to remember what they observe in the form of either
mental images or verbal symbols. Third, after attending and retaining, the
person needs *reproduction processes* so that memories can be converted into
behaviors at appropriate times. The last requirement is a *motivational process* that justifies the performance of observationally learned behaviors.
Motivation is usually provided by an expectation that the subject will receive reinforcement similar to that received by the model from whom the
behavior was learned.

The four-process system of modeling can be applied to our understanding of the development of patterns of abnormal behavior. Many irrational fears or phobias probably are learned observationally. For example,
more people are afraid of snakes than have actually been hurt by snakes;
most of these snake-phobic people have learned to be afraid by observation.
Assume a child accompanies her father to the woods for a walk. The father
sees a snake and cries out in fear. The child *attends* to the fear response of
her father and notices that the fear disappears when he runs from the snake.
The reduction of fear seems reinforcing to the parent. The child *retains* the
image of the snake, her frightened father, his running away, and the subsequent diminution of fear. Weeks later the child sees a snake in the woods,
feels afraid because her father was, has the ability to *reproduce* her father's
running behavior, and is *motivated* to do so by her own fear. Although she
has never been hurt by a snake, the child has learned to respond to them
with fear and avoidance via the process of modeling and observational
learning.

CONCLUDING COMMENTS

Beginning with the same basic data, psychological theorists seem to
have arrived at a number of very different explanations of normal and abnormal behavior. According to the psychological theories, people may be good,
bad, free, enslaved, reasonable, irrational, developing, stagnating, governed

internally, governed externally, and so forth. Specific to many of the psychological theories is also a primary reliance on some single characteristic of human behavior. For example, Freud emphasized sexual needs, whereas Rogers's bias was toward self-actualization. However, an appreciation of the variety of theories offered to explain human behavior suggests that, more than any single determinant, a combination of various factors may be most effective in explaining why people do the things they do. You may be able to consider such combinations more easily after you've read about the sociological and biological theories in the chapters that follow.

CHAPTER SUMMARY CHART

In this chapter on psychological explanations of behavior, we first described the theory of Sigmund Freud:

Catharsis
Free association
Psychoanalysis
Hysterical patients
	The unconscious
	The psychic triumvirate
	Psychological
	  development
	Ego defense mechanisms
		Weak ego and ab-
		  normal behavior
		Hydraulic theory
		  of symptoms

After Freud's, we described two other analytic perspectives:

Sullivan:	*Erikson:*
Interpersonal focus Life stages Chums Consensual validation Security operations	Psychosocial stages of development Developmental conflicts Identity crisis

The humanistic and existential theorists focus more on people as basically good:

Rogers:	*Maslow:*	*Binswanger:*

Innate drive toward
  self-actualization
Evaluative behavior
  patterns
Unconditional
  positive regard
	Hierarchy of
	  needs
		Umwelt, Mitwelt, Eigenwelt
		
		Kierkegaard:
		
		Free choice
		Authentic versus
		  nonauthentic modes

The learning theories of behavior are based upon a belief that stimuli and reinforcers control behavior:

Classical conditioning:

CS, UCS, CR, UCR
Acquisition, extinction
Spontaneous recovery
Higher-order conditioning
Stimulus generalization
Discrimination
Conditioned emotional response

Operant conditioning:

Shaping, successive
   approximation
Primary and secondary
   reinforcers
Continuous versus inter-
   mittent reinforcement

Dual process:

Classical and operant conditioning combined to produce models for symptom
   development

Observational learning:

Not all behaviors learned
   through direct
   experience
Imitation
Modeling

CHAPTER 5
SOCIOLOGICAL
EXPLANATIONS

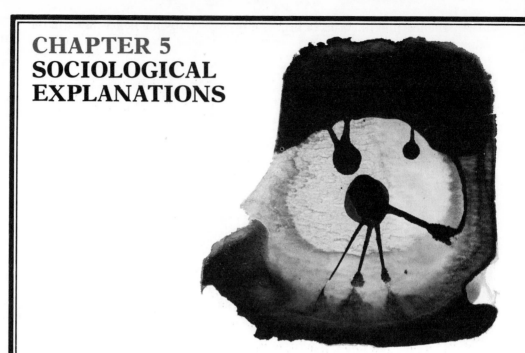

Whereas psychological theorists focus primarily upon intrapsychic, interpersonal, and reinforcement factors to explain behavior, sociological theorists generally consider social or environmental determinants more important. To these theorists, people do not exist in isolation. Rather, most people live within a social structure that they affect and are affected by. These theorists believe that the stresses associated with living in certain civilizations may be related to the occurrence of emotional disturbances. Indeed, many people consider our society to be at fault for the mental problems we face today. Many sociological theorists regard modern cities as spawning grounds for a wide variety of behavioral aberrations. The search for "the simple life" may demonstrate a need to escape from the stresses that we face daily.

Sociologists and social psychologists have contributed much to our understanding of mental disorders. We will describe several explanations of being different that have been proposed by socially oriented theorists. These explanations include *societal-reaction theory*, a *sociopsychological formulation*, and *socioenvironmental theory*. These theories of psychopathology assume that the social context in which behaviors occur is the most important factor in the labeling and development of behavior. As James Thurber humorously demonstrated in his fable of the unicorn in the garden, the context of a behavior can have much to do with society's definitions of it. Following a discussion of the theories, we will present some of the significant relationships between certain social characteristics and the occurrence of behavioral problems. We will examine the frequency of abnormal behavior as it relates to such characteristics as social class, religion, marital status, age, race, and geographical location.

The Unicorn in the Garden

James Thurber

Once upon a sunny morning a man who sat in a breakfast nook looked up from his scrambled eggs to see a white unicorn with a gold horn quietly cropping the roses in the garden. The man went up to the bedroom where his wife was still asleep and woke her. "There's a unicorn in the garden," he said. "Eating roses." She opened one unfriendly eye and looked at him. "The unicorn is a mythical beast," she said, and turned her back on him. The man walked slowly downstairs and out into the garden. The unicorn was still there; he was now browsing among the tulips. "Here, unicorn," said the man, and he pulled up a lily and gave it to him. The unicorn ate it gravely. With a high heart, because there was a unicorn in his garden, the man went upstairs and roused his wife again. "The unicorn," he said, "ate a lily." His wife sat up in bed and looked at him, coldly. "You are a booby," she said, "and I am going to have you put in the booby-hatch." The man, who had never liked the words "booby" and "booby-hatch," and who liked them even less on a shining morning when there was a unicorn in the garden, thought for a moment. "We'll see about that," he said. He walked over to the door. "He has a golden horn in the middle of his forehead," he told her. Then he went back to the garden to watch the unicorn; but the unicorn had gone away. The man sat down among the roses and went to sleep.

As soon as the husband had gone out of the house, the wife got up and dressed as fast as she could. She was very excited and there was a gloat in her eye. She telephoned the police and she telephoned a psychiatrist; she told them to hurry to her house and bring a strait-jacket. When the police and the psychiatrist arrived they sat down in chairs and looked at her, with great interest. "My husband," she said, "saw a unicorn this morning." The police looked at the psychiatrist and the psychiatrist looked at the police. "He told me it ate a lily," she said. The psychiatrist looked at the police and the police looked at the psychiatrist. "He told me it had a golden horn in the middle of its forehead," she said. At a solemn signal from the psychiatrist, the police leaped from their chairs and seized the wife. They had a hard time subduing her, for she put up a terrific struggle, but they finally subdued her. Just as they got her into the strait-jacket, the husband came back into the house.

"Did you tell your wife you saw a unicorn?" asked the police. "Of course not," said the husband. "The unicorn is a mythical beast." "That's all I wanted to know," said the psychiatrist. "Take her away. I'm sorry, sir, but your wife is as crazy as a jay bird." So they took her away, cursing and screaming, and shut her up in an institution. The husband lived happily ever after.

Moral: Don't count your boobies until they are hatched.

From *Fables for Our Time*, by James Thurber. Copyright © 1940 by James Thurber and © 1968 by Helen Thurber. Published by Harper & Row, Inc. Originally printed in *The New Yorker*. Reprinted by permission of Helen Thurber and Hamish Hamilton, Ltd., London.

SOCIOLOGICAL AND SOCIOPSYCHOLOGICAL EXPLANATIONS OF ABNORMAL BEHAVIOR

The sociological formulations of abnormal behavior generally describe people as embedded in culture and sensitive to social pressure. The social-contextual emphasis, which first sprouted in the work of neo-Freudians such as Sullivan and Erikson, reaches full bloom in the sociological theories of mental disorder. From among a host of such social-oriented approaches, we have chosen three as representative and useful to our later discussions of specific disorders and their treatments. Societal-reaction theory is purely sociological, whereas the sociopsychological formulation and socioenvironmental theory are promising mergers of the sociological and psychological perspectives.

Societal-Reaction Theory

Also known as labeling theory, societal-reaction theory was developed in the early 1960s and owes much of its impetus to the thinking of sociologist Thomas Scheff (1966, 1975). Societal-reaction theorists identify two types of being different that they term *deviance. Primary deviance* refers to behavior leading to a person's being labeled as different by society. Examples of primary deviance are stealing or exhibiting oneself sexually to small children. Primary deviance may develop for cultural, social, psychological, or biological reasons. However, according to this theory, primary-deviance behavior in itself does not cause one to become a problem to oneself and others. Rather, it is society's reaction to primary deviance that is most crucial to the development of disordered behavior. *Secondary deviance* occurs when a person is placed permanently in a deviant role by society's reaction. With regard to society's role in producing deviance, Becker (1963) has stated: "Social groups create deviance by making rules whose infractions constitute deviance and by applying these rules to particular people and labeling them as outsiders" (p. 9). It should be noted that simply breaking society's rules does not constitute secondary deviance: to be so classified a person must break a rule *and* be reacted to as deviant for his actions.

Why do people break rules in the first place? The answer to this question comes from Gove (1970). Although he opposes societal-reaction theory, Gove clearly states its basis:

A person may commit primary deviant acts because:
1. he may belong to a minority group or sub-culture whose values and ways of behavior may lead to violations of the rules of the dominant group.
2. he may have conflicting responsibilities in that the adequate performance of one role may produce violations in a second role.
3. he may violate rules for personal gain, usually with the expectation that he won't get caught.
4. he may be simply unaware of the rules and violate them unintentionally. Primary deviance is thus attributed to inconsistencies of the social structure, to hedonistic variables or to ignorance while personality or psychiatric disorders are ignored. . . . Usually the most crucial step in the development of secondary deviance is the experience of being caught and publicly labeled deviant [p. 874].

According to societal-reaction theorists, the label of deviant, once applied, is all but indelible. The difficulty in reversing the labeling process leads to the stable secondarily deviant behavior patterns known as mental disorders, as the following example illustrates.

A seven-year-old boy was brought to a psychologist with his parents' major complaint being that he showed little interest in school. He was constantly being teased and upset by his peers. His teacher complained that he would daydream in class, fail to complete homework, and often pick fights with other students. After extended evaluation, the investigator determined that informal testing by an inexperienced kindergarten teacher had resulted in the child's being labeled as having a learning disability (see Chapter 18). Consequently, teachers working with the young boy were more likely to see him as having some difficulty that in reality he did not have. Although they provided him well-meaningly with special help, they also produced in him a belief that he had special problems. The children in his class came to see him similarly and teased him about being a "dummy." Soon he saw himself as different, the children saw him as different, his teachers saw him as different, and his parents saw him as different. As a result, the child was severely disturbed and upset each day in school, and his work suffered immensely. His major problem was that he had become what he originally was erroneously labeled as being.

Scheff (1966) has discussed the application of societal-reaction theory to abnormal behavior. He states that in the development of mental disorders, the rules broken during the primary-deviance phase are quite special. They are rarely, if ever, openly stated, and are not formal rules or laws like those concerning robbery or violence. Rather, they are rules *left over* after all the usual categories of specific societal regulations are exhausted. They are therefore termed *residual rules,* and it is their violation that leads a person to be labeled "mentally ill."

A good way to generate a list of residual rules for yourself would be to consider those social guidelines that we take so much for granted that we notice them only when they are broken. Some examples of residual rules are "an adult must be involved in some task when in public"; "one should not stand too close to another person when speaking to him"; "one does not spit in people's faces"; "one does not sing songs in church during a somber funeral eulogy"; "one does not stand on the seat at a football game and expose himself"; and so forth. According to Scheff, the list of residual rules is virtually endless, and *residual deviance* (as violation of residual rules is termed) seems to include just about every possible type of what society considers to be "crazy behavior." For example, Scheff proposes that *primary* residual deviance, the simple one-time violation of residual rules, may be common among a wide sector of the population. Most of these one-time offenders are normal people who know where and when to violate residual

One way to handle anxiety generated by residual-rule breakers is to ignore them. (Photo by Joseph Czarnecki.)

rules appropriately. In fact, most residual-rule violation is harmless to those involved in it. The main point of Scheff's argument is that the *stabilization* of residual deviance into a diagnosable mental disorder is usually the result of societal reaction to that deviance in the form of labeling. If, by some stroke of bad luck or poor judgment, a person is observed in an act of residual-rule violation, he or she may be pulled into a social-labeling process beyond his or her control. A former professor of one of the authors described this social process as the game of "Pass the Anxiety"; our version of the game is presented in the accompanying box.

Societal-reaction theory is intriguing in its simplicity and would seem to be a fine explanation for the fact that criminals tend to stay criminals because they are forever labeled as ex-convicts. The same may be true

---

Pass the Anxiety: A Game for an Indefinite Number of Players

Players and playing surface: The players of *Pass the Anxiety* include a Primary Deviant, any number of nonprofessional but socially respectable Observers, one or more Authority Figures, several Professional Labelers (psychiatrists, psychologists, or social workers), a couple of Lawyers, and an Institution. The playing surface represents Society, which, much like the psyche, doesn't tolerate tension well and seeks homeostasis.

Routine of play: Play begins when the Primary Deviant is observed violating a *residual rule* by one of the nonprofessional Observers. The classic opening gambit, known as the Kraepelinian Kickoff, involves a person of middle- or lower-class social standing (upper-class people usually are disqualified from playing the Primary Deviant because their behavior is hidden or explained away as eccentric), who is standing outside a store talking to a mannequin in the window about a lacrosse game between the Cincinnati Reds and the Houston Oilers.

The Primary Deviant's behavior arouses *anxiety* on the part of the storekeeper (Observer), who worries that the presence of the Deviant may hamper business or that some property damage will occur. The storekeeper now has the anxiety but doesn't want to keep it (note the resemblance to Hot Potato). He or she therefore decides to pass it to someone else, a maneuver learned through specialized preseason training called "growing up in our society."

The storekeeper calls the police (Authority Figures) and upon their arrival suddenly feels calm again. The police say words similar to "We'll take care of this," a move that signals their acceptance of responsibility for the social tension. They take the Deviant, and the anxiety, with them, and the storekeeper goes about his or her business. (Going about one's business after the anxiety has been passed is specifically allowed for in Rule 14, which states "Having passed the anxiety, the passer may go about his or her business with little personal upset or permanent damage.") Meanwhile, the police, having exhausted all explanations of the Deviant's behavior known to them (drunkenness or drug use), can't deal with the anxiety either. They therefore execute the next phase of play, called *nonprofessional authority-based nonspecific labeling*, or the Adlerian Power Play. The rules governing this move are quite complex but generally prescribe calling the person a weirdo, crazy, nuts, bananas, crackers, and so forth. This move is available to any player in the game but can be used for societal-tension reduction only by players with *clout* (issued via orange jerseys at the beginning of play). Once the labels are applied, the police can justifiably pass the anxiety on. Since they have called the Deviant "sick," they naturally take the Deviant to a hospital emergency room and present him or her to the intern or resident on duty. The physician (another Authority Figure) says words similar to "I'll take care of this." The police breathe a sigh of relief—the usual response of players when they successfully pass the anxiety—and go about their business.

Now the physician has the anxiety, especially if his or her specialty isn't psychiatry. If, after speaking with the Deviant, the physician feels unable to handle the anxiety effectively, he or she hands it to a Professional Labeler of deviant behavior, the on-call psychiatrist. This play is called the Freudian End-Around and can be initiated only by a player who has had years of medical school and clinical experience. The psychiatrist soon appears in the emergency room and accepts the anxiety from the resident, who then goes about his or her business.

The psychiatrist proceeds to carry out the crucial play entitled *specific labeling and formal societal recognition of deviance*, or the DSM-II Double Reverse. Only players listed as Professional Labelers can perform this move. On behalf of society, the psychiatrist is permitted to remove the Deviant temporarily from the social scene; that is, he or she hospitalizes the person. If the deviance is severe, according to the label assigned to it (schizophrenia, psychotic depression, and so on), the psychiatrist may make a lateral pass to the Lawyers, who carry out the final play of the game, *commitment*. This play involves the further removal of the Deviant as a source of societal tension through consignment to an Institution (End Zone). There, the final holders of the anxiety are charged with doing one of two things: either to fix the Deviant and return him or her to society without the anxiety-producing behaviors or to keep the Deviant out of society for good, so that no more anxiety is produced. In either event, the object of the game is achieved when the Deviant is no longer a Problem. All players go about their business (Rule 14), and the Deviant is faced with the prospect of a lifetime of secondary deviance; he or she is the Loser.

An example of the Kraepelinian Kickoff: Anxiety is passed from a primary deviant to a nondeviant member of society. (Photo by Joseph Czarnecki.)

for formerly hospitalized mental patients. However, labeling theory doesn't consider adequately the reasons that deviance occurs and generally doesn't deal with specific aspects of people who deviate, or situations in which they do so. In a combination of Scheff's theory and basic psychological learning theory, Ullmann and Krasner (1969, 1975) have attempted to resolve these theoretical shortcomings.

The Sociopsychological Formulation

Ullmann and Krasner (1969, 1975) have presented a sociopsychological view of abnormal behavior that combines the societal-reaction perspective we have just described and basic learning theory (Chapter 4). Their position is that abnormal behavior is in no way different from normal behavior in its development and maintenance, or in the manner of its alteration. They agree with Scheff that the main difference between normal and abnormal behavior lies primarily in people's reactions to deviance. "The person whose behavior is called maladaptive is probably acting in a manner *unexpected* by his observers. The abnormal person's behavior is not disturbed; it is *disturbing*" (1969, p. 93; italics ours). Because of their emphasis on societal reactions and the interrelationship of their ideas with those of Scheff, we have included Ullmann and Krasner's theory under sociological rather than psychological perspectives.

In Ullmann and Krasner's view, "correct" behavior usually requires a certain sequence of events. First, a person must attend to and correctly interpret a situation, or *receive a stimulus*. Next, the person's behavioral repertoire must include the skill to *respond* appropriately and the person must make that *appropriate response*. Finally, the person must be *rewarded for the response* by the environment or independently. If any of these four steps is missing, then the person's reaction in a given situation may be seen by others as maladaptive or abnormal. For example, a man may find himself being told a joke. His friend says "My wife said that on our vacation she wanted to go somewhere she'd never been. I said, 'How about the kitchen?'" If the man doesn't pay attention to the story (doesn't receive the stimulus) he may not laugh. If the joke is considered funny by all those around him and he doesn't laugh, he may be considered to have responded inappropriately. Perhaps he never learned how to laugh (which is unlikely, but bear with us as an example). Or he may receive the joke stimulus and have the ability to laugh, but for some reason he doesn't emit the response (perhaps he doesn't find it funny or has heard it before). In any case, his behavior will be considered inappropriate to the situation. Alternatively, all may go well and he may laugh at the joke only to find that others aren't amused and don't laugh. In this case he isn't rewarded for his behavior and may be considered "different."

From the sociopsychological perspective, a given behavior (such as laughing in our example) is not in itself normal or abnormal. It is the *situation* and the *expectations of society* that determine the label placed on a specific act. According to Ullmann and Krasner, then, we must learn *how* to act in certain situations and we must know *when* given behaviors are appropriate or inappropriate in order to maintain our social label of normal. It is how and when we do things, and not what we do, that are of crucial importance. To be acceptable as normal, behaviors must be emitted at the *appropriate time*, in an *appropriate place*, and under *appropriate circumstances*. A final requirement is that there be a respectable (powerful) *observer* present to determine for society the acceptability of one's behavior. Even when the time, place, and circumstance requirements are violated, if no one observes the behavior, it is *not* considered abnormal. Thus, if a man who dresses in women's clothes every single day for ten years stays in his house, he may not be considered different, because his behavior doesn't bother anybody. He creates no disturbance and thus produces no social anxiety. On the other hand, if a man who dresses in women's clothing is obvious about it, goes out into the street, and is observed, he probably will be labeled as "sick" and dealt with as in the game of "Pass the Anxiety." As you think about this sociopsychological explanation, you may realize that every day of your life you probably emit behaviors in private that, emitted before an observer, could get *you* labeled as abnormal. Some examples we obtained from our students are sitting in a bathroom stall making believe you are a jet pilot, talking to your pet plant Marvin, or examining your nude body in the mirror. However, those who are labeled normal usually are aware of the presence of observers and can change their behavior accordingly.

Outside observers may not always be needed to label one's behavior as normal or different. To some extent we *do* evaluate ourselves, and if we perceive ourselves as violating residual rules, we may *self-label* and cause ourselves to experience all the same detrimental effects of secondary deviance as a person labeled by a powerful other. An example of the power of self-labeling is shown in the following case history of a young man who was involved in normal adolescent homosexual sex play for years with no societal labeling but who deteriorated as a result of self-labeling.

During early adolescence a young man and a close male friend sporadically engaged in mutual masturbation. Neither thought anything of it at the time, and such behavior often was accompanied by their poring over pornographic magazines depicting nude females. During the patient's third year of high school, his basketball coach discussed the "horrors" of homosexuality during a team meeting. Trying to instill a masculine image in his players, he described behaviors such as mutual masturbation as "sick" and "girlish," and told his players that if they were approached regarding such behavior they should take violent action against their accoster. Although he laughed and joked along with everyone else about the discussion, the young man began to feel anxious and guilty on his way home. By the time he arrived home he had convinced himself that he was indeed a homosexual of the type spoken of by his coach. He labeled himself as sick and sexually disturbed. From that point on he avoided dating girls (something in which he had been active prior to this) and became a loner. He feared that his friends would discover (via his looks or actions) that he was homosexual. Although he had lived with his sporadic mutual masturbatory behavior for several years, it was not until he had labeled himself as disturbed that his psychological problems began.

Besides the situational and labeling components of being different, Ullmann and Krasner include the concept of *expectations*. Certain behaviors often are expected by society in given situations, and the rules governing these circumstances can be very rigid. This is especially true for adults, whose socially acceptable repertoire is very limited. Children aren't expected always to behave in a clearly circumscribed manner and may be allowed a much broader range of acceptable behaviors. For instance, a young boy won't be labeled, arrested, or hospitalized for urinating on an automobile tire in a shopping-center parking lot, but let a grown man try it and away he goes. Generally, the older we get, the more rules we must follow, the more rigid

Social rules for children are much more flexible than those for adults. (Photo by George Lazar.)

society's expectations, and the narrower the path of normality. If we don't behave as society expects in a given situation, we are liable to be labeled abnormal.

Socioenvironmental Theory

The theories we have discussed thus far offer explanations for the development and labeling of abnormal behavior with the major focus on the individual and his interaction with society. The socioenvironmental theorists

(Dohrenwend, 1975; Kohn, 1972; Meyers, Lindenthal, & Pepper, 1971, 1974, 1975) focus more on the effects of society and social factors than on the individual's behavior per se. Because it is clear and easily applicable, we will describe a theory of mental disturbance offered by Kohn.

Kohn (1972) has noted that living in the lower class may produce great stress and that this great stress in turn can be related to producing mental disturbance. He states that lower-class position is among the greatest stressors in society because it "affects people's ability to deal, not only with conditions defined as stressful, but also with many other dilemmas and uncertainties in a rapidly changing, complex society" (p. 298). He goes on to say that the *family* is important because of its role in transmitting to children conceptions of reality that the parents have learned from their own experience. Kohn believes that lower-class families transmit attitudes to their children that aren't always conducive to success in society at large. Specifically, he speculates that the lower a person's social position, "the more likely he is to value conformity to external authority and to believe that such conformity is all that his own capacities and the exigencies of the world allow . . . the more likely is his orientation system to be marked by a rigidly conservative view of man and his social institutions, fearfulness and distrust, and a *fatalistic belief that one is at the mercy of forces and people beyond one's control, often beyond one's understanding*" (p. 298, italics added).

Kohn feels that many lower-class people do not learn an adaptive attitude system for coping with society and that this lack of coping ability is a primary reason for the development of an inordinate number of severe cases of psychoses in the members of the lower class. Some support for this point of view may be found in the related concept of *locus of control of reinforcement* (Rotter, 1966). Generally, locus of control reflects the degree to which people believe in their own ability to control what happens to them. Consistent with Kohn's speculations, researchers (Duke & Mullens, 1973; Nowicki & Hopper, 1974; and others) have found that as compared to normal people, severely disturbed individuals tend to believe that what happens to them is most likely the result of fate, powerful others, luck, chance, or circumstances too complex to understand. Further, lower-class people tend to feel less in control of their lives than middle- and upper-class individuals (Nowicki & Strickland, 1973).

Other sociological theorists, such as Meyers, Lindenthal, and Pepper (1971, 1974, 1975) emphasize the relation between specific life events and the development of psychopathology. They have found that the greater the number of significant life events (see Table 5-1) experienced by an individual in a given time period, the greater the likelihood that the person will develop psychological problems. From this perspective, *any change* in life pattern—be it positive or negative—represents a stress that challenges one's ability to cope. Among the group of people rated as mentally unimpaired in Table 5-2 (p. 117), only 7% reported five or more life-crisis events. On the other hand, among the very impaired group, 30% reported five or more life-crisis events. These data demonstrate a reasonably clear relationship

When sociopsychological needs are not met, there can be devastating consequences. (Photo courtesy of the Department of Housing and Urban Development.)

between the reporting of significant life events and psychological maladjustment.

Note in Table 5-2 that in each area, the greater the degree of impairment, the larger the percentage of people reporting significant life events. Thus, among the very psychologically impaired, three out of ten reported education-related events, nearly five out of ten reported health-related events, and so forth. Among the psychologically unimpaired, life events do occur. For example, 29% reported health-related events, 32% reported family-related events, and so forth. From these data it seems clear that the mere occurrence of significant life events does not *always* lead to

Table 5-1. *A categorization of major life events*

   I. Education-related events
     a. start school
     b. graduate from school
     c. fail school
     d. change schools
     e. problems in school
  II. Relocation-related events
     a. move to same type of neighborhood
     b. move to better neighborhood
     c. move to worse neighborhood
     d. build a new house
 III. Marriage-related events
     a. engaged
     b. married
     c. divorced
     d. separated
     e. intermarried
     f. major change in relationship with spouse
 IV. Family-related events
     a. engaged
     b. married
     c. member enters armed forces
     d. pregnancy
     e. birth of a child
     f. adoption of a child
     g. new person moves into household
     h. family member leaves household
     i. change in number of family get-togethers
  V. Interpersonal-related events
     a. major change in relationship with spouse
     b. trouble with in-laws
     c. trouble with boss
     d. change in relationship with friends
 VI. Health-related events
     a. birth of a child
     b. serious physical illness
     c. accident or serious injury
     d. pregnancy
     e. stillbirth
     f. frequent minor illness
     g. mental illness
VII. Work-related events
     a. start work for first time
     b. change to same type of job
     c. promoted to more responsible job
     d. demoted to less responsible job
     e. laid off temporarily
     f. expanded business
     g. business failed
     h. trouble with boss
     i. trouble at work
     j. fired
     k. out of work over a month

Table 5-1. *A categorization of major life events (continued)*

        l. any large reorganization at work
       m. retirement
       n. success at work
  VIII. Finance-related events
       a. laid off temporarily
       b. business failed
       c. out of work over a month
       d. improvement in financial status
       e. financial status a lot worse
       f. foreclosure of mortgage or loan
   IX. Legal-related events
       a. being in court
       b. detention in jail
       c. being arrested
       d. law suit or legal action
       e. loss of driver's license
    X. Community-related events
       a. fire
       b. burglary
       c. redevelopment of neighborhood

emotional disturbance. Many people experience several major life events per year and yet remain relatively well adjusted. Meyers and his colleagues have found that the degree to which people are socially accepted and feel integrated into society affects their response to stressful events. The more integrated the person is, the less adverse are the effects of significant life events.

SOCIOLOGICAL CORRELATES OF BEING DIFFERENT

Having looked at the selection of sociological and sociopsychological theories, we may conclude safely that social factors are important in thinking about abnormal behavior. We will now consider some of the correlates of behavior disorders identified by sociological researchers.

These researchers focus on the occurrence, cause, and treatment of mental disorders. *Demographic variables* (characteristics of people used in statistical analyses of human populations) are examined to determine their relationship to the *incidence* and *prevalence* of disorders. The *incidence rate* tells us the number of new cases of a particular pattern of symptoms within a given period of time (usually a year) per a given number of people in a population (usually 100,000). Thus, the incidence rate for a specific disorder for the year 1974 might be stated as 2.3/100,000. The *prevalence rate* reports the total

Table 5-2. *The relationship between significant life events and psychopathology*

Percentage of Persons of Varying Mental Status as a Function of Number of Life Events Reported

	Mental Status		
Number of Events	Unimpaired	Moderately Impaired	Very Impaired
0	27	18	11
1	34	24	24
2	22	21	16
3	6	13	12
4	4	8	7
5	3	6	6
6	1	4	5
7	2	2	2
8	1	1	6
9	0	3	11

Percentage of Respondents by Type of Event and Mental Status

	Mental Status		
Type of Event	Unimpaired	Moderately Impaired	Very Impaired
Education	18	24	30
Relocation	15	16	19
Marriage	12	20	24
Family	32	37	40
Interpersonal	5	7	20
Health	29	41	47
Work	21	34	40
Financial	13	24	35
Legal	3	5	16
Community	4	9	11

From "Life Events and Psychiatric Impairment," by J. Meyers, J. Lindenthal, and M. Pepper, *Journal of Nervous and Mental Disease*, 1971, *152*, 149–157. Copyright 1971 by Williams & Wilkins Company. Reprinted by permission.

number of cases of a type of disorder in existence at any point. For example, the prevalence rate for the same disorder might be stated as 5.8/100,000. The prevalence rate for any disease usually is higher than the incidence rate. Higher prevalence rates usually are found in long-term disorders such as schizophrenia, and lower rates are the rule in short-lived syndromes such as the common cold. We hope the data in the sections to follow will provide you with some feeling for the wide variation in incidence and prevalence rates of disordered behavior and the importance of social variables in the understanding of being different.

Social Class and Being Different

In an 1855 study of insanity in Massachusetts, Jarvis said, "the pauper class furnishes, in ratio to its numbers, 64 times as many cases of insanity as the independent class" (pp. 52–53). One hundred years later a classic study by Hollingshead and Redlich (1958) also found a relationship between social class and the incidence of various types of emotional disturbances (see Table 5-3). Dividing the population of New Haven, Connecticut, into five socioeconomic classes, they found that as you move from the upper to the lower classes the proportion of disordered behavior that is psychotic also tends to increase. In Class V, the lowest socioeconomic group, about nine out of ten psychologically disturbed individuals were diagnosed as psychotic, while in Class I, the highest socioeconomic group, only about one out of two psychologically disturbed individuals was so diagnosed. However, these results may be questioned for several reasons. First, people in the upper classes have more power and wealth than those in the lower socioeconomic classes and therefore may more easily "cover up" psychotic family members or friends. Further, powerful or wealthy psychotic people are more likely to be labeled "eccentric" rather than "crazy" and therefore may not be counted in the Hollingshead and Redlich data. Unfortunately, lower-class people usually are diagnosed and treated at overcrowded state facilities, where professionals often make quick, unsophisticated diagnoses and where the label of "psychotic" may be more the expectation than the exception.

Despite these reservations, there are other sources of evidence that social class may be related to disordered behavior. Several researchers have reported attempts to determine the *latent* prevalence of emotional disturbance

Table 5-3. *Relationship between social class and diagnosed mental illness in New Haven, Conn.*

Social Class	Percentage of Disturbed Individuals Diagnosed as Neurotic	Percentage of Disturbed Individuals Diagnosed as Psychotic
Class I (wealthy, high-society professionals)	53	47
Class II (managers, paraprofessionals)	67	33
Class III (small businessmen, skilled and white-collar workers)	44	56
Class IV (semiskilled workers)	23	77
Class V (unskilled workers and laborers)	8	92

From *Social Class and Mental Illness: A Community Study*, by A. Hollingshead and F. Redlich. Copyright 1958 by John Wiley & Sons, Inc. Reprinted by permission.

in the population, which would include those who have been "covered up" or never treated. In such studies, hospitalization and diagnosis are not used as the only indicators of mental disorder. Rather, attempts are made to survey other indices in the total population to determine the extent and degree of emotional disturbance. Termed *epidemiological investigations*, these studies are exemplified in the work of Leighton (1959) and Srole, Langner, Michael, Opler, and Rennie (1962).

Leighton studied the incidence of disordered behavior in a small town (population 3000) in Sterling County, Nova Scotia. He first determined that 47 of every 1000 adults were receiving psychiatric care in local hospitals and clinics. However, he realized that this figure didn't adequately answer his question regarding the *true* prevalence of symptoms in the general population. To determine the true prevalence, 283 people were interviewed by psychiatrists for at least an hour to determine the presence and degree of mental symptoms. On the basis of these interviews, Leighton reported that 37% of the participants were considered to have symptoms indicative of severe mental disorder. An additional 30% were considered to have some probable or definite mental disorder. His final estimate indicated that 370 individuals per 1000 of the population *needed* psychiatric treatment, but only 47 were *receiving* it. Although limited in scope, Leighton's work suggests that more intensive study may be needed if we are to find *all* people with psychological problems.

With a similar purpose, but on a more massive scale, Srole and his colleagues examined an area of midtown Manhattan for the presence of mental disorder (Srole, Langner, Michael, Opler, & Rennie, 1962, 1975). A sample of 1660 people was chosen from a population of over 100,000. On the basis of numerous interview questions, each person was assigned one of four mental-health ratings. *Well* indicated that no diagnosable symptoms were observed. People manifesting mild tensions or depressions, but who were rarely bothered by them, were said to have *mild symptoms*. *Moderate symptoms* were indicated when some specific area of life function was hampered. For example, a fear of crowds in an otherwise healthy person would be termed a moderate symptom. The last category, *impaired*, was used to describe those who couldn't function adequately due to mental symptoms; that is, they couldn't easily hold jobs or rarely could leave their homes.

Generally, according to ratings made by the trained interviewers, only one person out of five was found to be "well." Remember that this study was dealing with people living their day-to-day lives as "normal," functioning individuals. The similarity of the data from central Manhattan, with all its crowding and pressures, and data from a small, rural Canadian town adds to the generalizability of the findings.

A glance at Srole's data on social class (Table 5-4) reveals several interesting relations. The first of these is the reduction in the percentage of people considered "well" as we move from the upper to the lower class. Also note that even in the upper class, two out of three individuals manifested some discernible disturbances. However, even this high number is sur-

Table 5-4. *Socioeconomic level and mental symptoms*

	Parental Socioeconomic Level		
Mental-Health Category	Upper	Middle	Lower
Well	34.1%	21.4%	12.9%
Mild symptoms	35.5	38.1	39.6
Moderate symptoms	20.5	23.7	27.7
Impaired	9.9	16.8	19.8

From *Mental Health in the Metropolis,* by L. Srole et al., New York University Press, 1978. Reprinted by permission of Dr. Srole.

passed by those in the lower class, where nearly nine out of ten exhibited some problems.

More recent support for the relationship between social class and psychological disturbance has been provided by Gove and Howell (1974). Using family income as an indicator of social level and more descriptive mental-health categories, Gove and Howell clearly demonstrate the greater incidence of severe impairment among lower socioeconomic groups than in higher groups (Table 5-5). It should be noted that in this sample of mental patients, as in the Hollingshead and Redlich sample, the *higher* the economic level, the *less* likely was it that the symptoms experienced were severe. These data lend support to the idea that when lower-class individuals suffer psychological disturbances, they usually suffer more severe impairment than those from other social classes. The reasons for this differential social-class effect aren't clear, but theories such as Kohn's (1972), described earlier, may be applicable.

Table 5-5. *Type and severity of mental symptoms by income (percentages)*

Severity of Symptom	Almost Nil	Mild	Moderate		Severe
Type of Symptom	No Symptoms	Some Distress	Disorganized but Not Disruptive	Disruptive but Not Disorganized	Disorganized and Disruptive
Income $0–3999	1.9	12.3	27.4	13.2	45.3
Income $4000 up	0.7	32.4	33.1	11.7	22.1

From "Individual Resources and Mental Hospitalization: A Comparison and Evaluation of the Societal Reaction and Psychiatric Perspectives," by W. R. Gove and P. Howell, *American Sociological Review,* 1974, *39,* 93–97. Copyright 1974 by the American Sociological Association. Reprinted by permission.

Research into the relationship between social class and mental disorder continues. That the relationship is reliable, there is little doubt. After reviewing a number of studies of the relationship, Dohrenwend and Dohrenwend (1974) reported:

The highest rates of psychiatric disorders have been found in the lowest social class in 28 out of 33 studies. This relationship is strongest in the studies conducted in urban settings (where stress is assumed higher). The relationship is more consistent for the subtypes of schizophrenia and personality disorder, than it is for neuroses or depressive psychoses [p. 439].

Religion, National Origin, and Being Different

Just as social class is clearly related to the frequency and type of being different, there also is evidence that religion and national origin may be related to prevalence rates. There are certain religious or national groups that many in our society believe possess certain general psychological and personality characteristics. Data compiled by Srole and his colleagues (1962, 1975) suggest that there are in reality few differences among the three major religious groups in the United States with regard to overall percentage of disturbance (Table 5-6). However, one significant difference is that although Jews tended to experience more mild and moderate problems than Catholics and Protestants, they had fewer severe problems. Other data indicated that Jews suffer significantly less alcoholism than Catholics and Protestants.

Although few differences in mental-disturbance rates related to religion, other data led Srole and his colleagues to suggest that there may be definite nationality differences (Table 5-7). However, the data on nationality and mental disorder must be viewed in terms of variations in what Srole et al. call *detachment level:* the degree to which the nationality group had

Table 5-6. *Presence of psychological symptoms as a function of religious origin*

Mental-Health Category	Religious Origin		
	Catholic	Protestant	Jewish
Well	17.4%	20.2%	14.5%
Mild	34.5	36.4	43.2
Moderate	23.4	19.9	25.1
Impaired	24.7	23.5	17.2

From *Mental Health in the Metropolis*, by L. Srole et al., New York University Press, 1978. Reprinted by permission of Dr. Srole.

Table 5-7. *Mental-health classification by national origin*[a]

Nationality Group	Mental-Health Category			
	Well	Mild	Moderate	Impaired
British	21.6%	39.7%	19.0%	26.7%
German-Austrian	18.3	32.9	24.4	24.4
Irish	12.5	35.0	22.5	30.0
Italians	15.0	32.5	15.0	37.5
Hungarians	13.6	36.4	31.8	18.2
Czechoslovakians	13.3	41.7	18.3	26.7
Puerto Ricans	0.0	39.1	8.7	52.2
All others	19.2	39.7	19.2	21.9
Total group	16.1	36.0	21.2	26.7

[a]Arranged in order of increasing detachment levels.
From *Mental Health in the Metropolis*, by L. Srole et al., New York University Press, 1978. Reprinted by permission of Dr. Srole.

been assimilated into the dominant culture at the time of the survey. From their data, Srole et al. suggested that the degree of *belongingness* seemed to be related to the occurrence of disordered behavior. If the various nationality groups examined in Table 5-7 were examined in their homelands, they probably would show incidence rates for impairment similar to those of the Americans in the Manhattan sample.

Marital Status and Being Different

The Manhattan study (Srole et al., 1962, 1975) has provided some information on variations in the severity of symptoms as a function of marital status (Table 5-8). Most striking is the higher rate of psychological impairment among divorced than married people. More recent data pro-

Table 5-8. *Distribution of mental-health categories of married and divorced respondents 30–39 years of age*

Mental-Health Category	Males		Females	
	Married	Divorced	Married	Divorced
Well	24.8%	4.0%	19.2%	7.0%
Mild	37.8	36.0	39.9	19.3
Moderate	18.1	20.0	21.0	31.6
Impaired	19.3	40.0	19.9	42.1

From *Mental Health in the Metropolis*, by L. Srole et al., New York University Press, 1978. Reprinted by permission of Dr. Srole.

vided by Gove and Howell (1974) are consistent with these findings (Table 5-9). These investigators concluded that married people experience fewer and less severe symptoms because their families provide help and support. Notice in Table 5-9 that married people suffer more minor or moderate irritations than single people. However, the single and divorced or disrupted groups tend to experience more severe difficulties. In Gove and Howell's data, single people tend to come out worst; but before most of you panic, remember that these data are collapsed over all ages and both sexes and therefore include older as well as younger unmarried people.

Age and Being Different

Recently there has been an increase in the amount of concern for and research into the problems of aging, and we will discuss the specific symptom patterns of the elderly in Chapter 21. For now, Table 5-10 indicates that there is significant variation with age in the "well" and "impaired" categories. Members of the three older age groupings are less often "well" than the people in the younger group, and the frequency of impairment rapidly increases with age.

Race and Being Different

The relationships we have discussed thus far are usually seen as cold statistics that most of us accept as fairly accurate. However, the attempt to identify race as a correlate of mental disturbance is fraught with emotional overtones. Racists and nonracists alike can find support for their positions in the same sociological data. At present, we cannot state definitely whether there is a relationship between race and mental disorder. In 1913, a psychia-

Table 5-9. *Type and severity of symptoms by marital status (percentages)*

Severity of Symptom	Almost Nil	Mild	Moderate		Severe
Type of Symptom	No Symptoms	Some Distress	Disorganized but Not Disruptive	Disruptive but Not Disorganized	Disorganized and Disruptive
Single	0.0	8.6	17.1	17.1	57.1
Disrupted	2.0	18.4	24.5	10.2	44.9
Married	1.1	28.2	35.1	12.6	23.0

Note: Values represent percentages of mental patients classified by marital status and symptomatology.

From "Individual Resources and Mental Hospitalization: A Comparison and Evaluation of the Societal Reaction and Psychiatric Perspectives," by W. R. Gove and P. Howell, *American Sociological Review*, 1974, *39*, 93–97. Copyright 1974 by the American Sociological Association. Reprinted by permission.

Table 5-10. *Distribution of mental-health classifications by age groups*

Mental-Health Category	Age Group			
	20–29	30–39	40–49	50–59
Well	23.6%	16.8%	19.3%	15.0%
Mild	37.5	37.6	37.0	33.1
Moderate	23.6	22.4	23.2	21.1
Impaired	15.3	23.2	23.2	30.8

From *Mental Health in the Metropolis*, by L. Srole et al., New York University Press, 1978. Reprinted by permission of Dr. Srole.

trist made the following statement in an article in the then respected *Psychoanalytic Review:* "During its years of savagery, the ["colored"] race had learned few lessons in emotional control, and what they had attained during their few generations of slavery left them unstable. For this reason we find deterioration in the emotional sphere most often an early and persistent manifestation" (Evarts, 1913, p. 396). Much research has been spurred by Evarts's supposition.

Maltzberg (1956, 1959) reported that in New York City during the period 1949–1951, the incidence rate for "mental disease" for Whites was 173.6 per 100,000; for Blacks, it was 340.4 per 100,000. From these findings he concluded that Blacks suffered more emotional disturbances than Whites. However, J. Fischer (1969) noted that Maltzberg had used hospital admissions as a criterion for defining people as disturbed. From our previous criticisms of research on incidence and prevalence as a function of social class, you know that first, not all those in need of treatment seek it (Srole et al., 1962; Leighton, 1959), and second, people from lower socioeconomic levels usually go to hospitals where the sort of research Maltzberg was doing is more likely to be permitted. Thus, it is probable that Maltzberg's samples were severely biased and may not reflect the true incidence of disordered behavior in the groups he studied.

Rates of disturbance usually are higher in urban than in rural areas. The higher incidence in urban areas has important implications for an accurate assessment of the relation between race and mental disturbance. In 1939 Faris and Dunham divided a map of Chicago into areas representing increasing distance from the center of the city and calculated incidence of disorder as a function of that distance. Although rates of mental disorder generally increased as one moved toward the center of the city, *both* Black and White rates were higher in central areas. Further, Blacks living in the suburbs had lower incidence rates than Whites living in the center city. In the center of the city, which was predominately Black, rates for Blacks were *lower* than those for Whites. Faris and Dunham's results were supported by Klee (1967) in Baltimore. Such studies suggest that social isolation and crowding may be more important than race in explaining the higher rates of disorder usually found among Black people.

Research in crowding and inner-city life has implicated social class as the crucial variable mediating the mental disorder–race relationship. That is, regardless of race, it seems to be people in lower-class groups who show more disturbances. Support for this conclusion comes from Pasamanick (1963), who initially did an analysis of race and mental disorder based on the usual criterion of mental-hospital admission. He then recalculated prevalence rates on the basis of adjusted scores derived from *all* sources of treatment (such as private practice and community mental-health centers). He found prevalence rates based on hospital admissions to be 357 per 100,000 for Whites and 650 per 100,000 for Blacks. Recalculating the figures for all sources of treatment, he obtained "corrected" rates of 12,974 per 100,000 for Whites and 7,395 per 100,000 for Blacks. Thus, these "true prevalence" rates actually showed Blacks to have *fewer* disturbances than Whites. Data such as these have caused J. Fischer (1969) to conclude that "the notion that there is a higher proportion of mental illness among Negroes than among whites can, indeed, be described as a *myth*" (p. 444).

In the centers of many cities studied by sociologists, conditions are found that contribute to a sense of isolation and loneliness. (Photo by Sherry Suris.)

CONCLUDING COMMENTS

In many ways, the sociological perspective on people who are different is based on the concept of deviance. We have described primary and secondary forms of deviance and the manner in which they may be related to abnormality. However, there are some social theorists who believe that, if society looked closely enough, deviance would be so common that most people could be classified in some way as abnormal. For example, Simmons (1969) discriminates between "divergence" and deviance, noting that although it is normal to diverge from socially acceptable behavior, true deviance needs to be redefined as "simply divergence that is much greater than the divergence of the majority" (p. 44). However, even given a more realistic definition of deviance, it may not be true that mentally disturbed people are considered deviant by the majority of society—the supposed source of labeling of residual-rule violations and the like. For example, Simmons reports that in answer to the question "What is deviant?" only 12% of a group of people mentioned "mentally ill," whereas 49% said "homosexuals," 47% said "drug addicts," and 46% said "alcoholics." In fact, mentally ill people were seen as no more deviant than "beatniks" and "communists"! Results such as those of Simmons suggest that, for certain disorders, the concept of mental illness as deviance may be more popular among sociologists and sociopsychologists than it is among lay people.

CHAPTER SUMMARY CHART

In this chapter on sociological explanations of behavior we first described three theories:

Societal-reaction theory	*Sociopsychological theory*	*Socioenvironmental theory*
Scheff: labeling Primary deviance Secondary deviance Residual-rule violation Residual deviance	Abnormal people disturbing, not disturbed Abnormal behavior learned, just like normal behavior Violations of expectations Time, place, observer, circumstance	Abnormality caused by stress from life-change events Inability to cope related to social class

We then presented information on sociological correlates of abnormal behavior:

Social class

Lower class—more psychosis
Upper class—more neurosis
Lower-class people generally more impaired
Midtown Manhattan study

Religion

Jews have more symptoms at the moderate level and fewer at the impaired level.

National origin

Little relation to nationality, but degree of detachment from major culture related to rates of disorder

Marital status

Mixed indicator
Divorcees have highest disorder rates; married people the lowest.

Age

Older people have highest incidence rates.

Race

Early research suggested Blacks have higher rates, but recent work indicates that social-class variables explain race factors.

CHAPTER 6
BIOLOGICAL
EXPLANATIONS

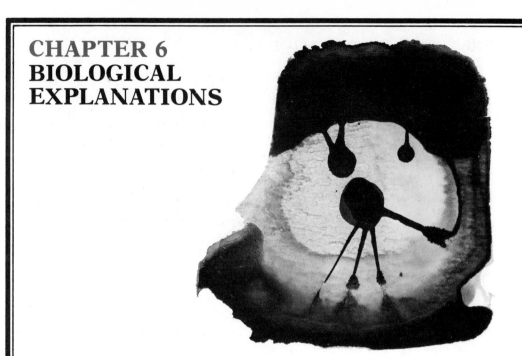

The biological approach to human behavior is generally based upon the belief that the way people act can be explained by some genetic or physiological mechanism. From the biological perspective, mental disorders—like physical disorders—are seen as the result of some identifiable physical dysfunction, hereditary defect, invading organism, foreign substance, or disease of the nervous system. Few biological theorists completely discount the importance of the psychological and social factors we described in Chapters 4 and 5, but they consider that biology is primary and personality and environment are secondary.

In this chapter we will present information basic to your understanding of later specific explanations of various forms of being different, beginning with descriptions of the nervous and endocrine systems. Both of these systems clearly are involved in normal as well as abnormal human behavior. We also will present an overview of the search for toxic, genetic, and biochemical factors in the development of abnormal behavior.

THE NERVOUS SYSTEM AND BEHAVIOR

The nervous system is involved in directing and controlling human behavior (see Figure 6-1) and is composed of a network of communication lines within the body that may be divided into two major parts. The first part, the *central nervous system* (CNS), is composed of the brain and spinal cord (see Figure 6-2). The second component, the *peripheral nervous system* (PNS), includes receptor nerves carrying sensory information from the body to the CNS, effector nerves carrying directives from the CNS to muscles, and a group of specialized nerves called the *autonomic nervous system* (ANS). The autonomic nervous system, composed of the *sympathetic* and *parasympathetic* systems, is intimately involved in determining emotional behavior.

Basic Characteristics

The nervous system is responsible for a wide variety of activities. However, all of these activities are carried out by basically the same type of specialized cells, called *neurons*, whose messages are transmitted from one cell to another by similar electrochemical means at sites called *synapses*.

Neurons. Neurons are the basic building blocks of the nervous system. As shown in Figure 6-3, a neuron is composed of a *soma*, or body of the cell; an *axon*, a single, often quite long fiber; and several shorter fibers called *dendrites*, which resemble tree branches. The axon is involved primarily in carrying messages away from the cell and the dendrites are generally "receivers." However, this distinction isn't always accurate

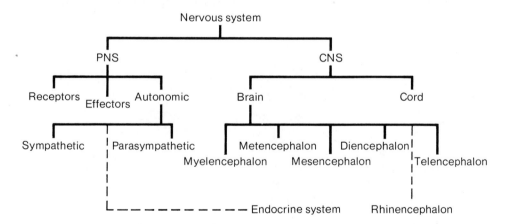

Figure 6-1. *The organization of the nervous system. From* Brain and Behavior, *by H. Brown. Copyright © 1976 by Oxford University Press, Inc. Reprinted by permission.*

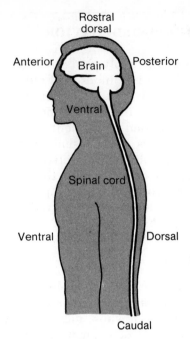

Figure 6-2. *The brain and spinal cord*

(Brown, 1976). Rather, as we will see below, there may be a variety of ways in which neurons can affect one another.

Synapses.   Neurons must communicate with one another in order for behavior to occur, yet it is a peculiar characteristic of the nervous system that "every neuron is an *independent unit,* having no apparent direct connection with any other neuron" (Brown, 1976, p. 246). Communication

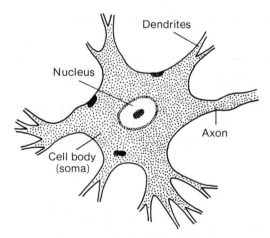

Figure 6-3. *A neuron and its major structures*

between neurons usually occurs across tiny spaces between them called *synapses.* Some synapses are between axons and dendrites (axo-dendritic synapses), others are axo-somatic (from the axon directly to the cell body). Any one neuron in the human brain can have as many as 200,000 synapses with other cells. We will see later that problems in the transmission of a neural impulse between cells may have much to do with disordered behavior.

Although we now know that there is an actual space at the point where one neuron meets another, experts once believed that communication across synapses was electrical. This assumption was based upon the knowledge that transmission of nerve messages (impulses) *within* neurons is electrical. Since electrical transmission occurred within cells, it seemed logical to assume that similar transmissions occurred between cells. When the space between nerve cells was discovered, those assuming an electrical means of communication proposed that electrical impulses "jumped the gap" from cell to cell like a spark.

The presently accepted alternative to the electrical theory, the *neurohumoral transmission theory* (Eckstein, 1970), proposes that synaptic transmission is not primarily electrical. Within the end of the axon on the transmitting neuron are small sacs (synaptic vesicles) of chemicals called *neurotransmitter substances* which, when electrically stimulated by the nerve impulse, break open and release the neurotransmitters into the space between the neurons. The neurotransmitters stimulate receptors on the dendrites of the "receiving" cell, and an electrical impulse builds in that second cell until it is sufficiently strong to produce a new impulse. Following transmission, the neurotransmitters generally are inactivated, either by being broken down and dissipated or by being taken back into the synaptic vesicles for reuse. As Brown (1976) states, it is now known that this chemical system of transmission "has profound significance for physiological psychology because it is apparently the primary mechanism by which neural activity is regulated. The extent to which behavior is related to neural activity involves, in large measure, chemical actions at the synapses. In that sense the synapse has been viewed as the locus of the mind" (p. 28).

Transmitter substances and their availability seem to have much to do with the occurrence of a variety of severe psychopathology. As we will see in later chapters, difficulties in neurotransmission, as reflected by abnormal variations in neurotransmitters such as *norepinephrine, serotonin, dopamine,* and *acetylcholine,* have been implicated in the patterns of psychotic depression and mania and in schizophrenia. We will discuss these implications in Chapters 7 and 8.

The Central Nervous System (CNS)

Effective neurotransmission is essential to the efficient operation of the central nervous system, the largest systematic collection of neurons and synapses in the body. The system is composed of the brain and spinal cord and is the master controller of physical and mental functions. Composed of nearly 12 billion neurons, the brain may be divided into several structures or divisions. Most of these structures aren't relevant to our understanding of abnormal behavior and won't be discussed here. However, the *limbic system*, a structure located near the middle of the brain, has been seen by many as critically important in the regulation of emotions such as rage, fear, and sexual arousal. Once thought to represent the "seat of emotion" (Papez, 1937), the limbic system is now known to be but a part of the overall neurological system for the regulation of feelings. From the perspective of abnormal psychology, perhaps more important than the limbic system and other components of the CNS are the activities of the peripheral nervous system.

The Peripheral Nervous System (PNS)

Parts of the nervous system not contained in the brain and spinal cord may be considered constituents of the peripheral nervous system (PNS). There are three major components of the PNS: the sensory system, the motor system, and the autonomic nervous system (Brown, 1976). The sensory system collects information from receptors such as the eyes, ears, and skin and sends it to the CNS for processing. The motor system carries messages from the CNS to the muscles of the body. The autonomic nervous system is involved with control of the "involuntary" systems of internal organs such as the heart, lungs, stomach, and so forth. Since the ANS is important for the understanding of abnormal emotional behavior, we will describe it further.

Generally, the autonomic nervous system is responsible for maintaining physical balance or homeostasis. For example, when the body is hot, the ANS controls sweating and other body changes which bring about cooling. Likewise, when the body is cold, the ANS may produce shivering and alteration of blood flow, which increase body heat. To aid in maintaining the functioning and safety of organisms, the ANS is composed of two structurally and functionally distinct components, the *sympathetic nervous system* and the *parasympathetic nervous system*. As seen in Figure 6-4, each major "involuntary" organ of the body is connected to both of these systems, allowing these systems to work antagonistically to maintain homeostasis. For example, while impulses from the sympathetic system typically *speed up* the heartbeat, impulses from the parasympathetic may *slow it down*. For another example, impulses from the sympathetic system may *dilate* the pupil of the eye, while impulses from the parasympathetic system *constrict* it.

The sympathetic system is a dominant determinant in emotional reactions, such as fear and flight, while the parasympathetic tends to be more dominant in sedentary functions such as the stimulation of digestion. Another look at Figure 6-4 will suggest how the sympathetic and parasympathetic systems are built appropriately for their special functions. Notice that the "switching stations," or ganglia (groups of neurons clumped to-

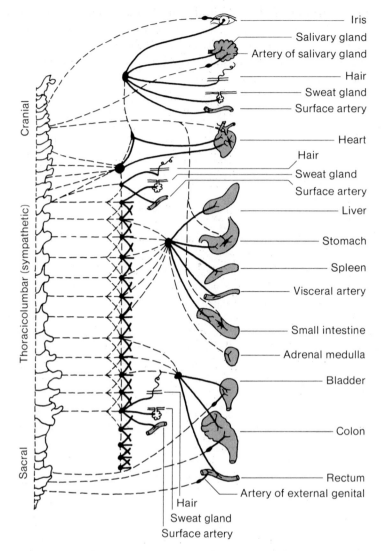

— Iris
— Salivary gland
— Artery of salivary gland
— Hair
— Sweat gland
— Surface artery
— Heart
Hair
— Sweat gland
— Surface artery
— Liver
— Stomach
— Spleen
— Visceral artery
— Small intestine
— Adrenal medulla
— Bladder
— Colon
— Rectum
— Artery of external genital

Cranial

Thoracicolumbar (sympathetic)

Sacral

Hair
Sweat gland
Surface artery

Figure 6-4. *The autonomic nervous system and its connections. From* Brain and Behavior, *by H. Brown. Copyright © by Oxford University Press. Based on a drawing by W. Cannon in* Bodily Changes in Pain, Hunger, Fear, and Rage, *copyright 1929 by Appleton, Century, Croft. Reprinted by permission of Oxford University Press, Inc. and Prentice-Hall, Inc.*

gether), for the sympathetic system are near the spinal cord and connected with one another in what is called the *sympathetic chain.* One result of this chaining means that when one of the ganglia is stimulated by the brain and spinal cord, *all* of them tend to be stimulated. Thus, the reaction of the sympathetic nervous system is general and diffuse. Most innervated organs probably are affected in the preparation for emotional expression or experience. Thus, when you are anxious, all organ systems affected by the sympathetic nerves become involved—your palms are sweaty, your heart beats faster, your digestion stops, your pupils dilate, your kidneys work faster, and so forth.

In contrast to the sympathetic system, where ganglia are near the spinal cord and interconnected, the ganglia for the parasympathetic system are located near the organ they control and are *not* interconnected in a chain. Because the parasympathetic ganglia are not connected, they usually affect only one organ at a time. Thus, after you have eaten a large meal, the parasympathetic system can signal your stomach to start digesting food with little or no effect upon your other organs.

We will see in Chapter 11 that the autonomic nervous system may be involved in the development of some psychologically based physical symptoms, such as migraine headaches. Constant tension may produce extended activity of the sympathetic system, thereby shutting down some important parasympathetic functions. For example, a person who is angry and upset much of the day may not be able to digest food properly; nutritional and gastric symptoms may appear after a lengthy period of such sympathetic-nervous-system dominance.

THE ENDOCRINE SYSTEM AND BEHAVIOR

The nervous system shares control of emotional behavior with the endocrine system, which affects behavior through glandular secretions called *hormones*. Endocrine-system effects are governed to some extent by a neurohumoral-transmission process similar to that found in the nervous system.

In contrast to the billions of neurons involved in the nervous system, there are only a few glands in the endocrine system. However, as seen in Figure 6-5 and Table 6-1, these relatively few glands exercise a wide range of behavioral control. The *pituitary*, like the brain, is the primary organizer of its own behavioral control system; but since it is regulated by a higher brain center, the endocrine system is itself an agent of the central nervous system (Brown, 1976). Under normal conditions the endocrine system significantly affects sexual behavior, maternal behavior, growth, sexual development, and stress reactions. For example, the endocrine system produces the release of adrenaline (epinephrine) that can give us a surge of energy during physically or emotionally stressful activities.

If the endocrine system functions properly, smoothly integrated behavior activities are usually observed. However, malfunctions of the endocrine glands have been related to a variety of physical disorders with psychological concomitants. For example, hypoactivity of the thyroid gland during early life may produce *cretinism*. Cretinism involves retarded

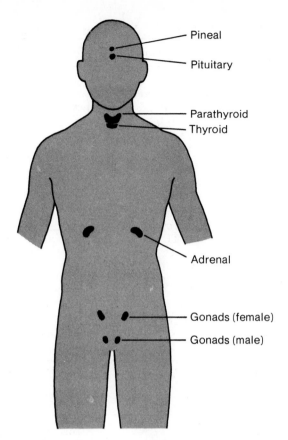

Figure 6-5. *Endocrine glands in the human body*

growth and intelligence, distorted body features, and psychosocial disabilities. Hyperactivity of the thyroid may result in Basedow's disease, usually characterized by irritability, anxiety, frequent changes in mood, and general emotional discomfort.

Abnormal variations in the secretion of other endocrines, such as the adrenals, parathyroids, and gonads, may also be accompanied by abnormal behavior patterns. For example, reduced levels of adrenal corticoids (Addison's disease) may be related to psychological symptoms such as fear, hallucinations, irrational beliefs, and depression, as well as to physical symptoms, which include muscular weakness, stomach upset, and pallor of the skin. Excess of adrenal corticoids may result in Cushing's disease, characterized by psychological symptoms such as crying, jitteriness, agitation, and irritability. In most instances of endocrine-based disorders, medical alteration of abnormal hormone levels may result in disappearance of psychological symptoms. However, in some instances, such as cretinism, the effects of endocrine imbalance are irreversible.

Table 6-1. *Functions of the endocrine system*

Gland	Locus	Hormone	Target	Function
Pituitary	Base of hypothalamus			
Neurohypophysis		Antidiuretic	Kidney	Stimulates reabsorption of water
		Oxytocin	Uterus	Stimulates contractions
			Mammary glands	Stimulates milk secretion
Adrenohypophysis		Somatotropic	Bone	Stimulates growth
		Thyrotropic	Thyroid gland	Activates thyroid secretion
		ACTH	Adrenal cortex	Stimulates steroid secretion
		Gonadotropic	Gonads	Stimulates secretion of estrogens and androgens
Thyroid	Neck, around pharynx	Thyroxin	Energy-expending tissues	Regulates metabolism
Parathyroid	Thyroid gland	Parathormone	Blood	Regulates calcium and phosphate levels
Adrenal	On kidneys			
Cortex		Adrenal steroids	Cell membranes	Electrolyte balance
Medulla		Epinephrine	Cardiovascular system	Increases blood flow
Pancreas	Below stomach	Insulin	Energy-expending tissues	Stimulates glucose absorption
Gonads	Sex organs	Estrogens (ovaries) Androgens (testes)	All tissues	Sex arousal, primary and secondary sex characteristics
Pineal	Third ventricle of brain	Melatonin	Gonads	Inhibits gonadal secretions

From *Brain and Behavior*, by H. Brown. Copyright © 1976 by Oxford University Press, Inc. Reprinted by permission.

BIOLOGICAL FACTORS IN BEING DIFFERENT

With this introduction to relevant neuroanatomy and neurobiochemistry, we may now turn to an examination of attempts to find biological bases for some psychological disorders. Three of the most popular approaches have been the search for a toxic factor, the search for a genetic factor, and the search for a biochemical factor.

The Search for a Toxic Factor

It isn't surprising that the first efforts to identify the biological causes of behavioral deviations would focus on *toxicity*. After all, it had been known for a long time that invading organisms such as bacteria and their accompanying toxins were associated with disease. Basically the search for toxic factors involved attempts to find some foreign substance or organism in the bodies of disordered people, to extract it, and to assess whether the substance or organism could produce the disease in others.

The history of the search for toxic factors in disordered behaviors is replete with "miracle" discoveries. A description of one of the earliest so-called miracles will demonstrate why many of those involved in the study of disordered behavior treat such findings with great caution. In 1932, Freud (not Sigmund) and Dingemanse published an article in which they reported the isolation of a specific biochemical in the blood of schizophrenics. The substance, which they called *catatonine*, was not usually found in the blood of nonschizophrenics whom they sampled. The optimism generated by their discovery was dampened a year later when they embarrassedly reported that their mystery substance was *nicotine* (Dingemanse & Freud, 1933). Indeed, what these researchers had "discovered" was biochemical evidence that the smoking habits of a certain group of mental patients were different from those of certain groups of normal people!

However, the search for toxic substances hasn't been without benefits. Through such investigations, a number of factors have been identified that may confound and mask relationships being investigated. For example, the possible confounding effects of eating habits, physical surroundings, and drug use now are tightly controlled in biochemical experiments, with the result that some possible "toxic factors" have been suggested more clearly.

Two such toxic substances once thought to be related to schizophrenia were *ceruloplasmin* and *taraxein*, biochemicals isolated by Heath (1954) and his co-workers (Heath & Mickle, 1960). Initially Heath attempted to find the cause for abnormal brain waves in schizophrenic patients. In his early attempts, he searched for ceruloplasmin (literally, blue plasma protein), also reported to be present in disordered people by Akerfeldt (1951). Heath could not isolate the substance in schizophrenic plasma, but he did find a somewhat similar substance, which he called *taraxein*. Reportedly, monkeys injected with taraxein produced abnormal brain waves and prison volunteers injected with taraxein produced abnormal behavior. Unfortunately, researchers outside Heath's group could not replicate these results even when the taraxein was supplied by Heath himself (Robins, Smith, & Lowe, 1957).

A second strategy suggests that body biochemistry malfunction, rather than a toxin, is the basis of behavioral difficulties. In this research approach, the goal is to determine whether the production or metabolism of certain *normal* biochemicals has gone awry. For example, one such biochemical substance, adrenochrome, is a normal metabolite (by-product) of adrenaline. In large amounts, adrenochrome has been shown to impede web-spinning in spiders and to produce psychoticlike behaviors in pigeons. Hoffer and Osmond (1958, 1959) proposed that psychotic people produce more adrenochrome during the normal course of their adrenaline metabolism than nonpsychotics. Consistent with his assumption, Hoffer and his associates (Hoffer, Payza, Szara, & Axelrod, 1960) found higher concentrations of adrenochrome in schizophrenics' blood. Again, though, as is so often the case in physiological research, this finding hasn't been easy to replicate (Szara, Axelrod, & Perline, 1958).

Although research directed at isolating specific metabolic abnormalities or toxins continues, much of it is now confined to particular disorders such as schizophrenia. Instead of discussing these studies here, we will consider them when we provide biological explanations for schizophrenia later in the book.

The Search for a Genetic Factor

Proponents of the genetic role in mental disorders generally believe that being different may be a hereditary characteristic. We know that some physical characteristics are inherited; each of us looks somewhat like his or her parents and siblings. It was once thought by proponents of Lamarckianism that many personality characteristics and learned skills also could be inherited, but it is clear to modern geneticists that inheritance is not so simple. Most genetic theorists accept the inheritability of physical characteristics but believe that personality characteristics are primarily the result of the environment in which a person develops. Some experts in behavior claim that heredity ("nature") is most important, and other experts favor environment ("nurture") as the crucial determinant of behaviors. This nature-nurture debate has raged for decades. Results of research suggest that there may be some inherited component in such disorders as schizophrenia and the affective psychoses (Chapters 7 and 8).

Naturally Occurring Genetic Experiments: The Kallikak Family.   One possible method of studying genetic effects on abnormal behavior is to observe naturally occurring cases of behavior disorder. In 1919, psychologist Henry Goddard published a report about a family he called the Kallikaks, which had a higher proportion of mental defectives and social problems among its members than would be expected on the average. To put his study of this family in perspective, we must note that Goddard was a Social Darwinist and believed that *eugenics*, the application of genetic knowledge to alter a species, should be applied to the human race. In fact, Goddard was psychological advisor to a group that published such papers as "Report of the Committee to Study and to Report on the Best Practical Means of Cutting Off the Defective Germ-plasm in the American Population" (1914). Specifically Goddard studied the Kallikak family to demonstrate the manner in which this "defective germ-plasm" could pass itself from generation to generation according to known laws of genetics.

Goddard's presentation begins with Martin Kallikak (see Figure 6-6 for a sketch of the Kallikak family tree), who had seven normal children with his lawful wife. But Martin apparently "fooled around" some, because Goddard reported that Martin had sexual relations with a "nameless feeble-minded girl." As seen in Figure 6-6, his indiscretion resulted in a feeble-minded son named Martin Jr., who married a seemingly normal woman, Rhoda, who gave birth to eight living children, five of whom deviated into sexual promiscuity, alcoholism, and feeble-mindedness. Figure 6-7 shows that when one of these children, Old Sal, married a feeble-minded husband, the coupling of both "defective germ-plasms" resulted in severe retardation among almost all of the descendants.

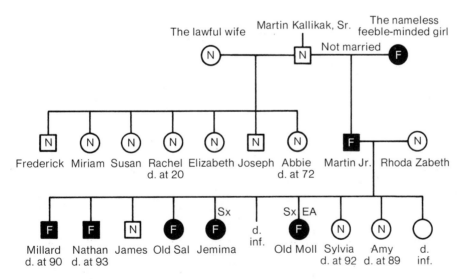

N = Normal. F = Feeble-minded. Sx = Sexually immoral. A = Alcoholic.
D = Deaf. d. inf. = died in infancy.

Figure 6-6. *Martin Kallikak's family tree. From* The Kallikak Family, *by H. Goddard. Copyright © 1919 by Macmillan Publishing Co., Inc.*

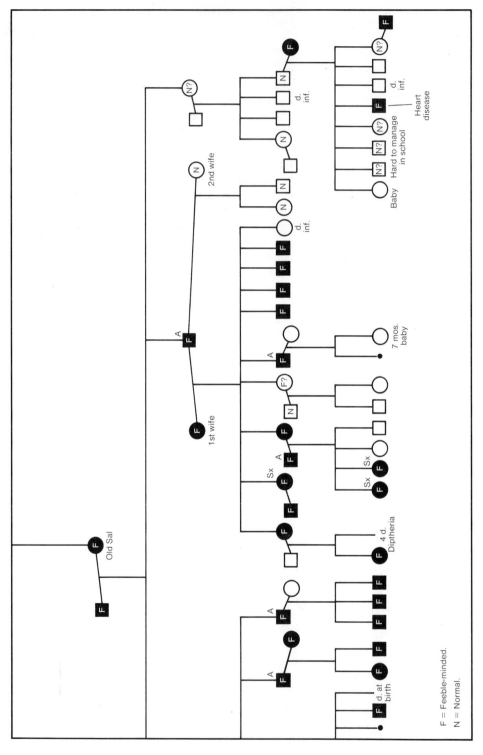

Figure 6-7. *When feeble-minded marries feeble-minded. From The Kallikak Family, by H. Goddard. Copyright © 1919 by Macmillan Publishing Co., Inc.*

F = Feeble-minded.

N = Normal.

After proposing that "a-sexualization" of Martin Jr. would have prevented so much "bad blood" from entering the human race, Goddard's conclusion is as follows:

> We find on the good side of the family prominent people in all walks of life and nearly all of the 496 descendants owners of land or properties. On the bad side we find paupers, criminals, prostitutes, drunkards, and examples of all forms of social pest with which modern society is burdened [1919, p. 116].

Goddard tended to lump deviant behavior together, without differentiating between, say, schizophrenia and retardation or alcoholism. Although some of the data from naturally occurring "experiments" do support the notion that aberrations run in families, controlled research with animals and people provides us with a more realistic evaluation of the significance of inheritability of disordered behavior.

Planned and Controlled Genetic Experiments. The storylike presentation of Goddard's data may be interesting, but it lacks the scientific validity available through controlled studies of animals and people. We all know that there may be different temperaments among animals, such as dogs. For example, Dobermans are potentially more vicious than terriers. Essentially, types of "personality" may be bred for in animals. Research-based genetic explanations of abnormal behavior share the belief that people, like lower animals, inherit various emotional traits and behavioral propensities that may lead them to be abnormal.

C. Hall (1934), a pioneer in psychogenetics, studied the inheritance of emotionality in rats. He used ratings to describe the emotional responsiveness of rats when they were placed in a large, open area. For nine generations, those animals rated high on emotionality were inbred, as were those with low ratings. The strain of animals rated high in emotionality became more emotional with each ensuing generation. However, the low-emotional rats reached a low point of emotionality within one generation and didn't reduce their level of emotionality further with subsequent breeding. Hall concluded from these findings that it was possible to breed selectively for psychological characteristics and that, were controlled studies in humans possible, similar results would be obtained.

Unfortunately the time required to repeat Hall's study with humans is prohibitive. Within their own lifetimes, researchers cannot follow five or ten generations of people, nor can they "inbreed" people deliberately. One possible solution might be to use family histories of currently diagnosed people to determine what their hereditary line has been. Exemplified in its grossest form by Goddard's work with the Kallikaks, this retrospective methodology has recently attained a higher level of sophistication. However, before describing the results of these more recent studies, let us provide you with some of the language necessary for understanding genetic data.

A case of a particular behavior disorder usually is identified by traditional diagnostic means (see Chapter 2). When the genetic background of the particular person comes under research scrutiny, the person is labeled a *proband.* A proband is the person about whom hereditary information is sought and with whom concordance and discordance are assessed. *Concordance* means that a given relative has the same disorder as the proband; *discordance* means that the relative does not. *Percentage risk* or *heritability* refers to the statistical chance that a given relative of a proband will inherit the disorder in question.

Most of the significant research relating genetics to abnormal behavior has been done with twins as the basic population. The reason for using twins may be obvious to you. Identical or *monozygotic* (MZ) twins share the exact same genetic endowment. Therefore, if a disorder is passed through the genes, one would expect that if one MZ twin is a proband, the other twin should be concordant for the aberration; that is, if one identical twin is schizophrenic, so should the other be. *Dizygotic* (DZ) or fraternal twins do *not* share the same exact genetic programming, but they do experience somewhat the same environment at the same times in their lives; genetically, they are no more similar than *full siblings* (brothers and sisters born at different times to the same parents). As you can see, in twins, we have a naturally occurring experimental design: MZ twins control primarily for genetics, and DZ twins control primarily for environment. If concordance rates for a given disorder are higher for MZ, we conclude that heredity probably is more important; if DZ concordance is high, then environment may be a more potent factor.

Given this basic information, let us now take a look at some of the early data relating inheritance to disordered behaviors. Because it is the most widely occurring of all the psychoses, most of the studies dealt with schizophrenia. A classic genetic research began with the impressive efforts of Franz Kallmann (1938, 1946, 1953). In his original study, 1087 schizophrenic probands (twins, siblings, and so on) were identified and the concordance among over 12,000 of their relatives was calculated. Generally, results suggested that schizophrenia tended to "run in families"; the closer the blood relationship, the more likely it was that concordance would occur. According to Kallmann (1946), the chances of concordance in monozygotic twins reared together could be as high as 91.5%. That is, if one twin was diagnosed as schizophrenic, then nine times out of ten so was the other. Further, as the blood relationship became more distant, the risk of the disorder also became lower.

Inferences drawn from such data created a mild sensation. If inheritance could explain the incidence of severe disordered behavior, then merely by stopping "defective" individuals from reproducing, schizophrenia might be prevented. However, closer inspection of Kallmann's data reveals some methodological problems. For instance, many of those who diagnosed probands and their relatives may have been given faulty data. Some patients may have been diagnosed as schizophrenic simply because their relatives were so diagnosed. Further, there was some question as to whether patients were being reliably and accurately classified as schizophrenic. As suggested in Chapter 1, there are some serious problems in our classification systems. More telling than these criticisms, better-controlled research usually failed to replicate Kallmann's high figures.

A summary of the data relating genetics and schizophrenia is presented in Table 6-2. The synthesis of results of a large number of studies shows that MZ concordance is significantly higher than is DZ for both schizophrenia and the affective psychoses (manic and depressive), suggesting a definite genetic influence in these disorders. In fact, MZ rates are usually higher than DZ for every severe behavioral aberration studied.

While research with twins has continued from Kallmann's time to the present, a significant amount of recent research has used a methodology in which adopted children with behavior problems are compared to their biological and adoptive parents. The rationale for the method seems sound. If behavior disorders are primarily transmitted genetically, a child born of one or two disturbed biological parents would be expected to develop a disorder even if adopted by normal parents. A basic research question is, "If a child with schizophrenic inheritance is raised by adoptive nonschizophrenic parents, are his chances less or the same for developing schizophrenia?"

Shields (1973) has concluded that the results from adoption studies such as those done by Rosenthal and Kety (1968) generally support the hypothesis that "the raised incidence of schizophrenia in the families of schizophrenics is to be accounted for by shared genes and not by having been reared by a mentally ill parent" (p. 583). Considering the data on adoptees and twins, we find it difficult to deny the importance of genetics in the occurrence of some abnormal behavior. In later chapters we will see that the recent evidence for a relationship between heredity and severe mental disturbance is substantial.

Table 6-2. *Selected studies of concordance rates in schizophrenia of monozygotic and dizygotic twins*

Investigator	Year	Country	Percentage of MZ Twins Both Diagnosed Schizophrenic	Percentage of DZ Twins Both Diagnosed Schizophrenic
Gottesman and Shields	1966	England	42	9
Kringlen	1967	Norway	25–38	8–12
Fischer, Harvald, and Hauge	1969	Denmark	29–48	10–19
Tienari	1975	Finland	15	7

Adapted from "Twins—Still Our Best Method," by E. Kringlen, *Schizophrenia Bulletin*, 1976, *2*, 429–433. National Institute of Mental Health, U.S. Department of Health, Education, and Welfare.

A Genetic-Environmental Explanation: Diathesis-Stress Theory. Although it is supported by research data, a relationship between genes and behavior still tells us little about the specific mechanics of the development of behavior disorder. For example, why do some children grow up with parents who are psychotic and yet not develop psychoses? Conversely, how can a person develop a psychosis when the parents and family are not so disturbed? The need to take into account both heredity and environment in the development of disordered behavior seems logical. *Diathesis-stress theory* represents an attempt to elucidate the contributions of heredity as well as environment. Since concordance rates in MZ twins are rarely perfect for abnormal behavior, environment must play some role in determining the occurrence or nonoccurrence of disorders. Kallmann (1953) reported that for schizophrenia, concordance rates for MZ twins reared apart were lower than for twins reared together. Others (for example, Shields & Slater, 1961) also have reported that among discordant MZ pairs, environmental factors appear to play a significant role in whether both twins manifest the disorder. To explain these findings, the diathesis-stress theory makes the assumption that people are endowed genetically with a predisposition (diathesis) toward developing a particular behavioral disorder. Given sufficient environmental stress, the predisposition may manifest itself behaviorally. Twins, both diathetic for schizophrenia, and both raised in the same stressful environment, should both develop the disorder. However, if they are separated at birth, the twin living in the less stressful environment may not develop the disorder.

Perhaps the best application of the diathesis-stress theory to explain behavior disorder was offered by Paul Meehl (1962). Meehl proposed that there was an inherited neural defect in schizophrenics that he called *schizotaxia.* When the schizotaxic individual's predisposition toward schizophrenia is combined with normal learning from society, it sometimes produces a *schizotypic personality structure.* This personality structure usually includes four core behavior patterns: *anhedonia* (a defect in pleasure capacity); *ambivalence* (inability to choose, or mixed feelings about things); *autism* (a withdrawal into the self); and *dereism* (a tendency toward fantasies and hallucinations). Meehl states that all of these patterns are "universally" learned by schizotaxic individuals no matter where they are reared. He further states, "Only a subset of schizotypic personalities decompensate into clinical schizophrenia. It seems likely that the most important causal influence pushing the schizotype toward decompensation is the *schizophrenogenic mother*" (p. 380). Thus, Meehl concluded that the multiple factors contributing to the development of mental disorder were the genetic predisposition for schizophrenia, the development of the four core behavior patterns, *and* a particular kind of mother.

Diathesis-stress theory allows us to explain why two siblings raised in the same home might be discordant for psychosis: one may be schizotaxic, while the other is not. The theory also explains why identical twins (if one is schizotaxic, both must be) reared apart seem to have lower concordance rates: some of the twins have gone into nonschizophrenogenic environments. A more involved and complete statement of the diathesis-stress theory can be found in Rosenthal and Kety (1968). We will describe more recent evidence for the role of genetics in schizophrenia and other psychoses in Chapters 7 and 8.

The Search for a Biochemical Factor

Unlike genetic researchers, who deal with gross aspects of behavior and physical characteristics, those seeking biochemical factors in abnormal behavior have attempted to focus on a more specific level of investigation: discovering defects in the biochemical functions involved in normal neural synaptic transmission.

Earlier in this chapter, we described some of the neurotransmitter substances and their role in nerve communication. Researchers have noted that there are certain parts of the brain where specific transmitter substances usually are found in greater concentrations. These sites of greater concentration have led some investigators to conclude that the transmitters may be crucial to brain functioning in that particular area. Different research approaches have been used to delineate exactly how neural transmitters affect behavior. In one such approach, the quantity of transmitter substance may be depleted or elevated by using drugs and the ensuing effects observed. For example, it is known that administration of certain antidepressant medications (see Chapter 24) normalizes the level of the transmitter norepinephrine. With greater amounts of norepinephrine, neurons tend to fire more smoothly and elevation of mood may be observed.

In a second approach to studying the role of neurotransmitters in behavior, levels of neurochemicals may be altered via *implantation*. By means of a delicate surgical procedure, a small tube called a *cannula* may be lowered into a specific site in the brain. The chemical to be studied is then passed through the tube until it reaches the area under study and the subsequent effects can be observed. In an early demonstration of the effects of the implantation of different neurotransmitters on behavior, S. Grossman (1960) administered the neurotransmitters acetylcholine and norepinephrine to rats. When a specific brain area was stimulated with acetylcholine, animals acted as if they were hungry and ate a great deal; when the very same area was implanted with norepinephrine, the animals appeared thirsty and drank a lot of water. The important point here is that neurochemicals may be clearly involved in the control of eating and drinking, as well as most other "normal" bodily functions. Some researchers reason that any difficulty in the normal biochemical function of the nervous system may also be reflected in abnormal behavior; that is, in the same way that an acetylcholine-depleted animal may not be able to move even if it "wants" to, a schizophrenic may not be able to think clearly, even if he or she wants to. If the "chemical stuff" needed for nerve transmission is unavailable or chemically out of balance, messages may go out but never arrive at their destination.

CONCLUDING COMMENTS

There have been several very exciting discoveries of biochemical factors in schizophrenia and manic-depressive psychosis in recent years. Much of the biochemical work in disordered behavior seems to have been spurred by the advent of the tranquilizers and antidepressant drugs. In searching for better medications, researchers have learned an immense amount about what happens neurochemically in severely disturbed people. We will discuss some of the specifics of these findings in Section III. Suffice it to say here that if a biological cause of psychosis is to be found, then the most likely place to find it is in the neurotransmitters and their interaction with physical and psychological experience.

CHAPTER SUMMARY CHART

In Chapter 6 we have discussed the basic information necessary for an understanding of biological explanations of abnormal behavior:

Central nervous system	*Peripheral nervous system*	*Endocrine system*
Brain Neurohumoral transmission Neurotransmitters Spinal cord	Autonomic nervous system: sympathetic parasympathetic Antagonistic and involved in involuntary function	Hormones Pituitary gland—the master disorders associated with endocrine imbalance

We then described three basic methods of searching for biological factors in abnormal behavior:

The toxic factor	*The genetic factor*	*Biochemical factors*
Invading poisons Taraxein Metabolic problems	Nature versus nurture The Kallikaks Psychogenetics Kallmann: twins Adoption studies Diathesis-stress theory	Neurotransmitters and neural communication Abnormality related to excesses or dearth of neurotransmitters

SECTION III
THE PSYCHOSES

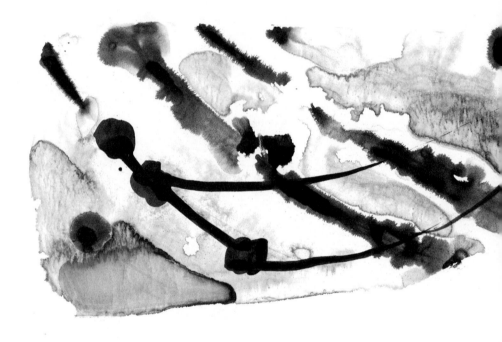

Chapter 7
Schizophrenia

Chapter 8
Affective Disorders

Chapter 9
**Paranoid Conditions and
the Rare Psychological Disturbances**

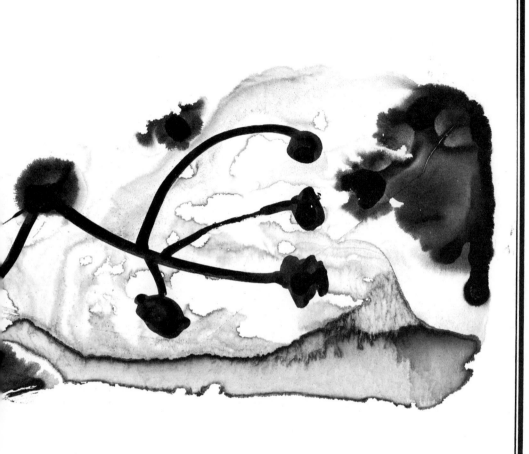

In Section III we will look closely at the psychoses, an extremely severe form of behavior disorder. Psychotic people are characterized by a lack of contact with the reality around or within them. The majority of psychotic people are so involved with severely distorted thoughts or feelings that it is often impossible for them to relate effectively with others. The psychoses affect a surprisingly large number of people in the United States and the rest of the world. We will discuss these disturbances in three separate chapters. First, in Chapter 7, we will describe the most widely occurring psychotic patterns, the schizophrenias. In Chapter 8, we will discuss the affective psychoses, and Chapter 9 will cover the paranoid psychoses and a selection of other, more unusual severe disturbances.

151

CHAPTER 7
SCHIZOPHRENIA

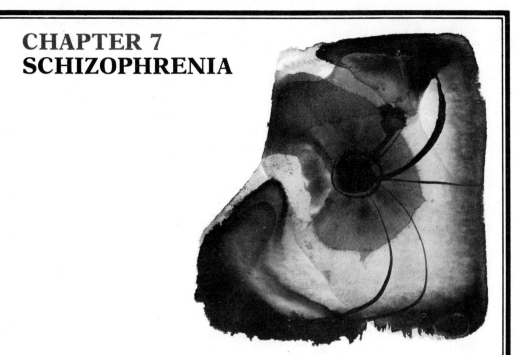

     The most common form of psychotic behavior is schizophrenia. Schizophrenia is characterized by "breakdown of integrated personality function, withdrawal from reality, emotional blocking, distortion, and disturbances of thought and behavior" (Coleman, 1974, p. 772). However, no professional or clinical description of the set of disorders referred to as the schizophrenias can begin to make one appreciate the seriousness of this psychosis.

     In fact, schizophrenia is an extremely serious disorder that is very widespread. It has been estimated (Babigian, 1975; Mosher & Feinsilver, 1971) that between 180,000 and 200,000 new cases of schizophrenia are diagnosed each year in the United States. Counting previously diagnosed cases, approximately 2 million Americans suffer from some form of schizophrenia at any time; the odds are 1 in 100 that a given United States citizen may be diagnosed as schizophrenic during his or her lifetime. Worldwide, it has been estimated that there are over 10 million schizophrenic people (Lehmann, 1975a). Schizophrenia is obviously not a rare behavioral aberration. With over half of all mental-hospital beds being occupied by schizophrenic patients, the schizophrenias represent a major challenge for those dealing with behavioral disorders.

Owing to its status as a major problem, schizophrenia has attracted a large amount of theoretical and research attention. In a text focusing only on the schizophrenias, it might be possible to describe all the possible theories and research concerning this disorder. However, in our text, we have had to select the more prominent and promising explanations for schizophrenic behavior. In what will be our pattern in most chapters on specific disorders, we will present descriptions of the schizophrenias, followed by a series of explanations offered for the disorder. We close the chapter with a brief look at therapies specifically directed at schizophrenic disorders.

DESCRIPTIONS

The different types of schizophrenia share some general characteristics. We will present those characteristics often used by diagnosticians in identifying schizophrenia across all subtypes. After introducing the general features of schizophrenia, we will describe the differences that typically separate its various subcategories.

Fundamental Characteristics

Bleuler (1930) pointed out four common fundamental characteristics of schizophrenia: disturbance of *affect*, disturbance of *association*, disturbance of *activity*, and presence of behavior that is *autistic* (detached from reality). Although of historical interest, these characteristics (known as the four A's) bear little specific similarity to characteristics of schizophrenia as viewed by modern diagnosticians. Current experts (Sartorius, Shapiro, & Jablensky, 1974; Schneider, 1957) usually consider schizophrenia to be a conglomerate of dysfunctions (see Table 7-1) in the general, behavioral, perceptual, cognitive, affective, and verbal realms of human behavior. We will now describe in more detail the dysfunctions in each of these six realms.

General Dysfunctions.   Observed in almost all schizophrenic people (Lehmann, 1975a), the general deficiencies associated with schizophrenia are a group of five special characteristics. *Symbolism*, the first characteristic, is the pronounced use of indirectly related patterns in speech, thought, and behavior. The use of symbolism in schizophrenia may be exemplified by a woman who used the sun as a symbol of important people in her life and thus spoke of the "sunshine," rather than the love, of her family.

Schizophrenics also show increased *sensitivity* to sensory and emotional stimulation. Because of this hypersensitivity, schizophrenics may be more responsive to sensory stimulation than normal people.

Table 7-1. *Core characteristics of schizophrenia*

Characteristics	Frequency among Patients
Lack of insight	97%
Auditory hallucinations	74
Verbal hallucinations	70
Ideas of reference	67
Suspiciousness	66
Flatness of affect	66
Voices speaking to patient	65
Delusional mood	64
Delusions of persecution	54
Inadequate description	64
Thought alienation	52
Thought spoken aloud	50

From "The International Pilot Study of Schizophre-nia," by N. Sartorius et al., *Schizophrenia Bulletin*, 1974, *1*, 21–34. National Institute of Mental Health, U.S. Depart-ment of Health, Education and Welfare.

In addition to symbolism and increased sensitivity, schizophrenics exhibit *social withdrawal*. With few exceptions, the schizophrenic person is isolated and alienated from others and frequently cannot establish close relationships.

Schizophrenics also show a *loss of ego boundaries* and are unable to know where *I* ends and *you* begins. Thus, schizophrenics may believe others can read their minds or understand their bizarre speech. Conversely, some schizophrenics may feel they can read others' thoughts. In extreme cases of loss of ego boundary, people may see themselves as being merged or fused with inanimate objects such as rocks or TV sets.

A fifth general characteristic of schizophrenia, *variability*, refers to the frequent unpredictability and inconsistency of schizophrenic behavior. In contrast to "normal" people, whose behavior is ordinarily predictable, schizophrenic people can make us uneasy because we don't know what they will do next.

Behavioral Dysfunctions. Whereas the general dysfunctions are common to most schizophrenic people, additional specific dysfunctions are possible in a variety of areas. The schizophrenic person may show too much or too little activity, and the activity may be bizarre and unpredictable. Behavioral dysfunctions vary from person to person, but we can delineate four general kinds.

Grotesque grimacing and flailing of the arms or legs are examples of the first kind of behavioral dysfunction, called *psychotic mannerisms*. In some cases, the schizophrenic person's eyes may be held in either a down-ward or a skyward gaze and he or she may exhibit a wry smile. Although

Isolation and withdrawal are common characteristics of the schizophrenias. (Photo by Robert Foothorap.)

these mannerisms hold little communication value for an observer, they may be very meaningful to the schizophrenic person.

Besides strange mannerisms, the schizophrenic may show *echopraxia*, or the mimicking of behavior seen in others. Patients rarely seem to realize the negative effect of such behavior on those around them, even though it may be maddening to the "mimickee." Verbal requests or demands to stop the echopractic activity are usually ineffective.

In *stereotyped behavior*, the schizophrenic repeats self-initiated behaviors, such as pacing back and forth between two doors, for hours on end. One of the authors remembers a patient who for a year and a half rubbed her index finger up and down on her forehead every minute by the clock. Her stereotyped behavior resisted repeated attempts at alteration.

While the previous behavioral dysfunctions affect speech or movement, the last kind is the typical *slovenly appearance* and *poor social manners* of schizophrenic people. In some mental hospitals, one can still observe patients who haven't bathed or washed in days, whose clothing is soiled with feces or urine, and who walk about with no recognition of those around them. Social skills are rarely used by schizophrenics; for example, they usually don't smile when you smile at them. Although not frequent today, public masturbation and public sexual activity have been observed among long-term hospitalized schizophrenic patients.

Perceptual Dysfunctions.   In addition to deviations in behavior patterns, schizophrenic people may manifest *perceptual dysfunctions.* Distortions in, or absence of, accurate perceptions of the real world have been described by Lehmann (1975a):

> [The schizophrenic] frequently sees objects and people change their dimension, their outline and their brightness . . . before his eyes. . . . Time may become devoid of any structure or meaning and the experience of passing of time may extend or contract. . . [Perceptual] disturbances include hypersensitivity to light, changes in perception of other people's faces, misperception of movement, hypersensitivity to sound or smell or taste [p. 892].

The most common form of perceptual dysfunctions seen among schizophrenics is the *hallucination.* Hallucinations may be defined as sensory experiences for which there are no external stimuli. For example, the lines from a song by Irving Berlin, "I hear singing and there's no one there; I smell blossoms, and the trees are bare," are an excellent example of hallucinations. You remember, however, that the characters who sing these lines aren't *sick,* they're just in love.[1]

The most frequent types of hallucinations are *auditory.* Most often people hear voices (their own, God's, their family's) talking, screaming, whispering, or singing at or about them. With the loss of ego boundaries described earlier, it is frequently impossible for hallucinators to know whether the voices come from inside them or from such commonly claimed sources as radiators, TV sets, furniture, and the like.

Next in frequency of occurrence are *visual* hallucinations. Some schizophrenic people may claim to see things of a frightening or symbolic nature, usually in conjunction with an auditory hallucination. Thus, the person who *hears* God screaming may also *see* God or an angel in the room.

Although they are far less frequent than auditory and visual misperceptions, hallucinations of smell, taste, and touch also can occur.

Cognitive Dysfunctions.   Parallel to hallucinations, cognitive dysfunctions are ideas or thoughts that have no basis in reality. We can delineate two types of cognitive disturbances, *delusions* and *dysfunctions of thinking.*

---

[1] Excerpt from "You're Just in Love," by Irving Berlin. © Copyright 1950 by Irving Berlin. © Copyright renewed 1977 by Irving Berlin. Reprinted by permission of Irving Berlin Music Corporation.

A common feature in some sorts of schizophrenia, delusions are incorrect beliefs that cannot easily be corrected by discussion or logical argument. The content of delusions can vary widely. Table 7-2 is a listing of the types of delusions most frequently encountered. Remember that most of us have some false ideas not soundly based in fact. For example, many left-wingers probably feel that extreme right-wing political groups are "paranoid about communism," and the right-wingers may feel that the leftists are "blind pawns" of communism. It is likely that neither group is completely correct—each is deluded a little. Pathological delusions are different from such everyday political beliefs, however, for the psychotic person is quite alone in his or her misperception of the world. There is usually little or no basis in fact for the schizophrenic person's delusional ideas, and their bizarreness is apparent to most people—even to other patients with different delusions!

Dysfunctions of thinking differ from delusional thinking in that they emphasize the manner in which schizophrenics mentally process information, rather than the content of such information. One example of thought disturbance is the use of special rules of logic called *paralogic* (Arieti, 1966). An illustration of paralogical thinking is the following: "The Virgin Mary was a virgin. I am a virgin: therefore, I am the Virgin Mary" (p. 37). Matte-Blanco (1959) described what is called the *pathological symmetry* of schizophreniclike logic: "John is Peter's father, therefore Peter is John's father" (p. 254).

Disturbances in thought also have been ascribed to factors other than faulty logic. For example, Payne (1966) has shown that schizophrenics cannot easily filter out unnecessary stimuli and therefore have difficulty in

Table 7-2. *Delusions common among schizophrenics and other psychotic people*

Delusion of influence	A belief that others are influencing one by means of wires, TV, and so on, making one do things against one's will.
Delusion of grandeur	The belief that one is in actuality some great world or historical figure, such as Napoleon, Queen Victoria, or the President of the United States.
Delusion of persecution	The belief that one is being persecuted, hunted, or interfered with by certain individuals or organized groups.
Delusion of reference	The belief that others are talking about one, that one is being included in TV shows or plays or referred to in news articles, and so on.
Delusion of bodily change	A belief that one's body is changing in some unusual way—for example, that the blood is turning to snakes or the flesh to concrete.
Delusion of nihilism	A belief that nothing really exists, that all things are simply shadows; also common is the idea that one has really been dead for many years and is observing the world from afar.

focusing on the important components of a situation. Shakow (1971) believes that the schizophrenic person has difficulty responding to irrelevant stimuli and therefore may experience constant interruption in thought processes. For this reason, it is characteristic of many schizophrenics to stop in the middle of a thought and change to a new topic.

Affective Dysfunctions. Although primarily a disorder of thought and perception, schizophrenia also can include alterations in affective or emotional responsiveness. Most notable among these affective alterations is reduced emotional responsiveness or *blunting.* Many schizophrenics exhibit "flat" affect; that is, they tend not to respond to situations with normal levels of feeling. Venables and Wing (1962) theorize that schizophrenic people may be so involved with responding to internally generated stimuli that they can't respond to anything else. In contrast, Mednick (1958) proposed that schizophrenics actually protect themselves from stimuli with which they can't cope by "turning themselves off."

Perhaps even more common than emotional blunting in schizophrenic people are *inappropriate emotional responses.* For example, a schizophrenic person may smile or laugh while talking about the horrible way his or her mother died. Generally, the more pronounced the inappropriateness of emotion, the more severe the schizophrenia. Indeed, the re-

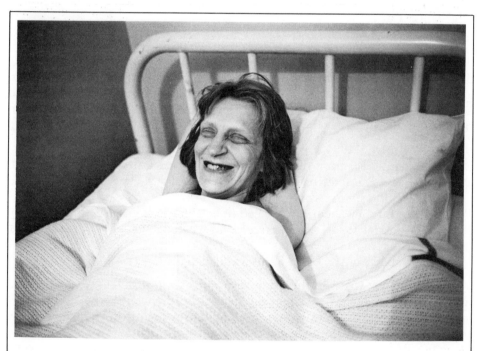

Inappropriate and uncontrolled elation may accompany severe psychological disorders. (Photo by Mary Ellen Mark/Magnum.)

turn of appropriate affect and reduction of blunting are often significant signs that the patient is on the road to recovery.

Verbal Dysfunctions. The verbal deficits typical of schizophrenia are probably the first to be observed and the most disconcerting. Verbal dysfunctions can take a variety of forms, each representing some degree of deviation from normal conversation.

In one bizarre speech behavior called *mutism,* the schizophrenic may not utter a sound for anywhere from a few hours to several years. Typically, encouragement or prodding has little to do with the return of normal speech.

In *echolalia,* a second bizarre speech pattern, the schizophrenic person answers questions in such a way as to repeat most of the words of the questions. For example:

Therapist: How are you today?
Patient: Today I am fine.
T: When did you come to the hospital?
P: I came to the hospital two days ago.

Echolalia may also take the form of total repetition of another's speech:

Therapist: Today is a nice day.
Patient: Today is a nice day.
T: How do you feel today?
P: How do you feel today?

Incoherent speech differs from echolalia in that the schizophrenic person may speak as if he or she were saying something very definite, but in actuality it makes little sense. Often the speaker becomes quite animated and awaits some reply. The following example demonstrates what we mean by incoherent speech:

Therapist: Why are you here?
Patient: I cannot fail to let him see that I am barren and wasted. The Prime Minister is raving and yelled at me but I feel cold.
T: But why are you here?
P: You don't hear me or need to hear me. I cannot see the trees any longer for they are barren and wasted. The leaves are dead and my mother. Witches are Halloween Eve. The sky is black and shoe polish. Hail to the walfordstefkin.

The final word in the above example, *walfordstefkin,* exemplifies a fourth form of verbal dysfunction in psychotic people, the creation of *neologisms.* Literally "new words," neologisms probably are constructed by schizophrenics because no word in the normal language can express the idea they're trying to convey. For example, upon investigation, the word *walfordstefkin* was found to mean the patient's brother Walter's car (a Ford) was being kept by his wife Stephanie's relatives. However, most neologisms aren't so easy to decipher and remain logical only in the private domain of the schizophrenic's disturbed thoughts.

Verbigeration refers to the senseless repeating of the same word or phrase for hours or even days. Thankfully, verbigeration is rare. It is the verbal equivalent of the stereotypic repetition of certain behaviors that we described earlier.

DIAGNOSTIC SUBTYPES

Now that we have described the general and specific dysfunctions often seen in all subtypes of schizophrenia, we will describe the specific subtypes themselves. The diagnostic subtypes of schizophrenia are determined primarily by the *content* of symptoms and variations in the fundamental characteristics of schizophrenia. Discrimination among the various subcategories often is difficult, not only for students, but for professional diagnosticians as well.

Catatonic Schizophrenia

Motor involvement usually distinguishes catatonic schizophrenia from other forms. Further, differences in disturbed motor behaviors differentiate the two kinds of catatonic schizophrenia: *stuporous catatonia* and *agitated catatonia.*

In stuporous catatonia, spontaneous motor activity is reduced markedly, and automatic obedience, waxy flexibility, and mutism are present. *Automatic obedience* refers to the catatonic person's tendency to follow all instructions, no matter how absurd. For example, a patient who was told to stand on one foot and pat his or her head would do so without hesitation. In *waxy flexibility*, there is compliance of a more passive sort. Here, the person may be placed in a wide variety of awkward postures and usually will remain in such a position until moved out of it. Catatonic schizophrenic people may also manifest mutism or be unable to speak or respond spontaneously.

Completely opposite from the reduction of activity seen in stuporous catatonia is the motor excitement characterizing agitated catatonia. Here the patient manifests wild, uncontrollable verbal behavior and very destructive motor behavior. In these destructive episodes, some patients have gouged out their eyes and pulled sinks off walls. In fact, prior to the advent of the psychoactive drugs (see Chapter 24), agitated catatonia also was known as fatal catatonia (Stauder, 1934), because without effective methods of halting the wild excitement the patient often died of exhaustion.

Hebephrenic Schizophrenia

More talkative and active than most catatonic people, the hebephrenic schizophrenic is a bundle of energy characterized by primitive, disorganized, and regressive behavior. Hebephrenic people often are slovenly dressed and incoherent in speech. There is usually little real reason for the "joy" they manifest, and their behavior can best be described as "silly." The following personal experience of an actively hallucinating hebephrenic patient shows a lack of clear response to our initial question and a special type of thinking distortion called *clang*. In clanging, the person speaks in rhymes; new thoughts or topics emerge as a result of a rhyming relationship with the previous thought. Thus *knees* leading to *nephew* (probably via *niece*) is an example of a clang association, an association made on the basis of sound rather than content.

PERSONAL EXPERIENCE: *A Hebephrenic Speaks in Clang*

Interviewer: How does it feel to have your problems?

Patient: Who can tell me the name of my song? I don't know, but it won't be long. It won't be short, tall, none at all. My head hurts, my knees hurt—my nephew, his uncle, my aunt. My god, I'm happy . . . not a care in the world. My hair's been curled, the flag's unfurled. This is my country, land that I love (singing), this is the country, land that I love.

I: How do you feel?

P: Happy! Don't you hear me? (Mumbles some incomprehensible things.) Why do you talk to me? Rowf! Rowf! (Barks like a dog.)

Paranoid Schizophrenia

Whereas the catatonic person's major difficulty is in movement and the hebephrenic's is in emotion, the paranoid schizophrenic person is characterized by strong delusions of persecution, influence, or grandeur. These characteristics are shown in the personal experience that follows.

PERSONAL EXPERIENCE: *The Fears of a Paranoid Schizophrenic*

I felt that a group of people were banding together to destroy my life. I remember feeling that the mail I received was coded in some way that my wife could understand and I couldn't. Once I saw an advertisement addressed to my wife from a car dealer. It said "Come and see our new line of small cars." I was sure that my wife was having an affair with the car dealer and that the ad was a message telling her when and where to meet with him. I felt almost like I had a fever; my face got flushed and I felt warm all over. My heart was pounding. I was so angry I had trouble breathing. I ran into the house and threw the card at my wife. I started screaming at her. She started to cry and I knew that I was right; I started to hit her and she ran to our neighbor's house. I don't remember what happened then. I woke up here at the hospital. I'm still not entirely sure I was wrong about her, but she does say I thought it all up. I don't really know.

Generally, paranoid schizophrenics seem to be more intelligent and to manifest a "healthier" life than the other subtypes. Approximately half of all schizophrenic first admissions to mental hospitals are diagnosed as paranoid. Of course, the paranoid schizophrenic *is* basically schizophrenic and therefore may also exhibit the general characteristics of personality deterioration and thought disorders.

The category of paranoid schizophrenia also includes people who are so disoriented that they believe they are important people such as Joan of Arc, Napoleon, or Jesus Christ. Often the belief that one is a famous person represents the schizophrenic's attempt to understand why others are "persecuting" him. The normal person would say, "I'm not important enough to be really persecuted so I must be wrong about my suspicions"; the paranoid schizophrenic may say, "I'm being persecuted. There must be a reason. Only famous, important people are persecuted. Therefore, I *must* be such a person."

Other Schizophrenias

In addition to the three major subtypes we have just described, there are several other patterns of schizophrenia. *Simple schizophrenia*, which occurs fairly frequently, doesn't usually involve the gross behavioral deviations described thus far. Rather, the simple schizophrenic person is characterized by a lack of motivation for basic living and general loss of interest. These people rarely manifest hallucinations and delusions, but they may be characterized by avoidance of others, lack of appetite, difficulty in holding a job, increased sleeping, fatigue, vague nervousness, and the like. Many simple schizophrenic people don't require hospitalization and live out their lives on the periphery of society as derelicts or hoboes. They often drift from place to place, rarely establishing a residence or any acquaintances.

Latent schizophrenia (sometimes also known as *borderline schizophrenia*) is a classification reserved for those who exhibit only occasional episodes of thought disorder and personality disorganization, but who are usually able to function fairly well. *Schizoaffective schizophrenia* includes a strong depressive *or* manic component. Thus, a schizoaffective person may have delusions of grandeur but react to them with delirious happiness. Fear appears to be the primary differentiating symptom in *pseudoneurotic schizophrenia* (Hoch & Polatin, 1949). More specifically, it is a syndrome characterized by "diffuse pan anxiety, a vague, all encompassing ever present fear which sometimes is attached to phobic objects and other times is not attached to anything specific" (p. 249). The pseudoneurotic schizophrenic may be misdiagnosed as an anxiety neurotic or phobic.

ALTERNATIVE CLASSIFICATIONS

As diagnosticians attempted to apply the symptom-based DSM-II, they found little common ground. One expert might conclude that a given set of symptoms meant a person was hebephrenic, whereas another might conclude that the symptoms described an agitated catatonic. To overcome the unreliability of diagnosis and to add more scientific accuracy to diagnosis in schizophrenia, alternative or modified classifications and diagnostic methods have been developed. We have chosen four alternative systems to review on the basis of their historical importance or future promise. Many of the proposals included in these alternatives are encompassed in DSM-III (see Chapter 1).

Process versus Reactive Schizophrenia

An early alternative subtyping of schizophrenia was based on the process-versus-reaction dimension (Kantor, Wallner, & Winder, 1953). According to this system, only two subgroups can be delineated within the population of schizophrenics. *Process schizophrenia* is characterized by a long history of coping problems, slow insidious onset of symptoms, family history of schizophrenia, and a poor chance of recovery. In contrast, *reactive schizophrenia* is usually defined by little or no history of maladjustment, rapid and sudden onset of symptoms, and a good chance of recovery. A summary of some of the differences between process and reactive patterns is provided in Table 7-3. Note that these groups tend to differ throughout their lives. In fact, many experts believe that process schizophrenia may be biologically caused, whereas reactive schizophrenia may be induced by psychological stress. In other words, these two types of schizophrenia share similar symptom patterns, but they may have different causes.

Acute versus Chronic Schizophrenia

Instead of being based on the developmental characteristics of the disorder, the acute-versus-chronic dimension focuses on the manner of onset of psychiatric symptoms. Professionals working in clinical settings

Table 7-3. *Developmental differences between process and reactive schizophrenics*

Process Schizophrenic	Reactive Schizophrenic
Birth to Fifth Year	
Early psychological trauma	Good psychological history
Physical illness—severe or long	Good physical health
Odd member of family	Normal member of family
Fifth Year to Adolescence	
Difficulties at school	Well-adjusted at school
Family troubles paralleled by sudden changes in patient's behavior	Domestic troubles unaccompanied by behavior disruptions. Patient "had what it took."
Introverted behavior trends and interests	Extroverted behavior trends and interests
History of breakdown of social, physical, mental functioning	History of adequate social, physical, mental functioning
Pathological siblings	Normal siblings
Overprotective or rejecting mother; "Momism"	Normally protective, accepting mother
Rejecting father	Accepting father
Adolescence to Adulthood	
Lack of heterosexuality	Heterosexual behavior
Insidious, gradual onset of psychosis without pertinent stress	Sudden onset of psychosis; stress present and pertinent. Later onset.
Physical aggression	Verbal aggression
Poor response to treatment	Good response to treatment
Lengthy stay in hospital	Short course in hospital
Adulthood	
Massive paranoia	Minor paranoid trends
Little capacity for alcohol	Much capacity for alcohol
No manic-depressive component	Presence of manic-depressive component
Failure under adversity	Success despite adversity
Discrepancy between ability and achievement	Harmony between ability and achievement
Awareness of change in self	No sensation of change
Somatic delusions	Absence of somatic delusions
Clash between culture and environment	Harmony between culture and environment
Loss of decency (nudity, public masturbation, and so on)	Retention of decency

have long known that the symptom picture during the initial phase of schizophrenia is often quite different from that presented in later phases. In the initial or *acute* phase, the person is usually struggling to solve his or her problems and, as a result, may be agitated, perplexed, confused, and highly anxious. However, after this acute phase passes, the person may either recover or deteriorate further. If further deterioration occurs, *chronic schizophrenia* may result. The chronic patient is typically apathetic and seems resigned to living a maladjusted life.

Acute and chronic schizophrenia differ in several other significant ways. In acute schizophrenia, onset of the disorder is rapid and usually associated with some clearly observable set of life stresses. Moreover, these people usually seek help. Their chances for a rapid recovery and return to normal life are very good. In chronic schizophrenia, instead of a sudden onset of symptoms, the disorder appears slowly and insidiously. The person rarely seeks help and seems to lack the desire to fight the developing problems. The prognosis for chronic schizophrenic people is usually very poor, and many such patients are in and out of hospitals for most of their lives. As we shall see later in the chapter, the differences observed in the onset and patterns of symptoms in acute versus chronic schizophrenia may reflect their being two distinct disorders, not one. It may well be that acute schizophrenia is psychogenic and chronic schizophrenia, biogenic.

Symptom Clusters as Subtypes

The approach of Lorr, Klett, and McNair (1963) involves an attempt to isolate clusters of psychotic symptoms. These researchers found that, although not all of the symptom clusters appear in any one particular type of psychosis, on the basis of combinations of the ten clusters shown in Table 7-4, they could identify six basic subtypes of psychotic patterns. For example, schizophrenia represented a combination of the symptom clusters of perceptual distortion, disorientation, motor disturbance, and conceptual disorganization. Manic psychosis was seen as a combination of the symptom clusters of hostile belligerence and grandiose expansiveness. As an alternative to DSM-II, the work of Lorr and his colleagues represents a sophisticated and scientifically accurate effort that deserves more attention.

Schizophrenia-Spectrum Classification

The DSM-II and the alternatives we've presented thus far describe schizophrenia as a specific disorder with definable symptoms of extreme severity. However, researchers are aware that there may exist a *set* of related disorders, less severe than schizophrenia, that reflect loss of reality contact, difficulties in thinking, perceptual disturbances, and the like. Called the *schizophrenia spectrum,* these disorders include a variety of disturbances ranging from definite schizophrenia to uncertain schizophrenia (Kety, Rosenthal, Wender, & Schulsinger, 1968, 1976).

Table 7-4. *Ten psychotic-symptom clusters*

Hostile belligerence	Person verbalizes resentment and hostility, is irritable, easily annoyed, complaining, critical, and suspicious.
Paranoid projection	Delusions of influence, persecution, and reference
Grandiose expansiveness	Feelings of superiority, belief in special powers or reasons for living, self-exaltation
Excitement	Loud speech, boisterous attitude, hyperactivity, elevated mood, and feelings of power
Anxious intropunitiveness	Anxiety and depression, vague worries or fears, self-blame, guilt feelings, low self-esteem
Retardation and apathy	Quiet voice, slow speech, lack of interpersonal responsiveness, slow movement, lethargy, indifference, bland facial expression
Perceptual distortion	Primarily hallucinations
Disorientation	Lack of knowledge of time or place
Motor disturbances	Mannerisms and bizarre postures, silly smiling and grimacing
Conceptual disorganization	Incoherent speech, irrelevant answers, repetition of words and phrases

Adapted from *Syndromes of Psychosis*, by M. Lorr, C. Klett, and D. McNair. Copyright 1963 by Pergamon Press, Ltd. Used by permission.

As seen in Table 7-5, the schizophrenic spectrum encompasses mild, moderate, and severe thought disturbances and includes disorders traditionally seen within DSM-II as personality disturbances or even neuroses. Spectrum diagnosis is especially important in research into the genetics of schizophrenia. For example, close relatives of schizophrenics may not be concordant for schizophrenia, but they may be concordant for other schizophrenia-spectrum disorders.

An Evaluation

Having described a selection of classifications of schizophrenia that have been offered as alternatives to DSM-II, we would like to comment on them briefly. In practice, the acute-versus-chronic continuum seems to be the most widely adopted and applied, but it is less firmly researched than the process-reactive dimension. The complexity of the symptom-cluster approach probably reduces its wide application. The schizophrenia-spectrum alternative is popular in research, since it allows for clear and reliable diagnosis over a wide range. However, in clinical practice, the spectrum is so wide as to make diagnosis often meaningless. In spite of the numbers of replacements, DSM-II seems firmly entrenched with those using diagnostic categories.

Some experts have offered the controversial idea that schizophrenia may not even exist. For example, Van Praag (1975) has said, "I believe that the schizophrenia concept no longer meets any of the criteria of the disease entity. In fact the term signifies hardly anything more than psychosis. I

Table 7-5. *Diagnostic system used in schizophrenic-spectrum classification*

A. Definitely not schizophrenia (specify diagnosis).

B. Chronic schizophrenia (chronic undifferentiated schizophrenia, true schizophrenia, process schizophrenia).
Characteristics: (1) Poor prepsychotic adjustment; introverted; schizoid; shut-in; few peer contacts; few heterosexual contacts; usually unmarried; poor occupational adjustment. (2) Onset: gradual and without clear-cut psychological precipitant. (3) Presenting picture: presence of primary Bleulerian characteristics; presence of clear rather than confused sensorium. (4) Posthospital course: failure to reach previous level of adjustment. (5) Tendency to chronicity.

B2. Acute schizophrenic reaction (acute undifferentiated schizophrenic reaction, schizoaffective psychosis, possible schizophreniform psychosis, [acute] paranoid reaction, homosexual panic).
Characteristics: (1) Relatively good premorbid adjustment. (2) Relatively rapid onset of illness with clear-cut psychological precipitant. (3) Presenting picture: presence of secondary symptoms and comparatively lesser evidence of primary ones; presence of affect (manic-depressive symptoms, feelings of guilt); cloudy rather than clear sensorium. (4) Posthospital course good. (5) Tendency to relatively brief episode(s) responding to drugs, electroshock therapy, etc.

B3. Borderline state (pseudoneurotic schizophrenia, borderline, ambulatory schizophrenia, questionable simple schizophrenia, "psychotic character," severe schizoid individual).
Characteristics: (1) Thinking: strange or atypical mentation; thought shows tendency to ignore reality, logic, and experience (to an excessive degree) resulting in poor adaptation to life experience (despite the presence of a normal IQ); fuzzy, murky, vague speech. (2) Experience: brief episodes of cognitive distortion (the patient can, and does, snap back, but during the episode the idea has more the character of a delusion than an ego-alien obsessive thought); feelings of depersonalization, of strangeness, or of unfamiliarity with or toward the familiar; micropsychosis. (3) Affective: anhedonia—never experiences intense pleasure—never happy; no deep or intense involvement with anyone or anybody. (4) Interpersonal behavior: may appear poised, but lacking in depth ("as if" personality); sexual adjustment—chaotic fluctuation, mixture of heterosexuality and homosexuality. (5) Psychopathology: multiple neurotic manifestations that shift frequently (obsessive concerns, phobias, conversion, psychosomatic symptoms, etc.); severe widespread anxiety.

C. Inadequate personality.
Characteristics: A somewhat heterogeneous group consisting of individuals who would be classified as either inadequate or schizoid by the APA (1968) *Diagnostic Manual.* Persons so classified often had many of the characteristics of the B3 category, but to a considerably milder degree.

D1, Uncertain B1, 2, or 3 either because information is lacking or because even if
2, enough information is available, the case does not fit clearly into an appro-
or 3. priate B category.

From "The Types and Prevalence of Mental Illness in the Biological Families of Adopted Schizophrenics," by S. Kety, D. Rosenthal, P. Wender, and F. Schulsinger. In D. Rosenthal and S. Kety (Eds.), *The Transmission of Schizophrenia.* Copyright 1968 by Pergamon Press Ltd. Reprinted by permission.

consider the concept to be obsolete. The term should either be reoperationalized or dropped altogether" (p. 2). The world-renowned psychiatrist Karl Menninger has long protested the use of the term *schizophrenia*, calling such a diagnosis "a twentieth century version of witchcraft" (Lehmann, 1975a).

EXPLANATIONS

At this point, we hope you have some appreciation of the herculean task of trying to explain schizophrenia. The wide range of dysfunctions common to all types of schizophrenia doesn't fit into a clearly definable pattern of problems. Schizophrenia is so complex, so puzzling a phenomenon that theorists from many disciplines have joined in a massive effort to explain it. We have organized our discussion of explanations for schizophrenia into five major groups. We will consider schizophrenia as a disorder based upon psychological, social, genetic, biological and biochemical (including neurological and viral), and biopsychological dysfunctions. All of these explanations have their strengths and weaknesses, but as yet none seems to be the final answer.

Psychological Explanations

The first collection of explanations for the schizophrenias, the psychological approaches, share the belief that schizophrenia is caused by or expressed in behavioral, cognitive, perceptual, or experiential dysfunctions. One of the psychological explanations to follow, the psychoanalytic theory, is important currently and historically, whereas the others are more modern hypotheses on the psychogenic basis for schizophrenia.

Schizophrenia as Regression: The Psychoanalysts. Psychoanalytic theorists see schizophrenia as a return to an earlier level of functioning. According to Freud, the earliest stage of personality development involves the id with an ego not yet differentiated from it (Chapter 4). In this theory, infants are unable to discriminate between self and outside because only primary-process thought exists. Schizophrenia is seen as a loss of contact with reality and regression to the oral stage of psychosexual development. The regression occurs because of either an uncontrollable increase in id demands or an unbearable degree of guilt or moral anxiety produced by the superego.

Regardless of the specific internal or environmental precipitator of regression, schizophrenic symptoms are thought to be caused by a sequence of events that follows the initial break with reality. In the first phase of this progressive sequence, *regressive symptoms* reflect the return to the infantile level. These regressive symptoms include feelings of depersonalization, sense of loss, delusions of grandiosity and self-importance, passivity and vegetative existence, and primary-process thought. When regression is complete and contact with reality has been surrendered, the schizophrenic person attempts to regain reality through *restitutional symptoms*: to replace the lack of perceptions grounded in reality, hallucinations may develop; to replace reality-based beliefs, delusions emerge; to reestablish verbal communication, bizarre and incoherent speech occurs. Usually when the person is seen for diagnosis, he or she shows primarily restitutional symptoms. These restitutional symptoms reflect intrapsychic conflicts that have led to regression in the face of unbearable stress.

Freud wasn't the only psychoanalytic theorist to conclude that schizophrenia represents regression to an earlier level of function. The noted psychoanalytic theorist Silvano Arieti (1955) also proposed a regression hypothesis. Based upon the neurological fact that higher brain centers tend to control lower, more primitive centers, Arieti believed that, in the face of extreme stress, a *teleological* or purposive regression occurs. People experience a "functional paralysis" of higher brain centers, forcing them to readjust downward to a lower level of function where stress is reduced to a degree with which they can cope. According to Arieti, schizophrenics regress further and further back until they reach a point at which high mental functions, such as logical thought and speech, break down and the typical symptoms of psychosis are clearly observable.

Schizophrenia as an Arousal and Attention Dysfunction. Whereas the regression theorists tend to focus upon complex intrapsychic conflict, the majority of other psychological explanations of schizophrenia focus on one or two specific causative dysfunctions. For example, there are a great many data regarding specific dysfunctions in arousal and motivation among schizophrenics. Motivation theorists generally perceive schizophrenia as an inability to receive, process, or respond to internal and external stimulation.

An early arousal theorist, Mednick (1958), believes that preschizophrenia is characterized by excess arousal in the form of massive anxiety. Because of stimulus generalization (see Chapter 4), a great number of stimuli become associated with this massive anxiety. This means that more and more stimuli have the power to make the person anxious and afraid. A vicious circle then may develop in which more and more stimuli are associated with anxiety, and soon the person is so aroused that he or she must respond to nearly every occurrence with anxiety. According to Mednick, when this point is reached, the person is suffering from acute schizophrenia.

To cope with the intense anxiety of acute schizophrenia, Mednick believes, the person tries to find ways to *reduce* the aversive feelings. One way to deal with the anxiety is to stop responding to the real world and to attend to a small number of irrelevant tangential events and stimuli. The result of this attentional shift is a dramatic reduction in arousal to a lower-

*The Development of Acute Schizophrenia via Stimulus Generaliza-
tion and Classical Conditioning*

Remember Little Albert? Well, imagine that we can vary his degree of anxiety while we present the white rat and the loud noise
together. If his fear is at a level of, say, 25 on a scale of 100, his fear may
generalize to bearded people and fuzzy clothes. But, as you can see in
the diagram, if we increase the fear, more and more situations will be
encompassed by his generalized anxiety. According to Mednick (1958),
each of these new anxiety producers adds to the ever-increasing level
of arousal in the preschizophrenic person. Eventually, in an effort to
avoid being made anxious by just about everything, the person will
stop responding and become an underaroused chronic schizophrenic.

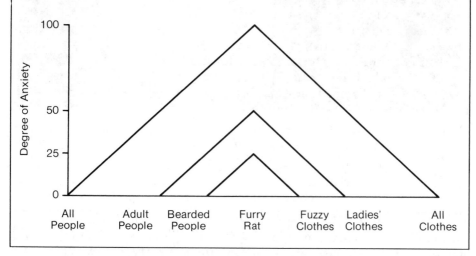

than-normal level; the behavioral result is that the person now is considered a chronic schizophrenic who is underaroused and unresponsive. Research evidence for poor arousal levels among schizophrenics comes from
the work of Zahn (1975), who found that schizophrenics are not aroused by
important environmental stimuli as are normal people.

As an explanation of schizophrenia, attentional-interference theory
focuses, not on arousal and motivation per se, but on problems associated
with thinking and meaningful attention and perception. A leading researcher in interference theory, Shakow (1962), believes that the schizophrenic has difficulty in attending to and focusing on relevant aspects of a
situation and can't avoid attending to peripherally important aspects. The
net result is that unimportant stimuli interfere with the ability to process
and deal with important stimuli. McGhee and Chapman (1961) believe that
schizophrenic symptoms are the result of the schizophrenic's basic inability to select, process, and control the stimuli impinging upon internal or
external sensors. Further clarification of interference theory also comes

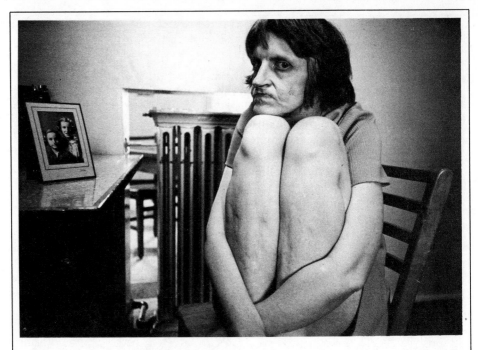

Although some experts believe that schizophrenia may be a withdrawal to a safer place, the boredom, loneliness, and separation from family experienced by many institutionalized persons hardly seems attractive. (Photo by Mary Ellen Mark/ Magnum).

from Payne (1962), who states that the major problem of schizophrenics is an inability to *exclude* unimportant stimuli: they respond to everything, and often their responses are inappropriate or bizarre. For example, if you were unable to exclude looking at the pictures on the wall of your room while trying to read, you might find yourself staring at the wall and turning the pages of your text—a highly abnormal-looking behavior.

Recent evidence (Holzman, Proctor, & Hughes, 1973) indicates that attentional deficits may be reflected in schizophrenics' inability to attend visually to moving stimuli. An interesting addition to this finding is that 44% of close relatives of schizophrenics also have trouble in attending to and tracking visual stimuli (Holzman, Proctor, Levy, Yasillo, Meltzer, & Hurt, 1974). Attentional deficit in schizophrenic people also has been demonstrated by Wohlberg and Kornetsky (1973), who reported that, on a simple measure of attention, both active *and* remitted schizophrenics made more errors than normal people.

Interference theory generally states that, due to a tendency to over-include, schizophrenics are unable to attend to stimuli and to focus normally on them. Thus, bizarre speech and thought occur because weak associations attract as much attention as strong associations. Thus, it wouldn't be surprising if, in response to the word *table*, instead of the expected association *chair* a schizophrenic were to say *tangerine*.

Schizophrenia as Caused by Unhealthy Family Life. We now move from the theorists who deal with cognitive dysfunction to those who see family pathology as the source of schizophrenia. These theorists believe that, as a result of a disturbed early family life, schizophrenics don't learn the interpersonal skills necessary to communicate effectively. Haley (1959) stated that, because of these destructive family relationships, schizophrenics may manifest one or more of four different communication problems. First, schizophrenics may deny being the source of a communicative message by saying, for example, that God is talking through them or that they are Napoleon. Second, schizophrenics may indicate, through incoherent speech, that their words aren't really a communication. Or schizophrenics may refuse to receive the message by denying that they are themselves. Finally, schizophrenics may mislabel the context of the message and respond as if they were someplace else. For example, upon hearing someone say "Time to go," schizophrenics may believe that they are to be led to their deaths in a prison or the like. Any or all of these four problems in communication can be perceived by the outside observer as schizophrenic behavior. The basis for such communication problems is believed to be early family pathology.

Bateson, Jackson, Haley, and Weakland (1956) theorize that families of schizophrenics engage in what they call double-bind communications. With such communications, children may find themselves in a "no win" situation with their parents. The mother may be seen as seductive and seeking love from her child, yet when the child approaches her, she withdraws. In contrast, the father is often ineffective, passive, and unable to mollify such mother-child interactions. The result can be that the child may never feel secure in other close relationships, or feel capable of accurately receiving or sending messages to others. A solution to such interpersonal conflict is to withdraw into psychosis.

Also focusing on family members as the source of schizophrenia, Lidz, Cornelison, Fleck, and Terry (1958) have described an interpersonal formulation of the cause of schizophrenia. These investigators describe two types of pathological characteristics found among families of schizophrenics. *Marital schism* refers to the situation where parents remain together yet bicker and argue constantly, thereby producing a highly tense, volatile home environment. In a second pathological characteristic called *marital skew,* overt happiness and harmony frequently mask deep parental dissension and hatred. In such a home, usually one parent is deeply emotionally disturbed, and the other family members are forced to sacrifice their growth and happiness to help the disturbed member function. A child being reared in a skewed home often finds it difficult to develop a sense of self-importance and feeling of security. The end result of this inability may be schizophrenia. In a study of 256 families, half of which had produced at least one schizophrenic child, Friedman and Friedman (1972) reported that parents of patients manifested more psychopathology and thought disturbances than parents of normal children. Further, Wynne and Singer (cited by Keith, Gunderson, Reifman, Buchsbaum, & Mosher, 1976) have also found a significant statistical relationship between parental psychopathology and level of schizophrenic symptomatology among offspring. From a theoretical perspective with empirical data, Heilbrun (1974) has argued that schizophrenia is related to the presence of aversive control in the mother-child relationship.

Schizophrenia as Learned Behavior. Although the family theorists have found numerous relationships between early home life and schizophrenia, their approaches have rarely included explanations of the specific mechanisms of the development of the psychoses. A learning-theory attempt to describe such mechanisms has been made by Ullmann and Krasner (1969, 1975). In their *sociopsychological* formulation of schizophrenia, these authors have provided plausible and testable descriptions of the development of schizophrenia.

Ullmann and Krasner hypothesized that schizophrenia results from the *"extinction* of attention to social stimuli to which 'normal people' respond" (1975, p. 357). Put another way, schizophrenics haven't been reinforced by others for attending to appropriate social cues; they may even have been actively punished for doing so. In a self-protective manner, the attentional response is extinguished and the person begins to respond to asocial, culturally unaccepted stimuli. For example, instead of attending to what his wife is saying and speaking with her, a schizophrenic may speak with a TV set. As inappropriate responding continues, he may be considered deviant by those around him. Ullmann and Krasner suggest that societal reaction can change this primary deviance into more permanent secondary deviance, thereby firmly establishing the nonattender as schizophrenic (see Chapter 5).

Social Explanations

The social approaches to schizophrenia emphasize the effects of sociocultural and environmental life stresses. As stated by Dohrenwend (1975) and Dohrenwend and Dohrenwend (1974), the social perspective assumes that environmental stress can produce failure to cope, which may lead to schizophrenic symptomatology.

One line of evidence presented by Dohrenwend is that normal people exposed to the extreme stress of war are known to develop psychotic symptoms. It is indeed clear that severe stress can produce behavioral deterioration, but it's also clear that stresses as severe as war are not everyday events. Normal life events also must be shown to be stressful if the social-stress hypothesis is to be supported. Using the scale of stressful life events devised by Holmes and Rahe (1967), several researchers have found relationships between psychological distress and the occurrence of divorce, death of a spouse, loss of a job, and the like (Dohrenwend, 1973; Markush & Favero, 1974). Further, Gersten, Langner, Eisenberg, and Orzek (1974) have reported similar relationships between stress and symptom development among children as well as adults.

Although it is plausible, the social-stress theory doesn't adequately account for the fact that many people develop schizophrenia who have never experienced significant life stresses. Further, the fact that certain disorders run in families is hard for social theorists to explain. Although the stresses in the lower social classes will be shared by members of the same family (Kohn, 1972), research indicates that children of schizophrenics adopted out of their social class of origin still are more likely to develop schizophrenia.

Genetic Explanations

The genetic theorists propose that schizophrenia is physically inherited. Generally, such explanations hypothesize that schizophrenia tends to run in families, *not* because the children experience similar maladaptive atmospheres or maladaptive learning, but because they have similar genetic endowment. With the background of support for the general genetic argument acquired in Chapter 6, we will now present modern data specific to the genetic transmission of schizophrenia.

Studies of Close Relatives and Twins. The most obvious requirement for a genetic explanation of schizophrenia is that the disorder occur more frequently among people who are related. Further, the closer the genetic similarity (with identical twins being most similar), the greater should be the concordance rates. For example, in his study of schizophrenics, Rosenthal (1971) found a definite relationship between degree of relatedness and increased chance of developing schizophrenia. Shields and Slater (1961) also have reported higher concordance rates among siblings and parents of schizophrenics than would be expected in people not genetically related. Although we discussed research with twins in Chapter 6, we would like to reiterate here that there seems to be ample evidence to support the conclusion that certain kinds of schizophrenia have some genetic basis. Kallmann's (1950) concordance figure of 0.86 is high; better-controlled studies have produced concordance figures among monozygotic twins of 0.56 (M. Fischer, 1973) and 0.31 (Kringlen, 1967, 1976). When concordance rates for schizophrenia-spectrum disorders among twins are calculated, the genetic component is even clearer. For example, Shields, Heston, and Gottesman (1975) have been able to show that, using spectrum diagnoses, concordance rates for dizygotic twins as well as monozygotic twins could be elevated above the 50% level.

Studies of Adoptees. Besides studying twins, Kety et al. (1968, 1975) and Rosenthal, Wender, Kety, Welner, and Schulsinger (1971) have used their system of diagnosing schizophrenia-spectrum disorders to study adopted children who develop schizophrenia. The study of adoptees (Heston, 1966) is a well-controlled approach to the assessment of genetic involvement in schizophrenia. The study of identical twins always has been hampered by the fact that twins were reared in similar family environments that might have interacted with genetic endowments to facilitate schizophrenic symptoms. An adopted child, however, receives genetic endowment from one family and life experiences from another.

Kety (1975b) has reported on a study of adopted individuals who have become schizophrenic, and his results further support genetic involvement in the transmission of schizophrenia. As shown in Table 7-6, the percentage of schizophrenia-spectrum disorders in biological relatives of schizophrenic adoptees is significantly greater than in nonbiological relatives. Kety also reported that half of the adoptees he studied had no biological or adopted relatives with schizophrenia-spectrum disorders. He concluded from the data that there may be *two* different types of schizophrenia, one with a strong genetic basis and the other with little or no genetic basis.

Kety's proposal that there may be two types of schizophrenic disorders has historical precedent. In the early part of this century, Bleuler spoke of two types of schizophrenia, as have present-day geneticists such as Stromgren (1975). Stromgren believes that there are *true schizophrenias*, which are genetically transmitted, and *schizophreniform psychoses* (schizophrenic reactions), which are caused environmentally. He concludes that many of the contradictory findings involving the genetic basis of schizophrenia would have been clarified if true schizophrenia and schizophreniform psychoses had been distinguished diagnostically.

Table 7-6. *Prevalence of schizophrenia-spectrum disorders in biological and adoptive relatives of schizophrenic and control adoptees*

	Diagnosis of Schizophrenia in Relatives (Percentage)			
	Chronic	Latent	Uncertain	Total
Biological relatives of schizophrenics	2.9	3.5	7.5	13.9
Biological relatives of controls	0	1.7	1.7	3.4
Adoptive relatives of schizophrenics	1.4	0	1.4	2.7
Adoptive relatives of controls	1.1	1.1	3.3	5.5

From "Mental Illness and the Biological and Adoptive Families of Adopted Individuals Who Have Become Schizophrenic," by S. Kety. In H. M. Von Praag (Ed.), *On the Origin of Schizophrenic Psychoses.* Copyright 1975 by De Eruen Bohn, BV. Reprinted by permission.

The study of adoptees has dramatically affected the field of genetic research in schizophrenia. Until the late 1960s, the dominant belief was that child-rearing patterns and other social and psychological factors were most important in the development of schizophrenia. The work of Kety, Rosenthal, and their Danish colleagues has significantly altered this perception. After reviewing the studies of adoptees, Gottesman and Shields (1976) stated "that the burden of proof has shifted from showing that genes are important to showing that environment is important" (p. 367).

Populations at High Risk.   To demonstrate further the importance of genetic components in the development of schizophrenia, some researchers (Garmezy, 1974; Garmezy & Streitman, 1974) have studied populations in which the risk of schizophrenia is considered to be extremely high due to various genetic factors. For example, close relatives of schizophrenics show higher concordance rates than distant relatives. Further, the chances of becoming schizophrenic given one parent who is schizophrenic are higher than if both parents are normal. Slater and Cowie (1971) have noted that the risk of schizophrenia in children with one psychotic parent is 13.9, whereas the risk for so-called dual matings (where both parents are schizophrenic) is 46.3. Further, if both parents are schizophrenic, the concordance rates among nontwin siblings is higher than in cases of single schizophrenic parents or normal parents (Odegaard, cited by Gottesman & Shields, 1976).

Diathesis-Stress Theory.   Both the pure genetic approach and the pure environmental approach have difficulty in satisfactorily explaining the occurrence of schizophrenia in some twins and not in others, or in some adoptees and not in others. To account for these facts, explanations that consider both heredity and environment have been generated. These diathesis-stress theories generally state that it isn't a specific abnormality that a person inherits, but rather a *predisposition* to develop the schizophrenic disorder, given the proper environmental conditions (stress). One diathesis-stress theory that effectively explains much of what is known about the occurrence of schizophrenia among relatives is that proposed by Meehl (1962). According to Meehl's theory, an inherited predisposition, *schizotaxia,* must interact with a *schizophrenogenic environment* to produce schizophrenia.

In response to the findings of the Danish adoption studies, the environmental theorist Dohrenwend (1975, 1976) has stated that we must recognize a standoff between the genetic explanations and the environmental theories. Gottesman and Shields (1976) argue that the resolution of genetic findings and social factors results in a "sophisticated detente known as diathesis stress theory" (p. 371). These authors believe that *liability* to schizophrenia is inherited, not schizophrenia itself, and that the development of schizophrenia is dependent upon the existence of severe life stresses and inability to cope in people diathetic for schizophrenia.

Biological and Biochemical Explanations

The genetic theorists have provided convincing evidence that *something* is inherited in schizophrenia, and the psychological-social theorists make a good case for environmental stresses aggravating genetic predispositions. However, neither group says very much about the exact nature of the biological defects that may be associated with schizophrenia. From the biological-biochemical perspective, several physical aberrations may be seen as a source of bodily expressions of inherited or environmentally produced schizophrenia. Among these aberrations are neurological disease, a slow-acting viral infection, an imbalance of neurotransmitters, and self-generated hallucinogenic chemicals.

Schizophrenia as a Neuromuscular Dysfunction. Given that schizophrenia may be considered a disorder of the nervous system (Meltzer, 1976), we may expect that it would be accompanied by some physically observable neural dysfunctions. Meltzer has presented evidence that such neuromuscular dysfunctions do exist in schizophrenics. Using as an indicator of skeletal muscle deterioration the presence of the enzyme creatine phosphokinase (CPK), Meltzer has found disease-indicating elevations of CPK in a variety of psychiatric patients (see Table 7-7).

In addition to chemical signs, Meltzer has used muscle-tissue abnormalities as indicators of the presence of nerve disease in schizophrenics. He reported that such muscular problems tend to run in families in much the same way as schizophrenia. As seen in Table 7-8, the percentage of schizophrenic patients with abnormal musculature is very high as compared with normal people. Further, close relatives of schizophrenics manifest higher-than-normal levels of abnormal muscle tissue.

Meltzer's work suggests that something may be physically wrong with the schizophrenic person. As evidenced by several indicators, neurological disease may be present, yet the mechanism by which such

Table 7-7. *Percentage of patients with creatine phosphokinase (CPK) elevations*

		Time of CPK Elevation			
Diagnosis	N	Admission	Later	Any Time	Never
Nonpsychotic	19	0	5.3	5.3	94.7
All psychotic	187	47.1	60.4	75.9	24.1
Acute schizophrenic	123	50.4	61.0	78.9	21.1
Chronic schizophrenic	40	42.5	65.0	70.0	30.0
Bipolar—manic phase	12	33.3	58.3	75.0	25.0
Psychotic—depression	12	41.7	41.7	66.7	33.3

From "Neuromuscular Dysfunction in Schizophrenics," by H. Meltzer, *Schizophrenia Bulletin*, 1976, *2*, 106–135. National Institute of Mental Health, U.S. Department of Health, Education and Welfare.

Table 7-8. *Percentage of psychotic patients and relations showing abnormal muscle biopsies*

Group	N	Abnormal (%)
Controls	34	14.7
Nonpsychotics	19	5.3
All psychotics	166	69.3
acute schizophrenics	108	69.9
chronic schizophrenics	36	38.3
First-degree relatives	26	50.0

From "Neuromuscular Dysfunction in Schizophrenics, by H. Meltzer, *Schizophrenia Bulletin*, 1976, *2*, 106–135. National Institute of Mental Health, U.S. Department of Health, Education and Welfare.

physical-neurological disease is translated into schizophrenic behaviors is unknown.

The Viral Hypothesis. In addition to the hypothesis that an inherited or acquired nerve disorder is present in schizophrenia, there is some evidence that this psychosis is caused by a long-acting virus (Torrey & Peterson, 1976). Generally, the viral hypothesis of schizophrenia states that certain "slow viruses" (active over long periods of time, as opposed to 24-hour viruses and the like), such as those known to exist in Parkinson's disease, may combine with genetic predispositions to produce schizophrenia. Initial infection with the virus may occur prior to birth in the same way that german-measles virus causes damage to unborn children. Acquisition of the virus prior to birth would account for the higher concordance rates for schizophrenia among monozygotic twins than dizygotic twins, inasmuch as MZ twins share the same placenta and are more likely to be simultaneously affected.

Evidence for the viral hypothesis is sparse. Penn, Racy, Lapham, Mandel, and Sandt (1972) have isolated a viral infection in a case of fatal catatonia, a disorder characterized by schizophrenic behavior, high fever, and cerebral hemorrhage. Further, Torrey and Peterson (1976) report that data from over 4000 schizophrenic patients indicate a significantly high incidence of abnormal finger, foot, and palm prints. Such abnormalities are similar to those produced by german measles during early fetal development.

A final bit of evidence for viral involvement in schizophrenia is that births of schizophrenics aren't randomly distributed throughout the calendar year, as would be expected of a purely genetic disease. Rather, worldwide, more schizophrenic people are born in January through April than at any other time of the year (Dalen, 1974; Hare, Price, & Slater, 1974). Torrey and Peterson (1976) point out that many viruses, such as rubella and measles, show peaks of occurrence at the same times. The hypothesis is that infants are infected during their mothers' late pregnancy or shortly after their birth and only manifest symptoms many years later.

The Dopamine Hypothesis. Although well supported, the neurological-disease model and the viral hypothesis tell us little about the mechanisms whereby abnormal thoughts, feelings, and behavior occur. In the *dopamine hypothesis* and the *transmethylation hypothesis,* we find attempts to explain the physical bases for schizophrenia at a molecular level.

Dopamine, a neurotransmitter found in differing amounts in different parts of the brain and nervous system, has been implicated in schizophrenic behavior (Meltzer & Stahl, 1976; Usdin & Bunney, 1975; Usdin & Snyder, 1973). Specifically, several lines of evidence suggest that an excess of dopamine-dependent neuronal activity in certain brain synapses is associated with the occurrence of schizophrenia.

The first line of evidence for the dopamine hypothesis stems from studies of the action of antipsychotic drugs such as chlorpromazine (Thorazine) and haloperidol (Haldol). For example, Carlsson and Lindqvist (1973) found that these drugs reduced psychotic behavior by reducing dopamine's effectiveness via a blockade of dopamine receptors in the brain. Further, Snyder, Banerjee, Yamamura, and Greenberg (1974) have reviewed a variety of studies which show that dopamine levels are reduced by antipsychotic drugs parallel to the remittance of schizophrenic symptoms.

The role of dopamine in the production of certain types of schizophrenic patterns of behavior is fairly well documented. However, several types of schizophrenic symptoms—such as mutism, social withdrawal, blunting of emotion, and lack of ability to experience pleasure—don't seem to be related to excess dopamine alone. Biochemically, these symptoms seem to be produced by a reduction at the synapses of the neurotransmitter norepinephrine. The *dopamine-norepinephrine-imbalance hypothesis* thus proposes some faulty neural mechanism in schizophrenics that simultaneously increases dopamine and decreases norepinephrine levels. In his review of the dopamine-norepinephrine hypothesis, Kety (1975a) states that there is evidence that inhibition of the enzyme dopamine-B-hydroxylase at certain sites of the brain causes a release of dopamine and a reduction in availability of norepinephrine. Wise and Stein (1973) also have reported that postmortem examination of brains of schizophrenic patients revealed that there had been a marked reduction of dopamine-B-hydroxylase activity in these people as compared with normal people. However, the reason for the original inhibition of the dopamine-metabolizing enzyme isn't clearly addressed by the proponents of the dopamine-norepinephrine-imbalance hypothesis.

The Transmethylation Hypothesis. Whereas the dopamine hypothesis is based upon variations in levels of normal body chemicals, the transmethylation hypothesis reflects the belief that schizophrenia is the result of internally produced hallucinogenic chemicals similar to LSD, mescaline, and psilocybin that aren't normally found in the body (Rosengarten & Friedhoff, 1976). First proposed by Osmond and Smythies (1952), the transmethylation hypothesis is based upon the observation that a small chemical change in catecholamine and norepinephrine, which occur normally, would result in a compound very similar to the hallucinogen mescaline (see Figure 7-1). It was hypothesized that a genetically caused aberration in the metabolic system might cause norepinephrine to break down and create schizophrenia-producing hallucinogens. Later research suggested that other normal biochemicals such as serotonin (Woolley, 1962; Woolley & Shaw, 1954) also could be transformed into hallucinogenic compounds.

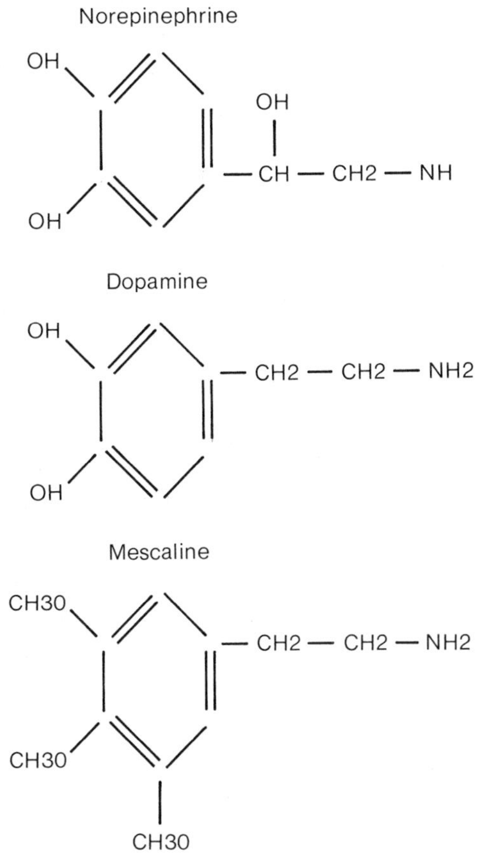

Norepinephrine

Dopamine

Mescaline

Figure 7-1. *Similarities between normal biochemicals and the hallucinogenic substance mescaline. Via complex biochemical processes, both norepinephrine and dopamine can be transformed into mescaline or other hallucinogenic substances. The transmethylation hypothesis of schizophrenia states that self-produced hallucinogens cause the symptoms of psychoses.*

Woolley noted that serotonin is chemically similar to the hallucinogenic drug LSD. One action of LSD in the brain is to block the neuraltransmission function of serotonin. Woolley and Shaw proposed that, when serotonin was insufficient or blocked, psychotic symptoms (such as those caused by LSD) would be produced:

> Schizophrenia is regarded as starting with a failure to form enough serotonin in the brain, and this is seen in the shyness and depression which are usually forerunners of the disease. With increased emotional strain, the control mechanism which governs the level of serotonin in the brain begins to fail. The production of serotonin may increase sharply . . . and this probably coincides with the agitated phase. Subsequently, decreased production may again take place [Woolley, 1962, pp. 183–184].

In further specifying the role of serotonin variation in schizophrenia, Woolley proposed that an *excess* of serotonin would be associated with hallucinations and acute schizophrenic excitement; a serotonin *deficiency* would be related to the lethargy and withdrawal seen in chronic schizophrenics. Although Woolley's hypothesis is a logical explanation of schizophrenia, subsequent strong research support has been lacking.

The major problem with the idea that the bodies of schizophrenic people produce hallucinogenic chemicals is that there are several differences between drug-induced and naturally occurring psychoses. First of all, drug-induced psychoses usually are observed in normal volunteers who are aware of the nature of the drug they are taking and may have an understanding of their temporary mental impairment; they would tend to be less disturbed by this "temporary" impairment than a truly schizophrenic person. Second, it is known that people often develop increased tolerance for hallucinogenic drugs, so that their effectiveness decreases after repeated doses. If schizophrenics are producing hallucinogens, it isn't clear why they don't also acquire increasing tolerance (Rosengarten & Friedhoff, 1976). These two problems are among several facing the acceptance of the transmethylation hypothesis. Like all of the others we have discussed, this hypothesis is not a sufficient explanation for schizophrenia, but it may well be a part of the final answer.

A Biopsychological Explanation

By this time, it should be obvious to you that no single psychological, social, genetic, or biological-biochemical theory can yet explain schizophrenia. Some approach combining these theories will probably be most useful. One of the world's leading researchers on schizophrenia, Kety (1969), has pointed out the dangers of pursuing a purely biological approach in trying to discover the basis for this disorder:

Those interested in explaining the biological aspects of schizophrenic disorders cannot with impunity ignore the psychologic, social and other environmental factors which operate significantly at various stages of their development. Leaving aside etiologic considerations, it is clear that exogenous [outside of the individual] factors may precipitate, intensify or ameliorate the symptoms and confound the biologic picture [p. 165].

In this section we will present a recent attempt to integrate genetic, biochemical, and psychosocial factors into a meaningful etiological explanation of schizophrenia.

A. R. Cools (1975) proposes a theory of schizophrenia that includes the major biochemicals implicated separately in other research. In addition, he hypothesizes that life experiences such as family, stress, trauma, and the like could cause biochemical alterations that in turn would be expressed in the *final common pathway* called schizophrenia.

Cools has proposed that dopamine, serotonin, and norepinephrine are *all* involved in a set of connected pathways within the brain. If something affects the dopamine system, the other two systems will subsequently be affected. Abnormal functioning of each system yields a different subgroup of schizophrenic symptoms. For example, if the dopamine system is *hyperactive* and produces too much dopamine, neologisms, motor dysfunctions, and impaired ability to attend to relevant stimuli may result. Similarly, the serotonin system is considered abnormal if it is *hypoactive.* Reduced availability of serotonin results behaviorally in an inability to maintain newly acquired thoughts and motor patterns and an inability to habituate to (learn to ignore) irrelevant internal and external stimuli.

Cools next describes the effect of norepinephrine-system abnormality. He notes that reduced availability (hypoactivity) of norepinephrine is associated with an inability to terminate verbal and motor patterns such as may be observed among chronic schizophrenics. Excess norepinephrine has been isolated among acute schizophrenics and is associated with hyperactivity, high anxiety, and confusion.

Although the biochemical pathways described by Cools can be used to explain the occurrence of schizophrenic behavior, previous theorists have been unclear as to *how* the various chemical imbalances come about. Cools's attempt to explain this leads him to integrate psychological theory with biochemical theory. He postulates that stressful life experiences alter normal metabolism of dopamine, serotonin, and norepinephrine. As evidence for such a relationship, he cites the work of Welch and Welch (1971), who showed that the long-term isolation of animals from their groups resulted in altered and abnormal variation in these catecholamines. Breese and his colleagues (1973) have shown that mother-child separation in infant monkeys has adverse effects upon catecholamine levels. Although not conclusive, the evidence cited by Cools and others seems to support his contention that life events can affect biochemical balance and that biochemical balance is associated with normal and abnormal psychological function. It may be that imbalances in dopamine, serotonin, and norepinephrine represent the final pathway for the variety of genetic, social, psychological, and biochemical deficits that can cause schizophrenic behaviors. Only time and further research will tell.

TREATMENT

Having described the various forms of schizophrenia and reviewed the variety of explanations offered for these psychoses, we are ready to take a brief look at the types of treatment that are more or less specific to this set of disorders. As in most chapters on specific disorders, we will leave all discussion of general outpatient therapeutic methods for Section VIII. Here we will describe various types of in-hospital approaches specific to the treatment of schizophrenia. As you read on, remember that only one-third of schizophrenics are "cured" by our present techniques; one-third actually worsen and become long-term chronic patients; and the final third tend to remain about the same. These figures are discouraging, not only for you who are learning about schizophrenia, but for professionals dealing with the disorder and for schizophrenics and their families as well.

Milieu Therapy

One way of dealing with the schizophrenic patient is through milieu therapy, a form of in-hospital treatment in which the individual's total environment is planned to be therapeutic. The ward, the staff, and all experiences are structured to be part of a healthy, corrective atmosphere or *milieu*.

Often known as a *therapeutic community*, the milieu may include not only traditional forms of one-to-one talk therapy, but also occupational or vocational rehabilitation, recreation, music, dance, and art therapies. The patients also govern their lives to some degree through ward elections. Every member of the hospital staff and every other patient is considered to be a part of each person's treatment program.

Many experts don't believe that the therapeutic milieu is universally helpful, in spite of its fine humanistic character. For example, Van Putten (1973) concludes that a therapeutic community can actually be harmful to some schizophrenic patients who can't perceive, attend to, or process social stimuli. These patients may be overwhelmed by a ward where parties, activity, and noise are the rule. Inappropriately placed in such an environment, many psychotic people may actually worsen. Probably no one treatment is best for all.

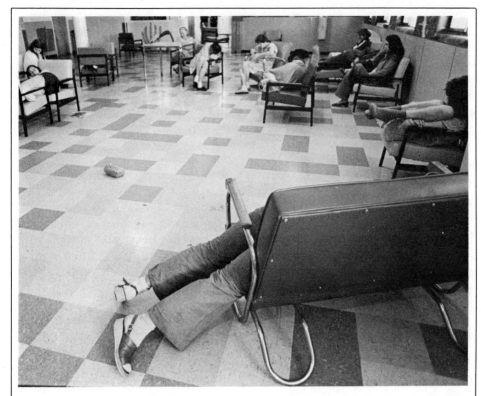

Even in the presence of others, those with severe psychotic disorders often act and feel quite alone. (Photo by Joseph Czarnecki.)

Drug Therapy

Milieu treatment emphasizes the person "learning" to behave appropriately as a result of exposure to the proper environmental conditions. This second mode of treatment for schizophrenics involves the use of drug therapy or *psychochemotherapy* to bring about appropriate behavior (see Chapter 24).

Although no known drug "cures" schizophrenia, in the sense of making the disorder disappear permanently, a variety of drugs reduce the occurrence or intensity of schizophrenic behaviors. The earliest and still the most widely used antipsychotic agents are the *phenothiazine* derivatives. These chemicals, such as Thorazine (chlorpromazine), can rapidly and effectively reduce the confusion, anxiety, and restlessness of acute schizophrenia. Other effective but less used agents are the *butyrophenones* (Haldol) and the *thioxanthenes* (Prolixin).

When used to treat hospitalized schizophrenics, drugs are usually administered very soon after admission. Starting with a low dose, the physician gradually increases the amount of medication until maximum antipsychotic effects along with minimum side-effects are obtained. This level is generally reached at very high doses. Once proper medication is identified, improvements may take up to six months, after which there is no guarantee that a relapse won't occur. Often patients who have manifested what is considered maximal improvement in their specific case will be given maintenance doses of antipsychotics permanently.

Psychotherapy

Besides total milieu treatment and antipsychotic drugs, there are some specific applications of psychotherapy to the treatment of schizophrenia. Because of the special problems in interpersonal communication and relating that often are part of the schizophrenic syndrome, it is difficult to use most of the more widely known psychotherapies such as psychoanalysis or client-centered therapy. Rather, special counseling techniques have been developed that lend themselves to the treatment of schizophrenia. We will present a selection of these particular forms of psychotherapy.

Direct Analysis. A technique devised and best applied by John Rosen (1953), direct analysis is a type of psychotherapy in which a psychotic person is "forced" to accept that he is psychotic and to accept the therapist as an omnipotent provider of all his needs and a loving, firm parent. Scheflen (1961) describes Rosen as using "with resourcefulness and persistence a dramatic barrage of powerful maneuvers to persuade the patient to relinquish his psychotic behavior, promising and rewarding, threatening and punishing, coercing, . . . using group pressure, ridiculing and shaming, . . . imitating and caricaturing . . . and using shocking interpretation."

Rosen's theoretical base is psychoanalytic, and he seems to believe that much of schizophrenia lies in faulty mother-child relationships. His goal in direct analysis is to replace the faulty parent of the schizophrenic person with himself as a benevolent, yet authoritarian, parent who will guide the person back to better adjustment. As seen in the sample of a Rosen-type interview below, some of his focus is upon sexual difficulties:

Patient: I don't know what you want.
Therapist: I want you to love me.
P: Huh?
T: That's right, I want you to love me. I want you to come right up to me and kiss me on the mouth!
P: I don't wanna do that.
T: What's the matter, does it scare you to think about loving a man—about kissing a man?
P: Yeah.
T: Does that make you a homosexual? Or me a homosexual? I love some other men and so do you.

P: No I don't.
T: How about your father? You loved your father, didn't you?
P: Uh-h.
T: Answer me! I can't understand you when you say "Uh-h."
P: Yes, I guess I loved my father.

Behavioral Psychotherapy.   A second type of psychotherapy widely used with schizophrenics is based on learning principles. In behavior modification, laboratory-tested techniques of altering behavior are applied in efforts to alter symptoms. In a classic example of behavior modification in schizophrenia, Isaacs, Thomas, and Goldiamond (1960) used chewing gum as a reinforcer to reestablish verbal communication in a mute, withdrawn patient. Each time the patient made an approximation to speech, he was rewarded with a piece of gum. After a time, the patient *asked* for gum prior to receiving it. Using the method of successive approximations (Chapter 4), the operant response of speech was reinstituted and generalized to numerous people throughout the hospital. Prior to the therapeutic intervention, this schizophrenic person hadn't uttered a word for 19 years!

In another, more complex, application of learning theory, Ayllon and Azrin (1968) developed the now widely used program called the *token economy*. A token economy is a small economic unit within a treatment setting. Behaviors of importance, such as attending therapy groups, cleaning rooms, and the like, are "paid for" by staff with tokens of various kinds (stamps, poker chips, stars, and so on). With earned tokens, patients are able to "buy" things they would really like (reinforcers). Common reinforcers on a psychiatric ward can include such things as TV time, sleep time, a new hair-do, candy bars, books, and extra recreation time. Ayllon and Azrin have reported that the institution of a token economy in the large hospital they studied resulted in drastic improvements in "target" behaviors such as serving meals, self-grooming, taking ward jobs, and cleaning rooms. Patients who previously sat by passively became excited to sign up for various token-rewarded chores around the hospital. In a review of the token economy and other behavioral techniques used in the treatment of schizophrenia, Liberman (1972) has stated:

> The token economy . . . has been shown to be effective in increasing the adaptive repertoire of institutionalized schizophrenics. Behavioral interventions are effective, even when phenothiazine medication is withdrawn from chronic psychotics [p. 47].

We can conclude from Liberman's statement and the research of others (Millby, 1975; R. Patterson, 1975) that at least at the level of basic hospital behavior, schizophrenic patterns can be altered. However, other evaluators of behavioral intervention (Gagnon & Davison, 1976; Kazdin & Bootzin, 1972) have noted that generalization of alteration of behavior from hospital to home may not occur, and complex behaviors such as abstract thought and language may not be amenable to behavioral manipulation.

CONCLUDING COMMENTS

In one sense we seem to know a great deal about schizophrenia, but in another sense we know very little. For example, the National Institute of Mental Health (1974) has noted that a treated and discharged schizophrenic patient has only a 50% chance of remaining out of the hospital for as long as two years. This alarming readmission rate has been termed the "nation's number one mental health problem" (p. 13). The seemingly dismal success rate for treatment of schizophrenics raises the question of whether there is really a "cure" for this disorder or set of disorders. So often in the past the hopes of professionals and of patients' families have been raised by the announcement of a "breakthrough" and impending cure. In each case it seems that the excitement has faded and the frustration increased when the discovery failed to deliver its "miracle." Perhaps schizophrenia cannot be truly cured; perhaps, much like the broken bone, which although no longer painful still is permanently scarred, schizophrenia can merely be repaired, controlled, or softened in its effects. We can only hope that future research will provide an answer to this most widespread of all serious mental disorders.

CHAPTER SUMMARY CHART

In this chapter on schizophrenia, we first described the schizophrenias:

Fundamental characteristics	*Diagnostic subtypes*
General dysfunctions	Catatonic
Behavioral dysfunctions	Hebephrenic
Perceptual dysfunctions	Paranoid
Cognitive dysfunctions	Simple, latent,
Affective dysfunctions	schizoaffective
Verbal dysfunctions	

Alternative types
Process/reactive
Acute/chronic
Symptom-cluster types
Schizophrenia spectrum

Then we provided a look at several explanations for schizophrenia:

Psychological explanations

Psychoanalytic theory
Arousal and attention
    problems
Unhealthy family life
Learned symptoms

Social explanations

Social-stress theory

Genetic explanations

Studies of relatives and twins
Studies of adopted people
Populations at high risk
Diathesis-stress theory

*Biological/biochemical
    theories*

Neuromuscular dysfunction
Viral hypothesis
Dopamine hypothesis
Transmethylation hypothesis
A biopsychological model

Finally, we considered the major special ways of treating schizo-phrenia:

Milieu therapy

Communities
Patient management

Drug therapy

Anti-psychotic drugs
Very large doses

Psychotherapy

Direct analysis

Behavioral therapy

Token economies

CHAPTER 8
AFFECTIVE DISORDERS

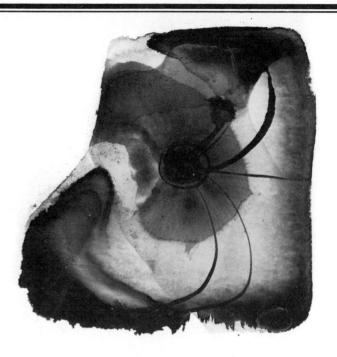

Just as schizophrenia may be seen primarily as a disorder of thought, the *affective disorders* may conveniently be classified as *disorders of feeling.* People with affective psychoses typically experience depressions far deeper and mood elevations far higher than do normal people.

The 1960s have been described as the Age of Anxiety, and there are those who feel that the 1970s may be the Age of Melancholy (Bliven, 1972). The resources of the earth are limited and, with world population rapidly increasing, there is a very real threat to our individual and collective survival. Many of our humanistic ideals have been dashed by the harsh realities of our complex political and social structures. Changes in the way we live may be significantly related to recent increases in the incidence of affective disorders and in the number of suicide attempts. There seems little doubt that the affective disorders are of major importance to us as students of abnormal psychology, for they touch most of us in some form or other. After all, moderate depression and elation are *normal* human emotions and, like anxiety, may be seen as serving an adaptive purpose. This adaptational view of affect derives from animal–human research in which it has been demonstrated that the signs of depression in a person tend to evoke parenting and caretaking behaviors in others (Klerman, 1975). In fact, the adaptive

190

function of depression may originally have been based upon animal infants being in need of a "mother" after their biological mother was killed. To ensure the survival of the species, often another animal, responding to the signs of depression (weeping, withdrawal, helplessness), would take over the care and nurturance of the youngster.

In this chapter we won't deal with the normal or adaptive aspects of depression and elation. Rather, we will focus upon instances where the adaptive function of emotion seems questionable and where loss of control of emotional responses seems to have occurred. As in the discussion of the schizophrenias, we will begin with descriptions, followed by theoretical explanations and treatments specific to affective disorders. Much more of our discussion will be about depression than about mania. This imbalance reflects the facts that depression is more common and more destructive and that more research attention has been devoted to depression than to mania.

DESCRIPTIONS

The affective disorders have in common an involvement with an individual's emotional reactivity. As a group, these disorders comprise a variety of symptom patterns with theoretically differing etiologies. In the

Signs of depression in a person tend to elicit caretaking behavior in others. (Photo by David Powers.)

present chapter we deal only with affective disorders of a psychotic degree. You will see in Chapter 10 that there is a neurotic form of depression, but this neurotic pattern is less severe. We will present the major DSM-II classifications of psychotic affect disturbances beginning with the most common, the *manic-depressive psychoses*. We will then describe some possible alternative conceptualizations of affective disorders.

The Manic-Depressive Psychoses

Manic-depressive psychoses may be classified into three subtypes: *manic type*, characterized by excess elation; *depressive type*, characterized primarily by excess depression; and a *circular type*, characterized by alternation between elation and depression. These psychoses are fairly common. For example, in 1970, about 70,000 manic-depressive people were admitted to psychiatric services. This number accounted for 3.5% of all psychiatric admissions during that year. Further, women patients outnumber men by a ratio of 2 to 1. In contradistinction to schizophrenia, which is more common in the lower classes, affective psychoses occur more frequently among the upper classes. More than half (58%) of the cases of the manic form of affective disturbances occur in young adults between the ages of 20 and 35.

Two characteristics of manic-depressive disorders set them apart from other forms of psychosis. First, there is a high rate of *spontaneous remission*. With or without treatment, the majority of affective episodes simply subside after a while; however, manic episodes usually remit much sooner than depressive ones. Second, after remission of one episode there is unfortunately a great likelihood of a recurrence of the disorder at some point in the person's life.

Manic Type. The manic subtype of manic-depressive psychosis may manifest itself in any one of three forms: *hypomania, acute mania,* or *delirious mania.* In each form, the major mood is one of elation out of proportion to reality. The person is in unusually high spirits and, in the less severe forms of elation, often will be thought of as the "life of the party." In actuality, however, the "good time" is out of control and the person can do little to slow down. In most cases, thoughts flit from one idea to another; things that usually are ignored may be treated as if they had great importance. Jokes, puns, and wild statements often spew forth from the patient in what has been called *logorrhea* (Mendels, 1970). Motor activity can also be affected, with dramatic increases in gesturing, grimacing, and general movement.

Variations in the degree of these manic behaviors are used to discriminate diagnostically among the three forms of the disorder. In hypomania, the least severe form, the person usually doesn't appear out of control, but rather seems to be in a jolly mood. R. Cohen (1975) describes a classic triad of symptoms in hypomania that includes an elevated but unstable mood; a "pressured" speech pattern in which words seem to want to

PERSONAL EXPERIENCE: *What Is It Like to Be Severely Depressed or Manic?*

What is it like to have your problems?

Oh, I don't know. It's like an empty feeling inside—just empty.

Like everyone else's problems. I worry about whether my children will be able to have children or if they'll find a cure for me.

It's like somebody making money but not me. I'm here for free now, but the federal government can only pay for so long, and then they'll be broke and I won't be able to get a job.

I feel like I'm an in-between going nowhere. I want a separation from my husband, but I'm afraid.

I just don't feel like doing anything. I wouldn't go out; I wouldn't do anything. I wouldn't talk to or see my friends; I just stayed home all the time. I worried about being rejected by my family. I just wasn't strong enough to handle the conflict I was going through.

I'm manicky, yeah, but it's a free country! I can be manicky if I want to; there's no law against it! I know a lot of people who are manicky, and they're not in a hospital. This isn't so much of a problem. I get a lot done and do a lot more things than most people I know.

You don't know what it feels like being nervous? I just feel so bad that I don't feel like living anymore. I wouldn't try to do anything to hurt myself, but I just didn't feel like there was anything to live for and I would be better off dead. I hope these shock treatments help.

Let me tell you, I'd rather have cancer than have a mental illness. Cancer you can either cure or it kills you but the mental illness I have is incurable . . . it's terrible. There's something wrong with my brain. I want them to operate on it and see what causes my depression and wildness. Otherwise, nothing helps.

It's terrible. I wouldn't wish this on anybody.

come out faster than the person can say them; and an increase in motor activity. Cohen describes the hypomanic as follows:

> He talks easily, winningly, humorously and he talks and talks and talks—and talks. He is warm, then friendly, and then uninvitedly intimate and unwelcomely personal. He radiates good health; his eyes shine, there is a sheen in his hair, a glow to his skin, a bounce in his stride; one can almost see the elasticity of his muscles.

He is constantly on the go and never seems to tire. Only as one stays with him does one become aware of his distractibility; of impatience and intolerance when his wish is not immediately gratified; of impulsive and ill considered actions; of unseemly self-indulgence; and of bland disregard of patent difficulties [p. 1018].

In acute mania, the characteristics of the hypomanic are present, but to a greater degree. The mood disturbance is usually very apparent to others. The acute manic may pun wildly, tease, make blasphemous comments, sing insane songs, and move about wildly. Cameron (1947) has provided an example of manic speech and its freewheeling form:

> "You go out and stand pat—pat, you hear! Who was Pat? What does he wear when he's in Ireland? This hair won't stay out of my eyes (brushes it aside and touches pillow). See this pillow (raising it behind head)? Now is it even, even or odd? Even or odd, by God; I take it even, by God. By God we live, by God we die, and that's my allegiance to these United States. See my little eagle (bedsheet wrapped around feet and stretched taut)? These are my wings. No, I have wings of a girl." Patient sings *Prisoner's Song*, making flying movements with her arms to accompany the lines, "Over these prison walls I would fly." Then sings, "One little Indian, two little Indians," and suddenly shouts, "Heap big Indian chief! I'm not afraid. I got a heart right there, I've got a key to my heart. I don't want instant death. No, not one little teensy, eensy, weensy, not one little teensy, eensy, wittsy, wonsy bit. Right is right, wrong is wrong, two rights don't make a wrong. So they are, all over the world. God made the world, but this isn't Adam speaking, it's me. Mr. Adam, you can't just walk out of here. It's O.K. by me, I've said my say. Out you go! Take me if you want to or leave me. Shoot if you want to. I have just one heart, a right heart. I'm so tired. So shoot, shoot, but only once. Point the gun at the right breast. I'll know him wherever I see him, dead or alive. Shoo-oot, 'Oh, Columbia the gem of the ocean' (sung). Shoot, I'm ready, 1-2-3, shoo-oot! (hand over heart, eyes closed). My husband, my heart aches, oh, it aches, I'm tired, I'm tired, I'm tired" [p. 205].[1]

The person with acute mania doesn't seem to care about the rights of others and may react violently to those who interfere. Frequently, ideas pour forth in a torrent, with hallucinations and delusions being freely communicated. The following personal experience is an account of a patient who has experienced this level of manic disturbance.

[1]This and all other quotations from this source from *The Psychology of Behavior Disorders,* by N. Cameron. Copyright 1947 by Houghton Mifflin Company. Reprinted by permission of the Executor of the estate of Norman Cameron.

PERSONAL EXPERIENCE: *Mania*

I just remember feeling wonderful . . . on top of the world. God I felt good—inside me it was like a glass of pop with too many bubbles—they just came busting out and I laughed and I sang. Everybody else had a good time. I know they did—we were all laughing until our sides hurt, and tears came running down our faces. Wow—what a time.

Yes I remember everyone else stopping, but I didn't—I couldn't—it was as if I was out of control. I was having a great time—but it was a little scary, too.

Delirious mania may occur after a person has passed through hypomania and acute mania, or it may appear independently. All of the usual manic symptoms are generally present to the most intense degree, but in addition there is typically a total loss of contact with reality. Speech is often incomprehensible, hallucinations and delusions may be rampant, and the person frequently has difficulty controlling bladder and bowel functions. Many times it is impossible to converse with such people because they are totally oblivious to their surroundings. The person in a state of delirious mania may fit the layman's stereotypic picture of a "raving maniac."

Depressive Type. The manic disorders are marked by elation, but the depressive psychoses involve the opposite end of the feeling continuum. The depressive subtype of manic-depressive psychosis is characterized by extremely depressed mood and mental and physical slowing. In some cases, uneasiness, apprehension, and agitation may appear (so-called *agitated depression*). Delusions of worthlessness and bodily change may occur, along with hallucinated voices describing the patient's misdeeds. Suicide is always a very real threat in the psychotically depressed. Symptoms of depression can be rated according to various clinical scales, such as that prepared by Zung (1965) (Table 8-1). Like the manic types of psychosis, depressions may manifest any of three degrees of severity.

The mildest form of psychotic depression is *simple depression*, characterized by a general slowdown of functioning associated with a loss of enthusiasm for mental and physical activity. To the individual, it often seems as if even the simplest task is too great to tackle; even eating can become a chore, and weight loss is probable. Conversation may be avoided, and interactions with people are minimized. A general heaviness seems to be associated with every minute of every day. At this level of depression, there is usually little or no problem with logical thinking processes, and hallucinations or delusions are rare. Many normal people experience this degree of depression (commonly called "the blues") and feel better within a

Table 8-1. *Zung's self-rating scale for depression*

	A little of the time	Some of the time	Good part of the time	Most of the time
1. I feel down-hearted and blue				
2. Morning is when I feel the best				
3. I have crying spells or feel like it				
4. I have trouble sleeping at night				
5. I eat as much as I used to				
6. I still enjoy sex				
7. I notice that I am losing weight				
8. I have trouble with constipation				
9. My heart beats faster than usual				
10. I get tired for no reason				
11. My mind is as clear as it used to be				
12. I find it easy to do the things I used to				
13. I am restless and can't keep still				
14. I feel hopeful about the future				
15. I am more irritable than usual				
16. I find it easy to make decisions				
17. I feel that I am useful and needed				
18. My life is pretty full				
19. I feel that others would be better off if I were dead				
20. I still enjoy the things I used to do				

few days. However, when depressive episodes return, aren't linked to any real occurrence, and increase in severity, the diagnosis of simple depression may apply.

More severe than simple depression is *acute depression*, in which the physical and motor retardation described earlier is intense. Typically, activity level drops sharply, interpersonal avoidance increases, and delusions of responsibility for world calamities and family tragedies may enter the picture. Thoughts of suicide are common, and feelings of guilt and worthlessness pervade every waking moment. Sleep is difficult, if not impossible, and rarely restful. The person often expresses little hope that better days are ahead and seems to feel helpless. Cameron (1947) provides the following example of an acutely depressed patient. Note the delusional beliefs and the general lack of faith in a cure:

> On admission to the hospital, the patient sat slumped in a chair, frowning deeply, staring at the floor, his face looking sad and drawn. When questioned, he answered without looking up, slowly and in a monotone. Sometimes there was such a long pause between question and reply that the patient seemed not to have heard. Every now and then he shifted his position a little, sighed heavily and shook his head from side to side. His first verbal response was, "It's no use. I'm through. All I can think is I won't be any good again." In response to further inquiries he made the following comments, relapsing into silence after each short statement until again asked a question. "I feel like I'm dead inside, like a piece of wood. . . . I don't have any feeling about anything; it's not like living any more. . . . I'm past hope. . . . There's nothing to tell. I've lied to everybody. My family is ashamed of me. I've messed up my life. I'm no good to anybody. . . . My memory is gone. I forget everything. . . . I can't look people in the eye any more. I've done everything wrong. You're wasting your time on me" [p. 508].

Depressive stupor differs from simple and acute depression in that, with few exceptions, people who suffer from it are *completely* inactive and unresponsive to people or things. They refuse to eat, are oblivious to bowel and bladder function, and often have to be hospitalized for maintenance through intravenous feeding and catheterization. Fortunately, modern treatment methods such as electroshock frequently alleviate the symptoms of depressive stupor quickly. If this treatment were not available, such patients would probably die.

Circular Type. People suffering from the circular type of affective psychosis experience alternating manic and depressive attacks as illustrated in the following personal experience. Frequently there is a brief period of normality during the passage from one feeling state to the other. Although many believe that these mood swings are common, in fact, only about one out of five manic-depressive people suffers from this circular variety (Coleman, 1976).

> **PERSONAL EXPERIENCE:** *Manic-Depressive Psychosis, Circular Type*
>
> When it's beginning to happen, I can feel it. It's like a wave of feeling suddenly overwhelming me. When I was depressed last year, all I can remember is the sense of worthlessness I felt. I couldn't believe that anyone could care about me or try to help me. I just wanted to die. My doctor gave me this note that I wrote then: "Dear Doctor ———, Please don't waste your time on me. Please help the ones who deserve to live. I wish you and your wife well in your new home in San Jose. When they take me to my grave I'll feel relieved. Death will be my punishment for the evil I've done to you and to my fellow man."
>
> It scares me to even read such a note and even more to realize that I wrote it. But my most recent episode was an uncontrollable high—I mean, happiness with no bound. It started at a party I was at over New Year's Eve—always a tough time for me to get through, anyway. I felt that wave, that uncontrollable surge of feeling, and I was there before I knew it. I couldn't stop myself from moving around, talking, singing, and carrying on. I felt like I could lick the world, I felt that the whole world thought I was something special. I really liked that feeling, but again, I've been told by Dr. ——— that I was acting crazy and out of control. He said that I went around making believe that I was a dog looking for a fire hydrant and that I wet my pants. It sounds funny to think of it now. Thank goodness for the lithium therapy—it brought me down. I wish I knew what prompted the attacks. . . . At least they've all gone away—so far.

Psychotic Depressive Reaction

Psychotic depressive reactions differ from the manic-depressive psychoses in that the depressive symptoms do not develop out of some long-standing disorder, but rather are a reaction to some type of environmental stress. Among those stressors identified as capable of inducing psychotic depressive reactions are death of a parent or spouse, loss of a job, destruction of one's home, and other life events similar to those we discussed in Chapter 5 (Meyers et al., 1971). In a person unable to cope with extremely stressful occurrences, stressful life events could precipitate a depression of psychotic proportions. Most frequently, psychotic depressive

Some forms of reactive depression result from the loss of loved ones or property. (Photos courtesy of the American Red Cross.)

reactions are diagnosed on the basis of history. If there is a specific precipitator and no other manic-depressive disorder in the person's past, it is most likely a reactive depression. The chances of recurrence of a psychotic depressive reaction as a rule aren't nearly so high as for the slower-developing manic-depressive form of the affect disturbances.

Involutional Melancholia

The major differences between involutional melancholia and the other types of affective psychosis lie in the age of onset of depression and the lack of significant history of depressive episodes. *Involutional* (meaning, literally, without control) *melancholia* occurs three times more frequently in females than in males; typically the disorder strikes women between the ages of 50 and 60 and men between the ages of 60 and 70. In women, the onset of the disorder usually follows menopause by a maximum of seven or eight years.

Generally, as involutional melancholia develops, people begin to experience periods of insomnia and feelings of inner tension. They become easily fatigued, both mentally and physically, and show a reduced need for food or sexual activity. Fears for personal health and complaints of a continuous headache are frequent. Gradually, the person with involutional melancholia may develop a sense of despondency accompanied by constant weeping and loss of interest in favorite activities. As involutional melancholia deepens, insomnia worsens, weight loss increases, and numerous bodily ills may be imagined. The person typically presents a picture of extreme sadness mixed with agitation, often in the form of hand-wringing, pacing, repeated pleas for help, and self-deprecating statements. In severe cases, the person may experience delusions of guilt and bodily changes. For example, those suffering from involutional melancholia may believe that their insides have turned to concrete or that future bowel movements will be impossible. The following personal experience of involutional melancholia demonstrates many of the characteristics we have described.

PERSONAL EXPERIENCE: *Involutional Melancholia*

I don't know what went wrong with me. I had always been strong and stable, but now I feel so terrible and frightened. I can't sit still, and I'm always so tense and irritable. I cry at the drop of a hat. My children try to get me to do things, but they only succeed in making me mad. Even my grandchildren irritate me—can you imagine that? Nobody can stand me anymore. I nag and cry and nag and cry and can't be satisfied. I feel like nobody can help me and I really don't deserve to be helped.

Other Patterns

The various types of manic-depressive psychoses and reactive depression make up the greatest number of instances of the affective psychoses. However, included in DSM-II are other, less frequent kinds of affective disorders that deserve some comment as well.

Postpartum Depression. Postpartum depression shares with reactive depression the fact that it comes in response to a specific occurrence, in this case, childbirth. Often, following childbirth, women experience severe temporary depressive reactions that in some instances can reach psychotic proportions. Winokur, Clayton, and Reich (1969) have stated that these postpartum depressions are probably the result of endocrine changes pursuant to delivery interacting with a predisposition in some women to develop an affective psychosis under stress. These researchers found that the probability of postpartum depression in women with previous histories of depression was higher than normal. The personal experience that follows is a description of postpartum depression as it was experienced by a 21-year-old mother.

Being a mother can sometimes be a lonely and frightening experience, as well as a joyful one. (Photo by George Lazar.)

PERSONAL EXPERIENCE: *Postpartum Depression*

I think the "blues" started right there in the hospital. I felt unable to relax at all. Now that I was a mother I had many important duties. I didn't feel sure I could live up to these responsibilities and at night in the hospital bed I didn't sleep but outlined my daily schedule in my mind. I knew that when the baby and I got home I would have to be busy keeping the place in such a condition to be a "wholesome environment" for a child. I decided that I would have to force myself to stick to this schedule.

After we were home for awhile I began to feel like a shell. I did the same thing every day. While the baby was awake I was his servant and when he was asleep I cleaned and checked on his breathing. Nothing could upset my routine. If I knew a friend might call I took the phone off the hook or simply didn't answer its ring. I couldn't see anyone or go anyplace because it would upset my routine and I would be an unfit mother.

Although it's called postpartum *blues* I remember feeling incapable of being blue. I just felt profoundly *empty*. There was no feeling for anything. I was quite sure that I didn't and couldn't love my husband or child.

The very worst day was when our baby was baptized. It was a bright spring day. I remember that a shaft of sun shone in from the porch that morning and I somehow saw it as a symbol that there was light and life somewhere but *I* would never be part of it.

After about six months I began to have bad stomach aches and diarrhea. Everytime I went out (which was not often and only to the grocery store or on some short errand) I would develop severe stomach pains and have to come home. Soon I began to think that I'd probably die.

By this time my husband, who had been very patient and kind, insisted that I see a doctor. The doctor found nothing wrong with me and spent quite a while talking with me—gently prodding. At last I cried, sobbed in fact, and told him that I felt nothing, loved nothing, and was nothing.

After this visit to the doctor I realized that I had a "real problem." Somehow just knowing this helped. Maybe I wasn't just empty, maybe I was unwell. Very, very slowly I started to feel better. I think I could have gotten better faster with some professional help. Now that the "baby" is six, I am better than I ever was but I do regret that I never let myself enjoy his babyhood.

Manic-Depressive Disorders in Childhood. Far less common than postpartum depression are affective psychoses that occur in young children. Kraepelin (1896), a trailblazer in the classification of mental disorder, observed that the prime time for onset of the first attack of a manic-depressive disorder was in the age period of 15 to 20 years. He noted that it was rare to find such cases in children younger than 13. However, according to Winokur and his colleagues (1969), cases of manic-depressive psychosis have been recorded in children as young as ten years of age. An example is provided here:

> Mary W., 12 years old, was seen in the clinic in a state of hyper-activity, exhilaration, and extreme talkativeness. Menstruation at that time had not yet begun. She had had her first attack of affective disorder at the age of 10 years, which was 15 to 24 months before she was seen in the clinic for the first time at age 12. At 10 years she would not go out of the house and was afraid that people were watching her. She had feelings of derealization and expressed the feeling that she did not belong to the world. There was little in the way of spontaneous talk. This depression (which started at the age of 10 years) continued for 7 months, after which she became excited, talked excessively, sat in peculiar positions, and had flighty thoughts. She then went into a period of 4 months in which phases of depression and excitement alternated every 2 weeks. This, in turn, was followed by a depression that lasted for 3 months. A normal mental state intervened for a month, and her illness recurred. It was then that she was seen in the clinic (age 12 years), showing alternating periods of depression and excitement. Her illness remitted in 9 weeks, and she was well for 2 years, during which time the first menstruation occurred. At 14 years of age she again entered the clinic in a state of excitement that had developed after a period of depression; this time she was exhilarated, distractible, boisterously overactive, and continuously talking. In a period of 3 months she improved and was home until the age of 19 years, when she again became excited and had to be admitted to a state hospital. This excitement disappeared in a few weeks, and she regained her normal health. Eight years later another attack requiring hospital admission occurred. This particular case appears to be one in which affective disorder, showing both mania and depression, started considerably before puberty (17 months to 4 years prior to menstruation). There is an adequate follow-up to indicate that the patient's illness was indeed a rather typical manic depressive psychosis [pp. 23–24].[2]

Reactive Mania. Although reactive depression is frequent, the opposite pattern, *reactive mania,* is rarely observed. The manic reaction is usually in response to the removal of some clearly definable environmental stress. For example, one woman experienced a manic attack following the death of her elderly mother, who had become a tremendous burden in her failing years. The pattern also has been observed in some patients following a surgery about which they had been anxious. Of course, all of us would feel relief at surviving drastic surgery, but the reaction we are discussing is of psychotic proportions.

ALTERNATIVE CLASSIFICATIONS

To this point we have discussed the forms of affective psychoses following the DSM-II classification system. However, you will remember from Chapter 1 that not everyone is satisfied with DSM-II. This dissatisfaction is especially marked with regard to the affective psychoses. Over the past 30 or 40 years, at least ten alternative systems for classifying affective psychoses have been proposed. Several of these different ways of looking at affective disorders have gained wide popularity and will be described here.

Primary versus Secondary Affective Disorders

A significant problem facing diagnosticians is whether emotional symptoms are reflections of an affective psychosis or are simply part of some other disorder, such as hebephrenic schizophrenia. In an effort to resolve the confusion, Robins, Muñoz, Martin, and Gentry (1972) have divided affective disorders on the basis of chronology of symptoms and presence of other psychiatric disorders. *Primary affective disorders* are those occurring in patients who have previously been well or whose only previous problems were of mania or depression. *Secondary affective disorders* are those appearing in mentally ill people with other types of diagnosable problems, such as schizophrenia. Using this classification, Robins and his associates have been able to categorize satisfactorily up to 90% of patients they have studied. Whether the primary–secondary distinction is useful in research and in guiding treatment has yet to be determined.

Bipolar versus Unipolar Affective Disorders

Unlike Robins, who was concerned with differentiating affective disorders from other disorders, Perris (1966) was concerned with different categories *within* the affective psychoses. Perris separated patients on the basis of whether they had experienced *both* manic and depressive episodes, or just one or the other. Those experiencing both types of episodes were referred to as *bipolars,* and those with pure symptom histories of a single affective disorder (either manic or depressive) were termed *unipolars.* Research has shown that these groups actually differ in a number of significant ways (Table 8-2). Bipolars tend to be younger and to recover more quickly than unipolars. Although there is no conclusive evidence, we may be dealing with two separate, biochemically based disease entities in bipolar and unipolar affective psychoses.

Table 8-2. *Characteristics of unipolar and bipolar depression*[a]

Variable	Bipolar Depression	Unipolar Depression
Genetic investigation	If two members of one family become depressed, then it is probable that both will develop either a bipolar or a unipolar illness.	
Childhood environment	No significant differences concerning childhood bereavement between the two groups. Higher incidence of unfavorable home conditions in the bipolar group.	
Precipitating factors	No significant differences between the groups. Tendency to more frequent somatic factors among unipolars.	
Celibacy	Significantly higher number of celibates among male bipolar patients than male unipolars. No difference concerning women.	
Fertility	No significant differences between the groups.	
Personality traits	Significant predominance of syntonic personality pattern.[b]	Significant predominance of asthenic personality pattern.[c]
Median age at onset	About 30 years.	About 45 years.
Body build	No significant differences between the groups.	
Color-form preference	More pronounced color preference during both depressive phase and remission.	More pronounced color preference during depressive phase.
Flicker threshold[d]	Lower than controls both during depressive phase and remission.	Somewhat low during depressive phase. Higher than in bipolar patients.
Clinical rating	No significant differences either in anxiety-depression or in retardation scores.	
Response to treatment	Require fewer ECT.	Require more ECT.
Course	Somewhat shorter episodes, more frequent relapses.	Somewhat longer episodes, less frequent relapses.
Suicide	No significant differences between the groups.	

[a]From *Concepts of Depression*, by J. Mendels. Copyright 1970 by John Wiley & Sons, Inc. Reprinted by permission.
[b]*Syntonic personality:* Individual characterized as sociable, active, easy to get along with.
[c]*Asthenic personality:* Individual characterized as somewhat withdrawn, easily fatigued, hypersensitive, obsessional.
[d]*Flicker threshold:* Perceptually, the point at which a rapidly flashing light, previously seen as constant, is seen as flickering.

Endogenous versus Exogenous Affective Disorders

Similar to the useful differentiation between process and reactive schizophrenia (Chapter 7), subclassification of depressions also has been attempted on the basis of patient history. In this third alternative to DSM-II, depressions occurring with slow onset and no clear precipitating life stresses are called *endogenous*. Among the characteristics of endogenous depressions are early morning awakening, weight loss, guilt, and reduced reactivity. On the other hand, *exogenous* depression (also called reactive depression) occurs with rapid onset in younger people and typically is associated with more clearly definable life stresses. Although useful clinically, this distinction has not been officially recognized.

EXPLANATIONS

Given the variety of points of view regarding the description and classification of affective psychosis, it shouldn't be surprising that an unusually large number of explanations have been proposed for these disorders of mood. We have organized the multiple theoretical approaches into the psychological, the biological and biochemical, and the integrated bio-psychological explanations.

Psychological Explanations

The wide range of psychological explanations of affective psychoses began in the early work of the psychoanalysts and continues through the current efforts of learning theorists. The psychological approaches share the belief that depression and mania can be explained on the basis of learning, life experiences, and internal psychological events. As you will see, each set of these theories tends to focus on a different aspect of psychological function.

Loss of Love Object and Inward Aggression: The Psychoanalysts. One of the first psychological conceptualizations of manic-depressive disorder was provided by the early psychoanalyst, Karl Abraham (1948). Abraham felt that people prone to affective psychosis are similar to the neurotic type called obsessive compulsives; that is, they are ambivalent, egocentric, and so taken equally by love and hate that they can't express one feeling in the absence of the other. Their inability to express pure love leads to feelings of inner impoverishment. This impoverished feeling is the result of fixation at the oral stage of psychosexual development caused by an ambivalent attitude toward the mother. Such people grow up being unable to relate adequately to *love objects* (parent, spouse, lover, and so on) and experience intense frustration when trying to obtain gratification from them. In reaction to problems in relating to others, in later life they regress to the oral level and relate to themselves with the same love-hate ambivalence: sometimes they hate themselves (depression) and sometimes they love themselves (mania).

Freud also entered the theoretical debate. He noted in *Mourning and Melancholia* (1957) that the behavior of grieving was similar to that of depression. Just as bereaved people mourn the loss of important others, depressed individuals mourn the loss of their own egos. After all, the ego had been deeply involved with the love object itself (mother, for example) to the extent of becoming identified with it. Thus, when a loved person or realized goal is lost, the ego "feels" the loss and depression results. Freud also proposed that depression represented a turning inward of aggressive feelings that may have been felt toward another person. In people unable to express aggression effectively, a sense of despair ensues and may lead to suicide (see Chapter 15). In support of this view, Kendall (1970) found that in societies where aggression is permitted, there is a lower incidence of depression.

Loss of Self-Esteem and Lack of Self-Value: The Ego Analysts. More focused than the early psychoanalysts on specific function of the ego, many ego analysts see *loss of self-esteem* as the most crucial psychological factor in depression. Jacobson (1953) states:

> Manic-depressives manifest a particular kind of infantile narcissistic dependency on their love object. What they require is a constant supply of love and moral support from a highly valued love object, which need not be a person, but may be represented by a powerful symbol, a religious, political, or scientific cause, or an organization. . . . As long as their "belief" in this object lasts, they will be able to work with enthusiasm and efficiency [p. 67].

As a result of what Jacobson describes, such people overly value their love objects and thus undervalue themselves. When loss of the love object is threatened or actual, then all that is left is the depression associated with the low self-esteem of the undervalued ego.

Another ego analyst, Bibring (1953), has added a variation on Jacobson's point of view. He states that the basic mechanism in depression is the ego's shock-filled realization that it is helpless in regard to its aspirations. The person realizes that something he or she has made very important can never be attained, and the result of this realization is a sort of grieving process. Depressive people set unrealistic goals for themselves, and their self-esteem is attached to the achievement of these goals. When self-esteem drops, it is a signal to the ego that a state of helplessness is imminent. In the psychologically stable individual, the loss of self-esteem leads to activities designed to reduce the threat to self-esteem. These activities may involve lowering of goals or perhaps mildly distorting one's

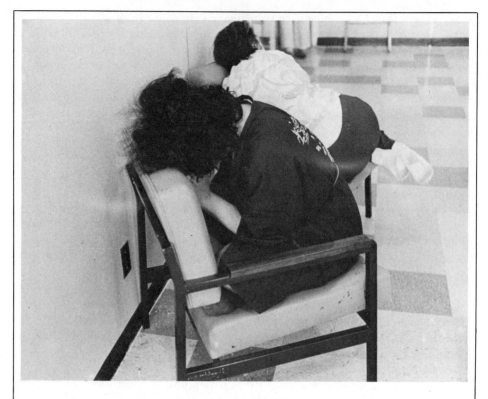

The pain of depression often prevents people from reaching out to one another. (Photo by Joseph Czarnecki.)

perception of events through the use of defenses. However, in the depressed individual, instead of constructive activities, a state of helplessness and depressed feelings ensues. Manic episodes, in contrast, are the result of excitement surrounding a belief that the unrealistic goals are being met, when in reality they aren't.

Interpersonal Ambivalence and Faulty Social Learning: The Neoanalysts. The theories of Abraham and Freud dealt primarily with intrapsychic conflict and gave great importance to the concepts of hostility, inward aggression, and the loss of love objects. The neoanalysts, however, have recognized an interpersonal basis for affective disorders and lay the responsibility for disturbance on faulty social learning and the generalizing into later situations of maladaptive habits learned from parents. M. Cohen, Baker, Cohen, Fromm-Reichmann, and Weigart (1954) attempted to assess the interpersonal and sociocultural aspects of manic-depressive psychosis. They determined that manic-depressives generally were brought up by mothers who were dissatisfied with their family status and concerned with elevating it. These mothers were further described as ambitious, aggressive, and blaming; the fathers usually were seen as weak, dependent, and self-deprecating. The characteristic ambivalence of manic-depressives is attributed to their mothers' rewarding them for dependency and conformity while punishing them for assertiveness and autonomy. Cohen et al. state that "an important authority is regarded as the source of all good things, provided he/she is pleased; but he is thought of as a tyrannical and punishing figure unless he is placated by good behavior" (p. 117). For the neoanalyst, then, the psychological focus is more on what has happened *to* the person than on what has happened *within* the person's psychic apparatus.

Thought Disturbance: The Cognitive Theorists. The cognitive theorists take the position that all psychogenic disorders are thinking disturbances. A. Beck (1967) has proposed that *schemas* are crucial to understanding the origins of depression. Schemas are organized clusters of attitudes, beliefs, and assumptions about events in the internal and external world that mediate between what the person perceives and the responses to those perceptions. Supraordinate (higher-order) schemas influence subordinate (lower-order) schemas. For example, whereas a supraordinate schema may have to do with authority in general, a lower-order schema may have to do with attitudes about a person's boss. Beck believes that psychological disorders result from some biased set of schemas that adversely affect the person's ability to see the world accurately and to function adequately. In manic-depressive disorders, specific powerful supraordinate schemas about the self, the outer world, and the future typically are involved. The most significant and damaging of these distorted schemas involves the negative evaluation of the self in which people view themselves as worthless and helpless. Associated with this negative self-evaluation are supraordinate schemas that yield negative interpretations of current life experiences and negative views of the future. For example, a depressed person faced with a term paper would filter this problem through all of his or her distorted schemas. The resultant perception might be "I can't write good term papers, I'm no good at them [self-schema]; I'll never do it with all the other stuff I must do [outer-world schema]; I'll fail—I know it [future schema]." As a result of these three schemas, the depressed individual theoretically finds the world filled with unreachable goals, unscalable obstacles, and hopelessness.

According to Beck, manic people, by contrast, possess a different set of distorted schemas. They see themselves in a very positive light, see the future as unrealistically bright, and find a bit too much goodness in all their experiences. For Beck, the difference between the manic and the depressive—or among all psychological disturbances for that matter—lies, not in different processes, but in the *content* of their distorted schemas.

Reinforced Mood Alteration: Operant Theorists. Differing from Beck's perspective in its focus on less complex forms of learning, an operant conditioning–reinforcement analysis of depression was proposed by Charles Ferster (1965). Ferster concluded that the main characteristic of depression is a "reduced frequency of emission of positively reinforced behaviors." To emphasize his point, Ferster presents the example of two spinster sisters: one dies, and the other falls into a psychotic depression. In operant terms, the reason for the surviving sister's becoming depressed is that the source of reinforcement (her sister) for a large number of her behaviors is now gone, and she is no longer rewarded for her usual daily behavior. His explanation works well for reactive depression in that any significant change in a person's life can result in change of reinforcers. We can understand the stress and ensuing depression associated with loss of a spouse, loss of a job, change of neighborhood or friends, and so on. However, the operant approach doesn't explain clearly and easily why a reactive *mania* would follow the same types of life events.

The learning-theory approach of Lewinsohn and Atwood (1969) is slightly different from Ferster's. They state that, due to early learning, depressives are the kind of people who evoke very little reinforcement from those to whom they relate; that is, they generally receive little attention, love, interest, and the like. Depressives are thought to receive little reinforcement because of their poorly developed social skills and often aversive personality characteristics. Low positive-reinforcement schedules tend to result in depressive behavior such as guilt, self-deprecation, and fatigue. Lewinsohn and Atwood's formulation states, then, that depression is brought about by an individual's characteristics and societal reaction to those characteristics. We must emphasize that this explanation, like Ferster's, seems to work better for reactive depressions than for the endogenous states. In fact, another behaviorist, Lazarus (1971), clearly states that operant formulations of depression are best suited for the neurotic-reactive types and that the endogenous depressions are most likely physiological in nature.

Although the operant theorists say disappointingly little about manic behavior, we can speculate that such behavior derives from a distorted perception of a high rate of positive reinforcement from others, resulting in a higher rate of emission of all behaviors. For example, a person may see the laughter of others as an inordinately strong reinforcer and may therefore continue to act silly. Furthermore, from the perspective of Lewinsohn and Atwood, we can hypothesize that people prone to mania tend to evoke much attention and interest from others and that this produces a higher-than-normal rate of responding. This fits in with the idea that manic people are often the life of the party but can't stop their outlandish behavior in a more serious setting.

Learned Helplessness: An Animal Model of Depression. The psychological theories of affective psychoses we have discussed thus far are based primarily upon work with humans. The model we will describe now, however, is based upon research with animals in which behavior *similar* to that of depression in humans has been experimentally produced and observed. On the basis of their work with animals, Maser and Seligman (Maser & Seligman, 1977; Seligman, 1975) have presented a theory of *learned helplessness* as the precursor to depression:

> Learned helplessness undermines motivation to respond and so it produces profound interference with the motivation of instrumental behavior. It also proactively interferes with learning that responding works when events become controllable, and so produces cognitive distortions. The fear of an organism faced with trauma is controllable; if the organism learns that trauma is uncontrollable, fear gives way to depression [Seligman, 1975, p. 74].

In the original experimental indication of learned helplessness, Seligman and his colleagues were studying shock-avoidance learning in dogs. They restrained dogs and submitted them to shock that some of them could never avoid. Thus, they didn't learn to avoid, but learned that they were *helpless.* Later in the experiment, the dogs were placed in a divided box on one side of which they received a shock. They could escape this shock merely by jumping over a barrier into the other side. However, when the "helpless" dogs were introduced to this task, they behaved differently from those who had initially learned to avoid shock.

At first, much like the untrained dogs, the "helpless" animals ran around frantically for about 30 seconds; but unlike the naïve dogs, who would discover by accident that they could escape the shock by scrambling over the barrier, most of the conditioned dogs simply stopped moving, lay down in the corner, and whined. Even though the shock continued for a full minute, the experimentally prepared dogs continued to lie in the corner. On the next trial, the "helpless" dogs tended to move about for an even shorter amount of time before once again plopping down and whining in the corner. Previous learning in the early stages of the experiment apparently prevented the "helpless" dogs from finding out that they had some control over what happened to them in this new set of circumstances. Learned helplessness has been observed in cats, fish, primates, rats, and people (Roth & Bootzin, 1974).

Once induced, the state of "learned helplessness" often has tremendous staying power, as Seligman discovered during his attempts to "cure" his affected dogs. First, he removed the barrier to allow the dogs easy access to the side away from the shock, but the dogs didn't move. Next, he made the dogs hungry and dropped food on the safe side, but still the dogs tended just to lie there, absorbing the shock. With few exceptions, attempts to seduce the dogs to go to the safe side were unsuccessful. Finally, at the suggestion of a behavior therapist, whose clinical experience with descriptively similar human patients led him to prescribe a "swift kick," Seligman and his colleagues placed leashes around the necks of the dogs and *dragged* them across to the safe side. After between 25 and 200 draggings, the dogs began to respond on their own. Apparently, the inability to control outcomes had lowered the motivation of the dogs to respond and to initiate new responses that were adaptive. They had to be forced to see that they had some control over what happened to them.

Generalizing from these experimental findings, Seligman speculated that, due to an unfortunate and uncontrollable set of life experiences, some people learn to perceive themselves as being unable to control what happens to them. These people see aversive situations as unavoidable and under the control of others. As a result of such an attitude, they may react to pain and disappointment by acting lethargic and depressed. Even though *learned helplessness* seems an intriguing explanation of affective disorders, there is no biochemical support for its parallel with actual psychotic depression. Seligman himself seems to believe that the behaviors he observed are more like exogenous than endogenous depression.

Biological and Biochemical Explanations

Unlike the psychological explanations, in which etiology is based upon learning and life experience, the biological perspectives deal with internal, physical changes and their possible relation to depression and mania. Our discussion of neurotransmitters in Chapter 6 now becomes important, for much of the flurry of biochemical research in the affective disorders since the early 1960s has focused on neurotransmitter substances and their role in psychotic behavior.

The Catecholamine Hypothesis. The first group of neurotransmitter substances thought to be involved in affective psychosis were the *catecholamines*, the most important of which is *norepinephrine.* Schildkraut (1970) proposed that depression may be associated with a *deficiency* in brain norepinephrine, whereas manic behavior reflects an *excess* of norepinephrine. As support for his theory, he noted that psychoactive drugs that elevate mood tend to produce an increase in norepinephrine at synapses, but those which produce depressed mood cause a reduction of this biochemical. An appropriate amount of neurotransmitter substance allows smooth and normal neural transmission, but the presence of too much norepinephrine at synapses typically allows nerves to fire too frequently. Conversely, if too little of the substance is available, the neurons may be unable to respond to normal impulses impinging upon them.

Research on antidepressant medications and their mode of action contributed much support to the catecholamine hypothesis. Different types of antidepressant drugs (see Chapter 24) work in different ways to affect the presence of norepinephrine. For example, a group of antidepressant drugs called the monoamine-oxidase (MAO) inhibitors halts the action of the enzyme that metabolizes norepinephrine, thereby elevating the concentration of this neurotransmitter at the synapses. However, some antidepressants, called tricyclics, inhibit the reuptake of norepinephrine into the synaptic vesicles after neurotransmission. A higher-than-normal level of norepinephrine has been correlated with an increase in manic mood level. A drug called lithium carbonate, now widely used in the treatment of manic psychosis, produces a marked *decrease* in available norepinephrine at brain synapses. It is thought that this reduction in available norepinephrine in turn decreases the hyperresponsivity of the nervous system and slows down neurotransmission to a more normal level.

While much of the information concerning the function of neurotransmitters derives from research with animals, there is some confirmation of these findings from research with mental patients. For example, Kety (1975a) found low levels of norepinephrine in the urine of depressive humans and high levels in manic patients. Further research by Maas, Fawcett, and Dekirmenjian (1972) has shown that reduced catecholamine availability, evident in depressed people, returns to normal with successful treatment by antidepressants. These investigations further support the catecholamine hypothesis, but we still don't know the *cause* of neurotransmitter variations, only that they exist. Further, as we will see, the catecholamine hypothesis by itself doesn't seem adequate to explain the biochemistry of affective psychosis.

The Indoleamine Hypothesis. In addition to the catecholamines, another group of neurochemicals, the *indoleamines*, has been implicated in the affective disorders. For example, one indoleamine, *serotonin*, has been shown to be deficient in the brains of suicidal, depressed people (Shaw, Camps, & Eccleston, 1967). However, serotonin levels have also been found to be lower than normal in manic psychosis as well as in psychotic depression (Coppen, 1972; Van Praag, Korf, & Schut, 1973). Since serotonin is depleted in *all* cases of affective psychosis—not lower in depression and higher in mania—the indoleamine hypothesis seems more complicated than the norepinephrine explanation. That serotonin affects behavior differently than norepinephrine has been stated by Kety (1975a), who reported that increases in serotonin produce drowsiness, lethargy, and marked sedation; decreases yield aggressive behavior, increased locomotion, and increased sexual behavior. These effects are the opposite of those observed with norepinephrine imbalances.

The Permissive-Amine Hypothesis. The regular and predictable variations in indoleamine and catecholamine levels in affective disorders suggest that neither of these hypotheses alone can explain fully the biochemical involvement in manic and depressive behaviors. In light of this, they have been combined into what is called the *permissive-amine hypothesis*. With evidence mounting for lowered serotonin in all affective disorders and for catecholamine elevation in mania and its deficit in depression, theorists such as Prange, Wilson, and Lynn (1974) proposed the permissive-amine hypothesis. In this theory, it is proposed that the biological (genetic) predisposition to affective psychosis is a serotonin deficiency.

Kety (1975a) states that, in normal amounts, serotonin regulates the degree of reactivity of synapses and exerts a stabilizing effect upon variations in available catecholamines. If serotonin is deficient, catecholamines are "permitted" to vary without suitable control and can reach pathogenically high or low levels. Kety states that "a deficiency of serotonin at central synapses is an important generic or constitutional requirement for affective disorder, permitting what might otherwise be normal and adaptive changes in norepinephrine activity and the resultant mood states to exceed the homeostatic bounds and progress in an undampened fashion to depression or excessive elation" (p. 184). Thus, variations in mood in affective psychosis would be attributable specifically to norepinephrine variation, but the predisposition to overreaction in the form of extreme variations would be the result of a genetic lack of the dampening effects of serotonin. This intriguing hypothesis has yet to be tested fully enough to make suitable evaluation possible.

A Biopsychological Explanation

While each of the psychological and biological explanations of affective disorders seems plausible, neither approach satisfactorily accounts for all types of mood disturbances. For example, there are depressions caused by life stresses such as the death of a spouse or the failure to achieve an important goal. Further, there are people who develop affective psychoses for which there seems to be no satisfactory psychological or environmental cause. In an attempt to reconcile these problems and to take into account all research implicating various factors, Akiskal and McKinney (1973, 1975) have proposed an *integrative model of affective disorders*.

In the integrative model of depression, the symptom itself is defined as an interaction of three levels of function: the experiential, the biochemical, and the behavioral. As seen in Figure 8-1, many different components make up what is generally termed *depression*. Depression (or mania) is seen as a "biological final common pathway" for a variety of interacting expe-

Experiential	Chemical	Behavioral
Nonrelatedness Anhedonia Hopelessness Loss of control	Alternation in functional level of catechotamines and indoleamines Electrolyte disturbance	Disturbances in sleep or appetite Psychomotor dysfunction (slowing or agitation)

Figure 8-1. *Definition of depression as a multilevel interaction. From "Overview of Recent Research in Depression," by H. Akiskal and W. McKinney,* Archives of General Psychiatry, *1975, 32, 285–305. Copyright 1975 by the American Medical Association. Reprinted by permission.*

riences and events. As Figure 8-2 shows, the initial cause of an affective disturbance may be biological and/or psychological. For example, psychological stress in the form of adult object loss, physical disease, learned helplessness, and the like can begin the process of depression. Regardless of its source, once a depressive reaction has begun, *biologically* it is the same as all others. Hence, deficits in norepinephrine may be observed whether depression is physiologically or developmentally based. Although Akiskal and McKinney's model is much more complex than we have presented it here, our purpose is to demonstrate the manner in which they have combined seemingly disparate research and theory into a promising and meaningful integrated explanation of the affective disturbances. It is our opinion that only an integrated approach will bear fruit and, if not Akiskal and McKinney's, some similar model will ultimately provide the best description of the etiology of depression and mania.

TREATMENT

There are characteristics of affective psychoses that make them different from other psychological disturbances. Specifically, with or without *any* intervention, depression will generally disappear within nine months

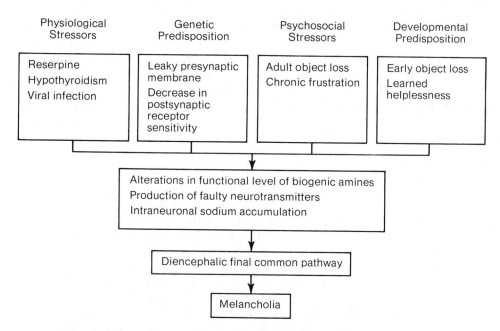

Figure 8-2. *Depression as a final biological pathway. From "Overview of Recent Research in Depression," by H. Akiskal and W. McKinney,* Archives of General Psychiatry, *1975, 32, 285–305. Copyright 1975 by the American Medical Association. Reprinted by permission.*

of onset, and manic episodes will generally abate within three months of onset. As a rule, only within the realm of affective disturbances can a person and his or her family be assured of recovery in this way.

Regardless of this assurance of remission, however, attempts at treatment are made for several reasons. First, if an episode can be shortened, the person can return to a productive life much sooner. Second, especially in depressed people, there is a risk of suicide if severe symptoms are allowed to continue. Finally, avoidance of extended hospitalization is highly desirable, for it minimizes the chance that the patient will become dependent on the hospital.

We will briefly describe methods of treatment specifically important for the affective disorders. General methods of therapy that may also be used in depression or mania will be described in Section VIII. For now, we will look at hospitalization, psychochemotherapy, and electroconvulsive therapy.

Hospitalization

The decision to hospitalize a person is a serious and difficult one. For a depressed or manic person, hospitalization may be necessary when there is a risk to self or others, a pathogenic relationship with family that could worsen the episode, a need for physical therapies such as shock, or expected difficulty in engaging the person in a psychotherapeutic outpatient relationship (Mendels, 1970).

Recent developments in antidepressant and antimanic drugs have made hospitalization less frequent, but short inpatient treatment periods are still often desirable. Since antidepressants often take up to seven days to take effect, severely depressed people who are suicidal may be hospitalized briefly while they await chemical relief of their symptoms. Due to the nature of the affective disorders and their rate of spontaneous remission, it is rare to find long-term hospitalized people with primary diagnoses of affective psychosis.

Psychochemotherapy

The main reason for the significant reduction in hospitalized affective-psychotic people in recent years is the advent of chemical treatment for depression and mania. Fuller descriptions and discussion of this treatment will be provided in Chapter 24, but we will mention a few relevant points here.

Antidepressant drugs are of several classes, each with different biochemical ways of varying the level of catecholamines and indoleamines at the nerve synapses. Typically, the drugs require a few days to take effect, and proper dosage is usually determined via trial-and-error adjustment called *titration*. Mendels (1970) has noted that, due to the availability of antidepressants, the use of electroshock has decreased, chronically ill patients have been released from hospitals, and many previously unreachable people have been made more responsive to psychotherapy.

While drugs for depression have been available since the 1950s, only within the last decade has *lithium carbonate* been used as a treatment for manic episodes. Apparently affecting the catecholamine levels in opposite ways from the antidepressants, lithium has been successfully used to reduce the duration of manic episodes in many people and to prevent their recurrence.

Electroconvulsive Therapy

Electroconvulsive therapy (also known as ECT or electroshock) will be discussed in depth in Chapter 24. Here it will suffice to note that ECT is extremely effective in halting depressive episodes; it usually has little or no effect upon manic symptoms, schizophrenia, or any other forms of psychological disturbance.

Following six to eight ECT treatments, most people manifest a lifting of depression. Modern ECT is performed under medical supervision and is considered by experts (Kalinowsky, 1975a) to be physically safe even for people with heart conditions. Adverse concomitants of ECT may include amnesia concerning the events of several days before and after the treatment, difficulty in concentrating, and some confusion. Even with these contraindications, many psychiatrists feel that ECT is the preferred treatment in cases of extreme depression associated with severe suicidal ideas. They reason that it is better to begin ECT than to wait for antidepressant drugs to take effect.

CONCLUDING COMMENTS

In many ways, the affective disorders are enigmatic. On the one hand, they are more likely than the other psychoses to go away with—or at times without—treatment. On the other hand, they are also more likely to recur throughout the lifetime of an afflicted person. Although both the manic and depressive disorders share the unique characteristics of the affective psychoses, only the depressive disturbances generally have been viewed as significantly dangerous. Called by some "the only potentially fatal mental disorder" (NIMH, 1975), depression has often been associated with suicide. In fact, it has been estimated that up to 75% of suicide attempts occur in people with depressive symptoms. Further, the chances of suicide in a person with a history of severe depression can be as much as 36 times higher than in people without such a history. The impact of these alarming facts may be tempered by the awareness that psychological and chemical/physical treatments for the affective disorders seem to be among the most effective for any of the varieties of being different.

CHAPTER SUMMARY CHART

In this chapter, we first described the various types of affective psychoses:

Manic-depressive psychoses

Manic type	Depressive type	Circular type
Hypomania	Simple depression	Alternating manic
Acute mania	Acute depression	and depressive
Delirious mania	Depressive stupor	episodes

Psychotic depressive reactions

Definite precipitating life stress
Low chance of recurrence

Involutional melancholia

Occurs with increasing age
Depression about life events and fears
Severe depression that doesn't
  abate easily

Other patterns

Postpartum depression
Childhood depression
Reactive mania

Alternative classifications

Primary versus secondary
Endogenous versus exogenous
Unipolar versus bipolar

We then offered a variety of explanations for affective disorders:

Psychological explanations

Psychoanalysis: loss of love object;
  aggression turned inward
Ego analysts: loss of self-esteem
  and lack of self-value
Neoanalysts: interpersonal
  ambivalence and faulty social
  learning
Cognitive theorists: schema
  distortion
Animal models: learned helplessness
Operant theorists: reinforced mood
  alteration

*Biological and biochemical
explanations*

Catecholamine hypothesis:
  increased neurotransmitters
  yield elation; decreased,
  depression.
Indoleamine hypothesis: serotonin
  is deficient in affective disorders
Permissive-amine hypothesis:
  lack of serotonin "permits"
  abnormal variation of
  catecholamines

Finally, we described some forms of treatment especially important in affective psychoses:

Hospitalization

Indicated when there is:
risk to self and others
pathogenic relation-
ships at home
need for shock therapy
expected noncoopera-
tion in outpatient
therapy

Psychochemotherapy

Antidepressants:
alter catecholamine
availability
trial-and-error
titration
Antimanics:
lithium carbonate
alter catecholamine
levels
help prevent
recurrence

*Electroconvulsive
therapy*

ECT, electroshock
therapy
Very useful in depres-
sion, not in other
psychiatric
disorders
A safe technique
Treatment of choice if
suicide risk is high
and rapid reduc-
tion of depression
is sought

CHAPTER 9
PARANOID
CONDITIONS
AND THE
RARE
PSYCHOLOGICAL
DISTURBANCES

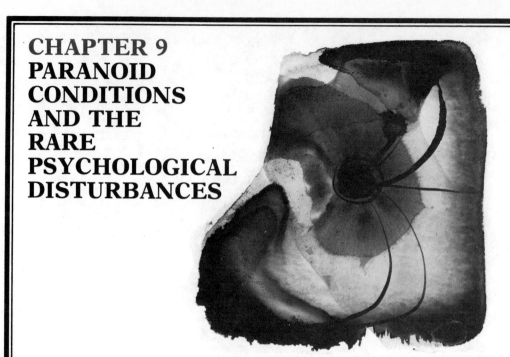

We have included a chapter on the paranoid conditions and rare psychiatric disorders because we have learned that our students in abnormal psychology are very interested in them. Also, we believe that a knowledge of the rare psychological disorders may help you to appreciate the wide range of psychological deviation. Only the paranoid disorders are specifically included in DSM-II; the rare disturbances usually are included in "wastebasket" categories such as *unclassified* or *atypical* patterns.

THE PARANOID CONDITIONS

Paranoid conditions are psychoses characterized by stable delusions of grandeur, influence, and persecution. Typically, no hallucinations are involved and the delusions aren't usually so bizarre as those found in other forms of psychosis. In fact, paranoid delusions are often highly organized and systematic. People classified as paranoid typically show appropriate affect, maintenance of social behavior, and minimal personality deterioration. Clinical observation suggests that paranoid people are usually more intelligent than those suffering from other psychotic disturbances

221

CHAPTER 9:
PARANOID
CONDITIONS AND THE
RARE PSYCHOLOGICAL
DISTURBANCES

and can express their ideas and beliefs effectively, often convincingly. Quite often, paranoid people behave and sound basically normal except in the area of their delusional beliefs.

The paranoid conditions include a variety of patterns varying in content, severity of disorganization, and age of onset. We will describe the major paranoid patterns and then discuss explanations of and treatments for this set of psychotic disorders.

Descriptions

There is much disagreement about the best classification for paranoid psychoses. We have chosen to reconcile various points of view and present a range of paranoid conditions, some of which are undoubtedly psychotic, others of which may be merely personality disturbances. All show the basic symptom of suspiciousness-turned-delusion that characterizes the paranoid person.

Paranoia. In the most severe paranoid condition, *paranoia*, a person develops a chronic, extremely well-systematized delusional state. Hal-

Although not always of psychotic proportions, suspiciousness is a part of daily life for many people. (Photo by Joseph Czarnecki.)

lucinations and mental deterioration usually don't occur. Most frequently, the delusional system is based upon *one* basic false belief from which a complex network of misinterpretation develops. Paranoia can exist for many years and, outside of their delusional systems, such people may appear normal and emotionally healthy. However, within the paranoid system, they often express a belief in their own superiority and a conviction that, due to this special status, they are being persecuted. The following personal experience describes the development of a paranoid delusional system in a 48-year-old woman.

PERSONAL EXPERIENCE: *Paranoia*

I felt for a long time that I could not tell anyone about how I was thinking. I felt very isolated and withdrawn. I went to work and came home as usual, but I never really felt comfortable any more. It all started, I guess, when I was 17 or 18—I'm not sure. I and some of my girl friends were sitting around at a little restaurant we used to go to. We were talking about boys, as usual, when one of the girls said that

Child in Forest 1951, Wynn Bullock

223

CHAPTER 9:
PARANOID
CONDITIONS AND THE
RARE PSYCHOLOGICAL
DISTURBANCES

she thought that God had made boys differently so that they could control the women as well as all other things on earth. To me what she was saying at first seemed ridiculous. . . but she was a very bright well-read girl and I respected her. I thought about what she had said and noticed that there were great similarities between women and all of nature in that all of us could easily be destroyed by men and their strength. I noticed that even the strongest and most vicious of animals could be easily killed by a man with a gun. I sensed a oneness in the weakness and vulnerability of women and the rest of nature.

Soon I became very involved in protecting all of the other "weak" members of my new group. I felt that men were innocent victims of a grand design but still I feared them. I prayed that they would not destroy the flowers in my garden or the trees in my yard. I began to believe that I had to protect and preserve for posterity the last remnants of the earth. I felt that after the men had unknowingly destroyed everything only I and my garden would remain. I built a very tall fence around my home, telling everyone that it was because I wanted privacy. I spent large amounts of my salary to buy samples of every type of plant and flower seed I could find. I kept all the seeds catalogued in a special room in my house and I kept the room locked—only I could enter it. Soon, I became very wary of any men who came to the house—I felt sure that they knew about the "seeds for the future" that I kept in the house and that they were going to destroy them and me. I put in an alarm system, which made me feel better for awhile, but I soon feared that the man who put in the system would tell other men how to bypass it.

I lived in worry for over 30 years, guarding the seeds, guarding my garden, hiding behind the tall fence around my house. I could find no one I could really trust with my burden. I had few friends and I rarely went out. But I was sure that I had to protect the "weak" in the earth . . . I was very sure.

In this account, we can see the way in which the paranoid woman's delusions developed from an innocent teenage comment to a need to protect all of nature from extinction. Remember, her intellect remained intact and, for most of the 30 years, she seemed able to function normally and realistically outside her belief system.

Paranoid State.   Like paranoia, *paranoid states* are characterized by delusions but no hallucinations; unlike paranoia, the delusions aren't nearly so structured or well organized. Instead, the beliefs are numerous, fragmented, distorted, and obviously bizarre to observers. However, the degree of distortion and bizarre ideation (thinking) is far less extreme than that of the paranoid schizophrenic person (Chapter 7).

Paranoid states usually last only a short time (a few weeks or months); however, they tend to recur throughout a person's life. People who are prone to manifest paranoid reactions are usually overly sensitive to the thoughts and feelings of others; they are often insecure and may feel inadequate and worthless. In trying hard to gain others' respect and admiration, they tend to exaggerate and misinterpret meaningless events and then may become suspicious, belligerent, and hostile. This sequence is shown in the following personal experience.

PERSONAL EXPERIENCE: *A Paranoid State*

Patient: It's funny now to talk about it, but I really believed it then.
Therapist: What happened, exactly?

P: About five years ago, I was in business with a cousin of mine . . . a clothing store. We sold men's and boys' ready-to-wear on 38th Street in New York. It was a small store, but it did well. Both of us were taking home about 28 or 30 thousand a year, and we got along well. One month, when I was doing the books, I noticed some erasures in some of the columns. It seemed that, when I looked back, there were erasures on each page that my partner worked on and none on mine. I couldn't get those erasures out of my mind—why were they there? What was erased? I started watching my cousin and he seemed to act strange. He would always count the day's receipts alone in the back room. I always took this as OK, but I began to think that he was taking more "funny money" [nonrecorded, out-of-the-till income] than usual. It's a long story, but before I knew it I was following him home and hiding in alleys. I was sure he was stealing me blind and changing the books. Everything came to a head when I accused him of robbing 2000 dollars over a one-month period. I was sure he had done it. We got into a fist-fight—nearly wrecked the store. The cops came and took me to a hospital; my cousin said I was completely out of control.

T: And now what do you believe?

P: Now . . . Ha! . . . My cousin is a sloppy bookkeeper—he takes as much from the register as I do—he counts the receipts in back 'cause who should count it in front where who knows who the customers are? I'm OK.

Minor Patterns. In addition to paranoia, paranoid states, and paranoid schizophrenia, there are a number of rarely seen paranoid patterns that usually reflect very limited or *circumscribed delusions*. For example, in the condition called *paranoid litigious state*, the individual is

225

CHAPTER 9:
PARANOID
CONDITIONS AND THE
RARE PSYCHOLOGICAL
DISTURBANCES

deluded specifically about the fairness or unfairness of the legal system. Usually an adverse legal decision leads the person to initiate an unending series of legal battles to overturn the decision. Important to the diagnosis of this disorder is that most of the legal proceedings are instigated against the advice of lawyers and the courts. Such people seem to feel that they *must* win their case. Since they have little realistic chance of winning, their litigation often continues indefinitely.

Paranoid eroticism differs from the paranoid litigious state in that, instead of law, sex is involved. In paranoid eroticism, the person (most often a female) may believe that she is deeply in love with some other, often famous person. According to the delusion, the other person, for reasons of career, family, or honor, can't reveal his true love for her. This fact explains why, when she writes to him, he doesn't answer, or when she calls him, she can't get through to him. Victims of paranoid erotic states often are lonely, sad people who live with their fantasies and hurt no one.

Unlike the litigious and erotic states, which may occur at any age, *involutional paraphrenia* occurs only in the elderly. Until the appearance of this state, such people typically show no history of paranoid ideas and manifest little disturbance of thought or affect. However, with the onset of the involutional paranoid state, they show intense suspiciousness, defensiveness, secretiveness, and hypersensitivity. Because older people often feel slighted, ignored, and victimized by others, they may arrive at delusional explanations for their problems. For example, a common paranoid delusion is that one's children are banding together with doctors and nurses to help get rid of one.

Explanations

The variety of paranoid conditions we've just described have in common that the person exhibits delusional thinking and feelings of persecution, suspiciousness, and grandiosity. However, explanations for these types of behavior patterns are sparse. Unlike the search for causes of the schizophrenias and the affective disorders, remarkably little effort has been expended by theorists and researchers in the quest for an understanding of paranoid disorders. There are no acceptable biological, biochemical, or genetic theories of paranoia. Only psychological explanations of paranoid disturbances seem worthy of discussion, and even these are few in number and lacking in empirical support.

Psychoanalytic Theory. To the Freudian theorist, paranoid psychoses differ from schizophrenia in that, in paranoia, the ego is still intact. However, the ego defenses of projection, denial, and repression are overly active and can result in paranoid patterns of thought and action. Freud proposed that paranoia is the result of repressed homosexuality. On the basis of his famous "Schreber" case, Freud (1925) concluded that repressed homosexual urges were projected onto others; these others then were seen as desirous of "attacking" the paranoid, thereby justifying a hostile, suspicious demeanor. Although interesting and theoretically plausible, Freud's explanation for paranoid delusion is unsupported by research evidence. In fact, some researchers have concluded that there is *absolutely no relationship* between homosexuality and paranoid psychoses (Planansky & Johnston, 1962).

Developmental Factors.   Whereas Freud emphasized the defense of projection and the development of homosexuality in the paranoid, others have directly or indirectly implicated developmental-childhood experiences in the later appearance of paranoid conditions. For example, Erikson (1963) describes the initial developmental conflict, *basic trust versus mistrust,* which may be involved in paranoid disorders. To Erikson, basic trust is crucial to a sound, healthy parent–child relationship. Without trust, parents and powerful others may be seen as incapable of helping, so the child can develop a belief that he or she may be betrayed and controlled by a hurtful world.

As the child grows, the early pattern of mistrust may intensify and expand, leading the child to stay away from other people. This avoidance is returned, because few people like the angry suspiciousness of the pre-paranoid. The child's behavior ensures that his or her initial ideas will be confirmed; other people come to be seen as not nice, not accepting, or not worthy of trust. For self-protection, the budding paranoid may become supersensitive to the thoughts and actions of others. He or she may come to believe that no one else can be trusted. According to the Eriksonian line of thinking, when life stresses build up, the person is unable to acquire the help of others. As a result, such a person may either deteriorate into paranoid schizophrenia or withdraw into a closed delusional system such as the *pseudocommunity* proposed by Cameron (1943) (to be discussed below). Paranoid symptoms may be said to serve the purpose of helping very suspicious people to cope with problems with which they cannot easily deal.

The Paranoid Pseudocommunity.   One possible outcome of pre-paranoid development is the paranoid pseudocommunity, or fantasied world, first clearly described by Norman Cameron (1943). Although not a total explanation of paranoid conditions, the concept of pseudocommunity provides a feeling for the development of the impenetrable delusional system of the paranoid person.

According to Cameron, prior to the development of the pseudocommunity, paranoid people are mistrusting and confused about life events or the reasons for their being persecuted. After dwelling on these problems for awhile, they may have an "Aha!" experience that takes the form of creating a pseudocommunity: "The paranoid pseudocommunity is a reconstruction of reality. It organizes the observed and inferred behavior of real and imagined persons into a conspiracy, with the patient as its focus"

227

CHAPTER 9:
PARANOID
CONDITIONS AND THE
RARE PSYCHOLOGICAL
DISTURBANCES

(Cameron, 1963, p. 486). After the pseudocommunity crystallizes, every-thing seems explainable; the person "knows" *who* is persecuting him (for example, the Communists), *why* they are persecuting him (perhaps because he is President of the United States), and *what* he must do to stop them (buy rifles and build a wall around his house). *Everything* "makes sense."

The concept of the pseudocommunity also can explain why paranoid disorders are so difficult to treat. Each new bit of information, each new experience, is incorporated into the delusional system. For exam-ple, if the paranoid person meets a psychiatrist, he may immediately con-clude that the doctor was sent to drug him and deliver him to his perse-cutors. If *you* believed this about your doctor, would you let him or her touch you? Wouldn't you act in a "paranoid" manner?

Treatment

Treatment of paranoid conditions can be very difficult, primarily because the delusional system of the paranoid often counteracts attempts to establish a therapeutic relationship. Although we will describe hospitaliza-tion, psychochemotherapy, and psychotherapy for a paranoid person, no treatment is universally effective. As in the case of other psychoses, acute and sudden paranoid reactions tend to remit easier and faster than chronic delusional disorders, regardless of the type of treatment administered.

Hospitalization. Although the most effective, immediate stress-re-ducing treatment for most other psychoses is hospitalization, it isn't al-ways easy or advisable in the case of the paranoid disorders. From the perspective of a paranoid delusional system, a hospital may be seen as a prison, concentration camp, or execution site. In response to such delusions, peaceable people often will become violent to protect themselves from being "imprisoned." In some cases, then, attempts to hospitalize paranoid people can worsen rather than improve their condition.

With acutely disturbed paranoid people, hospitalization in an in-stitution with a trusting, open staff, coupled with relaxation and relief from life stress, can result in rapid reduction of delusional thinking. Once such distorted beliefs are attenuated, therapeutic relationships can develop and psychotherapy may be pursued. Among paranoid people who suffer little or no personality disorganization, rapid release from the hospital is the rule; typically, the only paranoid people who are hospitalized for long periods are severely disturbed paranoid schizophrenics.

Psychochemotherapy. Normally used in combination with hos-pitalization and other modes of therapy, *psychochemotherapy* with paranoid psychotics usually involves major tranquilizers (see Chapter 24) such as the phenothiazine derivatives, thioridazine (Mellaril), and chlor-promazine (Thorazine). Soon after being hospitalized or brought to a psy-chiatrist, the paranoid person may be placed on relatively large amounts of tranquilizers to reduce the fear and agitation that usually accompany hospitalization. If the person continues to improve, psychotherapy can begin and drug dosages can be lowered. Drugs are rarely, if ever, the *only* form of treatment for the paranoid person. They usually are used as adjuncts to hospitalization or psychotherapy.

Psychotherapy.   Psychotherapy with paranoid people can be a very frustrating, frequently fruitless endeavor. Unlike neurotic or schizophrenic individuals, the paranoid person may not experience severe distress. In addition, the paranoid person usually doesn't trust others, including psychotherapists. Kolb (1973) describes some of the stringent requirements for successful therapy with the paranoid:

> Treatment should initially be as permissive as possible. The therapist should maintain an open, courteous, considerate attitude, coupled with scrupulous truthfulness and good faith. Recalling the essential pathology, attention should be paid to the patient's delusions, but no attempt should be made to criticize or convince the person that he is in error in his conclusions. . . . Nor should any efforts be made to convince him that he is among friends who are kindly disposed to him or that he has a warm, attractive personality himself. All forms of ingratiation should be avoided, as they will be interpreted as evidence that the patient is again dealing with persons similar to those whom he believes have betrayed him in the past [p. 411].

Given these basic requirements, we may consider as examples psychotherapeutic approaches that have been proposed specifically for paranoid individuals. The first method was developed by Sullivan (1956), whose specific expertise was in dealing with the psychotic disorders. Sullivan theorized that interpersonal anxiety is at the root of paranoid feelings. He believed that paranoid ideas were a type of security operation developed by the individual in order to defend against apprehensions. The goal of therapy is to *destroy* the irrational delusion and return the person to the point where he or she again experiences severe anxiety. When this most difficult therapeutic task has been accomplished, the therapist can foster a realistic, strong relationship with the client so that adaptive growth and anxiety reduction can occur.

While Sullivan's approach advocates attacking delusions and increasing anxiety, Cameron (1943) believes that the initial task of the therapist is to *lower* anxiety by manipulating the client's environment. From such a perspective, Cameron would remove the person from a stressful home life, job, or community setting to reduce anxiety. When anxiety is sufficiently reduced, the therapeutic relationship may begin.

In the attempt to establish a relationship with a paranoid individual, the psychotherapist must be a "safe confidant," according to Cameron.

229

CHAPTER 9:
PARANOID
CONDITIONS AND THE
RARE PSYCHOLOGICAL
DISTURBANCES

She or he should be a nonjudgmental, accepting, and relaxed person who won't become upset or anxious in the face of the paranoid's delusional, often angry material. If the client can learn to trust the therapist—and the therapist's perception of the world—he or she can begin to look at life events differently and form healthier, more realistic attitudes.

RARE, UNUSUAL, AND EXOTIC DISORDERS

The rare psychiatric patterns are so unusual that they have no specific place in the DSM-II classification system. When observed, these disorders usually create great excitement among professionals, but they are officially recorded as unclassified types. There is much disagreement as to whether these rare disorders are actually different, or simply "plain old" neurotic or psychotic patterns with unusual symptoms. Limited effort has been expended in theory and research regarding the rare syndromes. We will mention such efforts when they exist, but for the most part this section will be descriptive.

Gilles de la Tourette's Syndrome

In Gilles de la Tourette's syndrome, the person manifests uncontrollable body movement and verbal utterances in the form of swearing, epithets, and obscenities. These verbalizations are at times accompanied by spitting, blowing, and barking sounds. Such behavior is termed *coprolalia* ("feces-speech") and typically occurs without warning. As a result of this unpredictability, people who show this behavior often must remain at home and frequently cannot take part in normal social, academic, or work activities. Some researchers (Bruun & Shapiro, 1972) suggest that there is an organic basis for the disorder, whereas others (Morphew & Sim, 1969) claim the problem is functional. In either case, the cause of Gilles de la Tourette's syndrome is unknown. The syndrome is rare, occurring about six times in every 100,000 psychiatric patients (Ascher, 1948). Recently, the use of the tranquilizer haloperidol dramatically reduced the symptoms of Gilles de la Tourette's syndrome in nine out of ten patients to whom it was administered (A. Shapiro, E. Shapiro, & Wayne, 1973).

Ganser's Syndrome

In Ganser's syndrome, the individual is in a "twilight state" that produces the prime characteristic of the syndrome, *passing beside the point.* This phenomenon is manifested in patients' giving wrong answers to most questions. However, the wrong answers aren't usually out of context; they are "near misses." Thus, when asked how many legs a table has, the patient might answer five; when asked his or her age, a 35-year-old may say 38;

when asked the month, he or she may say January rather than December. The distorted thinking in Ganser's syndrome is different from that of the schizophrenic in that the disorganized psychotic's answer is rarely "in the ballpark"; the Ganser patient is usually very close, but wrong.

Ganser's syndrome is believed to be a functional disorder that occupies an intermediate position between neurosis and psychosis and between disease and malingering (Lehmann, 1975b). The psychotic aspect may be seen in the frequent occurrence of auditory and visual hallucinations and disorientation. Such people are often suspected of malingering because they appear to be *consciously* giving incorrect answers. Also, the fact that Ganser's syndrome frequently is seen among incarcerated individuals, such as prisoners, would suggest that "faking" is a possibility. However, since similar Ganser patterns are found among people in different parts of the world, and since most people trying to fake mental disorders would probably exaggerate bizarre thought rather than "just miss" normality, the malingering conceptualization is improbable.

Ganser's syndrome usually lasts less than a month and rarely requires lengthy treatment. Lehmann (1975b) reports that drugs, hospitalization, and electroshock can shorten the duration of the disorder, but such measures hardly seem necessary.

Folie à Deux

The rare disorders discussed so far involve single individuals, but *folie à deux* involves two people. Literally meaning "double insanity," folie à deux is characterized by psychotic symptoms, such as delusions, that are transmitted by some means from one person to another. As a result, both people share the same psychotic beliefs. The contagiousness of the delusion appears to be purely psychological and not biological, and it occurs only under specific circumstances. The two people involved must live in close, intimate circumstances; one of them must be a true psychotic; and the "receiver" must be very dependent upon the delusional "donor."

Folie à deux usually involves paranoid delusions that are easy to believe because the people involved live in a sheltered atmosphere. Without outside reality-testing, the delusions of the psychotic partner can't easily be assessed by the initially nonpsychotic partner. An interview with two women who share a folie à deux follows:

> *Interviewer:* How are you today?
> *Mary:* No good!
> *Jane:* No—no good!
> *I:* Why?
> *M:* You saw the newspaper—you saw what the president said about us.

231

CHAPTER 9:
PARANOID
CONDITIONS AND THE
RARE PSYCHOLOGICAL
DISTURBANCES

J: Yes—you saw what he said.

I: What?

M: Don't make believe you don't know—he said that we would have to pay more taxes—you know what that means!

J: Yes, it means that Mary and I will have to move to a different ward. It means we will have to have operations.

M: Yes, and we don't want to have operations. The president can't make us have operations.

J: No—he can't. Will you help us?

I: How?

M: Call the president. Call the newspaper!

J: Call Dr. ——. He'll know what to do.

M: Yes, call him. He'll know!

In this example, you can see that the two women share their misinterpretation of the newspaper headline and have similar goals and ideas.

Shared psychoses needn't be limited to two people. There are cases on record (Waltzer, 1963) of *folie à douze,* a shared psychotic delusion among 12 people in the same family!

Although classed among the rare disorders, folie à deux occurs more frequently than the other patterns described in this section. Once identified by society, both people are usually removed from their isolation and hospitalized. In the hospital, treatment typically involves the passive partner's being separated from the psychotic partner. The passive partner usually returns to a normal, intact state within a few weeks or months simply by being in contact with a reality-based environment. The psychotic partner must be treated more intensively. After treatment, if the passive partner is reunited with the still-disturbed psychotic partner, the shared delusion may be reestablished rapidly.

Autoscopic Experiences

Autoscopic experiences are characterized by hallucinations in which a part of the individual's own body is projected outside himself and is being looked at as if it were in a mirror. The person's mirror-image may move about in a reflection of the person's own movements and generally is vague and transparent. Autoscopic experiences in themselves aren't conclusive evidence of psychosis, but they may be seen as symptoms in specific forms of severe disturbances, such as schizophrenia.

Lukianowicz (1958) suggests that autoscopic experience may be similar to the fantasy of infantile imaginary companions, in which a playmate is conjured up to satisfy some psychological need. No specific treatment is usually necessary, because autoscopic perceptions are usually fleeting and rarely return.

Capgras' Syndrome

Capgras' syndrome involves a delusional belief that important people in one's life are impostors. The victims of Capgras' syndrome may come to their erroneous conclusions by seeing insignificant characteristics in the faces or manner of friends as evidence that different people are now disguised as these friends. The misperceptions needn't be limited to people; Klempel (1973), for example, reports that dogs and other animals can be perceived as doubles and that people can view their own handwriting as a forgery.

Explanations of Capgras' syndrome seem as infrequent as the disorder itself. However, Arieti and Meth (1959) have proposed an interesting psychodynamic conceptualization. These theorists believe that psychotic people wish to reject important others in their lives but fear losing them. By making these others impostors, they can reject the doubles without having to admit to the rejection of the real people. These theorists reason that, in this way, the people need never face the guilt they would have felt had they turned against or become suspicious of their spouses, parents, or best friends.

Atypical Cycloid Psychoses

The last of the rare disorders we have chosen to discuss, *atypical cycloid psychoses*, are marked by alternating episodes of bipolar symptom patterns. Bipolar patterns are characterized by alternations in opposite kinds of behavior, such as mania and depression.

The first type of cycloid psychosis, *motility psychosis*, is marked by alternating *hyperkinetic* (much movement) and *akinetic* (no movement) phases. In hyperkinetic psychosis, uncontrolled, abrupt autonomous gestures may be observed. However, these gestures usually aren't stereotyped or repetitive but appear as random movements. Opposed to this excess movement, akinetic motility psychosis involves behavior similar to that of stuporous catatonia (described in Chapter 7). The main difference is that akinetic motility psychosis rarely accompanies severe mental deterioration and typically remits soon after onset.

The *confusional states*, a second type of atypical cycloid psychosis, are also bipolar. One extreme, *excited confusional psychosis*, is marked by anxiety and agitation combined with incoherent speech and frequent misidentification of important others. The other extreme, *inhibited confusional psychosis*, is characterized by mutism and greatly reduced motor behavior, as well as confused thoughts and perceptions.

A third atypical pattern is *anxiety-blissfulness psychosis*. On the anxiety pole, the degree of fear may be so strong as to render the person incapable of even moving; paranoid ideas and hallucinations may accompany the overwhelming anxiety. In the blissfulness phase, ebullient, expansive behavior is frequently combined with a belief that the individual is on a

233

CHAPTER 9:
PARANOID
CONDITIONS AND THE
RARE PSYCHOLOGICAL
DISTURBANCES

divine world-saving mission. The blissfulness typically derives from a sense of being so good to all of mankind.

All the varieties of the atypical cycloid psychoses are rare, but the motility psychosis is the most common of them. Needless to say, the diagnostician may find it hard to see the difference between catatonic schizophrenia and an inhibited confusional psychosis or akinetic motility psychosis. For most practicing professionals, the difference is frequently moot, and the atypical cycloid psychotic person is usually treated in much the same way as other severely disturbed individuals. However, there is one big difference: people with atypical cycloid disorders typically recover quickly and completely, whereas those suffering from other forms of psychosis may remain hospitalized for years after the onset of the disorder.

CONCLUDING COMMENTS

Although it is most often cast as a "disturbance" worthy of treatment, paranoia isn't always a bad thing. For one thing, some delusions can make people and their families happy rather than miserable. For example, the belief that one is destined to greatness and is guided by some beneficent force can spur an individual on to significant achievements. Because her son was "born in a cowl" — signifying to some a life of greatness — Sigmund Freud's mother treated him specially. His many brothers and sisters had to sacrifice so that Sigmund could go to school and "reach his destiny." It may very well be that his mother's delusion contributed significantly to Freud's eventual stature.

Paranoia may also be seen as an adaptive pattern of behavior. For example, Hertzberg and McClelland (1974) have noted that paranoid beliefs may result from the complexity of modern culture in that such beliefs allow one to "substitute a rigorous (though false) order, for chaos" (p. 60). Further, delusions of self-reference and the like may help people to dispel a sense of individual insignificance. Thus, to Hertzberg and McClelland, paranoia is a "natural response to the confusions of modern life" (p. 60).

CHAPTER SUMMARY CHART

In this chapter, we discussed the paranoid conditions:

Description	Explanations	Treatment
Paranoia Paranoid state	Psychoanalytic theory: repressed homosexuality	Hospitalization Drug therapy

Description (continued)	*Explanations* (continued)	*Treatment* (continued)

Minor patterns
  litigious state
  eroticism
  involutional
    paraphrenia
	Psychosocial theory:
	  developmental
	  factors; paranoid
	  pseudocommunity
		Psychotherapy
		  Sullivan
		  Cameron

We then discussed the rare psychoses:

Gilles de la Tourette's Syndrome	*Ganser's Syndrome*	*Folie à Deux*

Uncontrollable tics
Verbal abusiveness
Coprolalia
	Twilight state
	Passing beside the
	  point
	Possible malingering
		Insanity for two (or
		  more)
		Shared delusions

Autoscopic Phenomena	*Capgras' Syndrome*	*Atypical cycloid psychoses*

Projection of body parts
  outside body
	Friends and relatives
	  are impostors
		Motility psychosis
		Confusional states
		Anxiety-blissfulness
		  psychosis

SECTION IV
DISORDERS RELATED TO ANXIETY AND STRESS

Chapter 10
Psychoneuroses

Chapter 11
Psychophysiological Disorders

Unlike psychotic behavior, which many lay people see as unintelligible and strange, the symptoms of disorders associated with anxiety and stress are familiar to most people. Probably each of us, at times, has experienced some degree of the kind of feelings that plague those suffering from such disorders. Although we're not saying that to experience such feelings is to have a diagnosable disorder, we do suggest that when such worries, fears, and pressures become pervasive and inappropriate much of the time, we are probably dealing with an abnormal state of affairs.

Anxiety, the experience of a sense of impending harm or doom, is important to the understanding of much of abnormal behavior. Anxiety is one of the most common symptoms reported by people who are different. The majority of the disorders we will describe in this section may be seen as partially the result of attempts to deal with the discomfort and stress of anxiety.

Psychoneurotic people (Chapter 10) share a common pattern of developing maladjustive means of dealing with anxiety. These maladjustive means may solidify into a neurotic disorder characterized by "self-defeating" patterns of behavior.

Most theorists would probably agree that anxiety is involved significantly in the psychoneuroses, but in the etiology of psychophysiological disorders (Chapter 11) more emphasis is placed on stress than on anxiety. However, we believe that anxiety also can be involved to some degree with the wide range of psychophysiological disorders. In psychoneuroses, anxiety is usually diffuse in its physiological effects; in psychophysiological disorders, the effects of anxiety seem more specific.

CHAPTER 10
PSYCHONEUROSES

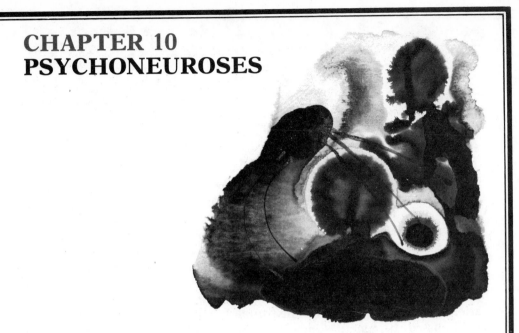

Being blessed or cursed, as the case may be, with the ability to remember and anticipate physical or emotional dangers, human beings can experience *anxiety,* a form of fear based not upon the present alone but on actual or fantasied experiences in the past and future. To the observer, a person experiencing anxiety appears to be fidgety, pale, irritable, sweating, having difficulty breathing, frequently needing to urinate, and the like. The anxious person seems to be in physical pain, but few physical pains could be worse than the emotional pain of anxiety as described in the following personal experience.

PERSONAL EXPERIENCE: *Anxiety*

At times I felt that it would never stop. It hurt, like a burning in my guts . . . like a knife ripping away at my flesh . . . like a scream inside me that couldn't get out. I couldn't sit still, I walked around the house, looked at the walls, tore up magazines. I would start to cry, then choke back the tears 'cause they frightened me more. I thought that I was falling apart. I can remember hearing Mary [his wife] say something to me. I yelled at her to go away. God . . . I can't even talk about it without feeling scared. It's like being afraid of something so terrible that no power in the world can help you. It's like being sure that you are going to die a horrible death and knowing that it is going to happen today. It's worse than dying, I'm sure. I wanted to die to make it stop. The medicine helped a little, but just remembering . . .

To avoid such feelings, a person may be motivated to develop a variety of behaviors calculated to solve the problems creating the anxiety. Many of these behaviors are adaptive and help the person to halt the difficulties he or she faces. However, other behaviors may be self-defeating; that is, the price of reducing the immediate level of anxiety may be paid in the future by the acquisition of patterns of living that themselves produce other psychological problems or physical dysfunctions. As self-defeating behaviors, the *psychoneuroses* may be viewed, in part, as the result of a variety of strategies (defenses) instituted to handle overwhelming anxiety. We discussed the general kinds of defenses in Chapter 4; their purpose, as you remember, is usually to soften and deflect the negative effects of anxiety. With few exceptions, neurotics seem to have a knack for substituting *self-deceptive defenses* for conscious coping with anxiety. The defenses may help the neurotic to avoid coming to grips with the events or conflicts producing the anxiety, but the cost of such maneuvers, which rarely are completely successful, is high. Most neurotic people show continual or episodic signs of fatigue and tension. Still, the typical neurotic manages to utilize defenses with enough finesse that, in spite of being maladaptive, neurotic patterns become stabilized, self-perpetuating, self-defeating—and very difficult to change.

DESCRIPTIONS

In describing the neuroses, we will attempt to portray the particular experiential misery neurotics feel as they attempt to handle their anxiety. Since most neurotic disorders may be seen as different ways of dealing with anxiety, we have organized our descriptions to reflect those different styles. In the anxiety and phobic neuroses, anxiety is most obvious. In the hysterical neuroses, the anxiety is most often compartmentalized or converted to physical disorders. In obsessive and compulsive neuroses, anxiety is *almost* neutralized by ritualized thinking and behavior. When anxiety is turned inward, it may result in a form of depression, as in depressive neurosis. Finally, we will mention three neurotic disorders—neurasthenia, deper-

Intense anxiety can lead to further problems when an individual can't attend to work or other daily requirements of life. (Photo courtesy of the American Heart Association.)

sonalization, and hypochondriasis—that are seen less frequently in clinical practice than the other patterns we will discuss.

Anxiety Neurosis

The person classified as an *anxiety neurotic* appears to be lacking any effective means of dealing with anxiety (Marks & Lader, 1973). As a result, any one of three forms of anxiety neurosis may appear. The first form, *free-floating anxiety*, is characterized by mild, constant apprehension for which the person typically can find no good reason. More severe anxiety may occur in the form of an *anxiety attack,* or a sudden experience of intense anxiety, usually in some specific circumstance. These attacks are frequently accompanied by difficulty in breathing, chest pains, restlessness, and other signs of extreme fear. A third and most intense form of anxiety disorder is the *panic reaction,* a state marked by such uncontrolled and unbearable anxiety that actual physical pain may be experienced. Some people have attempted suicide to escape the anguished feeling. Estimates suggest that anywhere from 6% to 27% of psychiatric inpatients are diagnosed as anxiety neurotic (Marks & Lader, 1973).

The personal experience of intense anxiety is difficult to communicate through the written word. Some writers have tried to describe the particular dread and terror that comes with experiencing raw anxiety. We want to share with you a most articulate attempt. Though the report is somewhat dated, the experience of anxiety the writer describes is not. He was an English professor whose fear of locomotives set off his anxiety attacks.

PERSONAL EXPERIENCE: *Anxiety Neurosis*

I light a cigar in the doorway . . . just as a train is passing over beyond the meadows . . . my eye sees the horrible phantom in the map once more. I suffer the intensest seizure of terror sensations . . . I say nothing . . . try to "walk it off" . . . within a hundred feet I throw the cigar away, saying it seems to make me feel worse (a truth uttered by the subconsciousness, with different purport from that intended, while the throwing away was an attempt to get rid of the unknown factor of torment). I recover a little. I feel a sinking loneliness, an uneasy, a weird isolation. The locomotive-phase of road-house and cigar of less than an hour before has already lapsed from consciousness. I take off my hat; I mop my head; I fan my face. Sinking . . . isolation . . . diffused premonitions of horror. "Charlie" . . . no answer. I am alone, alone, in the universe. My subconscious knows what the torture is; and makes my voice shriek, as I rush back and forth on the bluffs: "My God, won't that go; my God, won't that train go away!" I smash a wooden box to pieces, board by board, against my knee to occupy myself against panic. I watch the train . . . it seems so slow . . . so slow . . . if it will only get across the flats . . . out of hearing.

The account demonstrates that anxiety neurotics may be particularly miserable people whose experiencing of terror testifies to the failure of their attempts to handle anxiety. Typically, although the origin of the anxiety may be hidden by the defense of repression, the emotional impact of the unfounded fear is not. As a result, the person may experience a number of physiological symptoms; he or she may feel weak, faint, or sweaty, and may sigh, pant, and frequently show coronary symptoms varying from an intense pounding to a skipping of heartbeats. Under the bombardment of these general physiological effects, anxiety neurotics may be frightened and want to run somewhere to hide; but everywhere they go, they take the source of the anxiety right along with them, and their flight is to no avail.

Phobias

Whereas anxiety neurotics may not know the source of their tension, people with phobias attach their fear to something that realistically is minimally harmful. The individual usually recognizes consciously and rationally that the feared object or situation is safe, but if it isn't avoided, intense anxiety occurs nevertheless. This fact is depicted in the next personal experience.

PERSONAL EXPERIENCE: *Fear of Flying*

I don't remember when it started; all I know is that I've never really been calm around airplanes. When I was younger, just the thought of having to take an airplane trip would hurl me into a panic. If I knew that I'd have to fly somewhere, I would be unable to think about anything else until the trip was over. If possible, I avoided flying at all costs. . . . Sometimes this avoidance led me to do some pretty shameful things. Once, when my father had a heart attack, I made up some story to convince my mother that it would be best if I did not fly home to see him. When my grandmother died, I did not attend her funeral to be at my mother's side, because I was afraid to get on a plane.

My fear is a strange one. . . . I am willing to let my wife and children go on airplanes, and I never worry about them, but I believe that if I were to go on a plane it would become "ill-fated Flight 417" or the like. When I have to fly, I sit tightly in my seat, feel tense for every moment (my longest flight was eight hours), and constantly need to urinate from nervousness. I wish I could overcome this. It makes me feel so miserable and ashamed.

A major difference between anxiety neurotics and neurotic phobic people is that phobic people have a definite, identifiable source for their fear; the fear is not free-floating as it usually is in anxiety neurosis, but rather is attached to something.

The terror experienced by neurotic phobics when coming in contact with the object of their fear is often very similar to that described in the following personal experience.

PERSONAL EXPERIENCE: *Fear of Moths*

Terror is the only thing that comes close to how I feel when I think of moths. Their willowy, see-through wings always seem filthy. I remember being stuck in a car with a huge moth and my date, not knowing how terrified I was of moths, thought I was kidding when I told him I was afraid. It was terrible! I can feel it right now . . . the . . . feeling trapped and the moth with its ugly body flitting around so quickly, I couldn't anticipate where it would go next. Finally that creature hit me in the arm and I screamed—it felt dirty and sleazy and then it hit me in the face and I began to scream uncontrollably. I had the terrible feeling it was going to fly into my mouth while I was screaming, but I couldn't stop. By this time, my date believed my terror and stopped the car. I jumped out and ran screaming down the street. Finally I stopped by a tree, sat down and began to cry. It took me 15 minutes to calm down and to feel foolish.

Although nondisabling phobias are common in the general population, affecting about 77 out of every 1000 people, disabling phobias are relatively rare, affecting only 2 out of every 1000 people (Agras, Sylvester, & Oliveau, 1969). According to outpatient-clinic data, phobias make up only about 5% of neurotic patients seen, and there are slightly more male than female phobic people. Phobias usually become incapacitating only when the feared object or event is constantly present in the environment or interferes with the performance of valued tasks. Having a phobia of snakes, as a number of us do, isn't incapacitating unless one's job or leisure activities involve potential contact with snakes. A fear of closed places (claustrophobia) may be disabling to a coal miner or an elevator operator, but probably not to a person living on a farm. Although the number of possible phobias is infinite, among those most frequently encountered in practice are fears of streets, open places, crowded enclosed places, and flying.

Phobias may be of two types: *neurotic phobias* and *traumatic phobias*. Neurotic phobias are characterized by a strong tendency for the fear to generalize to similar objects and events. For example, over time, a fear of cocker spaniels may become a fear of all dogs, then of all four-legged animals, then of places where animals live (such as kennels), and so on. The tendency of neurotic phobias to generalize stands in contrast to traumatic phobias, which usually can be traced to a single traumatic event and in which the fear often remains fairly well encapsulated. For example, fear of a particular amusement-park ride may remain limited to that ride and not generalize to others.

The naming of phobias is based upon Greek and Latin derivatives. The object of the phobia forms the first part of the term; the suffix *phobia* forms the second. Thus, *agoraphobia* represents fear of going out in open places alone; *hematophobia*, fear of spilled or drawn blood; *ailurophobia*, fear of cats; and *triskaidecaphobia*, fear of the number 13. The possibilities are endless, but some representative phobias are listed in Table 10-1.

Hysterical Neurosis

As opposed to anxiety neurosis and phobias, where anxiety usually is easily observed, in hysterical neurosis, attempts to reduce anxiety may involve compartmentalizing the fear or converting it into a physical symptom. As you've read in Chapter 3, the history of hysteria is closely related to the history of the psychogenic approach to disordered behavior. Hippocrates and the ancient Greeks viewed hysteria as an important disorder occurring only in women. The source of the hysterical disorder then was thought to be the uterus (in Greek, *hyster*) as it wandered through the

Table 10-1. *Some representative phobias*

Name	Object(s) Feared
Acrophobia	high places
Agoraphobia	open places
Ailurophobia	cats
Algophobia	pain
Anthropophobia	men
Aquaphobia	water
Astraphobia	storms, thunder, and lightning
Claustrophobia	closed places
Cynophobia	dogs
Hematophobia	blood
Monophobia	being alone
Mysophobia	contamination
Nyctophobia	darkness
Ocholophobia	crowds
Pathophobia	disease
Pyrophobia	fire
Syphilophobia	syphilis
Thanatophobia	death
Xenophobia	strangers
Zoophobia	animals or a single animal

woman's body in search of a child. Freud's insightful investigation of hysterical disorders made for clearer conceptions of this form of being different by showing, for example, that it occurred in males as well as females.

The basic hysterical personality, according to McCall (1963), includes a "child-like immaturity, self-centeredness, poor insight, a notably weak psychic integration and an extraordinarily high degree of suggestibility" (p. 2). There are two general types of hysterical neuroses: *dissociation* and *conversion*. McCall points out one important difference between the two: dissociatives have a propensity to become overtly anxious under stress, a tendency usually not shown by those with conversion hysteria.

Dissociative Type. Hysterical dissociation disorders are characterized by a blocking off from awareness of significant portions of one's present experience. This blocking-off process, or *compartmentalization*, is similar to the defense of denial, in that it excludes from awareness specific activities. A person functioning under the influence of an isolated portion of awareness is said to be in a state of dissociation. Within the general type of hysteria known as dissociation, there are three subtypes: *amnesia and fugue states*, *somnambulism*, and *multiple personality*.

Amnesia, or total loss of memory, is the most common of the dissociative reactions. Janet (1925) pointed out the different types of amnesia, ranging from *localized amnesia*, in which the person suddenly becomes aware of having lost memory for a period of time, to the more rarely seen *systematized amnesia*, in which the person forgets only selected events. An interesting amnesiac phenomenon is called *continuous amnesia*, in which the person forgets each successive behavioral event as it occurs. Continuous amnesia is portrayed in this classic comedy routine:

> *Patient:* I have this terrible problem. I can't seem to remember important things that happen to me.
> *Doctor:* How long have you had this problem?
> *Patient:* What problem?

Janet reported a patient with continuous amnesia who attempted to read a novel, but ended up reading only the first page over and over again. After an entire day's reading, the patient couldn't remember even the name of the book.

Fugue states are related to amnesia and occur when people under psychological stress lose their sense of identity and literally leave the situation. In some cases, the person may reappear thousands of miles from home with a new name and a new life. Some of these individuals come to the attention of the police when they become disorganized in the face of new stress and, under questioning, can't trace their lives past a certain point. Rarely do people in a true fugue state question the fact that they can't remember their past. They may be the "amnesia victim" you have read about in the paper or have seen characterized in detective stories, soap operas, and melodramas. Individuals who develop a fugue reaction usually have histories of being dependent, anxious, and inadequate. They seem to have difficulty keeping themselves together under the normal stresses of everyday living. When additional stress is introduced, they seem to fragment into the resulting flight from the scene.

Somnambulism refers to a state similar to sleep during which the individual may experience or reexperience a traumatic event. Somnambulistic people may or may not have conscious awareness of the event in their waking state. Behaviorally, somnambulists may appear to others to be out of contact with reality and preoccupied with their own private thinking. Once people "snap out" of the somnambulistic state, they usually have no memory of its occurrence.

Many people erroneously believe that sleepwalking and somnambulism are the same. Several differences may be specified, however. First, somnambulistic episodes can occur while the person is either asleep or awake. Further, sleepwalking is fairly common, occurring in about 1 out of every 20 people. While it is safe to say that sleepwalking may occur in hysterical people, certainly only a few sleepwalkers should be classified as hysterical. Sleepwalking may be a natural phenomenon of the young and occurs frequently in children through college-age young people. Sleepwalking also differs from somnambulism in that somnambulism is usually associated with dreams and is believed to be purposive, whereas sleepwalking is typically more random and directionless.

A folklore of which many of you probably are aware has grown up around the sleepwalker. The folklore suggests that one should never awaken sleepwalkers or that if one leaves sleepwalkers alone, they won't hurt themselves. Neither of these folk beliefs is well supported by the facts. Probably the best course of action to take with sleepwalkers is to awaken them gently and make sure they get safely back to bed.

Unlike amnesia, fugue, and somnambulistic states, which affect a part of a person's thinking, multiple personality affects the person's entire self. Multiple personality may be what the public thinks of when schizophrenia is mentioned, but this is incorrect. Multiple personality is a neurotic disorder in which an individual alternates between two or more personalities. "Dr. Jekyll and Mr. Hyde" is a literary example of multiple personality. As you may remember, Dr. Jekyll's personality splits into "good" and "evil" parts with the aid of a chemical potion. However, real-life cases of multiple personality don't always show a split into good and evil parts, and these individuals don't need a chemical to achieve their personality transformations. Generally, in multiple personality the new *secondary personalities* that develop are less conservative, inhibited, and morally constrictive than the original *primary personality*. The change from one personality to another can be abrupt and dramatic. Although each of the multiple personalities typically has its own set of memories and behavior patterns, usually the secondary personality is aware of the primary

248

SECTION IV:
DISORDERS
RELATED TO
ANXIETY AND
STRESS

personality but not vice versa. The primary personality generally has amnesia for the time that the other personalities are in control.

One of the earliest reported cases of multiple personality (Prince, 1906) is that of a Miss Beauchamp. Her therapist described her personality makeup in the following manner:

> Each varies in these respects from the other two, and from the original Miss Beauchamp. Two of these personalities have no knowledge of each other or of the third, excepting such information as may be obtained by inference or second hand, so that in the memory of each of these two there are blanks which correspond to the times when the others are in the flesh. All of a sudden one or the other wakes up to find herself, she knows not where, and ignorant of what she has said or done a moment before. Only one of the three has knowledge of the lives of the others. . . . The personalities come and go in kaleidoscopic succession, many changes often being made in the course of twenty-four hours [p. 2].

Two of the most famous recent cases of multiple personality also involve women, "Eve" and "Sybil." Both cases have been popularized in book and movie form (Schreiber, 1973; Sizemore, 1977). Both women developed a number of personalities. The origin of these personalities has been the subject of some debate, with certain investigators believing that some of the personalities of Eve and Sybil were *iatrogenically* formed; that is, the personalities may have been produced by the patient in an unconscious attempt to please the psychiatrist. However, the completeness and vividness of the personality changes in multiple personality are difficult to dismiss as mere attempts to please a therapist. In addition, therapists dealing with those showing multiple personality have provided evidence that the secondary personalities had been developing long before therapy began (Thigpen & Cleckley, 1954).

On the question of who develops multiple personality, one early writer (F. Alexander, 1930) went so far as to say that the potential for developing multiple personalities was in all of us. Although there are now numerous theories of the etiology of this disorder, none is compelling, and there is no agreed-upon treatment process.

Conversion Type. Conversion reactions, the second major type of hysterical disorder, differ in a number of ways from the dissociative neuroses. The most salient difference is that, in conversion hysteria, a physical incapacity appears without an appropriate physical basis. This psychological copy of physical disease often is symbolically related to the individual's psychological conflicts. It is as though the conversion hysteric were able to *convert* the anxiety and psychological conflict into physical disability or disease. This conversion works so well that the conversion hysteric may lack much of the overt tension observed in dissociative hysterics. The

All about Eve

The headline in the newspaper read "Identity Revealed: 3 Faces of Eve," reintroducing us to "Eve" in 1977. For nearly 20 years after the release of the motion picture about a woman with three distinct personalities and the difficulties she faced as a result of her personality transformations, "Eve" lived in obscurity. But in 1977, "Eve" published a personal account of her experiences (Sizemore, 1977). We now know that "Eve" is Mrs. Chris Sizemore, a housewife from Fairfax, Virginia, with a son (who, by the way, didn't know of his mother's affliction until he was 13) and daughter (who has a daughter of her own).

Mrs. Sizemore revealed that, in fact, she had 21 different complete personalities. Oddly enough, the personalities appeared in sets of three. The three personalities would resolve eventually into a primary personality, and then a different set of three personalities would begin to form. The personalities varied in character from quiet and rather

"Eve" (Chris Sizemore) revealed that she had worked through considerably more than the original "three faces" in her book I'm Eve. *(Photo by Jim Lingstrum.)*

mousy to wild, life-of-the-party types. Mrs. Sizemore has once again resolved into a stable primary personality that has been present for some time.

Mrs. Sizemore's first experience with multiple personality occurred when she was only 2 years old. During her teenage years, the disorder wasn't identified, and Mrs. Sizemore was considered a chronic liar and a bit "weird" by her peers. As she says, "I would be in school as one personality for a lecture or class discussion . . . and then when I came back the next day for a test I was a different personality. That personality hadn't been to the lecture and didn't have any idea what the answers were to the test" (Shields, 1977, p. 7).

Needless to say, the personality transformations led to many embarrassing moments, and she couldn't complete high school with her peers. The inability to transfer memory of experiences from one personality to another made life very difficult for her. For example, what she learned in one personality, such as sewing, often wouldn't transfer to another personality.

Mrs. Sizemore's personality transformations would be named according to the primary trait of the behavior shown. For example, there was the "spoon lady," who collected all sorts of spoons; the "blue lady," who liked everything to be blue; and the "phonograph lady," who loved records. Several of the personalities even made out wills; one can hardly imagine the legal complexities these wills could cause!

Mrs. Sizemore believed that her disorder sprang from her emotional inability to handle death. She always remembered being forced to kiss her dead grandmother and believed that the separate personalities were safety valves developed to handle her fears.

Mrs. Sizemore's chief therapist first met her when she came in for marriage counseling. However, he soon realized that Mrs. Sizemore presented some extraordinary problems. As a result, he instituted a process of intensive treatment that included hypnosis, drugs, and a variety of verbal psychotherapies. She related her fear of personality transformations. "I would get up when I felt a personality change starting and just run, run wildly anywhere. I ended up running into a tree and cutting myself pretty badly" (Shields, 1977, p. 22).

One wonders whether the saga of "Eve" is over. Will she develop more personalities? How will the publicity she is going to receive affect her life? All these and many more questions await the test of time.

relative lack of tension or anxiety in the face of an apparently debilitating physical ailment gives the disorder the characteristic of *"la belle indifference"* (noble lack of concern). To meet an individual whose arm is hanging useless and witness "la belle indifference" may lead one incorrectly to suspect the person of *malingering* or consciously faking disease. However, the fact is that, although conversion hysterics may receive a great deal of *secondary gain* from others for their apparent illness (such as attention, sympathy, or being excused from work or the military), they don't seem to be consciously aware of the connections among their physical disorder, the psychological conflict, and the attention received.

Over the past 75 years there seems to have been a steady decline in the frequency of conversion hysteria, probably related to the rise in the level of education of the general population. Only in areas where these educational gains have not yet been achieved can one still find conversion hysterias in any great numbers. It seems the brighter and more educated a person is, the less likely he or she is to develop this type of neurosis.

Having presented general information about conversion hysteria, we now turn to the specific kinds of conversions—sensory, motor, and autonomic—which differ primarily in the body systems involved.

Sensory conversion involves the loss or distortion of the ability to receive sensory stimuli. The sensory conversions have a place in history and were well described during the time of the *Malleus Maleficarum* (Chapter 3). For example, the "devil's claw," a patch of skin insensitive to touch, often was used as damning evidence that an individual was a witch. Many a poor conversion hysteric probably met grisly tortures and death for nothing more than showing this particular sensory conversion.

The presence of a *tactual anesthesia* (inability to sense touch) has long been among the primary diagnostic signs of hysterical reactions, and in World War II, tactual anesthesias were found in many of those soldiers diagnosed as hysteric. In one tactual disturbance, glove anesthesia, people lose feeling in their hands up to the wrist—a physically impossible occurrence. Confronting conversion hysterics with the physical improbability of their symptoms often does little to dissuade them from their particular way of dealing with psychological problems.

Besides the anesthesias, where there is a *loss* of sensitivity, there are also the hyperesthesias, in which the person is *oversensitive.* Like the princess in the nursery story of the "Princess and the Pea," the hyperesthesic person may be supersensitive to touch. A man seen by one of the authors could wear only light cotton clothing because of the discomfort any other clothing would cause. Although no physiological basis could be found for this disorder, the subjective experience of pain was no less real, as the following personal experience reveals.

PERSONAL EXPERIENCE: *Hyperesthesia*

Patient: You know you asked me how it feels when I put on heavy clothes. Well, it's sorta like once when I was a kid and we all went to a lake for a picnic. I got out in the sun and really got sunburned and I couldn't sleep all that night. Everybody was up with me and all I could wear was a T shirt and shorts. The pain was really hard to take but I didn't cry. And that's how I feel now when I put on anything but these real light clothes. I must really be a sight walking around on these cold days like this.

Therapist: But aren't you cold?

P: Sure, but I can take it.

T: Didn't this difficulty begin about the same time you were divorcing your wife?

P: Sure did.

T: Do you see any connection?

P: What connection?

In this brief dialogue we can see some of the chief characteristics of the conversion hysteric: the *secondary gain* (attention), *"la belle indifference"* ("I can take it"), and the inability to connect consciously the physical symptom to the psychological conflict.

Motor conversions involve disabilities of the musculature of the body, including "fits" and muscular contractions or tremors occurring without physical basis.

The person manifesting motor conversions may mimic several of the common epileptic or other convulsive seizures. However, the hysterical "fit" can be differentiated from a real seizure in a number of ways. First, the hysterical "convulsion" is not characterized by rhythmic movements, as are physically based seizures, but rather by chaotic thrashing about. Moreover, hysterical patients will rarely be incontinent of urine or feces and won't bite their tongues, as true seizure victims often will. Last, when conversion hysterics fall to the ground, they usually fall in a safe, comfortable place.

Besides hysterical fits, the motor conversions include *astasia-abasia*, in which the individual may be bedridden because of difficulties in walking. The gait of such a person is characterized by wild thrashing of the arms and staggering steps as the person searches for support from furniture, walls, or other people. However, physical examination reveals that the person has control of those muscle groups needed for standing and walking. In astasia-abasia there is usually an absence of the muscle atrophy or impairment of blood flow found in true neurological disorders marked by loss of muscle use.

Other motor conversions can mimic a number of different paralyses. For example, in *writer's cramp*, muscle pain occurs in the hands of individuals who need to write to make a living or pass in school. Typically, these "paralyzed hand muscles" operate quite well when they aren't involved in a stressful task. Writer's cramp may be one effective way to escape the anxiety generated by the possibility of failing a course or losing a job. A primary diagnostic sign that the writer's cramp is a motor conversion is the relative unconcern of these affected individuals as they inform you, for example, that they may lose their jobs or their place in medical school.

The last motor conversion we will describe is *hysterical aphonia*, in which an individual can't speak above a whisper. Like many conversion hysterics, the person manifesting hysterical aphonia often can be tricked into behaving normally, as shown in the following incident:

> A forty-five-year-old married woman felt badly treated and neglected by her husband. This had been particularly aggravated following the departure of their two grown children from the home. After one in a series of angry scenes with her husband, she suddenly developed aphonia. Following examination, the physician spoke to another person present. In a whispered tone, but loud enough to insure the patient's overhearing, he said, "That old gal is an awful fake. There is nothing wrong with her. Of course she could talk if she really wanted to."
>
> The angry response of the patient was an indignant vocal denial. This proved the doctor "right," and announced her cure [Laughlin, 1956, p. 263].

Besides sensory and motor conversions, there are conversions that involve the autonomic nervous system (see Chapter 6), which controls the digestive, eliminative, respiratory, and circulatory systems. *Autonomic conversions* may affect any one or a combination of these systems. Although the conversion hysteric may mimic a variety of respiratory and visceral disorders, among the most complex jobs of duplication is the autonomic conversion *pseudocyesis*, or phantom pregnancy. In pseudocyesis, women not only may cease menses but also may suffer "morning sickness" and manifest enlarged breasts and abdomen. There are cases where physicians have been temporarily fooled because of the nearly perfect physical similarity to an actual pregnancy. It is as though the woman desires a child so much that she, in essence, "becomes pregnant"—fooling herself as well as others. It would be interesting to listen in on a conversation between a patient and her doctor during her 11th month of pregnancy, but we will have to settle for the following personal experience, which took place six months into a "phantom pregnancy." It is a conversation between an interviewer and a woman who had just been told she wasn't really pregnant.

PERSONAL EXPERIENCE: *Pseudocyesis*

Interviewer: How do you explain the fact that you had all the signs of pregnancy and now find that you're not?

254

SECTION IV:
DISORDERS
RELATED TO
ANXIETY AND
STRESS

Woman: (calmly): I guess God willed it to be so. Probably there was something wrong with the baby.

I: Then you still believe you were pregnant?

W: Sure . . . didn't you see my belly . . . I had a baby.

I: But the doctors said they could find no proof of a baby.

W: Well, they're wrong. Don't worry, I'll get pregnant again.

In *anorexia nervosa,* another autonomic conversion, the primary dysfunction is of eating behavior. Typically, patients eat less and less until, in one out of ten cases, they die of complications brought about by malnutrition. Based on a survey of the reported cases of anorexia nervosa, Bliss and Branch (1960) describe the average victim as a woman between the ages of 18 and 25 weighing 122 pounds before her illness and 78 pounds at the height of the disorder. However, this description of the average case of anorexia nervosa doesn't communicate the fact that nearly 20% weigh between 60 and 70 pounds, or that 10% weigh *less than 60 pounds.* Women have been reported to weigh as little as 37¾ pounds (Seidensticker & Tzagournis, 1968). We can be thankful that anorexia nervosa is uncommon, occurring in only 1 of every 100,000 people. The following case history may be considered typical.

The case involved a 22-year-old, very beautiful woman. She was tall and dark, with good features, and presented a picture of sophistication, sexuality, and grace. Her appetitive difficulties began when she met her husband in Hawaii on his Rest-and-Relaxation leave from Vietnam. She engaged in oral sex with her husband for the first time during her stay. When she returned home, she began to show signs of lack of appetite. By the time the author met her, her weight had dropped from 136 to 98 pounds over a four-month period. She was still stunning, and it was not hard to imagine how attractive she must have looked at her normal weight. True to the code of the conversion hysteric, she showed no signs of anxiety about her weight loss or her apparent lack of appetite. She had come to the hospital because of her mother's concern and not her own. Psychological testing indicated that she had some real problems with sex and that the act of oral sex had become symbolically entangled with her eating behavior.

The last time one of the authors saw this woman she had continued to lose weight and was down to 76 pounds. Traces of her beauty were still left. Even with this continued weight loss, the hospital staff was optimistic about her future because of her age, intelligence, and the fact that she was showing signs of anxiety about her condition.

Obsessive Reactions

In contrast to the hysteric person, who either compartmentalizes or converts anxiety in attempts to control it, the obsessive person intellectualizes in what may be seen as an attempt to think the anxiety away. Obsessive neurosis is the diagnosis in about 5% of all psychoneurotic patients. There seems to be no significant difference in incidence with regard to sex, but a large proportion of obsessive people are unmarried and come from the middle and upper classes (Nemiah, 1975a).

The obsessive neurosis often begins in adolescence or early adulthood; its central characteristics are usually persistent and unshakable thoughts and sexual or hostile impulses of an unpleasant and unwanted nature. Although the feelings or impulses are rarely, if ever, acted upon, the subject often lives with the constant fear that the dreaded impulses may break through. This fear is shown in the following personal experience.

PERSONAL EXPERIENCE: *Obsessive Neurosis*

I can tell you how it is when I'm being obsessive. It is a tiring experience. I've always been an organizer . . . so that from the time I get up in the morning until I go to sleep at night I'm thinking about what's going to happen. I worry, but I can take it and it's not too bad . . . but it's when those terrible thoughts come into my head that I become afraid. The thoughts are all different, and they're sickening and terrible. Like when I was outside with my child, I thought of what would happen if my metal rake slipped and flew over and hit my child in the head. I don't know why I would think of this. It made me feel like a crazy person, and then I'm worried sick the rest of the day that I'm going to think that thought again. Here's another example of what I mean. While eating dinner the thought suddenly came to me . . . how would it look if I drove my fork through the eye of my husband . . . I mean my husband's eye. I can see the fork puncture the eye and the liquid squirts out . . . and then I break out in a cold sweat and have to leave the table. Why in God's name would I think such things? I love my child and my husband. I'm a kind person . . . I go to church. . . . It makes me feel crazy and different. Even telling you makes me feel weird about myself.

Compulsive Reactions

A *compulsion* may be viewed as a felt need to carry out certain admittedly senseless sequences of actions or to think certain peculiar and "magical" thoughts, as a way to reduce anxiety. Compulsions can take many forms, perhaps the most famous of which is the hand-washing com-

256

SECTION IV:
DISORDERS
RELATED TO
ANXIETY AND
STRESS

pulsion of Lady Macbeth. A number of compulsions are related in some way to guilt about sex, as is shown in the following personal experience of an adolescent girl responding to the beginning of menses.

PERSONAL EXPERIENCE: *A Compulsive Reaction*

I remember how embarrassed I was when I found that my panties were soiled. I was at school. My mother really never prepared me for this happening and I get mad at her even now. Anyway . . . ever since then I've had to go through the same washing order or I get so uptight that I cry. Although it means I have to get up two hours earlier than I used to, I get up so that I can have enough time to complete the washing. I start with my toes, washing each individually, and then I have to go over every inch of my body twice. For every major part of me I have to use a new washcloth. It takes from 10 to 12 washcloths to complete the washing. The morning washing only makes me feel OK until the afternoon. I couldn't wait until I could get home and wash. It got so bad that I used to carry washcloths and soap to school so that I could slip into the lavatory and wash. I lived in fear that one of my friends would see me, but I just had to do it. My parents don't understand . . . and I guess I don't either . . . but I have to wash . . . I just have to or I feel so dirty and slimy and junky. I hate that feeling.

In addition to repeated single behaviors such as washing, there are also *serial compulsions* in which anxiety is handled by specific ordering procedures. To the person doing the ordering, one activity must be followed by a designated other; typically, the more anxiety, the more widespread, pervasive, and complex the ordering procedure. Ordering rituals can take the form of magical arranging, in which clothes, for example, must be put in a certain place, in a certain way. One of the authors had a friend in college who nearly flunked out of school because of what approximates an arranging compulsion. After supper, he would return to his room and spend time readying himself to study. By the time he had showered, organized his books (always in the same order), sharpened his numerous pencils, arranged his papers, and attended to other tasks, two hours were used up, and he would often fall asleep at his desk. Perhaps you have acquaintances who behave in a similar fashion. It is characteristic of most compulsive neuroses that they take up more and more of a person's time, behavior, and energy. The authors have encountered people whose compulsions require up to 16 hours a day. The following case-history excerpt reveals some of the frustration of a person being forced to do things that she believes to be senseless and even stupid:

A young unmarried woman developed an irresistible need to think of a different person with each separate act she performed in a given series, until she finally reached a point at which gainful employment and marriage were both out of her reach. This magical practice began originally as a technique of distraction from sex preoccupations, which had induced severe anxiety reactions in the patient as she walked each morning to work. She established a rule that each step on or off the curb at a corner must be accompanied by the thought of some adult she knew, the adult must be a different one for each step on or off the curb, and she must have one clearly ready in her imagining ahead of time. If she thought of the same person twice on the same street something terrible might happen. The provisions of her ritual made a frequent change of street convenient and this obliged her to start to work earlier and to shun company, both because talking interfered with preparation for the curb crises, and because her changes of course were hard to justify to someone else.

Because her anxiety over possible lapses continued, the patient's magical practice spread to other situations. As she put on or took off each article of clothing she had to think of a different person, and the same rule eventually applied to eating, to washing and drying dishes, dusting and tidying the house, inserting typewriter paper and carbons at work, opening and sealing envelopes or filing letters. She had to give up her job, finally, when the ritual crept into her typing in spite of everything she did to prevent it. She could not help daydreaming as she typed and sooner or later forbidden thoughts would start up her protective device. This first cut her speed down and later destroyed her accuracy also. Of her complicated ritual, she said, "For a long time I couldn't break it, and now it just seems easier to go on" [Cameron, 1947, p. 296].

Compulsive magical behavior may be related in some ways to superstition. There is more than a little similarity between the behavior of the compulsive neurotic arranging his clothes in a certain fashion and the basketball player who has to wear the same "lucky" socks (unwashed) for every game. The authors have observed some of the superstitious rituals performed by those in sports and in the theater. Although performers may admit their superstitious behavior is senseless, they also feel that stopping such behavior would produce much anxiety. For example, a famous baseball player has to touch second base running on to the field and first or third base running off the field; an Olympic gold-medal runner has to run wearing a golf hat; and a famous actress has to wear the same bra when beginning a movie.

However, in contrast to superstitious people, compulsive neurotics seem never quite sure that their rituals will succeed, and this may force

258

SECTION IV:
DISORDERS
RELATED TO
ANXIETY AND
STRESS

them to keep expanding their rituals. More than anyone else, the compulsive neurotic person is usually aware of the frailty of people and of the imperfection of their behavior. It is this uncertainty that long ago led Janet to call compulsive neurosis the "doubting sickness."

Depressive Neurosis

The depressive neurotic is believed by some theorists to turn anxiety inward in the form of depression. Neurotic depression typically involves an excessive reaction of depression to an internal conflict or to an identifiable event, such as the loss of a loved one or valued goal or possession. Although we all may feel pain in reaction to such unfortunate happenings, neurotic depressives typically react with *too* much sadness for *too* long a time. They may react with appropriate feeling, but they overdo it. Neurotic depressive disorders differ in many ways from the depressive psychoses discussed in Chapter 8 (see Table 10-2), but the most important differences are that neurotic depression usually occurs in response to some environmental stimulus and is characterized by insight into the condition and by a virtual absence of disordered thought processes.

A vivid example of the loneliness and despair of neurotic depression is nicely captured in the following excerpt from a man's diary (Barbellion, 1919). The man began keeping a diary from the age of 13. He suffered from a terminal disease that finally took his life at the age of 23.

December 21.

This continuous preoccupation with self sickens me—as I look back over these entries. It is inconceivable that I should be here steadily writing up my ego day by day in the middle of this disastrous war. . . . Yesterday I had a move on. To-day life wearies me. I am sick of myself and life. This beastly world with its beastly war and hate makes me restless, dissatisfied, and full of a longing to be quit of it. I am as full of unrest as an autumn Swallow. 'My soul,' I said to them at breakfast with a sardonic grin, 'is like a greyhound in the slips. I shall have to wear heavy boots to prevent myself from soaring. I have such an uplift on me that I could carry a horse, a dog, a cat, if you tied them on to my homing spirit and so transformed my Ascension into an adventure out of Baron Munchausen.' With a gasconnade of contempt, I should like to turn on my heel and march straight out of this wretched world at once [p. 83].

The possibility of attempting suicide is high in depressive neurosis, but there is some disagreement over how lethal and serious these attempts may be. Nemiah (1975c) believes that the danger of successful suicide is relatively low, but McCall (1963) cautions that the potential is high. We

Table 10-2. *Usual clinical features of neurotic versus psychotic depression*

Clinical Feature	Neurotic Depression	Psychotic Depression
Quality of depression	Normal despondency	Abnormal melancholy
Variability of depression	Much	Little or none
Delusions	Absent	Sometimes present
Depersonalization	Absent	Present
Anxiety component	Strong	Weak
Neurotic component	Strong	Weak
Diurnal variation	None	Worse in morning or evening
Concentration	Intact	Poor
Guilt	None or insincere	Intense remorse
Reaction to self	Pity	Pitiless
Weight loss	Variable	Invariable
Constipation	Variable	Invariable
Health	Usually poor	Good, except during episode
Precipitating event	Clear and strong	Absent or weak
Family history of depression	Absent	Present

From "Independence of Neurotic Depression and Endogenous Depression," by L. Kilch and R. Garside, *British Journal of Psychiatry*, 1963, *109*, 451-463. Copyright 1963 by Hendley Bros., Ltd. Reprinted by permission.

believe that, in any case of depression, it is wiser to overestimate than underestimate the suicide danger.

Other Neurotic Patterns

The neurotic disorders we have described thus far are conceived by most professionals as clear-cut syndromes. However, neurasthenic neurosis, depersonalization, and hypochondriacal neuroses often are seen as indistinct syndromes. There is a good chance that these patterns won't be included in DSM-III, but since they are part of DSM-II, we will describe them briefly.

Neurasthenic Neurosis. The major symptoms of neurasthenic neurosis, or neurasthenia, are generally chronic weakness, fatigue, and sometimes exhaustion. Literally, the word *neurasthenia* means "nerve weakness," but there is little proof that the nervous system is involved in any significant manner. Neurasthenic people often share with hypochondriacal people the symptoms of self-preoccupation, constant physiological and psychological complaints, and the tendency to place the responsibility for care on others. However, the neurasthenic's reactions usually are more selective than the hypochondriac's, especially in terms of fatigue. Some neurasthenic people may appear to be at death's door when at home or interacting in ordinary situations, but then spring to life when involved in interesting outside activities.

260

SECTION IV:
DISORDERS
RELATED TO
ANXIETY AND
STRESS

Hypochondriacal Neurosis. Hypochondriacal neurosis is marked by preoccupation with the body and with fear of presumed diseases of various organs. There usually are no actual losses of systemic functions.

Hypochondriacal neurosis frequently is considered to be a chronic disorder with a small possibility for improvement. Some physicians may be driven by hypochondriacal patients into prescribing medicine or performing surgery that appears, in retrospect, probably unnecessary. The hypochondriac is often a self-centered, self-preoccupied attention getter who fits snugly into the role of a sick person. Sickness can evoke secondary gain in the form of sympathy and attention from others, as well as provide a convenient excuse for failure. An example of an attention-getting maneuver is shown in the following letter:

Dear Mother and Husband:

I have suffered terrible today with drawing in my throat. My nerves are terrible. My head feels queer. But my stomach hasn't cramped quite so hard. I've been on the verge of a nervous chill all day, but I have been fighting it hard. It's night and bedtime, but, oh, how I hate to go to bed. Nobody knows or realizes how badly I feel because I fight to stay up and outdoors if possible.

I haven't had my cot up for two days, they don't want me to use it.

These long afternoons and nights are awful. There are plenty of patients well enough to visit with but I'm in too much pain. The nurses ignore any complaining. They just laugh or scold.

Eating has been awful hard. They expect me to eat like a harvest hand. Every bite of solid food is agony to get down, for my throat aches so and feels so closed up [Menninger, 1945].[1]

EXPLANATIONS

The explanations for neurotic behavior patterns may be seen as tied inseparably to the explanations for anxiety itself. Since neurosis is conceptualized by most theorists as reflecting styles of dealing with intense anxiety, we will present current explanations of the development of anxiety. We will emphasize psychological explanations, because there is little evidence that biological factors are involved in neurosis to the same degree as in psychosis.

Before we describe the theories of anxiety, we want to reiterate that we are dealing with ways in which anxiety can produce behavioral, emo-

[1]From *The Human Mind*, by K. A. Menninger. Copyright 1945 by Alfred A. Knopf, Inc. Reprinted by permission.

tional, and physical malfunctions. In Chapter 4, we described several theoretical perspectives on the development of normal and abnormal behavior. As you read through this section, recollect that many psychoanalytic theorists believe that the particular pattern of neurotic behavior may depend upon the specific defensive maneuvers chosen by an individual in the effort to protect the ego. For example, the use of displacement as defense tends to give phobic people their characteristic style of dealing with their fears. (See Table 10-3 for other proposed relationships between defenses and neurotic styles.) Counter to the analytic view, most learning theorists see specific neurotic behavior more as a function of imitation, superstition, or other factors involved in the selection of an anxiety-reducing (and thereby self-reinforcing) response to repeated exposure to a fearful stimulus. We believe that, if you understand how anxiety can come about, you may understand more easily how it can be differentially experienced or expressed in disordered behavior.

Psychoanalytic Theory

Early in his career, Freud regarded anxiety primarily as a physiological reaction to a chronic inability to reach orgasm in sexual relationships. However, based on the information he had gleaned from the continuing analysis of his patients, Freud (1936) later changed his theoretical view of anxiety. He theorized that anxiety was more likely a specific state of "unpleasure" that functioned as a danger signal. The earliest anxiety felt by a person was *primary anxiety*, which was possible just after birth and reflected a failure to have basic physiological needs met. Freud went on to delineate three other types of anxiety *(realistic, neurotic,* and *moral)* differing from primary anxiety, not in the experiential character of the feeling, but in its source.

Realistic anxiety is both sensible and adaptive; its source is generally in the external world. Realistic anxiety helps to protect us from real dangers in our environment and is an early-warning system that alerts us to potential harm from the world around us. Examples of realistic anxiety are the fear of cobras in India and of muggers in dark alleys.

Table 10-3. *Probable conceptual relationships between defense mechanisms and neurotic styles*

Neurosis	Defenses Involved
Anxiety neurosis	Failure of defenses, except for repression
Phobias	Displacement, projection
Dissociative reactions	Denial, repression
Hysterical neurosis	Denial, somatization, projection
Obsessive-compulsive neurosis	Isolation, undoing, reaction formation
Depressive neurosis	Failure of repression, displacement

262

SECTION IV:
DISORDERS
RELATED TO
ANXIETY AND
STRESS

To understand *neurotic anxiety,* it is necessary to recall the tripartite personality structure of id, ego, and superego. Neurotic anxiety arises from the ego's realization that, if the aggressive or sexual urges of the id aren't checked by consideration of reality, the psychological existence of the individual may be threatened. Freud believed there was a constant struggle between the ego and the id for the determination of an individual's behavior. In Freudian theory, it is from this basic conflict of ego and id that neurotic anxiety is thought to arise.

Moral anxiety involves the ego's interactions with the superego. The superego is usually an early ally of the ego in controlling the id, but it may create its own difficulties. Like the id, the superego isn't in good contact with reality and, because of this, even the person's *thinking* of taboo id-directed activities may bring quick punishment from the superego in the form of guilt or shame. Moral anxiety represents the feelings encountered when a superego "rule" is about to be violated. Generally, the more rigid a child's upbringing, the more likely it is that moral anxiety will occur. If there are no "rules" to violate, moral anxiety is less likely.

Although they are no different experientially, any of the three types of anxiety can occur in a specific situation. Knowledge of the individual's personality and past may delineate the type of anxiety experienced. For example, let's assume a boy is anxious about stealing a toy from a small store. If he is anxious because he is afraid of getting caught by the watchful storekeeper, he probably is experiencing *realistic* anxiety. If he is anxious because his ego perceived the stealing as the expression of hate toward his father (symbolized by the storekeeper), the feeling most likely is *neurotic* anxiety. If he is anxious because he has always been taught that stealing is a sin to be punished by burning in hell, he probably is feeling *moral* anxiety.

In psychoanalytic theory, the primary function of the ego is to maintain the individual's emotional stability and avoid severe anxiety by mediating among the id, the superego, and reality. To aid in accomplishing these tasks, the ego defense mechanisms are sometimes used. When defenses are imperfect, they may result in behavior patterns described as neurotic (Table 10-3).

Neo-Freudian Theory

To the neo-Freudians, primary anxiety is basically a fear that dependency needs will not be met. The greatest threat to a person is the possibility of a loss of protection and security from the "parenting ones."

Some neo-Freudians (R. W. White, 1964) believe that children go through a socialization process that begins some time in their first year. Parents may enforce social mores and customs by means of threats to withdraw love. The withdrawal of love is conceptualized as the source of primary anxiety. To avoid primary anxiety, the children restrict their behavior and conform, fearing that otherwise their "parenting ones" will no longer love them. The restriction of their basic impulses may frustrate the children and make them angry. To most neo-Freudians, the core of neurosis lies in how the children deal with this anger. Since parents often respond with severe disapproval to expressions of aggression from their offspring, the children may have to learn further to control any direct expression of such hostility toward their powerful caretakers. Aggressive impulses may be controlled through the development of defenses such as repression or denial. However, when defenses are threatened (when the child fears that aggression may break through and he may lose his security), anxiety is experienced. Anxiety that results from defenses being threatened is usually referred to as secondary anxiety. Secondary anxiety is most closely associated with neurotic behaviors.

Learning Theory

Learning theorists see anxiety primarily as the result of environmental factors. Present-day learning theorists such as Skinner (1938), Eysenck (1957), and Ullmann and Krasner (1975) believe that they may be able to explain the occurrence of anxiety in simpler terms than those used by psychoanalysts. The learning-theory concept of anxiety is tied very closely to the basic phenomena of motivation, learning, and reinforcement discussed in Chapter 4.

Primary and Secondary Drives. To the learning theorist, physiologically based *primary drives*, such as sex, thirst, and hunger, are important motivators of basic, survival-oriented behavior. However, it is the learned or *secondary drives* that are often psychologically most crucial in determining complex normal and abnormal behavior. Such learned drives may be exemplified by needs for money, prestige, and security. These secondary drives usually are seen to develop as the result of association with a primary drive.

A significant primary drive in consideration of the development of anxiety is pain avoidance. The pain-avoidance drive appears to be biologically programmed into all animals and seems crucial to species survival. Pain is associated with the occurrence of many stimuli, and the anticipation of this pain may be equated with anxiety. Thus, most of us feel anxious before receiving an injection, an event associated with pain. However, the experience of anxiety itself is unpleasant, so we usually are motivated to avoid the anxiety and, if possible, the situation causing it. The anxiety we feel is a *secondary avoidance drive*, the strength of which may vary on the basis of such factors as the number of times a situation has been associated with pain and the intensity of the aversive stimulus in question. Mild anxiety may help us discriminate between choices and motivate us to do better on most tasks (Spielberger, 1966). However, the greater the strength of the secondary avoidance drive called anxiety, the more likely it is that the experience will have deleterious rather than beneficial effects.

264

SECTION IV:
DISORDERS
RELATED TO
ANXIETY AND
STRESS

The concept of a learned avoidance drive was exemplified in Watson and Rayner's (1920) study of Little Albert. As you remember, Watson and Rayner placed Albert in a crib with a pet white rat, and then Watson stalked up behind Albert and loudly banged a steel bar. Albert cried! After several of these sessions, Albert finally began to act *anxiously;* just the sight of the furry animal was enough to send him into tears. The animal seemed to have become a secondary source of fear for him through association with the primary stimulus (aversive sound).

Generalization of Anxiety. If anxiety were associated only with the specific situation to which it was first related, it wouldn't be so pervasive a phenomenon. However, anxiety may spread or *generalize* to other aspects of our experience in at least three major ways. First, an organism can learn to react, not only to the stimulus originally causing a secondary avoidance drive, but to objects associated in time, place, and circumstance with the originally feared object or situation. These once-neutral objects or circumstances can then become anxiety-evoking cues in themselves. Little Albert, for example, developed an intense fear of the crib in which the conditioning occurred, of the room in which the crib was located, and probably of John Watson and his colleague.

Besides generalizing across time, place, and circumstances, anxiety can generalize along the dimension of *stimulus similarity*. Here, an organism learns to fear objects or situations that are experientially or descriptively similar to the originally feared events. Returning again to Albert, we find an example of the adverse effects of this type of generalization. It seems that Albert didn't just remain fearful of the fuzzy rat. He soon manifested signs of anxiety in the presence of other furry animals, his mother's furry handwarmer, Watson's hair, and even a mask of Santa Claus. Albert's fear seemed to generalize to a wide variety of fuzzy and hairy objects and people.

Anxiety can also generalize according to people's ability to label, categorize, and abstract their behavior verbally and mentally. For example, *mediated generalization* helps us to generalize that a stove, match, and fire are all hot and shouldn't be touched. Without this sort of verbal generalization, the education of a young child would be very difficult. However, this ability also allows anxiety to generalize to seemingly unrelated areas of a person's life. If bitten by a dog, a person may learn to fear not only dogs, but perhaps words beginning with the letter *d,* or words that sound like *dog,* such as *hog* or *bog.* Depending upon the abstract class of things to which the person assigns his experience, and the intensity of the feared experience, anxiety can spread in complex ways that are often difficult to understand.

In most instances, generalization of anxiety is adaptive and allows the organism to avoid dangerous situations and to profit from experience. A major distinction between fear as adaptive and fear as disruptive may lie in the intensity of the fear and, in turn, the degree of the generalization. To spank a child is adaptive if spanking helps alert the child to what is dangerous in the environment. Spanking may not be adaptive, however, if the child is struck for no apparent reason and thus learns to fear everything.

Drive Reduction. Since anxiety appears to have the qualities of most secondary drives, it follows that it should respond to procedures that reduce the strength of secondary drives. Behaviors that are followed by the reduction of an aversive stimulus usually are reinforced and tend to occur again under the same or similar circumstances. Some learning theorists see neurotic behaviors as responses that are maintained because they result in the reduction of the secondary drive of anxiety. Thus, compulsive people who wash their hands continuously may do so because the hand-washing behavior reduces anxiety temporarily. Hysterical people may develop bogus physical disabilities because that makes it possible to remove themselves from stressful situations. Most learning theorists don't believe that these behaviors are consciously chosen, but think that they probably derive from a variety of sources beyond the person's immediate awareness. Anxiety-reduction behavior may be discovered by chance, as in some magical compulsions, or they may be learned by imitation, as is probable in phobias of snakes, mice, and the like.

Conflict Theory

Based on Freudian and neo-Freudian theory, but also associated with learning-theory explanations of anxiety, Dollard and Miller (1950) introduced a conflict theory of anxiety. They believe that conflict occurs when a person is motivated simultaneously by two strong competing drives. When there is conflict, there is often anxiety; and the more difficult the conflict is to resolve, the greater the degree of anxiety.

Conflicts typically arise from an encounter between two fairly equal drive tendencies—approach and avoidance (see Figure 10-1). There are four basic types of conflict conceptualized by Dollard and Miller. One type of conflict occurs when an organism is motivated simultaneously to pursue two desirable but incompatible goals. Called an *approach-approach* conflict, this type rarely gives rise to much anxiety. Greater anxiety is typically produced in an *avoidance-avoidance* conflict, in which there is no positively valued choice; the organism must choose between a rock and a hard place. The avoidance-avoidance conflict is represented in the film *Butch Cassidy and the Sundance Kid,* in which two cowboy outlaws are trapped at the edge of a chasm, with the choice of being shot by the approaching posse or jumping off a hundred-foot cliff.[2]

Anxiety also can be produced by an *approach-avoidance* conflict. In humans, an approach-avoidance conflict may be created when a person is both attracted to and frightened by sexual involvement with another. In *multiple approach-avoidance* conflicts there are several goals, each with a

[2]They jumped.—*Ed.*

266

SECTION IV:
DISORDERS
RELATED TO
ANXIETY AND
STRESS

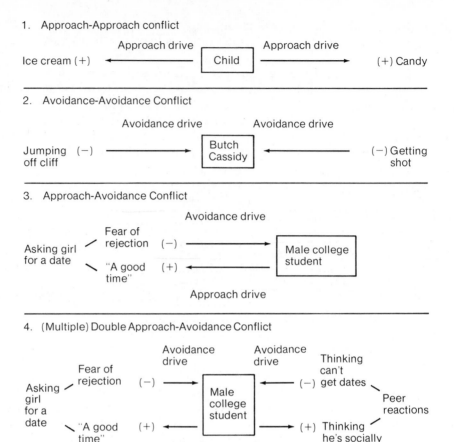

FIGURE 10-1. *Types of conflicts*

number of desirable *and* undesirable features that a person must somehow sum up and compare before choosing a goal. The multiple approach-avoidance conflict probably approximates the real world more closely than the single approach-avoidance conflict. Rarely are we faced with choices so simple that we can clearly identify approach-approach or avoidance-avoidance conflicts. As you can imagine, the complexities of multiple goal conflicts are such that they are nearly impossible to identify clearly. To the conflict theorist, however, if conflicts can be resolved, anxiety and its negative neurotic consequences may be reduced.

TREATMENT

Procedures that are effective in dealing with anxiety by and large should be useful in treating psychoneurotic disorders. Many of the traditional individual psychotherapies (such as psychoanalysis and the client-centered and Gestalt therapies) came into existence primarily to deal with neurotic disorders. More recently, other procedures have evolved to deal with anxiety and its expression in the psychoneuroses. These newer procedures—behavior modification, biofeedback, and chemical treatments—appear to be differentially beneficial, depending on the type of psychoneurotic disorder.

Psychological Approaches

The individual psychotherapies for the neuroses are similar in that they require psychoneurotics to talk about their problems and critical life events to a therapist, and in that the prognosis for psychotherapeutic success depends on a number of factors. For such therapy to succeed, the psychoneurotic person should show some evidence of stability in relationships within the family and at work, should be able to deal with emotions without becoming unduly depressed or anxious, and should have a well-defined set of symptoms that are clearly tied to direct stresses from the environment. In other words, neurotic people who aren't very disturbed and can focus on and deal with a clearly defined set of problems probably will do best in individual psychotherapy. It should come as no surprise that, among the neuroses, the clearly delineated phobic disorders respond well to individual psychotherapies. In psychoanalysis, a major form of individual therapy, people are taught to free-associate (speak whatever comes to mind) as a way of uncovering underlying conflicts. Therapists can also use hypnosis or drugs to reach the underlying conflicts that may have led to the particular formation of symptoms.

Whereas the analyst's goal is generally to search out the underlying conflicts leading to the formation of symptoms, behavior modifiers typically view the symptoms themselves as the most important component of a disorder. To the behavior modifier, the person showing the particular behavior we have called neurotic does so because of learning. Although they never had the opportunity to treat Albert, Watson and Rayner (1920) did present a number of possible remedial procedures. They suggested, for example, repeatedly presenting the feared object alone and then presenting it paired with pleasurable events, to neutralize the fear response. These two approaches are now called *habituation* and *reciprocal inhibition,* respectively, and both have been used successfully, especially with phobic individuals (Wolpe, 1973).

In habituation, phobics may be forced to experience the feared object until they get used to it. However, in reciprocal inhibition, the presentation of a weakened form of the feared object is paired with an antagonistic response, such as relaxation. For instance, in the treatment of the fear of flying, one might first have the client compose a list of items graded from being very distant from the flying experience to actually being in the airplane. The client is also taught to relax. When the graded list and relaxation training are completed, the person typically is given the weakest item on the list to imagine and is then told to relax. The first item might be the

268

SECTION IV:
DISORDERS
RELATED TO
ANXIETY AND
STRESS

following: "You are told that when you complete your project in a year you will have to fly out to the coast to sign the contracts." The therapist reads such an item aloud and then asks the client to imagine it happening but at the same time to relax. When the client can experience a particular item without feeling anxious, he or she may then move on to the next, more anxiety-provoking item, until the entire list can be experienced without anxiety.

Of all the neurotic disorders, phobic disorders appear to be the most amenable to behavior modification such as the reciprocal inhibition we just described (Goldfried & Davison, 1976). However, other behavioral techniques have been successfully applied to other neurotic symptoms. For example, *response prevention* has been used with some success in obsessive-compulsive individuals. In response prevention, people are placed in the type of environmental situation that produces the obsessive-compulsive behavior, but they are prevented from expressing the behavior (Thorpe, Schmidt, Brown, & Castell, 1964). In *flooding*, the patient may be forced to experience the fear or obsession a number of times. After repeated trials in which the feared object or obsessive thought is experienced, the person appears to adapt to the presence of the fear or obsession. As a result of such adaptation, the person may no longer need to use the phobic or obsessive strategy (Rachman, Marks, & Hodgson, 1973).

Biofeedback

Neither of the psychological approaches just described deals directly with nervous-system functioning. Instead, they approach anxiety through cognitive or behavioral means. In these psychological approaches, autonomic anxiety responses usually are viewed as the targets of change through some suggestion or relaxation. In biofeedback, the person is more directly taught to control autonomic functioning, and this control decreases the feelings of anxiety. For example, Blanchard and Young (1974) present a case of a 50-year-old man diagnosed as an anxiety neurotic. He had symptoms of anxiety and weakness, as well as a speeded-up heartbeat. The man was attached to biofeedback equipment that sounded a change in audio tone when he was able to relax enough to slow his heartbeat. As reinforcement, the man was paid one cent for every ten seconds his heart beat was below a certain rate. At the beginning of training, the man had a rate of 96 beats per minute; at the end of 19 trials his rate was 14 beats slower and remained so even after training and rewards were stopped. Moreover, the man reported that he *felt* less anxious and stronger. Single cases don't prove the overall worth of a treatment, but it would appear that biofeedback is a promising approach for dealing with anxiety.

Biological Approaches

There is a debate between proponents of the psychoanalytic and learning-theory approaches over whether the behavioral "symptom" should be the focus of treatment or is merely the result of a core conflict, but both would probably agree that tranquilizers deal only with the symptoms of the neurosis. The majority of the tranquilizing drugs are effective only against the feeling of anxiety itself and don't have much effect on the other symptoms that may accompany a specific neurotic disorder. For example, although tranquilizers such as meprobamate and Valium would probably decrease the anxiety level of a dissociative hysteric, the person might still show the characteristic symptom picture of dissociative hysteria—minus the anxiety. Barbiturates may alleviate the symptom of insomnia in anxiety neurosis, and antidepressants such as imipramine may elevate mood in depressive neurosis.

Most who prescribe drug therapy are quick to point out that drugs should be used only in conjunction with a therapeutic program that includes some form of psychotherapy. Without such a therapeutic relationship, the danger of becoming psychologically and, in some cases, physiologically addicted to the tranquilizing drugs increases dramatically. As Nemiah (1975c) states: "Drugs should never be allowed to become a substitute for a relationship with a doctor" (p. 1263).

CONCLUDING COMMENTS

We have spent a good deal of time on the neuroses, but we must note that there is some question as to whether they truly exist. It may strike you as strange that we would question the utility of the concept of neurosis at the end of such a lengthy chapter. However, Szasz's criticism of the entire idea of disease entities in abnormal behavior (see Chapter 1) reminds us that neurotic symptom patterns were thought by some past diagnosticians to be due to physiological sources, such as wandering uteruses and weak nerves. Today, neuroses are seen as sharing a potpourri of behavioral symptoms, styles of interaction, and inferred internal dynamics. Clinical experience suggests that there are not so many *pure* neurotic disorders as one would expect from the amount of space devoted to them in this and other texts on abnormal behavior. McCall (1963) has taken an extreme stance in regard to the utility of the classification of neurosis:

> It would generally be more reasonable to speak not so much of psychoneurosis, but of neurotic reaction or neurotic tendencies which may be present in psychosis, in the so-called character disorders, in situational disturbances which affect basically normal individuals subjected to severe physical illness, an intolerable homelife, or political tyranny. Take away from the sum total of diagnosed neuroses all those instances which can be attributed to incipient or latent psychosis, character disorder, or situational stress, and there would probably remain only a few examples of pure neurosis, i.e.,

270

SECTION IV:
DISORDERS
RELATED TO
ANXIETY AND
STRESS

autonomous syndromes of stable groups of symptoms, describable without reference to another underlying or precipitating disturbance [p. 12].

Although we wouldn't go this far in questioning the utility of the category of neurosis, it does seem that McCall's opinion deserves serious consideration by researchers and theoreticians. In fact, the early drafts of DSM-III (American Psychiatric Association, 1977) have dropped the category of neuroses altogether.

CHAPTER SUMMARY CHART

In this chapter, we discussed the psychoneuroses, beginning with descriptions of disorders associated with anxiety:

Anxiety neurosis	*Phobias*	*Hysterical neurosis*
Free-floating anxiety	Irrational fears	Dissociation: amnesia, somnambulism, multiple personality
Anxiety attack	Neurotic phobias	
Panic reaction	Traumatic phobias	Conversion: sensory, motor, and autonomic

Obsessive neurosis	*Compulsive reactions*	*Depressive neurosis*
Persistent, unshakable thoughts	Need to carry out certain acts	Reactive depression milder than affective psychosis

Other neuroses
Neurasthenia
Hypochondriasis

We then considered several explanations for the neuroses:

Psychoanalytic theory	*Neo-Freudian theory*	*Learning theory*
Neurotic anxiety	Primary and secondary anxiety	Primary and secondary drives
Failure of defenses		Pain avoidance
		Secondary avoidance drives
		Generalization of anxiety
		Drive reduction

Finally, we looked at methods of treatment for the psychoneuroses:

*Psychological
    approaches*

Individual therapy
Psychoanalysis
Reciprocal inhibition
Habituation
Flooding

Biofeedback

Conscious control of
"involuntary"
expression of
tension

Biological therapy

Minor tranquilizers

CHAPTER 11
PSYCHOPHYSIOLOGICAL DISORDERS

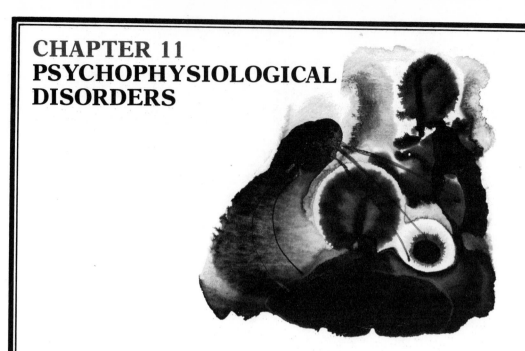

In the previous chapter, we described some of the possible maladaptive attempts to reduce anxiety shown in the neurotic disorders. Another set of disorders that may result in part from different, but still unsuccessful, means of dealing with anxiety are the *psychophysiological disorders* (PPD). In this type of anxiety-related disorder, a person's means of handling psychological difficulties seems to be expressed physiologically. Although people with psychophysiological disorders may exhibit physiological disease symptoms similar to those of the conversion hysteric, there are several significant diagnostic differences. For one thing, psychophysiological disorders usually involve changes in internal organs such as the heart or lungs, whereas conversion hysteric reactions more often are marked by changes in peripheral systems such as eyes and muscles. For another thing, in the psychophysiological disorders, there usually is a *very real* physical disease accompanied by actual physical damage; such physical damage is singularly lacking in conversion hysterias. Finally, PPDs are believed by most professionals to be multiply determined; that is, rather than being primarily psychological, these disorders are thought to be based upon an interaction of social, biological/genetic, and psychological factors.

DSM-II defines the psychophysiological disorders as "characterized by physical symptoms that are caused by emotional factors and involve a single organ system, usually under autonomic nervous system innervation" (American Psychiatric Association, 1968). Psychophysiological patients make up a small proportion of admissions to state mental hospitals or of those visiting private psychiatric practitioners (less than 1%). Yet, due to their often life-threatening consequences, these disorders demand a great deal of theoretical and research effort. Much of the theoretical effort is devoted to investigating the reasons why different individuals "choose" different organ systems as sites for psychophysiological disturbance. For example, we don't know exactly why some individuals suffer respiratory-system breakdowns (asthma) and others, gastrointestinal-system break-downs (ulcers). There are at least three major "guesses" made by researchers and clinicians as to why a particular psychophysiological disorder might be "chosen." One view is that the specific psychophysiological disorder occurs in the organ system that is physically the weakest. The weakness in a specific organ system may have a genetic or environmental cause. Thus, for example, if the respiratory system is a person's weakest organ system and the person experiences continued stress, this could lead to a breakdown of that system in the form of asthma.

A second explanation suggests that there are differences in inherited patterns of response to stress that may predispose people to develop specific system breakdowns. For example, some people respond to stress with elevated blood pressure, whereas others respond with increased acid production in the stomach. Lacey and Lacey (1958) have shown these differences in individual physiological reactivity to stress to be fairly stable over time. Some of the varieties of physiological responses to anxiety are shown in Table 11-1. To get an idea of what normal college students saw as "physiological symptoms" of anxiety, we asked students in our classes to write down what physiological behavior they experienced as anxiety. Table 11-1 is a list of "symptoms" experienced by these students, arranged according to frequency. You will see that there are some unique and varied indicators of anxiety.

A third theory suggests that specific types of personality—and *not* weak organ systems or inherited response patterns—are the chief reasons for the development of certain psychophysiological disorders. For example, people who have dependence-independence conflicts may be more prone to develop ulcers (F. Alexander, 1934). Consistent with this personality explanation, research has found that people tend to express different attitudes, depending on the type of psychophysiological disorder they have. Table 11-2 shows that, although an ulcer patient most often "feels deprived," the hypertensive person "feels threatened with harm." However, you should realize that these data don't tell us whether these attitudes are the cause or the result of the psychophysiological disorder, and they give us little help in evaluating the merit of the three theories.

We can now describe specific patterns of symptoms in psychophys-

274

SECTION IV:
DISORDERS
RELATED TO
ANXIETY AND
STRESS

Table 11-1. *Physiological correlates of anxiety in college students*

Physiological Response	Percentage of 300 Subjects Mentioning the Physiological Reaction
Increased heart rate	20
Digestive upset	17
Sweat, cold sweat	15
Sweaty palms	15
Increased breathing rate	11
Alertness, heightened senses	11
Muscular tension	10
Tire easily, weakness	9
Knots or butterflies in stomach	8
Pulse-rate increase	6
Whole body tense, tight	6
Hypertension	6
Weak legs, legs buckle	6
Light-headed, faint, dizzy	5
Shaky	5
Cry easily	5
Lose appetite	5
Nauseated	5
Hands and feet tap	5
Can't sit still	4
Sudden movements, twitches	4
Talk a lot, fast, loud	3
Headaches	2
Jittery laugh	2
Can't sleep	2
Mind blanks	2
Frequent urge to go to bathroom	2
Break out in blemishes	2
Flushed	2
"Cotton mouth," tough speaking	2
Clenched fists	2
Increased metabolism	2
Cold hands	2
Hot ears	1
Tension behind eyes	1
Burning inside	1
Teeth grind, sore jaws	1
Chilled	1
Loss of feeling	1
Hair on legs stands out	1
Skin rash	1
Bite nails	1
Smoke	1

iological disorders. However, we will depart from the format used in previous chapters. The psychophysiological disorders involve widely disparate system dysfunctions and may best be seen as a set of separate disorder

Table 11-2. *Psychological characteristics of four psychosomatic types*

	Ulcerative Colitis	Peptic Ulcer	Essential Hypertension	Bronchial Asthma
General neurotic traits	Immature Insufficiently balanced Passive-dependent Egocentric Oversensitive and vulnerable Impaired adaptability Insecure Inadequately regulated discharge of aggression Difficulty in interpersonal communication	Immature Insufficiently balanced Passive-dependent Egocentric Oversensitive and vulnerable Impaired adaptability Insecure Inadequately regulated discharge of aggression Difficulty in interpersonal communication	Immature Insufficiently balanced Passive-dependent Egocentric Oversensitive and vulnerable Impaired adaptability Insecure Inadequately regulated discharge of aggression Difficulty in interpersonal communication	Immature Insufficiently balanced Passive-dependent Egocentric Oversensitive and vulnerable Impaired adaptability Insecure Inadequately regulated discharge of aggression Difficulty in interpersonal communication
Outward appearance	Mild, "average," sometimes pseudovirile Sentimental, polite Ambition / Activity / Honesty / Diligence / Reliability } Moderate Neat Obedient-dutiful ("Conventional superego," middle-classy) Compliant Socially moderately successful	Driving, self-asserted Businesslike Ambition / Activity / Honesty / Hard-working / Reliable } Marked Careful, orderly Conscientious-dutiful (Highly developed superego, idealistic) Dominant Often successful	Controlled, driving Correct Ambition / Activity / Fanatically honest / Hard-working / Reliable } Marked Careful, orderly Compulsive-dutiful (Strict superego, rigid-normative) Partly docile, partly aggressive Often successful	Sometimes shy, often exacting, and stubborn At times docile, at times irritable and impatient Ambition / Activity / Honesty / Diligence / Reliability } Marked } By outbursts Compulsive Dutiful by outbursts (Superego insufficiently incorporated) Exacting, often in protest, tyrannical Sometimes successful, often social failures

276

SECTION IV:
DISORDERS
RELATED TO
ANXIETY AND
STRESS

Table 11-2. *(continued)*

	Ulcerative Colitis	Peptic Ulcer	Essential Hypertension	Bronchial Asthma
Social behavior pattern	Imitation of standards of other people	Living up to high ideals	Rigid, living on principles	Poorly adapted, feel easily wronged, often in protest Impulsive, unpredictable
Preferred pattern of abreaction or aggression	Transferred to parental figure	Competitive	Destructive ("hot-tempered") ("throw the truth in one's face")	Domineering
Attitude toward marriage partner	Overtly dependent, often frigid or impotent. Marriage often late or not at all	Ambivalent: dependent but overtly protective and dominant. Loyal to partner Sex life usually normal	Ambivalent: on one hand conforming to partner's standards, on the other hand dominating and aggressive Sometimes promiscuous	Ambivalent: on one hand tyrannical and exacting; on the other hand dependent Often frigid or impotent Sometimes promiscuous
Basic mood	Insecure and anxious	Insecure and driving	Insecure and aggressive	Insecure and oppressed

From "The Place of Personality Traits in Specific Syndromes: Cause or Effect," by J. Bastiaans. In J. Wisdom and J. Wolff (Eds.), *The Role of Psychosomatic Disorder in Adult Life*. Copyright 1965 by Pergamon Press, Ltd., Oxford, England. Reprinted by permission.

types. The explanations and treatments for one type of psychophysiological disorder are usually irrelevant to the other types. Therefore, we will present descriptions, explanations, and treatments for each type of disorder. Although DSM-II defines nine separate types of psychophysiological disorders, we will describe what we consider to be four of the most important: cardiovascular disorders, gastrointestinal disorders, respiratory disorders, and headaches.

CARDIOVASCULAR DISORDERS

The psychophysiological cardiovascular disorders involve diseases of the heart and blood vessels. The two most destructive and prevalent of these cardiovascular disorders, *coronary heart disease* and *essential hypertension*, account for untold loss of years of life, as well as a number of psychological difficulties.

Coronary Heart Disease

Ranking first as a cause of death, coronary heart disease (CHD) may account for as many as *half* the deaths in the United States. CHD is not a cause of death only in the aged; it is responsible for one out of four deaths of people between the ages of 35 and 64. Many more men than women are victims of CHD, and a healthy male child in the United States has one chance in five of developing some form of CHD before he is 60 years old.

Description. The most common deadly form of coronary heart disease, *myocardial infarction*, is what we commonly refer to as a heart attack. These attacks usually are caused by obstruction of one of the coronary, or heart, arteries and can lead to the death (necrosis) of a portion of the heart muscle. If that part of the heart muscle is crucial for maintaining heart functions, then the person will probably die. The experience of a myocardial infarction is uniquely frightening, as is shown in the next personal experience.

PERSONAL EXPERIENCE: *Heart Attack*

I probably would not have been able to talk about my heart attack right after it happened, so it's better that it's been some time since it happened. I know that I will probably be very intellectual in my description, but let me assure you that I can still feel how it was to experience a heart attack. I'm not a young man, being 63 years of age, but then one never really thinks of oneself as being old. I was fairly active. I played golf about two or three times a week, cut the grass, and the like. My father had a bad heart but I really had no inkling that I would have heart trouble. Then one night in October it began. Business had really been rough; competition with another firm was making work a living hell. Everybody was always trying to do something to someone else. So I had to think about the business night and day. Anyway, it was just after dinner and I wasn't feeling very well. But my stomach had been acting up lately anyway so I didn't make very much out of it. It felt like gas and I wondered if maybe I ate too fast. About an hour later it was still there but getting worse. I began to get flushed and to feel very uncomfortable. I couldn't sit but it was getting to be painful to walk. I did not want to alarm my wife so I didn't make very much out of it. I managed to stand the pain until about one o'clock in the morning. That's when my arm began to hurt like I threw it out playing ball. When I found that I could not move it without severe pain, I called out to my wife and she got help from the hospital. By the time I got to the hospital, I knew it was serious and that I might not live through the night. I thank God I survived; it has made me appreciate life again.

Explanations. The lethality and prevalence of CHD has stimulated a search for explanations of why some people develop these diseases and others don't. One explanation supported by research data suggests that there is a significant interaction of physiological and psychological factors in producing CHD. A second explanation deals with the existence of a "coronary personality."

Lipowski (1975) has identified six major factors that appear to be related to the development of CHD:

1. *Dietary factors:* diets that are habitually filled with high levels of saturated fats, cholesterol, and calories
2. *Blood chemistry:* elevated levels of various chemicals such as cholesterol
3. *Organ disease or dysfunction:* kidney disease, high blood pressure, or diabetes mellitus
4. *Living habits:* a deadly trio of smoking, overeating, and physical inactivity
5. *Psychosocial factors:* chronic dissatisfaction with life and work
6. *Familial factors:* family history of CHD and related disorders

Although these six factors are *known* to be significantly related to CHD, the incidence of the disorder hasn't decreased. We believe that inability to use this knowledge to prevent CHD is due, in part, to people's resistance to changing the controllable factors related to CHD. The fact that smoking, overeating, and remaining inactive are known to be dangerous doesn't seem to reduce these practices. There are many possible reasons for a lack of responsiveness to such a realistic threat; people may deny the possibility that the disorder could happen to them, they may be lazy, or they may even have a need for self-destruction.

The resistance of CHD to attempts to reduce its frequency may also be due to the fact that relatively little is known about the natural history of the disease. We do know that there are signs of arterial pathology in some children who may later develop adult CHD. Further, studies of Vietnam veterans revealed that nearly half (45%) showed some evidence of coronary arteriosclerosis (the presence of fatty tissue in the arteries) (Lipowski, 1975). We don't know whether the stresses of war caused a greater degree of arteriosclerosis or whether the same percentage of disease is present in the general population.

In addition to the physical factors known to be related to CHD, certain personality characteristics seem to be associated with an increased incidence of these disorders. One significant investigation into the personality characteristics associated with CHD was begun by M. Friedman and Rosenman (1959). They concluded that there was a major behavior pattern, which they called "Type A Personality," associated with CHD. Those categorized as Type A individuals seemed to live as though they were con-

The stress associated with the pressure of business has often been thought to be related to the occurrence of heart attacks. (Photo by David Powers.)

tinually under pressure. These men had difficulty relaxing and felt as though they were always under some time demand to complete a task that only they were good enough to do. Type A men not only tended to suffer greater numbers of myocardial infarctions but also had more severe attacks than did non–Type A men. The assessment of whether men are Type A or Type B (primarily characterized by a lack of the factors found in Type A) is usually accomplished through a structured interview.

From the foregoing description of the Type A individual, one might expect that CHD would be most prevalent in middle- and upper-class businessmen. On the contrary—and indicative of the lack of an absolutely clear and reliable relationship between psychosociological factors and CHD—it is the members of the lowest socioeconomic and educational groups that appear to have the highest incidence of CHD. For example, a study of 106 consecutive myocardial-infarction patients seen at a cardiac-care unit showed that these patients tended to come from large families, had only a smattering of formal education, worked more hours per week than required, and had difficulty getting along with peers and superiors. It appeared from this sample that CHD patients had been nonadapters to their social environment for some time before they developed CHD. Although they showed a high need and drive for work, the CHD patients seemed to derive little satisfaction from it. One investigator concluded that CHD patients may engage in competitive striving for defensive reasons: "For them striving is liable to be subjectively related to a need for approval" and a "defensive strategy against anxiety, depression or guilt feelings" (Lipowski, 1975, p. 1662). Thus, it may be competitive striving for defensive reasons that is related most clearly to the development of CHD.

Treatment. Just as the stresses and emotions generated by psychological conflicts may be a significant cause of CHD, the treatment of CHD should take into account the psychological response of the victim to his or her disease. Lipowski (1975) lists four general coping responses to CHD: *realistic appraisal* of the damage and realistic attempts at rehabilitation; *excessive dependence,* accompanied by symptoms of anxiety and depression; *denial* of the illness and living as though it had not happened; and use of the illness to *manipulate* others. The denial of danger to life has potentially fatal consequences. However, it is often difficult for myocardial-infarction patients to accept the fact they they are to some degree helpless and sick. More than half of those hospitalized for CHD exhibit significant signs of depression and anxiety. However, the most severe reactions usually occur in those who were tense and upset before being hospitalized. Of the more than 2 million myocardial-infarction cases occurring each year, about one out of six victims cannot return to a normal, productive life for *psychological* reasons.

Since psychological factors seem to play a significant role in the patient's adjustment to CHD, a victim's family and doctor should help the patient walk the narrow line between denial of the disorder, including resumption of a life-style and habits not conducive to health, and psychological invalidism, in which activity is phobically avoided. The proper attention given by significant others in the CHD patient's life may be crucial to effective recovery.

Psychological factors also may play a significant role in the success of the three major innovations in the treatment of CHD: the cardiac-care unit, implantation of pacemakers, and cardiac surgery. In the first two approaches, there seem to have been few negative psychological consequences (Lipowski, 1975). Research shows that most patients are reassured rather than frightened by being placed in cardiac-care units. Likewise, it has been found that most patients make a good psychological adjustment to pacemakers. However, severe psychological difficulties are sometimes created by open-heart surgery. About half of those who have open-heart surgery experience postoperative psychiatric difficulties ranging from delirium to paranoid psychosis. Although most of these psychological difficulties clear up in a week, any treatment of the heart-disease patient must certainly deal with the occurrence of such disorders (Lipowski, 1975).

Essential Hypertension

No apparent organic cause is easily found for the chronic high blood pressure that characterizes essential hypertension. The blood pressure reflects the ability of the blood vessels to remain flexible. Should the blood vessels become rigid due to disease, age, or other causes, the possibility of strokes and other disorders increases.

Description. About nine out of every ten cases of essential hypertension are believed to be psychophysiologically caused. More frightening may be the fact that, of the estimated 23 million people with hypertension, *half* are unaware of it. Unlike the often spectacular effects of myocardial infarction, hypertension can work its destruction insidiously and often without the awareness of the victim. Although prevalent in all ages and socioeconomic groups, hypertension affects, proportionately, about twice as many Blacks as Whites, with Black males being the most affected group. The effect of even moderately high blood pressure that persists for an extended time is frequently to shorten life expectancy dramatically. If the presence of hypertension is combined with such factors as smoking or high cholesterol levels, then the death rate for these individuals can be five times that for individuals who don't possess these indicators. High blood pressure is more frequent in populations undergoing rapid cultural change, migration, or socioeconomic mobility, and in urban as opposed to rural populations.

Explanations. Although we know that hypertension is a major health problem, and that abnormally high blood pressure can result from either an acceleration of the heart rate or constriction of blood vessels, we don't know exactly the mechanisms by which psychological factors make the heart beat faster or the blood vessels constrict. Some theories have been proposed to account for the occurrence of hypertension, however, and we will now describe a few of them.

Theorizing from their clinical experience with hypertensive patients, psychoanalysts offer the explanation that these people have few effective outlets for aggressive impulses. They may be afraid to show these impulses, which then may have to be expressed through the symptom of hypertension. According to most psychoanalysts, hypertensive people, unlike neurotic people, may be unable to make efficient use of defenses and must rely on constant, conscious monitoring of their aggressive impulses for control.

Some support for the analytic explanation of hypertension was obtained by M. Davies (1970). He acquired the cooperation of 128 factory workers, whom he divided into high, middle, and low blood-pressure groups. Davies found that subjects who had a history of neurotic traits in childhood and scored in the neurotic direction on a personality inventory had the *lowest* blood pressure. These results are consistent with the explanation that these individuals had neurotic defenses available to deal with anxiety and hostility and thus did not have high blood pressure.

In other research, Hokanson and his colleagues at Florida State University have taken as a starting point the explanation that inhibition of aggressive impulses is related to hypertension. In a series of studies (Hokanson & Burgess, 1962; Hokanson, DeGood, Forrest, & Brittain, 1971), an experimental situation was set up in which two subjects were to cooperate in completing a task. In reality, one of the subjects was always a colleague of the experimenter whose function was to engage in behavior that frustrated the subject and hampered the completion of the task. This experimental procedure was successful in raising the subject's blood pressure. Afterwards, the subject was placed in one of a number of experimental situations that differed primarily in the available method of dissipating frustration and thus lowering blood pressure. Hokanson found that, if males could aggress against the source of their frustration (their work partner), their blood pressure usually decreased, but if they could not, it generally remained high. Interestingly, females' blood pressure decreased when they were able to *reward* the source of their frustration.

This apparent sex-related divergence in dealing with the source of frustration led Hokanson to look for some common denominator between the two sexes. He hypothesized that males and females who had lowered their blood pressure had exercised control over the source of their frustration, but had done so in the socially acceptable ways dictated by their sex roles. In an experiment to test this hypothesis, two groups of subjects performed a symbol-matching task in which they were shocked for wrong responses. One group of subjects had control over how many one-minute rest periods they wanted to take. Their blood pressure was compared to that of a second group of subjects, who were given the same rest periods and number of shocks, but had no control over when they could take their rest periods.

Consistent with the hypothesis that control over the source of frustration is related to lowered blood pressure, Hokanson found that the group with no control over the occurrence of their rest periods showed higher blood pressure, regardless of sex.

Although Hokanson doesn't deal with long-term effects of frustration or high blood pressure, the results of his studies suggest that, if people have to "sit on" their anger for long periods of time, their blood pressure may rise and stay high even after the cause of their frustration has been removed. The fact that suppressed anger can raise blood pressure even when the source of frustration is gone may explain why such a large proportion of Black males are hypertensive. Hokanson's conclusions regarding inhibited anger and high blood pressure are in agreement with the conclusions of Black psychiatrists Grier and Cobbs, as reported in their book *Black Rage* (1968). On the basis of clinical observations, these psychiatrists concluded that past and present treatment of Blacks, especially males, by an oppressive White society causes them to feel rage. However, the Black man's rage has few avenues of acceptable expression and thus must be suppressed to protect him from the possibility of retaliation from the White society. Blacks living in unpleasant and unsatisfactory situations, experiencing feelings of rage they cannot express, should be especially vulnerable to hypertension. In support of this hypothesis, research results suggest that it is more likely race and not membership in the lower social class that is most significantly related to hypertension. For example, a study of people in the city of Detroit (Gentry, Harburg, & Havenstein, 1973) selected "high-stress" and "low-stress" areas of the city. White males and Black males were compared within each area, thus controlling for social class. It was found that when environmental stress was low, White and Black males did not differ in blood pressure; but in the high-stress areas, Black males had significantly higher average blood pressure than White males.

Treatment. Although the explanations of essential hypertension include significant psychological and social factors, treatment of the disorder is largely based on drugs. Medications that lower blood pressure may be combined with early detection to produce a community-medicine approach to treatment. However, maximum benefit to the hypertensive person usually is gained by focusing on the psychological pressures contributing to the disorder. Psychotherapy with hypertensive people typically emphasizes adaptive methods of handling crises or conflicts. It isn't usually true that merely allowing the hypertensive free rein to his angry feelings will decrease blood pressure. Hypertension is a complex condition that, with few exceptions, won't be relieved by such simple treatment approaches.

An attractive alternative to chemotherapy in treating essential hypertension is the use of operant-conditioning techniques to help people obtain control over their blood pressure. For example, in one study (Benson, Shapiro, Tursky, and Schwartz, 1971), seven patients with hypertension

284

SECTION IV:
DISORDERS
RELATED TO
ANXIETY AND
STRESS

were administered 22 training sessions in which they were attached to biofeedback machines that gave a certain tone when blood pressure was lowered. The subjects were told to try to make the machine produce the tone reflecting the lowered blood pressure. All but one subject showed a decrease in blood pressure after reinforced training. The authors believed that these results suggested a good basis for therapeutic intervention, but Brener (1974) cautioned that, for a treatment to be effective, there must be generalization from the laboratory to the outside world, and that the control must be maintained in the *absence* of feedback from machinery. In any case, the biofeedback approach has many possible applications to the problem of essential hypertension (see Chapter 24).

GASTROINTESTINAL DISORDERS

Like the cardiovascular system, the gastrointestinal (GI) system is a common pathway through which humans express their emotions and is therefore a primary site of possible psychophysiological disorders. For example, many of us have experienced "fear in the pit of my stomach" and the like. In this section we will describe ulcers and colitis, two of the more prevalent and destructive of the many GI psychophysiological disorders.

Ulcers

Gastric ulcers may be the most widely known of psychophysiological disorders. In everyday conversations, we hear people say such things as "If he doesn't slow down he'll get an ulcer." Some of us may joke about the relationship between stress and ulcers, but, as the following personal experience demonstrates, ulcers are no laughing matter.

PERSONAL EXPERIENCE: *Ulcers*

I thought I would be different from everybody else. I wasn't going to let the pressure of the office give me ulcers like everybody else. But, God, was I ever wrong. They started a few years after I came to work here. At first it was just indigestion, especially after lunch and spicy foods like pizza and other stuff with tomato sauce in it. It was like a burning in my stomach, lots of belching and discomfort.

As far as I can tell I never really started getting tense at work, but others were getting promoted ahead of me. I tried harder . . . still other *younger* people were moving up. I worked at home, got to work early, skipped meals. I wanted to show the supervisor that I was solid, dedicated executive material, too. When the stomach pains and indigestion were joined by black bowel movements with blood in them I knew I had real trouble. At first I thought it was cancer; knowing it was "only" an ulcer was a relief at first, but sometimes I feel so bad that I wish I were dead.

Description. An ulcer may be thought of as a hole in the lining of the stomach wall that has been burned out by excess amounts of gastric secretions. Gastric secretions primarily are made up of *mucus*, which protects the stomach lining; *pepsin*, which breaks down proteins; and *hydrochloric acid*, which aids in digestion. In the development of an ulcer, gastric secretions (especially pepsin) may be produced in amounts well beyond what is needed to digest food adequately, and the excess secretion destroys stomach-lining tissue.

Explanations. The explanations for the development of ulcers may be divided into the physiological and the psychological. Physiological theories are based on innate physical differences in people. Psychological theories emphasize the effect of conflict and stress upon the development of stomach-lining irritations.

Physiological theorists propose that there is a physiological state in some people that predisposes them to develop ulcers under prolonged stress. The predisposing biological condition for an ulcer is thought to be acquired genetically. For example, it has been found that people with certain types of ulcers have larger, hypersecreting stomachs compared to normal controls. Further, we know from other studies (Weiner, Thaler, Reiser, & Mirsky, 1957) that those who, under normal conditions, produce more acids and pepsin than the average of the general population later develop ulcers. It appears, then, that the biological conditions necessary for the creation of an ulcer may be present long before the ulcer actually forms. This partly explains why, when two people experience the same degree of stress, only one may develop an ulcer.

We know from research with animals that certain psychological situations productive of conflict can be related to increased acid production and, in turn, to generally greater frequency of stomach disturbances. Devised first by Sawrey (1961), the basic ulcer-producing procedure entailed placing rats in a situation where they were shocked every time they attempted to eat or drink. Present-day refinements of this procedure can cause an ulcer in certain kinds of rats in as little as six hours (Wald, MacKinnon, & Desiderto, 1973). Supporting what is theorized to occur in humans, autopsies of rats subjected to ulcer-producing procedures show that their ulcers seem to be caused by a higher percentage of pepsin in the gastric secretions. However, the exact cause of oversecretion of pepsin in higher animals such as primates is still largely unknown. One hypothesis offered is that only specific kinds of stress may produce destructive kinds of acid production. An animal experiment often cited in support of the explanation that specific kinds of stress cause ulcers was done by Brady (1958). Brady had two monkeys sit next to each other in restraining chairs. Both monkeys received electrical shock, but only one, called the *executive monkey*, could prevent the shock from occurring by pressing a certain lever. The other monkey also had a lever, but it had no effect on whether the shock occurred. Both monkeys received the same number of shocks. After 23 days of such experience, the executive monkey died. An autopsy revealed that he had developed a severe ulcer. A subsequent autopsy of his partner monkey showed him to be ulcer free. The results of Brady's experiment were quoted in the popular press, and it was easy for the layperson to see the similarity between the stress placed on the executive monkey and the stress placed on the business executive. Seligman (1975) has criticized Brady's results on methodological grounds. He points out that, in Brady's procedure, the more active monkey was likely to become the executive monkey; and the monkey that was more active might also be more prone to develop ulcers. Further, in contrast to Brady's findings, Seligman has found that, in higher animals, those subjects who do not have control of the aversive stimuli are more likely to develop ulcers.

Work done with human subjects suggests that specific types of emotions may be related to ulcer production. Observations pertinent to human ulcer production have been gathered fortuitously from people who have suffered physical accidents. For example, Wolf and Wolff (1947) had a "ringside seat" to observe what was going on in one man's stomach. At the age of 9, the man had drunk a bowl of scalding soup that burned out the end of his esophagus. Some time later, physicians attempted to insert a tube into his stomach so he could be fed, but the operation had to be stopped because the patient was in danger of dying. The incomplete operation left the man with a large hole through which part of his stomach protruded. Amazingly, the patient adjusted fairly well to such inconvenience. For example, he reportedly first chewed his food for taste and then deposited it into a funnel that carried the food down a rubber tube into his stomach. The patient worked at the hospital and, in return for his medical care, he allowed doctors to observe his stomach activity. From observations of this man's stomach, it became clear that the type of stomach secretions varied, depending on the emotion the man was experiencing. When the man was angry, there was an oversecretion of gastric fluids. This was not the case when the man was sad or otherwise emotionally aroused. The observation that primarily anger produced oversecretions of gastric acid is consistent with the hypotheses of some psychoanalytic theorists (F. Alexander, 1952).

Treatment. Like the explanations for their development, treatment for ulcers reflects physiological and psychological biases. Although psychotherapy may be effective in helping the patient handle stress more effectively, counseling probably won't change the underlying physiological determinants that predispose an individual to develop an ulcer: the person who tends to hypersecrete stomach acids probably will always be vulnerable to developing ulcers under stress. In light of this, people who develop ulcers should know that the proneness to ulcers doesn't necessarily indicate a psychological defect or weakness, but reflects a way of handling stress involving gastric hyperactivity. In serious cases of ulcers, surgical cutting of the vagus nerve may be performed. The vagus nerve stimulates the stomach to secrete gastric juices, so cutting it reduces the production of such juices. Because of the numerous side-effects often accompanying vagus-nerve surgery, it is done only as a last resort in treating ulcers.

Colitis

Less well known and less studied than stomach ulcers, *colitis* can be just as painful and potentially as damaging a gastrointestinal disorder.

Description.   There are two kinds of colitis: *mucous colitis* and *ulcerative colitis*. In mucous colitis, the mucous lining of the colon is dissolved and may be eliminated in the stools. As a result, the patient may experience pain whenever eating or eliminating. To avoid such discomfort, the person with mucous colitis typically eats less and, as a result, becomes tired, listless, run-down, and irritable. In ulcerative colitis, an ulcer forms in the mucous membrane of the colon, causing bleeding. Colitis may develop at any age and, once present, can become chronic.

Explanation.   As with ulcers, there appears to be an intimate linkage between emotions and colitis such that the symptoms of colitis typically worsen when the person is experiencing certain stresses. Engel (1975) describes colitis patients as neat and orderly, with an almost "uncanny perception of hostility or rejecting attitudes on the part of others" (p. 1645). In addition, he sees colitis patients as usually having a dependent relationship with one key person, most often a parent, and few (if any) other satisfying or deep relationships.

From the psychoanalytic perspective, the mother may be extremely important in determining whether the biologically predisposed person will develop colitis. In what could almost be termed a symbiotic relationship, the patient may be extremely sensitive to the mother's feelings and needs. Typically, in the family of colitis patients, the father may be unable to stand up to the mother and cannot protect the child from her. In the person who already has either genetic or prenatal potential to develop this inflammatory bowel disease, these stress-producing, damaging family relationships can lead to the development of colitis.

Treatment.   Treatment methods for colitis include psychoanalytic therapy and drugs. In psychoanalytic therapy, the therapist seeks to become the "key" person in the colitis patient's life and, through this relationship, to help the patient learn new, more effective ways of relating to people. If psychological methods and drugs don't calm the colon, then surgery may be indicated. Surgical treatment of colitis usually involves an *ileostomy* (an opening in the ileum, which is the lowest part of the small intestine opening into the large intestine) or a *colectomy* (removal of all or part of the colon or large intestine leading to the rectum), but is suggested only if there is intractable diarrhea or threat of further disease such as cancer.

RESPIRATORY DISORDERS

Although they are not so lethal as cardiovascular disorders or so frequent as digestive disorders, psychophysiological respiratory disorders strike a significant number of people. There are three major types: *hyperventilation, dyspnea,* and *asthma.* Hyperventilation, or overbreathing, is most clearly a consequence of anxiety. The individual who overbreathes may begin to feel light-headed, dizzy, and tingly in the fingers and feet. These behavioral sensations are frightening and tend to make the hyperventilator even more anxious. Shortness of breath, or dyspnea, also seems to have a psychogenic cause. Hyperventilation and dyspnea are usually mild and may occur within other disorders, such as anxiety neurosis. We will focus the rest of the section on asthma, a more severe and disabling respiratory disorder.

Description. In asthma, there is a narrowing of the airways of the trachea, major bronchia, and bronchioles. This narrowing of airways may be caused by increased sensitivity to substances ingested or inhaled, by bacteria, or by stress. Asthma attacks usually are characterized by *wheezing* and *rales* (whistling sounds emitted when air is expired) and can be very frightening, as shown in the following personal experience.

PERSONAL EXPERIENCE: *Asthma*

I had asthma as a child. I no longer have asthma attacks, but I can remember quite vividly what they were like. One attack I remember especially clearly because it took place just before my seventh birthday party. My mother was getting everything in readiness for the party. My friends from school were going to come over at four o'clock, and I was putting out their party stuff . . . you know, the plates and favors and decorations. About quarter to four—I remember the time because I was asking my mother the time at five-minute intervals—I suddenly began to have a hard time catching my breath. The more I tried to take a deep breath the less I was able to succeed. I stopped and sat down and tried to take a breath and found that I could not; no matter how hard I tried to get that breath that I needed to feel like I was getting enough air, I could not. I began to gasp. My mother was in the kitchen and so did not know my plight. I felt really frightened at that point . . . all alone, unable to get any air. My gasps became louder and more labored, and that's when my mother heard me and came rushing into the room. By that time I was on the floor and if my mother's expression was any indication of how I looked, I must have looked bad. By the time the emergency police van arrived I was nearly blue and making the most horrible noises. I remember them and so does my mother to this day. The feeling of being able to breathe again after the oxygen was given to me was absolutely wonderful. I was so tired, though, that I slept on the way to the hospital. It's funny, even telling you this, you know, makes my palms sweat and makes me feel very uncomfortable.

Explanations. Because it is such a frightening set of symptoms, asthma has always enjoyed a great deal of theoretical interest. To explain and be able to cure asthma would be important to the parents of asthma victims and to the victims themselves.

Attempts to find a higher incidence of psychiatric symptoms in asthmatics have largely been unsuccessful. In one investigation, Graham, Rutter, Yale, and Pless (1967) studied the personality structure of a large population of 9-, 10-, and 11-year-old youngsters. Although psychiatric difficulties were more frequent in asthmatics than in physically normal children, these symptoms were no more frequent than in children who were normal but suffered from some other *physical* disorder. In essence, asthmatics seem to be a bit more neurotic and nervous than those who aren't asthmatic, but they have no consistent set of unique "asthmatic" personality traits (Tamarin, 1963; Van der Valk, 1960).

Psychodynamic theorists postulate that asthma may be caused by an unconscious fear of loss of the mother. Based on the findings of a study of 27 asthmatic patients undergoing psychoanalytic treatment, it was concluded that the central emotional component of asthma was "the repressed cry for the lost mother" (F. Alexander, 1952). Other psychological theorists believe that the major emotions prior to an asthma attack may be anger or anxiety caused by the loss of the "mothering one" (Knapp, Mushatt, Nemetz, Constantine, & Friedman, 1970).

Instead of focusing on personality traits or internal conflicts, physiological explanations for asthma focus on central-nervous-system functioning. More specifically, the physiological explanations have linked asthma to abnormal brain-wave patterns as measured by electroenceph-

290

SECTION IV:
DISORDERS
RELATED TO
ANXIETY AND
STRESS

alograms (EEGs). Although some investigators believe that abnormal EEG readings mean that asthma may be related to a specific nervous-system defect, most investigators don't say exactly what these abnormal EEG findings mean. However, there seems to be substantial agreement among researchers that nerve centers controlling respiratory activity may become hyperexcited for some unknown reason, triggering asthmatic behavior. If one could quiet these hyperactive nerve centers, then asthma attacks might be prevented. In support of nervous-system involvement in producing asthma, chemical means to calm nerve centers often have reduced the number and intensity of asthma attacks. The physiological explanation for asthma is supported by research showing that asthmatic children tend to have a higher mean heart rate and higher skin temperature than nonasthmatic children (Hahn, 1967).

There appears to be some support for both a psychological *and* a physiological explanation of asthma. However, this apparent dilemma can be resolved by assuming that *both* theories are accurate and that asthma may very well be produced in more than one way. Rees (1964) proposed that there may be three major causes of asthma: an *allergic* cause (a biological sensitivity to substances such as dust), an *infective* cause (as a result of some infective disorder), and a *psychological* cause (an emotional instigator such as anxiety, anger, or tension). All three causes are believed to be responsible for a significant number of asthma attacks.

Separating asthmatics into three separate etiological groups has allowed for a more accurate testing of hypotheses concerning the development and maintenance of asthmatic behavior. For example, although French and Alexander's (1941) dynamic explanation of asthma is much referred to, there is little empirical or research support for their theoretical hypotheses. However, etiological distinctions among asthmatics may yield specific groups in which the interaction or dynamics of the family is more predictive of asthmatic behavior.

Treatment. The treatment of asthmatic behavior generally has mirrored the psychological and physiological explanations offered for its development. The results of psychological treatments for asthma are equivocal. For example, Kelly and Zeller (1969) conclude that findings on the effectiveness of psychotherapy in treating asthma are inconclusive. However, behavior-modification techniques appear to enjoy some success.

Phillip, Wilde, and Day (1971) investigated the differential effects of hypnotism and relaxation training on the respiration of asthmatics. They assumed that asthmatic people could be separated into groups based on the different triggering mechanisms for their asthmatic attacks. They reasoned that psychological treatment in the form of hypnotism would be more effective in changing respiratory behavior of those subjects who had a psychological cause for their asthma attacks than for those subjects who had an infective cause. As they hypothesized, asthmatics who didn't respond to skin-testing for an allergic basis for their symptoms were more responsive to suggestion and behavioral relaxation procedures than others. In addition, they found that, regardless of the triggering source, almost all asthmatics benefited from relaxation training in terms of gains in respiratory efficiency. This suggests that such therapeutic procedures could help break up the vicious circle of perceived shortness of breath, tension, feelings of loss of control and fear, and back to shortness of breath. Relaxation training may help asthmatics gain some control over the occurrence, or at least the severity, of attacks (Kotses, Glaus, Crawford, Edwards, & Scherr, 1976).

The Phillip, Wilde, and Day study placed asthmatic subjects into certain therapeutic groups according to whether they could be treated successfully by a specific technique. In a large-scale application of this procedure, Peshkin (1959) identified a group of children as asthmatic primarily for psychological reasons. His major criterion for including a child in this group was the lack of improvement after a year's chemical treatment of physiological desensitization. Peshkin reasoned that asthmatic children who didn't respond to such extended treatment probably had asthma with a psychological cause that originated in the home, between the children and their parents. Based on the assumption of a defective parent-child relationship as a cause of asthma, Peshkin performed a "parentectomy," moving the child from the home into a carefully supervised milieu-therapy program. The results were impressive: in 99% of the cases, the asthmatic children were discharged as being either "completely or substantially recovered." Even more impressive was the fact that 97% of the asthmatic children maintained their improvement after three years.

HEADACHES

Headaches are not so destructive as our first three groups of psychophysiological disorders, but they are more frequent. Relatively few of us will experience the distress of ulcers or suffer through an asthma or heart attack, but all of us have headaches. We often can point readily to the psychological precipitants of our own headaches—the big exam, the baby crying, or the abnormal-psychology book that has to be completed by a certain deadline. Headaches seem to be one of our common, shared psychophysiological experiences. Most headaches may be classified as *muscle-contraction headaches*, caused by long-sustained tension in the skeletal muscles of the scalp, shoulders, neck, and face. The muscle-contraction headache may be part of the cost of living in our high-powered society and won't be discussed further here. A less frequent, but far more serious, painful, and disabling kind of headache is the *migraine*.

Migraine

Description.   More correctly called a vascular headache of the migraine type, the migraine typically has the following symptom pattern (Frazier, 1969):

292

SECTION IV:
DISORDERS
RELATED TO
ANXIETY AND
STRESS

1. recurrent throbbing headaches, usually on one side of the head at onset
2. nausea, vomiting, and irritability commonly occurring at the height of the attack
3. temporary visual disorders preceding the headache
4. history of migraine in the immediate family
5. dizziness, sweating, and other vasomotor disorders during an attack
6. response to taking ergotamine tartrate if administered early in the attack
7. attack duration variable but commonly two to eight hours

The following personal experience allows us to see how much more serious a migraine headache is than the muscle-contraction headaches most of us experience.

PERSONAL EXPERIENCE: *Migraine Headaches*

I'm describing how it used to be when I had an incapacitating migraine (while I still get headaches, they're no longer severe enough to be incapacitating). The pain was confined to my right temple and would radiate outward from there. Any movement of my head or exposure to light or noise would amplify the pain. Consequently, I was forced to lie down in a dark and quiet room for hours at a time—often 6 to 8 hours—unable to sleep. Occasionally, I would drift into sleep but awaken with the headache still there. I am fortunate in that I do not suffer concomitant nausea and vomiting, a frequent complaint.

The forced inactivity in a dark, silent place tended to produce feelings of frustration, depression, and occasionally intense self-pity. These feelings were especially likely when the attacks clustered within a short period of time, which often they did. When the headache at last disappeared, I felt absolutely flat—great fatigue and no emotion. I would sleep a dreamless sleep—sort of a sleep of the dead.

Explanations. There has been substantial documentation of the role of psychological factors in the etiology of migraine headaches. L. C. Kolb (1963) and Selinsky (1939) described a typical migraine-headache victim as a tense, driving, obsessional perfectionist with an inflexible personality maintaining a store of bottled-up resentments that can neither be expressed nor resolved. Consistent with this description, when asked to report the circumstances preceding their migraine attacks, many victims state that they were in an emotionally stressful situation and felt tremendous amounts of rage.

In an attempt to find support for a psychological explanation of migraine headaches, Henryk-Gutt and Rees (1973) compared office workers who had migraine headaches with those who did not. They found that migraine sufferers *subjectively* experienced more symptoms of emotional distress than controls, but they didn't differ in the degree of real-life stresses that were objectively assessed. Although there is little argument with the conclusion that psychological stresses may be a significant precipitant of migraine attacks, migraine subjects appear to be predisposed by constitutional and *not* environmental factors to experience a greater reaction to the same quantity of stress than those who don't have migraine headaches.

Although there may be some debate concerning the role of psychological factors in the etiology of migraine headaches, there is agreement that the headaches are the direct result of the autonomic nervous system's dilating cranial blood vessels, including pain-sensitive arteries of the scalp. Migraines often can be induced in those prone to them by injecting substances (such as histamines) that dilate these arteries. A common treatment of migraine headaches involves administering chemical substances that constrict these same cranial arteries.

Treatment. Migraine headaches seem to be due to an interaction of a learned overreaction to stress with an inherited hypersensitivity of the cranial nerves and arteries. Treatment of migraine headaches typically focuses on either the physiological or the psychological component of the etiological pattern. Some of the more successful physiological treatments for migraines are tranquilizers, antidepressant drugs, histamine desensitization, surgery, and special diets. However, the most effective physiological treatment for migraine headaches has been the administration of *ergotamine tartrate* and its derivatives (trade name, Cafergot or Migral). Administration of ergotamine tartrate early in the migraine-headache attack usually restores the dilated vessels to their original state and reduces the severity of the headache. Some attempts have been made to find drugs that would prevent headaches, but few have been found that are worth the danger, the side-effects, or the risk of addiction.

Recently, behavior-modification techniques used separately or in combination with medication have shown promise in treating migraine headaches. These techniques are based on the assumption that, if a person could relax in response to the cues that a migraine headache was developing, this might lessen the response of the endocrine and autonomic neurons. Using a population of 17 migraine-headache sufferers, Mitchell and Mitchell (1973) found that pitting relaxation against the tension of migraine-headache cues was successful in reducing the number of migraine episodes and the duration of migraine headaches. Biofeedback methods also have enjoyed some success in lessening the impact of migraine pain.

CONCLUDING COMMENTS

Tension, stress, or anxiety can have tangible effects on our bodies. Some researchers estimate that about one-third of all working days lost to illness are attributable to the kind of anxiety-related psychophysiological disorders we have discussed. Whether there actually is more anxiety and stress now than in the past is really beside the point. The hundreds of thousands of people who are turning to self-relaxation techniques such as Zen, Yoga, and transcendental meditation seem to perceive themselves as burdened by stress and anxiety. Psychophysiological disorders such as ulcers and coronary heart disease used to be the domain of male adults. However, women and children now seem to be showing up with these disorders with alarming frequency (G. Alexander, 1975). For example, 20 years ago, males were 12 times more apt to die of a heart attack than females of the same age. Today that ratio has shrunk to four to one. As we discussed in Chapters 10 and 11, the control of anxiety and stress has become a problem

The increasing number of women and children reporting ulcers and heart disease underlines the increasing stress on these groups of people. (Photo by George Lazar.)

of great significance for all of us in the mental-health field. In the section to follow, we will continue to examine the role of control, but in the behavioral rather than in the feeling realm.

CHAPTER SUMMARY CHART

In this chapter, we discussed ways in which actual physiological disorders can arise out of psychological dysfunction:

Cardiovascular disorders	*Gastrointestinal disorders*
Coronary heart disease	Ulcers
Coronary personality	Stress produces excess
High-risk factors	stomach secretion
Essential hypertension	Executive monkeys
High blood pressure	Colitis: mucous and
More common in Black people	ulcerative
Suppression of anger	
Chemical treatment	

Respiratory disorders	*Headaches*
Hyperventilation, dyspnea,	Muscle-contraction headaches
and asthma	Migraine headache
Asthma is major form	Intense pain
Unconscious fear of	Perceptual symptoms
loss of mother	Nausea, weakness
Smothered cry	Drug treatment and
Abnormal EEG	behavioral methods
Parentectomy	

SECTION V
DISORDERS OF BEHAVIORAL SELF-CONTROL

Chapter 12
Personality-Development Disturbances

Chapter 13
Drug and Alcohol Addiction and Dependence

Chapter 14
Disorders of Sexual Behavior

Chapter 15
Calamitous Death: Suicide and Murder

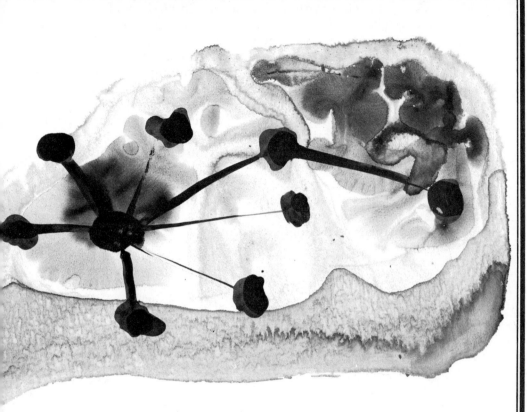

The disorders of behavioral self-control comprise a group in which overt maladaptive *behavior*, rather than thought and feeling disturbances or anxiety reactions, is the rule. The disorders of behavioral self-control differ from the psychoses and the neuroses in that they reflect a faulty development of the personality more than a change in an already formed personality under stress. In a parallel to physical disorders, a psychotic or neurotic person may be similar to a very good tennis player who is suddenly unable to play because he or she has developed a tennis elbow. People with disorders of behavioral self-control are similar to people who can't play tennis now because they never learned how to play at all or because they learned to play incorrectly. Within the group of patterns of behavior we call the disorders of behavioral self-control, we typically find people encountering difficulties because of some character flaw or distortion rather than because of any "disease process." In this classification of disorders, a *behavior*, and not a *feeling* such as anxiety, depression, or the like, is usually the focal symptom. From the perspective of most professionals, people classified as exhibiting disorders of behavioral self-control "act out" their problems against society rather than suffer personal distress and discomfort. Unlike those suffering from psychoses or neuroses, people with disorders of behavioral self-control often don't seek help for their "problems" until forced to do so by a society with which they are in direct conflict.

Disorders of behavioral self-control may be expressed in four general realms: crime, chemicals, sex, and violent death. When socially acceptable means of satisfying needs are not freely available, the possibility for developing the disorders of behavioral self-control may be increased. For example, people who have learned to care only for themselves and not for others may manifest the behavior pattern called *sociopathy*. People who can't use drugs and alcohol in socially acceptable moderation may become addicts. People who can't satisfy their sexual needs maturely may express sexual needs in a deviant way. Finally, people who can't find adaptive ways to cope with the stresses of life may choose to deal with the stress by ending their own lives or the life of another. These socially unacceptable responses to problems are usually more prevalent among men than women. For the most part, and for reasons that are not yet clear, disorders of behavioral self-control are primarily the domain of males.

CHAPTER 12
PERSONALITY-DEVELOPMENT DISTURBANCES

The personality-development disturbances are included as disorders of behavioral self-control because they represent instances in which social-behavior patterns most of us possess are either lacking or distorted in some way. One result of these developmental misfortunes can be that people with personality-development disturbances often find themselves unable to relate to other people or to society in continuously productive ways. Sooner or later, most people with such developmental disturbances come into conflict with society and are alienated from others or ridiculed. We have divided the personality-development disturbances into two major categories. In the first category, the *personality disorders*, we will describe patterns in which a person has a rigid personality style that he or she uses regardless of changes in situational requirements. Second, we will discuss the *socialization disturbances*, the most dramatic and troublesome forms of personality-development disturbances, which include dyssocial reactions and psychopathy, a pattern in which moral development may be so faulty that the person often experiences no sense of guilt. We will offer explanations for both categories of personality-development disturbances, but since these disorders are usually resistant to treatment, they allow for only limited discussion of corrective efforts.

PERSONALITY DISORDERS

In the personality disorders, a particular personality style is over-used. Most normal people have different types of behavioral responses available, depending on the situation; people with a personality disturbance typically use only one general style of response in most situations. The use of a single style often results in an inappropriate or rigid response. Further, the style that is adopted also may be seen as a milder form of patterns that, in their severest forms, could be considered psychoses or neuroses. The tendency to use one style of behavior to deal with a variety of situations may not be serious enough to bring the person to the attention of mental-health personnel and agencies, but it does reflect a less-than-optimal adjustment.

Descriptions

Paranoid Personality.   In *paranoid personality*, the individual's primary interpersonal style is marked by rigidity, unwarranted suspicion, jealousy, envy, interpersonal hypersensitivity, and a tendency to blame others and ascribe malicious intent to them (DSM-II) (American Psychiatric Association, 1968). Paranoid personality typically results in a person's being unable to establish close, trusting interpersonal relationships and often leaves him or her with a sense of isolation. The suspiciousness of the paranoid personality often puts others off, which can further reinforce the suspicious style. The effect of the paranoid style on others is shown in the following personal experience.

PERSONAL EXPERIENCE: *Paranoid Personality*

When I moved into my new neighborhood, I was pleased to find that most of my neighbors were quite friendly. That is, all except the guy in the house on the right of ours. About a week after we moved in, I got up real early and went out to start work on a fence for the yard. It must have been about seven o'clock when I got out there and drove in the first fencepost. Well, I couldn't believe it but, about ten minutes later, here comes this guy with a ball of string and some papers. And he tells me that he wants to help me not to violate the county ordinance about how fences have to be 6 inches on the land of the builder of the fence and that the lay of the land out back was such that it was hard to know the boundary without a line and survey drawings. He pulls out the survey drawings and shows me where our land meets and then goes about stretching a string from one corner of the property to the other. I just stood there . . . I actually felt a little afraid of him. . . . After he finished, he wished me luck and went back into his house. Later on he came out to check how I was doing, and he told me about the "hippies" that sometimes come through the neighborhood and he has lots of guns in the house just in case they start doing damage or going wild on drugs. I smiled. . . . We still live there and I know that the guy is a little strange, but he keeps a high-level executive job and seems basically stable . . . he's just a little more suspicious than the rest of the world.

Affective Personality. Just as the individual with a paranoid personality may be seen as the normal counterpart of the paranoid psychotic, the person with an *affective personality* may be considered similar to those with affective psychoses. The affective personality may exhibit alternating and recurring episodes of depression and elation not related appropriately to what is actually occurring. In the periods of depression, such people may be overly worried, pessimistic, and listless; in the elation phase, ambition, enthusiasm, and energy usually characterize their behavior (DSM-II). Those with whom affective people interact often feel uncomfortable in their presence. There is something unnerving about dealing with people whose moods are unpredictably up or down and who don't seem to respond emotionally to the realistic variations in the everyday world. When faced with undue stress, the affective personality can deteriorate into a pattern of affective psychosis such as those described in Chapter 8. From the person's own point of view, being at the whim of inordinate feelings isn't comfortable, as shown in the following personal experience.

PERSONAL EXPERIENCE: *Alternating Affective Personality*

Other people usually joke about me, but I just can't control the way I act. Sometimes I feel as high as a kite . . . ten minutes later I'll be sitting in my office feeling like I want to die. I've always been like this as long as I can remember. When I was a kid I used to fool around a lot with the other guys and then I'd come back to the house and my mother would say that she heard me laughing "like an ass" and that I'd made a fool of myself again. I'd sit down and feel just crappy. I notice now that after I really have a good time, I feel bad. It's almost as if I have to pay for the good feelings with an equal amount of bad feelings. Sometimes, when I feel bad, even a nice thing won't give me pleasure. When I'm up, though, everything looks good and I can't believe that anyone or anything can hurt me. Some of my friends think I'm the strangest person they ever met. Sometimes I like that and sometimes I'm hurt by it.

Schizoid Personality. The schizoid personality is characterized by withdrawal from others, shyness, reticence to interact, and often "eccentric" behavior (DSM-II). The schizoid person seems out of step in a group and often has little to do with peers. If intensified, the behavior of the schizoid person can become similar to that of the chronic schizophrenic person we described in Chapter 7 (extreme social isolation, inappropriate affect, and inability to communicate effectively). Schizoid personalities are often found among people raised in very sheltered environments or by parents who perhaps were schizoid or schizophrenic themselves. The following personal experience shows how a schizoid person appears to others.

PERSONAL EXPERIENCE: *Schizoid Personality*

My class had one boy in it who was really strange. He would stare at you with the weirdest look when you talked to him. He was usually dressed like a slob, usually he smelled like he hadn't taken a bath in weeks. Nobody talked to him . . . he never came to dances, football games, or club meetings. He did badly in school, never knew the answers when he was called on. He always made me nervous when I was around him. I really don't know why, but he made me uncomfortable. He made us all uncomfortable. I never knew what happened to him after we graduated. I guess I never really cared.

Hysterical Personality. Unlike the paranoid, affective, and schizoid personalities, which are similar to psychotic patterns, the *hysterical, obsessive-compulsive,* and *asthenic* personality patterns are similar to the neuroses. A hysterical personality style is marked by emotional instability, excess excitability, overreactivity, and a tendency to overdramatize (DSM-II). Frequently, hysterical people depend on others to feed their vanity. Hysterical people quite often "tell a good story" about their life events, making good things sound fantastic and bad things sound devastating. Nothing seems to please hysterical people more than to have others be jealous of successes and sympathetic to pain. They seek an audience; and, if attention-seeking at the level of a personality disorder isn't successful, there is some chance that more severe neurotic symptoms (such as hysterical conversions, dissociations, and the like) may develop. The characteristics of the hysterical personality style are shown in the following personal experience.

PERSONAL EXPERIENCE: *Hysterical Personality*

I have been so upset lately that I welcome this chance to tell about my problems. You ask what it's like to have my problems? I'll tell you . . . it's hell on earth . . . it's the pits . . . it's like a slow death at the hands of a torturer. My God, I cry myself to sleep each night, I wake up feeling lousy . . . I can't eat. Sure, I can go to work and most of the time I do fine, but when the worries about promotion hit me I stall like a car that's out of gas. I can't get going. All I can think about is that some of the other people will get promoted before me. If M—— gets promoted first, I'll just die . . . I really mean it. She got here two years after I did . . . it wouldn't be fair if she got promoted first. I mean I work and slave trying to keep the office running . . . everybody knows that. When I'm sick that place just stalls . . . nobody knows what to do . . . why they've even had to call me at home . . . from my sickbed I've had to get them out of jams nobody but me could solve. I mean, nobody.

Obsessive-Compulsive Personality. In contrast to the hysterical personality style, which is characterized by a dramatic overreaction to events, the obsessive-compulsive personality is marked by an excessive concern with sameness and the application of rigid standards of thought and behavior. Typically, compulsive people are most concerned with *behaving* in certain ways, and obsessive people, with *thinking* in certain ways. Many of us are aware of compulsive homemakers who clean the ashtrays almost before the ashes fall into them; such people aren't always compulsive neurotics, but the rigid adherence to rules of cleanliness may qualify them as compulsive personalities.

Like compulsive people, obsessive people frequently find it difficult to relax and enjoy life. However, obsessive people generally express their rigidity in terms of constant rumination, self-doubt, and undue conscientiousness. When people with an obsessive style find that they cannot control the degree to which they ruminate and that anxiety occurs in the absence of such rumination, the first step has probably been taken toward the development of obsessive neurosis.

Asthenic Personality. The *asthenic personality* most frequently is characterized by fatigue. Rather than becoming energized to activity by the presence of everyday stresses, the asthenic person seems to become tired. As shown in the following personal experience, the asthenic is typically without enthusiasm, often incapable of enjoying things that most people enjoy, and overly sensitive to physical and emotional stress.

PERSONAL EXPERIENCE: *Asthenic Personality*

I almost slept my way through college. I was always that way, but *then* it really hurt me. I failed out of school because I couldn't stay awake for my tests. I couldn't study. Every time I had some work to do, I felt sleepy and lay down for a while. The next thing I'd know, it'd be morning and I didn't study at all. The guys in my dorm used to call me "Womb-man." The name came from the idea that one of them got in a psych course that frequent sleeping represented a desire to go back to the safety of the womb. I guess I did feel secure in bed, but a womb? That was a lot of crap.

Explosive Personality. The people who exhibit the personality styles we've described thus far as a rule aren't dangerous. However, the explosive personality is frequently marked by dangerous episodic outbursts of physical aggression (DSM-II). The people who experience such outbursts usually interact nonaggressively and are bewildered as well as embarrassed by their sporadic explosive behavior. However, regardless of how bad they feel after an outburst, they usually can do little to prevent future occurrences of this rage reaction. The following personal experience typifies this sort of behavior.

PERSONAL EXPERIENCE: *Explosive Personality*

I'm basically a calm man. I try to be soft-spoken and kind. I make it my business not to hurt animals or living things of any kind. I have always tried to be a good husband and a good father to my daughters. But there's something that happens to me, something I can't explain and can't anticipate. I lose control of myself—I get angry and hurt the kids, I hurt my wife. The last time it happened, I had brought some work home from the office and was trying to get it done. My wife asked me if we had any money in the checking account, my younger daughter asked if I'd read her a book; I was getting very tense. A little later my older daughter hit the little one and the little one came crying to me. That was it! I blew up. I grabbed the older one and threw her to the floor and kicked her. She started to cry and my wife screamed at me. I took out after her and threatened to hit her, too. She took the kids out of the room and left me alone. After a few minutes I calmed down and felt like crying. That kind of thing happens to me about once every couple of months. I can't help it. If I could stop it, don't you think I would?

Explanations

The personality disorders may be precursors of many of the more serious disorders we discussed in earlier chapters. Because these styles aren't fully developed disorders, they seem not to have stimulated a large amount of theoretical interest. However, these disorders are ways of coping with life and of relating to others, and it is clearly important to understand them theoretically. In our opinion, David Shapiro (1965) has offered a fine theoretical explanation for personality styles.

Shapiro's perspective on psychological styles grows out of the tradition of psychoanalysis. According to Shapiro, the basic motivator for the development of different personality styles is the need to deal with, organize, and safely discharge *tension*. As you remember from Chapter 4, the psychoanalytic perspective assumes that behavior is motivated by a need for tension reduction, whether the tension is biological (as in the case of hunger) or psychological (as in the case of interpersonal anxiety). To Shapiro, different psychological styles represent different *tension-organizing systems*. These systems develop to help individuals make sense of what is going on around them. Thus, for example, some people may develop a paranoid style because dealing with others makes them anxious; if they keep their distance from others they won't become anxious. Such a view of the world can help people to make sense of what happens and to deal effectively with daily tensions. However, if an unusual or severe kind of tension is experienced, the paranoid style may need to become a *defense* against ego deterioration. When this occurs, the paranoid personality style may deteriorate into a diagnosable psychotic paranoid reaction.

According to Shapiro, psychological styles develop in order to process internal and external stimuli. People develop their unique ways of processing such stimuli as the result of *innate organizational configurations*. These innate configurations are composed of the basic psychological (mental, perceptual, physical) equipment with which each individual is born. From birth on, information from various sources and the tension resulting from too much conflicting information are dealt with in an individualistic way. Although the specific style of the adult isn't always clearly present in the child, even at early ages some children show the beginnings of a personality style by the manner in which they respond—or don't respond—to particular novel situations. Innate patterns result in each person's placing a unique "stamp" on all of his or her experiences. This "stamp" helps to shape the specific psychological defensive style of the adult. For example, one of us brought a frog to his son's preschool class as part of a class project. The frog elicited a wide variety of reactions from the children (consistent with the teacher's perceptions of them). Some children came forward and wanted to touch the frog and find out more about him. Some children spent most of the time screaming about how "yucky" frogs were and dramatically covered their eyes and made motions as if they were going to vomit. Other children totally ignored the frog and kept doing what they were doing. Still others began to yawn and act as though they didn't care. The varied reactions of the children to the frog may be viewed as indicators of potential personality styles in adults.

Generally, we may consider all of the personality disorders as reflections of individualized ways of dealing with the world. Each of us, in his or her own way, sees the world slightly differently than other people. What

Some people may seem to act in eccentric and inappropriate ways but are actually dealing with their world as best they can. This man brings two pet rabbits to the beach in his bicycle basket. He says they like the beach. (Photo by George Lazar.)

is stressful to one of us may be enjoyable to another. The nature of any person's reaction to events in the world must not be seen as independent of that person. Shapiro notes, in this regard, that people respond to the outcome of severe stress differently, depending on their previous styles of coping with stress. The same stress can produce a compulsive neurosis in one individual and a hysterical conversion in another. It is in this context that the personality styles take on their greatest importance in our study of people who are different.

SOCIALIZATION DISTURBANCES

People with personality styles such as those described in the first part of this chapter rarely are formally diagnosed, because they generally don't cause much trouble for themselves or others. Socialization disturbances, however, are characterized by behavior patterns that are frequently of concern to society and that, if identified, frequently warrant incarceration, rehabilitation, and treatment. Within the group we have called the socialization disturbances, we include dyssocial personality and psychopathy.

Dyssocial Personality

Dyssocial personality represents a type of disorder in which faulty socialization is the primary contributor to a person's being different. The dyssocial person isn't considered truly abnormal from the perspective of DSM-II, for although such a person typically commits crimes against society, he or she is not seen as having any basic psychological defect. Rather, the dyssocial individual is thought to have developed in a setting in which crime or other activities judged by the larger society as unacceptable were accepted as "normal." People raised in such "deviant subcultures" are considered different from the perspective of the major culture, but from the point of view of their own group they may be appropriately adjusted. Just as we see the dyssocial person as different, were we to enter the dyssocial subculture, we would stand a good chance of being considered deviant and of being treated as such.

In terms of explanations, the dyssocial personality really requires none other than the fact that the person has adequately adopted the rules and values of his or her subculture. The problem is not the person, but the values of the subculture that are in opposition to those of the major culture.

Psychopathy

Psychopathy is more widely known than dyssocial personality. One reason for this notoriety may be that the term *psychopath* is often used in descriptions of criminals; for example, a newspaper account of a murder may refer to a "psychopathic killer." The general public frequently holds the misconception that all criminals are psychopaths and vice versa. In truth, however, psychopathy, which is also known as *antisocial personality*, is a specific pattern of personality-development disturbance that may sometimes be associated with criminal behavior.

Description. Although there are a variety of points of view regarding exactly what makes a person a psychopath, one very clear descriptive statement comes from the work of Hervey Cleckley (1976). In *The Mask of Sanity*, Cleckley notes that the psychopath is characterized by superficial charm and intelligence, absence of any signs of irrational thinking, absence of any signs of neurosis or anxiety, insincerity and unreliability, incapacity for loving or relating to others, inability to learn from punishment, and the lack of a meaningful life plan. Generally, psychopaths don't seem to be governed by such things as morals, guilt, or shame. They seem to be driven by the philosophy "I want what I want when I want it and nothing and nobody will stand in my way."

Dyssocial people are considered deviant by the major culture but may be appropriately adjusted within their subculture. (Photos by Marc Rattner.)

Psychopaths often use extraordinary insight into the workings of others to charm and manipulate them into doing what is wanted. Many psychopathic people are likable at first. However, if they want something, they will rarely hesitate to use any means to manipulate you and use you, without regard for your feelings, to get what they want. When wit and charm don't succeed, some psychopaths will turn to violence.

The psychopath's skill at manipulation is pointed out by Karpman (1961), who noted that psychopaths can simulate emotional reactions and affectional feelings for others when it will help them to obtain their goal. Karpman delineates two basic kinds of psychopaths: the *aggressive-predatory* type, who is aggressive and callous in the active pursuit of desired goals; and the *passive-parasitic*, who tends to "bleed" others of whatever he or she wishes from them through passive manipulation.

There are several alternatives to Karpman's categorization of the psychopathic person. Arieti (1967), for example, has suggested that there are *simple psychopaths*, who exhibit an inability to delay gratification of needs for any length of time, and who will not or *cannot* alter their current behavior in order to avoid later punishment. *Complex psychopaths* also exhibit an inability to delay gratification, but they differ in having a desire to "get away with" doing whatever they wish. The complex psychopathic person tends to be intelligent and to be able to wield and manipulate power. This group may include very successful and imaginative criminals, as well as some politicians and high-level businessmen. The view of events from the perspective of the psychopathic person is shown in the following personal experience.

PERSONAL EXPERIENCE: *Psychopathic Personality*

I have agreed to write this only because I am safe from any prosecution and cannot be harmed if this remains confidential. Anyway, most of what I will recount happened over 30 years ago. I am a professor of biology and have been for over 35 years. When I first began my teaching career, I had a great many things I wanted to do. I wanted to become a well-known and respected microbiologist, I wanted to attain a tenured faculty position at _____ University, I wanted to be chairman of my department someday. Lots of things. But I had always wanted lots of things; as a child I can remember wanting a bullet that a friend of mine had brought in to show the class. I took it and put it into my school bag and when my friend noticed it was missing, I was the one who stayed after school with him and searched the room, and I was the one who sat with him and bitched about the other kids and how one of them took his bullet. I even went home with him to help him break the news to his uncle, who had brought it home from the war for him.

But that was petty compared to the stuff I did later. I wanted a Ph.D. very badly, but I didn't want to work very hard—just enough to get by. I never did the experiments I reported; hell, I was smart enough to make up the results. I knew enough about statistics to make anything look plausible. I got my master's degree without even spending one hour in a laboratory. I mean, the professors believed anything. I'd stay out all night drinking and being with my friends and then the next day I'd get in just before them and tell 'em I'd been in the lab all night. They'd actually feel sorry for me. I did my doctoral research the same way, except it got published and there was some excitement about my findings. The research helped me get my first college teaching job. There my goal was tenure.

The rules at my university were about the same as at any other. You had to publish and you had to be an effective teacher. "Gathering" data and publishing it was never any problem for me, so that part was fine. But teaching was evaluated on the basis of forms completed by students at the end of each semester. I'm a fair to good teacher, but I had to be sure that my record showed me as excellent. The task was simple. Each semester, I collected the evaluation forms, took out all the fair to bad ones and replaced them with doctored ones. It would take me a whole evening, but I'd sit down with a bunch of different-colored pens and pencils and would fill in as many as 300 of the forms. Needless to say, I was awarded tenure.

This account demonstrates psychopathy in a controlled environment and involves a pattern of noncriminal behavior performed by a person who, as McCord and McCord (1964) note, feels little or no *guilt*. While no one psychopath manifests all of the signs identified by Cleckley and others, the professor we have just heard from certainly exemplifies, from a clinical perspective, this socialization disturbance.

Clinical examples, however, are but one source of descriptive information about psychopathic behavior. There is ample research evidence as well that differentiates psychopaths from normal people. For example, in research on psychological factors, Lykken (1957) found that psychopathic criminals tend to manifest less anxiety than other criminals. In addition, Kingsley (1956) reported that psychopaths showed more impulsivity, aggressiveness, hostility, and immaturity than normal people on the Rorschach inkblot test. In studies of physiological factors, Hare (1968a, b) has found that sympathetic-nervous-system arousal is lower among psychopaths than among normal people. Hare (1970) reports other data that indicate that psychopaths may be less responsive to emotional experiences and that, if they do respond to stress, the responses can only be seen in their behavior—not in their physiological functioning, as would be the case in a normal person. Thus, a psychopath may *act* frightened, if fear is a response appropriate to his current need, but his biochemistry will show little sign of actual sympathetic arousal (see Chapter 6).

In addition to the research evidence on psychological and physiological differences between psychopaths and normal people, there are data indicating that psychopaths may be *cortically* underaroused. In other words, at the level of the functioning of the cortex, the psychopath has a lower level of brain activity than normal people and, as a result, tends to seek more stimulation. Further, psychopaths don't learn such things as conditioned fears as well as normal people (Hare, 1970).

Explanations. Several explanatory perspectives—the biological-genetic, the psychological, and the family-process—have made significant contributions to a better knowledge of the origins of psychopathy. Each perspective, however, has fallen short in one way or another.

There is some evidence for a genetic component in psychopathy. For example, Slater and Cowie (1971) have reported a higher-than-normal concordance rate for psychopathy when one member of a set of identical twins is psychopathic. Further, recent studies of adopted children in Denmark and the United States (Crowe, 1974; Schulsinger, 1972) indicate that adoptees isolated from biological parents who were diagnosed as psychopaths showed increased rates of sociopathy and criminality compared to normal people.

Although these data suggest a genetic component, they still don't adequately explain the physical mechanism through which psychopathy develops. Some researchers have suggested that psychopaths have lower levels of cortical arousal (Quay, 1965) and therefore need greater levels of stimulation. It is this search for stimulation that drives psychopaths and gets them in trouble. The level-of-stimulation hypothesis is supported by research suggesting that one early manifestation of psychopathy may be hyperactivity in children (Cantwell, 1972; Morrison & Stewart, 1973). Both hyperactivity and psychopathy in turn may be related to some as yet unidentified brain disorder. We do know that abnormal brain waves are more frequent in psychopaths and in others with known organic involvement than they are in normal people (Arthurs & Cahoon, 1964).

Counter to the biological theories, the psychological theories hold that psychopathy is not physical, but can be explained on the basis of some failure in proper learning and socialization. From the psychoanalytic perspective, for example, Greenacre (1945) suggested that the psychopath never develops a superego and that the lack of a conscience results in the lack of ability to feel guilt. Without a superego, id instincts can be satisfied by the psychopath's ego without regard to the ethical, moral, or cultural limitations felt by most individuals. Solomon, Turner, and Lessac (1968), in a further refinement of Greenacre's perspective, believe that the psychopath fails to learn to experience resistance to temptation and guilt because he is disciplined for misbehavior long after undesirable behaviors have been emitted. These researchers note that such delay of punishment is crucial to the development of the psychopath's later behavior patterns, in which the threat of punishment seems meaningless.

In addition to the focus on lack of conscience, some theorists believe that psychopaths have never learned to *role-play*. Gough (1948) theorized that, since psychopaths seem unable to learn to adopt the roles of others, they manifest only a "facsimile" of personality. They don't really feel the things they show, nor can they empathize with the internal feelings of others. This lack of ability to empathize with others may make psychopaths unable to judge their own behavior from the point of view of another and unable to experience embarrassment, loyalty, group identification, and the like. According to Gough, psychopaths can't be considerate of the needs and wishes of others because they can't in any way identify with them.

The inability of the psychopath to delay gratification of needs has also been posited as a causative factor (Mischel, 1966). Most normal people can put off gratification of needs. If given a choice between one candy bar today or five next week, most of us would choose to wait to get the larger reward. However, psychopaths typically don't delay rewards; with few exceptions, they want what they want *now*, and not a week later. Mischel feels that inability to delay rewards may originate in a childhood where promises were rarely kept by parents and, unless the child got what he could when it was offered, he rarely got anything. Such a history of empty promises can result in the inability to control impulses and delay need-gratification in normal, socially acceptable ways.

Although the psychological theories are intimately tied to family experiences such as child-rearing practices, the family-process theorists focus more on the adverse effects of a child's family experience as a whole than on any particular component of it. Hare (1970) has noted, "Perhaps the most popular generalization about psychopathy is that it is related to some form of early disturbance in family relationships, including parental loss, emotional deprivation [and] parental rejection" (p. 95). Greer (1964) found that six out of ten of the psychopaths he studied had lost a parent, and the majority of these had lost a parent before the age of 5. The frequency of parental loss was also shown in a study by Oltman and Friedman (1967), in which the authors concluded that it was not *death* of parents that caused the child's problems, but separation: the stresses and conflicts in the home prior to divorce or separation of the parents seemed to result in a greater frequency of psychopathy than did the death of a parent.

Some researchers have attempted to identify other family patterns in the childhood experiences of antisocial people. One thorough effort has been the work of L. Robins (1966), who isolated a large number of factors that differentiated psychopathic childhood and family characteristics from those of various psychotic patients. In Table 12-1 we have reproduced these factors. Generally, we can see that antisocial behavior is present from an early age and that conflict with the law is quite common. It must be remembered, however, that more sophisticated psychopaths are usually not included in the kinds of studies we have reported, because they go unidentified. The college professor

Table 12-1. *Childhood and family characteristics of sociopaths and other patients*

Characteristics	Percentage of Sociopaths (N = 94)	Percentage of Other Patients (N = 342)
Male	85	70
Referred for any antisocial behavior	95	66
For theft	40	20
For sexual problems (girls only)	29	11
Symptoms		
Theft	81	49
Incorrigible	79	52
Running away	71	39
Truancy	66	36
Bad companions	56	36
Sexual activity and excessive interest		
(Boys)	56	44
(Girls)	79	62
Stay out late	55	35
School discipline problems	53	31
Aggressive	45	26
Reckless	35	23
Impulsive	38	20
Slovenly	32	17
Enuretic	32	21
Lack guilt	32	14
Lying without cause	26	11
Median age at referral	(14)+	(13)+
Median age of onset	(7)+	(7)+
Girls only	(13)+	(8)+
Juvenile court case	79	39
Sent to correctional institution	51	17
School retardation at referral	68	55
Final school level, eighth-grade graduate	62	36
Antisocial toward		
Parents	73	50
Teachers and other authority figures	83	57
Strangers	39	21
Businesses	41	20
Family patterns		
Father sociopathic or alcoholic	53	32
Broken home, all causes	67	63
Divorce and separation	44	33
Impoverished home	55	38
Patient is only child	18	14
Patient is 1 of 4 children	27	17

+Numbers are ages, not percentages.
From *Deviant Children Grow Up*, by L. Robins. Copyright © 1966 by Williams & Wilkins Co., Baltimore. Reprinted by permission.

whose personal experience you read, although psychopathic, would probably not fit the childhood pattern of law-breaking and delinquency suggested by Robins's research. Nevertheless, he does fit the classic description of the psychopathic person. Any explanation of psychopathy and research into its cause must take into account the fact that it isn't so easy to find and study a broad sample of antisocial people as it is to study schizophrenic individuals.

Treatment.   Most of the disorders we have described in this text are in some way amenable to traditional forms of treatment. Unfortunately, this is not true of psychopathy. In fact, as Hare (1970), McCord and McCord (1964), and Cleckley (1976) have noted, traditional forms of psychotherapy are usually less effective with the psychopath. Chemical, biological, and other forms of physical therapies have no better record. Indeed, the psychopathic individual is extremely difficult to treat by any method.

The reasons for the difficulty are several. First of all, psychopaths often see nothing wrong with themselves, since it is society that is uncomfortable, not them personally. Second, traditional psychotherapy tends to be based upon the relationship between the therapist and the client. The psychopath, who is unable to form *any* relationship easily, certainly cannot form a strong therapeutic bond with a professional. Further, many psychopaths talk their way out of trouble or therapy by appearing to be normal and in control of themselves. Many therapists have been fooled into giving a psychopath a clean bill of health because the client "convinced" them that he or she had recovered and reformed. Finally, psychopaths may not be good candidates for psychotherapy, especially group psychotherapy, because many of them cannot empathize with others and may say and do things that are harmful to fellow group members.

Some attempts have been made to find special treatments for psychopaths. These attempts include *therapeutic communities,* or *milieus,* with strict behavioral regulation and firm authority. As opposed to the treatment of other mental problems, where self-government and self-direction are generally most effective, psychopathic children tend to respond more to authoritative leadership and firm discipline. For example, Craft, Stephanson, and Granger (1964) found that such children treated under an authoritarian regime got into trouble with the law far less than another group that had received more democratic treatment. Although not widely used or extremely successful, the therapeutic-community approach is one treatment available for the psychopath. The majority of these individuals unfortunately are sent to penitentiaries rather than hospitals, and many leave prison as they entered it—driven by impulse, feeling no guilt, and caring for no one.

CONCLUDING COMMENTS

Some theoreticians have expanded the idea of personality style to explain the existence of other behavior disorders. For example, Robert Carson (1969) views personality disorders as a direct result of persistent and potentially maladaptive styles of behaving. Like Harry Stack Sullivan, Carson believes most of the maladaptive personality styles result because disordered people are "hung up" in the maintenance of their styles regardless of situational demands. Carson reasons that a prime motivator for the adoption of such rigid behavioral styles is avoidance of anxiety. That is, people behave in a certain rigid style because it helps them feel safe and secure. To maintain such safe feelings, these people try to control events by always behaving in the same manner. Much like a broken clock which, although not running, is correct twice daily, the rigid maintenance of a specific behavioral style can result in a person's acting appropriately in *some* settings, but inappropriately in most.

CHAPTER SUMMARY CHART

In this first chapter on disorders of behavioral self-control, we discussed the personality disturbances, a group of diagnosable yet rarely treated patterns of being different:

Descriptions	*Explanations*
Paranoid personality	Shapiro:
Affective personality	Psychological styles
Schizoid personality	Tension-organizing systems
Hysterical personality	Innate configurations
Obsessive-compulsive personality	
Asthenic personality	
Explosive personality	

We then discussed the socialization disturbances, including *dyssocial personality*, which occurs when a normal adjustment is made to an abnormal culture, and *psychopathy:*

Descriptions	*Explanations*	*Treatment*
Cleckley	Biological-genetic theory	Traditional forms
The mask of sanity	Adopted children	of treatment
No guilt or shame	Cortical-arousal problems	not effective
Simple psychopath	Hyperactivity	Authoritarian
Complex psychopath	Psychological-social theory	milieus
	No superego	
	No resistance to temptation	
	Inability to role-play	
	Family theories	
	Parental rejection	
	Parental loss	

CHAPTER 13
DRUG AND ALCOHOL ADDICTION AND DEPENDENCE

Drug and alcohol abuse involves poor control over the ingestion of foreign substances into the body in order to achieve some change in mood state. People who possess a certain personality style may be more prone than others to ingest chemicals to change their mood, but there is not yet any conclusive evidence that personality type is related clearly to drug and alcohol abuse.

The use and abuse of mind-altering chemicals such as alcohol, marijuana, cocaine, opium, heroin, nicotine, LSD, and a host of other psychoactive substances, legal and illegal, has had significant effects on our society. Although some would argue that alcohol should be placed in a different class from the other drugs, it is our position that alcohol is no different from or less dangerous than other often abused chemicals.

Unlike people manifesting other forms of disordered behavior, drug users are considered by many as responsible for their own problems and often aren't seen or treated as "ill." Many social stigmas have been associated with the abuse of chemicals, and the concept of drug addiction as a "disease" hasn't been widely accepted. Regardless of how the drug problem is perceived, however, we cannot deny its existence or its effect on large numbers of people in our population.

317

CHAPTER 13:
DRUG AND
ALCOHOL
ADDICTION
AND
DEPENDENCE

In this chapter, we first will familiarize you with some of the special language of drug use and the specific classifications of drug behavior. Next, we will deal with alcoholism. Although similar to other addictive drugs in its social and interpersonal effects upon its victims, alcohol use is so widespread that it merits separate consideration. In a third section of the chapter we will describe other psychologically or physiologically addictive chemicals.

THE DEFINITIONS AND CLASSIFICATIONS OF DRUG USE

The majority of forms of abnormal behavior are usually defined by observation of behavioral symptoms, but abnormal drug use also may include significant physiological manifestations. The traditional categorization of drug abuse is based primarily upon the kind and degree of these physiological reactions. A newer typology of drug usage, prepared by the National Commission on Marihuana and Drug Abuse (1973), is based upon *frequency* and *context* of drug use.

A significant number of "down and outers" reached their place in life because of alcohol addiction. (Photo by David Powers.)

Current Definitions and Classification

The current official classification system defines physiological addiction to drugs as characterized by *habituation* (increased bodily tolerance to the drugs) and *withdrawal symptoms*. Habituation leads to an increased dosage requirement: more and more of a drug is needed to maintain a given level of effect. Withdrawal symptoms occur when a person suddenly stops using the chemical to which he or she is addicted. The severity and form of withdrawal vary from drug to drug, but they may be ordered generally from greatest to least danger to life thus: minor tranquilizers (such as Valium), barbiturates (such as Seconal), alcohol, and heroin or morphine. The placement of minor tranquilizers first and heroin last in terms of lethality may surprise some of you, but it reflects the available data.

Different from physiological addiction, *psychological dependency* refers to the need for a given drug under certain situational or circumstantial conditions. For example, the student who feels the need to take amphetamines to remain alert prior to an exam *and* who feels anxious about the exam if he or she hasn't taken the drug would probably be considered psychologically dependent on that drug. Such psychological dependence can occur with substances such as chewing gum, Life Savers, and various foods, as well as drugs, and may exist with or without true physiological addiction.

Besides the possibility of being physiologically addicted or psychologically dependent on drugs, people can also *abuse* drugs when using them in a manner for which they were not meant or at a dose or frequency level higher than is medically appropriate. The homemaker or businessman who has a prescription for two Valium every four hours and who takes six may not be addicted, but she or he is abusing the drug. Likewise, many instances of getting very drunk can be defined as drug abuse.

The three classifications of addiction, dependence, and abuse have frequently been misapplied to drug-taking behavior and effects. For example, some believe that people who use marijuana frequently are addicted in the same sense that heroin users are, but evidence suggests they may only be "dependent."

A Typology of Drug-Using Behavior

In an attempt to clarify the frequent confusion and misuse of the traditional labels for drug usage, the National Commission on Marihuana and Drug Abuse (1973) developed a new classification of drug-usage patterns. The commission defined five classes of drug usage, based primarily upon situational factors, frequency, and physiological involvement.

Experimental use, the first of the five classes, is defined as a short-term trial of one or more drugs with a maximum frequency of usage of ten times per drug. It is believed that this type of drug use is usually motivated by the person's curiosity and desire for new experiences and most often

319

CHAPTER 13:
DRUG AND
ALCOHOL
ADDICTION
AND
DEPENDENCE

occurs in the company of other experimenting friends. Experimental use may be seen as low-risk drug usage in that it rarely involves physiological or psychological addiction. Sitting around at a party trying some marijuana for social reasons is an example of experimental usage.

Social-recreational use is similar to experimental use in that it typically occurs in group or social settings. However, it differs in that the drug use is typically more formalized and regular. The risk of addiction is considered low in users of drugs such as marijuana but higher in social-recreational users of cocaine or heroin.

In *circumstantial-situational* drug use, rather than experimenting or indulging in recreational use, people take a drug in order to obtain a specific effect necessary for coping with a specific situation. For example, the student who uses an "upper" or stimulant to study for every exam or the professional athlete who must take some drug before each game would fit this category. Generally, drug use is halted when the task for which the drug was taken is completed. In most cases, little or no physical or psychological dependence occurs. The greatest danger in circumstantial-situational drug use is that the necessity for the drug-provided boost may spread to new situations and circumstances, and the user may find that he or she requires the effect more frequently. If the drug use spreads or increases in frequency, then it may be classified in one of the more severe categories.

Intensified drug use differs from the first three classes because of the presence of *long-term* drug usage. The user in this group usually takes a drug a minimum of once per day to maintain some constant level of drug effect. The most frequent format is persistent self-medication, such as the taking of daily tranquilizers or barbiturates. Another manifestation may be the executive who *needs* a drink every day at lunch and upon arriving home. People entrenched in intensified use often perceive their drug use as a normal part of everyday life; often there is moderate physiological and psychological addiction, but daily functioning is usually not hampered severely.

Compulsive drug use, the fifth and most severe class, includes both high-frequency and high-intensity drug usage continuing over a long period of time. Typically, the person is psychologically and physiologically dependent on chemical substances. If attempts are made to stop drug intake, withdrawal symptoms generally occur and severe illness and even death may result. Individual and social functioning in this class of user typically deteriorates, and the motivation to continue drug use seems stronger than the person's ability to deal with the addiction. The compulsive user often becomes preoccupied with obtaining drugs and may be forced to resort to crime in order to support the drug habit. However, not everyone in this category is a "junkie" or "down-and-outer"; many people who are in high-status positions or are wealthy enough to support this degree of drug usage aren't identified and can continue their destructive patterns, unhampered, for years.

Individuals who fall into the first three categories of drug usage prepared by the commission don't usually present problems in terms of disordered behavior. However, serious behavioral difficulties do occur in people who are intensive and compulsive drug users. As we will see, the alcoholic may be classified as either intensified or compulsive; the heroin addict is probably compulsive. It is our belief that the commission's typology is clear and helpful and may do much to put drug use in its proper perspective.

ALCOHOL

Most of us have heard about and perhaps snickered at the activities of groups such as the Women's Christian Temperance Union (WCTU) earlier in this century. In their battle against "Demon Rum," these women attempted to save family and home from the ravages of alcoholism. The WCTU, despite all its efforts, and Prohibition, with all its legal and social nightmares, did little to stem the tide of alcoholism. One out of every 20 people now living in the United States is an alcoholic. If we assume that, on the average, the alcoholic affects the lives of at least three other people, the staggering extent of the alcoholism problem becomes even clearer. Yet, in so many ways, we calmly accept what has been called "the national addiction." The drunk is a favorite subject for many comedians and story tellers. To drink alcohol is to be accepted in many social groups. Many young people are introduced to drinking by rock-music stations that offer up a combination of popular singers and advertisements for cheap soda-pop-flavored "youthful" wines. A whiskey company once offered a bicentennial special—a gallon of whiskey for $17.76, as if to say that, to be patriotic, you also have to be a heavy drinker.

In many ways, our society teaches us that alcohol use is acceptable. How many of us remember the cowboy movies in which, just before a gunfight in the street, one of the participants takes a quick gulp of whiskey in the saloon for "courage"? Many wine and beer commercials on television and radio suggest that alcohol is somehow different from and less dangerous than the other drugs we misuse. As we will see, however, nothing could be further from the truth.

Description

Alcohol addiction, or alcoholism, is but one of a variety of possible complications associated with the abuse of this chemical. Since it seems that the disorder appears in more than one form, there have been several attempts to classify the variations of the alcohol addictive pattern. Indeed, the percentage of alcoholics who fit the "down-and-out" stereotype is small (about 5%). The great majority of alcoholics are members of the working class or a higher class, live with their families, and hold down a good job.

321

CHAPTER 13:
DRUG AND
ALCOHOL
ADDICTION
AND
DEPENDENCE

Alcoholics–Who Are They?

The National Institute of Alcohol Abuse and Alcoholism (NIAAA) has published (1972) a lengthy report on the occurrence of drinking problems. We will mention some of the more stable of their findings so that you may see how alcohol-related problems manifest themselves.

Consumption rates: Americans consume, on the average, 2.61 gallons of alcohol per year. The Pacific states and New England lead with averages of around 3 gallons per year; the south-central states (Alabama, Mississippi, Louisiana, and Arkansas) trail with a rate of 1.63 gallons.

Sex: Men drink more than women and are much more likely to become alcoholics. Heavy drinking is most likely to occur in both men and women between the ages of 45 and 49.

Occupation: Most professionals and businessmen (83% of them) drink, but they are less likely to become heavy drinkers than people lower on the occupational ladder. Generally, the lower the occupational level, the more likely alcoholism is to develop out of heavy drinking.

National origin: Americans whose fathers were born in Ireland, Italy, or Great Britain report the highest percentage of drinkers among them (around 90%). Of these three nationalities, the Irish claim the highest percentage of *heavy* drinkers (33%).

Socioeconomic level: Among both men and women, the lowest socioeconomic group had a *smaller* percentage of drinkers than the highest group. The percentage of *heavy* drinkers, however, did not differ according to socioeconomic status.

National drinking patterns: France and Italy are by far the leaders in world alcohol consumption (6.53 and 4.01 gallons per year per person respectively). The United States is in the middle of the pack (2.61), with Finland (1.03), Iceland (0.96), and Israel (0.82) claiming the lowest alcohol intake. Occurrence of alcohol-related problems seems to parallel these consumption rates fairly closely.

One useful classification system has been proposed by Jellinek (1960), who places alcoholism on a continuum of degree of severity and incapacitation. The Alpha alcoholic, the first of four types, tends to rely upon alcohol to reduce or relieve emotional or physical pain but doesn't usually lose control over use of the drug. Interpersonal relationships may deteriorate when the person finds that use of alcohol is frequently more important than relating to others. In the second type, the Beta alcoholic, physical problems caused by the use of alcohol occur in addition to interpersonal difficulties. These physical diseases may include cirrhosis of the liver and ulcers, but physical or psychological *dependence* is not present. Gamma alcoholism is one step worse than

The typical alcoholic American

young · old · male · female

black · white · rich · poor

employed · unemployed · executive · laborer

student · doctor · immigrant · native born

**There's no such thing as typical.
We have all kinds. Nine million alcoholic Americans.
It's our number one drug problem.**

FOR INFORMATION OR FOR HELP, WRITE: NATIONAL CLEARINGHOUSE FOR ALCOHOL INFORMATION, BOX 2345, ROCKVILLE, MARYLAND 20852
U.S. DEPARTMENT OF HEALTH, EDUCATION, AND WELFARE · PUBLIC HEALTH SERVICE · ALCOHOL, DRUG ABUSE AND MENTAL HEALTH ADMINISTRATION

NIAAA
NATIONAL
INSTITUTE
ON ALCOHOL
ABUSE AND
ALCOHOLISM

Beta. There is physiological dependence such that cessation of drinking produces physiological withdrawal symptoms. Gamma drinkers have usually lost control of their drinking and may exhibit significant signs of physical, psychological, and social deterioration. The last and most severe form Jellinek describes is the Delta alcoholic. Here the drinker *cannot* abstain from drinking for any period of time and usually doesn't experience the brief periods of

323

CHAPTER 13:
DRUG AND
ALCOHOL
ADDICTION
AND
DEPENDENCE

WHAT KIND OF DRINKER ARE YOU?

TAKE THIS TEST AND FIND OUT FOR YOURSELF.

☐ 1. Do you think and talk about drinking often? ☐ 2. Do you drink more now than you used to? ☐ 3. Do you sometimes gulp drinks? ☐ 4. Do you often take a drink to help you relax? ☐ 5. Do you drink when you are alone? ☐ 6. Do you sometimes forget what happened while you were drinking? ☐ 7. Do you keep a bottle hidden somewhere — at home or at work — for quick pick-me-ups? ☐ 8. Do you need a drink to have fun? ☐ 9. Do you ever just start drinking without really thinking about it? ☐ 10. Do you drink in the morning to relieve a hangover?

If you had four or more "yes" answers, you may be one of the nine million Americans with a drinking problem. For a free booklet, write: N.I.A.A.A., Box 2045, Rockville, Md., 20852.

NIAAA

NATIONAL
INSTITUTE
ON ALCOHOL
ABUSE AND
ALCOHOLISM

U.S. DEPARTMENT OF HEALTH, EDUCATION, AND WELFARE • Health Services and Mental Health Administration

DHEW Publication No. (HSM) 72 9087   For sale by the Superintendent of Documents, U.S. Government Printing Office, Washington, D.C. 20402 · Price 18 cents; $11.25 per 100   Stock Number 1724-0188

The National Institute of Alcohol Abuse and Alcoholism has launched a public-education program to make people more aware of the negative effects of alcohol.

sobriety of the Gamma drinker. In the Delta alcoholic, cessation of drinking usually leads to severe physiological withdrawal symptoms. Although not universally accepted, Jellinek's system does provide a useful means of conceptualizing the several varieties of alcoholism. People commonly progress through these states of drinking behavior, and the Alpha alcoholic of today may be the Delta alcoholic of tomorrow.

The special misery of the alcoholic is underlined in the following personal experience, offered in response to the question, How does it feel to be an alcoholic?

PERSONAL EXPERIENCE: *Alcoholism*

That's a tough question. . . . It's miserable. . . . You work all day . . . at about four-thirty you start getting a craving for the bottle. You stop on the way home from work and get a bottle. . . . You go home, turn the tube on and start drinking. You pass out . . . wake up about one o'clock in the morning and can't go back to sleep. My stomach started hurting so bad that I could hardly move. . . . I was doubled over in pain. Doc told me it was my liver and pancreas all swollen up. My family's gone. . . . My wife was crazy anyway, but after she left two years ago the drinking got worse. I had to leave the house I lived in since I was a kid. . . . I lost my job . . . had to live in an apartment with a friend. That's no way to live; I didn't ever see my kids. God, do I miss 'em. Sometimes I don't feel like I've got anything to live for. . . . Sometimes I wish I was dead. I drink mostly whiskey, about 10 fifths a week when I'm really rolling. . . . Last time, I went five straight days without eating . . . my mind was foggy and I knew it. I've been off of the stuff for about 40 days now and I'm determined not to go back to it. I hope I can do it.

A chart depicting the usual progress of alcohol addiction and recovery, if it occurs, has been provided by Glatt (1974). As seen in Figure 13-1, physical, psychological, and social effects may be rampant as the person slowly progresses to the depths of the disorder. Although generalized, the figure is a useful description of the consequences of alcoholism.

In addition to creating social, familial, and occupational devastation, the alcoholic may place himself in great physical jeopardy. A specialist in the treatment of alcoholics (Talbott, 1974) has stated that death may be more likely in withdrawal from alcohol than in withdrawal from such drugs as heroin and morphine. The picture of a person going through alcohol withdrawal is not pleasant. Hallucinations may occur as the body is hurled into physiological upheaval. In addition, the body's temperature-regulating system can be thrown off and, if unchecked, body heat can continue to rise to levels at which a significant percentage of brain cells may be destroyed. The nervous system can be so disturbed that normal functioning cannot automatically continue; breathing may stop and convulsions can occur. After the early crucial phase has passed and life signs are again stable, the person frequently suffers temporary brain damage and is often unable to perform ordinary

325

CHAPTER 13:
DRUG AND
ALCOHOL
ADDICTION
AND
DEPENDENCE

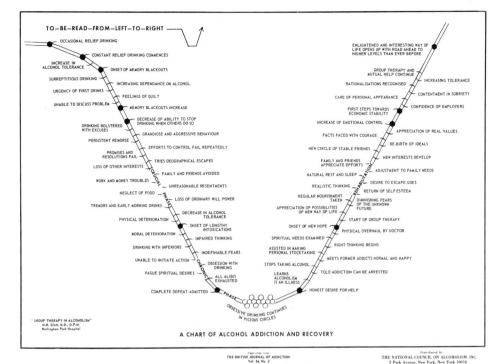

Figure 13-1. *A chart of alcohol addiction and recovery. From* A Guide
to Addiction and Its Treatment, *by M. Glatt. Copyright 1974 by MTP
Press, Ltd. Published in the U.S.A. by John Wiley & Sons, Inc. Reprinted
by permission.*

motor tasks such as writing, drawing simple diagrams, and the like. Although
many of these symptoms usually disappear rapidly, the so-called alcoholic
toxicity may remain for several weeks after the onset of withdrawal. It has
been said that, if one is left unattended by medical personnel, the chance of
dying during alcohol withdrawal is higher than that of a patient in an
intensive-care unit with a coronary condition (Talbott, 1974).

In addition to the physical symptoms, the most severe psychological
symptoms related to withdrawal from alcohol are *delirium tremens,* or DTs.
These hallucinations usually occur in people over 30 years of age who have
been consistently drinking for at least four years. L. Kolb (1973) states that DTs
are usually caused by a sudden drop in intake of alcohol and are usually
precipitated by the onset of withdrawal. The delirium may be preceded by
restlessness, sleeplessness or nightmares, and terrifying hallucinations and
delusions. A common hallucination is seeing spots becoming horrible insects
that grow in size. Alcoholics may be so panicked by such psychoticlike hallucinations that they may attempt to kill themselves or others. To avoid or halt
DTs, a drink is often the alcoholic's only short-term answer.

Other Disorders Associated with Excess Alcohol Use

Korsakoff's psychosis is a syndrome that may develop after delirium ceases. First described by Russian psychiatrist Sergei Korsakoff in 1887, it is characterized by amnesia, disorientation in time and place, and distortion of memory. It is primarily thought to be due to a deficiency in Vitamin B and to deterioration of the nerves of the cerebrum and the peripheral nervous system. One of the special characteristics of Korsakoff's psychosis is *pseudo-memory,* a condition in which the person reminisces about things that never happened. Interestingly, this disorder occurs more frequently in women; no clear explanation for this phenomenon is available. The psychosis may clear up in a couple of months, but many people experience permanent memory loss that they attempt to fill with their pseudo-memories. The symptom pattern can occur in reaction to other neurological diseases, but it is associated primarily with alcoholism.

Alcoholic paranoia may develop in people who have become addicted to alcohol and who are predisposed to faulty adjustment and suspiciousness. With the continued abuse of alcohol, weak coping mechanisms are stressed, and jealousy, irritability, fault-finding, and defensiveness may occur. These reactions can lead to the development of a delusional system that friends, relatives, and professionals cannot easily break into. When alcohol-related paranoia occurs, the prognosis is especially poor, and repeated paranoid and alcoholic episodes are usually expected to continue.

Explanations

Regardless of the specific categorization of alcoholism that one prefers, it is necessary to try to understand the occurrence of this disorder of impulse control. Major explanations for alcoholism may be divided into three basic types: psychoanalytic, behavioral, and biological.

Psychoanalytic Theory. From the Freudian point of view, alcoholism reflects a fixation at the level of *oral dependency.* Stress or trauma associated with unfulfilled id-level needs is thought to be reduced through oral-incorporative means. Although there is little empirical support for this contention, it is true that most alcoholics are also heavy smokers. In addition, some analysts believe that a drive to self-destruct (thanatos) exists in the alcoholic. Specifically, alcoholics may have incorporated hated aspects of a parent and, in an attempt to destroy that parental part of the personality, may also destroy themselves. At times, the self-destructive drive of the alcoholic is obvious to professionals and laypeople alike. The authors know of an instance in which an alcoholic with a severely deteriorated liver was

327

CHAPTER 13:
DRUG AND
ALCOHOL
ADDICTION
AND
DEPENDENCE

told that one more drink would result in death. The person took the drink and died the day after being released from the hospital.

Within the analytical framework, symptoms are usually seen as attempts to satisfy basic needs. Excessive drinking can produce numerous "rewards" not obtainable in more appropriate ways. For example, people who have a great need for acceptance by others and who don't have sufficient interpersonal skills to gain it when sober may find that the reduction of inhibition produced by alcohol makes it possible for them to get along better.

Behavioral Theories.   Unlike the analytic view, which includes underlying, hard-to-observe variables, in the behavioristic view, alcoholism can be described in terms of reinforcement theory. As seen in Figure 13-2, anxiety from a variety of sources may be reduced by the intake of alcohol. Since anxiety reduction is a positive reinforcement (see Chapter 4), the behavior that immediately precedes it is likely to occur again. Drinking behavior therefore can be strengthened as a response to stress each time a person drinks and feels better. Of course, as the alcoholism becomes more severe and there is tissue dependence upon the chemical, withdrawal symptoms begin if the person stops drinking. These withdrawal symptoms can be relieved by more drinking. Thus, even after the original stressors are gone, the alcohol dependence itself can keep the pattern going. However, the person now drinks to avoid the pain of withdrawal, not just to reduce anxiety.

Biochemical and Genetic Theories.   In addition to the intrapsychic-conflict explanation of the Freudians and the reinforcement explanation of the behaviorists, there are those who believe that alcoholism, or the tendency to develop it, may be inherited. Research results such as those of Eriksson (1968), Rodgers (1966), and Schlesinger (1966) present evidence that there is some *genetic* component in the occurrence of alcoholism.

Other evidence that alcoholism may be inherited comes from the observation that there is a similarity in the patterns of alcoholism and diabetes, a metabolic disorder that is often genetic in origin (Shoemaker, 1975). As a way of thinking about alcoholism, this theory suggests that the body of the alcoholic may not be able to process alcohol, much as the diabetic cannot process sugar. As in the diabetic, the difficulties with processing alcohol may not appear until later in life. Thus, we frequently find alcoholics who complain that they used to be able to drink all they wanted

Figure 13-2. *A reinforcement explanation of alcoholism*

without any addiction but that, as they grew older, they became unable to control their drinking.

Treatment

It is a safe bet that sooner or later alcoholism will touch each of us in some way. However, one of the greatest difficulties associated with the identification and treatment of the alcohol addict is the defense mechanism of *denial*. People with drinking problems frequently go to great lengths to deny to themselves and others that they have a drinking problem. In fact, many mental-health professionals feel that accepting the fact that one is alcoholic is a very significant step toward improvement.

Alcoholics Anonymous (AA). Probably the best-known psychological treatment for alcoholism is Alcoholics Anonymous (AA). Started in 1938 by a physician who had beaten his own problem with alcohol, AA is based upon a Christian religious philosophy but has been used interdenomina-

---

The Twelve Steps of Alcoholics Anonymous

1. We admitted we were powerless over alcohol . . . that our lives had become unmanageable.
2. [We] came to believe that a power greater than ourselves could return us to sanity.
3. [We] made a decision to turn our will and our lives over to the care of God *as we understood Him.*
4. [We] made a searching and fearless moral inventory of ourselves.
5. [We] admitted to God, to ourselves and to another human being the exact nature of our wrongs.
6. [We] were entirely ready to have God remove all these defects of character.
7. [We] humbly asked Him to remove our shortcomings.
8. [We] made a list of all the persons we had harmed, and became willing to make amends to them all.
9. [We] made direct amends to such people wherever possible, except where to do so would injure them or others.
10. [We] continued to take personal inventory and when we were wrong promptly admitted it.
11. [We] sought through prayer and meditation to improve our conscious contact with God *as we understood Him,* praying only for knowledge of His will for us and the power to carry that out.
12. Having had a spiritual awakening as the result of these steps, we tried to carry this message to alcoholics, and to practice these principles in all our affairs.

329

CHAPTER 13:
DRUG AND
ALCOHOL
ADDICTION
AND
DEPENDENCE

tionally with success. AA's approach to treating alcoholism as a disorder is broken down into twelve steps, which are usually traversed according to a loosely defined time schedule. Typically, AA members meet in groups in which they admit that they are addicts and cannot regulate their drinking. With support from other alcoholics, some of whom have recovered, new members can learn to gain control over their own drinking patterns. One AA innovation involves a kind of reinforcement system in which members

With the Twelve Steps in full view, an Alcoholics Anonymous meeting begins with a brief prayer. (Photo courtesy of Alcoholics Anonymous.)

are given different-colored poker chips to represent the length of time they have remained sober. For example, obtaining a blue chip for one year of sobriety has become a valued goal for many members. The success of Alcoholics Anonymous has led to the creation of similar organizations for people with other kinds of problems. There currently exist such groups as Neurotics Anonymous and Gamblers Anonymous, both of which have their own equivalents of the Twelve Steps and use similar treatment procedures. In addition, groups such as Al-Anon, for spouses of alcoholics, and Ala-Tot, for children of alcoholics, help people cope with problems associated with alcoholism.

Group and Milieu Therapy. AA provides a type of group treatment, but its meetings are rarely directed by a professional. Formal group therapy, led by professionals, has also been effective with alcoholics. Modern alcohol-treatment centers often attempt to provide their patients with a therapeutic environment (*milieu*) in which formal and informal treatment goes on. In the formal setting, group therapists typically meet with patients and discuss the problems of adjusting to a life without alcohol. In the informal meetings, patients may casually talk about drinking experiences and their attempts to overcome addiction. Our experience indicates that a combination of this milieu approach along with the Twelve Steps of AA can be extremely beneficial.

Behavioral Approaches. The behavioral approaches use learning-theory principles to "zero in on" the behavior of drinking. Such approaches generally conclude that drinking, like any other behavior, is maintained by positive reinforcement. The learned associations to drinking are usually pleasurable, and the immediate consequences of drinking behavior are often positive in terms of anxiety reduction and "good feelings." From the behavioral perspective, correction for faulty learning in the alcoholic consists of altering the alcoholic's reinforcement system so that drinking becomes associated with immediate *unpleasant* consequences. One such behavioral procedure is *aversive conditioning.*

Some of the more popularized versions of aversive conditioning of the alcoholic entail a patient's being wired to some sort of shock apparatus and given an electric shock every time he attempts to take a drink. As a result of this conditioning, the alcoholic may develop an aversion to drinking but often *only when wired for shock.* When he or she is aware that no shock is possible, drinking may continue. In other words, the treatment rarely generalizes to situations outside the therapy room.

One solution to this lack of generalizability has been developed by Cautela (1970b). Cautela's approach to aversive conditioning is called *covert sensitization,* and its goal is to produce in the individual a permanent aversion to drinking. When we have an intestinal virus that nauseates us, we often review in our minds the foods we ate just before the onset of the illness. It is not uncommon for us then to avoid those foods for quite a while afterwards. Covert

331

CHAPTER 13:
DRUG AND
ALCOHOL
ADDICTION
AND
DEPENDENCE

sensitization is based upon setting up a similar aversion to alcohol. In essence, Cautela has his patients imagine feeling nauseated and vomiting, and then associates these feelings with the act of drinking. By producing graphic, detailed mental scenes of drinking and negative reactions to drinking, the therapist tries to produce a new association in the alcoholic's mind: alcohol is no longer associated with pleasure, but with discomfort. After the aversive stimuli are presented and emphasized, the therapist asks the person to imagine himself throwing the drink away. This act of throwing the drink away is followed by an imaginary good feeling (*covert reinforcement*) in which the drinker feels clean and warm. When the covert reinforcer follows the throwing away of the drink, avoidance of liquor is believed to be strengthened. Thus, Cautela attempts not only to reduce the probability of drinking but to simultaneously increase the probability of avoiding alcohol intake.

Recent Innovations. The assumed goal in the treatment of alcohol addiction described up to this point is total abstinence from alcohol. Davies (1962) has gone so far as to state that there was unusual agreement among those who treated alcoholics that these patients would never again be capable

---

A Covert-Sensitization Scene

I want you to close your eyes and imagine the scene I'm about to describe. See yourself clearly doing all the things I suggest. You are walking down the street. It is a sunny day and you're feeling particularly good. Suddenly, you pass in front of your favorite bar. You stop for a moment and decide to go in and get a drink. You walk toward the door of the bar and just as you open it, you get a queasy feeling in your stomach. Sort of like you ate some food that disagreed with you. You say to yourself, "Maybe a drink will settle my stomach." You walk up to the bar and ask the bartender for a scotch and water. [This part is tailored specifically to the patient's own habits and preferences.] Just as you do this you kinda burp up some food. Little chunks of sour food are in the back of your throat. You swallow the chunks down but that sour smell and taste are still in your mouth; the queasy feeling is even stronger now. The bartender brings you the drink and you grasp the glass and take it to your lips. Just as it touches your lips—[therapist makes a vomiting sound] you vomit. You vomit all over your hands and into the drink. You look down into the glass and see the pieces of food and mucus floating around in the scotch and water. You can smell vomit mixed with the smell of the scotch. You vomit again. This time you spurt some vomit onto the bartender. He's looking at you in horror and disgust. You can smell the vomit and see it floating in your drink. You take the drink and throw it away. Suddenly you are outside again. You are clean and fresh-smelling. The sun feels warm on your back and the air is clear and stimulating.

of normal drinking and must abstain totally for the rest of their lives. However, some researchers and workers don't agree with the narrow and rigid criterion of total abstinence. Schaefer (1971) concluded that patients who believed the adage that one drink leads to drunkenness were less able to drink in a socially acceptable manner than those who didn't believe the adage. The possibility that a belief or expectancy might be responsible for the relatively low improvement rates of 30–40% (Popham & Schmidt, 1976) has led to programs that have modification of drinking rather than total abstinence as a goal (Sobell & Sobell, 1974). There appear to be enough successes with teaching some alcoholics to be moderate drinkers that the approach merits further research.

OTHER DRUGS OF DEPENDENCE

Although alcohol is the major drug of abuse and dependence in terms of the number of people affected, other drugs, such as the opiates, cocaine, amphetamines, barbiturates, psychedelics, and marijuana, also affect a significant number of people. Some authors have suggested that Americans favor the use of drugs to deal with a variety of personal, social, and biological problems. In 1973, more than 275 million prescriptions were written by U.S. physicians for tranquilizers, sedatives, and energizers. When coupled with drugs available illegally, this adds up to a substantial pool of available chemicals. A summary of the most common drugs of dependence and the description of the symptoms of their abuse are presented in Figure 13-3.

Since the theoretical explanations for addiction to or dependence on various drugs are often similar from substance to substance, we divert in this section from our usual pattern of description, explanation, and treatment. Instead, we will present descriptions of the various drugs and treatment for their abuse prior to a discussion of some general theories of drug misuse.

Opium and Its Derivatives

In contrast to alcohol, whose negative effects have been acknowledged by professionals for hundreds of years, the effects of opium addiction weren't clearly described until the writer Thomas de Quincey published *Confessions of an Opium Eater* in 1821. Since then, opium seems to have been either widely hailed as a cure-all or condemned. In the 19th-century United States, opium and its derivatives (collectively known as the *opiates*) were sold legally. Grocery and general stores often sold opium preparations over the counter without prescription, and they were readily available by mail order! Numerous patent medicines containing opiates were used for pain, coughs, and diarrhea. Physicians, in fact, often spoke of opium as "G.O.M.—God's Own Medicine" (Brecher, 1972) and used it as the drug of choice in at least 54 diseases including diabetes, insanity, nymphomania, tetanus, and nausea during pregnancy.

333

CHAPTER 13:
DRUG AND
ALCOHOL
ADDICTION
AND
DEPENDENCE

In fact, opium was used to treat chronic alcoholism in the early 1900s. It seems that opiates were used as frequently and indiscriminately in the past as we often use aspirin now.

Description. Opium itself is a raw product of nature and is obtained from the dried juices of an unripe opium-poppy capsule. *Morphine* is the active ingredient, and *heroin* is obtained by heating morphine in the presence of vinegar. Upon injection into the body, the heroin is rapidly converted once again to morphine. Another derivative of opium, *codeine*, is widely used in cough-control preparations. Opiates as a group are classified as narcotics primarily because of their sleep-inducing properties.

Opium may be either eaten or heated and its vapors inhaled. Morphine and heroin are sniffed, injected just under the skin (popped), or injected directly into a vein (mainlined). All of these narcotics are addicting, leading to increased physical tolerance, need for higher doses, and severe withdrawal symptoms. There are estimated to be 500,000 heroin addicts in the United States, half of whom reside in New York City. The following personal experience reflects the "style" of life the addict may be forced to lead.

PERSONAL EXPERIENCE: *Heroin Addiction*

Everything's a hassle. . . . Man, my whole life is devoted to one thing . . . smack. Nothing else matters anymore. And the whole thing is that it's no longer a kick. See, that's how I got started . . . it was the biggest kick of anything. But then after a while, it got to be like . . . no longer getting high . . . can you dig it? But, it's just like being kinda sick . . . till I can get some and then everything feels OK again. The worst times are when it's hard to get enough money or when I can't find a connection. . . . Then I just feel sick all over and real scared. What's it like shooting up? Well, at first it was pretty exciting. Ya know like this is it man, . . . this is the baddest thing you could do. So that kinda added to the thrill of it. When you get the stuff and you heat it up and when that needle first hits your vein, I get this fantastic warm sensation right here in my guts and then it just kinda spreads all over me and then nothing matters.

The subjective reaction to the intake of heroin may vary with the individual. A "rush," "kick," or "bang" is experienced most often by early users who inject the drug. Chronic users of heroin seem to use the drug more to avoid withdrawal symptoms than to experience the "rush." Even after "kicking the habit," some addicts report that the craving for heroin continues for a long time and that they never again feel "normal" without it. Heroin appears to be rapidly addicting if used continuously, but a few users report that infrequent usage ("chipping") without permanent addiction is possible. How-

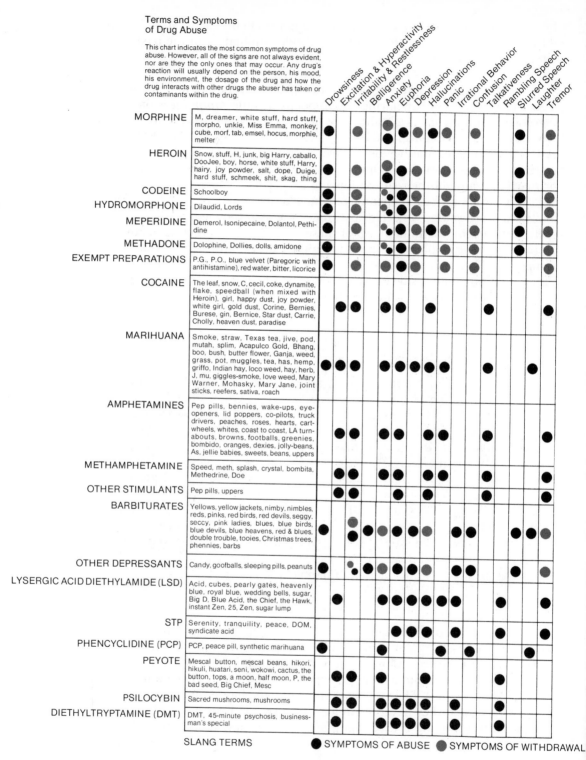

Figure 13-3. *Terms and symptoms of drug abuse.*

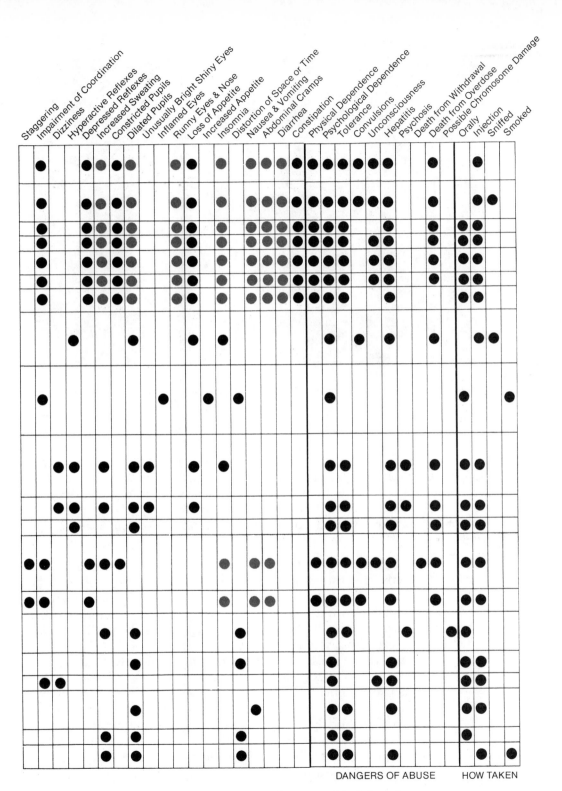

DANGERS OF ABUSE   HOW TAKEN

Source: United States Department of Justice, Drug Enforcement Administration.

335

Heroin use is no longer restricted to the back alleys of cities; it also occurs in middle- and upper-class homes. (Photo courtesy of the Department of Housing and Urban Development.)

ever, chipping is a dangerous game of "heroin roulette," in that statistics don't support a person's being able to limit heroin use to every once in a while.

In spite of present-day knowledge, there still are disputes about the results of heroin addiction. One of these is exemplified by an excerpt from the transcript of a Supreme Court decision in the 1962 case of *Robinson* v. *California:*

> To be a confirmed drug addict is to be one of the walking dead. . . . The teeth have rotted out, the appetite is lost, and the stomach and intestines don't function properly. The gall bladder becomes inflamed; eyes and skin turn a bilious yellow; in some cases membranes of the nose turn a flaming red; the partition separating the nostrils is eaten away—breathing is difficult. Oxygen in the blood decreases; bronchitis and tuberculosis develop. Good traits of character disappear and bad ones emerge. Sex organs become affected. Veins collapse and livid purplish scars remain. Boils and abscesses plague the skin; gnawing pain racks the body. Nerves snap; vicious twitching develops. Imaginary and fantastic fears blight the mind and sometimes complete insanity results. Often times, too, death comes much too early in life. . . . Such is the torment of being a drug addict; such is the plague of being one of the walking dead.

337

CHAPTER 13:
DRUG AND
ALCOHOL
ADDICTION
AND
DEPENDENCE

The results of research studies have rarely supported this description. An extensive survey of the effects of morphine addiction in British Columbia (Stevenson, 1956) suggested that neither physical nor psychological deterioration was observable in many long-term heroin users. Brecher (1972) goes so far as to conclude: "By far the most deleterious effects of being a narcotics addict in the United States are the risks of imprisonment, infectious disease and impoverishment" (p. 22).

Treatment. Parallel to the lack of consensus on the overall effects of heroin addiction are wide differences of opinion on how to treat the condition. The most popular treatment approach capitalizes on the opiate property of *cross-tolerance.* That is, the withdrawal symptoms from any one of the opiates may be delayed or abated by administration of any one of the others. Cross-tolerance led to the development of a very successful and controversial form of treatment for heroin addicts—methadone-maintenance therapy. In the mid-1950s, Vincent Dole, a specialist in metabolic diseases who first worked in the area of obesity, began a study of the metabolism of heroin. He later met Marie Nyswander, a specialist in addiction to heroin. Their research led to the discovery of a technique for detoxifying (withdrawing) heroin addicts through the administration of a synthetic opiate, methadone (Dole & Nyswander, 1968). They found that addicts maintained on methadone for a long time often became "normal, well-adjusted, effectively functioning human beings—to all intents and purposes they were *cured* of their craving for an illegal drug" (Hentoff, 1969).

The success of methadone maintenance seemed excellent. Through 1970, the dropout rate from the Dole-Nyswander program was less than 20%. Further, with the necessity of obtaining expensive and illegal heroin removed, the crime rate among methadone patients dropped markedly. However, in addition to the positive features of the methadone treatment program, there are some negative aspects. For one thing, the addict has traded one drug addiction for another. Furthermore, although methadone has fewer side-effects than heroin, sleepiness, constipation, excessive perspiration, weakness, and sexual impotence can occur. It has also been found that, as with many pregnant heroin addicts, pregnant women on methadone maintenance have children who usually experience withdrawal symptoms for some months after birth.

Other negative features of the methadone program include the increasing number of deaths from methadone overdose, the fact that the majority of methadone patients can and do take other drugs such as heroin and opium while in treatment, and the growing traffic in black-market methadone. Since there are nearly 100,000 people in methadone-maintenance programs at present, these negative features suggest that further proliferation of such programs needs to be critically evaluated.

Whereas methadone has been the drug treatment of choice for heroin addiction in the United States, Britain experimented with a program in which heroin addicts were provided with real heroin. This program was possible because heroin is legal in England and the number of addicts is much smaller than in the United States (only 2000 compared to 500,000). Recently, however, even the English have begun to switch to methadone for their addicts because it has fewer side-effects than heroin.

In contrast to treatment programs using primarily drugs to deal with heroin addiction, therapeutic communities such as Phoenix Houses use psychological and social means to break the addict's drug habit. Staffed by a large proportion of former drug users, Phoenix Houses use a number of confrontative techniques to break down the excuses offered by the drug user for his life-style. Although methadone programs have only 20% dropout rates, Phoenix House dropout rates are 50% or higher. This may be partially explained by the fact that nearly one-third of Phoenix House residents are less than 18 years old.

The relative effectiveness of methadone maintenance or Phoenix House treatment pales in importance next to the fact that as few as one out of five addicts is in any treatment program. The search for effective treatment for heroin addiction must consider the possibility that Samuels (1971) may be correct when he points out: "The vast majority of addicts don't want to get off heroin."

Cocaine

Not so widely used as the opiates, cocaine is a powerful central-nervous-system stimulant obtained from the leaves of a shrub known as *Erythroxylon coca*. Cocaine has enjoyed a long history of use. The Incas, for example, valued coca leaves so highly that they often used them to pay taxes and other debts. Probably the most famous instance of the use of coca leaves in the United States was by an Atlanta druggist, John Pemberton. In 1885, Pemberton combined extracts from the coca leaf with flavoring from the cola nut and produced what we now know and love as Coca-Cola. Of course, with its bit of cocaine, the drink caught on very quickly. By 1906, however, the Pure Food and Drug Law was passed forbidding the use of cocaine in the beverage, and the manufacturers began to use coca leaves with the cocaine removed.

Description. Unlike the opium or alcohol abuser, the cocaine user typically does *not* suffer any physical withdrawal symptoms even after long-term usage. However, cocaine withdrawal is often accompanied by the psychological feeling of depression. Further, cocaine users can often suffer severe psychotic reactions while still taking the drug. (Alcohol abusers generally experience psychotic episodes only when withdrawal begins.)

Cocaine may be sniffed in very small amounts or can be taken orally in combination with heroin or morphine in what is known as a "speedball." This drug mixture is said to improve the "rush" associated with heroin and to increase the mood elevation derived from cocaine.

For a long time, the high cost of cocaine and legislative controls had restricted its use. However, recent years have seen a sharp increase in the use

339

CHAPTER 13:
DRUG AND
ALCOHOL
ADDICTION
AND
DEPENDENCE

of cocaine, especially among those in the middle and upper classes, where it often is valued as a sexual stimulant (Harwood, 1974).

The search for the euphoric feelings associated with cocaine may be seen in the following account by a young cocaine user:

PERSONAL EXPERIENCE: *Cocaine Use*

I got a mental craving for more and more, buying additional "coke" from other addicts and occasionally exchanging "H" for extra "C." I could use all my supply of "C" [5 g] within four hours and I had none left in the afternoon. . . . I kept shooting it up. . . . Many people gave themselves overdoses of "C." . . . I once nearly killed myself through such an overdose: I felt a terrible explosion in my head and my heart beat violently. On that occasion the "C" crystals were damp so I didn't know how much I was using . . . the effects were much stronger than usual. Ordinarily after mainlining "C" the "flash" came within seconds: my heart started beating fast, there was a nervous excitement which usually scared me. . . . The first time when I took "C" I got the "flash," although I only took very little, perhaps ⅓ g, but later on I needed more to get the "flash." I liked the stimulation but every time I took "C" I had a fear of overdosing myself.

From *A Guide to Addiction and Its Treatment*, by M. Glatt. Copyright 1974 by MTP Press, Ltd. Published in the U.S.A. by John Wiley & Sons, Inc. Reprinted by permission.

Treatment. At present, treatment for cocaine users primarily involves therapy groups such as Synanon (see Chapter 23). Many cocaine users seem to have little desire to stop cocaine use and, even if discovered and treated, may return to it. No drug has been proved to have a cross-tolerance with cocaine.

Amphetamines

The opiates and cocaine are naturally occurring substances that have been used for hundreds of years. Amphetamines, however, are a product of modern-day chemical technology. Originally developed as stimulants (for example, Benzedrine in 1932), the amphetamines are usually used to lift the mood and energy level. The chemicals are widely used medically and are very inexpensive to manufacture. Although their main action is to stimulate and increase energy levels, one of the side-effects of amphetamines is to curb appetite. Many unsuspecting overweight men and women in the 1940s, 1950s, and 1960s were unknowingly introduced to heavy use of amphetamines as part of their weight-reduction programs.

Description.   The prolonged use of amphetamines doesn't necessarily lead to physiological addiction. However, psychological effects such as depression, agitation, and fear may accompany cessation of amphetamine use (Innes & Nickerson, 1970).

Taken orally and in small doses, the amphetamines typically are not extremely dangerous. However, many amphetamines, such as *methamphetamine* (Methadrine), or "speed," can be extremely dangerous when injected intravenously. People who inject amphetamines may also indulge in "binges" in which they may use enough of the drug to cause periods of sleeplessness of a week or more. Following one binge, the person may sleep for a day or two ("crashing"), awake, and begin another binge. Experts (Brecher, 1972; Glatt, 1974) state that a paranoid psychosis is a nearly inevitable result of a long-term, high-dose, intravenous amphetamine-injection habit. Since death may also result from such drug use, the slogan "Speed kills" is accurate.

Treatment.   Often nontraditional psychotherapy such as Synanon or the like is indicated for users of amphetamines. The problem with treatment here is often that the drug-induced psychological symptoms must be dealt with long after drug use has ceased. Thus, the goal of therapy may be not simply to stop the addiction behavior, but also to try to undo its vestigial damage.

Barbiturates and Other Sedatives and Tranquilizers

In contrast to the amphetamines, which primarily energize people and elevate their moods, the barbiturates and sedatives lower activity and mood levels. Nevertheless, barbiturates can be just as dangerous as amphetamines.

Description.   The addicting potential of a barbiturate depends on whether it is long-acting or short-acting. Long-acting barbiturates (those which take effect slowly and wear off slowly) rarely present a great abuse problem; they are usually used as medically intended. However, the short-acting barbiturates (rapid effect, rapid wearing off) are often misused. Examples of short-acting drugs are secobarbital and pentobarbital ("barbs"), which have been used widely as mood-altering drugs in social settings and as self-medication.

Severe addiction to the short-acting barbiturates is possible, but there seems to be an upper limit to the physical need. Regardless of this upper limit, however, experts (Glatt, 1974; Nowlis, 1967) note that physical dependence on barbiturates can be more lethal than dependence on opium, morphine, or heroin. Withdrawal from barbiturates often results in convulsions, coma, stupor, or death. It is estimated that over 3000 deaths occur annually as a result of barbiturate overdoses or withdrawal. Indeed, these freely available and widely produced drugs (400 tons per year in the United States) seem to be more dangerous than most of us would expect.

The so-called minor tranquilizers, such as Valium, Librium, and Miltown (see Chapter 24), may be as dangerous as barbiturates. Seemingly

341

CHAPTER 13:
DRUG AND
ALCOHOL
ADDICTION
AND
DEPENDENCE

dispensed almost like candy, these chemicals are used by millions of people in the United States for every slight tension and worry. Minor tranquilizers have tension-reducing effects similar to the barbiturates, but they don't usually produce fatigue and sleep. Addiction to these tranquilizing agents is possible, and both increased dosage requirements and *severe* withdrawal symptoms are common. Withdrawal from minor tranquilizers or barbiturates can be more dangerous to life than withdrawal from heroin or alcohol.

Treatment. In the long run, the best treatment for the abuse of barbiturates and the minor tranquilizers would seem to be public education. The vast majority of the 275 million prescriptions for "mood-altering" drugs are prescribed by nonpsychiatric physicians to deal with a wide variety of complaints. However, curing daily tensions by using these drugs can be more harmful than the original feelings of distress. Were professionals and laypeople more aware of the potential danger these drugs present, their inappropriate use would certainly be diminished.

Treatment programs similar to those described for alcoholics also are appropriate for barbiturate abusers. Group therapy and milieu treatment can be quite effective, as are various forms of aversive conditioning such as covert sensitization.

Psychedelic and Psychotomimetic Drugs

Whereas the drugs we have described thus far primarily affect mood levels, energy levels, and physical feelings, the psychedelic chemicals typically affect thinking and perceptual functioning. The *psychedelic* (mind-expanding) and *psychotomimetic* (psychosis-mimicking) drugs are not physically addictive but do produce psychological dependence (Glatt, 1974; Osmond, 1966). The most widely known of these drugs is probably lysergic acid diethylamide, or LSD, but the list also includes peyote (mescaline), psilocybin, tetrahydro-cannabinol (THC), and morning-glory seeds. Historically, psychedelic drugs were used in religious and mystical rites. For example, the Aztecs are known to have eaten parts of the peyote cactus to achieve a spiritual "high" and to experience a kind of "nirvana." In modern times, the peyote religion is still practiced by many American Indian groups that continue to use the drug legally.

Description. The psychedelic effects of LSD were accidentally discovered in 1943 by Dr. Albert Hoffmann, a Swiss chemist (Cashman, 1966). While attempting to derive a new compound of lysergic acid, Hoffmann accidentally ingested a small amount of the chemical. He experienced mild dizziness and sank into a state characterized by "extremely excited fantasies." To determine whether the cause of this state was the LSD, he undertook an experiment in which he ingested one-quarter of a milligram of the compound (a very large dose, as he was soon to find out). Within 45 minutes he was no longer able to write in his notebook and had to be taken home; a doctor was summoned and he found Hoffmann with a very weak pulse and

The sixties saw the rise of the flower children, who helped popularize the use of marijuana and other consciousness-affecting drugs. (Photo by Robert Foothorap.)

unable to speak coherently. About six hours later Hoffmann was able to describe his LSD experience:

> I can remember the following were the most outstanding symptoms: vertigo, visual disturbances, the faces around me appeared as grotesque, colored masks; marked motoric unrest, alternating with paralysis; an intermittent feeling in the head, limbs, and entire

343

CHAPTER 13:
DRUG AND
ALCOHOL
ADDICTION
AND
DEPENDENCE

body, as if they were filled with lead; dry, constricted sensation in the throat; feeling of choking; shouting half-insanely or babbling incoherently; I sometimes felt as if I were out of my body [p. 31].

Although the need for increased dosages of LSD is rare and physical withdrawal symptoms are not observed, psychological difficulties can occur. In an otherwise stable person, LSD-induced psychoses can create sufficient stress to cause long-term psychotic adjustment patterns. The occurrence of "flashbacks," or hallucinationlike perceptions, long after the drug has worn off often contributes to this extended stress. The experimental use of LSD was widespread in the 1960s and seems to have lessened in the 1970s, but *compulsive* use of LSD probably occurs infrequently.

Before concluding this section, we must mention that LSD also has been widely studied as a *psycholytic* agent—that is, a chemical that can help to reduce resistances in the psychotherapy process. An early study of the psycholytic use of LSD was reported by Busch and Johnson (1950), who concluded that the drug seemed helpful in reaching severely withdrawn patients and in shortening the psychotherapy process. In spite of numerous other studies of LSD as a therapy aid, S. Cohen (1965) has concluded, "No method of using LSD therapeutically has yet met rigid scientific requirements which include long-term follow-up and comparisons of patients receiving LSD with identically treated control groups" (p. 71).

Marijuana and Its Derivatives

Marijuana has changed the recreation and social habits of large numbers of Americans. A derivative of the wild-growing hemp plant known as *Cannabis sativa*, marijuana has perhaps one of the longest recorded histories of usage. A very early reference to the use of marijuana was found in a Chinese pharmacological treatise nearly 5000 years old. Recently, an urn filled with marijuana leaves and seeds dating from about 500 B.C. was discovered near Berlin, Germany. Historians have conjectured that marijuana was used extensively by ancient peoples because of its dual utility in making cloth and making people feel good.

Like the other drugs in this chapter, marijuana was once used medically. In the United States in the late 19th century, the drug was used to treat such disorders as migraine headaches, gout, rheumatism, cholera, convulsions, depression, DTs, insanity, and uterine hemorrhage (Brecher, 1972). In fact, many major drug companies sold over-the-counter cannabis preparations in the late 19th and early 20th centuries. Manufactured marijuana cigarettes were even available as an asthma remedy! As better, dose-controlled drugs became available for the treatment of illnesses, however, the medicinal use of cannabis dropped markedly. Its social-recreational use, however, remains common.

Description. In contrast to the opiates, which typically are injected, or cocaine, which usually is sniffed, cannabis leaves most frequently are smoked in cigarettes or a pipe. Eating the leaves in cookies or brownies also is quite common. The active ingredient in the marijuana plant is actually a resin which has formed on the leaves. Through a simple process, the resin can be removed and purified into cubes of pure resin called *hashish*. Hashish is much more potent than raw marijuana, and smaller amounts of its inhaled smoke usually produce greater emotional effects. Marijuana is not physiologically addictive. In fact, some regular users report that *lesser* amounts are often required after constant use.

Although there are few physical withdrawal symptoms from long-term use of marijuana, it is possible for a person to develop a psychological dependence. That is, the use of the drug may become situational or circumstantial, with the person needing the marijuana to relate effectively to others, to sleep, or to take care of personal problems.

Until the mid-1930s, when federal and state regulations were passed placing it in the same category as the opiates and cocaine, cannabis was a legal drug. Physicians were still permitted to dispense it by prescription, but it was no longer sanctioned for personal or recreational use. Since it became illegal, the black-market traffic in marijuana has increased, and today a vast number of people use the drug in spite of the threat of felony or misdemeanor charges. Its widespread use has prompted agitation for legalization. Whether marijuana use will once again be legalized is unknown, but the facts seem to be that, as a drug, it is not nearly so dangerous physically or emotionally as tobacco, alcohol, heroin, or cocaine. Dependence upon marijuana does, however, constitute a diagnosable condition within DSM-II, and its use is therefore a potential mental-health problem.

Explanations

It is safe to say that any one set of explanations has difficulty dealing with the wide variety of reasons people indulge in drugs. Such explanations must describe not only the initiation but the maintenance of drug use. Some theorists have attempted to develop a theory of drug use general enough to be applicable to most forms of drug addiction and dependence, yet specific enough to be helpful in understanding why particular chemicals are used. Glatt (1974), a major proponent of such a theory, believes that, rather than any one specific cause, it is the interaction of three separate factors that contributes to the development and continuance of drug misuse. These three factors are the "host," or the personality and physical makeup of the individual; the "environment," or the social, cultural, and economic atmosphere in which the person lives and grows; and the "agent," or the chemical and pharmacological nature of the drug involved.

The Host. According to Glatt, a person's psychological makeup is probably the most important factor in the *initiation* of drug-dependent behavior. However, physical characteristics—including physical tolerance of

345

CHAPTER 13:
DRUG AND
ALCOHOL
ADDICTION
AND
DEPENDENCE

drugs, genetic predispositions, and the like—are more clearly implicated in the *maintenance* of drug dependence. Host factors may contribute to drug misuse in at least three different ways. First, a *preaddictive personality* may predispose a person to try to escape from life stresses. If there actually is such a thing as the preaddictive person, he or she might be characterized by low frustration tolerance, lack of socially acceptable, nonchemical escape routes from stress, and a need to attain immediate relief from pain and discomfort. However, it is difficult to assess whether such a personality pattern is the result or the cause of drug abuse.

In addition to the possibility of a preaddictive personality, Glatt also proposes that *genetic factors* might affect the drug-taking behavior of the host. Although there now may be more evidence of a genetic predisposition for alcohol addiction than for the other drugs, there is some evidence that drug dependence may tend to run in families in a genetically explainable fashion (Glatt, 1974).

There is also the third possibility that the host may indulge in *relief drug-taking*. Usually drugs are taken to obtain relief from emotional pain or to maintain a desired, nonnaturally occurring level of mood or energy. Thus, rather than trying to alter his or her interpersonal relationships or life-style in order to achieve personal emotional comfort, a person may choose the more immediate solution of drugs. Glatt has stated that among "drug abusers one may find a higher proportion of inadequate, immature and insecure personalities than among the general population" (p. 25).

The Environment. In *social dependence*, drugs are used simply to obtain contact with and approval from drug-using peers. It is not uncommon for people who haven't used marijuana for several years to smoke some at a college reunion because they are with old college friends with whom they smoked in the past.

In addition to the phenomenon of social dependence, there are other ways the environment can affect drug-taking behavior. For example, the availability of drug "supplies" varies from social class to social class. More expensive drugs such as hard liquor and cocaine more frequently are abused by affluent people simply because they can afford them. For this same reason, "cheap" chemicals such as mass-produced beer and wines, heavily cut heroin, and poor grades of marijuana tend to be more common in the lower classes.

The values of the subculture in which a person lives also can exert a powerful influence on both the initiation and maintenance of drug behavior. Although somewhat similar to social-dependence effects, subculture effects are usually more powerful. In some cases, a dominant culture may be opposed to drug use, but a subculture may favor such behavior. The relative strength of the peer group vis-à-vis the dominant culture is often most evident during adolescence. Adolescents may perceive drug use, not only as a physical experience, but as an expression of their rejection of society as well. The special "secret language" of drug usage may help the adolescent to establish the identity and independence necessary for entry into adult life.

The Agent.   It is clear that personal and environmental factors contribute to drug dependence, but variations in the degree and danger of such dependence are usually a function of the specific chemical, or *agent*, involved. The agent can play a decisive role in the initiation *and* maintenance of drug excess. For example, Glatt notes that "the great majority of individuals introduced to the opiates for even a relatively brief period, however stable their personality, will become physically and psychologically dependent, and this even with the (initial) use of small *therapeutic* doses" (1974, p. 114). Accidental addiction has occurred infrequently among hospital patients treated for pain with morphine. Relative to the opiates, the other drugs we have discussed are less likely to produce such rapid dependence.

A Trifactorial Interaction.   The factors of "host," "environment," and "agent" may be seen as interacting to produce the variety of drug-dependent patterns we have described in this chapter. Glatt suggests that psychological and environmental factors may be most important in the *initiation* of drug use, but that agent factors may be more crucial in the maintenance of drug habits. Wikler (1973) proposed an explanation of drug use that is similar to Glatt's in its emphasis on an interaction of factors. However, in contrast to Glatt, Wikler separates factors influencing initiation and maintenance. Wikler sees the initiation of drug usage as based upon *social reinforcement;* that is, the person is under the influence of peer groups, drug subcultures, and the like. Once drug use has begun, however, it is continued on the basis of *pharmacological reinforcement.* Such pharmacological reinforcement may be of two types: pleasure obtained from the use of certain drugs (psychological dependence); or reduction of physical pain resulting from attempted withdrawal from drugs for which a physical need has developed (physical dependence). Thus, once a drug habit is initiated, mere alteration of the personal and social conditions that contributed to its inception won't always result in curing the habit; both the physical *and* psychological reinforcement components must be dealt with. An understanding of Wikler's dual-process theory allows us to understand more clearly the complexities of the development and treatment of the drug-associated disorders.

CONCLUDING COMMENTS

There seems to be a bias in some sections of our society in favor of handling "problems in living" by means of drugs. As we have pointed out, use of various sorts of drugs seems to be increasing, not decreasing. A significant reason for increased use may be the tensions of a modern, high-pressure style of life that takes its toll in terms of energy and anxiety. However, another significant reason may derive from the impact of the media on the way we live.

347

CHAPTER 13:
DRUG AND
ALCOHOL
ADDICTION
AND
DEPENDENCE

There is some reason to believe that showing drugs in a favorable light in songs and on television can have a significant impact on the initiation and maintenance of drug use. For example, a survey of 80 prime-time hours of television viewing showed that there was only one announcement that could be termed antidrug, as contrasted with 127 persuasive appeals promoting the use of licit drugs (Winick, 1973). Alcohol was the drug most often presented, and invariably it was shown in a positive social context. With such constant media bombardment, people probably find it difficult to assess accurately the value and meaning of drug use. We hope there will be a more rational and accurate presentation of drugs and their positive and negative features in the years to come.

CHAPTER SUMMARY CHART

In this chapter, we discussed drug dependence, beginning with a look at methods of classification of drug use:

Current definitions	*A new typology*
Physiological addiction	Experimental use
Psychological dependence	Social-recreational use
Drug abuse	Circumstantial-situational use
	Intensified use
	Compulsive use

Next, we considered alcoholism:

Description	*Explanations*	*Treatment*
Jellinek's Alpha, Beta, Gamma, and Delta alcoholics	Psychoanalytic: oral dependency	Alcoholics Anonymous
Delirium tremens	Behavioral: tension reduction due to chemical properties	Group therapy
Alcoholic toxicity		Milieu therapy
Withdrawal reactions	Genetic: similarity with diabetes	Behavioral therapy: Covert sensitization
		Aversive therapy

Finally, we discussed the other drugs of dependence:

Description

Dependence on:
    Opiates
    Cocaine
    Amphetamines
    Sedatives and tranquilizers
    Psychedelics
    Marijuana

Explanations

Glatt
Trifactor-interactional explanation:
    Host
    Environment
    Agent

CHAPTER 14
DISORDERS
OF
SEXUAL BEHAVIOR

The disorders associated with difficulties in controlling sexual impulses differ in several ways from the impulse disorders associated with crime and the use of chemicals. First of all, sexuality is not in itself an unnatural or socially unacceptable form of behavior. Crime may be considered "bad," and the introduction of chemicals into the body is unnatural, but sex is a vital part of life and is crucial to the continuation of our species. Second, although other impulse disorders occur in both males *and* females, sexual disturbances are almost completely a male phenomenon. Some reasons for this imbalance will be discussed later in this chapter. A third unique characteristic of the sexual dysfunctions is that they represent a much wider range of specific symptoms than other impulse disorders. Whereas drug reactions are physiologically limited in nature and variety, and crimes may fall into a small number of categories or types, sexual deviations include an almost infinite set of culturally unacceptable and often dangerous modes of impulse gratification. A last characteristic of sexual disorders is that they seem to be a part of a major social phenomenon. "Adult" bookshops, pornographic films, and "men's" magazines are common. Sexual "aids" such as vibrators, inflatable love-dolls, delaying creams, vitamins, and the like are a multimillion-dollar mail-order business. Sex is more a part of *normal* life than crime and drugs; it is more a part of *abnormal* life as well. In this chapter, we will focus on people in whom sexual deviations and difficulties represent the primary reason for their being different.

Before beginning our discussion of disorders of sexual behavior, we must digress for a moment into a discussion of classification. The DSM-II classification system of sexual behavior seems to assume that heterosexual intercourse is the single most important and "normal" sexual behavior and that all other sexual behaviors range from the unusual to the deviant. However, such a perspective leaves us with problems in dealing with these "other" sexual behaviors. For example, are all homosexuals disordered? How about the 95% of males who report that they masturbate at some time? Are they also to be considered disordered? According to DSM-II, we would be forced to answer yes to these questions. In light of such problems with DSM-II, and in order to clarify our description of these disorders, we have chosen to reclassify the traditional sexual disorders into three categories. *Sexual dysfunctions* involve the inability to carry out acceptable sexual behavior for either psychological or physical reasons. *Sexual deviations* are sexual behaviors that are undesirable to the individual or society and that fit the traditional DSM-II categorization of "those persons whose sexual interests are directed primarily toward objects other than people . . . , toward sexual acts not usually associated with coitus or toward coitus performed under bizarre circumstances" (p. 44). Finally, *sexual-orientation disturbances* include patterns in which there is a mismatch between physical and psychological sexuality. The major form of sexual-orientation disturbance is homosexuality.

We consider these three categories to be separable. Not only are their specific characteristics different, but so are the explanations and treatment for them. To reflect these differences, we will discuss each in a separate section of the chapter.

SEXUAL DYSFUNCTIONS

The first major category of sexual disorders, the sexual dysfunctions, involves a psychogenic inability to perform sexual intercourse. Difficulties can occur in both males and females, making the sexual dysfunction clearly different from the sexual deviations we will describe later. Further, dysfunctions occur primarily in people with heterosexual orientations, thus distinguishing them from the sexual-orientation disturbances.

Descriptions

Although sexual dysfunctions in males have been studied for many years, similar problems in women have been largely ignored. In the past, it seems to have been assumed that women were not supposed to enjoy sex. Few people asked women whether they were enjoying the sexual experience. For example, in the past, men may not have recognized premature ejaculation as a problem, because as long as the male experienced orgasm, it often didn't matter whether the woman was fulfilled. However, this is not the case today, for *both* male and female sexual dysfunctions are more commonly observed, studied, and treated.

Orgasmic Dysfunctions in Males.   Also known as impotence, orgasmic dysfunctions involve the male's inability to achieve or maintain an erection sufficiently firm to complete intercourse. In *primary* dysfunction, the man has rarely, if ever, experienced a successful erection; in *secondary* dysfunction, he was previously able to achieve an erection but presently is not. Although there are a wide number of possible physiological causes for inability to achieve an erection (such as diabetes mellitus, cardiorespiratory disorders, certain drugs, and alcohol), the majority of occurrences are psychogenic. Nearly eight out of ten men maintain the physiological capacity to consummate the sexual act at age 70. Because an episodic inability to maintain an erection is a normal occurrence for most men, Masters and Johnson (1970) have defined true dysfunction as a *failure in 25% of attempts* at intercourse. Psychological causes of impotence may involve a repressive upbringing in which the person was taught that sex was dirty and immoral. Cultural pressures on the male to

Some early sexual experiences take place in less than ideal circumstances. (Photo by Michael P. Dumont.)

perform in keeping with society's "masculine image" and initial failures in intercourse also may be significantly related to the later occurrence of erectile dysfunctions.

Even if erection is possible, *ejaculatory disturbances* also can be seen as a dysfunction. In an ejaculatory disturbance, the male can't control his ejaculatory process for a sufficient length of time during intercourse to satisfy his partner in at least 50% of their coital connections (Masters & Johnson, 1970). Although in a few instances there may be a somatic cause for premature ejaculation, most cases are caused psychologically. These psychological causes usually involve anxiety about the ability to "perform" the sex act. This anxiety may be due to the fact that, for many males, the first experience with sexual intercourse takes place in a situation where tension and anxiety abound, such as the back seat of a car or a blanket at the beach—situations where speed may be an important factor!

PERSONAL EXPERIENCE: *Impotence*

This is tough to talk about . . . but I guess since it's over with I should be able to look back. I . . . I remember when it started . . . or rather when I first got upset about it . . . uh . . . not being able to . . . uh . . . get an erection, you know. It was in my junior year in high school. I didn't . . . uh . . . date much, ya know, and the junior class was having a . . . uh . . . autumn dance and the other guys kept asking me if I was gonna take . . . uh . . . Janie M. 'cause they knew that I liked her. They all told me how Janie was . . . uh . . . easy . . . and that I'd be sure to get laid. Well, I had never . . . uh . . . had sex with a girl all the way before, ya know . . . and I couldn't let on that I was afraid, so I . . . uh . . . asked Janie out and she said OK. Everything went OK at the dance, except every time we got real close I sorta got a little erection and felt very excited and . . . uh . . . I tried to hide it and think about scary things to make it go away. During the dance lots of the other guys came by and . . . uh . . . winked at me, ya know, like they knew what was gonna happen later. Anyhow, after the dance, we went out for some food and then it was . . . uh . . . time to take Janie home. I drove her to a street nearby her home, ya know, and . . . uh . . . parked the car. She looked at me like she knew what I wanted and . . . uh . . . she started to kiss me. I felt all excited, but scared, too. I . . . uh . . . wow, I can't really talk too much more . . . I tried . . . I couldn't get an erection . . . she tried to make it hard, but she got disgusted . . . uh . . . she called me a fairy, a waste . . . and she was real mad. I felt so bad I dropped her off, went home . . . uh . . . and cried and punched myself in the head till it hurt. I couldn't even think about girls or get an erection with one for seven years after that. Now . . . uh . . . with this treatment, ya know, I'm OK. If ya know what I mean.

The opposite of premature ejaculation, *retarded ejaculation,* occurs infrequently and involves the inability to achieve a climax during intercourse. Masters and Johnson report that only 5% of their cases involved such a disorder. In most cases of retarded ejaculation, psychological causes are very similar to those found in premature ejaculation. However, there are also certain neurological disorders that can cause this problem, and their possible involvement should be determined before psychological treatment begins. For example, long-term use of certain antidepressant medications can produce an inability to ejaculate even though an erection and a sensation of climax are experienced.

Orgasmic Dysfunctions in Females. Once called "frigidity," sexual dysfunctions in women vary from a complete lack of response, to pain, to a variety of reactions that hamper full experiencing of the pleasures of sex. Until recently, orgasmic dysfunction was erroneously defined as a woman's inability to experience a "vaginal" orgasm. Freud believed that the clitoral orgasm was an "immature orgasm," and that only a mature woman could experience a vaginal orgasm. We now know from the work of Masters and Johnson that the clitoris is the major source of the orgasmic experience for women and that the belief in the superiority of the vaginal orgasm is nonsense.

Masters and Johnson (1970) separate *primary* from *secondary* orgasmic dysfunctions. In primary dysfunction, the woman never has experienced an orgasm, either by intercourse or by masturbation. Secondary dysfunctions are those in which orgasmic difficulties have appeared in a female once capable of normal orgasm. Data indicate that some women have experienced few or no orgasms (Kinsey, Pomeroy, Martin, & Gebhard, 1953). In fact, according to Kinsey's data, one out of every three women has never experienced orgasm before marriage. This lack of orgasmic experience may have been acceptable to women in the past, but apparently not today. In a recent survey of college students' behavior, Edwards (1977) reported that only one out of five college females reports never experiencing orgasm during sexual intercourse.

Explanations

Sexual dysfunctions may be either biologically or psychologically caused. Biological causes generally involve the presence of certain neurological diseases or disorders of the genitourinary system. If, because of disease, pain accompanies erection in the male or intercourse in the female, sexual contact will tend to become aversive and probably will be avoided. Other biological causes of dysfunctions include certain tranquilizers and antidepressants whose side-effects in males include suppression of the ability to ejaculate.

Although the biological causes of sexual dysfunctions frequently result in anxiety and concern about one's sexual adequacy, the psychological components in these cases are often secondary to the physical causes of the dysfunction. However, there are purely psychological bases for sexual dysfunctions. At the core of psychogenic sexual inadequacy, there often is a need to meet some standard of performance. If one's standard of performance isn't met, or there is a perceived threat that it won't be met, anxiety may occur. Anxiety is reciprocal to sexual arousal: if one is present, the other can't be. Thus, if a male becomes anxious, he may not be able to achieve an erection; if he can't achieve an erection, he is sure not to live up to his standards; if he doesn't live up to his standards, he becomes even more anxious. As you can see, the anxiety-dysfunction association can result in a vicious circle in which worries about inadequacy only make matters worse.

Sources of anxiety associated with sexual behavior are varied. Trauma, such as a partner ridiculing one's genitals or other body parts, can produce a loss of confidence that can compound itself into poor performance. In addition, fatigue and normally occurring temporary loss of erectile ability can be misinterpreted as lack of interest or lack of masculinity. In females, fears of losing control or of seeming "cheap" can result in inhibitions of sexual response. The psychological ways in which dysfunctions may evolve are legion. As has been true of many of the disorders we have discussed in this text, many different events can produce the exact same symptoms.

Treatment

Until the 1950s and 1960s, psychoanalysis or psychoanalytically oriented psychotherapy most frequently was used for treating sexual dysfunction, but the results of such approaches were often unsatisfactory. More recently, therapeutic programs initiated by such therapists as Masters and Johnson (1970) and Kaplan (1975) have shown considerable success in treating sexual dysfunctions.

Masters and Johnson used data gathered from their original research on the physiological correlates of intercourse and sexual pleasure to develop an effective treatment program. In essence, this treatment is based on the assumption that the causes for sexual disorders are to be found primarily in the interaction between the partners. Masters and Johnson reasoned that, at some time in the past, pressures probably changed a spontaneous interaction into one in which either one or both partners adopted a spectator role; in other words, sex has taken on the character of a command performance. To rectify this situation, the couple must typically leave home and come to stay near the treatment center. In this new situation, the couple is interviewed, both separately and together, by professionals of both the same and the opposite sex. They are given complete physical examinations to eliminate the possibility of physiological causes for their sexual problems. The couple then meets with the therapists, where they are confronted by what the therapists believe is the core of their problems.

Most often, the problem involves the sex act having become a spectator-performer interaction rather than a spontaneous one. To begin the treatment process, the couple may be instructed to undress in front of each other when they return to their room. While undressed, they are supposed to explore by touching each other to find what is pleasurable. However, they are instructed *not to have intercourse.* Psychotherapy counseling sessions are usually run concurrently with the exploring activity, and they focus on the couple's major problems. Although sexual techniques may be discussed in these sessions, there are no demands made for any particular level of sexual performance. Within a supportive atmosphere, the process of interviewing that focuses on interpersonal aspects and sexual exploration with no demand for performance appears to be extremely successful in eliminating the disorders of vaginismus (involuntary closing of the vaginal opening due to muscle spasm—100% success), premature ejaculation (98% success), and primary erectile disturbances (70% success). In terms of follow-up, the program shows an impressive 80% success rate over a year, for sexual dysfunctions in both women and men. We don't yet know which parts of the program are necessary and sufficient for its success, because there hasn't been enough work done with control groups or variants of the program. However, we do know that it is a very successful treatment approach for sexual dysfunctions.

SEXUAL DEVIATIONS

Although people suffering from sexual dysfunctions often are unhappy and troubled, they usually are not in conflict with the laws and mores of society. However, the *sexual deviations* typically run contrary to the established laws of society, in addition to engendering a significant degree of disdain from society as a whole. Many people may feel sorry for the man or woman who can't perform sexually but feel disgust toward a man who rapes women to satisfy his sexual needs.

Description

The sexual deviations are considered by some experts (Edwards, 1977; Storr, 1964) to be modes of sexual release that males use when normal modes of release aren't available. In instances of true deviation, the male typically is unable to establish intimate, love-related relationships with mature female peers. Because of this inability, and given a biologically based sexual drive, alternative nonintimate and impersonal channels of expression may be chosen. These channels compose the specific types of sexual deviations we observe. Sexual deviations may be manifested in an abnormal choice of sexual object or an abnormal choice of method of sexual gratification.

Disordered Choice of Sexual Object.   In deviations involving a disordered choice of sexual object, individuals have chosen or used for their sexual fulfillment objects not generally chosen or used by others. Rather than achieve sexual satisfaction through complete intimate sexual intercourse with opposite-sex peers, the sexual deviant may achieve satisfaction from physical or imaginary contact with objects that act as substitutes for normal sexual objects. Although many people use objects and situations such as those we will describe as *adjuncts* to sex, it is their use as a *primary* channel of satisfaction that is considered deviant.

The center of sexual interest in *fetishism* is some inanimate object, most often an article of clothing, which typically is used as a stimulus while masturbating. Usually stolen, the objects include common articles of women's clothing such as bras, shoes, or stockings, and other more unusual items. In one case, a man collected hair he cut off unsuspecting young girls, and he acquired quite a nice collection before being arrested. Another fetishist collected cardboard tubing found inside of such items as paper toweling or waxed paper. Fetishes for exhaust pipes, baby carriages, baby-food jars, and noses also have been reported. It is important to note that the sexual excitement caused by the fetishist's object is usually increased if the object is stolen. For example, providing the young man who collected tubing with all the cardboard tubes he needed probably wouldn't satisfy or excite him in the least. Some of the excitement engendered by stealing the prized object is shown in the following personal experience.

PERSONAL EXPERIENCE: *Fetishism*

I was about 14 when my friend Bobby and I used to have a clubhouse in a storage building behind my father's store. We kept a lot of stuff in there, mostly dirty books and stuff . . . we had quite a collection, some classics in fact—Jayne Mansfield and Marilyn Monroe. I started collecting girls' panties when I found a pair in the trash in the alley down the block from my house. I told Bobby about it, but he didn't really get as excited about it as I did. I don't know, just the idea that those panties were once right next to the ass of a girl really turned me on . . . and the thought that she didn't know that I was kinda sneaking a sniff without her saying it was OK really got me hot. After a while, just like the dirty books, I lost interest in the first pair of panties, but it wasn't easy to get newer ones, especially since I really didn't get off on them unless they were unwashed. I finally found a way to get them by hanging around the laundromat on the avenue. . . . After a woman would bring in her basket of clothes, I would wait till she went to the soap machine and while she was busy I would quickly run by and pick out a pair of panties and stick it inside my shirt. I don't know how many pairs I got that way but I got a lot. Bobby always complained that the clubhouse wasn't the same because of what I was doing, but I didn't care.

The *transvestite* obtains sexual gratification and pleasure by wearing the clothing of the opposite sex. Although homosexual and transsexual people also may dress in the clothing of the opposite sex, the transvestite is the only one who obtains primary sexual excitement by the "feel" of such clothing. A fetishist can develop into a transvestite by having the female objects with which he masturbates increase into a complete cross-sex clothing outfit. Usually, dressing in cross-sex clothes is done in private and is an isolated part of the person's life. Most transvestites are male, married, and maintain their masculine identity in the family except for the fact that they frequently dress in cross-sex clothing for sexual excitement. It is one of the wonders of human adaptability that many wives learn to live with their husbands' strange dressing habits. Usually masculine in appearance, the male transvestite rarely indulges in homosexual activity, for he is generally heterosexual in orientation.

Unlike transvestites, who maintain cross-sex orientation, *transsexuals* feel as though they are trapped in the body of the wrong sex. Unable to accept the fact of their own physical sex, transsexuals may dress in the clothing of the opposite sex although, unlike the transvestite, they will *not* be excited by this act. The opposite-sex clothing simply seems to feel more appropriate to the manner in which these people think about themselves. Transsexualism is rare and occurs more in males (about 1 in 100,000) than in females (about 1 in 400,000). These individuals usually have histories of gender and sex-role confusion: males are likely to have been "sissies" and girls, "tom boys." However, in physical appearance and by most other criteria of hormonal and sexual attributes, transsexual males and females don't differ from nontranssexuals. The differences lie in the manner in which transsexuals think of themselves. Transsexual males may be seen as physically male and psychologically female, whereas the reverse holds true for transsexual females. For example, the typical transsexual male thinks, feels, and believes he is a woman. He doesn't value the secondary sexual characteristics of males, but may be in constant anguish that he can't fulfill himself as a woman and may fantasize about having breasts and a vagina. The need to fulfill himself as a woman may eventually drive him to sex-change surgery. Similar drives and conflicts exist among female transsexuals, who wish to live as physical males.

Incest, or sexual relations among blood relatives, is unlike the deviations discussed thus far in that the deviation includes other people.

Dr. Richard Raskind (left), a professional tennis player, underwent a sex-change operation to become Dr. Renée Richards (right), who played as a woman in the U.S. Open. (Photos by Wide World Photos.)

Healthy contact among relatives differs from incestuous contact in that a feeling of sexual excitement accompanies the latter. Incest has always been nearly universally prohibited (although intermarriage among Egyptian pharaohs and their sisters or other immediate relatives was condoned). Cross-cultural data show that the punishment of incest usually is severe. Estimates of its incidence are confounded by many factors, but in Sweden, for example, it is estimated that there are only 0.73 cases per million population, and in the United States, only 1.1 cases per million (Weinberg, 1955). Father-daughter incest is most often reported, and mother-son incest is more rare. Most of the reported cases of incest are among lower-class people, but one researcher concluded that aspects of lower-class life such as overcrowding, social isolation, and poverty need not be the only contributory factors (Henderson, 1975).

Lukianowicz (1972) studied 26 cases of father-daughter incest and described the fathers as slightly above average in intelligence, and to some degree psychopathic. Most often, incest begins with the oldest daughter when the father is about 40 years old. Once begun, the incestuous relationship may continue for some time. Lukianowicz concluded that daughters often share some of the responsibility for the relationship and, in some cases, may be the initiators.

Thus far, we have described disorders that are frowned on by society, but rarely lead to physical injury or harm. However, in *pedophilia*, the gratification of sexual needs with children, victims are often harmed or even killed. As a group, pedophiles may be described as a potpourri of mental defectives, alcoholics, and senile individuals. Generally, pedophiliacs try kissing and petting with children under 10 and sodomy, fellatio, or coitus with older children. The law generally defines the pedophile as one whose sexual contact is with children up to the age of 14, and who is 10 years older than the child. According to Gebhart, Gagnon, Pomeroy, and Christenson (1965), *aggressive* pedophiles usually are strangers to the child, tend to be in their 30s, and have a background of crime and drinking. They are among the *most dangerous of all sex offenders* and have in many cases murdered the children they've molested. However, the greatest number of pedophiles are *nonaggressive*. Typically, they know the child or the family, make no show of force, and tend to be either young, immature boys or older, lonely men. Although nonaggressive offenders will choose either boys or girls, aggressive male offenders typically choose boys. Most pedophiles are men, and most children molested are girls (a ratio of 2 to 1). The punishment for child molestation is explicit, and of all sex-related crimes, pedophilia is usually reacted to most strongly by society, especially if aggression is involved.

Seen much less frequently than the deviations just described, sexual involvement with animals and corpses has also been observed. *Bestiality*, sexual gratification through contact with animals, is relatively rare in spite of the abundance of myths and stories describing humans having sexual relations with everything from orangutans to swans. Most contacts are fleeting and involve dogs, cats, or farm animals. Most sexual contacts with animals take place during adolescence and usually indicate a transition to more acceptable means of sexual gratification. If sexual satisfaction is achieved *only* with animals, the behavior pattern is considered a deviation.

Unlike bestiality, which does occur in normal people, *necrophilia*, or sexual gratification through intercourse with a corpse, is always indicative of severe psychopathology. A patient seen by one of the authors had intercourse with his mother after she had died. In a continuous state of sexual excitement, he stayed with her for 24 hours after her death. Needless to say, he was severely disturbed, and the necrophilic behavior was but a small part of his overall psychopathology.

Disordered Choice of Method of Gratification. As opposed to deviations in which abnormal sexual objects are involved, the second major group of sexual deviations involves normal heterosexual sex objects but disordered methods of obtaining such contact. As was true of the disorders of sex object, the people we are about to discuss typically cannot achieve sexual satisfaction in intimate, love-related relationships. Instead, they must resort to substitutes for or approximations to actual intercourse. Again, while each of these deviations can be used in normal sexual stimulation, when they become the primary source of gratification, they are considered abnormal.

Frottage refers to obtaining sexual gratification by touching or rubbing another person. Although most forms of normal sexual interaction include some touching, the typical frotteur touches strangers of the opposite sex only in public places such as crowded sidewalks, subways, trains, and shopping centers. He may touch the breasts or buttocks of women while in these situations, and then flee. These men usually are harmless and rarely engage in dangerous or harmful sexual activity.

PERSONAL EXPERIENCE: *Frottage*

I don't see that much wrong with it, but if you want me to tell about it, OK, here goes. I grew up in New York City and spent a lot of time as a teenager on the subways. One of the ways that we used to get some action was to ride the trains during rush hour . . . you know, between 4 and 6. Well, we used to ride the IRT out of Broadway and go to the end of the line and then, for another token, we'd come all the way back. When the trains were packed, people used to be piled on top of one another. I would try to get close to some nice-looking girls and when the trains would come to a stop, I'd kinda let myself fall into them a little. I'd be able to cop a lotta feels that way and never really have any heat for it. Just being close to these women really drove me up a wall.

Somewhat more severe than frottage, *exhibitionism* involves the exposing of one's genitalia to strangers, usually females or children. The exhibiting most often occurs in inappropriate places and at inappropriate times, subjecting the observer to an upsetting and often repulsive scene. Police report that the *modus operandi* of the exhibitionist is usually consistent and individualistic, and that the danger of being caught seems to add to the excitement of the act. An extensive study of exhibitionists (Gebhart et al., 1965) indicated that only 10% of people imprisoned for sex crimes were exhibitionists, in spite of the fact that one-third of all arrests for sexual misbehavior involved exhibitionism. This suggests strongly that exhibitionism is a relatively harmless class of disorder. We say *relatively*, for about one out of every ten exhibitionists is involved in more violent forms of sexual offenses such as pedophilia and rape. Although two-thirds are married, exhibitionists appear to have difficulty in adjusting heterosexually and obtain much of their sexual satisfaction through masturbation or prostitutes.

The exhibitionist seems to have an overpowering "compulsion" to engage in his deviant behavior, and it appears that this compulsion occurs

Some forms of exhibitionism are considered acceptable. (Photo by Robert Foothorap.)

more in response to some kind of stress. Often this stress is caused by one of the interpersonal failures such people continually seem to experience. The exhibitionist may seek to provoke a strong reaction in women to prove his masculinity. Even though exhibitionism is usually harmless, it can be very upsetting to those who witness it, as the next personal experience shows.

PERSONAL EXPERIENCE: *The Victim of an Exhibitionist*

It's rare to be able to remember something as if it were yesterday, but when you mentioned in class that you wanted to know about reactions to exhibitionists everything came back. It happened when I was about 7 or 8 years old. I had just gotten a new BB gun and my friend and I went out to the local park where there were some woods . . . a strange thing in the middle of the city . . . we went out to shoot some birds. We were walking through the woods and taking unsuccessful potshots at squirrels and birds . . . the gun was so weak that we hit a squirrel dead on and he didn't even bat an eyelash. Anyway, we were walking up this path and turned a corner, when there was this guy . . .

he had red hair and was really big. . . . I guess he looked bigger cause I was so small, but I remember him as a giant. He had his penis in his hand and was waving it at us and mumbling something I never to this day can remember nor could I make it out at the time. I was so unbelievably scared that I aimed my BB gun at his penis, shot him with it and ran. We kept running until we got home, a good ten blocks away. For weeks after that I was afraid that the guy was gonna come after me and kill me for shooting a hole in his penis. I never went back to that park for as long as I lived in _____ .

Whereas the exhibitionist wants others to see him, the voyeur "works" secretly. A mild disorder, *voyeurism*, or *scoptophilia*, involves a male's obtaining sexual gratification by observing others (without their awareness) in various stages of undress or lovemaking. The "peeper" isn't usually interested in making any additional contact with the "peepee," and his sexual release typically comes through masturbation either during or after his observations. The danger of being caught makes the peeping all the more exciting. A large number of arrests made for sexual disorders involve voyeurs and, combined with exhibitionists, they make up the majority of all arrests for sexual misbehavior. Like the exhibitionist, the voyeur rarely becomes involved in any aggressive or dangerous actions.

PERSONAL EXPERIENCE: *Voyeurism*

I'm really upset about what I've done. . . . I feel like a freak or something. I was brought up in a religious family, and I shudder to think what my pastor would say if he knew about me. But I think that my strict upbringing had a lot to do with what I wound up doing . . . looking into dorm windows. I've never really gotten along well with girls . . . I'm sort of frightened by them. Look at me . . . I'm not very good looking . . . very few girls would really want to go out with me. But I'm a male, too, and I have a sex drive. I used to be able to satisfy myself by looking at *Playboy* pictures and all and then masturbating, but those girls weren't real . . . they're not alive. When I came to school, I learned from certain places it was easy to see into the girls' bathrooms in the dorm on the ridge . . . especially on hot spring nights when they open the windows. So, I got . . . binoculars . . . and would tell my roommate I'd be studying late at the library. Then I'd go up and watch the girls take showers and fantasize that they were having sex with me. I'd masturbate while I watched and after I reached a climax, I'd go home . . . and I'd feel real bad . . . kind of dirty and sick, but in two or three days, I'd be right back doing it again.

While they differ in their chosen method of communication, *obscene phone callers and letter writers* seek to provoke the same effect as exhibitionists. The obscene telephone caller may ring at any time of the day or night and fill the ear of the listener with heavy breathing or obscene sexual comments. Both men and women obscene callers apparently prefer to call females. If the obscene caller can engage the listener in conversation for any length of time, chances are he or she will call again. The telephone company estimates that there are 2 million obscene phone calls a year. There are also people who enjoy *receiving* obscene phone calls, and there are businesses on the fringe of society that provide this service for a fee. Obscene letter-writing also involves obscene and arousing messages. It is not so widespread as obscene calling (perhaps because of the slower service of the post office). If not apprehended, obscene letter writers have been known to carry on such activity for a long time.

Whereas the disorders of method presented up to now seldom involve physical harm, *sadomasochism* is characterized by aggression. In sadomasochism, the objects of sexual needs usually are confronted directly, and sexuality often is used to express primitive aggressive and hostile needs. In many instances, we believe this kind of aggressive sexual behavior reflects severe underlying psychopathology.

Generally, the *sadist* experiences sexual excitement when harming another person, whereas the *masochist* becomes sexually excited by being harmed. Sadism is named after the Marquis de Sade, an 18th-century nobleman who was known for his literary descriptions of brutal, cruel attacks on women. *Masochism* is named for the pain-loving character type developed by Leopold von Sacher-Masoch, a 19th-century Austrian author. Although some aggressiveness is shown in most normal sexual interactions, it usually is more a *result* of the sexual passion than the cause of it. However, in the case of the sadist and the masochist, hurting or being hurt is *the source* of sexual excitement. Sadomasochistic individuals can be very creative in coming up with ways to inflict or receive pain. Long-lasting relationships may develop when a sadist links up with a masochist; or, in some instances, the partners take turns being sadistic. There seem to be far fewer sadists than masochists. As a result, houses of prostitution frequently do a land-office business in serving those who need to be hurt. As a matter of fact, consistent with present-day professional specialization, there are prostitutes who "specialize" in pain-giving and pain-receiving.

PERSONAL EXPERIENCE: *Sadism*

I've only agreed to talk to you about this because I'm concerned that you are writing about sadism in an abnormal-psychology book. I want it known that sadism *is not* abnormal, but is the expression of a deeper sense of feeling for another person than is possible with routine sexual patterns. I am not an uneducated person and I've not come to these conclusions out of lack of knowledge or experience. To me sadism is the icing on the cake, the cherry on top of the sundae . . . it adds a special something to sex. The inflicting of pain upon another person is the inflicting of your existence upon them; when you kiss another person she need not remember that kiss nor the feelings associated with your presence, but when you cut a person with a razor ever so lightly and you share the drops of blood which result, the relationship is sealed and never to be forgotten.

Unfortunately, some sadists graduate to murder. Some of the most bizarre and spectacular mass murders have been committed by sadists who have punished and mutilated their victims before killing them. These "lust murders" can be either heterosexual or homosexual. In some cases, there may even be intercourse with the victim after death, which adds necrophilia to the pathological picture.

Rape may be seen as the fusion of sex and aggression and can be defined as the forcing of intercourse or fellatio by a man on an unwilling other, usually a woman. About 50,000 cases of rape are reported each year. Of all sexual crimes, rape seems to have shown the greatest increase during the past two decades. The data become even more disconcerting when we realize that for every reported rape, it is estimated that at least four go unreported! If these estimates are accurate, they suggest that nearly 250,000 women are raped each year.

In the eyes of the law, there are two kinds of rape: *statutory rape* and *forcible rape*. In statutory rape, the victim is under a certain age (17 in most states) and is assumed to have been "persuaded" or seduced by the man even if she had willingly cooperated in intercourse. Forcible rape is a different story. As the law now stands in most states, to convict a rapist, it must be proved that the offender used force or threats of force; the woman must have protested and resisted; and there must be medical evidence of vaginal penetration and injuries. Typically, the woman must then submit to an open trial where a frequent defense for the accused is to attempt to slander the woman and to show she titillated the man. Many women's groups have protested the entire legal procedure. In response to what they feel is inappropriate handling of many rape cases, women have spearheaded the opening of "rape-crisis centers" in many cities across the country. They have also worked for changes in the law that would make prosecution easier and reduce the humiliation victims often suffer in the courtroom.

FBI Uniform Crime statistics (1975) show that most rapists are young (33% under 20 years of age) and over half are married. Rape isn't usually a one-time crime; rapists tend to repeat their behavior. Men who rape girls under the age of 17 do not differ significantly in personality or description from those who rape older women. Rapists seem to be strongly heterosexual, with low impulse control. In fact, many rapists closely fit the description of the psychopath whom we described in Chapter 12. Their approach to life can be summed up by the statement "I wanted it, so I took it" (Kopp, 1962).

Although most rape victims are under 25, rapists, because of their low impulse control, often attack any woman who happens to come along. Women 80 years old have been brutally attacked and raped. Some rapists actually believe that all women secretly wish to be raped, and that the more the women fight, the more they really desire to be violated. If the woman does fight, she stands a good chance of sustaining an injury or of being killed. If she doesn't fight, she can be accused in the courtroom of inviting the attack. It becomes even more difficult for a woman to prove rape when the attacker is a friend or acquaintance, as is true in up to 50% of the cases. The courtroom scenes can be extremely embarrassing. One of the authors viewed such a proceeding, and it suggested what the Star Chamber inquisitions must have been like in the Middle Ages. The defense attorney asked questions about the woman's sexual behavior, from the time she was 6 years old and played "dirty doctor" to the hearsay evidence of whether she was thought to be "easy" in high school. In all, it was a distasteful procedure that made it clear why so few women report a rape, and why rape-crisis centers have come into existence.

Explanations

Considering the variety of sexual deviations, it should come as no surprise that explaining all of these aberrations within a single theory is impossible. Indeed, there are specific explanations for several of the sexual patterns, and we have mentioned some of these along with our descriptions. In this section, we would like to take a general explanatory look at sexual deviations. Our perspective will be multitheoretical and will reflect our belief that the various specific deviations merely represent modes of sexual gratification alternative to normal heterosexual intercourse. These alternative modes are abnormal in the sense that they don't contribute to the continuation of the species (the biological reason for sex) and are considered culturally unacceptable.

According to Edwards (1977) and Storr (1964), sexual deviations may be seen as simple exaggerations of normal male sexual tendencies. For example, normal males "exhibit" their masculinity in body-building, athletics, sports cars, and the like; deviant males "exhibit" their masculinity by exposing their genitals. Further, many normal males are easily aroused by the sight or touch of female undergarments; the fetishistic male achieves gratification *only* through such objects.

If sexual deviations are exaggerations of normal patterns, we are still left with the question of why these modes of sexual expression are chosen. Edwards (1977) has noted that the reasons may be found in either *sexual guilt* or *sexual inferiority*. The rare deviations in females are due to sexual guilt, a reaction to the violations of introjected rules of parents and society. Thus, the female who has been taught that sexual excitement is bad may become so guilty upon experiencing normal sexual arousal that she tries to deny her own sex orientation and may become a transvestite.

Since deviations are very rare among females, guilt must be seen as playing a minor role as compared with sexual inferiority. From what can be seen as a Freudian and neoanalytic perspective (see Chapter 4), Edwards (1977) believes that males who don't live up to their ego ideal sense themselves as inferior in terms of masculinity. If such males don't have the ability to relate in a normal, mature, and intimate manner with a member of the opposite sex, they are forced to opt for less acceptable alternatives for reinforcing their self-perception of masculinity. Essentially, when a normal channel is blocked, an abnormal channel is chosen. For example, in a fetishist, an object such as a bra takes on the power of the female who wore it and substitutes for her. The fetishist is guaranteed success in his interaction with the substitute and thereby increases his sense of masculinity. In pedophilia, the male is typically afraid of mature females and therefore chooses a child as an object. The child's powerlessness emphasizes the deviant's strength and masculinity, and his inferiority feelings are assuaged. According to theorists such as Edwards and Storr, sexual deviations may be understood as exaggerated normal patterns that may be used to satisfy needs for a sense of masculinity without the requirements of intimate personal relationships.

Treatment

Unlike most people who are different, some people who are sexually aberrant aren't uncomfortable about their behavior. Rather, it is society or the law that is upset by them. Thus, some sexually disturbed people seek help only because others have forced them to do so. Needless to say, this state of affairs often results in unmotivated and uncooperative clients. Although traditional forms of individual and group psychotherapy may be helpful in sexual problems, generally the behavioral-treatment approaches work best. As one behavior therapist put it, "All that is necessary for change to occur is that the client agree to take part in the conditioning procedures; his degree of motivation during the procedures is not crucial" (Cautela, 1968).

Generally, behavioral intervention is based upon the precept that biological sexual needs serve as motivators for behavior that satisfies them.

The reduction of the biological sex drive is a reinforcing event (orgasm is pleasurable) and can strengthen any behavior that precedes such reduction. In people who have learned how to relate on a mature heterosexual level, sexual fulfillment reinforces that level. In people who cannot relate in biologically adaptable or socially acceptable ways, other sexual behaviors must serve as the *primary* tension reducer. Behavior therapy is directed at two aspects of misdirected sexuality. First, the positively valued abnormal sex object or behavior must be made aversive or negative. Second, the difficulties faced when trying to satisfy biological drives through normal intercourse must be resolved.

The first type of therapy, producing aversion to abnormal sex objects, can be exemplified by *covert sensitization* (Cautela, 1968, 1970a). Mahoney (1974) has stated that this approach is consistently effective with sexual deviance. In covert sensitization, sex objects that initially are positively valued are associated in the client's imagination with aversive feelings such as nausea and anxiety. The procedure is similar to the one we described in the treatment of alcoholism in Chapter 13. The abnormal sex object or mode of expression is associated not with pleasure but with discomfort. In this way, the frequency of the deviant behavior may be reduced.

Once the deviant pattern is halted, it becomes necessary for treatment to focus on the development of more adaptive social-interpersonal-sexual skills. Successful development of these skills may be achieved through a variety of structured and unstructured individual and group therapies. In unstructured therapy, clients usually are allowed to develop new skills in their own way and at their own pace. In structured therapy, by contrast, various assignments are usually made by the therapist. For example, a client might be assigned simply to make a date with a woman. In a safe group setting, the client will be allowed to practice by role-playing himself asking another group member who role-plays a woman friend to go out with him. In this way, social skills that were absent may be learned, and the necessity for deviant modes of sexual expression may disappear in the face of more mature modes of expression. The combination of such new modes of expression and the acquired aversion to the deviant behavior provides an effective treatment program for sexual deviations.

SEXUAL-ORIENTATION DISTURBANCES

Until the early 1970s, the sexual pattern of homosexuality was included among the sexual deviations we have just discussed. However, homosexuality is different from the sexual deviations in several ways. First of all, many homosexuals are capable of mature, intimate interpersonal and sexual relationships. Second, their choice of object and mode of sexual satisfaction is primarily based, not upon distorted sexual abilities within their physically determined sex, but on the fact that emotionally and psychologically they experience themselves as oriented differently. Thus, many homosexual people *can* be intimate and loving only with a member of the same sex.

Description

Homosexuality seems always to have been a subject of debate. Regardless of personal sexual orientation, few seem to be unbiased about this class of sexual behavior. Therefore, we must keep certain facts about homosexuality in mind. First, data from survey studies suggest that there are *not* two distinct groups of people, one called heterosexual and one called homosexual, but rather a continuum of people who engage in sexual behaviors ranging from primarily homosexual through bisexual to primarily heterosexual. Second, homosexual behavior in men is typically more severely condemned by society than is homosexual behavior in women. In this respect, homosexuality is like most of the disorders we have discussed in this chapter—primarily a problem for males.

Originally, homosexuality was included in the DSM-I manual under sociopathic personality disturbances; in DSM-II, it was included under the section on personality disorders. However, in a recent decision (1974), the American Psychiatric Association voted to stop considering homosexuality in and of itself a mental disorder. In place of the previous classification, they substituted a category called *sexual-orientation disturbance*. This category is intended to be for individuals whose sexual interests are directed primarily toward people of the same sex and who are in some way disturbed by their sexual orientation. As a diagnostic category, sexual-orientation disturbance is explicitly distinguished from homosexuality as such, which is considered to be one among many forms of sexual behavior that are not, by themselves, psychiatric disorders.

This new classification fails to take into consideration the fact that human sexual behavior usually doesn't fall into neat, independent homosexual or heterosexual groups. Kinsey, Pomeroy, and Martin (1948) assumed that sexual behavior could best be conceptualized as a continuum from homosexuality to heterosexuality. Using a seven-point scale to represent this continuum, Kinsey described the various types of sexual behavior, as shown in Table 14-1. It is clear that most people manifest more than a single kind of sexual behavior. In homosexuality we generally are referring to individuals who fall in group 5 or 6 and who spontaneously are aroused by members of the same sex. It is usually the arousal pattern, and *not* the manifest behavior, that is the most significant diagnostic sign.

Further support for the idea that much homosexual behavior may be considered normal comes from Ford and Beach (1952), who reported that among 76 societies they studied, 64% considered homosexuality to be normal. In fact, in some of the societies, male homosexual behavior was nearly universal; of course, males also were involved in heterosexual relationships and could probably best be described as bisexual. These researchers also

Table 14-1. *Percentage of males and females engaging in homosexual and heterosexual activity*

Scale Point	Females	Males
0: Entirely heterosexual experience		
Single	61–72%	53–78%
Married	89–90	90–92
Previously married	75–80	—
1–6: At least some homosexual experience	11–20	18–42
2–6: More than incidental homosexual experience	6–14	13–38
3–6: Homosexual as much as or more than heterosexual	4–11	9–32
4–6: Mostly homosexual experience	3–8	7–26
5–6: Almost exclusive homosexual experience	2–6	5–22
6: Exclusive homosexual experience	1–3	3–16

Based on data from *Sexual Behavior in the Human Female*, by A. Kinsey et al. Copyright 1953 by W. B. Saunders Company. Used by permission of the Institute for Sex Research.

found evidence that, even in the societies where homosexuality was condemned, it existed in secret. It appears that homosexuality is a part of most civilized societies.

Most data for the incidence of homosexuality in the United States come from the work of Kinsey et al. (1948, 1953). Of over 5000 men surveyed, nearly 40% had at least one homosexually oriented orgasmic experience between adolescence and old age, and 10% were exclusively homosexual in their orientation (as rated by a 5 or 6 on Kinsey's scale) for at least three years. In addition, another 10% felt erotically aroused by other males. Of the nearly 5500 women interviewed, only 4% of unmarried women and 1% of married women were exclusively homosexual. However, 30% reported some homosexual experience or arousal during the course of their lives, one-third of them to the point of experiencing an orgasm. Unlike males, 20% of unmarried women and 10% of married women had experienced *no* sexual response, whether heterosexual or homosexual, between the ages of 20 and 35. Essentially, these women were sexually neuter.

Studies of the style of homosexual behavior usually reflect significant differences between male and female homosexuals. Saghir and Robins (1969a, b) gathered data from members of gay groups who had never been hospitalized for psychiatric reasons or arrested for criminal offenses. They found that male homosexuals usually began masturbating earlier and masturbated more frequently, engaged in homosexual experiences earlier, had a higher number of homosexual contacts, were more promiscuous, and engaged in more oral-genital sex than female homosexuals. Both males and females reported that they were erotically aroused by people of the same sex before adolescence and usually alternated between active and passive roles in lovemaking. In all, women tended to engage in fewer and longer homosexual relationships than males, who had more "one-night stands." These "one-night stands" often were engaged in compulsively. A homosexual male may have had as many as ten homosexual contacts in one night at

"I feel that the radicals are necessary, and I feel that we are necessary."
Mark is an executive vice-president of a New York corporation.

"You go through a lot of hurt when someone calls you a Chinaman, so
that in one sense you are more able to deal with someone calling you a
fag." Dennis, the son of immigrant parents, lives in San Francisco and
has been active with gay-Asian support groups.

"I was the American dream daughter—cheerleader, Prom queen, straight-A student, president of the honor society, newspaper editor. . . . I was miserable." Linda grew up in the South, married and put her husband through school, was divorced, and now works as a secretary in North Carolina.

As these examples show, homosexual people don't fit a single stereotype. (Photos from Word Is Out, Stories of Some of Our Lives, *published by New Glide Publications, Inc. Used by permission.)*

a variety of places such as public washrooms, public baths, autos, and public parks. The danger in these interactions seems merely to add to the excitement of the encounter. However, there is a self-defeating quality to one-night-stand behavior. There have been instances in which religious leaders, college administrators, and doctors have had their careers shattered when they were caught by police in public bathrooms engaging in homosexual activities.

Studies of men who participated in the impersonal sex of the public-bathroom circuit (called "tearooms") show that half were married and lived with their wives and children in generally middle-class homes (Humphreys, 1970). As a group, these men tended to be politically conservative and religious. Nearly half saw themselves as heterosexual and viewed the public-restroom meetings as a quick way of meeting their sexual needs. Although married, many of these men probably had unsatisfactory sexual relationships with their wives. Women homosexuals rarely engage in such impersonal interactions as the tearoom circuit. It appears that there probably are true differences between male and female homosexuals in their expressed sexual behavior—differences that parallel the sexual behavior of male and female heterosexuals.

Explanations

The explanations for sexual-orientation disturbances may be categorized as either biological or psychological. Biological theorists generally hold that some physical defect produces same-sex attraction. Psychological theorists think that faulty learning and harmful early-childhood experiences contribute most to the development of homosexual behavior.

Biological Theories.   Until recently, homosexuality was thought by some to be caused by defective genes or some degeneration of the nervous system. However, attempts to support such physiological theories have been largely unsuccessful. Although Kallmann (1952) found a concordance rate of 100% for homosexuality in a sample of monozygotic twins and only an average rate for dizygotic twins, his findings haven't been confirmed by others. In fact, L. S. Kolb (1963) found *no* concordance in homosexuality of twins in a sample of seven sets of monozygotic twins. If there is a genetic relationship in homosexuality, most theorists now believe it is a hidden predisposition for the individual to become homosexual if he or she encounters supportive environmental conditions. Certainly, though, there is no unequivocal evidence for a direct genetic link in homosexuality.

The other popular somatic explanation for homosexuality has been a hormonal one. Generally, hormonal theorists assume that imbalances in the levels of sex hormones (testosterone in males and estrogen in females) are related to homosexuality. Simply stated, the hormonal hypothesis is that homosexual men have lower levels of testosterone and homosexual women, lower levels of estrogen. For example, Loraine, Ismael, Adamopoulos, and Dove (1970) found low testosterone levels in homosexual males as compared to heterosexual controls, and Margolese (1970) found similar differences between healthy homosexuals and healthy heterosexuals in the presence of breakdown products of testosterone. Both results are consistent with the general hormonal hypothesis. However, many hormonal studies are characterized by major methodological difficulties that make it difficult to obtain clear results. Because of these difficulties, results obtained in one study generally fail to be replicated elsewhere.

Psychological Theories. Whereas the biological theorists believe that homosexuality can be caused by some inborn physical defect, the psychological theorists think that sexual-orientation disturbances may arise from the environment and psychological experiences. Freud proposed an early psychological explanation for homosexuality. In his "Three Essays on the Theory of Sexuality" (1930/1953), he suggested that all people were bisexual (attracted to both sexes) at the point in their normal development when they loved both of their parents. Homosexuality is seen as the result of an arrest of normal development at this bisexual (*homoerotic*) stage, or as a regression back to such a point. Freud further believed that we maintain vestiges of this homoerotic stage as we develop. Remnants of bisexual urges are felt in some as "homosexual panic," in which feared homosexual impulses arise in heterosexual people and produce severe anxiety.

Freud implicated the mishandling of the Oedipal stage and the failure of the male child to form a satisfactory relationship with his father as a major cause for the retardation of normal sexual development. Freud believed the presence of a detached, cold, and even hostile father, together with a close, binding, seductive mother sets the stage for the development of a homosexual orientation. However, the presence of a truly loving and caring father probably could prevent the development of a homosexual orientation, regardless of what the mother was like. In the case of homosexual development, a boy must deal with his incestuous feelings toward his mother. From his attempts to handle these incestuous feelings, he may develop a fear of sexual contact with the opposite sex (*heterophobia*). This fear develops because the boy may observe that women have "lost their penis" and that the very same thing might happen to him if his father learned of his feeling toward women in general, and his mother in particular. Freud suggests that sex with a woman awakens male fears of castration and may lead one to adopt a homosexual orientation.

Support for the Freudian explanation has been gathered by Bieber and his colleagues (1962). Bieber's group obtained the cooperation of 77 psychoanalysts who provided access to the case histories of 106 male homosexuals seen in analysis. On the basis of these case histories and information gathered through interviews of the patients by their analysts, Bieber concluded that the most significant factor in the genesis of homosexuality in this patient group was the particular parental constellation of cold father–seductive mother as hypothesized by Freud. As was also suggested by Freud, homosexual patients reportedly showed castration fears and an apparent aversion to female genitalia.

Generally, the data gathered by Bieber's group and others (Evans, 1969) hold only for males. As is true with much of Freudian theory, women are mentioned only in passing, and explanations presented for their behavior seem more convoluted than those presented for men. In fact, Freud offers little about the development of homosexuality in women. Perhaps we can assume that, parallel to the explanation for males, there may be an inadequate identification with the mother and a fear of sexual relationships with males as a result of a poorly resolved Electra complex (see Chapter 4).

A second psychological approach stems from learning theory. Learning theorists believe that the reinforcement of inappropriate sex-role behavior is an important contributor to the development of a person's homosexual orientation. In our culture, there is usually pressure on youngsters to adopt same-sex relationships for an extended length of time in their development. Most often, boys play with boys and girls play with girls in such activities as sports, scouting, and social interactions. It often takes youngsters some time and great courage to overcome the embarrassment of peer pressure in order to make cross-sex contacts. Then they must learn that such cross-sex contact brings more satisfaction than that obtained in same-sex interactions.

It would seem that a plausible psychological explanation of homosexuality would include the pathological family patterns proposed by Freud as they interact with other factors. For example, based on the description of parental relationships just given, we would expect more male homosexuality in ghetto-type living situations, where there is a higher proportion of absent fathers. However, examination of the incidence of homosexuality in ghetto populations doesn't show this to be true. Such factors as peer associations, availability of a homosexual milieu, and ability to find other outlets for sex appear to be important determinants of whether a person adopts a homosexual orientation. Most theorists would agree that learning a homosexual orientation includes both the reinforcement of behaviors in youngsters that are consonant with homosexuality and aversive conditioning to heterosexual behavior.

Treatment

Unlike people manifesting sexual deviations, people with sexual-orientation disturbance are capable in many instances of functioning publicly as not being different. Indeed, many homosexuals say that they are very happy and emotionally well adjusted. However, controversy has long existed over whether sexual-orientation disturbance is actually a sign of psychopathology. Prior to discussing the treatment of those who are homosexual *and* disturbed, we would like to examine the general nature of the relationship between homosexuality and emotional disturbance.

Freud described homosexuality as occurring in "people who exhibit no other serious deviation from the normal . . . whose efficiency is unimpaired, and who are indeed distinguished by specially high intellectual development and ethical culture" (1930/1953). Although he considered it no advantage to be homosexual, Freud certainly didn't classify homosexuality as a mental illness. However, other analysts have taken issue with the master on this subject. Bieber et al. (1962) view homosexuality as incompatible with obtaining a reasonably happy life and as the result of disordered sexual development. Others see homosexuality as inconsistent with the biological norm of procreation and cite data showing the relative scarcity of homosexuality in animals (Beach, 1948).

Those countering the argument that homosexuality is related to mental illness suggest that homosexuals aren't all that distraught and unhappy. They believe that the conclusion that homosexuals are unhappy is based on the perceptions of therapists who see only homosexuals who are dissatisfied enough with their life-style to seek psychological help. As for biological norms, Beach (1948) points out that, as one moves up the evolutionary scale, sexual behavior becomes more affected by learning. The fact that homosexuals usually show no predominately different incidence of other psychopathology suggests that this sexual orientation isn't necessarily related to a disordered sexual development.

However, it should be pointed out that, although there is no greater relationship between homosexuality and disordered behavior than between heterosexuality and such behavior, there certainly is no less. Some professionals and spokespeople for homosexual groups tend to give the impression that homosexuals are brighter, more loving, and typically superior to heterosexuals. This is most likely not the case; there probably are proportionally as many murderers, schizophrenics, and unhappy people among homosexuals as there are among heterosexuals. Being a homosexual is no safeguard against developing disordered behavior, nor is it a reliable concomitant of abnormality. Many homosexuals are disturbed and need treatment, and many are well adjusted.

There is little hope of success in changing a homosexual person's sexual orientation unless he or she is motivated to change. Attempting to force treatment on an unwilling or uncooperative homosexual person probably is morally unjustified, in the first place, and notoriously unsuccessful, in the second. Among homosexuals motivated to change their sexual orientation, psychotherapy has been successful, especially with clients under 35 years of age who have experienced some heterosexual satisfaction at some time in their lives and whose homosexuality is recent. The traditional forms of individual and group therapy to be discussed in later chapters can be applied to problems of sexual-orientation disturbance, and a combination of behavioral means and structured behavior change also has been found to be effective in altering homosexual orientation.

Aversion therapy has been used to deal with homosexual behavior. In this approach, the pleasurable association between sexual behavior with people of the same sex is replaced with a negative association. Through classical conditioning, an aversive stimulus such as an electric shock or a nausea-inducing drug comes to be associated with homosexual arousal. In one typical setting, a client is seated in a chair and connected to a safe, yet noxious, electric-shock device. Often a penile plethysmograph (which measures blood flow in the penis) is also applied. A series of slides is shown to the client. Pictures of same-sex nudes may be shown initially. When arousal is indicated by penile blood flow, a shock is applied. This shock becomes associated with arousal in response to homosexual stimuli. Typically, the client tenses up and shows obvious signs of discomfort while being shocked.

As the shock ends, a heterosexual stimulus appears on the screen. The reduction of shock is a positive stimulus and represents the relief of tension and anxiety. In this *anxiety-relief* paradigm, the heterosexual stimulus becomes positively valued by association with reduction of shock, while the homosexual stimulus is simultaneously made aversive by association with the shock itself. Using aversive therapy with homosexuals, behaviorists have reported success rates of 69% and above for up to three years (Feldman & MacCulloch, 1965). Although more traditional techniques may be used with homosexuals, data suggest that behavior therapies may be up to five times more effective in permanently altering sexual orientation (Ullman & Krasner, 1975). However, significant ethical reservations concerning the use of aversive techniques have slowed their application to the area of homosexuality.

CONCLUDING COMMENTS

We have attempted to present the sexual disorders generally as independent syndromes. However, many clinicians have assumed that sexual difficulties are neuroses and have treated them as such. H. S. Kaplan (1974) has pointed out that the neurosis model of sexual difficulties may become a deterrent to effective therapy when applied universally to all clinical situations. There are numerous avenues by which a person can arrive at sexual problems, and only one of these possible paths is neurosis. At the same time, because sexual problems may be one of the results of a more severe disorder, professionals should be involved in the diagnostic process. The diagnosis of the exact role of the sexual problem in a person's life is most significant and shouldn't be handled lightly. Recently, there has been an increase in the number of so-called sex therapists, whose training and expertise may be limited. We caution you that some of these "experts" may not have the training to deal adequately with all the aspects of a sexual disorder.

CHAPTER SUMMARY CHART

In Chapter 14, we described three groups of sexual disturbances. The first group was the *sexual dysfunctions:*

Description	*Explanations*	*Treatment*
Impotence in males Orgasmic dysfunction in females	Avoidance of sex due to fear, pain, genetic inability, or faulty learning	Masters and Johnson Traditional therapies

The second group of disorders was the *sexual deviations:*

Description	*Explanations*	*Treatment*
Disordered choice of object Fetishism Transvestism Incest Pedophilia Bestiality Necrophilia Disordered choice of method Frottage Exhibitionism Voyeurism Obscene communication Sadomasochism Rape	Sexual inferiority Sexual guilt Deviations as substitutes for acceptable modes of expression Deviations are male-dominated—need to prove masculinity	Behavioral therapy, covert sensitization Social development of more acceptable modes of sexual expression

Finally, we described the *sexual-orientation disturbances,* or homosexuality:

Description	*Explanations*	*Treatment*
Not a disorder, but an orientation Homosexual experiences common in normal development	Biological theory: hormonal imbalance Psychological theory: Freud	Not all homosexuals want or need help. Traditional psychotherapy

Description
(continued)

Many homosexuals are not unhappy, disturbed, or in need of treatment.

Explanations
(continued)

All people are homosexual early in development.
Faulty resolution of psychosexual crises
Psychological theory: learning
Homosexuality learned and maintained by reinforcement

Treatment
(continued)

Behavioral therapy, anxiety-relief therapy

CHAPTER 15
CALAMITOUS
DEATH:
SUICIDE
AND MURDER

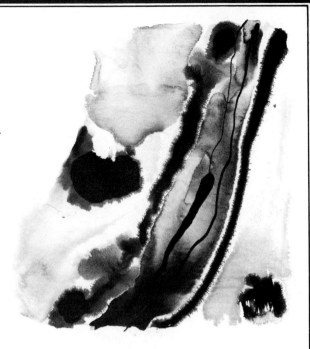

I am a student nurse. I am dying. I write this to you who are, and will become, nurses in the hope that by my sharing my feelings with you, you may someday be better able to help those who share my experience.

I'm out of the hospital now—perhaps for a month, for six months, perhaps for a year—but no one likes to talk about such things. In fact, no one likes to talk about much at all. Nursing must be advancing, but I wish it would hurry. We're taught not to be overly cheery now, to omit the "Everything's fine" routine, and we have done pretty well. But now one is left in a lonely silent void. With the protective "fine, fine" gone, the staff is left with only their own vulnerability and fear. The dying patient is not yet seen as a person and thus cannot be communicated with as such. He is a symbol of what every human fears and what we each know, at least academically, that we too must someday face. What did they say in psychiatric nursing about meeting pathology with pathology to the detriment of both patient and nurse? And there was a lot about knowing one's own feelings before you could help another with his. How true.

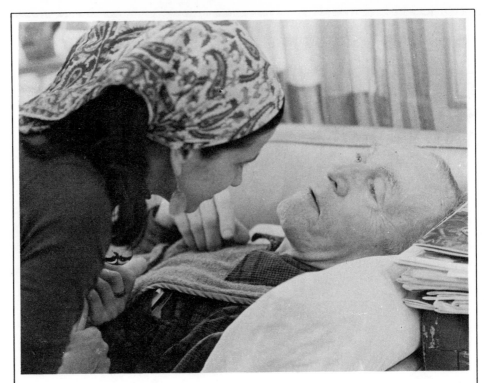

Those nearing death need attention and caring. (Photo by Joseph Czarnecki.)

But for me, fear is today and dying is now. You slip in and out of my room, give me medications and check my blood pressure. Is it because I am a student nurse, myself, or just a human being, that I sense your fright? And your fears enhance mine. Why are you afraid? I am the one who is dying!

I know you feel insecure, don't know what to say, don't know what to do. But please believe me, if you care, you can't go wrong. Just admit that you care. That is really for what we search. We may ask for why's and wherefore's, but we don't really expect answers. Don't run away—wait—all I want to know is that there will be someone to hold my hand when I need it. I am afraid. Death may get to be a routine to you, but it is new to me. You may not see me as unique, but I've never died before. To me, once is pretty unique!

You whisper about my youth, but when one is dying, is he really so young anymore? I have lots I wish we could talk about. It really would not take much of your time because you are in here quite a bit anyway.

If only we could be honest, both admit of our fears, touch one another. If you really care, would you lose so much of your valuable

381

CHAPTER 15:
CALAMITOUS
DEATH:
SUICIDE
AND MURDER

professionalism, if you even cried with me? Just person to person? Then it might not be so hard to die—in a hospital—with friends close [Kübler-Ross, 1969, p. 7].[1]

Among the living, death may produce waves of emotion that can cause disordered behavior. Even natural and expected death can have emotional ramifications that leave individual survivors vulnerable to a number of abnormal behaviors. Elizabeth Kübler-Ross (1975), a renowned writer and lecturer on death and dying, has been responsible for pointing out that

---

The Thinking of Elizabeth Kübler-Ross

It is easy to see that those suffering from a terminal illness appear to need people to be with them in a very genuine way, but this sort of interaction is difficult for most people, who often would rather leave the dying person alone.

Kübler-Ross has studied the "stages of dying" through which patients with a terminal illness usually pass. These are as follows.

Denial: "No, not me." This is a typical reaction when patients learn that they are terminally ill. This defensive action helps cushion the impact of the realization.

Rage and anger: "Why me?" Here patients rage against doctors and God for having such a thing happen to them. Why should others be happy and healthy and they die? Kübler-Ross sees this as not only permissible but inevitable.

Bargaining: "Yes, me, but . . ." Although patients accept the fact of death, they try to get more time by bargaining with God. For a month they will attend church regularly and engage in other such bargaining jousts with God.

Depression: "Yes, me." First there is a mourning of things not done and sins committed. Then comes a state of "preparatory grief," a movement toward a positive acceptance of death. This is followed by a time when patients do not want visitors. They are ready to die peaceably.

Acceptance: "My time is very close now and it's all right." This is a stage of resignation and what Kübler-Ross calls "really a victory."

The mental-health worker can be of tremendous help in aiding people through these stages. In helping patients deal more effectively with their coming death, the worker is also helping those touched by patients to deal more effectively with their feelings.

---

[1]From *On Death and Dying*, by E. Kübler-Ross. Copyright © 1969 by E. Kübler-Ross. Reprinted by permission of Macmillan Publishing Co., Inc. and Tavistock Publications, Ltd.

physicians and mental-health workers can significantly help others deal more appropriately with either their own anticipated death or the death of a significant other person. However, we in abnormal psychology are especially interested in the effects of what Weisman (1975) has called *calamitous death*. In calamitous death, the death is not only premature or unexpected but may also be violent and, in most cases, degrading. It is this kind of death that often causes the most emotional upheaval and creates the greatest potential for disordered behavior in survivors. Weisman believes that suicide and murder qualify for inclusion in the category of calamitous death. He disagrees with Szasz (1971), who believes that self-destruction is one of man's freedoms. Instead, Weisman sees suicide and murder as depriving people of dying a "dignified death." We agree, and we further believe that the emotional state one is in before inflicting a calamitous death on oneself or someone else, and the resulting emotional upheaval caused by such acts, are within the domain of abnormal psychology. For these reasons we have included this chapter on suicide and murder.

SUICIDE

The first form of calamitous death is suicide. The following account shows many of the characteristics of suicidal thought and behavior.

PERSONAL EXPERIENCE: *Excerpt from the Diary of a Suicide Victim*

I am tired of living, of fighting and arguing. . . . Oh, God, if anyone needed me, was dependent upon me, if even I had work to do, I would never think of death. But I have always thought of that since I've been ten or twelve, and I certainly am not made to be happy. . . . They say it is only a coward who commits suicide. There once was a race in Julius Caesar's time, the Romans, who thought it honorable death. I think it is not cowardly, and I know many people who have not nerve or bravery to do it. Myself is one, otherwise I would have been dead long ago, long ago. I lack either courage or despair. I believe it is the former, which will show to what extent I pity myself.

I looked around at my pretty things and longed for someone to appreciate them with me. . . . I am sad and lonely. Oh, God, how lonely. I am starving. Oh, God, I am ready for the last, last chance. I have taken two already, and they are not right. Life was the first chance, marriage the second and now I am ready for death, the last chance. It cannot be any worse than it is here [Cavan, 1926, pp. 298, 300–301].

Source: *Suicide*, by R. Cavan. Copyright 1926 by the University of Chicago Press. Reprinted by permission.

383

CHAPTER 15:
CALAMITOUS
DEATH:
SUICIDE
AND MURDER

On the average, every 20 minutes someone in the United States takes his or her life. The victim may be rich or poor, a city-dweller or a country-dweller, young or old, and different in almost an infinite number of ways from any other person who committed suicide. John Doe shares the experience of suicide with such personalities as Adolf Hitler, Sylvia Plath, Marilyn Monroe, Nero, Amy Vanderbilt, Vincent Van Gogh, Virginia Woolf, Hannibal, Cleopatra, Ernest Hemingway, Brutus, Tchaikovsky, James Forrestal, Marc Antony, Lenny Bruce, and Freddie Prinze. All of these victims seem to have shared a feeling of unbearable anguish that pushed them to the dramatic act of killing themselves.

Why do people kill themselves? Although the question is intriguing, only recently has there been a concerted effort to provide an answer. *Suicidology,* the study of suicide, has grown significantly over the past two decades. Despite the growth of scientific interest in suicide, you will have to be satisfied with only a smattering of solid information to use in your attempt to understand suicide and its effect on others surrounding the victim. What information we have concerning suicide will be provided in the following manner. First, we will present a historical perspective, emphasizing the views of suicide taken in religion, philosophy, sociology, and law. Next, we present some statistical information that underlines the extent of the suicide problem. Finally, we will describe the explanations offered for the occurrence of suicidal behavior and some of the preventive measures now in use.

Descriptions

The act of suicide itself is basically the taking of one's own life by any one of a variety of more or less violent means. To describe suicide is not an easy task; different people and groups consider the ending of one's own life from different perspectives. In this section we will present several of these different perspectives from historical and current points of view and will describe the facts we have about this form of calamitous death.

Historical and Current Perspectives on Suicide. Historically, various disciplines have often professed quite different attitudes toward suicide. We will first consider the religious perspective on self-inflicted calamitous death.

Many present-day religious views of suicide in Western countries have been affected by Judaeo-Christian beliefs. Some early Christians appear to have chosen their own deaths in the form of martyrdom. Roman lions killed a great number of Christians, many of whom were actually martyring themselves to quicken the process of getting to heaven. One of us visited an ancient Roman amphitheater in present-day Germany where over 4000 men, women, and children lost their lives, some by martyring themselves in what may be seen as a form of mass suicide. As part of an effort to stop this slaughter, the early church theologians decided to classify suicide as a sin. They reasoned that, since life was sacred and since only God gave life, only God had the right to take life away. Even though there is no admonition against suicide in the Bible, it soon became classified as a *mortal sin*, punishable by excommunication from the church. By the use of excommunication, thus, the Roman Catholic church hoped to stem the increase in suicide. However, as was true of many good deeds in the Middle Ages, this humanitarian policy became convoluted and was often used in later times as the basis for punishing both would-be suicides and those who survived suicide victims.

Until the 18th century, philosophers generally agreed with the theologians' view of suicide as a sin. In the 18th century, however, there was a significant split from church thinking. Jean-Jacques Rousseau (1712–1778), for example, put the blame for sin on society rather than the individual, whom he saw as naturally good and unspoiled. Another philosopher, David Hume (1711–1776), wrote the famous essay "On Suicide," in which he rebutted the notion that suicide was either a crime or a sin.

These philosophical attempts to modify the meaning and punishment of suicide attempts had relatively little impact on public policy, and until the 20th century, suicide was still considered by many to be a sin or a crime. Those who committed suicide were often refused burial in consecrated grounds, and the church taught that they were committed to the lowest reaches of hell. There was a general belief that the person who committed suicide was possessed by the devil. This belief led to elaborate and at times strange burial procedures. For example, a popular method of interring a suicide victim was burial at a crossroads with a stake through the heart. The purpose of the stake was to keep the victim in the coffin, and the choice of the crossroads site was calculated to confuse the ghost of the victim should it ever be freed from the stake.

In the eyes of the law, the suicide victim was historically better off than his survivors. The goods of the victim and those of his nearest kin could be confiscated at the discretion of legal authorities. Those who failed at suicide would have been better off dead. Family and friends frequently had to go through the extended anguish of watching the attempter be tried in court and probably sentenced to death anyway. During some trials, the attempter would change his mind about suicide as a solution to his problem only to find the hangman's noose waiting for him.

The Suicide Act in England (1961) was a dramatic legal breakthrough. It abolished criminal penalties for suicide, eliminated the liability of survivors to prosecution, but increased the penalties for those aiding and abetting the suicide act. Shneidman (1975) recently reported that, while some 27 states have laws against attempting suicide or against aiding a person attempting suicide, these legal restrictions are rarely enforced. It appears that the legal objections to suicide are nearly gone in Western society; only the social and psychological ones remain.

Statistics of Suicide.   Having described for you the significant historical views of suicidal behavior that affect our present ways of dealing with this act, we would now like to present some numerical data. The

385

CHAPTER 15:
CALAMITOUS
DEATH:
SUICIDE
AND MURDER

statistical findings we report are subject to many sources of inaccuracy. For example, to save family members embarrassment, many cases of suicide are "covered up" and called something else by the family doctor or the college health-center physician. Likewise, the single-passenger, fatal car crash under perfect weather conditions on a straight stretch of road may or may not be an accident. Given these kinds of distortion, we must assume that the frequency-of-suicide data we report are probably underestimates of the true occurrence of suicide.

According to World Health Organization statistics (1975), Finland, Austria, Czechoslovakia, Japan, and Hungary show the highest suicide rates, and Ireland, Italy, the Netherlands, Canada, and Poland show the lowest rates. These rates are surprisingly stable, and first-generation immigrants to the United States from these countries tend to maintain the same rates as those in their mother country (Sainsbury & Barraclough, 1968).

Although the rate of suicide in the United States places it only in the middle of the countries of the world, suicide still has been one of the top ten causes of death within the United States for well over 100 years. Suicide varies as a cause of death from third place in people 15–34 years of age to ninth place in people 55–74 years of age (Vital Statistics of the United States, 1971). More men than women committed suicide in 1975, in spite of the fact that well over three times as many women as men *attempted* suicide. This general relationship between gender and suicide frequency has existed for decades. The higher degree of successful suicides in males may be due to the fact that men typically choose more lethal means of attempting suicide than do women. Men most often use guns, whereas women most often use poison or drugs.

As well as differing by sex, the suicide rate varies considerably with age. Beginning in adolescence, there is a steady increase in the suicide rate, which reaches a peak in the 45-year-old-and-above age group. However, suicide is responsible for a greater proportion of all deaths in younger than older age groups, because death due to physical illness is less frequent among young people. In terms of attempted suicide, the peak frequency is in the 15-to-24-year-old age group; after 24, the number of attempts generally decreases with increasing age. Likewise, though many more younger than older people attempt suicide, the older the attempter is, the greater is the chance that the attempt will be successful.

In addition to sex and age, race, social class, and marital status have been significantly related to suicidal behavior. Proportionately more Blacks than Whites attempt and complete suicide. Because Blacks are over-represented in the lower socioeconomic classes, we don't know if it is race, socioeconomic level, or an interaction of the two characteristics that leads to more frequent suicide attempts among Blacks. The relation of marital status to suicide frequency suggests that those who are married have a lower suicide rate than those who are single. One exception to this statement is married teenagers, who show the highest suicide rate of all (Peck & Seiden, 1975).

Clues to Suicide. Among the numerous myths surrounding suicide is the belief that it is an impulsive act. In fact, the vast majority of those who commit suicide leave clues that, in retrospect, pointed clearly to their future self-destruction. Generally, these clues to the possibility of suicide involve changes in the person's life-style. Shneidman and Farberow (1961) present five basic clues that can help us to see whether a person is planning suicide so that we can "head him off at the pass":

1. Of those who commit suicide, three out of four see a physician four months or less before they kill themselves. Although there is no single trait or emotion that characterizes all suicidal people, the most frequent feelings are depression, hopelessness, and helplessness. The most predictive clues of a forthcoming suicide are verbal threats to do away with oneself. Verbal threats such as "I won't be around to bug you any more" or "This is the last straw . . . I can't take any more" should be taken seriously.

2. There are also behavioral clues indicating a future successful suicide, the most significant being an actual suicide attempt. Often seen by others as manipulation or as ploys to obtain attention, suicide attempts can be important indicators of future suicidal behavior. The fact that nearly four out of five suicide victims have previously attempted suicide underlines the importance of all suicide attempts.

3. People who have finally made the decision to kill themselves often begin to act differently. As a clue to the decision, the person may suddenly become calmer or behave as though he or she were about to go on a trip. Many people who have decided to commit suicide will give away their most prized possessions. For those who have made the decision to kill themselves, there are typically changes in sleep and eating habits, with sleep and food often losing their ability to refresh.

4. Another clue indicative of a possible suicide is when a life situation produces stress. For example, learning of a severe illness, or losing a significant person such as a parent, may bring a person to the point of contemplating suicide.

5. Last, one line of research has shown that there are a number of life-course clues to suicide that appear to predispose a person by 29 years of age to commit suicide by the age of 55. They are: early evidence of instability while in school, early rejection by the father, multiple marriages, alcoholism, unstable occupational history, ups and downs in income, a crippling physical disability (especially one involving difficulty in breathing), disappointment in the use of one's potential, a disparity between aspiration and accomplishment, any talk or hint of self-destruction, and a competitive or self-absorbed spouse. These indexes appear to reflect

387

CHAPTER 15:
CALAMITOUS
DEATH:
SUICIDE
AND MURDER

Suicide: Myths and Realities

Shneidman and Farberow (1961) have compiled a list of the prevalent myths surrounding the emotion-laden behavior of suicide. The myths—and the realities—are as follows.

1. *Myth:* People who talk about suicide don't commit suicide.
   Reality: Eight out of ten persons who completed suicides made previous attempts, and retrospective studies of suicidal persons show most gave ample warning through verbal and other behavior signals.
2. *Myth:* Suicide happens without warning.
   Reality: Most suicidal people give ample warning of what they are contemplating.
3. *Myth:* Suicidal people are fully intent on dying.
   Reality: Most attempters of suicide are ambivalent about dying, and, as just mentioned, most will let others know about their plans in various ways.
4. *Myth:* Once a person is suicidal, he or she is suicidal forever.
   Reality: Research has shown that the critical period within which suicidal behavior will probably occur is brief.
5. *Myth:* Improvement after a suicidal crisis means that the suicidal risk is over.
   Reality: Most suicides occur three months after a previous attempt when the people have the energy to carry out their objective of killing themselves.
6. *Myth:* Suicide occurs more often among the rich, or conversely, it occurs almost exclusively among the poor.
   Reality: Suicide occurs in all strata of society.
7. *Myth:* Suicidal tendencies are inherited or run in the family.
   Reality: There is no support for the assumption that suicidal behavior is genetically determined.
8. *Myth:* All suicidal persons are mentally ill, and suicide is always the act of a psychotic person.
   Reality: Data show that there is no necessary connection between mental illness and suicidal behavior.

personality weaknesses that show themselves in a suicide attempt when a person approaches the end of his or her productive life.

Suicide and Mental Disturbance. In addition to those who erroneously believe that suicide is an impulsive act, there are those who hold that a person must be "insane" to commit suicide. Certainly, if we measure the amount of distress and anguish experienced by the individual before the act of suicide, and by survivors afterward, then suicide qualifies for the label of disordered behavior. However, the relationship of suicidal behavior to what is officially viewed as disordered behavior is not so clear. If we compare occurrence of suicide with simultaneous occurrence of official APA-classified disorders, there is a relatively small amount of overlap. World Health Organization statistics suggest that about one out of every four suicide victims also has some evidence of "mental illness." Conversely, one can view these data as showing that three out of every four people who commit suicide are probably *not* mentally ill. The relationship with disordered behavior is most significant between suicide and the depressive disorders: among severely depressed people, the rate of suicide is 20 times higher than it is among the general population (World Health Organization, 1968).

Explanations

Modern attempts to explain suicidal behavior have had to take into account both the historical perspectives and the statistical facts we have just discussed. In the main, these explanations are either psychological or sociological; attempts to find a genetic or physiological explanation of suicide seem to have been largely unfruitful. We will first discuss the psychoanalytically based and social-learning psychological explanations, followed by the sociological and biological explanations.

Psychological Theories. The major psychological explanation of suicide comes from the analytic school of thought. Freud postulated that people have an innate need to be aggressive and that this aggressive drive may be expressed in fights, arguments, and wars. Like hunger and thirst, aggression is a drive that needs satiation. Freud thought of the aggressive drive as a part of what he postulated to be the death instinct, thanatos. He stated:

> A more fruitful idea was that a portion of the death instinct is diverted towards the external world and comes to light as an instinct of aggressiveness. In this way the instinct itself could be pressed into the service of Eros, in that the organism was destroying some other thing, whether animate or inanimate, instead of destroying its own self [Freud, quoted in Litman, 1967, p. 324].

To Freud, restriction of the aggressive drive by either the environment or psychic structures such as the superego could result in self-destructive behavior. He believed that suicide is in large part the result of repressed hostility that can find no other outlet.

In addition to the explanation of repressed hostility based on a death instinct, suicidal behavior is postulated to occur when a person who

389

CHAPTER 15:
CALAMITOUS
DEATH:
SUICIDE
AND MURDER

is both loved and hated by the victim is "introjected," or psychologically incorporated into the person. If this introjected "other" should do something that leads to the removal of the love component of the attachment, then the subject is left with only introjected hate, which he or she annihilates through the act of suicide. The following example may make the psychoanalytic explanation of suicidal behavior clearer: A man loves and hates his mother, and introjects her into his own psyche so that she now becomes part of him. Later, he finds that his mother has run away with another man, leaving him and his father alone. At this point, the love part of the introjection is neutralized, and all the man has left is the introjected hate, which he gets rid of by killing himself.

Freud pointed out that aggression can take either an outward or an inward route. A later analytic thinker, Menninger (1938), pointed out that the inward turn of aggression can indeed take many forms, but that only one of them is suicide. As support for his view, Menninger cited the self-destructive behavior of drug addicts and alcoholics (which he called *chronic suicide*), the need for self-mutilating surgery expressed by some neurotics (which he called *focal suicide*), and the psychosomatic disorders of frustrated rage such as high blood pressure (which he called *organic suicide*). The self-destructive component of these disorders is often obvious to outside observers. According to Menninger's view, most suicides are due in one way or another to a diverting of the aggressive drive back into the self.

Freud and Menninger assumed that the higher number of completed suicides found in the middle and upper classes was probably due to the fact that these individuals had stronger superegos, which blocked the expression of aggression and turned it back onto the person in the form of depression. Freud and Menninger seem to have reasoned that lower-class individuals, modeling after their parents and their environment, were used to a more immediate expression of aggression and therefore probably didn't require other channels of release. Perlin and Schmidt (1975) point out, however, that depression may not be the major source of suicidal behavior:

Although suicide is said to be the mortality of depressive illness, many suicidal individuals do not appear to be clinically depressed and many depressed patients are not suicidal. Recent reports suggest that hopelessness may be a better indicator of intensity of current suicidal ideation and the risk implied thereby than depressions [p. 149].

Social-Learning Theory. Unlike psychoanalytic theory, which seems to recognize only grudgingly the effect of the environment on suicidal behavior, social-learning theory assumes that suicidal behavior is highly dependent on learning from the environment. Like any other behavior, suicidal behavior is learned. A person may learn that indulging in self-destructive acts frequently attracts attention and care from other people.

This is especially true if the individual has had family members or friends engage in such behavior and thus was able to observe the effect of suicidal behavior on others. In this way, the person may learn that suicidal behavior can control and affect others in a very powerful manner. To the social-learning theorist, this observational learning can explain why there seems to be a greater likelihood of suicidal behavior in an individual if he or she has known someone who has committed suicide. From such a perspective, a person about to indulge in suicidal behavior may expect that this behavior will have the desired effect on others and probably is the most efficient way of dealing with "the problem"—regardless of what the problem may be.

Societal-Integration Theory. In his explanation of suicide, Emil Durkheim (1951) shifted the emphasis from what was going on inside the person to what was going on *around* the person. In so doing, Durkheim created a sociological model to explain the incidence and prevalence of suicidal behavior. Durkheim believed strongly that there was a connection between suicide rates and social conditions. Simply, Durkheim proposed that suicide frequency was inversely related to the integration and organization of society. When society is loosely organized and the individual is isolated, the suicide rate should therefore be higher. Durkheim classified three basic kinds of suicide, differing primarily according to the victim's relationship to society: egoistic, altruistic, and anomic.

In Durkheim's first class of suicide, *egoistic*, victims are individualistic and thus not a part of society. Either they have rejected society, or society has rejected them; but in any case they are not really a part of the general cultural group.

Altruistic suicide is directly opposite to egoistic suicide and occurs when individuals are too closely bound to society and feel required for the common good to perform some act of sacrifice. If they were not to perform the act of sacrifice, the societal pressures could cause them to experience unbearable shame. Altruistic suicide may be exemplified by the behavior of kamikaze pilots in World War II, who used their airplanes as bombs in attempts to destroy enemy ships.

Anomic suicide differs from egoistic and altruistic suicide in that it occurs when the victims' usual relationship to society is shattered and they find themselves alienated from a society of which they used to be part. For example, when Hitler took power in Germany, many educated people suddenly found themselves outside society. Their choice was often either to flee or to experience *anomie* (not feeling part of established society). Similarly, many poor people are subject to anomie, especially if they perceive that they were once in a better situation and thus are aware of a difference between their present situation and their goals. However, if poor and disadvantaged people accept their lot, prize what they have, and are satisfied, they aren't considered to be anomic, and aren't more prone to suicide.

Henry and Short (1954) attempted to combine Durkheim's sociological theory with psychological components. They reported that individuals

391

CHAPTER 15:
CALAMITOUS
DEATH:
SUICIDE
AND MURDER

For some World War II kamikaze pilots, altruistic suicide was both an honorable and a joyous death. (Photo courtesy of the U.S. Naval Institute, Annapolis, Maryland.)

who felt more responsible for their behaviors, especially their negative ones, seemed more likely to commit suicide. Those who didn't take responsibility for their actions were more prone to blame others for their ill fortune and thus seemed to escape the shame of failure. These individuals would be more likely to focus their anger on others. Middle- and upper-class people, Henry and Short concluded, were more inclined to take responsibility for their actions. Rather than jeopardize parental nurturance, these people would be likely to turn their anger and frustration inward, becoming, in time, frustrated adults.

Biological Theory. Neither the psychological nor the sociological explanations of suicidal behavior mention the possibility of biological etiology in suicidal behavior. However, Snyder (1975) reviews the biological work most closely related to suicide and concludes that "many biological factors may be construed as 'relevant' to the study of suicide" (p. 126). The major focus on biological factors generally involves the neurotransmitters, such as norepinephrine, and their functioning in the brain. Citing the catecholamine hypothesis of depression (see Chapter 8), Snyder concludes, "If there is a unique biological substratum of that state of mind that eventuates in a person taking his own life, our present knowledge of brain function might elect a possible alteration in catecholamine disposition as the major candidate" (p. 127). The major assumption in this explanation is that catecholamine dysfunction may be the cause of depression, which in turn is the cause of suicidal depression. Snyder points out that the majority of such research has been accomplished with animals and that one shouldn't conclude that human depressive states are caused by or are identical with lowered brain catecholamine levels. Nevertheless, he believes that the elucidation of brain mechanisms may hold the key to explaining suicide.

Treatment and Prevention

The best treatment for suicide is prevention, and effective prevention of suicide depends upon three factors. First is the accurate assessment of suicide potential. Second is some guideline for dealing with those considered to be probable suicide victims. Third is the availability of people who are trained in working with those considered to be dangerously suicidal. In this section, we will discuss these three factors and then reflect upon the aid needed by people who survive those who evade preventive efforts and successfully complete suicide.

Assessment of Suicide Potential. The determination of the seriousness of suicidal intention is literally a matter of life and death. According to experts (Shneidman, 1969, 1971, 1975), a person's potential for suicide consists of three components: *lethality, perturbation,* and *inimicality.*

The first component of suicide potential, *lethality,* refers to the probability that the person will commit suicide. How "lethal" a person is at any given time is a combination of past and present experiences, especially as they relate to death. Table 15-1 presents a scale composed of items relating to past experiences that is often used by assessors of a person's lethality.

Perturbation refers to a person's feeling of distress, or how disturbed or agitated he or she is. Although lethality and perturbation are interrelated, they are also independent components of suicide potential and should therefore be assessed individually. As Shneidman points out:

> One can be highly perturbed—in an acute schizophrenic episode, for example—and not necessarily be suicidal; the converse is, in a curious sense, also true. Although, admittedly, no one in his normal mind commits suicide, it is perfectly possible—indeed, it happens much too often—that a person need not be in a discernible state of high perturbation in order to kill himself [1975, p. 1778].

Thus, one can be upset (perturbed) and yet not really suicidal; more importantly, one can appear to be relatively unperturbed and yet be lethal

393

CHAPTER 15:
CALAMITOUS
DEATH:
SUICIDE
AND MURDER

Table 15-1. *A scale for determining chances of suicide*

Neuropsychiatric Hospital Suicide Prediction Schedule

Name .... Hospital .... Date ....

Sex ..... Age ..... Race ..... Marital S. ..... Diagnosis: ....

....

Admis. date of current hospitalization .... Length of stay ....

Prediction: High .... Moderately high ..... Moderately low ..... Low .....

[Check the appropriate level within each item and note its assigned weight in the column on the right. Add the weights assigned and check where subject falls in prediction.]

Item No.	Item Title	Check One	Scores	Weight	Assigned Weight
1.	Depressed in hospital most of the time	0	No	11.00	....
		1	Slightly	17.32	....
		2	Moderately	23.64	....
		✓.3	Severely	29.96	....
2.	Warm interdependent relation-ship	1	Inability	9.06	....
		✓.2	Limited	7.12	....
		3	Good	5.18	....
3.	Hope	✓.0	Yes	11.00	....
		1	Slightly hopeless	15.91	....
		2	Moderately	20.82	....
		3	Severely	25.73	....
		4	None despite opportunities	30.64	....
4.	Somatic problems leading to last hospitalization	0	No	11.00	....
		✓.1	Slight	9.50	....
		2	Moderate	8.00	....
		3	Severe	6.50	....
		4	Delusional	5.00	....
5.	Age at release from hospital	✓.0	25	11	....
		1	26–30	10	....
		2	31–35	9	....
		3	36–40	8	....
		4	41–45	7	....
		5	46–50	6	....
		6	51–55	5	....
		7	56–60	4	....
		8	61–65	3	....
		9	65+	2	....
6.	Under influence of drugs or alcohol during last hospitalization	0	No	11.00	....
		✓1	Yes	0.87	....
7.	Returned early to hospital after leaves or visits	0	No	11.00	....
		✓1	Yes	20.72	....
8.	Ever elope (escape from hospital)	0	No	11.00	....
		✓1	Previously	13.33	....
		2	Currently	15.66	....
		3	Both	17.99	....
9.	Going through divorce during last hospitalization	✓.0	No	11.00	....
		1	Yes	22.43	....

Table 15-1. *(continued)*

10. History of suicidal behavior	..✓.0	No	11.00	....
	1	Once	13.13	....
	2	Twice	15.26	....
	3	Three or more	17.39	....
11. Anxiety during last hospitaliza-tion	1	About usual	8.15	....
	..∿2	High	5.30	....
			Total	....

	High	Moderately High	Moderately Low	Low
Sum of assigned weights	189.36 to 130.00	129.99 to 117.45	117.44 to 107.67	107.66 to 84.35

enough to kill oneself. In fact, often it is this relative lack of perturbation that keeps people close to a possible suicide from intervening. Significantly, it is the lethality and not the perturbation dimension that is most closely related to the completion of a successful suicide.

The third component of suicide potential, *inimicality*, refers to the person's general life-style. It is here that we look for general and pervasive self-defeating patterns of behavior. These patterns, if continued, might significantly shorten the person's life. Alcoholics, smokers, drug abusers, and those who refuse to follow prescribed medical regimes are considered to be high in inimicality.

Besides the accurate assessment of a person's suicide potential, prevention must take into account three additional features of the suicidal state: its brief duration, the ambivalence of the suicidal person toward whether to live or die, and the dyadic nature of suicide (Shneidman, 1975). We will discuss each feature briefly.

First, the period of high lethality for suicide lasts only a brief time, but it is during this brief state of crisis that the person may complete the suicide act. A person will not stand on a window ledge for two and a half months deciding to jump, nor will anyone stand for a week in a room with a gun pointed at his or her head. The crucial period for completing suicide is usually brief, and during that brief time means of prevention must be applied.

Second, many of those who attempt suicide are ambivalent as to whether they want to live or die. At the same time the suicidal person is planning to die, he or she may be fantasizing about being rescued from the brink of death. The suicide act can frequently be a "cry for help"; and for this reason, prevention must always be addressed to the portion of the person that wants to live.

Besides being brief and a cry for help, suicidal behavior is a *dyadic event*. That is, although the psychological conflict may be waged within the

395

CHAPTER 15:
CALAMITOUS
DEATH:
SUICIDE
AND MURDER

victim's head, the conflict typically involves *someone else*, such as a mother, a loved one, a child, or a colleague. A person's death is not an isolated event; it leaves lasting marks on those who survive. As Toynbee (1968) concluded, "The two-sidedness of death is a fundamental feature of death . . .the sting of death is less sharp for the person who dies than it is for the bereaved survivor" (p. 23). Suicide has a way of stigmatizing the survivors, who often must deal with their guilt from within and accusations from without. For this reason, Shneidman concludes emotionally:

> On these grounds alone the psychiatrist is advised to minimize or totally disregard those well intentioned but shrill writers in the field who naively speak of a person's right to commit suicide . . . as though the suicidal person were a chronic, univalently self destructive hermit [1975, p. 1780].

Guidelines for Management of High-Lethality People. Once assessment procedures have identified a person whose suicidal motivation is very strong and who has a high probability of succeeding in self-destructive acts, we must have some way of trying to prevent the suicidal act. Shneidman (1975) suggests a number of management hints for dealing with the high-lethality patient:

1. Continuously monitor the patient's lethality.
2. Actively take the side of "life" by helping the patient deal with his problems in a realistic manner.
3. Mobilize community resources such as the Veteran's Administration on the side of the "life" part of the patient.
4. Obtain consultation from peers to help in deciding on the right course of action for the patient.
5. Hospitalize the patient only after careful consideration, because hospitalization tends to complicate treatment. It should be used only when necessary, and then for as brief a time as possible.
6. Use all the benefits the therapist can gain from transference. Here the "magic" of the patient-therapist relationship can be a very positive force in keeping the patient alive.
7. Involve the significant others in the life of the suicide attempter. Assess the influence and role of others in the occurrence of suicidal behavior as well as mobilizing the positive factors in the patient's life.
8. Bend the rules of confidentiality between the therapist and patient when necessary. Shneidman feels that suicide plans cannot always be treated as secrets.
9. Limit yourself to seeing only a few lethal patients. The tension generated in interacting with a self-destructive patient takes much energy. When a therapist loses a patient through suicide, studies show, he or she reacts much like anyone else. Litman (1965) questioned 200 therapists who had recently had a patient

commit suicide. These therapists felt guilt, grief, anger, inadequacy, and self-blame. A suicidal attempt, successful or not, by a patient can leave the therapist drained of the energy needed to deal adequately with other patients.

Suicide-Prevention Centers. Along with traditional mental-health professionals dealing with the possibility of suicide in their psychotherapy clients, a modern and promising approach specific to suicide prevention is the *crisis-center* movement. Historically, the Salvation Army was among the first to found centers to help both suicide attempters and their families deal more effectively with the conflicts surrounding suicide. Begun at the turn of the century, these Salvation Army centers flourished for a time both in North America and in Europe and then, inexplicably, disappeared. It was not until the 1960s and the reawakening of community responsibility for mental health (see Chapter 25) that centers to deal with suicide crises were reestablished.

Based on the assumption that not all crises occur between 9:00 A.M. and 5:00 P.M., modern-day crisis centers offer service 24 hours a day. The telephone is the main means of communication between the center and the person in crisis. Usually a majority of the telephones are staffed by volunteers, laypeople who are specially trained by professionals.

Most modern crisis centers operate on the basis of *crisis-intervention theory* as introduced by Lindemann (1944) and expanded by Caplan (1964) (see Chapter 25). According to crisis theory, a person is most malleable and vulnerable to helping efforts when in a state of crisis. However, the state of crisis is usually brief, so that whatever intervention is undertaken must be done quickly. Later may be too late, as shown in the following personal experience of one of the authors.

PERSONAL EXPERIENCE: *Suicide Prevention*

As a graduate student, one of us worked at a suicide-prevention center in a rural area. Most of the work of the crisis center was done by volunteers from the largest town in the area. These volunteers participated in long hours of workshops, honing their phone skills, before beginning to work at the center. Most of their work wasn't very dramatic. Phone calls came in at a fairly constant rate, but most involved routine requests for information about other mental-health facilities. Although valuable, answering phones and giving information isn't the world's most exciting work. However, not all calls are routine.

A man phoned and told the counselor who answered that he was going to kill himself. The telephone counselor, a woman in her 40s, used all of her considerable counseling skills to try to talk this man out of suicide. She was able to collect enough information from him to know

397

CHAPTER 15:
CALAMITOUS
DEATH:
SUICIDE
AND MURDER

that, by all indexes, the caller was highly lethal and probably would kill himself. No matter what verbal ploys she tried, the man appeared to be moving inevitably to killing himself with a .45-caliber pistol he had next to the phone. The call went on for nearly two hours, and police and hospital emergency facilities were alerted and ready to move in when needed. At the end of this tense two hours, the caller wished the phone counselor good luck and goodbye, and declared that he was now going to kill himself. All held their breath, waiting for the fatal shot to be fired. At this point, the phone counselor broke down and began to cry. Sobbing, she told the caller that he couldn't kill himself . . . that she cared too much about what happened to him for him to commit suicide. With tears rolling down her cheeks, this reserved middle-aged woman was begging a man whom she had never met not to kill himself. In response to this rather unorthodox and unplanned counseling approach, the man also began crying. With both parties sobbing, the caller's resolve to kill himself melted, and he told the counselor where he was.

This man is alive today because of the availability of the phone and people who cared enough about others to be willing to answer the call when it was made. Although these sorts of spectacular occurrences don't happen hourly, they happen often enough to warrant keeping the centers open. There is no other work in the field of mental health quite so valuable as that focused on saving another's life.

Although the theory underlying the development of crisis centers seems sound, there still is not enough empirical support for their effectiveness in lowering the frequency of attempted and completed suicides. One reason for the fragmentary data available is that the primary duty of the phone counselor is to help the caller, not to gather research information. However, some research data have been compiled. In one study, Litman (1965) analyzed a random sample of 1000 callers to the Los Angeles Suicide Prevention Center. He found that twice as many women as men called and that depression, alcohol, and drugs were the most frequent problems. Interestingly, Litman found that less than half the calls to the center were directly from the troubled person; many were from concerned family members. Further clouding the picture of the crisis center is research such as that of I. Weiner (1969), in which it was found that the introduction of suicide-prevention centers may have been correlated with an *increased* rate of suicide.

Regardless of the equivocal scientific support, we do know that the suicide-prevention centers are used a great deal, as shown by the millions of contacts made every year. The phone is apparently a less threatening means of communication than face-to-face interaction, and it is an easier first step for many troubled people. Although conclusive support for crisis-center effectiveness has not yet been obtained, given our limited mental-health resources, this approach appears to be a very promising means of meeting the massive problem of suicide.

Help for the Survivors. Despite preventive efforts, many people do succeed in taking their own lives. However, the emotional effects of suicide frequently extend beyond the individual victims. As we mentioned previously, suicide is, with few exceptions, a dyadic event. Those who survive the victim are often left with the many emotions generated by the suicide act. Shneidman (1973) believes that the survivor-victims of suicides constitute a monumental mental-health problem. To help the thousands of people who are affected by suicide every year, Shneidman proposes a process of *postvention*. The goal of the postvention process is to lessen the aftereffects of the suicide and to facilitate the recovery of the surviving members of the family and of close friends. Survivors of a suicide can experience a potpourri of negative emotions such as grief, guilt, and shame. Those experiencing grief have been found to be more vulnerable to both physical and mental illness (Wallace, 1973).

Although there are traditional religious procedures such as holding wakes or sitting shiva that approximate postvention, the concept emphasizes that grieving is a long-term process that takes months, not days, to be completed. On the basis of his clinical experience with the grieving process, Shneidman (1975) suggests that postvention work should begin immediately after the suicide, because most survivors want to talk to a helping person then. He further suggests that the survivor needs rational discussion rather than a focus on feelings toward the suicide victim. Lastly, Shneidman believes that the medical state of the survivor-victim should be constantly monitored, for he or she is more vulnerable at this time to a variety of physical disorders such as heart attack or high blood pressure. Keeping these guidelines in mind should allow one to deal more effectively with a survivor-victim of a suicide.

The Psychological Autopsy. Although it is not "treatment" in the true sense of the word, a psychological autopsy of the suicide victim can more clearly delineate the person's motives and activities so that the basic motives for his or her death can be understood. Weisman and Kastenbaum (1968) state that the purpose of such a technique is "to reconstruct the final days and weeks of life by bringing together available observation, fact and opinion about a recently deceased person in an effort to understand the psychosocial components of death" (p. 1). This technique is useful in looking at many types of death, and Shneidman modified the psychological autopsy specifically for suicide victims. In essence, information is gathered about the person's background characteristics (age, marital status, and so on), method of dying, history (such as medical treatment, psychotherapy), family (has anyone else committed suicide, for example), life-style (drinking, drugs, race cars, and so on) and methods of responding to previous stress.

399

CHAPTER 15:
CALAMITOUS
DEATH:
SUICIDE
AND MURDER

One of the authors participated in a psychological autopsy of a young college student who had driven her car into a structural support of an overpass. The road was perfectly straight, it was early in the evening, she hadn't been drinking or taking drugs; yet she drove directly into the pole at a speed in excess of 90 miles per hour and had never put on her brakes. After a preliminary investigation, the death was declared a suicide. Shortly thereafter, one of the authors was asked to participate in her psychological autopsy. The psychological autopsy took place in a fairly large room in which all those who could shed some light on the life of this young woman were assembled. In attendance, for example, were the woman's physician, lawyer, dormitory counselor, and brother (who was also in school), a counselor from the psychological center, two friends, and a number of other people who had had some contact with the victim, either through long-standing relationships or more recent interactions. In a procedure that was very painstaking and at times emotionally devastating, each of the members contributed his or her bits of information and opinion until, much like a giant jigsaw puzzle, this woman's life and motives became clearer and clearer. After about six hours of work it was apparent to all of us what had driven her toward the act of suicide. What was also apparent, but more difficult to take, was the fact that her movement toward suicide was as clear and straight as the highway she had driven off to end her life. The practical applications of knowledge gained from such a process were impressive to those of us who will deal with similar people in the future. In addition, places where interventions might have changed the course of the woman's movement toward the choice of suicide were found, and this led to certain changes in clinic procedures to benefit other clients who were in similar situations. In all, the procedure, though draining, resulted in a great deal of usable information for the prevention of such acts in others.

MURDER

Murder, a second source of calamitous death, is the taking of another's life. The taking of someone else's life, ending an opportunity for someone to fulfill himself or herself, is a uniquely heinous act. Murder has taken from us such people as Abraham Lincoln, Robert Kennedy, Martin Luther King, and John Fitzgerald Kennedy. Murder is made a more terrible psychological event by the fact that it is often an act of the young that takes place between loved ones and friends. Wolfgang (1964) has pointed out:

> More professional literature has appeared on homicide than on any other specific criminal offense, perhaps because murder has traditionally been viewed in most cultures as the most serious form of violation of collective life. Any injury short of death renders the

victim capable of at least some degree of return to his previctimized status. Neither individual nor societal homeostasis is possible with homicide; a piece of the island of humanity is violently torn away. Often the notions of retribution and compassion mingle in society's reaction both to the offender and to the offended [p. vii].

In spite of its appalling nature, or perhaps because of it, people have long been fascinated with murder. It has been a popular subject in literature, on television, and in the movies. At the time of this writing, there are 22 weekly crime, detective, or police stories on television. A count taken over one week of normal television viewing showed that 135 men, women, and children were murdered on the TV screen. Indeed, murder appears to be very popular. It is estimated that the average child watching an average amount of television will see 3047 people killed in a violent manner by the time he or she enters high school (Liebert, Neale, & Davidson, 1973).

Descriptions

In this section we will first present the historical background of murder. Next, we will describe some rather unsettling statistics concerning who gets killed, who does the killing, and how the killing gets done. Finally, we will consider the relationship between murder and the presence of diagnosable mental disturbance.

Historical and Current Perspectives on Murder. Society has almost always responded to murder with horror. Most historical-religious teachings forbid killing. This admonition was one of the Ten Commandments presented to Moses on Mount Sinai and has its equivalent in the laws of all major religions and societies. However, every culture has its exceptions to this law. In many cultures, for example, one may kill in self-defense or when engaged in war.

In the United States, murder is legally defined as any act of nonjustifiable homicide and can be classified as first- or second-degree murder, or as first-degree manslaughter. These three classifications of killing assume some degree of maliciousness in the killer. Classifying a killing as a murder typically assumes some premeditation on the part of the killer, whereas first-degree manslaughter assumes that the crime was provoked to some significant degree by the victim. First- and second-degree murder and first-degree manslaughter are behaviorally similar, but they are distinct in the eyes of the law and carry far different penalties.

Statistics of Murder. How does the United States compare with other countries in terms of frequency of murder? Statistics suggest that the United States is the "murder champion" among the countries of Western Europe and North America (World Health Organization, 1970). The United States has twice the murder rate of Finland and three times the murder rate

401

CHAPTER 15:
CALAMITOUS
DEATH:
SUICIDE
AND MURDER

of Canada (the closest competitors), and over 20 times the murder rate of Ireland. However, the United States is no match for its South American neighbors, who claim some of the highest murder rates in the world.

The United States experienced a "great murder wave" during the 1970s. The murder rate in the United States climbed from 5.3 per 100,000 in 1920 to almost 10 per 100,000 in 1973 (Federal Bureau of Investigation, 1975). It doesn't take a computer to figure out that this is nearly a 100% increase in the rate of murder. Simply stated, a greater proportion of people seem to be killing other people now than ever before. One murder is committed every 26 minutes in the United States.

Murder is a *male-dominated* crime committed by the *young*. About nine out of every ten murderers in the United States are male; almost half of the murderers are under 25 years of age, with one out of every ten below the age of 18. Murderers are also likely to be Black and from the lower socioeconomic classes. These characteristics also apply to victims, more than half of whom are Black, and nearly four out of five of whom are male.

There are also patterns of *methods* of homicide. Statistics show that about six out of ten victims are shot; about two out of ten are stabbed; and the remainder are murdered in a variety of ways, including strangulation, beating, hitting with blunt objects such as clubs and hammers, drowning, burning, poisoning, and exploding. Guns are the most popular weapon, and their popularity has increased with the easy availability of cheap handguns known as Saturday-night specials. Resistance to legislation to control such weapons is strong.

Murder and Mental Disturbance. Just as the majority of those who commit suicide are not mentally disturbed, the majority of murderers would not be considered insane. However, a number of people are not convicted of murder because of successful pleas of "insanity." The majority of those who are judged legally insane at the time they commit murder are diagnosed as schizophrenic. Schizophrenia can be characterized by intense hostility and anger, but most schizophrenics don't act out their hatred; instead, they dissipate it in fantasy. In fact, considering the large number of schizophrenics, murder is a relatively rare occurrence within this diagnostic classification. However, murder committed by a schizophrenic is an event to which the media give extensive publicity. We have all read headlines in the daily newspaper such as "Ex-Mental Patient Murders Housewife." With these kinds of prejudicing experiences provided by the media, it is no wonder so many people fear those who have or have had psychological problems.

The schizophrenic who murders has usually lost touch with where fantasies end and reality begins. This was true in the case of a man called Elmer that was reported by Guttmacher (1960). Elmer was described as a "sensitive, rather isolated youth who loved flowers and liked to watch birds" (p. 47). As Elmer passed through adolescence, he encountered failures in both social interactions and work, with the result that he was hospitalized with a "nervous breakdown" when he was 20. He was diagnosed at that time as a catatonic schizophrenic and treated with electroshock, but he returned home against the psychiatrist's recommendations. His only work when he returned home was taking care of the yard of a kindly lady named Mrs. Wise. One morning Elmer hid a butcher knife in a bouquet of flowers he had picked for her, went to her house, and "plunged the knife into her abdomen, disemboweling her." When interviewed later, Elmer related that he thought she was responsible for sexual dreams he was having that included her and his mother and sister. Voices had been urging him to put a stop to her influencing his dreams, and he gave in to the voices, as he explained:

As shown by the case of student Charles Whitman, a sniper who killed 15 people on the University of Texas campus in 1966, the horrendous act of murder is largely unpredictable. (Photo by Wide World Photos.)

403

CHAPTER 15:
CALAMITOUS
DEATH:
SUICIDE
AND MURDER

I felt that she had killed a lot of people. If I did not get her she'd kill more. I thought she had some ways like hypnotism to make people do things. One day I felt she was me. I acted like her. It was her voice, as though she was inside me. I bet that poor lady will hate me if there is a hereafter. The first question she will ask me is, "Why did you do it?" The first birthday that I was home from the hospital she and her old mother gave me so many presents that I cried. She seemed to get in my body and talk through me at times. . . . Do you think I tried to rape her? I don't think I did. I had that hateful feeling toward her then, I wanted to stab her [p. 142].

Treatment of the murderer who is legally declared insane usually must take place in a state institution. Typically, the individual has been adjudged not to know right from wrong and must receive psychological treatment until he or she does. What this treatment specifically entails is another question. At present, a wide variety of drug and physiological treatments such as electroshock and psychosurgery may be used in treating the "insane" murderer. As is true in noncriminal as well as criminally disturbed people, the success of the treatment varies with the severity of the disorder.

Explanations

Although there are severe religious and legal restrictions and punishment for maliciously killing another person, murder is not an infrequent occurrence in the United States. Attempts to explain why murder occurs may be classified as sociological or psychological. We will consider each in turn.

Sociological Theory. From the sociological perspective, factors such as social class are clearly related to the occurrence of murder. A large number of murders are committed by nonpsychotic young people who are members of the lower social classes. Of these young slayers, Schildre (1936) has observed:

It is rather that life and death do not seem to play an important part in the manifest content of psychic life. Persons of this kind seemingly kill as easily as children in their play, and they are no more concerned about their own death than children are. It almost seems that these "normal murderers," who are not otherwise so badly adapted to their reality, show particular infantile trends in their reaction to life and death. One may say they kill because they do not appreciate the deprivation they inflict upon others [p. 348].

More often than not, lower-class murderers come from what Wolfgang (1964) has called the *violent subculture*, where problems are usually solved by violence. In the violent subculture, there may be a lack of family cohesiveness that breeds frustration, which in turn often is handled by violence and aggression. Several studies present data to support the explanation that murderers were frustrated as children and learn maladaptive and violent means of expressing their frustration. For example, using maladaptive means of expressing frustration as a measure, Palmer (1964) looked at childhood differences between murderers and their brothers in regard to frustration. He studied 51 murderers and their closest (in age) brothers. He classified frustrations as being either physical or psychological. For example, indications of *physical frustration* were such things as a difficult birth or a beating given by one of the parents. On the basis of this scoring method, Palmer found that murderers had almost three times the number of physically frustrating events in their childhood as their brothers. To measure *psychological frustration*, Palmer used such indicators as toilet training begun before the age of 12 months, persistent bed-wetting during preadult years, and spending the majority of time playing alone during the first five years of life. He found that murderers had nearly *twice* as many psychologically frustrating events as their brothers had. When Palmer examined the kinds of aggressive behavior shown by murderers as they were growing up, he found that they tended to use more unacceptable and extreme releases of aggressive behavior, such as severely maiming animals.

Other work (Duncan, Frazier, Litin, Johnson, & Barron, 1958; Lamberti, Blackman, & Weiss, 1958) indicates strongly that many murderers were severely physically punished by their parents. For example, one murderer, as a child, had been held by his feet, stripped of all clothing, struck repeatedly with a belt, and then dropped on his head. Thus, there is some evidence to conclude that many murderers learned their aggressiveness by example from their parents.

Psychological Theory. The psychoanalytic explanation emphasizes internal drive states as the primary cause of one person's murdering another. As you remember, Freud postulated that we probably all have an aggressive drive that seeks fulfillment. At times, if it is not controlled by the ego and superego, this aggressive drive "spills" out in aggressive behavior. Depending on the situation, aggressiveness can be turned inward, as in the case of suicide, or outward, as in the case of murder.

Guttmacher (1960) presents the experience of a murderer that demonstrates aggression vacillating between turning inward and turning outward. The murderer's wife was threatening to leave, and he had returned at night to see her and his children.

PERSONAL EXPERIENCE: *Murder*

I was hoping against hope there'd be a man there. The lights were on, the shades were drawn—that was unusual. I rang the bell. I saw

405

CHAPTER 15:
CALAMITOUS
DEATH:
SUICIDE
AND MURDER

two shadows, then one, then two again. I hit the door with my fist and sprang it. There was no one there but her. . . . My wife was drinking beer. I put my cigarette out in it. Then we talked. She said she just didn't want me and I wasn't man enough to take it. I broke down and cried. She didn't cry, she went to bed. I wrote her a suicide note . . . and went into the bathroom and started to cut on myself with a razor blade. Then I thought of the children, especially my son, Thomas junior. He was all man. I felt so close to him then, I cannot explain it. I didn't want him to have pain in death. I would have thanked God if I'd had a gun. I tried to figure out which would be faster, to crush his skull or cut him to death. There is no easy way to kill anyone. I saw his face, he was dead in a minute. Irene was asleep, I don't think she ever woke up. . . .

I took the only tangible thing from her that she ever had—those children. I took them away. She has everything on her shoulders now, what a load.

Source: The Mind of a Murderer, by Manfred S. Guttmacher, M. D. Copyright © 1960 by Manfred S. Guttmacher. Reprinted by permission of Farrar, Straus, & Giroux, Inc.

This murderer seems to have experienced a loss of reality contact caused by his wife's leaving him, and he methodically went about destroying the "things" his wife would hate to lose—their son and daughter.

Whereas the Freudian explanation of murder emphasizes the internal drive of aggression, those espousing an observational-learning explanation of behavior (Bandura, 1977) assume that a person learns aggressive behavior primarily by imitating others. According to modeling theory, watching Daddy beat up Mommy, or a former football hero "beat up" someone in a movie, can reinforce that same style of problem-solving in the child. If those espousing a modeling theory of behavior are correct, then the high frequency of aggressive acts presented on television and in the movies may increase the chances that children will show these kinds of aggressive behavior in the future. This is a frightening possibility.

Prevention and Treatment

As was true of suicide, probably the most effective treatment for murder is prevention. To this end, the crisis centers described previously also can play a significant role in preventing people from reaching the point where they kill someone. If it is true that the greatest proportion of murders originates in the "violent subculture," then widespread social changes probably would have a significant effect on the incidence of murder as well. At present, society "treats" the nonpsychotic murderer primarily by imprisonment or execution. However, those nonpsychotic murderers allowed to enter psychotherapy of some sort often have a surprising amount of insight into their behavior, and often gain from both individual and group therapy. In therapy, the psychotic murderer may be dealt with in the same way as any disturbed individual. A wide variety of physical treatments such as electroshock, drugs, and psychosurgery have been used with some success with these individuals.

Very little seems to have been written concerning the effects of murder on those who know or are related to either the murderer or the victim. However, the emotional impact on family and friends probably is devastating. Those surrounding the murderer often have to deal with feelings ranging from anger that he or she took a life to guilt and shame that they were somehow responsible for the murderer's acts. Those surrounding the victim have to deal with feelings of loss, of guilt that they could have somehow prevented the death, and of anger at the murderer. When one considers that the murderer and his victim usually know each other and share friends or even relatives, the emotional consequences of this form of calamitous death can be far-reaching and complex. As Wolfgang (1964) stated:

> Often the notions of retribution and compassion mingle in the society's reaction both to the offender and to the offended. More attention has been focused on the one who remains after the deadly drama for he (or she) is exposed to the institutional processes of arrest, trial, and punishment, as well as being available for study [p. vii].

In spite of the social processes surrounding a murder, less research has been focused on the psychological consequences of murder than on suicide. Surely, the impact on the emotional lives of all those touched by murder may be as great as that of suicide. Perhaps the relative lack of psychological interest is due to the fact that murder occurs primarily among lower-class people or may be seen as a crime and thus not as a psychological problem. Few reasons justify the lack of attention given to the emotional stress and problems created in a vast number of people by the occurrence of murder. It seems apparent that postvention procedures are needed by those touched by murder as well as by those affected by suicide. Postvention procedures are especially needed in light of the fact that most murderers remain alive and become reminders of the murder to others. Perhaps the attention of suicidologists could be broadened to include the study of murder and its effects on the psychological well-being of those close to the murderer and the victim.

MURDER FOLLOWED BY SUICIDE

Although calamitous death usually involves either suicide alone or murder alone, a combination of the two, *murder-suicide*, is not an infrequent event. In the United States, about 4% of all murders are followed

407

CHAPTER 15:
CALAMITOUS
DEATH:
SUICIDE
AND MURDER

by a suicide; in Western European countries, where from one to two out of every ten murders are followed by a suicide, *more* murderers kill themselves than are executed by the state. The ratio of male to female cases of murder-suicide is about 11 to 1 in the United States, 3 to 1 in Australia, 1.7 to 1 in England, and 1 to 1 in Denmark. The countries with high suicide-murder rates are also those with a much higher suicide-to-murder ratio. For example, both in England and in Denmark, suicide is from 30 to 40 times as common as murder, and these countries also have the two highest percentages of murderers who kill themselves (West, 1965).

Description

Is there such an entity as a murder-suicide syndrome? Among others, Dorpat (1966) thinks there is, and he lists several identifying factors: the suicide followed immediately after the murder; there was an intimate relationship between a man and a woman; the man was disturbed, frequently psychotic; the histories indicated that the relationship was marked by prolonged, bitter conflict and that the murder and suicide came at a time of violent emotional struggle; frequently the act followed a real or threatened separation.

In the United States, whether a murderer is considered "sane" may be related to whether he or she is classified as a murder-suicide. Guttmacher (1960) found that suicide following murder was rare in the "nonpsychotic" group, but that one out of every five psychotic murderers also committed suicide. In most murder-suicide cases in the United States, a man killed a woman and then immediately tried to kill himself. This sequence is just the opposite of what occurs in Denmark, where more often a woman kills a man or a child and then herself.

The psychological components of murder-suicide are shown in the case of a man named James, described by Guttmacher. James had a long history of antisocial and assaultive behavior. Three marriages had ended unhappily. He began an affair with a married woman. Their affair was stormy, and, after he caught her making love with another woman in a car, he accused her of being homosexual. The emotional feelings that James experienced are revealed in the following account, obtained just before James killed himself:

> How in hell would you feel if the girl you loved turned out to be a goddamned fag? I have been in jails and I have known plenty of fags, but I never associated with the goddamned idiots. . . . The day I shot Mary I was on my way to return the gun to Bill _____ . I had to change buses two blocks from where Mary worked. I stood there for an hour. I didn't know what the Christ to do. I did not know whether to shoot myself or her or what to do. . . . Why did I do it? I know I am no damn nut or idiot. I have tried to figure out why I shot her, since I am here. I will never know.

An example of murder-suicide: This man leaped to his death after killing his business partner. (Photo by Wide World Photos.)

Explanations and Treatment

Explanations of murder-suicide are varied but usually center about the core feelings of anger and resultant remorse. Suicide can be the result of a predictable reaction of the individual to the murder he or she has just committed. Suicide also may be a means of escaping the punishment and social recriminations that probably will come as a result of the killing.

409

CHAPTER 15:
CALAMITOUS
DEATH:
SUICIDE
AND MURDER

However, the explanation most often applied for murder-suicide derives from psychoanalytic theory.

According to psychoanalytic theory, people possess an inborn aggressive drive that must find periodic satisfaction. The aggressive drive must find some outlet, either against the self or against others. To Freud, any restriction or blocking of outward aggressiveness increases the chances for the aggression to be channeled inward. A main difference between murder and suicide is that in the former, the aggressiveness is channeled outward, whereas in the latter, it is channeled inward. In the section describing suicide, we examined the presence of aggressiveness in many suicides—the tendency of the suicidal person to want to blame and hurt others. The choice—to kill oneself or someone else—seems at times to be arbitrary. A good example of the flexibility of the aggressive drive is in a case presented by Wood (1961):

> A man was constantly quarreling with his mistress. One quarrel developed when he objected to her dress as being too immodest. She refused to change the dress and the quarrel grew to be violent. He drew a knife and threatened to kill her and she promptly threw herself on her knees and begged him not to kill her. So he said, "All right! I won't stab you! I will stab myself!" He did so and died [p. 64].

Results of psychoanalytic studies suggest that those who murder also may have strong suicidal tendencies (Williams, 1964). Often the murderer was planning suicide and then decided at the last moment to kill someone else instead. A man may buy poison to kill himself and then give it to his wife; or he may decide to jump out of a window, change his mind, and push his mistress out. Conversely, suicide may represent a substitute for the murder of another person.

Dorpat (1966) agrees with the conclusion that murder and suicide seem to be part of the same psychological act. He argues further that if murder and suicide were governed separately by guilt or a need for punishment, then we probably would see two separate acts. Dorpat theorizes that in the murder-suicide syndrome the murderer may wish to die *with* the victim, thus gratifying fantasies connected with dying and sex. Folklore sometimes presents a rather romantic picture of reunion after death. One writer (Jones, 1968) has gone so far as to suggest that sex, birth, and death may be so intertwined that the fantasy of dying together is nothing more than the gratification of early childhood fantasies.

Treatment in cases of murder-suicide requires helping those who survive the double shock of murder *and* suicide. Extra stress may be placed on those close to the victim, because murder automatically involves various governmental agencies, social censure, and additional pressures.

CONCLUDING COMMENTS

It is difficult to imagine a worse consequence of a loss of control over feelings or behavior than the taking of a human life. Because of the present-day recognition of the psychosociological importance of death, there is a growing interest in the study of death-related issues. *Thanatology*, the study of death, calls for the comprehensive study of the aspects of death, dying, suicide, and life-threatening behavior. In this chapter, we have emphasized the last two aspects of thanatology, suicide and murder, rather than death and dying. Scientists are now moving into the realm of what used to belong exclusively to the clergy and philosophers. For example, studies have been launched into how people react to terminal illness. Kübler-Ross (1969) has accomplished pioneering work showing that terminally ill people generally move through identifiable stages in attempting to deal with their inevitable death. Other researchers, in attempts to gain more knowledge of how best to help those who are dying and those who survive, have studied the effects of untimely death and funerals. Today, the issues of death are being grappled with by professionals and laypeople alike. This debate has already led to more humane treatment of those facing death. We believe there will be no easy answers from such a painful and complex dialogue—only better ones.

CHAPTER SUMMARY CHART

In this chapter, we first described suicide, one form of calamitous death:

Historical perspectives	*Statistics*
Suicide as a sin	Men more than women
Suicide as a crime	Older people more than younger
The Judaeo-Christian ethic	Blacks more than Whites
Social and psychological objections still remain	Upper class more than lower class
	Single people more than married people
	Among top ten causes of death in United States

We then looked at several explanations for suicidal behavior:

411

CHAPTER 15:
CALAMITOUS
DEATH:
SUICIDE
AND MURDER

Psychoanalytic theory

Freud:
Aggressive instinct from id turned
inward
Thanatos
Ambivalent (love-hate)
relationships with self and others
Menninger: Different forms of self-
destructive behavior
Chronic suicide
Focal suicide
Organic suicide

Sociological theory

Durkheim: Suicide is inversely
related to integration in
society. People with
no place are more likely
victims.
Types of suicide:
Egoistic
Altruistic
Anomic

We also discussed ways to prevent suicide:

*Assessment of suicide
threat*

Cues:
Verbal threat
Sudden behavioral
change
Available means
Lethality,
perturbation,
inimicality
Ambivalence toward
life
Suicide as a
dyadic event

Prevention

Crisis centers—
24-hour phones
Lindemann's crisis
theory
Centers are success-
ful and widely
used, but not
really evaluated.

*Treatment for the
survivors*

Lessen aftereffects
Community inter-
ventions
Psychotherapy
Facilitate return
to full life
Postvention
Shneidman's
guidelines

We then looked at murder, a second form of calamitous death:

Description

Historical perspective
Religious dictums
against killing
Legal definitions
of murder
Statistics
U.S. second only to
South America
Men more than women
Young more than old

Explanations

Sociological
Violent sub-
cultures
Frustration (phys-
ical or psy-
chological)
Physical punish-
ment

Prevention and treatment

Crisis centers
Community and family
interventions
Psychotherapy
Imprisonment or
capital punishment

Description
(continued)

Blacks more than
    Whites
Friends more than
    strangers
Lower class more
    than upper class
Guns the most used
    weapons

Explanations
(continued)

Psychological
    Freud: aggressive
      instincts of the
      id turned out-
      ward; ambiva-
      lent (love-hate)
      relationships
      with self and
      others
    Learning theory:
      Children model
      after violent
      parents and
      TV shows

Finally, we described murder followed by suicide:

Description

Murder-suicide a real syndrome
Severely distraught people

Explanations and prevention

Psychoanalytic theory: in murder,
    aggression is turned outward;
    guilt can produce aggression
    turned inward and subsequent
    suicide.

SECTION VI
DISORDERS
PRIMARILY ASSOCIATED
WITH
BRAIN AND
NERVOUS-SYSTEM
DISTURBANCES

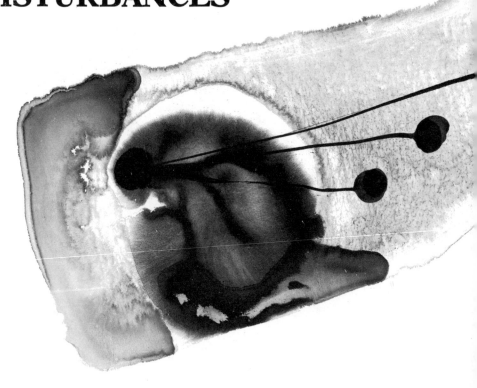

Chapter 16
The Brain Syndromes

Chapter 17
Mental Retardation

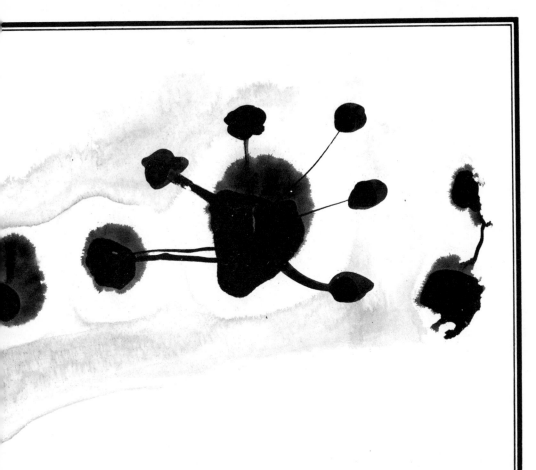

The lack of behavioral control in the disorders described in Section V is generally psychogenic. However, in the disorders primarily associated with brain and nervous-system disturbances, loss of control and other deficits in function are basically biogenic—that is, due to some organic dysfunction. Psychological aspects of a person do affect specific patterns of behavior seen in the brain syndromes and in most forms of mental retardation, but the primary causative factors seem to be neurological. Such neurological causation is more common in the brain syndromes (Chapter 16) than in the mental retardations (Chapter 17), where symptoms in some cases may be related to socioenvironmental conditions as well as biological and genetic factors.

While there are a number of treatments available to help with the physical consequences of neurological disorders, the significant positive effects possible through the use of psychological techniques are often overlooked. For this reason, we emphasize the psychological consequences of the brain disorders and describe the role of psychological counseling in the treatment of the brain syndromes and mental retardation.

415

CHAPTER 16
THE BRAIN
SYNDROMES

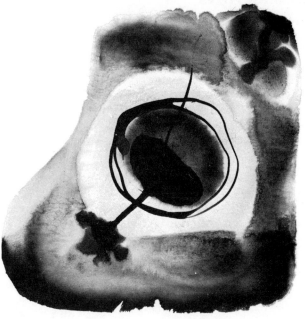

Psychological symptoms such as anxiety, delusions, hallucinations, and depression often are associated with brain syndromes. These symptoms may occur in psychogenic disorders as well, but in the brain syndromes they probably are more directly tied to a known physical cause. In fact, the primary cause of most brain syndromes is sufficiently clear that we can use the term *etiology*, which is generally reserved for specific, confirmed causes, instead of the more general term *explanation*. For example, mental symptoms that occur after a blow on the head are more clearly related to that blow to the head than they would be to a variety of unknown psychological factors. Treatment for the brain syndromes can be more direct than that for psychogenic disorders. For example, intense suspiciousness (paranoia) caused by a niacin deficiency can be treated directly by administering niacin, rather than by attempting to deal with the suspiciousness per se. However, although simple, direct treatment is possible in some cases, the effects of a number of brain syndromes remain largely irreversible.

SECTION VI:
DISORDERS
PRIMARILY
ASSOCIATED WITH
BRAIN AND
NERVOUS-SYSTEM
DISTURBANCES

DESCRIPTIONS

The brain syndromes are the patterns of behavioral disturbances associated with neurological damage to the brain or nervous system. They can be either *acute* (reversible) or *chronic* (irreversible). Brain syndromes may be characterized by both physical and mental disturbances in which basic social, emotional, intellectual, and physical skills can be affected. In contrast to some individuals with functional disorders, those with brain syndromes may be painfully aware that they no longer can do what they used to do. This realization of incapacity can contribute significantly to the anxiety and depression that often accompany the brain syndromes.

The following personal experience was obtained from a 49-year-old veteran with an above-average IQ who received significant brain damage in the Vietnam war. His response came after he had attempted unsuccessfully to put together a simple, four-piece puzzle.

PERSONAL EXPERIENCE: *Brain Damage*

Look at me . . . I'm sweating like a pig! Four f____ pieces and I can't even put them together. The harder I try the worse I do. You'd think I was doing the world's toughest puzzle. I try to be cool and not let it bother me, but my grandson could put this together. . . . You and I both know that. I can't tell you how frustrating it is to see something you could do easily before . . . you know. . . but something you can't do now. I feel like some kind of ass . . . some kind of stupid ass. But I know in my head how to do things. . . . Somehow when I start to put things together it just won't work. Tell me, will I be like this the rest of my life? What a helluva fix!

General Characteristics

Acute and chronic brain syndromes differ in many ways, but both types share several basic characteristics. Those suffering from brain syndromes, whether reversible or not, exhibit a variety of intellectual, emotional, and perceptual deficits (Goldfarb, 1967; L. Kolb, 1973). The symptom that is often first noticed by relatives or the victim is a disturbance in orientation. Whereas normal individuals are usually oriented in time, place, person, and circumstance, brain-damaged people often are not. They may not be able to tell you correctly the day of the week, or the month of the year. In more severe instances, they may not know where or who they are.

In addition to orientation problems, brain syndromes may involve disturbance of memory. Typically, memory for recent events is more impaired than memory for distant occurrences. For example, brain-damaged people may be able to recall things from their youth, but not from one or two hours earlier in the day. In some types of brain disorders, individuals may attempt to "fill in" memory gaps with fabricated stories and fantasied events (Korsakoff's symptom). Many times, brain-damaged people are embarrassingly aware of and upset by their memory disabilities.

Both perceptual and memory deficits due to brain damage may be revealed by figure-drawing tests such as the Bender Gestalt Test and the Benton Visual Retention Test (see Chapter 2). In these tests, persons may be asked to copy a figure directly from a drawing placed before them or to view the figure for five or ten seconds and, with the figure removed, to reproduce the design from memory. Brain damage may be indicated by an inability to copy figures directly or, even more importantly, to retain the figure in memory for a short period of time before reproducing it.

In disturbances in judgment, brain-syndrome deficits may be observed in the inability to apply moral, practical, or safety principles to the correct solution of daily problems. For example, to the question, "What would you do if a store were out of milk?" brain-syndrome people might respond that they

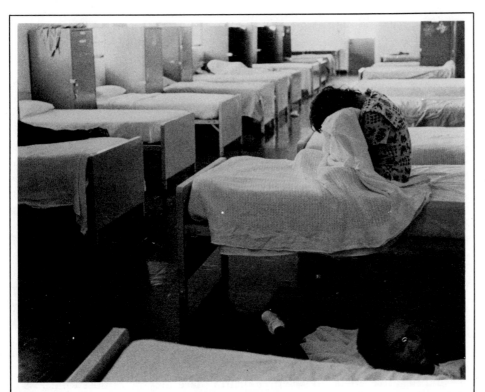

The loneliness that can afflict mentally disturbed people is no more apparent than with those patients whose symptoms are organic and irreversible. (Photo by Joseph Czarnecki.)

SECTION VI:
DISORDERS
PRIMARILY
ASSOCIATED
WITH BRAIN AND
NERVOUS-SYSTEM
DISTURBANCES

would wait until more milk came or perhaps go home. Before their difficulty, they probably would have correctly responded that they would go to another store.

People with brain syndromes may have difficulties not only in memory and judgment, but in the intellectual realm as well. One intellectual ability, vocabulary skill, is often among the most important bits of diagnostic information (Brosin, 1967). Lack of ability to use, recognize, or define everyday words can be a key indicator of brain dysfunction. Other intellectual indicators include inability to carry out mentally simple arithmetic calculations, such as subtracting 3s or 7s continuously, beginning at 100. Lack of general information, such as the name of the president of the United States or the individual's birthday, can also indicate intellectual deficit.

Whereas the first three deficits associated with brain syndromes may be loosely described as cognitive, the final deficit falls into the emotional-affective realm. In brain syndromes, mood alterations can take the form of either a flatness of feeling or rapid swings of emotion. Often, emotional reactions may be inappropriate in degree or content to the situation at hand. For instance, a brain-syndrome person may begin laughing hysterically when given a piece of gum or begin weeping when asked for the sum of 4 plus 2. However, these emotional reactions may also occur among people with functional disorders such as the schizophrenias or affective psychoses.

Acute Brain Syndrome

Acute, or reversible, brain syndrome is marked primarily by *rapid onset, reversibility,* and *delirium.* Delirium is a set of symptoms usually caused by acute cerebral insufficiency; that is, the brain stops functioning temporarily for one of a variety of reasons to be discussed shortly (Engel & Romano, 1959; Kolb, 1973). The delirium symptom complex typically includes clouding of consciousness, bewilderment, disorientation, dreamlike thinking, hallucinations, and fear. In *mild delirium,* the experience seems similar to that felt by most people after having been awakened suddenly in the middle of the night. For a few moments, everything may be hazy and unclear; the person may not know where he or she is. At such a time, the mind just doesn't work at its usual speed and efficiency. In contrast, people experiencing *moderate delirium* typically have longer-lasting, more severe disturbances in thinking and behaving. They often are aware of an inability to think and remember that can result in confusion, bewilderment, and signs of disorientation, first in time, then later in place, and finally in person. If the state of delirium progresses, the person may lose motor control and the ability to eat or drink unaided, become incontinent of urine and feces, and finally develop a coma or stupor.

The most serious effects on the functioning of the brain take place in *severe delirium.* Although in mild and moderate delirium there is some memory loss and negative affect, in severe delirium there may be almost total loss of memory, severe depression, and anxiety. The individual's attempts to reverse the delirium are usually to no avail. Because it is acute, delirium typically runs its course and then reverses itself. However, the rate and thoroughness of reversal often depend more upon the original cause of the cerebral insufficiency and the physical treatment provided than on any conscious personal efforts or psychological interventions.

Chronic Brain Syndrome

Chronic brain syndrome is characterized by *slow onset, irreversibility,* and *dementia* (see Table 16-1). The chronic, or permanent, brain syndromes can result from a variety of causes, including untreated or progressive acute disturbances. Dementia, the primary symptom complex seen in chronic brain syndrome, is usually of slow onset. Over time, a person's intellectual and problem-solving abilities may deteriorate, and his or her interests may narrow. Often, adjustment to new experiences may be more difficult to face. Frequently, the person may be aware of loss of skills and may try to compensate for such losses. As the insidious deterioration continues, memory defects may appear, and disorientation and confusion may occur more frequently. After a time, judgment usually is affected and emotional instability may become manifest. With few exceptions, the course of chronic brain syndrome or dementia is irreversible and eventually leads to death.

During the course of the disorder, multiple psychological symptoms can occur, ranging from psychotic patterns similar to schizophrenia, manic-depression, and paranoia to neurotic characteristics of intense anxiety, hypochondriasis, compulsions, and the like.

Table 16-1. *Comparison of acute and chronic brain syndromes*

Acute	*Chronic*
Associated with delirium	Associated with dementia
Reversible	Irreversible
Temporary cerebral insufficiency	Persisting damage to brain tissues
Symptoms may include clouding of consciousness, bewilderment, disorientation, confusion, hallucination, and fear.	Symptoms may include permanent loss of intellectual efficiency, impaired decision making, inability to use abstract ideas, and unstable or inadequate emotion.
Common causes are certain infections and high fevers, poisoning, head injuries, and cardiovascular insufficiency, and certain reversible nutritional deficiencies.	Common causes are brain atrophy with age, arteriosclerosis, degenerative brain disease, certain uncorrected nutritional deficiencies, and brain tumor.
Typically of brief duration but may last for several months. In some cases may become chronic.	Typically permanent and progressive, but may be marked by periods of lucidity.

Based on data from *Modern Clinical Psychiatry* (8th ed.), by L. C. Kolb. Philadelphia: Saunders, 1973.

SECTION VI:
DISORDERS
PRIMARILY
ASSOCIATED
WITH BRAIN AND
NERVOUS-SYSTEM
DISTURBANCES

ETIOLOGIES

Causative factors of brain syndromes may be grouped into those that primarily produce reversible (acute) symptoms and those that are often the precursors of irreversible (chronic) syndromes. However, it is possible for an acute disorder to become chronic due to lack of treatment or to the progressive nature of a particular disturbance. It is also possible for acute symptoms to occur in chronic disorders, as in the case of epileptic seizures that come and go yet may reflect a permanent brain disturbance.

Acute Brain Syndromes

In general, acute brain syndromes are induced by diseases or accidents that produce cerebral insufficiency, a reduction in oxygen available to the brain. Cerebral insufficiency may be compared with cardiac insufficiency, in that both may cause disabilities or even death. Further, just as there are a variety of causes for cardiac insufficiency (such as enlarged heart, hypertension, and the like) there may be a variety of causes for cerebral insufficiency. However, regardless of the cause, the effects of acute brain dysfunction are basically similar—delirium ranging from mild confusion to severe coma, stupor, or even death.

Head Trauma. A severe blow to the head may result in a number of possible organic disturbances. The mildest reaction, *concussion,* usually involves momentary interruption of brain function followed by a few moments or even hours of unconsciousness. Upon awakening, the individual usually experiences confusion and loss of memory for events that occurred a few minutes or hours before the trauma. Complete recovery is usual within a few weeks.

More serious than simple concussion, *traumatic delirium* may involve greater damage to the brain, resulting in a prolonged state of full-blown delirium. Haziness, dizziness, confusion, memory loss, and the like may appear, along with hallucinations and other psychoticlike behavior. If these symptoms last for more than a week, they may indicate severe brain damage that will require an extended period of time to remedy.

If a head trauma is severe, actual tissue damage may occur in the brain. Physical damage can take the form of *contusions* (a disruption of tissues accompanied by bleeding) or *lacerations* (gross tearing of brain tissue) that may result in *traumatic coma* lasting for 24 hours or more. Following this coma, individuals may awaken and experience the symptoms of traumatic delirium.

Drug Intoxications. In addition to severe head injury, acute cerebral insufficiency can be induced by the accidental or purposeful misuse of any of a large variety of drugs. In Chapter 13, we described some of the possible disorders associated with the use of many drugs and some of the effects on the brain brought about by drug overdose. In fact, among the most frequent clinical causes of delirium is misuse of the barbiturates and other sedatives (Kolb, 1973). Minor tranquilizers such as diazepam (Valium), chlordiazepine (Librium), and meprobamate (Miltown) are also major intoxicators. Delirium induced by drugs usually results from an overdose or an attempt to withdraw from an addictive chemical. It can lead to chronic brain damage or death.

Industrial chemicals such as mercury, lead, manganese, sulfur, and carbon monoxide can also cause acute brain syndromes that, in some cases, result in irreversible damage. Until the late 1940s, lead poisoning was widespread owing to the presence of the metal in paints on walls and toys chewed by infants and young children. Symptoms of lead poisoning include acute delirious episodes and, if uncorrected, progressive mental deterioration.

Infection. Besides trauma and drug overdose, acute cerebral insufficiency can be caused by intracranial infection. In meningococcal meningitis and tubercular meningitis, the meninges, or "wrappers," around the brain and spinal cord become inflamed. Common results are confusion, muttering, disorientation, and restlessness. The person may also be unable to remember recent events or to perceive accurately what is going on.

Chronic Brain Syndromes

Unlike the acute syndromes, the chronic brain syndromes are usually the result of severe or prolonged disease or extensive accidental damage. The chronically brain-damaged person often presents a picture of therapeutic hopelessness and progressive, inevitable deterioration. However, not all chronic disorders are hopeless; some, like epilepsy, can be controlled with proper treatment.

Presenile Brain Disease. Although the term *dementia* usually is associated with old age and so-called senility, several chronic disorders of the brain may produce presenile dementia. *Alzheimer's disease* is a presenile dementia whose average age of onset is somewhere in the mid-50s. (Senile dementias usually aren't diagnosed as such until age 65; see Chapter 21.) In addition to its relatively early onset, Alzheimer's disease most often has symptoms similar to those of general dementia described earlier. Typically, the deterioration begins slowly, with the first signs frequently being mild disorientation, forgetfulness, and loss of interest in daily living. In most cases, the disorder is insidious and unstoppable and results in death within about ten years after onset. Autopsies of victims indicate that Alzheimer's disease may be closely associated with brain atrophy and changes resulting in abnormal connections among neural fibers (Juel-Nielsen, 1975).

SECTION VI:
DISORDERS
PRIMARILY
ASSOCIATED
WITH BRAIN AND
NERVOUS-SYSTEM
DISTURBANCES

Pick's disease, a second type of presenile dementia, differs from Alzheimer's disease in being characterized by specific rather than general psychological and motor impairments. In Pick's disease, the primary signs often may be specific disabilities such as inability to read (dyslexia), to remember the names of familiar objects (agnosia), to perform specific motor acts (apraxia), and the like. Some patients may also show psychological symptoms of memory loss, flatness of affect, and inability to cope with new problems. Unlike victims of the other forms of dementia, people with Pick's disease usually don't exhibit hallucinations, delusions, or fantastic thoughts.

Syphilis. Whereas the primary reasons for the onset of the presenile disorders and their subsequent course of progressive dementia are not fully known, much is now known of the organic basis of *general paresis*, the chronic brain syndrome that occurs in 10% of cases of untreated syphilis. In fact, as we mentioned in Chapter 3, the discovery of the biological basis of general paresis gave early credence to the biological theories of mental disorders. The initial venereal infection, called primary syphilis, can be treated effectively with antibiotics. If untreated, the symptoms of primary syphilis usually disappear, and the individual may believe mistakenly that the problem has remitted. However, the absence of symptoms may signal the beginning of the incubation period, or secondary phase, of the disease that can last anywhere from 5 to 30 years. About two out of ten of those with secondary-stage syphilis will have their nervous system invaded by the syphilis-producing organism *Treponema pallidum*. Subsequent inflammation and degeneration of the central nervous system result in the outward signs of general paresis.

Among the first outward signs of this tertiary phase of syphilis are personality disturbances, in which people may become inconsiderate of others, lose their temper more easily, and show loss of control over sexual activities, rapid alteration of mood, increasingly frequent apathy, and depression. In time, psychotic symptoms such as delusions, hallucinations, and bizarre behavior may appear. Simultaneously, the signs of dementia may become manifest in the form of deficits in motor skills, memory, and judgment. As in the majority of cases of dementia, the usual result is death about four years after the onset of the tertiary symptoms. We now know that many such deaths are unnecessary and preventable. Possible signs and symptoms of venereal disease appearing a few days or weeks after sexual contact should never be ignored; they should always be evaluated by a physician.

Epilepsy. In most cases, *epilepsy* is believed to be primarily the result of chronic brain pathology reflected in unpredictable seizures and frequent states of delirium. Although epilepsy, like most other forms of chronic brain disorder, is irreversible, it usually doesn't involve the progressive deterioration and dementia common to the syphilitic, presenile, and senile dementias. Epileptic seizures are included as a chronic brain disorder because they involve loss or distortion of consciousness and frequently include psychological as well as physical symptoms. Some seizures may be produced by directly identifiable tumors, inflammation, or trauma in the brain; but about three out of four epilepsies (77%) are called *idiopathic epilepsies:* they seem to have no known cause. The following personal experience conveys what it's like to have an epileptic seizure.

PERSONAL EXPERIENCE: *Epilepsy*

But on October 31, just as I was going to eat my lunch, having done a whole morning's washing, I was shown abruptly that there was no truth yet in believing myself better.

The food was on the table, the oil stove lit. I picked up the coffee percolator to fill it. Just as I reached the sink and was standing in the doorway, I found I could not move, could not remember what I wanted to do. It seemed a long time that I stood there (actually perhaps a few seconds) saying to myself, "This is nothing. It will be all right in a moment and I shall remember *all the rest.*" Then I felt my head beginning to jerk backwards and my face to grimace. Then the percolator fell from my hand into the sink. But still some dogged part of me kept saying, "All this is really controllable." I was still conscious and felt violent gestures and spasms were shooting all over me, even till I felt my knees give and I fell down on the concrete floor. As I went, it shot through me, the astonishment: "As bad as this, then?"

The next thing I remember was the B____s' kitchen and Betty B____, God bless her, giving me tea and talking to me in the tone mothers use to little children coming out of nightmares. Rosie was by me, sitting at my feet. I asked the time. They said it was two o'clock. Half an hour had *gone.* I had not the slightest recollection of picking myself up or walking 100 yards up the road or going into their kitchen. Nor, for an hour or two, of what had happened before I fell.[1]

From *A Ray of Darkness*, by M. Evans.

The epilepsies may be categorized on the basis of the type of seizure manifested (Ervin, 1967). To some extent the specific type of seizure manifested seems to depend upon heredity (Ervin, 1967; Kolb, 1963), but the exact nature of the inherited defect is not yet known.

Grand mal seizures are what most people picture as epileptic seizures. The initial sign may be an aura, or sense of impending seizure, felt a few seconds prior to onset. The aura may consist of numbness, tingling, a

SECTION VI:
DISORDERS
PRIMARILY
ASSOCIATED
WITH BRAIN AND
NERVOUS-SYSTEM
DISTURBANCES

sense of distress in the stomach, hallucinated light flashes, voices, or odors, or motor symptoms such as twitching or stiffness.

As the seizure begins, air is suddenly expelled from the lungs, producing a crying-out sound. The individual loses consciousness and falls to the ground. The first phase of the seizure is called the *tonic* phase; as the person falls, his or her entire voluntary musculature goes into a continuous contraction lasting from 10 to 20 seconds. Breathing may stop momentarily, bladder and bowel control may be suddenly lost, and in males erection and ejaculation may occur.

Following the tonic phase, the *clonic* phase begins. This phase is characterized by intermittent periods of relaxation and contraction, resulting in jerking movements. During this time the individual can seriously damage the tongue by biting it. After the clonic phase, the person may sleep for a few hours and awaken confused and suffering a loss of memory for the events immediately preceding the seizure. In rare instances, instead of reviving, some people may begin another seizure and then another. Called *status epilepticus*, this condition is a medical emergency; it will cause death if it is not treated at once.

Less well known, and less frequent, are *petit mal* seizures. A petit mal seizure may be seen as an incomplete grand mal seizure. Usually, there is a loss of consciousness and awareness for 5 to 30 seconds. There is no aura, and the person doesn't fall down. In some instances, the individual isn't even aware that a seizure has taken place. To an observer, the person may merely look as if a glaze has covered his or her eyes. Petit mal seizures can occur up to 100 times per day. Some people experience both types of seizures.

Whereas grand mal and petit mal seizures may involve more general brain dysfunctions, *focal seizures* are related to abnormal EEG activity in specific parts of the brain. One example of focal involvement is the *Jacksonian seizure*. This type of seizure begins with a tingling or numbing sensation around the corner of the mouth or in a thumb. Usually, the sensation spreads to adjoining parts of the body until half the body is involved.

Like Jacksonian seizures, *psychomotor seizures* are related to abnormal EEGs in specific parts of the brain. However, psychomotor epilepsy may also produce changes in perception, self-awareness, thought patterns, and mood.

As in epilepsy, alteration of consciousness is the prime symptom in the brain syndromes of *narcolepsy* and *cataplexy*. In narcolepsy, the person may fall asleep involuntarily in the middle of an activity. The person may sleep anywhere from a few seconds to half an hour or more. The primary symptom of cataplexy is sudden loss of muscle control and power. Although conscious, the individual may fall limply to the ground and be unable to speak. Laughing sometimes may produce cataplectic attacks in those susceptible to them. The causes of narcolepsy and cataplexy are unclear at this time.

Other Causes. Less frequent than the presenile, general-paretic, and epileptic chronic brain syndromes are a number of disorders with a wide variety of causes. *Pellagra* is known to be caused primarily by a niacin deficiency. In addition to the physical sign of reddening of the skin, pellagra may include psychological symptoms of paranoid ideas, delusions, and hallucinations. If treated rapidly, pellagra-induced psychosis usually is reversible. However, if not quickly treated, permanent damage may result, in the form of chronic brain syndrome and dementia.

Like niacin deficiency, *cranial neoplasms* (tumors) also may produce chronic psychological and emotional symptoms. Early signs of a brain tumor may be impairment of consciousness, headache, loss of energy, and an exaggeration of existing personality disturbances. For example, people who were more anxious than normal before the tumors may become even more anxious. Specific symptoms will vary according to the type and placement of the tumorous growth. Generally, the more localized the neoplasm, the more likely it is that specific disabilities will result.

Nutritional deficiencies and neoplasms are two known causes of chronic brain syndromes. However, there are organically based disorders for which there are as yet no known causes. For example, *paralysis agitans* (Parkinson's disease) is characterized by muscular rigidity, difficulty in movement, and slow, rhythmic tremors of the hands and feet. There are no specific psychological symptoms associated primarily with paralysis agitans, but many people with this disorder become morose and irritable. However, these symptoms may be the result of the dependency and loss of behavioral freedom often caused by the disease.

Known to be hereditary, but also of unknown specific cause, *Huntington's chorea* usually manifests itself between the ages of 30 and 45. At first, the person may show mild irritability; later, suspiciousness, paranoid ideas, hallucinations, and dementia inevitably occur. The person may exhibit *choreiform movements* that are clumsy, jerky, and irregular. As the disease progresses, the muscles needed for speech, eating, and motion also may deteriorate. In Huntington's chorea, depression can become severe, and suicide may be a danger. Huntington's chorea usually results in death about 15 years after the first symptoms appear. There is no known cure.

TREATMENT

After reviewing the variety of acute and chronic brain syndromes, we are left with the feeling that many brain disorders are preventable, some are controllable, and a few are incurable. Administration of deficient nutrients, restoration of metabolic balance, and the like often can cure the delirium. In the case of trauma or intoxication, time and nature's own healing

SECTION VI:
DISORDERS
PRIMARILY
ASSOCIATED
WITH BRAIN AND
NERVOUS-SYSTEM
DISTURBANCES

Woody Guthrie, a popular folk singer of the 30s and 40s, died from Huntington's chorea. Statistics show that one-half of a victim's children inherit the disorder, and only time will tell whether his son, contemporary folk singer Arlo Guthrie, will also develop this dread disease. (Photo courtesy of Marjorie Guthrie and the Committee to Combat Huntington's Disease, Inc.)

processes seem to be the best treatment for the biological aspects of the disorders.

Psychological treatment of those who are experiencing acute brain syndromes is important in helping patients to adjust to new limits that may be imposed by the disorder, and preventing behavior (such as drug use) that may result in repetition of the acute brain syndrome. Especially in cases of accidental trauma, for which guilt or blame may be felt or applied, family counseling may be helpful in ventilating feelings, as is shown in the following personal experience.

PERSONAL EXPERIENCE: *Post-Trauma Family Counseling*

I will never forget that day. I was in the kitchen making dinner when Hal's friend came running in. He said to come quick, that Hal was hurt. I had been used to this kind of thing because Hal was always into something, but I went to look as usual. On the way, Hal's friend told me that the boys were playing golf and that Hal had been hit by Billy with a golf club. I expected a big cut, but when I arrived at the park, I saw Hal on the ground not moving and with a large bloody dent in his upper forehead. I almost fainted. Billy was crying and yelling "He's dead, He's dead!" I picked up Hal and rushed to the hospital. I fought back tears and fear all the way. . . .

Hal was in a coma for 18 hours. When he awoke he did not know who he was, where he was, or anything. Doctors said he was delirious and we would have to wait a few days to see how bad the damage was. John and I worried and worried. Hal seemed so far away, but the doctors said he was coming along OK. . . . John wanted to kill Billy. He was so angry I had to hold him back one night when he wanted to go to Billy's house. While Hal was in the hospital a social worker came to our house and talked with us about our feelings. First we said we were fine, but she said, "You mean you don't feel like hurting the boy who did it?" We laughed when she said this; it released so much tension. We talked things out. John was open with her. She said we would be abnormal if we didn't feel that way. But we know we couldn't *act* on the feelings. . . .

After three months, Hal got out of the hospital. Soon after, Billy and his family moved away. They did not say a word to us from the moment the accident happened until they left. We were sorry that we never were able to talk things out with them.

Psychotherapy for the family and the individual patient may be helpful in chronic as well as acute brain syndromes. Awareness of having an incurable disease and facing impending deterioration creates a great deal of stress and anxiety. The affected person, family, and friends may wish to deny the disorder, but fears need to be faced, discussed, and shared. Too frequently there is a tendency for family members and friends to withdraw from a person who is terminally ill. Although such behavior is understandable, it can do great harm to the disordered person, who needs more support than ever during the attempt to deal with the effects of brain syn-

SECTION VI:
DISORDERS
PRIMARILY
ASSOCIATED
WITH BRAIN AND
NERVOUS-SYSTEM
DISTURBANCES

drome. Isolation and avoidance might lead the ill person to become even more depressed and paranoid. However, much depression or paranoia need not be specifically associated with any particular disorder; each can be caused partially by the reaction of the victims or their families to the loss of ability. In other places in the text, we have used the words *sick* and *illness* cautiously, but people with chronic brain syndrome *are sick.* They have a progressive physical disease that requires care, support, and understanding; psychological adjustment needn't be sacrificed or forgotten because one's physical state is deemed untreatable.

CONCLUDING COMMENTS

Of all the disorders described in this textbook, severe brain disease is probably most often viewed as hopeless. With the continuing shortage of mental-health professionals, the situation for those with chronic brain syndromes becomes even more crucial. Nearly one out of every ten Americans has a mental disturbance severe enough to need professional help; of these, only one out of seven will obtain treatment. Our guess is that those with chronic brain syndromes are among the most likely to be ignored and to miss out on treatment.

However, there is some suggestion that a trend is developing toward a focus on the brain and on treatment of brain disorders. Although we don't agree completely with Andy (1976), who stated that "all abnormal behavior results from structurally abnormal brain tissue" (p. 54), we do believe that many of the answers to emotional behavior may lie in brain functioning. Defects in brain functioning may lead to intellectual as well as emotional difficulties. As you will read in the next chapter, brain dysfunctions can also play a significant role in mental retardation.

CHAPTER SUMMARY CHART

In this chapter on organic brain syndromes, we discussed patterns of behavior associated primarily with brain disease or damage:

Description	Etiology	Treatment
General characteristics: disturbances in judgment, memory, intelligence, and emotion	Acute brain syndrome: Head trauma Drug toxicity Infection	Few for the chronic syndromes Medical care for the acute syndromes

Description
(continued)

Acute brain syndrome:
rapid onset, delir-
ium, reversibility
Chronic brain syndrome:
slow onset, demen-
tia, irreversibility

Etiology
(continued)

Chronic brain syndrome:
Presenile disease
General paresis
Epilepsy
Vitamin deficiency
Tumors
Unknown causes

Treatment
(continued)

Psychological help
for victims and
their families

CHAPTER 17
MENTAL RETARDATION

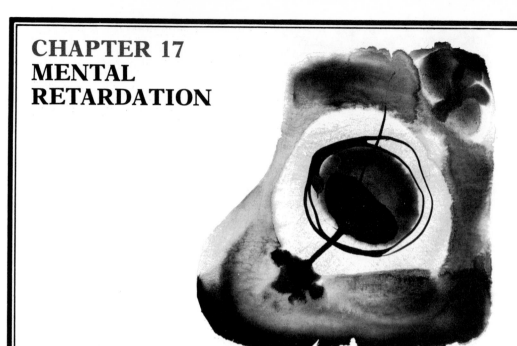

Mental retardation is defined by the American Association on Mental Deficiency as "significantly subaverage general intellectual functioning existing concurrently with deficits in adaptive behavior and manifested before the age of 18" (H. Grossman, 1973).[1] It is generally agreed that approximately 3% of the United States population, or about 6.5 million people, may be considered mentally retarded (Office of Mental Retardation Coordination, 1972). The mentally retarded person often is shunned, placed in separate schools, ridiculed, and even feared. However, mental retardation is merely a symptom (Robinson & Robinson, 1976) that may result from a variety of physically and socially based disorders, all of which manifest themselves in reduced intellectual functioning and hampered abilities to adapt to the requirements of everyday life. Because retardation may be multiply caused, we will describe the classifications of mental retardation by noting the general characteristics of people with this symptom. Next, we will present an overview of the genetic, physical-environmental, and social

[1]This and all other quotations from this source from *Manual of Terminology and Classification in Mental Retardation, 1973 Revision,* H. Grossman (Ed.). Copyright 1973 by the American Association on Mental Deficiency. Reprinted by permission.

factors known to be etiologically involved in the development of the symptom of mental retardation, followed by a discussion of several treatment approaches.

DESCRIPTION

The classification of mental retardation is fraught with problems of stigma and social involvement. Early scientific categories of mental retardation included such descriptive labels as "idiot," "imbecile," "moron," and the like. Although these terms are rarely used by professionals any more, they have found a place in our everyday language. The fact that these words are used to insult or denigrate others attests to the all too widely held attitude that the mentally retarded person is someone to be avoided and ridiculed. Because categorizing mentally retarded people is difficult, numerous attempts have been made over the years to produce a clear, easily applied classification system.

As we noted at the beginning of the chapter, the current definition of mental retardation is provided in the manual of the American Association on Mental Deficiency (AAMD) (Grossman, 1973). The AAMD defines each of the key terms in this definition as follows:

> MENTAL RETARDATION ... denotes a level of behavior performance without reference to etiology. Thus, it does not distinguish between retardation associated with psychosocial or polygenic influences and retardation associated with biological deficits. Mental retardation is descriptive of current behavior and does not imply prognosis [chances for recovery]. Prognosis is related more to factors such as associated conditions, motivation, treatment, and training opportunities than to the mental retardation itself.
>
> INTELLECTUAL FUNCTIONING may be assessed by one or more of the standardized tests developed for that purpose; SIGNIFICANTLY SUBAVERAGE refers to performance which is [significantly] below the average of the tests. On the two most frequently used tests of intelligence, Stanford-Binet and Wechsler, this represents I.Q.'s of 67 and 69 respectively.
>
> The upper age limit of the DEVELOPMENTAL PERIOD is placed at *18 years*.
>
> ADAPTIVE BEHAVIOR is defined as the effectiveness or degree with which the individual meets the standards of personal independence and social responsibility expected of his or her age and cultural group. Since these expectations vary for different age groups, DEFICITS IN ADAPTIVE BEHAVIOR will vary at different ages.
>
> During infancy and early childhood, sensory-motor, communication, self-help, and socialization skills ordinarily develop in a se-

SECTION VI:
DISORDERS
PRIMARILY
ASSOCIATED
WITH BRAIN AND
NERVOUS-SYSTEM
DISTURBANCES

quential pattern reflective of the maturation process. Delays in the acquisition of these skills represent potential deficiencies in adaptive behavior and become criteria for mental retardation.

The skills required for adaptation during childhood and early adolescence involve more of the learning process. . . . Attention should not only focus on the basic academic skills and their use, but also on skills essential to cope with the environment, including concepts of time, money, self-directed behaviors, social responsiveness, and interactive skills.

In the adult years, vocational performance and social responsibilities assume prime importance assessed in terms of the degree to which the individual is able to maintain himself independently in the community and in gainful employment as well as by his ability to meet and conform to standards set by the community. . . . Only those individuals who demonstrated deficits in both measured intelligence *and* adaptive behavior are to be classified as mentally retarded.

Within the framework of the definition . . . an individual may meet the criteria . . . at one time in his life and not at some other time. A person may change status as a result of changes or alterations in his intellectual functioning, changes in his adaptive behaviors, changes in the expectations of society, or for other known or unknown reasons [Grossman, 1973, pp. 11–14].

The AAMD definition of retardation is presented in such a way that it is possible to ascertain the degree of retardation by using standardized tests, such as the Wechsler Intelligence Scales (described in Chapter 2), and nonintellectual measures, such as the AAMD Adaptive Behavior Scales (Nihira, Foster, Shellhaas, & Leland, 1969). By administering these tests or suitable alternatives, one can determine the specific classifications of mental retardation.

There are four current categories of mental retardation. Classification is made according to severity of retardation and is expressed primarily in terms of intellectual ability. Given that the average IQ is 100 and that intelligence can be represented by a normal curve (see Chapter 1), four levels of retardation have been delineated: mild, moderate, severe, and profound.

Mild Retardation. One of the criteria for a diagnosis of retardation is an IQ of less than 70, because a person with such a score ranks higher than only 20% of people who have taken accepted IQ tests. People diagnosed as mildly retarded have IQs of 55 to 69, and 90% of retarded people score somewhere in this range. Only about 1% of mild retardates ever require institutional care. The remainder usually are able to complete schooling in special classes and, as adults, frequently can fill unskilled jobs. Actual brain damage and neuropathology are infrequent among the mildly retarded.

Moderate Retardation. Moderately retarded people have IQs in the range of 40 to 54 on the Wechsler scales. About 6% of retardates may be classified as moderately retarded. Unlike the mildly retarded, the majority of the moderately retarded show some sort of brain damage or other physical neurological disorder. Some moderate retardates may be institutionalized, but most of them are capable of living within the protective shells of their families and homes. Moderately retarded individuals may be capable of learning simple skills and often can earn money through jobs in sheltered workshops.

Severe Retardation. With IQs ranging from 25 to 39, severely retarded people represent more than 3% of retarded individuals. The majority of severely retarded people are permanently institutionalized and require constant care. They usually have difficulty learning even the simplest tasks. Severe retardation usually is associated with some genetic disorder or with severe brain damage due to accident, birth hazards, and the like.

Profound Mental Retardation. The profoundly retarded, who represent less than 1% of retarded people, have IQs of less than 25. Almost always hospitalized, profoundly retarded persons have difficulty attending to basic physical needs and usually require immense amounts of nursing care. Profound retardation usually is associated with severe disorders, where gross deformities of the brain, head, and body are often observed. Partially because of these physical problems, a large number of profoundly retarded people die at very early ages.

Although the four categories we have just described are associated with intelligence-test scores, the AAMD definition also includes adaptive behavior as a significant criterion for diagnosis. Thus, according to this system, a person with an IQ of 60 who scores very high on an adaptive-behavior scale might *not* be considered mentally retarded—or at least might be considered to be less severely retarded than the IQ alone would suggest.

ETIOLOGIES

There are several known causes for the development of mental retardation. We will attempt in this section to provide you with an overview of a variety of genetic, physical, and social factors that have been implicated in the occurrence of the symptom of mental retardation.

Genetic Factors

The symptom of mental retardation has been found to be associated with a number of genetic syndromes. In each of these syndromes, intellectual or physical abilities and often physical appearance are adversely

SECTION VI:
DISORDERS
PRIMARILY
ASSOCIATED
WITH BRAIN AND
NERVOUS-SYSTEM
DISTURBANCES

affected by some genetic difficulty. In some instances, the genetic difficulty is the result of extra chromosomes or mutant chromosomes; in other cases, dominant or recessive genes produce a disorder that is accompanied by retardation. A specific, detailed account of types of genetic syndromes associated with retardation is beyond the scope of this book. We will limit our discussion to two genetic syndromes whose role in producing retardation is reasonably clear: Down's syndrome and phenylketonuria.

Down's Syndrome.   Also known as *mongolism,* because of the oriental facial features of its victims, Down's syndrome is probably the single most common chromosomal cause of moderate to severe mental retardation (Robinson & Robinson, 1976). The disorder occurs once in about 660 births, with the risk dramatically increasing with the age of the mother. Down's syndrome is caused by a genetic defect at one of the chromosomes. With modern amniocentesis techniques, in which samples of the fluid surrounding the fetus can be taken and analyzed, it is often possible to determine whether Down's syndrome is present in an unborn fetus by the 17th week of pregnancy. However, such tests usually are performed only when there is reason to believe the disorder may be present.

The signs of mental retardation in a child with Down's syndrome can be present from about age 1. As the child grows, developmental milestones are typically reached later and later than by peers. Most Down's-syndrome children have IQs in the range of 40 to 54 (moderately retarded) and are capable of living at home. There is some evidence (Belmont, 1971) that Down's-syndrome children tend to show fewer signs of severe psychological disturbance than other types of retarded people. In fact, such children have been characterized as "lovable little creatures full of affection and tenderness" (Benda, 1946, p. 61).

The child with Down's syndrome manifests not only the intellectual and adaptive disabilities of the mentally retarded person, but also a well-documented set of particular physical features, such as floppy muscles, a small and flat nose, eyes that slant upwards, a short neck, small hands with short fingers, and sparse body hair. Most of these features don't affect the child's health directly, but they can be used as diagnostic criteria. However, physical defects such as the reduced size of the brain and the high incidence (40%) of heart malfunctions do represent serious threats to physical well-being. About 20-30% of Down's-syndrome babies do not survive their first two years; those who do are usually characterized by incomplete sexual development and infertility.

There are indeed many things that combine to make Down's-syndrome victims different. Note, though, that Down's syndrome is *not* a type of mental retardation; rather, mental retardation is one of the symptoms of the disorder.

Phenylketonuria (PKU).   Whereas Down's syndrome is caused by an extra chromosome, phenylketonuria (PKU) is caused by a genetic error in which the enzyme responsible for the metabolism of the biochemical *phenylalanine* is not present at birth. The result of this genetic error is that phenylalanine can build to dangerous levels, producing severe brain damage and consequently mental retardation. Incidence of PKU has been found to range from one in every 6800 births to one in every 14,000 births (Murdock, 1975). The average IQ of children with untreated PKU is about 50, placing the majority of them in the moderately to severely retarded range.

PKU was first described in 1934 by Folling (Robinson & Robinson, 1976), a veterinarian who developed an interest in a strange disorder present in a newborn child of a relative. The child's mother complained to several physicians that there was a strange odor emanating from the child's urine; dissatisfied with the physicians' claims that there was nothing to worry about, Folling went on to study the problem and to discover the PKU defect.

Generally, the PKU child appears normal for the first few weeks of life, but usually motor problems appear around 6 months of age. The child may not be able to sit at age 1, and may not walk by 4 years of age. About one-third of PKU children never learn to walk or to control defecation or urination, and about two-thirds never learn to talk. Unlike the usually friendly Down's-syndrome children, typical PKU children may be wild, uncontrollable, and generally unpleasant to be around. Psychologically, they may be fearful, restless, and so hyperactive that they require restraint and institutionalization.

Fortunately, the effects of PKU are preventable if the disorder is identified in the newborn infant. A simple urine or blood test for PKU given at birth is now a requirement in most hospitals. When PKU is identified, the infant can be placed immediately on a special phenylalanine-free diet. If done in time, this early dietary restriction usually prevents severe retardation. Berman and Ford (1970) report that successfully treated PKU children tend to perform within the average range of intelligence. The Collaborative Study of Children Treated for PKU (1975) reports that, in 95% of cases, neurological examinations are normal at ages 2 to 4, and that IQs are within the average range. Thus, simple control of diet can result in the avoidance of some of these devastating behavioral and intellectual deficits.

Physical/Environmental Hazards

The symptom of mental retardation can also result from damage by physical or environmental hazards. One way to categorize these environmental factors is according to the major developmental periods in which they occur. We will therefore consider environmental hazards to development at the prenatal, natal, and postnatal periods of life.

Prenatal Hazards. The unborn child is vulnerable to several types of hazards that may result in the symptom of mental retardation. One such hazard is *maternal undernutrition during pregnancy*. In a study of animals,

SECTION VI:
DISORDERS
PRIMARILY
ASSOCIATED
WITH BRAIN AND
NERVOUS-SYSTEM
DISTURBANCES

M. Winick and Rosso (1972) found that malnutrition in pregnant rats results in a reduction of as much as 15% in the number of brain cells in their offspring. The same authors also have noted that malnutrition in humans resulted in significantly lower birth weights in infants. These lower birth weights may reflect lower brain weight and reduced intellectual ability as well.

Maternal malnutrition may be controllable, but the presence of *acute maternal infection* is more difficult to avoid. About 5% of pregnancies may be accompanied by some viral infection (Hellman & Pritchard, 1971). These are most dangerous during the first three months of pregnancy. Although most viruses and bacteria are prevented from reaching the fetus by the placental barrier between mother and child, certain damaging agents can get through. Among these viruses are those causing measles, chicken pox, smallpox, polio, and rubella (german measles). Rubella is an acute infection that has been most frequently implicated in the production of birth defects and mental retardation. Of those fetuses whose mothers contract rubella, up to half become infected in the womb. The rubella-infected child can show growth deficiency, heart disorders, deafness, blood diseases, *and* mental retardation. Chess, Korn, and Fernandez (1971) reported moderate mental retardation in 25% of rubella-infected children and mild retardation in another 25%. As in the case of PKU, knowledge of the cause of rubella-induced retardation and disease has led to efforts to prevent its occurrence. Vaccination against rubella for women of child-bearing age has drastically reduced the incidence of rubella in pregnant women.

A prenatal hazard also may be present when there is a *chronic maternal infection.* Among the kinds of chronic infections that have been implicated in this group of hazards are herpes infection (Type II) and syphilis. Both of these can result in mentally retarded offspring. However, deleterious effects from both disorders can be avoided completely with adequate medical care, identification, and treatment prior to the 18th week of pregnancy.

Besides maternal malnutrition and infections, mental retardation can be caused prenatally by the mother's taking of *unsafe drugs and medications.* Shephard (1974) noted that at least 20 drugs can produce defects in the human fetus. In the 1950s, a drug called thalidomide produced eyeless, limbless, hopelessly retarded children in one out of five women using it. Such occurrences are grim reminders of the potential harmful effects of unsafe drug use during pregnancy. Alcohol also is counted among the damaging drugs pregnant women may not use safely. Researchers have shown that physical as well as mental deficiencies tend to be more common among infants born to female alcoholics (K. Jones, Smith, Streissguth, & Myrianthopoulos, 1974). Milkovich and Vandenberg (1974) have reported similar results among pregnant women who use some of the minor tranquilizers, such as chlordiazepine and meprobamate (Librium and Miltown).

The unborn child may encounter a variety of other hazards, such as radiation poisoning, Rh incompatibilities, and increased age and stress in the mother. Although these hazards may not always lead to a retarded child, each is capable of changing a normal, healthy fetus into a damaged one.

Natal Hazards. Natal hazards are those present during the birth process itself. Generally, these are responsible for mild retardation. The main natal hazards fall into three categories: prematurity, birth anoxia, and kernicterus.

Premature birth usually results in an infant whose birth weight is far below normal (under 5.5 pounds). Low birth weight is known to be related to a variety of possible physical and mental difficulties. For example, Niswander and Gordon (1972) have reported that the death rate for low-birth-weight infants is 25 times higher than for normal-weight infants. In addition, among those who survive low birth weight, the rate of neurological abnormality can be up to three times higher than in normal-weight babies. With modern medical care, a far larger proportion of premature and low-birth-weight infants are surviving into childhood. However, in a study of 55 such children who weighed less than 3 pounds at birth, it was found that at age 5, 58% had IQs of less than 80, and only 30% were attending regular schools (Goldman, Goldman, Kaufman, & Liebman, 1974). The exact reason for the relationship between low birth weight and its concomitant disabilities is not clear.

In addition to low birth weight, *anoxia* (lack of oxygen) during the birth process may result in mild retardation. Anoxia can occur as a result of an early separation from the placental blood supply during the birth process or from lack of spontaneous breathing immediately after birth. Robinson and Robinson (1976) note that, although there are few controlled studies of anoxia in humans, studies in monkeys have demonstrated that anoxia can be associated with permanent brain damage. In a study of human children with a history of breathing difficulties at birth, E. Graham, Ernhart, Craft, and Berman (1963) reported that these children exhibited more neurological abnormalities and intellectual disabilities than normal controls.

Kernicterus, a disorder resulting from inability of the liver to function adequately in the newborn, can also cause retardation. When levels of a biochemical called *bilirubin* reach too high a level in the child's body, it can produce the yellowness of the skin characteristic of liver dysfunction, severe destruction of brain cells, muscular disorders, and seizures—in addition to retardation. Careful medical treatment of such infants with blood transfusions and special lights to metabolize bilirubin now have reduced the damaging effects of kernicterus.

Postnatal Hazards. Even with uneventful prenatal and natal periods of development, physical hazards can occur shortly *after* birth in

SECTION VI:
DISORDERS
PRIMARILY
ASSOCIATED
WITH BRAIN AND
NERVOUS-SYSTEM
DISTURBANCES

several ways. Accidental head injuries account for a large number of the post-natal hazards; the degree of ensuing retardation and disability in these instances usually depends upon the extent of actual damage to the brain. Generally, the more the damage, the more severe the retardation.

In addition to head injuries, postnatal brain damage can occur as a result of infections involving the brain. *Encephalitis*, in which the brain itself is inflamed, and *meningitis*, in which the wrappings around the brain and spinal cord are infected, both may be implicated in the development of mental subnormality. Because of its viral nature, encephalitis often can't be treated with antibiotics, and the chances of permanent brain damage in severe cases may be as high as one in three. Common meningitis, however, is bacterial and can usually be treated with modern medications. Early diagnosis and treatment reduce the possibility that mental retardation will result.

Cranial neoplasms, or brain tumors, can also cause impaired intellectual functioning, seizures, loss of vision, a staggering gait, and headaches. With early identification and treatment, the negative effects of the tumor can be reduced.

Social Factors

Some forms of mental retardation (primarily of the mild type) can be caused by purely social factors. The name given to mental retardation not based upon clear cerebral pathology is *retardation due to psychosocial disadvantage* (H. Grossman, 1973). When mental subnormality and lack of adaptive ability are present in socially and culturally disadvantaged children, nonorganic causes are the rule rather than the exception.

The relation between socioeconomic level and lowered intellectual abilities is clear. For example, Vogt (1973) has reported that in children from families earning less than $3000 per year, illiteracy rates may be as much as three times the national average. Further, Cassell (1973) reports that the incidence of mental retardation is consistently higher in poor urban areas.

Physical Health. Among the possible factors implicated in the relationship between social disadvantage and mental retardation is the poor physical health of lower socioeconomic groups. Bauer (1972) notes that most of the physical or environmental hazards to development and the chances of contracting infectious diseases after birth occur more frequently among the poor. The health of children and pregnant women who are poor generally is at greater risk than that of people at higher socioeconomic levels. Without proper prenatal care, many avoidable hazards can do great harm to lower-class people.

Home Environment. Along with poor health, an inadequate home environment often is found in poorer segments of our society. Houses may be infested by disease-carrying rodents, and they may be overcrowded or unsafe and lack proper heating. These factors make it more likely that a child will suffer brain damage from disease or accident.

In addition, disadvantaged people may have attitudes that contribute to lower intellectual functioning in children. For example, adults may value a passive and conforming child who may fail to experience stimulating learning situations. Likewise, disadvantaged children have little preschool exposure to the kinds of things they will be doing when they get into formal classrooms. These children may not be able to adjust well to school,

Environmental factors are often implicated as the primary cause in instances of retardation. (Photo courtesy of the Department of Housing and Urban Development.)

442

SECTION VI:
DISORDERS
PRIMARILY
ASSOCIATED
WITH BRAIN AND
NERVOUS-SYSTEM
DISTURBANCES

may fall behind, and may deteriorate intellectually. Also, such children may be overloaded with input and may not be able to develop the attentional skills needed to learn. Lacking the proper kind of experience and necessary attitudes for learning, the disadvantaged child is handicapped in dealing with formal schooling.

A final factor associated with the higher rate of socially based retardation in disadvantaged children is the type of parent-child relationships that are more prevalent in lower socioeconomic groups. Because of financial pressures and a lack of highly sought after skills, heads of many lower-class families find that they are unable to support their families adequately. As a result, a large number (55%) of the mothers in lower-class families find it necessary to work full time outside the home. When mothers work, the responsibility for child care is usually passed to someone else, such as a babysitter, older sibling, neighbor, or relative. According to R. W. White and Watt (1973), one result of this arrangement is that the interchanges necessary for successful parent-child relationships often are missing, and intellectual, social, and emotional growth can be hampered.

TREATMENTS

Having considered the characteristics and the possible causative factors involved in the development of the symptom of retardation, we are ready to consider some of the ways in which professionals have tried to help mentally subnormal children and adults. Treatments for mental retardation represent a variety of techniques, ranging from educational, to psychotherapeutic, to institutional. Mental retardation due to brain damage or hereditary defect is not a symptom that can be completely cured. Often a goal is optimal adaptation to an unchangeable disability. However, in retardation due to psychosocial disadvantage, some "catching up" may be possible with large investments of time, effort, and money.

Education

Although limited in ability, some mentally retarded people are taught how to take care of many of their daily needs. Without such education, the majority of retarded individuals would probably sink lower and lower into intellectual and social deficit. Nevertheless, there is some controversy regarding the necessity of special training for retarded pupils. Some people believe the retarded child should be educated separately from normal children, but others feel such separation may be unnecessary and even harmful.

Special Education for Retarded People. From the perspective of those who believe in specialized education for retarded people, the scheme of classification proposed by the AAMD isn't sufficient. For special education, retarded people are usually classified into two groups, the *educable mentally retarded* (EMR) and the *trainable mentally retarded* (TMR).

EMR children generally fall into the IQ range of 55 to 70. They may be expected to reach a level of anywhere between third and sixth grade by the time they finish school. Social adjustment and ability to take care of themselves are the primary objectives of their schooling. Special classes for EMR children generally are small and emphasize social competence and occupational skills rather than academic achievement. There are special EMR classes and programs for people of different ages (Robinson & Robinson, 1976):

Infant stimulation class: For children from birth to 3 years of age, infant stimulation involves parents and teachers providing maximum healthy stimulation in the developing child.

Preschool class: For children 3 to 6 years old with mental ages from 2 to 4 years, preschool classes introduce group experiences and continue healthy stimulation.

Elementary primary class: For EMR children 6 to 10 years of age with mental ages from 3 to 6 years, primary classes are generally preacademic. Experiences such as those of a regular kindergarten are provided in hopes of building self-confidence, early language development, and security in the school situation.

Elementary intermediate class: For EMR children 9 to 13 years of age with mental ages of 6 to 9 years, intermediate classes are designed for children who cannot remain in regular classrooms due to inability to sit quietly and to exhibit other social skills necessary for regular schooling. Focus in class is on academic tools of reading, writing, and mathematics, as well as on practical everyday skills.

Secondary school classes: For EMR children at junior and senior high school levels, secondary school classes emphasize vocational training and domestic skills. Students are taught to apply basic tools to everyday problems such as use of money, reading of newspapers, application for jobs, and the like.

Postschool programs: For persons who have completed formal schooling, postschool programs provide a place where continued vocational and educational guidance is available. Examples of such programs are sheltered workshops and rehabilitation agencies such as the Salvation Army and Goodwill Industries.

With few exceptions, TMR children are more severely retarded than EMR children and present a different set of educational problems. TMR children have IQs in the range of 25 to 55 and may not be expected to achieve any more than the slightest mastery of academic skills. Primary goals for TMR children usually involve their being able to care for themselves and to sustain themselves in simple occupational endeavors. Regular

SECTION VI:
DISORDERS
PRIMARILY
ASSOCIATED
WITH BRAIN AND
NERVOUS-SYSTEM
DISTURBANCES

schooling is generally impossible for TMR children, and very few of them can function in the most liberally organized EMR classes. Contributing to the TMRs' difficulties in school is the frequency of physical problems in this more severely retarded group. Children who have seizures, who lack control over elimination, and who show other characteristics often associated with more severe retardation aren't readily accepted by regular schools.

Burton (1974) has stated that the term *education* may be a misnomer for the services needed by TMR children. The goal of the TMR class is to develop basic skills that normal and EMR children usually learn as they grow. TMR children must learn such "simple" tasks as washing themselves, eating properly, speaking, following simple directions, and the like. Instead of books, they must learn to read important signs: signs indicating "Danger" or "Stop" may be much more important to read than simple stories. Efforts to educate the TMR child can be frustrating. In some cases, there is evidence that special programs for TMR children are able to teach little more than the child could learn at home (Dunn, 1973). However, the sense of accomplishment that accompanies seeing a severely retarded child do something as basic as brush his teeth alone for the first time is hard to measure scientifically.

It may sound as if we're saying that special classes for TMR children do as much for teachers and parents as they do for the children themselves. In fact, Kirk (1972) has noted that relieving parents of some responsibility and helping them to see their children's disabilities more realistically are indeed two results of special classes. Kirk notes that the effects on children of TMR classes are hard to assess: "Invariably, the children improved from year to year, but whether this improvement stemmed from the programs or from maturation was hard to know" (p. 234).

Normalization of Education of Retarded Children. As we noted earlier, not all of the professionals involved in the care of mentally retarded children agree that EMR children need special education. Although it is obvious that TMR children need special attention, there is concern that special education for mildly retarded children may only make these children look and feel more different than they are. The proponents of *normalization,* or *mainstreaming,* believe that mildly retarded children should be integrated into regular classrooms and not placed in special classes.

The idea of mainstreaming retarded children gained impetus in the late 1960s. The beginning of the movement can be traced to the change of position effected by Lloyd Dunn, a long-time advocate of self-contained special classes for the educable retarded child. Dunn (1968) said the following:

> I have loyally supported and promoted special classes for the educably retarded for most of the last 20 years, but with growing disaffection. In my view, much of our past and present practices are morally and educationally wrong. We have been living at the mercy

of general educators who have referred their problem children to us. . . . And we have been generally ill-prepared and ineffective in educating these children. Let us stop being pressured into continuing and expanding a special education program that we know to be undesirable for many of the children we are dedicated to serve [p. 5].

Dunn's statement gave life to a movement away from special placement and toward integration of EMR children into regular classrooms for the majority of the school day. To be sure, all special education has not ceased. Rather, modern education for the EMR child involves a combination of special and regular classes. Special classes may be better while a child is learning to adjust to school, with regular classes tried a few hours a day in certain subjects, such as art or physical education. However, the goal of mainstreaming is to fit the EMR child as much as possible back into his normal peer group.

Several assumptions about the efficiency of mainstreaming may provide further support for its wider implementation (Robinson & Robinson, 1976). One assumption is that the "special classroom is an isolating experience" (p. 383). In general, children from special classes within regular public schools are avoided by the other pupils and often feel lonely, unwanted, and negatively valued. In the mainstream approach, EMR children tend to play with their normal classmates and feel more a part of the entire school group. Another assumption behind mainstreaming is that EMR children are "better able to achieve socially and academically if they are exposed to models whose achievement in both areas is more expert than their own" (p. 383). This assumption is supported by the fact that retarded children placed in regular classrooms may be less disturbed than those forced to remain in special programs. It's also true that a "regular classroom bears a greater resemblance to the real world" (p. 393). By being exposed to the realities of existence among other children, the mainstreamed student will be better able to adjust to life outside the protection of the special program. A final assumption behind mainstreaming is that "exposure to mentally handicapped children helps other children to understand and accept them" (p. 384). From the perspective of labeling theory and general societal reactions to those who are different, this seems a sound argument for normalization. If the prejudice against retarded children can be reduced by educating them alongside normal children, the threats to the emotional adjustment of the retarded child might be dramatically reduced.

The concept of mainstreaming is so recent that there is little conclusive research bearing upon its efficiency. Mesibov (1976) has noted that the data evaluating mainstreaming generally have been mixed. First of all, the hopes that normal children's attitudes toward retarded children will be improved by normalization haven't been fully realized. Furthur, MacMillan, Jones, and Meyers (1976) have noted that, regardless of specific components of a mainstreaming program, teachers' attitudes toward retarded

446

SECTION VI:
DISORDERS
PRIMARILY
ASSOCIATED
WITH BRAIN AND
NERVOUS-SYSTEM
DISTURBANCES

children in their regular classes may be the major determinant of the success of normalization programs. MacMillan et al. urge that the *principle* of mainstreaming be separated from its *implementation*. Although early research has shown that the implementation of mainstreaming may be ineffective, the principle still may be sound.

Psychotherapy

Although the major problem with many retarded people is irreversible physical damage and its concomitants, there may be emotional problems and maladjustment as well. With the greater stress placed upon the retarded person by even a simple daily problem, it is no wonder that a large number of retarded people also manifest some kind of psychological symptom. Often these symptoms take the form of acting-out behavior in which the person becomes violent, abusive, or irritable; other times, depression and anxiety may cloud the basic pattern of retardation. When the psychological components of the symptom pattern of the retarded person become so strong as to hinder efforts at education and adaptation, psychotherapy often becomes a major part of treatment. Generally, the therapeutic approaches are of four types: individual psychotherapy, group psychotherapy, behavior modification, and observational learning.

Individual Psychotherapy. Individual therapy with a retarded individual typically involves a professional trained in the areas of mental retardation and psychopathology engaging in a one-to-one relationship with the disturbed individual. Individual therapy with the retarded may be of either the nonverbal or the verbal type, depending upon the client's age and degree of retardation.

Nonverbal individual-therapy techniques represent a variety of approaches to the treatment of the retarded person. *Play therapy* (Chapter 18) has been adapted to the special problems of the retarded by Leland and Smith (1965, 1972). In their approach, differing combinations of structured or unstructured play materials and structured or unstructured therapeutic techniques are used in an effort to match the therapy to the level of the individual. With severely retarded and disturbed children, unstructured materials (water, finger paint) may be used in a free, unstructured therapy atmosphere. With mild retardates, structured materials (puzzles, coloring books) may be used in a more highly structured atmosphere. A child may be seated at a desk and required to relate more formally to the therapist. In addition to play therapy, other nonverbal techniques useful with adults include art therapy, occupational therapy, and music therapy.

Verbal psychotherapy can be used only with those who are capable of communicating in words. The majority of retarded people in this category will be mildly retarded adults. As is true of individual psychotherapy in general, treatment of emotionally disturbed retarded people may be directed at support, advice, insight, relaxation, or a number of other particular goals. The relationship between therapist and client is often the key factor in successful treatment and recovery.

Group Therapy. There is ample evidence that a group-therapy approach has advantages over the individual approach. Group therapy is a more economical mode of treatment, given the shortages of professionals qualified in therapy for the retarded. Further, the group atmosphere allows for safe practice in relating to peers, which may be problematic or ignored in individual therapy. Finally, group therapy affords members with models for better adjustment and re-creates a sense of safety and "family feeling" that can be extremely helpful to the frightened or depressed retarded person, regardless of age (Robinson & Robinson, 1976).

Behavior Modification. Behavior modification seems to be an effective form of therapy as well. Behavior modification involves the application of basic laboratory-derived principles of punishment and reinforcement to the alteration of behavior. To the behavior modifier, the behaviors present in the retarded child or adult can be altered in strength by applying suitable reinforcement.

Behavioral approaches in retarded people have included operant conditioning, in which reinforcers are given whenever desirable behaviors are performed; aversive conditioning, in which punishments are administered whenever undesirable behaviors are performed; and token economies, in which points or tokens earned for "good" behavior may be traded for candy, gum, movies, or the like. Many professionals believe that behavioral methods have been the most effective form of treatment for the problems of the mentally retarded (Gardner, 1970).

Observational Learning. Observational-learning approaches depend upon the presentation of new models after whom retarded people may pattern themselves. For example, researchers have shown that imitation learning (Bandura, 1969; see also Chapter 4) makes it possible to teach severely and moderately retarded children such basic skills as using the telephone (Stephan, Stephano, & Talkington, 1973) and communicating simple ideas to peers (Talkington, Hall, & Altman, 1973). Imitation learning seems to be a highly valuable asset to a therapist working with retarded children. With attractive models, almost all retarded children can learn via imitation.

Residential Placement

Residential placement of retarded people is different from education and psychotherapy in that it typically involves total control of the retarded person's life. Once known as *institutionalization*, residential placement involves removing retarded people from their homes and placing them in a setting where they may live either permanently or for some

448

SECTION VI:
DISORDERS
PRIMARILY
ASSOCIATED
WITH BRAIN AND
NERVOUS-SYSTEM
DISTURBANCES

extended period of time. Although many moderately retarded individuals live in residential facilities, the majority of those who are institutionalized fall in the severely and profoundly retarded categories. In 1972, the number of retarded people in residential centers in the United States was about 190,000. Since about 6 million people in the United States may be considered mentally retarded, the number in permanent residential status is relatively small. This testifies to efforts to maintain retarded people in the community as part of the mainstream.

The decision to place a child in a residential facility is a stressful and emotional one for most parents. Yet there comes a time in the life of some families with a retarded child when this decision must be faced.

PERSONAL EXPERIENCE: *The Father of a Severely Retarded Child*

We had Ronnie put in an institution a year ago . . . and my wife still cries whenever she sees his picture. We visit him a couple of times a year, but that doesn't seem to help 'cause it just brings back all the sadness that we feel because he's not with us and because he had to be born retarded. It's really not fair for something like that to happen to a kid or to the rest of the family. Maybe there's something we could have done to prevent it. . . . I don't know . . . the doctors don't know exactly what caused it. His brain didn't get enough oxygen when he was born. If it had, he would be living with us today. We just couldn't help him at home. He wasn't learning anything, and we were all pretty upset most of the time. We must have taken him to ten different specialists and tested him, but nothing helps. Maybe he's happier there, but it hurts no matter where he is. It would have been easier for him and us if he hadn't lived. . . . At least then the grief would have gone away.

The decision to place a child in a residential facility is complex. An extensive study by Saenger (1960) of factors related to the decision to institutionalize a retarded child suggests several basic conclusions. First, the more severely retarded a child, the more likely it is that residential placement will be chosen. Nearly nine out of ten of Saenger's sample of profoundly retarded people were hospitalized as opposed to one out of ten of the moderately to mildly retarded group. Saenger also noted that the presence of behavior problems *outside the home* was significantly related to institutionalization. A child who caused little or no such trouble for parents was less likely to be placed in a hospital. Another reason for institutionalization is that the retarded person causes unbearable stress and trouble at home. Finally, the fact that outpatient care is not readily available to many lower socioeconomic groups may leave institutionalization as the only recourse for the family of a poor retarded person. Many families probably

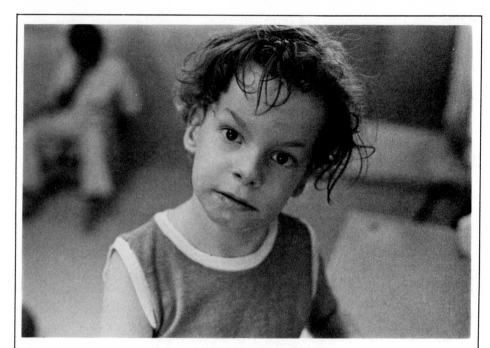

Institutionalized children like this retarded child need human contact and care in order to fulfill their limited potential. (Photo by George Lazar.)

would prefer to keep a retarded person at home, but when their choice is limited to no treatment or residential treatment, they frequently are forced to decide in favor of the latter.

Residential treatment can take any of several forms. There are the traditional state or private hospitals, as well as a variety of residential programs that can provide positive experiences. One example of an alternative to the state hospital is the *group home,* a sort of boarding house in which a limited number (perhaps 40) of retarded people live under the same roof with a staff of professionals. In this protected environment, home members can carry on simple vocational tasks, produce salable items in sheltered workshops, take part in group therapy, and live as nearly normal a life as possible. The group home can avoid many of the detrimental aspects of the large institution and maintain many of the characteristics of a real "home" for the retarded person.

CONCLUDING COMMENTS

In the past, retarded people often have been treated as second-class citizens. But name-calling and avoidance of the retarded may not have been society's worst offense against this group of people who are different. It

450

SECTION VI:
DISORDERS
PRIMARILY
ASSOCIATED
WITH BRAIN AND
NERVOUS-SYSTEM
DISTURBANCES

seems that the separation of retarded people from the rest of society also may have been fostered unwittingly by our public-education system. Traditionally, many parents of retarded children have been forced to seek special, often expensive, schools for their children, since few public-school systems were able to offer such educational opportunities. However, in the mid-1970s, federal legislation was passed that guarantees the right of *all* children to a free public education. One result of this legislation is that improved public-education programs for retarded people are becoming a reality throughout the United States. The availability of such programs can help integrate retarded children and adults into the educational, social, and cultural mainstreams. It is hoped that such integration will result in retarded citizens' no longer being the avoided minority group they seem to have been in the past.

CHAPTER SUMMARY CHART

In this chapter we discussed the symptom called mental retardation:

Descriptions	*Etiology*	*Treatment*

Intellectual deficit
Adaptive behavior
Mild, moderate, severe, and profound retardation
	Genetic factors:
	   Down's syndrome
	   Phenylketonuria
	Physical hazards:
	   Prenatal hazards
	   Natal hazards
	   Postnatal hazards
	Social factors:
	   Psychosocial disadvantages, physical health, environment
		Education:
		   Special education
		   Mainstreaming
		Psychotherapy:
		   traditional, music, occupational, and art therapies
		Residential placement

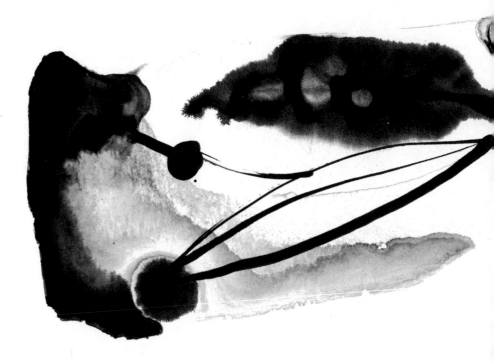

SECTION VII
DISORDERS OF SPECIAL AGE GROUPS

Chapter 18
Children

Chapter 19
Adolescents

Chapter 20
College Students

Chapter 21
The Elderly

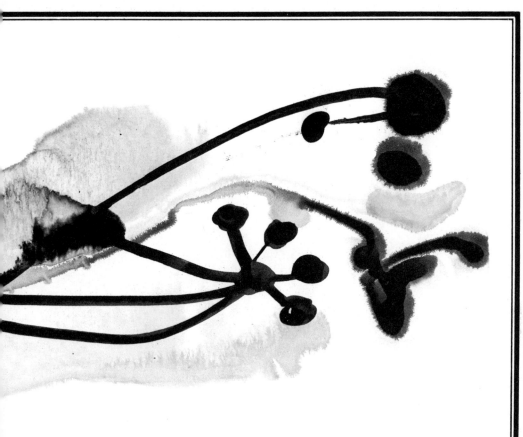

In previous sections on psychoses, neuroses, disorders of behavioral self-control, and brain disturbances, we have described patterns of being different that can occur in people of any age. However, a number of disorders seem to be limited to, and perhaps even causally associated with, membership in specific age groups. Although a few DSM-II classifications deal with such disturbances, numerous specialists working with children, adolescents, college students, and the elderly have gone beyond the limits of DSM-II to reclassify and reconceptualize the problems of the special people with whom they work. Reflecting this more focused attention, in Section VII we will consider problems of special age groups as they have been viewed by those specifically involved in their understanding and treatment.

453

CHAPTER 18
CHILDREN

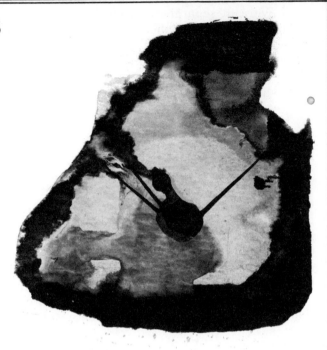

Writing a chapter on disorders in children is a difficult task for several reasons. First, many behaviors that may be considered abnormal among adults and adolescents are part of a child's normal behavioral repertoire. For example, as this is being written, one of our children (age 9) is sitting in her room talking to one of her dolls; in most 9-year-olds this is not cause for alarm. However, if one of us did this, it would be a different matter. A second difficulty in describing children who are different stems from the lack of an acceptable diagnostic system. For example, our guide throughout this text, DSM-II, provides only a few behavioral classifications for children. Because of the limitations of DSM-II, an independent classification system for children's disorders was developed by the Group for the Advancement of Psychiatry (GAP) in 1966. The GAP system seems to be more readily applicable than DSM-II to children's problems. In addition to incorporating psychotic and neurotic categories from DSM-II, the GAP system recognizes the fact that many childhood behaviors are developmentally understandable and often represent "temporary" disturbances.

The advantages of the GAP system argue for its use as a guide to our presentation of children who are different. Although the GAP system includes a description of neuroses in childhood, we believe that these patterns aren't sufficiently distinct from those of adults (described in Chapter 10) to warrant separate mention here. In this chapter, after we describe psychoses and present the major explanations for their occurrence, we describe developmental deviations. These are behavioral aberrations that are symptomatic of some blockage or temporary detour in normal development. We close by describing the types of appropriate treatment for children who are different.

PSYCHOSIS IN CHILDREN

Whereas the neurotic patterns in children are quite similar to those in adults, the psychotic disorders in children frequently are qualitatively different from their adult counterparts. One major difference is that hallucinations are rarely reported in psychotic children. Second, adult psychotics usually have developed psychologically to a mature state and then deteriorated back to a more basic level of functioning; psychotic children typically haven't matured psychologically in the first place.

The psychotic child isn't a rarity. For example, Milt (1963) reported that estimates of the number of psychotic children in the United States run

A child must travel a long and difficult road to become a well-adjusted adult. (Photo by Tony Grant.)

as high as half a million. Of further interest is the implication, based on the results of several studies (Kanner, 1948; Von Brauschitsch & Kirk, 1967), that childhood psychosis tends to occur more in the upper and middle classes than in the lower class. This is directly opposite to the usual relationship between social class and adult psychoses reported elsewhere (see Chapter 5).

Descriptions

There is some disagreement concerning the accurate description of categories of childhood psychoses. Although several categories have been proposed (for example, Wolman, 1972), most of the literature on childhood psychoses focuses on childhood schizophrenia, early infantile autism, and a group of other psychoses in children.

Childhood Schizophrenia. At first glance, childhood schizophrenia would appear to be simply schizophrenic behavior in young people. However, as we shall see, childhood schizophrenia is quite different from its adult counterpart and stands at the center of a controversy regarding the actual nature of childhood psychotic disorders. Reviewers of the childhood-psychosis literature (Laufer & Gair, 1969, for example) have noted that the term *childhood schizophrenia* often is used as a "semantic convenience," a label that may be applied to any or all of a broad variety of severe behavioral deviations in children. However, some (for example, Bender, 1956; Goldfarb, 1974) believe that a specific disorder called "childhood schizophrenia" does exist and that it is clearly distinguishable from the other forms of childhood disorders. Numerous controversial attempts to define clearly the diagnostic criteria for childhood schizophrenia (Bender, 1956; Bradley & Bowen, 1941; Potter, 1933) generally have been unsatisfactory. However, the GAP diagnostic system (1966) does yield a workable set of indicators of severe disturbance (Creak, Cameron, Cowie, Ini, MacKeith, Mitchell, O'Gorman, Orford, Rogers, Shapiro, Stove, Stroh, & Yudkin, 1961). Creak et al. have presented the nine indicators of "the schizophrenic syndrome of childhood," which may be summarized as follows:

1. Gross and sustained impairment of emotional relationships with people
2. Apparent unawareness of personal identity to a degree inappropriate to age
3. Pathological preoccupation with particular objects without regard to their accepted functions
4. Sustained resistance to change in the environment and a striving to maintain or restore sameness
5. Abnormal perceptual experiences, such as increased or decreased sensitivities
6. Acute, excessive, and seemingly illogical anxiety

7. Speech lost, never acquired, or age-inappropriate
8. Distortion in patterns of movement
9. A history of serious psychological deficit

These "nine points" (Quay & Werry, 1972) represent the distillation of a large amount of diagnostic information. The presence of an appreciable number of these indicators usually is considered sufficient to warrant a diagnosis of childhood schizophrenia. However, this diagnosis is typically made only after other possibilities have been ruled out. For example, if signs of neurosis are present, then the diagnosis of neurosis ordinarily will take precedence over one of childhood schizophrenia. However, there are those who argue that autism shouldn't be given precedence—that childhood schizophrenia may well be the only "real" form of childhood psychosis and that the other types of psychoses we will discuss are simply special cases. The following is a description of a childhood schizophrenic.

Gerald was an 11-year-old boy who had enjoyed a normal developmental history until the age of 6. He had learned to talk and walk at almost the same time as his peers, but had experienced a large number of minor physical ailments; he seemed pale and looked somewhat weak. Nevertheless, his parents reported that he played and romped with the other children in his neighborhood.

At the age of 6, upon entering school, Gerald began to change. His teacher reported that he would often sit in his seat and stare at the walls, apparently attending to things of which she was not aware. When she called on him, he often totally ignored her. She felt that he often "stared right past her" when he spoke with her. After one year in school, Gerald developed a host of other problems; his speech became noticeably hard to understand, and he manifested numerous aggressive and violent outbursts. These led to many trips to the principal's office, where Gerald began to spend more and more time. It was in the principal's office that Gerald first manifested the "saliva-throwing" behavior that led to his expulsion. As children passed him, he would put his fingers in his mouth, wet the tips with some saliva, and then flick the saliva at the children. The victims complained and Gerald was expelled.

At his first meeting with a psychiatrist, Gerald said nothing; he sat and stared at the doctor and flicked saliva at him. No attempt to stop him or talk to him was successful. Gerald had withdrawn almost completely, yet he wouldn't avoid company or ignore others—he would "relate" to them through his saliva-flicking habit. Finding Gerald intractable at home, his parents finally agreed to hospitalize him when he was 7½ years old. He remained withdrawn and unresponsive to treatment.

Early Infantile Autism. A form of childhood psychosis first clearly defined by Leo Kanner, early infantile autism is characterized by extreme withdrawal, unresponsiveness to social stimulation, and absence of development of an ability to relate to others. Kanner (1973) noted that autistic children are usually males (by a ratio of 4 to 1) who, during the first 10 weeks of life, are exceptionally healthy and often described as precocious. The earliest sign of autism usually occurs at about 6 months of age, when parents may notice that the child doesn't make typical movements anticipatory to being picked up. Between 6 and 18 months of age, the additional signs of autism, such as head-banging, apathy toward people and playthings, highly repetitive and situational play, unusual language patterns, and an insistence upon being left alone may appear. What Kanner called "autistic aloneness," the child's insistence on being left alone, is most significant for the diagnosis of autism. By the age of 2, the autistic child appears to have withdrawn into a world of inner fantasy, devoid of people.

Although most symptoms of autism are deficits, certain autistic children have specific abilities superior to those of normal children. For example, Kanner (1972) states that autistic children often have "uncanny ability to remember exactly situations and stimuli to which they have been exposed." Some autistic children have been found to be superior to normal children in musical ability. Rimland (1969) reported that one autistic child was able to reproduce an operatic aria in a foreign language after having heard it only once. Sherman (1953) reported an autistic child who, by the age of 14 months, could reproduce the entire musical scale with perfect pitch and, by the age of 3, sang a remarkable repertoire of music, including themes from symphonies by Mozart and Haydn, songs by Schubert and Brahms, selections from *Carmen*, material from a Tchaikovsky Piano Concerto "and diversified well-known songs" (p. 825).

Reports of special abilities among autistic children often receive widespread publicity. As a result, many people believe that some autistic children grow up to become noted artistic geniuses or that autistic children outgrow their autism and become creative and accepted people. Sadly, nothing could be further from the truth. In a follow-up study of his original sample of 11 autistic children, Kanner (1963) reported that, at the ages of 30 to 40, the majority remained hospitalized or in some other way isolated from society. However, one had completed a bachelor's degree and was working as a bank teller. Upon considering the fate of most of his original subjects, Kanner said: "After its nearly 30 year history and many bona-fide efforts, no one as yet has succeeded in finding a therapeutic setting, drug, method or technique that has yielded an amelioration and lasting results for all the children" (pp. 186–187).

According to Rimland (1964), who, with Kanner, has contributed much to our understanding of autism, this childhood psychosis differs from childhood schizophrenia in a number of ways. The summary of the differences between autism and childhood schizophrenia (Table 18-1) suggests that these are two distinguishable disorders.

To be the parent or grandparent of an autistic child is a painful, heart-rending experience. To see an infant, healthy and energetic, slowly

Table 18-1. *Comparison of early infantile autism and childhood schizophrenia*

Characteristics	Autism	Schizophrenia
Onset and course	Present from beginning of life	Disordered behavior follows period of normal development
Health and appearance	Excellent health, well formed, good-looking	Poor health from birth; somatic problems in all body systems
EEG	Normal	Over 80% have abnormal EEGs
Physical responsiveness	Do not adapt to being held; are stiff and unresponsive	"Mold" to parents—clinging
Aloneness	Withdrawn; demand isolation	Seem isolated, but wish contact and care
Preservation of sameness	Go to any length to keep things exactly as they are	Do not care about sameness; will throw things into disarray
Hallucinations	No hallucinations or delusions	Frequent delusions and visual and auditory experiences
Motor performance	Excellent	Poor coordination, balance, and locomotion
Language	Do not use the word *I* until age 7 or older; repetitious	Often incoherent, but use the words *I* and *yes* early in life
Personal orientation	*Un*oriented, detached, oblivious to environment; do not wish to relate	*Dis*oriented and confused; try to relate but can't
Conditionability	Difficult to condition classically	Easy to condition classically
Parents' background	Highly educated, higher class, intellectual	Poorly educated, lower class, nonintellectual
Family history of disturbance	Low incidence of disorders in relatives	Higher rate of disorders in families
Development	Arrested	Regressed
Fascination with mechanical objects	Fascinated by mechanical objects	Not fascinated by mechanical objects
Thoughts	Inhibition of thoughts	Confusion of thoughts
Spinning of objects	Deft spinning of objects	Clumsy spinning of objects

From *Infantile Autism,* by B. Rimland (Copyright 1964 by Appleton-Century-Crofts) and *Autism and Childhood Psychosis,* by F. Tustin (Copyright 1972 by Hogarth Press, Ltd.). Reprinted by permission of the publishers, Prentice-Hall, Inc. and Hogarth Press, Ltd.

withdraw and reject love and nurturance is a nightmare no parent would wish to experience. Since a personal experience from an autistic child was unavailable, we present next the poignant perspective of a woman describing her autistic granddaughter.

PERSONAL EXPERIENCE: *Living with an Autistic Child*

I awoke to a noise I couldn't mistake. I looked at the clock—5 A.M. Penny was flipping a shoe lace on the cold air register—up and down, up and down. She had finally gotten to sleep at midnight the night before. Five hours is all she seems to need. I need twice that. I changed her diapers; she's 3 but not toilet trained yet. It is almost impossible to train her, although she is upset if I drop milk on her dress giving her a drink. She likes to be neat.

She amuses herself quietly—doesn't demand attention as long as she can find a shoe lace, a drawer handle to flip, a piece of plastic to shake, paper that crackles. She'll hold the point of the shoe lace between her fingers and run it up and down a cold air register, a window, legs of furniture, or even the shoe that holds the shoe lace. She loves our plastic tablecloth because it makes a noise when she shakes it up and down. Now she has found a small ball with a rattle in it. She jumps up and down holding it in her hand and laughs as it rattles. Now she is on all fours, and each time she crawls forward the rattle makes a noise when her hand hits the floor. The faster she crawls, the more noise—and she laughs. She dropped it when she spotted a round plastic coffee lid and started biting it and letting go—this amused her for a minute—but started to flip at furniture with it, going from one piece to another, then bending down and stroking the floor with it. Now she has spotted her Raggedy Ann doll and sat on the floor with it in her arms not moving for five minutes. Looking at her sweet face with an expression of peace, contentment, a faint smile made her look like an angel—not a trace of a damaged child. She looks so perfect—how can anything be wrong? There should be some facial characteristic to show all this lack of normalcy. I can see none. Maybe it is self-willed rejection of our world. She moved, and I stopped my poor reasoning and watched as she wrapped the Raggedy Ann doll's dress around the finger of her left hand and used the other hand to pick at the covered finger. Her mouth moved in a sucking motion (mouth closed). Now she rubs her lips with the covered finger. This she does often. . . .

She will spread the fingers of her left hand and hold it about 3 inches from her left ear and make *ah ah* sounds. Sometimes loudly, sometimes not so loudly. Ah ha! I think, I bet there is something wrong with her left ear—maybe something bothers her and she is trying to clear the ear. I guess and guess and I am still puzzled with her.

Most of her day is spent flipping something onto some object. She'll flip a drawer pull if she hasn't a string, stick, spoon, pencil, or anything she can find like that. She seems fascinated with plastic garment bags. Often I find her in a closet shaking the bottom of a plastic garment bag. If I didn't get her she would spend hours doing that and be so content. . . .

The sound of water—in the sink or bathtub—draws her attention. She can hear that from a distance and runs to watch. If she has something in her hand, she will very quickly drop it in the sink or tub. I have to watch closely if she is in the bathroom, as she will walk into a filling tub with her shoes and clothes on. . . .

Her diet is milk and graham crackers. Peanut-butter bread—very little—and lately baby-food cottage cheese and bananas, and if that isn't Heinz, she compresses her lips and refuses. Sometimes she'll take vitamins—sometimes no. Every kind of food has been offered. She climbs out of a high chair—if she eats, it is while she is walking around. . . .

I wonder how much she remembers, how far back it goes and just what she remembers. Is she storing it up and when the "bin" is full it will all spill out and that is the "breakthrough" they talk about? I've heard of kids not talking until they were 4 years old and suddenly say everything in sentences. Please God let that be your will! I'm sure she has a working mind. Why is she hiding it from us—or trying to? She has a lot of normal impulses, and every once in a while they sneak out, which gives me hope and assurance that one day she will be normal and perhaps exceptionally bright.

Other Childhood Psychoses.   Although arguments abound that there are no true forms of childhood psychosis beyond schizophrenia and autism, there is some evidence that there may be other classifiable psychoses. To acquaint you with these rare yet clearly definable categories, we will briefly present them here.

Symbiotic psychosis is a rare form of childhood psychosis described by Margaret Mahler (1952). The term *symbiosis* is derived from the biological phenomenon in which two living things are mutually dependent upon each other for survival. In the case of the child who is classified as symbiotic, there is usually an intense, mutually dependent relationship with the mother. In fact, even the briefest separation from the mother can send waves of panic through the child. By the time most children are going off to nursery school and developing some independence, the symbiotic child typically manifests few signs of ability or willingness to leave home.

Special symptoms of symbiotic psychosis include intense fear of separation, conflict between craving for body contact and fear of being touched, and agitated catatoniclike panic behavior (Mahler, 1952). Although similar signs may be observed in many autistic children, the symbiotic child *needs* to be with the mother, whereas the autistic child wishes to be alone. In addition, the severity of symptoms and degree of incapacity in the symbiotic child are usually much less than in the autistic child.

Infantile psychosis, also called *psychosis of atypical development*, involves psychotic mothers who sometimes produce children manifesting signs of psychosis. The child may show signs of impairment of contact with reality, lack or impairment of meaningful verbal communication, withdrawal from social interaction, striving for sameness, and general age-inappropriateness of behavior patterns (Reiser, 1963). As you can see, many of the symptoms are similar to those of the autistic or schizophrenic child. However, the absence of the unusual skills of the autistic child and the involvement of a disturbed mother may make infantile psychosis a separate diagnostic pattern.

The last rare form of childhood psychosis we will describe is often given the difficult-to-pronounce name *propfhebephrenic psychosis* (Eisenberg, 1967). First coined by Kraepelin (1896), this term refers to psychotic behavior patterns superimposed upon, or concomitant with, mental deficiency. Eisenberg (1967) delineates three forms this disorder may take: (1) a psychosis may develop in a mentally retarded child who cannot adjust to environmental stress; (2) due to continual deterioration of organically disturbed children, a level of almost total psychological regression is reached; and (3) transient psychotic episodes may appear in retarded children who otherwise function at optimum levels, given their deficiencies. Propfhebephrenic psychosis may be seen as a schizophrenic reaction to stress produced by personal limitations and frustrations. However, given the special circumstances under which it occurs, there is some support for classifying it as a separate category of being different.

Explanations

It may be no surprise to you that there are few satisfactory theoretical explanations for childhood psychoses. Nevertheless, if we group these disorders together, we can uncover some promising explanations of severe disturbances in infants and young children. These explanations generally fall into two broad categories—psychological and biological (Rutter, 1968; Ward, 1970).

Psychological Explanations. Psychological explanations of childhood psychosis are characterized by their emphasis on environment and parent-child interactions as causative factors. Generally, the psychological theorists believe that, without the psychological stress produced by faulty environment or people such as "refrigerator-type" parents (Kanner, 1943), the psychotic child probably would have grown up to be basically normal.

In the psychoanalytic explanation, adult psychosis represents the deterioration of the ego, whereas child psychosis is the result of the failure of the ego ever to develop (Alanen, 1965). Theoretically, the psychotic child remains abnormally "fixated" at early levels of development. In the autistic child, normal development of the self and movement from primary- to secondary-process thought may never occur. Thus, the child remains withdrawn and entrenched in the fantasy of primary thought. In older children, faulty resolution of Oedipal conflicts can result in identification with abnormal parents, so that the child adopts the psychotic role of the mother or father.

Other psychoanalytic explanations suggest that personality distortion may occur in children when they experience the anxiety produced by anxious parents (Szurek, 1956), or when they perceive the world as a dangerous place (Bettelheim, 1967). In essence, because of parental neglect, rejection, or even brutality, the child experiences early psychological damage that may be reflected later in psychotic symptomatology.

The behaviorists typically believe that childhood psychosis can be explained in terms of learning principles that don't require such theoretical constructs as ego deterioration. An early learning-theory explanation for autism was proposed by Ferster (1965), who believed that the behavioral deficits of this syndrome were the result of failure on the part of parents to reinforce the child's appropriate behavior with praise or simple attention. Of course, most parents failed to reinforce, not out of malice, but probably because of their own personal difficulties. For example, a depressed parent might not respond to a child's request to play a game. If these social behaviors consistently are ignored by the parent, they eventually extinguish for lack of reinforcement. After a period of time, the only behaviors that remain may be those which are self-stimulatory and self-reinforcing, or those bizarre enough to get attention from the parents. These strong attention-getting behaviors found in psychotic children often involve activities such as smearing feces, screaming, head-banging, and arm-flapping. According to Ferster, parents of autistic children may "teach" their children that such extreme behaviors are necessary to obtain their attention.

Biological Explanations. As opposed to the psychological theories, which emphasize environmental or parent-induced damage, the biological explanations of childhood psychoses focus on organic deficits. As we concluded in the chapters dealing with adult psychoses (Chapters 7, 8, and 9), the biological theories frequently seem more tenable than psychological theories in explaining severely disturbed behavior. However, biological research in childhood psychoses lags behind its adult counterpart.

The possibility that childhood psychosis (among other childhood disorders) is genetically determined has been evaluated by Cowie (1965). As can be seen in Table 18-2, Cowie reports that, among monozygotic (identical) twins, concordance rates for psychological disturbances are much higher than among dizygotic (fraternal) twins. The higher rate of disturbance in fraternal twins of the same sex than in those of opposite sex suggests that the gender of the child and the resultant differences in parental reactions and treatments may play a role in the genesis of childhood disorders.

Table 18-2. *Psychological disorders in twin schoolchildren*

Condition Studied	Monozygotic		Dizygotic (same sex)		Dizygotic (opposite sex)	
	Concor-dant	Non-concor-dant	Concor-dant	Non-concor-dant	Concor-dant	Non-concor-dant
Juvenile deviancies	34	3	20	5	8	32
Behavior disorders in children	41	6	26	34	8	21
Severe childhood maladjustment	7	0	4	2	2	1

Note: Figures are the number of pairs of twins in each category.
From "The Genetical Aspects of Child Psychiatry," by V. Cowie. In J. Howells (Ed)., *Modern Perspectives in Child Psychiatry.* Copyright 1975 by Churchill Livingstone, Edinburgh. Reprinted by permission.

Evidence suggesting that a genetic link may exist for childhood psychosis doesn't explain the genetic mechanism by which such disorders are produced. An early, thorough attempt to describe a possible specific biological malfunction in childhood psychosis was made by Lauretta Bender (1956, 1960). To Bender, childhood schizophrenia is caused by a "pre- or perinatal deficit, trauma, or damage, or a physiological crisis which is the stress that decompensates the genetically vulnerable child" (1971, p. 667). She further postulates that the inherited weaknesses in the preschizophrenic child manifest themselves in the form of disturbances in perception, thought, language, motor behavior, and social behavior. Barbara Fish and her associates (Fish, Wile, Shapiro, & Halpern, 1966) have shown that the biological dysfunctions reflecting genetic vulnerability proposed by Bender may be present as early as 1 month of age in children who later develop childhood schizophrenia.

Other biologically based theories are similar to Bender's approach in their emphasis upon some basic biological dysfunction as the foundation upon which childhood psychosis develops. For example, Rimland (1964) believes that the source of autism lies in damage to the neurological system that "wakes up" a person and a resultant inability to attend to relevant stimuli long enough to relate one stimulus to another. Thus, the child may not be able to establish love for the mother because of an inability to associate her with relief of pain, satisfaction of hunger, and the like. Rutter (1968) suggests that the basic problem in psychotic children is damage to the speech area of the brain. As a result of this damage, psychotic children don't receive spoken information well and can't express themselves effectively. These deficits can interfere with the children's ability to interact with their environment in order to meet their basic needs. Finally, some researchers are seeking a biochemical basis for childhood psychosis. For instance, Sankar and his associates (Sankar, Cates, Broer, & Sankar, 1963) have reported that lowered levels of serotonin and other catecholamines seem to be related to the presence of psychotic symptoms in children. Although no definitive biological causative factor has been found as yet, the obvious parallels of these findings to those reported for adult schizophrenia cannot be ignored.

DEVELOPMENTAL DEVIATIONS

The developmental deviations differ from childhood psychoses in that they are not, per se, formally diagnosable disorders. Rather, they represent a wide variety of instances in which normal child development has "jumped the track" either temporarily or permanently. These deviations from developmental progress often cause great concern among parents. However, the majority of the developmental deviations are temporary, easily corrected, and give little cause for worry. An understanding of these deviations may be necessary so that caretakers can respond appropriately. Overreacting to a child's stuttering, for example, often can do more damage than the original stutter. In this section we will discuss disturbances related to bodily functions, disturbances of the musculature, habitual manipulations of the body, disorders of speech, and specific learning disabilities. Since there is no all-encompassing body of explanation or treatment for these types of developmental deviations, we will diverge from our usual presentation to include relevant theories or treatments when available for a specific disorder.

Disturbances Related to Bodily Functions

The developmental deviations in bodily functions involve sleep, intake of food, and elimination of waste materials. In these cases, parents may be concerned for the child's health and about the child being ridiculed by others.

Sleeping. It may be difficult for you to remember, but there was probably a time in your life when you never wished to sleep, even when exhausted, and couldn't remain in bed past seven in the morning. Sleep disturbances may represent an important source of potential conflict in a family. Indeed, a child can exercise great control over parents with a well-chosen sleeping problem. Not all such difficulties are consciously planned, of course, but they often produce many advantages for the child involved. A representative sample of sleep disturbances are bedtime rituals, nightmares, and night terrors.

Although not clearly abnormal in the strict sense of the word, bedtime rituals can become so complex and demanding that they create extreme stress for parents and children alike. One of us knew a child who, prior to going to sleep at night, required a certain pair of red and white striped socks on his feet, a bowl of peanuts in his bed, two small lights placed in specific positions in his room, a shade half-drawn on his window, three poems told to him in specific order, and three kisses on each cheek. If this order were not followed, he would become agitated and refuse to go to sleep. At first, parents may find such behavior cute, but later, when they try to stop the pattern, they find it firmly established.

Unlike bedtime rituals, which occur before the child goes to sleep, nightmares and night terrors occur after the child is asleep. Nightmares and night terrors occur in normal as well as disturbed children, but they are usually more severe and frequent in the latter. Although sometimes seen as similar, nightmares and night terrors are actually two separate events. However, in their most severe forms, both suggest that the child may be having difficulties in adjustment. Table 18-3 shows the differences between these two disturbances and indicates that nightmares are less severe than night terrors.

Eating. Mealtime, like bedtime, can become emotionally stressful if parents pressure their children to eat according to some set of rigid demands. Indeed, many parents equate a child's rejection of their food with a rejection of them. Further, some parents believe that a full stomach can make everything "all better." Some children soon learn that eating is a

Table 18-3. *Differences between nightmares and night terrors*

Nightmare	Night Terror
Fearful sleep experience followed by awakening.	Fearful experience occurs in sleep; awakening does not follow.
Slight moaning or movement are only noticeable signs.	Features are distorted; eyes wide open expressing terror; sits up or jumps from bed; cries out.
Child is awake when parents arrive and can tell what happened.	Child sleeps as parents watch child; cannot be awakened or attack shortened by parents.
After awakening, child recognizes parents and surrounding objects.	If child awakes, does not recognize parents or surroundings.
No hallucinations.	Child hallucinates actual dream objects.
No perspiration.	Profuse perspiration.
Long period of wakefulness and review of dream may follow.	Peaceful sleep instantly follows termination of terror.
Entire nightmare lasts no longer than one or two minutes.	Terror may last up to 20 minutes.
Contents are remembered fairly clearly.	Complete amnesia for contents of and occurrence of terror.

From *Child Psychiatry* (4th Ed.) by L. Kanner. Copyright 1972 by Charles C Thomas, Publisher, Springfield, Illinois.

potential source of control over parents. Two examples of severe eating disturbances are rumination syndrome and pica.

Occurring as early as the first few weeks of life, *rumination syndrome* is characterized by the child's frequent bringing up of food without vomiting or retching. Such infants may appear to be manipulating their palates with their tongues to make themselves vomit and typically don't respond to efforts to get them to stop. As a result of rumination, normal increases in weight and proper bodily function frequently don't occur, and the child's very survival may be threatened. Kanner (1972) reports that one out of five ruminative infants dies. Some experts (Clark, 1975) believe that rumination is a response to a "stressful environment." In these instances, the infant is often unwanted or may be the center of family conflict. The infant's expression of family tension may be reflected in the refusal to hold down food.

In rumination, the child rejects food; in *pica*, however, the child ingests a wide variety of inedible substances. Like a magpie (which, in Latin, is a *pica*), a bird reputed to eat anything, these children may eat paper, wool, plaster, paint chips, buttons, string, hair, soap, shoe polish, rags, dirt, sand, bugs, worms, leaves, wood splinters, and pebbles (Kanner, 1972). Although it is normal for very young children to place inedible materials in their mouths, children with pica don't outgrow this pattern and continue to place objects in their mouths with the intent of swallowing them. *Coprophagy*, a rare disorder in which children eat their own or others' feces, is associated with severe pathology.

Elimination. Disturbances in bowel- or bladder-training can also lead to problems. When toilet training begins, usually around age 2, parents often make demands upon the child to delay what had been a natural occurrence. Some children may be unable or unwilling to meet parental demands. In any case, this is a potential source of parent-child conflict.

When a child exhibits little or no control over bowel movements, the problem is called *encopresis*. In younger children, encopresis may simply be a reflection of incomplete training; but when a child is older than 5 or begins "soiling" again after a period of successful bowel-training, there may be a diagnosable disorder. At times, the reasons for the encopresis are clear. For example, a child seen by one of us had a two-month history of soiling himself between three and five each school-day afternoon. Although his house was always open, he seemed to prefer to have a bowel movement in his pants rather than enter the house while his mother was still at work. He finally related that someone had told him that creatures wait in empty houses to eat up little boys. Once this was clarified, his parents arranged for the boy to use the nearby house of a friend who was home, and the encopresis problem was solved. However, encopresis also may be a sign of more severe disordered behavior, and this possibility should be evaluated.

In *fecal retention*, the opposite of encopresis, children don't have regular bowel movements. Retention is often much more physically dangerous than encopresis, since impacted bowels and other disorders of the colon can ensue if the behavior isn't altered. The following case history provides an example of the development of a fecal retention syndrome.

A 4-year-old female was referred to a child psychiatrist by her pediatrician. The child had a history of bowel-training dating back to 18 months of age. The referring symptom was a bowel retention to the extent that the child would span up to two weeks without having a bowel movement. The child complained of severe headaches and stomach pains, and the parents and pediatrician were concerned about impacted bowels and the possible need for surgical intervention. Interviews with the parents revealed that the mother was extremely upset by the child's "refusal to cooperate"; she stated that she approached training from a firm standpoint and that she would get very angry whenever the young girl soiled her training pants. She admitted, quite emotionally, that she had beaten the girl several times after the girl refused to use the toilet. The situation had gotten so complex that the mother would place the child on the toilet and read to her for three hours or more, hoping that the child would move her bowels. Frustrated, she would allow the child to go in her room to play and would find that she had soiled her pants within five minutes after leaving the bathroom. This resulted in further beatings and emotional outbursts on the part of both parents. The child's only recourse seemed to be to stop her bowel movements altogether, which she did when she adopted her retention symptom. After a period of professional intervention, the retention pattern remitted, but the parents continue to avoid the thought of the toilet-training experience.

Encopresis and fecal retention are disconcerting symptoms, but they are by no means as frequent as the developmental deviation associated with lack of bladder control—*enuresis*. Normally, development of bowel control precedes bladder control. For unknown reasons, bladder control is usually more difficult and more sensitive to emotional states in children. Enuresis can be of two types: nocturnal or diurnal. Generally, nocturnal enuresis, or bed-wetting, is much more common and less cause for concern than wetting during the day—diurnal enuresis.

Nocturnal enuresis usually takes the form of wetting once per night. Often, the pattern persists in spite of parental efforts to control enuresis by withholding fluids prior to bedtime or having the child urinate before going to sleep. When bed-wetting becomes an actual enuresis problem is really a matter of opinion. Some early points of view (Kanner, 1943) hold that night wetting beyond the age of 3 is abnormal. However, modern thought (McCandless, 1975) is more flexible, suggesting that bed-wetting up to age 7 is within normal limits. Adverse parental reaction to wetting can sometimes turn normal bed-wetting into a problem. The manner of onset of night wetting may also be clinically important. In a child who has been dry for a time, the return of night wetting is often a sign of emotional upheaval.

For example, it isn't uncommon for a 3- or 4-year-old to regress temporarily to enuresis upon the birth of a new infant in the family.

In the understanding and treatment of enuresis, we find one of the earliest examples of the successful application of learning theory to the alteration of abnormal behavior. The behavioral-treatment approach is based upon the theoretical concept that waking to go to the bathroom is a response that must be associated with bladder distention as a stimulus. For whatever reason, this association may not have occurred in enuretics. To establish the needed association, Mowrer and Mowrer (1938) devised a system in which two copper screens separated by a cotton pad were laid on the child's bed. Each screen was connected to one pole of a buzzer attached to a battery power source. The device was hardly noticeable in the child's bed and quite comfortable when covered with an ordinary bed sheet. When a few drops of urine were passed, the cotton pad became wet and the salinity of the urine served as an electrical conductor completing the circuit between the copper screens. The completed circuit set off a loud buzzer that woke the child, who could then go to urinate. In this way, waking could be associated with bladder distention and the child could learn (in a few weeks or less) to get up and urinate rather than await the noxious buzzer. This method worked effectively in stopping bed-wetting, and follow-up of children treated in this way has shown that as many as 81% remained dry up to four years after treatment (Deleon & Mandell, 1966).

Disorders Associated with the Musculature

The body dysfunctions we have just discussed may be related to malfunctions of certain specific muscles, such as the gastric and eliminative sphincters, and these aren't the only muscle functions that fall prey to "track-jumping." Any of the voluntary or involuntary muscle systems can be involved in developmental deviations. We will describe two common types of muscular disturbances: tics and apraxias. As is the case with the majority of other children's syndromes we have described, these also occur in normally growing children.

Tics. Sudden, quick, *involuntary* repetitive movements of the muscles that cause blinking of the eyes, grimacing, shaking of the head, sniffing, moving of the ears, jerking of the shoulders, arms, or legs, hiccuping, or clearing of the throat are called *tics*. A greater rate of tic behavior is frequently related to a higher anxiety level. During normal development, 7- to 9-year-old children often develop ticlike behaviors that may frighten or anger their parents. Some children will make strange noises with their tongues or blink their eyes, totally unaware that they are doing so. If parents don't label or obviously respond to such behavior, most tics usually will disappear in a short time. However, if the parents insist that the child stop, the symptom may itself become a continuing source of anxiety and become more firmly established.

If a tic behavior does establish itself and becomes a source of discomfort to child and parent alike, one effective way of dealing with the pattern is *negative practice* (Yates, 1958). Through negative practice, parents may gain control and the child may become therapeutically aware of the involuntary tic. The procedure is simple: each time the parents find the child twitching, they *calmly* instruct the child to produce the behavior *voluntarily* for a period of about a minute. After a short time, voluntary production of the tic typically becomes aversive, and the behavior that leads to the minute of tic production (the involuntary tic) reduces in frequency. In the ideal, the child becomes aware of performing the undesirable behavior and can learn to curtail it.

Apraxias. Whereas tics generally reflect an inability to *stop* performing some motor action, apraxias are characterized by an inability to *begin* or perform some specific motor behavior. Apraxia can be of the muscles used in writing (writing apraxia) or speech (speech apraxia). Apraxia may be distinguished from *dyspraxia*, a condition in which things can be done, but not done well. For example, in writing apraxia, a child can't write at all; in writing dyspraxia, the child can write, but not clearly or legibly. When apraxia or dyspraxia is present from early in life, some organic defect usually is implicated. However, psychogenic apraxias (which are psychologically based or caused) may be suspected when an inability appears in a child with no history of previous difficulty or known accidental head or nerve injury. For example, a child who complains of difficulty or inability to write after a period of doing some difficult assignment may be suffering from a psychologically based apraxia, writer's cramp.

Disorders Associated with Habitual Manipulations of the Body

Habitual manipulations are difficulties in *conscious, voluntary* repetitive movements. These habitual repetitive manipulations are considered to be self-reinforcing, and children usually are *aware* of them (Kanner, 1972). Children can choose to manipulate a broad number of body parts. Some manipulations, such as thumb-sucking, are common and more or less normal; others, such as hair-pulling, often are indicative of more severe degrees of being different.

Thumb-Sucking. In the early 1900s, a number of devices and techniques were developed to halt thumb-sucking. Inventors produced wire cages that could be placed around the guilty finger, but resourceful children sucked the thumb, cage and all! Others developed foul-tasting preparations that were smeared on children's fingers in an attempt to make the behavior "distasteful," but many children soon learned to like the stuff because it was associated with the very pleasurable act of thumb-sucking. According to modern thinking, thumb-sucking in young children may be normal and, if the child is left alone, the behavior probably will disappear. However, when the behavior persists beyond the age of 6, chances increase that it may indicate an underlying problem.

Masturbation. Masturbation creates more adverse reactions than thumb-sucking. Masturbation often occurs in early infancy. Male infants only a few months old may have erections during the washing of the genital area. Female infants also may respond as if the sensations they experience in the bath are pleasurable. Later, self-manipulation frequently occurs. Most of the "problem" with masturbatory behavior lies in the reaction of parents and society.

One of the unfortunate truths of our society is that we reach physiological sexual maturity long before it is socially permissible to carry on sexual activity. Thus, some form of adaptation usually is necessary so that sexual release can occur in.the absence of heterosexual relationships. One obvious replacement is masturbation. If masturbation can be seen as developmentally appropriate in the light of our social customs, and not as something dreadful, we believe there will be fewer problems associated with the behavior. Sex education in our elementary and high schools is one means of improving this aspect of the adjustment of youngsters.

Other Body Manipulations. There are several less common forms of body manipulation, including tongue-sucking, lip-biting, nose-picking, ear-pulling, and ear- or nose-twitching. Each of these behaviors can occur in normal children and probably will disappear if ignored. However, there are two types of habitual manipulation that should be taken more seriously. The first of these, *trichotillomania,* or hair-pulling (Delgado & Mannino, 1969), usually occurs only in severely disturbed children. As a result of trichotillomania, affected children may be left with large patches of sore, bald scalp that often become infected.

Head-banging is also pathological body manipulation. Children may bang their heads against walls or furniture for hours, and it isn't uncommon for such children to receive concussions, severe headaches, or closed or open wounds. Gentle head-banging may occur spontaneously and normally in infants (in which case it is probably best ignored), but it usually disappears by the age of 2½. Beyond this age, children can produce great damage to themselves if the condition goes uncorrected.

Disorders Associated with Speech

The developmental deviations we have discussed so far are primarily physical, but disorders of speech and disorders of learning are related primarily to social and educational development. Speech involves communication with others and thus is related to the maintenance of acceptable social and interpersonal relationships. Absent, delayed, or problematic speech may be a source of concern to parents awaiting the baby's "first word," and speech disturbances can open the frightening possibility that their child will be different. We will describe two important abnormal patterns of speech—stuttering and mutism—that may be psychologically based.

Stuttering. A disturbance in the smooth flow of speech, stuttering occurs in about 1 of every 100 people. Half of all stutterers are children. Males usually outnumber females by a ratio as high as eight to one (Kessler, 1966). Van Riper (1953) distinguishes two types of stutterers. Unaware of their disability and not usually self-conscious, *primary stutterers* are developmentally normal. Most normal children exhibit this behavior between the ages of 2 and 5. There is some chance that, if the early, developmentally normal disfluencies are labeled a problem and overreacted to, the stuttering may become secondary. In *secondary stuttering*, children may be painfully aware of their problem and, if their attempts at self-control of stuttering fail, they may become anxious and stutter more.

Although there is little agreement as to a single cause of stuttering in children, many theories have been offered. One of the earliest is probably the theory of *mixed cerebral dominance* (Orton, 1937; Travis, 1931). According to this view, if one of the cerebral hemispheres is not dominant (as is normal), then the two sides of the brain are in constant conflict. One result of such a conflict can be inability to synchronize the speech musculature, which in turn can lead to stuttering.

An example of a psychological theory offered for stuttering is that of Johnson (1955), who believes that pathological stuttering is caused by parental reaction to normal *primary* stuttering. That is, parents may become anxious about speech disfluencies and force children to slow down, to repeat what they say, and to pay attention to their speech patterns. The result is that the children become very aware of the fact that there is something different about them. Moreover, because they learn that faulty speech will evoke parental anger, they may become anxious about beginning to speak. A high level of anxiety about speaking may produce even more stuttering, and the children may find themselves in the middle of a vicious circle. According to Engel and Helfand (1964; cited in Kessler, 1966), most instances of stuttering are best ignored by parents. Ignoring such primary stuttering can lessen the chances that secondary stuttering will develop. The list of situations that can cause increased stuttering in normal children (and some adults) is presented in Table 18-4.

Mutism. In stuttering, the child typically has articulate speech but is hesitant or anxious about speaking. In *mutism*, articulate speech is absent or nearly absent. Possibly the most common cause of mutism is the absence of hearing *(deaf-mutism)*, but several forms of the disorder are psychologically based. For example, mutism is common among schizophrenic or autistic children who have withdrawn to such a degree that they don't relate verbally to

Table 18-4. *Normal stuttering-inducing situations (based on Engel & Helfand, 1964)*

Being overstimulated
Having to compete to speak
Expecting to be interrupted before finishing
Feeling that what he is saying is being disapproved
Feeling that he won't be believed
Admitting to bad behavior
Being unable to see his listeners
Feeling the listener is angry
Being tired
Expecting punishment
Feeling the listener is impatient
Being asked to "perform" for people
Being afraid of something
Using words he isn't sure of
Not being positive he is correct
Being upset because parents are fighting
Telling a lie
Being compared unfavorably with other children

their world. At a less severe level, mutism can also reflect a hysterical reaction of childhood in which the speech apparatus is temporarily nonfunctional due to anxiety.

Mutism also can occur in basically normal children. However, as in the case of stuttering, the symptom may best be perceived as some kind of reaction to parental demands (Kanner, 1972). For example, the child whose parents require absolute perfection in speech may experience intense fear of talking. To avoid the possible wrath of disappointed parents, the child may choose to remain silent. Given this "parentogenic" mutism, it isn't uncommon for the child to speak freely with nonjudgmental others, such as peers or younger children.

Disorders of Learning

More vague and difficult to identify than the first four categories of developmental deviations, the learning disorders have received a great deal of attention from professionals working with troubled children since the 1950s. According to Ross (1974), three different patterns of learning problems can be distinguished: learning disorders, learning disabilities, and learning dysfunctions. Although Ross's categories are clearly distinguishable, the term *learning disability* has come to include learning dysfunctions as well.

Learning Disorders. A child with a learning disorder is one whose basic ability to learn isn't impaired, but who can't learn because of "acquired, incompatible responses" (Ross, 1974). For example, children who can't sit still and attend to a written page will be unable to learn what is on the page because their incompatible behaviors prevent them from attending long enough to read the material. Further, children may have learned that certain aspects of the school situation are aversive (kids pick on them and so forth), and, as a result, they avoid going to class or to school altogether. In the extreme learning disorder known as *school phobia*, children fail to learn, not because they are "dumb" but because of their avoidance and fear of school. The following case history is an example of school phobia.

John M., a cute 7-year-old boy, was brought to a psychologist on the advice of his pediatrician. His mother reported that John had not attended school for the previous two weeks because of a stomach ailment and that, even though he had recovered, the child would not go back to school. For three days, his mother had taken John out to the bus stop, where John had begun to complain about going to school. Each day when the bus approached, the child became visibly fearful and began to gag and choke. The gagging was followed by his vomiting his breakfast and returning home. John's father had become angry about this at first, feeling that the boy was just making himself sick so he wouldn't have to go back to school. His mother felt differently, and a strong conflict arose between John's parents. John's father refused to meet with the psychologist.

On the day of the first appointment, the psychologist took John and his mother to the school, where a meeting was held among the teacher, principal, psychologist, and mother. It was soon determined that, on the day before he became ill with the original stomach ailment (which may or may not have been psychosomatic), John had had a fight with a girl in the class—and had lost. In fact, he had been pinned to the ground by this girl, and she had spat on him while all the other children watched and laughed. As a final embarrassment, the boy had been forced to say numerous self-derogatory things before he was allowed to get up and go about playing. The teacher had learned of these happenings after John had been out of school for several days, but didn't think the boy had had such a severe reaction.

John was fearful about returning to school because of the embarrassment and the emotional pain associated with the fight with the girl. He believed the other boys would call him a sissy or a weakling (and he was unfortunately right). The psychologist, however, realized that after a few days of teasing the matter would be forgotten if John were able to face those trying few days. With the support and encouragement of his teachers, family, and psychologist, John was *forced* to attend school. Even if he vomited, he was cleaned up and taken to school. Two weeks later, the phobia had subsided dramatically and hadn't recommenced when followed up six months later.

Kennedy (1965) has described a program of treatment for school phobia. The program seems to be based on forcing the child to go to school. He describes six essential aspects of treatment:

1. Early identification of the problem—within two or three days after onset

2. Deemphasis of somatic complaints (I'm sick or I don't feel well)
3. Insistence upon school attendance, including the use of force when necessary
4. Matter-of-fact approach to the problem on the part of parents and support for attending school under any conditions
5. Discussions with the child *after* school hours, further emphasizing the importance of facing fear and going to school
6. Informal telephone follow-up to the child

Learning Disabilities. According to Ross (1974), the child with learning disabilities, like the child with a learning disorder, doesn't work up to levels expected on the basis of intelligence. However, the problem in learning disabilities doesn't reside in interfering responses such as school avoidance, but originates in psychological disorders that are unrelated to school or academic activities. Such disabilities may be seen in autistic children or childhood schizophrenics, where the symptoms of the disorder prevent the children from ever applying themselves to the learning process. An example of the difference between Ross's concepts of learning disorders and learning disabilities lies in school-avoidance behavior. As seen in the previous section, children who avoid school owing to some fear of the school or learning situation probably have a learning *disorder*. Children who avoid school because they are unwilling or unable to leave their mothers or home situations usually have a learning *disability*.

Learning Dysfunctions. The third type of learning problem, learning dysfunction, is defined by exception. Ross (1974) states:

> When a child does *not* manifest general mental subnormality, does *not* show an impairment of visual and auditory functions, is *not* prevented from attending to the educational tasks by unrelated psychological disorders and is provided with cultural and educational advantages, but is nonetheless severely impaired in his learning efficiency, we shall consider him to fall into the category of learning dysfunctions [p. 104].

Such children manifest a large number of difficulties with concept formation, attention, perception, coordination, communication, and motor control. They may be hyperactive and distractible, and may manifest school-related problems in reading, spelling, arithmetic, and verbal or auditory reception, association, and expression. Treatment of such conditions often involves assessment by a specialist in learning dysfunctions or learning disabilities, and remedial training carried out in the home and classroom. Emotional difficulties usually enter the picture only when the child is labeled by others as deviant or abnormal. The following personal experience shows the emotional strain on a mother whose child is different because of a specific learning dysfunction.

The Learning Dysfunction and Disabilities Specialist

A relatively new professional discipline in the overall effort to help troubled children is the *learning disabilities specialist* (LDS). The LDS holds at least a master's degree in learning and communication disorders and is specially trained in the identification and remediation of specific and general learning disabilities.

Learning disabilities have been defined as follows:

> A learning disability means a disorder in one or more of the basic psychological processes involved in understanding or in using language, spoken or written, which may manifest itself in an imperfect ability to listen, think, speak, read, write, spell, or do mathematical calculations. The term includes such conditions as perceptual handicaps, brain injury, minimal brain dysfunction, dyslexia, and developmental aphasia. The term does not include children who have problems which are primarily the result of visual, hearing or motor handicaps, of mental retardation, or of environmental, cultural, or economic disadvantage [*Federal Register*, 1976, p. 52,404].

Typically, the LDS assesses the presence of learning disabilities through the use of a variety of formal structured tests and informal evaluation procedures.

After identifying specific problem areas (deficits), the LDS may prescribe a remedial program of practice and guidance involving the school, parents, and other professionals such as child psychiatrists and psychologists. Such remedial programs may involve structured practice in areas of weakness while incorporating the strengths of the child (Johnson & Myklebust, 1967). For example, consider a child who has difficulty reading because of an inability to ignore irrelevant cues. Remedial efforts for this child might include practice in reading words one letter at a time, with other letters concealed to avoid distraction.

Although diagnosis and remediation of learning disabilities are the primary tasks of the LDS at present, one expert (Parrill-Burnstein, 1978) has said that the future role of the LDS will be as a general "learning specialist" rather than as a specialist who works with problem children only.

PERSONAL EXPERIENCE: *How Does It Feel to Have a Child with Specific Learning Disabilities?*

Michael was an adorable little baby. He was very quick to crawl and walk and though he was quite slow at speaking, I was told this was normal for a boy and a second child. By the time he was 4, we thought he was a mechanical genius and that he didn't chatter continually because he was basically quiet. Generally, Michael was easygoing, but he didn't seem to listen to us or do the little chores we asked of him. He went to nursery school that year and things went OK because it was the kind of place where kids just did what they wanted. But all hell broke loose in kindergarten. He couldn't follow instructions the teacher gave. His teacher said he became frustrated when the other kids would try to include him in activities. More and more he just wanted to be by himself, and he seemed to be so angry he'd hit and cry. My husband and I were very upset, but the teacher said he was just immature and should repeat kindergarten. Another year there just made everything worse. Now younger children were able to do things Michael couldn't. Our pediatrician didn't think much of the problem but suggested we might feel better seeing a psychiatrist. This started the summer after kindergarten and continued through a few months of his first grade. We spent a lot of money, learned more than we wanted to know about ourselves, but still it didn't help Michael. We were terribly guilty that Michael had so many psychological problems that he couldn't learn and couldn't have friends. He'd cry that he wanted to read and didn't know why he couldn't. The children didn't choose him for teams because he wouldn't follow the rules. He was so angry. We thought maybe he was retarded, but then how could he be so good with mechanical things and drawing? And sometimes he seemed to know so much. We were frantic, and his teacher said we'd better have him tested and that she thought he might have a specific learning disability.

Now Michael is in a self-contained learning disabilities class in the school and we know how much difficulty he has learning through hearing and planning and organizing things. It's good to know that he's not just stubborn and spiteful. We don't know how much Michael will ever be able to do, but at least all of us are less frustrated now.

TREATMENTS

In this section we will describe the general methods of treatment available for some of the disorders we have described. Not all the therapies are appropriate to all the psychoses, neuroses, and developmental deviations, but we have attempted to select the most common types used in treating the variety of children's disorders. These child therapies fall into two major groups: *play therapy* and *behavioral therapy*. Play therapy was developed specifically for children, but the behavioral methods are a subset of the large group of behavioral approaches to adult and child problems (see Chapter 22).

Play Therapy

Play therapy is a method for treating behavior disorders in children that takes advantage of the fact that children often can express themselves better in play than in other activities. Furthermore, because of children's limited verbal abilities, traditional "talk" therapies may be difficult with younger people. The theoretical and conceptual basis for play therapy has been stated by Woltman (1959):

> The spontaneous and self-generated activities of the child enable him to structure, to conceptualize, and to bring to tangible levels of activity his experiences and the feelings with which he invests them. Play, in this meaning, furnishes the child with opportunities to "act out" situations which are disturbing, confusing, and conflicting to him [p. 21].

As is the case in most forms of psychotherapy, there are several kinds of play therapy. Three representative approaches are the psychoanalytic, nondirective, and relationship play therapies.

Psychoanalytic Play Therapy. In psychoanalytic play therapy, play is used as a way of understanding and resolving Freudian phenomena such as transference, fixations, Oedipal blockages, and the like. Anna Freud and Melanie Klein perceive play as parallel to free association in the adult (Klein, 1955). Generally, the therapist's role in chld psychoanalysis is to identify problems in psychosexual development and to attempt to understand the symbolic nature of the child's play behavior. Through "corrective" play and interpretation, insights and behavior change may occur as the child is placed back on the normal track of psychic development.

The analyst may see the child as many as four or five times a week. The typical playroom has a toilet freely available, plenty of water, and toys that can be used to express feelings and levels of development. For example, finger paints are considered to be anal-level materials in which smearing and messing may be enjoyed. A child who spends much time washing at the sink may be showing guilt over sexual thoughts or taboo activities. Doll play may be used to identify mother-child attraction in boys or father-child attraction in girls, and so on.

By skillful interpretation of the use of play materials, the psychoanalytic therapist can gain an understanding of the child and can direct movement toward more developmentally appropriate play objects. If a child smears finger paints for the entire session, a therapist may try to move him or her toward the use of crayons, a more controlled mode of emotional expression. It is hoped that later the more controlled mode of expression will generalize to situations outside the playroom.

Nondirective Play Therapy. Whereas psychoanalytic play therapy requires that the therapist attempt to redirect deviant psychosexual development, in nondirective play therapy (Axline, 1947, 1964), the therapist provides an atmosphere of acceptance so that the child will be able to work out problems within the play setting with a minimum of direction and guidance. Sessions usually are held in a playroom furnished with items such as dolls, guns, paints, water, sand, and various other toys. Typically, the child is seen, not with parents, but rather in a one-to-one relationship with the therapist.

Axline (1964, p. 93) defines the role of the therapist in nondirective therapy by stating eight basic principles. These may be stated as follows:

1. The therapist must develop a warm, friendly relationship with the child as soon as possible.
2. The therapist accepts the child exactly as he or she is.
3. The therapist establishes a feeling of permissiveness in the relationship so that the child feels free to express his or her feelings completely.
4. The therapist is alert to recognize the *feelings* the child is expressing and reflects those feelings back in such a manner that the child can gain insight into his or her behavior.
5. The therapist maintains a deep respect for the child's ability to solve his or her own problems if given the opportunity.
6. The therapist does not attempt to direct the child's actions or conversations in any manner. The child leads the way; the therapist follows.
7. The therapist does not attempt to hurry the therapy along. It is a gradual process and is recognized as such.
8. The therapist establishes only those limitations that are necessary to anchor the therapy to the world of reality and to make the child aware of his or her responsibility in the relationship.

The last of Axline's guiding principles is perhaps the most important. Although the play-therapy relationship is a special one, children must learn to live with realistic expectations and limits if they are to transfer their progress in the playroom to their home environment. Some therapists consider limit-setting to be the essence of play therapy and the main source of its effectiveness.

Nondirective therapist Haim Ginott (1964) believed that setting limits is crucial to a realistic, healthy relationship with a child. Within an accepting, nondirective atmosphere, the child's ability to learn and deal with limits eventually leads to improvement. Ginott believed that limit-setting helps direct the child's energies into therapeutic channels and enables the therapist to maintain acceptance and empathy for the child. Limit-setting further helps strengthen self-control and enables a child to gain understanding and respect for laws, ethics, and social responsibility. Within the safe, accepting confines of the playroom, disturbed children may be able to relearn some of the behaviors they may have missed learning earlier and to express some of the feelings that are too threatening to express elsewhere.

Relationship Play Therapy. As presented by Moustakas (1959), relationship play therapy differs from nondirective and psychoanalytic play therapy in its premise that the past is less important than the present. Relationship therapists believe that the relationship established between child and therapist is the absolute key to successful treatment.

In the playroom, the focus is on the "here and now," and the accepting therapist attempts to help the child experience feelings as they occur or as they are reflected in play. Moustakas believes that children must learn to *individuate* themselves—to perceive themselves as mortal and able to live through separations and disappointments. According to relationship-therapy theory, if the child can establish a strong, open, intimate relationship with the therapist, self-worth will increase and maladjustment will decrease.

Behavioral Therapies

The therapies just discussed emphasize play as the vehicle for diagnosis and change. However, the behavioral therapies for children represent applications of laboratory-derived principles of learning to the modification of disordered behavior in youngsters. Through the manipulation of rewards and punishments, behavioral therapists are able to strengthen desirable patterns and weaken or extinguish (see Chapter 4) undesirable patterns. We have selected two types of behavioral approaches, the token-reinforcement system and the reward-and-punishment method used with psychotic children.

Token-Reinforcement Systems. Using stars, pennies, and poker chips as rewards isn't a new method of changing behavior. Teachers have long used stars and the like to reward pupils, providing perhaps the earliest applications of what are now called *token-reinforcement systems* (Ayllon & Azrin, 1968). A *token* is any object that has value because the owner can trade it for something reinforcing. Thus, a penny is a token that, when placed in a gumball machine, leads to the delivery of an enjoyable sweet. The token itself has no intrinsic value. Its value is derived only by association with the objects it can "purchase." In token-reinforcement systems, tokens are given for a desirable behavior, and the tokens can be used later to "buy" desired reinforcers. For example, children may be told that they will be able to get a comic book if they accrue ten stars. They can obtain one star each time they successfully clean their rooms. The stars are merely paper, but each one gains value because it represents one-tenth of a comic book.

Although there are numerous ways in which token systems may be applied to the alteration of normal *or* abnormal behavior, we will describe one representative approach. The first step in treatment usually requires the parents, child, and therapist to determine what are called *target behaviors*, behaviors that all agree need to be altered. Target behaviors may include "do's" such as doing homework and cleaning up rooms, or "don't's" such as not poking baby brother in the eye or not eating plaster from the walls. Once the target behaviors are clearly determined and understood, a *star road* may be prepared. As can be seen in Figure 18-1, a typical "road" has ten "toll booths" or "gates"; ten stars or tokens are required for passage through a gate. At the very end of the road is a representation of a previously agreed-upon reinforcer (a toy or a similar desirable object) that the child may obtain only by traversing the "road." Behaviors that will result in the awarding of a token are clearly set forth for the child. At each ten-token gate, a smaller reinforcer (a candy bar or comic book) may be given to the child. These *intermediate reinforcers* ensure the maintenance of behavior from the beginning of the program to the final reward as many as 100 tokens down the highway. Using the token-reinforcement star road, such behaviors as school avoidance, lying, irritating a younger sibling, refusing to eat, and the like may be effectively removed and replaced with more acceptable behaviors.

Emotive Imagery. In token systems, the emphasis usually is on formal, tangible reinforcers; in emotive imagery, imagination is used to reduce intense fears. In instances of more severe disturbances, such as those involving intense anxiety, token-economy systems may not be sufficient to guide behavior change. In such instances, some psychological difficulty may prevent a child from even getting into a position where he or she might earn the token offered. For example, children who are school-phobic can't earn stars for good school work if they can't get themselves to go to school in the first place. In these and similar circumstances, the method of emotive imagery, as developed by Lazarus and Abramovitz (1962), has been extremely successful. Emotive imagery is based upon the concept of *reciprocal inhibition*. This concept states that, since two reciprocal behaviors such as fear and relaxation cannot occur at the same time, the instillation of one will prevent the occurrence of the other.

Lazarus and Abramovitz report the use of emotive imagery in the treatment of a young boy with an intense fear of dogs. Through an interview, they determined that one of the boy's dreams was to own and drive an Alfa-Romeo. The therapist asked the boy to close his eyes and imagine that an Alfa-Romeo was outside his house. Little by little, the boy was asked to see himself getting into the car and driving it down the street, much to the admiration of everyone. After the boy was experiencing strong positive feelings, the therapist introduced a big dog into the scene. The boy was told that he was safe inside his car. After several sessions, the child was able to imagine himself next to the car and near the dog with no anxiety of note. Lazarus and Abramovitz report excellent success with emotive imagery in the treatment of childhood phobias, with three sessions being the average required for noticeable improvement.

A modification of the emotive-imagery technique was developed by one of us during an "invited" tour in the U. S. Army. The technique involves the identification of a superhero, such as Batman, Superman, or Wonder-

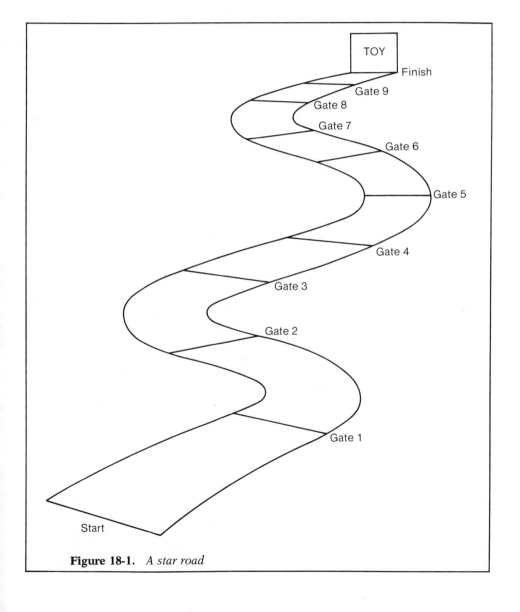

Figure 18-1. *A star road*

woman, and the establishment of an imaginary contract between the superhero and the child. The contract calls for the child to imagine that the superhero accompanies him or her during attempts to deal with difficult life events or feared situations. The therapist agrees to award a "superhero certificate" when the child has satisfactorily carried out the "deal" with the superhero. The following is a representative case example.

A 6-year-old boy was referred by his pediatrician due to a problem with daily soiling (encopresis). It was determined from the interview with the child that he was often unable to get to the bathroom quickly enough to prevent the "accident." His parents were very angry and concerned about the problem and had "tried everything" from rewards to thinly veiled threats of death and dismemberment. In a brief meeting with the child, the therapist found that his superhero was Richard Petty, the famous race-car driver. A contract was struck in which the boy was told to imagine that, when his "stomach told his head" that it had to go to the bathroom, he was to imagine that Richard Petty would be on the scene with a race car (good old number 1) and speed him to the bathroom in time. One week later, the child was seen again. His parents reported that the rate of soiling had dropped from seven times per week to two. Three weeks later the behavior was totally gone, and the child had been "clean" for a week and a half. The child was given his superhero certificate and cherished it dearly. Six-month follow-up revealed no recurrence of the problem.

Treatment of Psychotic Children. Whereas the reinforcement systems primarily emphasize reward, either through tokens or imagination, behavioral approaches to treating psychotic children often include very real punishment. The psychotic child frequently represents a special treatment problem because of withdrawal, mutism, uncooperativeness, and difficulty in relating. Thus, most forms of play therapy can't be applied easily to the psychotic child. In view of these problems, behaviorists dealing with psychotic children may have to return to basic concepts of reinforcement and punishment in the hope of treating the child. The successful application of basic punishment and reinforcement to psychotic children was developed by Ivar Lovaas (Lovaas, 1967; Lovaas & Koegel, 1973).

Lovaas's approach is simple: when children behave abnormally, they are punished; when they act normally, they are rewarded. Punishment in the form of electric shock following autistic or schizophrenic behavior, and rewards such as hugging and kissing following appropriate social-interpersonal behavior, may be employed. Lovaas attained national recognition ("Screams, Slaps and Love," 1965) for his work with autistic children. Lovaas places unresponsive children on a shock platform, surrounded by therapists. The child is called, and if he or she doesn't respond by approaching one of the therapists, a strong shock is applied. In discomfort, the child runs, often crying, to one of the surrounding therapists, who hugs and kisses him, thereby reinforcing his "approaching people" behavior. Admit-

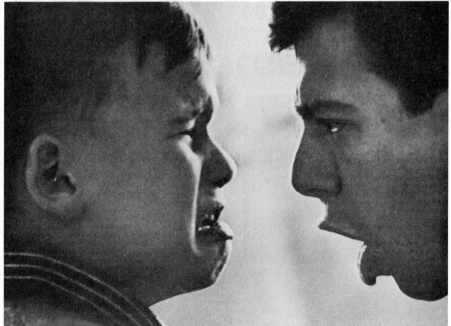

Breaking into the world of autistic children so that they can learn to feel and love can be an emotional and involving experience. (Photo by Allen Grant, LIFE magazine, © 1965, Time Inc.)

tedly, Lovaas's techniques may be drastic, but they are used only when all else has failed. Systematic manipulation of praise and punishment has helped many psychotic children to relate more effectively.

CONCLUDING COMMENTS

Many of the disorders observed in children seem to be transient developmental disturbances needing little or no treatment. Nevertheless, we must not lose sight of the fact that many disturbed children do need skilled professional attention, but may not get it. Conservative estimates place the number of children under the age of 18 in the United States who need *immediate* help at about 1.4 million (Clark, 1974). As many as 9 million more youngsters are believed to be in need of some form of psychological help. Trends suggest that the number of children who need such help is increasing. It is becoming more apparent to parents and professionals alike that the millions of children who are neurotic, hyperkinetic, depressed, or have personality disturbances can and should be helped. We must hope that adequate facilities and sufficient numbers of trained professionals will become available in the future to serve this increasing number of young people who are different.

CHAPTER SUMMARY CHART

In this chapter, we discussed the problems associated with children who are different. We first described children who are *psychotic:*

Descriptions	Explanations

Childhood schizophrenia
Early infantile autism
Symbiotic psychosis
Infantile psychosis
Propfhebephrenic psychosis
	Psychological:
	  Psychoanalytic—failure of ego
	    ever to develop
	  Behavioral—extinction of social
	    responses by ignoring parents
	Biological: genetically caused
	    problems in neurological
	    systems

The second group of children who are different are those with *developmental deviations*, a set of problems in which development has "jumped the track":

Disturbances related to bodily functions	*Musculature disturbances*
Sleep disturbances	Tics
Eating disturbances	Apraxias
Elimination disturbances	Dyspraxias

Habitual manipulations	*Speech disturbances*	*Disorders of learning*
Thumb-sucking	Stuttering	Learning disorders
Masturbation	Mutism	Learning disabilities
Hair-pulling		Learning dysfunctions
Head-banging		

We closed the chapter with a discussion of treatment methods especially useful with children who are different:

Play therapy	*Behavioral therapy*	*Treatments for psychotic children*
Psychoanalytic play therapy	Token-reinforcement systems	Lovaas's method of using shock to motivate autistic children
Nondirective play therapy	Emotive imagery	
Relationship play therapy		

CHAPTER 19
ADOLESCENTS

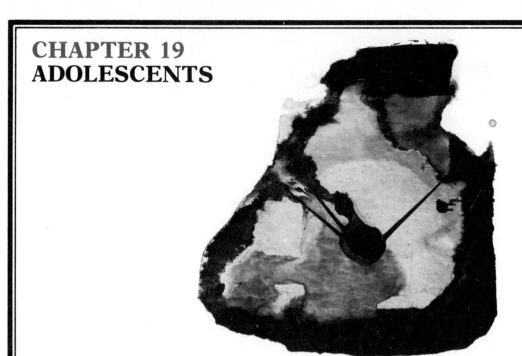

Adolescence is considered by most theorists to include the years between the onset of puberty and the age of 18. Formal psychological study of this developmental period was begun in 1904 by G. Stanley Hall, who realized the importance of this phase and the stress associated with it. We will begin our discussion of adolescence with a description of the abnormal behavioral patterns of this phase recognized by DSM-II. Following these descriptions, we will present an alternative system of classification derived by a specialist in adolescent psychiatry. This alternative has developed in much the same way as the GAP system for children (Chapter 18); that is, available classification schemes didn't seem to reflect accurately what clinicians saw in their patients, so the clinicians created a diagnostic system that did.

DESCRIPTIONS

Although we will limit our descriptions of adolescent disturbances to those not mentioned elsewhere in the text, most disorders are possible in adolescents. In DSM-II, the traditional categories of adolescent disorders are referred to as the Special Disturbances of Adolescence. These categories aren't meant to include all adolescent deviations; rather, they represent those reaction patterns specific to the age period between the onset of puberty and the age of 18. The categories are called *reactions* because they are seen primarily as responses to the transient stresses of the adolescent years.

Overanxious Reactions

In overanxious reactions, the person usually shows extreme self-consciousness, sleep disturbances, baseless fears, and hypersensitivity to other people. Most frequently, the adolescent's anxiety may manifest itself in restlessness, irritability, and generally high levels of arousal (Jenkins, 1968).

Runaway Reactions

In overanxious reactions, adolescents may not interact well with their parents, but runaways leave home without parental assent as a way of coping with home and family stresses. About 600,000 children run away from home each year ("Prostitutes," 1971). Jenkins (1971) suggests that running away is the result of an aversive life situation coupled with rejecting parents. Although it is a diagnosable behavioral disorder, runaway reaction is also a crime in several states. In these states, parents can have runaway children incarcerated for forced treatment.

Withdrawal Reaction

In withdrawal reaction, rather than becoming hyperanxious or running away, teenagers detach themselves from the outside world and turn into themselves for safety (Jenkins, 1968). The symptoms of withdrawal reaction, which can include daydreaming, shyness, listlessness, and unrealistic fantasies, are shown in the following personal experience.

PERSONAL EXPERIENCE: *Adolescent Withdrawal*

When I was 14—and I remember this very well—I felt very alone, unwanted by friends or by my family. I studied hard and did well in school . . . my teachers liked me. But I was afraid of most of the other kids. I was afraid to go out on a date—My God, what would happen if I asked a girl and she said no! I preferred to not ask and never be rejected than to ask and "maybe" be rejected. I sat in my house much of the time—the other kids went out—I didn't want to. They'd all hang out at the pizza place or the pinball hall, but I *never* went. I don't think my parents minded my not going either—they never said anything about it. I'm not sure they really cared anyway—as long as I wasn't a trouble-making teenager like "the rest of them" I was ignored. When I sat in the room studying I'd spend a lot of time just floating off—I'd think about being a great NBA basketball player (I can't play well at all) or a powerful politician or something. As I look back I can see that I wanted respect and importance and wanted people to like and value me. I never felt that then. . . . All I felt was isolation, loneliness, and sadness.

Unsocialized Aggressive Reaction

In contrast to the adolescent who withdraws, in the unsocialized aggressive reaction of adolescence teenagers can be described as openly or passively hostile, physically or verbally aggressive, vengeful, and destructive. Such adolescents frequently engage in vandalism and arson. It appears that the unsocialized aggressive adolescent has chosen to lash back at a rejecting environment rather than to withdraw or run away from it as in other adolescent reactions. In many ways, these youngsters resemble adult psychopaths. The response of others to such people reveals the fear these adolescents can create.

PERSONAL EXPERIENCE: *Unsocialized Aggressive Reaction*

I remember Larry, the toughest guy in my class. I think he's in jail for murder now, but it's no surprise to me. In fact it's a relief having a guy like him off the street! I still shudder to think that I spent four years in the same classroom with him—and lived! Larry had no respect for the teachers, no respect for the cops, not for anybody. He would take on anybody. I remember in tenth-grade English, we had a particularly passive teacher—Larry went right for his eyes. He'd say things like "That's a stupid looking jacket you have on today, Mr. F." and then see what would happen. Mr. F. came over and grabbed Larry by the shirt and Larry said, "My mother worked hard to buy that!" (He always seemed to invoke his mother as justification for his behavior.) Then he pushed Mr. F., punched him in the mouth, and the teacher began to bleed. We were scared stiff. Larry got thrown out of school, but he was back in one month, unchanged. He seemed angry all the time; nobody fiddled with him about anything.

Group-Delinquency Reaction

A teenager who, in response to a stressful life situation, becomes involved in delinquent groups such as street gangs and the like may be diagnosed as showing a group-delinquency reaction. Seeking acceptance

and security often unavailable at home or in social groups, the group delinquent seems to find a special place in the street gang. Within the street-gang
subculture, antisocial behavior is frequently rewarded by respect and admiration of the gang. A sense of security and status may be obtained by
identifying with the group through group jackets, emblems, and the like.
However, being a member of a delinquent group doesn't always indicate
group-delinquency reaction. Many youngsters belong to such groups, not
out of a need to cope with a poor family or home life, but for a variety of
other reasons.

Suicide

Although it is not a behavior limited to this age group, suicide occurs among adolescents with enough frequency to warrant mention here. In
his study of adolescent suicide, Haim (1974) has reported that suicide is the
third most frequent cause of death among people age 14 through 19. Suicide
may be perceived as the most extreme form of withdrawal from real or
perceived rejection and hurt. As in the typical adult suicide pattern, more
adolescent males succeed than females, and they usually use more violent
means than females.

An Alternative Classification
of Adolescent Disorders

As you remember from the previous chapter, DSM-II hasn't always
been successful in describing children's behavior and, in many settings, has
been replaced by the system proposed by the Group for the Advancement of
Psychiatry (1966). Professionals working with adolescents have also found
DSM-II to be inadequate, and alternative approaches have been proposed.
The system offered by the adolescent psychiatrist M. Robert Wilson (1971)
is based upon the concept that adolescence is a period in which struggles to
establish a *role identity* characterize development. Problems may arise in
any or several of five crucial developmental dimensions: dependence-
independence, impotence-omnipotence, passivity-aggressivity, altruism-
narcissism, and femininity-masculinity. To Wilson, psychopathology
occurs when a rigid polarization manifests itself along any of these dimensions. The polarization is motivated by a need to find a "safe anchor" in a sea
of emotional turmoil. For example, anchoring at the aggressivity pole results
in the aggressive teenager, while anchoring at the passivity pole may produce
the withdrawal-reaction type.

Wilson's system doesn't apply different names to syndromes with
different anchors, as is the case with DSM-II. Rather, he proposes that
diagnosticians consider five classes of one disorder—*adolescent crisis.* The
classes are generally differentiated on the basis of previous history of
psychiatric symptoms in childhood and of preadolescent vulnerabilities
(failure to resolve any or all of the five dichotomous dimensions).

Adolescent Crisis–Class I: "Healthy" reaction to adolescence. Reflects anxiety from working through of normal teenage problems. No current or past symptoms, no previous vulnerabilities.

Adolescent Crisis–Class II: Psychiatric disorders in which there was no evidence of emotional disability prior to adolescence. Class II represents a pathological reaction to normal adolescent issues in a teenager who has no psychiatric history.

Adolescent Crisis–Class III: Psychiatric disease with evidence of preadolescent vulnerability, but present symptoms are first diagnosable symptoms in child's life. Thus, psychological symptoms are reactions to specific stresses of adolescence.

Adolescent Crisis–Class IV: Psychiatric disorder with history of preadolescent vulnerabilities, *plus* preadolescent psychiatric symptoms. Symptoms seen in adolescence are only *amplifications* of preadolescent symptoms.

Adolescent Crisis–Class V: Psychiatric disorder with history of preadolescent vulnerabilities plus preadolescent psychiatric disturbances, *but with no change in symptoms with adolescence.* Represents a failure to enter or face adolescence: no rebelling, complaining, or fighting.

In Wilson's system, in addition to the class categorization, specific symptom manifestations usually are included in the total diagnosis. For example, a particular adolescent may be classified as exhibiting a Class III Adolescent Crisis with polarization in omnipotence and aggressivity as manifested by excessive rebellion, drug abuse, and running away. Such a diagnostic system gives a clearer picture of the problems being faced by individual adolescents and, therefore, more effective guidance for treatment of these problems.

EXPLANATIONS

Deviant adolescent behavior is most frequently seen as a result of a failure to cope effectively with the special developmental problems associated with the transition between childhood and adulthood. Generally, theoretical explanations of the disorders of adolescence are derived from conceptualizations of normal adolescent development. In an early theoretical treatment of adolescence, Hall (1904) characterized this period of life as a period of *Sturm und Drang,* or "storm and stress." Hall felt that inner turmoil and a type of second birth of the adult was the hallmark of adolescence, and that adolescent problems could be understood in terms of failure to cope with the natural turmoil of this period. Later theorists (Muuss, 1962, 1971) generally agreed with Hall's view.

Deciding on who they really are can be a bewildering experience for adolescents. (Photo by Joseph Czarnecki.)

The Theory of Anna Freud

Following in the footsteps of her renowned father, Anna Freud developed a theory of adolescence (1946, 1958) that was a major psychoanalytic statement of the psychodynamics of this stage of development. Like Hall, Anna Freud believed that adolescence is a period of storm and stress, but she assumed the specific source of the turmoil to be the onset of puberty and the arousal of long-unconscious sexual urges. When these sexual urges arise, strong id impulses may begin to bother a relatively weak ego and may threaten to overthrow the tenuous adjustment of the early adolescent. Usually, the ego can cope with the id's sexual demands on an adolescent through two special defense mechanisms: *asceticism*, or the repudiation of pleasure, and *intellectualization*, or using the intellect to distance oneself from impulses.

Anna Freud believed that turmoil among adolescents is inevitable; teenagers will experience a degree of storm and stress no matter what their family and life environment are like. Adolescence is a period of "developmental disturbance," a time of "normal abnormality" when behaviors that could be diagnosed as deviant in adults usually don't indicate permanent disturbance. Among these behaviors may be uncontrollable, frequent emotional outbursts, periods of deep depression and melancholy, inordinate fears, bizarre dress, drug use, and the like. In adults, these patterns could suggest severe disturbances; according to Anna Freud, in adolescents, they may suggest transitory "normal" patterns due to the deleterious effect of the reawakening of sexual id urges at puberty.

The Theory of Harry Stack Sullivan

Like Anna Freud, Harry Stack Sullivan (1953) saw adolescence as a crucial developmental stage. In Chapter 4 we described Sullivan's theory and his stages of psychological development in detail. Here we will focus on Sullivan's thoughts about adolescence.

In the first developmental stage, called *preadolescence*, Sullivan sees the crucial development of the *chum* relationship, an intense bond with a best friend of the same sex and age. From this relationship, preadolescents learn of "love," sensitivity, and validation of personal self-worth. If they fail to achieve these characteristics, they may enter the next stage, called *early adolescence*, quite ill prepared. Children who haven't had a "chum" may feel lonely, isolated, and unsure of themselves and can be quite vulnerable to later stresses.

According to Sullivan, the learning of intimacy is a crucial stage on the way to becoming a well-adjusted adult. (Photo by Robert Foothorap.)

Early adolescence is signaled by the onset of puberty and the appearance of needs to be physically intimate with members of the opposite sex. In this stage of development, the adolescent may feel stress as a result of what Sullivan calls "collisions," or conflict. One important collision is that between sexual desires and feelings of self-worth. For example, a teenage boy who pets with his girl friend and afterward experiences intense guilt may be involved in an early adolescent collision. If too many or too severe collisions are avoided, and if the adolescent is "lucky" in attempts at heterosexual intimacy, an integrated, well-developed pattern of "preferred genital activity" emerges and a stage called *late adolescence* begins.

In *late adolescence*, physical intimacy can be reached with members of the opposite sex, and emotional intimacy in the form of genuine interpersonal relationships can be attained with people of either sex. Being able to achieve such intimacy typically produces feelings of self-respect and maturity; but failure to establish strong relationships can leave the late adolescent morose, lonely, and maladjusted.

The Theory of Erik Erikson

Considered by a number of adolescent researchers and authors (Gallatin, 1975; Guardo, 1975) to be the most integrated and extensive description of the phenomenon of adolescence available, the theory of Erik Erikson (1950, 1968) focuses more on the social perspective than do the explanations of Anna Freud and Harry Stack Sullivan. For Erikson, adolescence is the crucial period of life when identity and a sense of being are obtained; one cannot have a feeling of being alive without a sense of identity.

According to Erikson, an individual passes through a series of eight psychosocial developmental stages (see Chapter 4). At each stage there is a "crisis," or turning point, at which the adolescent may choose adaptive or maladaptive behavioral solutions. Each stage represents a developmental task whose resolution is reflected in a balance between two opposing personality components (trust versus mistrust, autonomy versus shame and doubt, and so on). In the developmental stage of adolescence, the crisis is *identity versus identity confusion*. Within this stage, Erikson describes seven major developmental subtasks. Each of these subtasks has to do with identity versus confusion, and each is tied in some way to past and present crisis resolutions. A description of these seven developmental subtasks may clarify how adjustment or maladjustment in adolescent identity can arise.

1. *Temporal perspective versus time confusion.* The earlier resolution of the trust-mistrust challenge leaves children predisposed to different reactions to adolescence. If they are trusting, children usually enter adolescence with confidence in accepting the past and security in preparing for the future (good time perspective). If they were nontrusters, in adolescence they may be isolated and unable to view the past, present, or future in an integrated way.

2. *Self-certainty versus self-consciousness.* Autonomous children typically enter adolescence confident of their own abilities to face difficulties and accepting of themselves as good human beings. Shameful children often question their ability, may be self-conscious, and are probably not secure in their problem-solving ability.

3. *Role experimentation versus role fixation.* Children with initiative usually enter adolescence ready to experiment with new role identities and new experiences; they have the courage to face the task of seeking a new being. In contrast, guilt-ridden children may be "role-inhibited" and fearful of changing fixed patterns.

4. *Apprenticeship versus work paralysis.* Industrious children generally enter adolescence ready to master new tasks, to apply themselves to the problems of role identification. Children who feel inferior may see nothing worth trying, may feel frustrated, and may be unable to mobilize their energies to confront challenges.

A successful resolution of the adolescent stage can increase the chances of success in the three major life phases still to come. The three adolescent subtasks to follow lay the crucial foundations for later development.

5. *Sexual polarization versus bisexual confusion.* This subtask focuses on the attainment of a sex-appropriate identification. Sexually polarized adolescents usually are secure in their masculinity or femininity and thus ready for later intimate heterosexual relationships. However, sexually confused adolescents may be in store for later difficulty in establishing meaningful intimate relationships.

6. *Leader- and followership versus authority confusion.* Besides establishing their sexuality, adolescents must build the foundation for later professional, social, or familial productivity. To accomplish this goal, adolescents should develop an ability to see themselves alternately as leader and follower. Confusion about when to submit to authority may result in later difficulties in dealing with adult relationships.

7. *Ideological commitment versus confusion of values.* If the previous subgoals are resolved in the direction of "ideological commitment," the final adolescent subtask usually results in an adult with a set of values that can serve as guides to life. In late adulthood, such values allow for a more positive review of one's life and a sense of integrity. If confusion of values is the result of this adolescent subtask, a weakened guiding philosophy emerges, and later life may be filled with self-doubt, a sense of wasted years, and despair.

For Erikson, adolescence is a socially authorized *delay of adulthood.* Adolescence is a time when the limitations of childhood are lifted, but the responsibilities of adulthood are not yet imposed. Erikson sees this period of delay as a social *moratorium* in which adolescents may experiment with different values, attitudes, and patterns of behavior before committing themselves to an identity with which they may have to live for the rest of their lives. During this moratorium, the seven developmental subtasks must be successfully completed. If, because of fate, family needs, or other events, the moratorium ends too soon, adolescents may show identity confusion, feelings of failure, and fear of adulthood. Maladjustment in adolescence may reflect an inability to deal with the requirements of the moratorium. A failure to meet the requirements of adolescence may be due to a faulty resolution of preadolescent crises or an extreme lack of support and open rejection during the course of adolescence. According to Erikson, it is quite normal for adolescents to feel tumultuous and upset. Abnormality often appears when the adolescent chooses avoidance, denial, aggression, and the like as coping devices instead of confronting and resolving crises.

TREATMENTS

Many adolescent problems may be amenable to the usual kinds of adult psychotherapy discussed in Section VIII. Here, we will describe special applications of individual and group therapy to adolescents.

Individual Techniques

Staton (1963) describes three possible levels of helping relationships between adults and teenagers. The first level, *situational counseling,* can be performed by teachers, ministers, scout leaders, or any other person in whom the adolescent has faith. Situational counseling is usually brief and is directed primarily at specific, transitory problems of adolescence, such as not having done a good enough job on some important school task. When deep-rooted problems, such as a poor self-image, are troubling the teenager, more thorough *reeducational counseling* may be required. Staton describes this second level of counseling as one in which there usually are attitudinal or habitual problems, not just situational difficulties. In reeducation, teachers, guidance counselors, and the like can be the source of help by identifying and altering adolescents' faulty habits and beliefs about themselves and others. When personality "reconstruction" is indicated, Staton suggests the use of *adolescent psychotherapy.* Typically, "deep-seated" problems such as delinquency, psychotic behavior, severe anxiety, and depression require psychotherapy. Staton notes that reconstructive counseling is within the domain of trained mental-health professionals, and not guidance counselors, teachers, football coaches, and the like. In the remainder of this section we will describe the special characteristics of individual psychotherapy with adolescents; further details of the first two levels of counseling are provided by Staton (1963).

Usually, individual therapy involves an adolescent meeting once or twice a week with a trained psychotherapist. The particulars of the therapeutic process will vary according to the theoretical orientation of the therapist. For example, psychoanalytic therapy might be directed at resolving the crisis brought about by the reemergence of sexual urges; Erikson's theory might suggest that therapy be directed at identity development and the abolition of role confusion. However, regardless of the specific content of the treatment, individual therapy with adolescents has certain basic characteristics.

One-to-one treatment with teenagers usually is extremely difficult. Adolescents are notoriously uncooperative when it comes to attending sessions for which they often see no purpose. Uncooperativeness is especially evident when parents bring youngsters against their will. To deal with such negative attitudes, therapists must try to create trust between themselves and the adolescent. The therapist must convince the client that their discussions will be held in total confidence and that the therapist is out to help the adolescent and *not the parents*. In our own work with adolescents, we have found that the following points, if successfully made, can be of immense help in establishing a good relationship with an adolescent:

1. I am here to help *you*, not your parents.
2. I will not tell your parents or anyone else anything that goes on between us unless you and I both agree that I should do so.
3. I will tell your parents that they cannot tell me anything for my ears only. If they call me, I will tell them before they say anything to me that I will tell you everything they say to me when I report the call to you.
4. Even if it hurts or embarrasses me or you, I will always be straight with you and I will tell you what I am feeling.
5. I will never be late or miss appointments or not be ready to relate to you during our sessions (unless some personal emergency arises), and I expect the same commitment from you.
6. You can talk about terminating our relationship whenever you wish, but you must give me at least one week's notice. We must try to agree mutually as to when we stop seeing each other.
7. I am older than you and I realize it; don't let my age lead you to believe that I cannot understand *any* of your feelings.

Once the therapist and the adolescent client have reached the difficult goal of a trusting understanding, individual therapy can progress. Usually the client has the responsibility of bringing in topics to discuss; the therapist has to make sure that confidence is never violated and must offer support for the adolescent who is trying new roles and developing more effective attitudes.

Group Therapy

Another successful method for treating adolescent disorders is group therapy, a method of psychotherapy in which five to eight people joined together by common adjustment problems meet regularly with a professional counselor or therapist. Some experts in treating adolescents (MacLennen & Felsenfeld, 1968; Rosenbaum, 1972) believe that group therapy is the preferred mode of treatment for several reasons. First, many of the problems of adolescents are centered upon or associated with relationships with social peer groups. Thus, learning to relate well to an adult professional may not be as much help to an adolescent as learning to relate to similarly troubled peers. A second reason that groups may be preferred is that many adolescents don't easily trust one-to-one relationships with adults. Often they feel the therapist may be an agent of their parents who will force them to comply with parental wishes. Also, as mentioned earlier, adolescents sometimes are late to or absent from individual-therapy sessions. In group therapy, peer pressure can be brought to bear on such problems. Individual therapy with adolescents isn't impossible, but one-to-one treatment of adolescents may not be the optimal mode of helping for all.

The essentials of successful adolescent group therapy have been described by Berkovitz (1972), who feels that a "total spirit of acceptance and trust" is the key to effective therapy with teenagers. Berkovitz believes that the optimal group size is five to eight members. Outpatient adolescent groups meet once a week and residential groups (such as those meeting in halfway houses, group homes, and the like), up to five times a week. In both types of groups, Berkovitz suggests that males and females should be mixed together, but that younger adolescents (age 13 to 15) should usually not be mixed with older adolescents (ages 16 to 18). Berkovitz feels that two cotherapists, one male and one female, are the best combination to lead adolescent groups. Effective group leaders must be many things to the members—teachers, reflectors of feelings, transmitters of values, and sources of information, care, and respect (MacLennen & Felsenfeld, 1968). From the psychotherapeutic perspective, leaders of adolescent groups must be able to clarify reality, to confront hostility and lack of trust, to disclose personal information, to describe personal feelings, and to stand as a firm support for each member. As evidenced in the following interaction of an outpatient adolescent group, these tasks aren't easy to accomplish.

> *Therapist:* OK, let's begin. Anyone sitting on anything? [Use of jargon often helps adolescents feel more comfortable, but not always, especially if it appears forced.]
>
> *Bob:* Yeah, I'm really mad at you!
>
> *Therapist:* What's going on, Bob?
>
> *Bob:* We said that the stuff we say in here would stay in here, right? You said that we had confidentiality, right?
>
> *Therapist:* Yes, of course.

Bob: Well, how come somebody at school told me they heard I was afraid of girls? I've never said that anywhere except here . . . last week. I don't even know why I came back here. In a few days the whole damn school will know.

Therapist: And you think I told someone?

Mary: Somebody else in the group might have blabbed, Bob.

Bob: Who?

Mary: I don't know; don't look at me.

Jim: Me neither. I don't even go to your school.

Therapist: It looks like everybody is afraid of Bob. I must admit I am, too. He looks very angry and upset. But I know I didn't blow any confidence. How about the rest? Any slips of the tongue or loose conversations outside the group?

Fred: I spoke about the group to my mother . . . but I didn't mention names or anything.

Bob: Then you're the one. I oughta . . . (Gets up.)

Therapist: Bob, calm down. Blaming Fred won't help the situation at school. What's done is done and he's sorry it happened, but let's deal with the reality of some other kids knowing about your problem. What can you do about it?

Bob: F—k you! Now you're trying to make out like blowing our confidentiality isn't important. Well, I'm gonna tell everything about everybody in here and then they can see how I feel.

Mary: We can see how you feel without you doing that, Bob. We know you're upset. We care.

Fred: God, Bob, I didn't mean to hurt you. I mean . . .

Therapist: Bob, let's talk about this some more before you go and do something rash.

As can be seen from this excerpt, trust is often the crucial component of group therapy with adolescents. The trust in the therapist may be tenuous at best, and often the slightest indication of breach of trust can result in great anger, hurt, and threatened vengeance. Leaders of adolescent groups are frequently on thin ice; they may be accepted only conditionally and in many ways are expected to be perfect human beings. Therapists treating adolescents should be able to relate to teenagers, yet remain adults; and they should be ready to take a great deal of emotional confrontation, yet retain a commitment to helping their clients.

CONCLUDING COMMENTS

Parents of adolescents often ask whether there is any way they could have prevented the problems they face with their teenage children. However, some experts (Shopper, 1976) hold that avoiding these problems might actually be a disservice to the developing adolescent. Shopper believes that rebelliousness is a necessary part of achieving independence. Rather than trying to avoid conflicts, parents primarily should strive to ensure that the results of conflicts are minimally damaging. For example, Shopper notes that an adolescent who stays out until one when he or she was supposed to be home at midnight is indulging in a relatively harmless rebellion, compared to the teenager who crashes the family car into a school building. In either case, rebellion occurs and independence may be fostered, but in the former instance far less harm is done. Shopper notes that, although parents may be excellent caretakers for young children, the challenges of guiding an adolescent may be very taxing and result in problem-filled family relationships. Further, although many parents wish to give their children a different experience from the one they had, this often is impossible. For many parents, a superior-subordinate relationship may be the only way they know how to deal with a rebellious youngster. Conflict and turmoil seem inevitable, but Shopper feels that the key to a "successful" adolescence probably is a basically healthy parent-child relationship during the "twelve or thirteen years parents have to prepare for their child's adolescence" (p. 9).

CHAPTER SUMMARY CHART

In this second chapter on special age groups, we discussed problems of adolescence:

Descriptions	Explanations	Treatments
DSM-II:	Anna Freud:	Individual therapy
Overanxious reaction	inevitable turmoil	Group therapy
Runaway reaction	in adolescence	Greatest problem is
Withdrawal reaction	Sullivan: problems	gaining the trust
Unsocialized	in personal val-	of the adolescent
aggressive reaction	idation in the	
Group-delinquent	adolescent de-	
reaction	velopmental stage	
Suicide	Erikson: problems in	
Wilson's adolescent	resolution of the	
crises, Classes I-V	identity crisis	

CHAPTER 20
COLLEGE
STUDENTS

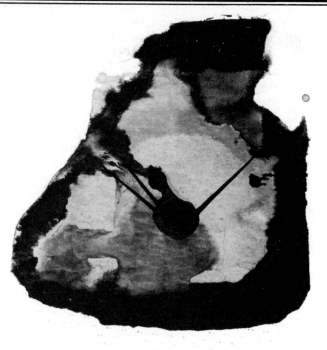

Having described for you the special problems associated with childhood and adolescence, we turn to the age group to which most of the readers of this text probably belong, college students. Erikson (1971), who is responsible for much of the present-day interest in difficulties associated with different developmental periods, describes the college situation thus:

> Colleges, of course, are foremost among the institutions which permit the study of comparable inner problems under demonstrable conditions. Students are men and women of the same age-group, who share a certain range of intellectual endowment and a converging set of motivations and who compete in life-tasks dictated by a known tradition which they have (more or less) freely chosen as a trusted style. . . . Colleges . . . [are not] only good study grounds, but breeding grounds for deviant behavior of all kinds [p. xx].

Most college students are in the final stages of dealing with the conflicts and crises of adolescence and are beginning to confront the issues unique to college age. However, not all students can cope with these issues. For example, it has been estimated that, during the undergraduate years, about 2 out of every 100 students will experience a psychotic disorder requiring hospitalization (Ryle, 1969). Further, an additional 15 out of every 100 college students are likely to have an emotional disturbance sufficiently intense to warrant treatment by professionals. Another 20 out of 100 may experience transitory symptoms as a result of one or more of the three major stressors of college life: examinations, social interaction, and career choice. Ryle notes that college students are more likely than their noncollege peers to seek psychological help during the ages 18 to 24. Whether the greater use of psychological assistance by college students is due to greater need or to free availability of campus mental-health services has not yet been ascertained. One fact is certain, however: in the college situation, students are subjected to severe stresses and are often ill prepared in terms of their own identity, self-confidence, and vocational direction to handle such stresses. Many of you reading the text probably have had some difficulties yourselves or know of fellow students who have had emotional troubles directly tied to the college experience.

Although Erikson asserts that feelings of alienation may be associated with all age groups, these feelings are rarely more salient and dramatic than among college students. "The college adolescent must learn

Although they are often among our brightest and most promising people, college students may suffer periods of great loneliness and anxiety.

to deal with a new body image, a new physical self as well as changes in body sensations. . . . Feelings that were unknown to the individual, or were experienced in modified forms now strike in all their rawness. The [college] adolescent senses he is different. Again he is *alien* to himself" (Josselyn, 1954, p. 223).

Our goal in the present chapter is to emphasize the special problems of college students. Some of these difficulties will most likely be familiar to you, and we hope that knowledge of them will allow you to face them more effectively if the need arises.

DESCRIPTIONS

In describing the disorders seen specifically among college students, we will not emphasize schizophrenia, manic-depression, neurosis, or the other disorders we have described elsewhere in the text. Suffice it to say that all of these disorders are possible in the college population, perhaps in even greater numbers proportionally than in other groups. An example of such severe disorders may be seen in the case history on page 506.

How College Students View "Insanity"

We asked college students some questions about insanity in order to find out how they viewed disordered behavior. Their responses were most interesting.

First we asked: "How many of you have felt you were going insane?" We found, surprisingly, that one out of two male undergraduates and two out of three female undergraduates had at some time felt as if they were going insane. These results have implications for those concerned with providing mental-health care to college students.

Second, we asked college students, "How do you think it feels to be insane?" We provide you with a sample of ten responses from males and females.

Males

1. Totally disoriented, unsure of who you are or of which various alternative personalities is the *real* you.
2. Would feel that the entire world is against you; however, to be able to retreat from the world is something which may be desirable for the person.
3. Would feel as though you are an outcast of society.
4. Detached from the world; an individualistic sort of trip that could be good or bad, depending on the person.
5. Probably very lonely.

6. Feels the same as someone who isn't "crazy."
7. No confidence in yourself, as well as being ill at ease with others, a feeling of helplessness.
8. Feel that what you see and perceive around you is not what everyone else perceives, or what everyone else tells you you should perceive.
9. Scary, don't know what's going on, confusing.
10. Probably frustration is the biggest problem. Frustration at people's reactions to you.

Females

1. Terror that most people can't comprehend, sort of like worst nightmare one can't get out of.
2. Feels rotten. Constant confusion, doubting your being, not happy with self.
3. Realize that you're different from everybody else and people would be constantly looking weirdly at you.
4. An indifferent feeling. Probably don't know they're insane.
5. Would be a feeling of not belonging in a normal environment. A feeling of confusion and not relating to those who are considered normal.
6. Highly confused and don't understand why.
7. Nothing seems to make sense anymore. You don't have a place in society.
8. Would feel bad because everyone around me would treat me poorly, ignore me, would not befriend me.
9. Feels uncomfortable since people treat you oddly and try to restrict your civil rights.
10. Feels like the world is against you. People abuse you but you feel like you are normal.

Third, we asked college students to list up to five adjectives describing an insane person. The list below includes the ten adjectives most frequently mentioned by males and females.

Males	*Females*
Confused	Confused
Disoriented	Abnormal
Disturbed	Strange
Sick	Sick
Irrational	Mixed up
Strange	Different
Crazy	Uncontrollable
Nuts	Frustrated
Wild-eyed	Out of touch
Depressed	Scared

A call was received by the psychiatric service from a worried faculty member about an undergraduate student who had become increasingly restless, excited, and confused over a period of days. He had expressed concern and suspicion about the telephone next door, which he thought could pick up sounds from his bathroom. He noted that certain electric bulbs in the corridor of his dormitory were not burning and felt this had some special significance that related to him. When the water in his shower began to run cold, he viewed the incident as part of a plot. His behavior grew increasingly strange.

Late one evening he emptied the contents of his wallet onto a sofa in a school library and left abruptly. This odd behavior was noted by some other students, who picked up the money, identification cards, and other contents of the wallet. They trailed the patient to his house, reported the incident to the housemaster, and gave him the discarded articles.

The housemaster called the psychiatric service at once. A psychiatrist and the housemaster went to the patient's room and found him busily engaged in throwing books and other effects out the door and down the hall. He said that the books were propaganda and that the money was materialistic and therefore he would have none of it. He was quite distractible and kept commenting upon casual happenings that he believed had specific reference to him. He talked in an expansive way of a mission he would perform which involved going to a foreign country and delivering it from the grip of communism. He tended to be somewhat jocular. Fortunately he recognized in a vague way that he was not well, requested medicine, and then agreed without question to admission to the college infirmary.

Soon afterwards he was admitted to a mental hospital and regressed to an utterly disorganized state in which he would lie on the floor naked, confused, and unable to care for his simplest needs. But he responded favorably to psychotherapy and treatment with tranquilizing drugs and was able to leave the hospital after about three months. He was readmitted to college and is making successful progress toward his degree.

Traditional classification systems are often difficult to apply to the college student. For example, in trying to use the traditional diagnostic categorization system to classify college students, Blos (1946) was forced to conclude, "When I tried to classify 387 cases, I was appalled to find that classification would indeed be fitting them into a procrustean bed for the sake of typology. I began to realize that I was dealing with case material which was basically different from cases seen in a mental hygiene or child guidance clinic" (p. 571). This statement is over three decades old, but it seems as relevant now as it was then. Reflecting the difficulty in classification, it is estimated that anywhere from one out of four to two out of four college students with psychological difficulties coming to the attention of helping personnel are assigned to the wastebasket category of "problem diagnoses" (Blaine & McArthur, 1971; Monks & Heath, 1954; Nowicki & Duke, 1978).

Our own work as clinicians and researchers in the college community has convinced us that the college student is indeed in a special situation that produces special problems. Erikson describes the college student as "a combination of explosive impulsivity and obsessive introspection" whose major problems appear to be motivation to stay in college and a great need for affection (in Blaine & McArthur, 1971). We agree, but we see college students as having other problems as well. In asking our students to list their major problems in dealing with the college situation, we find that grades, social life, and motivation frequently appear. (See Table 20-1 for a listing of some problems of "normal" college students.) In a two-year study of students applying for help at our university counseling service (Nowicki & Duke, 1978), we found that problems severe enough to merit students' coming for help other than vocational guidance could be subsumed under three groups. Clients involved in personal counseling had problems that could be called "existential depression." Examples of these problems were "I need to find out why I am not happy," and "Where am I headed in life?" A second group of personal problems could be called "social problems," in which many students complained of "lack of social life," "using sex as a way of relating," and difficulties in getting along with and establishing relations with members of the opposite sex. The last group of problems involved the clients' parents. Examples of "parental problems" were "How do I get my mother off my back?" and "How do I make my parents proud of me?" Synthesizing the results of various studies of college students' problems, we have decided to describe three groups of disorders: disorders associated with nonacademic personal concerns, disorders associated with academic mechanics, and disorders of academic progress.

Disorders Associated with Nonacademic Personal Concerns

Although many of the problems faced by college students are involved in some way with the task of completing college and beginning a

Table 20-1. *What are the greatest problems facing college students?*

Males	Females
Grades	What to do with their life
Social life	Developing sexual and emotional relationships
Vocational decisions	
Nervous about future	Strain from too much work
Sexual relationships	Grades
Peer pressures	Adjustment
Adjusting to new environment	Gaining independence
Leaving family for first time	Identity
Competition	Pressure from parents
Depression	Peer pressures
	Morals

career, three types of college-student disorders seem to be more personal than academic. These are the identity crisis, suicide, and apathy reaction.

The Identity Crisis.   It is Erik Erikson's theory that the main task of adolescence is to find an identity. For the college student, this usually means trying to find out who you really are. We find students in counseling grappling with such questions as "What am I on earth for?" "What do I really believe in?" "Is there a God?" "Is all I really want material things?" The conflicts that often characterize the identity crisis are revealed in the account offered by a student in the following excerpt from R. White (1952):

> I began trying to fit a personality to my make-up. I began acting out personalities and tried observing people and copying them, but I realized what I was doing and so carried that "how'm I doing attitude," that is, continually looking at and thinking about what I'd said or done, what impression I had made. But these personalities were all short-lived because they pleased some and not others and because they didn't produce that underlying purpose of making people like me; and every time unconsciously I would resort to my childish attitude to make myself noticeable. Examples of these "personalities" are independence (but I couldn't keep it up); arrogance (but people were only arrogant back at me); big shot in sex (but people weren't so much in love with it as I thought); hatefulness (people paid no attention to me); extreme niceness (people took advantage of it, kidded me about it because I did it to an ultra degree); humorous nature (but I was only being childish, silly); quiet and studious (but people were only passing me by and I kept feeling I was missing something). I became a daydreamer so intensively that up to the present I find I'm daydreaming almost all the time. I became conscious of a person's approach and would become fluttered, flustered, would try to make a friend of him no matter who he was but I overdid it [p. 154].[1]

It is likely that most students are bothered by questions of "meaning" at one time or another during their college years, but in some instances the identity crisis isn't easily solved and students may become incapacitated. Such students may stop doing course work or attending classes and, as a result, may find themselves in trouble with the administration. Because they can't find a comfortable niche in the social network of college, they may withdraw from friends and organizational activities as they search for meaning in their own existence.

In our own research (Nowicki & Duke, 1978), we reported that nearly one out of every three students coming for personal counseling had

---

[1]From *Lives in Progress: A Study of the Natural Growth of Personality,* by Robert W. White. Copyright © 1952 by Robert W. White. Reprinted by permission of Holt, Rinehart and Winston and Robert W. White.

The search for new roles and identities is an important part of the college years. (Photos by Joseph Czarnecki.)

what could be classified as a problem with identity. In the midst of such difficulties, these individuals tended also to show a great sensitivity to any occurrence that might reflect badly on their self-concept. Failure in either the social or academic realm was frequently magnified as the person searched for a sense of self.

Many parents have difficulty understanding what their children are experiencing in an identity crisis. From their perspective, it may seem that college has changed their youngsters from happy individuals who "knew what they were going to be when they grew up" into confused, questioning, dissatisfied people. In the fifties, the identity crisis was often associated with "beatniks" and in the sixties, with "hippies." In the seventies, however, there seems to be no particular group that reflects the identity crisis.

Suicide.   Although most identity crises are resolved successfully, or at least without much lasting difficulty, the search for identity, along with other college stresses, may sometimes lead a student to consider the drastic option of suicide.

Suicide is second only to accidents as a cause of death in college students. Within this group, the suicide rate has been increasing to the point that it may be up to 50% higher in some college-student groups than in the population as a whole (Stenzel, 1964). Ryle (1969) reported that the student suicide rate is approximately 4 out of 100,000 per year, but that the greater proportion of suicides occur in students who suffered in precollege years from severe depressive illnesses. In other words, rarely do student suicides occur in response to single psychologically disturbing events such as failure on a given test or lack of a date. Students who take their own life usually have had a history of difficulty in adjusting and may have experienced a long series of disappointments, failures, and other insidious stresses. Student suicides usually don't occur at one academic level (freshman, sophomore, and so on) more than any other, but suicides do occur more frequently in the spring (Ryle, 1969).

The following personal experience describes one person's reaction to a college student's suicide.

PERSONAL EXPERIENCE: *Suicide*

Charles lived on the second floor of my dorm, in the room above Mike's and mine. He was a strange sort of guy—kept to himself, yet we liked him and enjoyed talking with him. He wanted to be an accountant, but lord was he dumb! I don't know how he ever got into college, but he did—and he failed his entire first set of midterms. He was pretty upset, but he kept on trying. He failed all of his finals, too. We were worried about him—he seemed upset one day and calm the next. I remember the day it happened. I was lying on my bed about 3:30 in the morning think-

ing about going that day for the break between semesters. Suddenly I saw
something pass by the window—fast. Then I heard a thud and a moan. I
woke up Mike and we looked out. There was Charley lying on the cement
floor of the quadrangle, bleeding from his head and mouth—moaning. I
felt sick. He was still alive. We called the preceptor. He called the health
center. We covered Charley with a blanket. The moaning stopped. The
ambulance came and the doctor said he was dead. I went inside and
vomited—none of us said a word the rest of the day.

Two weeks later, school began. Charley's parents came to get his
things. They seemed shattered, sad people. They asked us if we knew
why he was so upset. We said, "No," but I still feel like maybe I did.
And maybe I didn't care enough about him to say something. And
maybe I could have stopped him or helped him. I'll remember that
morning forever—the sight of him lying there is burned into my mind.

In addition to those who actually attempt suicide, many students
think about it. A survey done at the University of Cincinnati found that
nearly three out of ten students sampled admitted thinking about their own
suicide during the academic year. Approximately one out of every ten of
these students rated these suicidal thoughts as very serious (Craig & Senter,
1972). Workers at one college crisis service reported that an average of six
calls per day involved serious talk of suicide (Skibbe, 1973). Suicide is
significantly more probable in college students than in their noncollege
peers, is more frequent in undergraduates than in graduate students, and is
more likely in those receiving either acceptable or above-average grades.

Seiden (1966) investigated the tragedy of suicide on college campuses where, he points out, the shock of suicide is especially great. "For
here are a relatively privileged group of persons enjoying valued advantages of youth, intelligence and educational opportunity. Why should persons, seemingly so rewarded, seek to kill themselves?" (p. 389). Seiden
found that students who committed suicide could be differentiated from
those who didn't in a number of ways. A sample of 23 University of California at Berkeley students who committed suicide over a ten-year period was
compared to students in general. Generally, it was found that suicide was
more frequent in older than in younger students, in males than in females
(more than three to one), in upper-class students than in under-class students, in single students than in married students, in foreign students than
in native, in language and literature than in other majors, in high-grade-
point-average students than in low-grade-point-average students, and in
those who came to a mental-health facility than in those who didn't.
Further, it appears that the peak months for suicides were October and
February. Surprisingly, only 1 of the 23 suicides occurred during the final
exam period. In fact, most suicides occurred during the first six weeks of the
quarter. The suicides were most likely to take place on a Monday or a
Friday and at the residence of the student.

According to Seiden, most students gave some warning that they were going to attempt suicide. For example, in completing a medical-history form, one student crossed out the word *emergency* and wrote in the word *death* in the question, "Whom shall we notify in case of emergency?" Clues aren't always this obvious, but Seiden reports that suicide victims often presented a similar symptom picture of "insomnia, anorexia, and extreme moodiness, especially moods of despondency" (p. 397). Among the particular crises precipitating suicides in college students were concern over grades, unusual somatic complaints, and difficulties with interpersonal relationships. This last precipitator usually involved students who were asocial and withdrawn. One extreme example is that of a withdrawn student suicide victim who was dead for 18 days before anyone found him in his room.

Apathy Reaction.   The complex of behaviors and feelings that reflect apathy is at once related to the disorders of identity and suicide and yet different. Walters (1971) defines apathy in college students as "a state of reduced emotional lability, preoccupation with current work difficulties to the exclusion of past experiences and future expectations, and an inability, in spite of constant effort, to study effectively" (p. 129).

Called "sophomore slump" by some, apathy reaction is much more than a slump and can affect the functioning of students during any year of school. Apathetic students are more than merely uninterested, as all students are at one time or another during their college years; such a student "is reacting with profound, generalized disinterest over a longer period of time to less defined and often obscure circumstances [and] frequently hangs on to his disinterest until academic indolence results in his withdrawal or severance from college" (Walters, 1971, p. 145). Walters also points out that, unlike depressed people, apathetic students don't seem to be trying to obtain love and attention from the outside world; rather, they seem to have decided that the outside world doesn't have what they need. Because of this conclusion, their problem usually isn't that they have the wrong educational or social goals, but that they have *no* goals. Apathetic students typically have spent little time thinking about or formulating goals and, as a result, they frequently are "committed to nothing."

We discovered in our own research (Nowicki & Duke, 1978) that all but one of our sample of apathetic students were male. They usually came to the attention of others during times of academic stress or decision and exhibited lack of interest in educational, social, and interpersonal matters. The most usual initial complaint involved the inability to concentrate on studies.

Walters (1971) concludes that apathy plays a defensive role and often may be used by the college student to anger and provoke others. He presents the following case history to show the characteristics of apathy and its provocative nature:

A 21 year old college junior was referred for therapy because of the conviction that he was intellectually inferior to his friends because something (either heredity or a disease) had impaired his memory. He was a potentially bright, innately warm young man who had long substituted these gifts with uneven, mediocre performance and a defensively reserved manner. Like the first patient he too was aggressive, but only in projects in gunsmithing and automobile mechanics where his considerable talents were well hidden from his outgoing and popular older brother and his eminently successful father with whom he was in passive competition. In therapy he soon worked through his feelings of intellectual inferiority and allowed himself academic success. His social defenses, however, proved more formidable. His innate warmth and compassion seemed to be sensed by fellow students and over his protests he was included in the usual social activities. In contrast, his view of this was that his friends only felt sorry for him; and he would cite their inevitable exasperation that his passivity would ultimately produce as examples of their untrustworthiness. A turning point in therapy, however, began with his insight into the following incident: The patient was playing hockey with friends. The score was close and competitive; spirit was high. The patient, however, reacted to this by a completely lackadaisical attitude. When the puck was passed to him, he would make a grossly ineffectual stab at it, miss it, and then slowly, even indolently, skate out of bounds to retrieve it. Quite naturally this soon reduced both sides into railing at the patient for his lack of spirit. The patient, quite predictably, assumed that they were angry and intolerant of his inadequacy. By clarifying this example, the therapist was able to point out how the patient had made both sides feel defeated, and thus was using "passive resistance" as a way of satisfying his own aggressive urges. By rationalizing this into inadequacy he protected himself from seeing the aggressive nature of his action [p. 139].[2]

From our own experience with college students, we can attest that Walters's interpretation is sensible. Many apathetic students end up irritating and angering a great number of people—suggesting that they very well might intend to do so.

Disorders of Academic Mechanics

The problems of academic mechanics—difficulties associated with the technical tasks necessary for successful college-level work—are most likely to come to the attention of counselors. Typically, a college student

[2]From "Student Apathy," by P. A. Walters. In G. B. Blaine Jr. and C. C. McArthur (Eds.), *Emotional Problems of the Student.* Copyright 1971 by Appleton-Century-Crofts. Reprinted by permission of Prentice-Hall, Inc.

may experience difficulties in studying or taking exams; either of these difficulties can be academically disastrous.

Daydreaming, inability to sit still for even short periods of time, inability to concentrate, memory impairment, lack of study skills, and the like can all be associated with difficulties in studying. Study disabilities

A major stress for college students is the experience of competition and continuous evaluation. (Photo courtesy of the University of California, Berkeley.)

can be either *general* (the student can study no subject at all) or *specific* (the student may do very well studying art, but can't study physics). Often referred to as a "mental block," the inability to study may begin a vicious circle that produces more anxiety and more difficulty in studying. Students may find that they can't finish their assignments, so they fall behind and worry even more.

It has been our experience that the sudden onset of a general inability to study is usually related to some transient life disturbance, such as family trouble or the break-up of a love relationship. However, specific study disabilities are most frequently related to career-choice conflicts. For example, a premedical student who really wants to be an artist may find herself at the top of her art classes yet unable to study organic chemistry. Inability to study often serves the purpose of calling parents' attention to the possibility that medicine or some other parentally approved career may no longer be the student's choice.

Unlike studying difficulties, in which the student doesn't learn the required academic materials, in *test-taking difficulties* the student may know the material but be unable to show this knowledge on an exam. Also referred to as *test anxiety*, these difficulties are characterized by extreme incapacitating anxiety either during exams or just before them. The test anxiety can result in the student's avoiding the anxiety by missing the exam or by taking it and doing poorly. Typically, test-anxious students study very hard for exams and believe that they "know their stuff." However, as the exam nears, these students usually experience a similar sequence of events. First, they begin to *doubt* their own knowledge—other students obviously know more than they do—they will *never* be able to pass. Second, the student tends to overvalue the importance of the test. That is, the test comes to be more than a measure of knowledge in a course; it becomes an indication of a student's self-worth. Facing a crucial task that reflects self-worth, feeling doubtful about one's knowledge—it's no wonder that test anxiety results.

It has been estimated that two out of ten students show adverse effects from anxiety about examinations (Ryle, 1969). Further, it has been our observation that, although general unhappiness and identity problems are more frequent among arts and humanities students, test anxiety seems to be much more frequent in the preprofessional group. An example of a severe reaction to a final exam will help you to appreciate the degree to which anxiety can affect some of your fellow students.

PERSONAL EXPERIENCE: *Test Anxiety*

Near the middle of a final exam in physics I was approached by a female student who looked disheveled, teary-eyed, and distant. She said that "it was all over for her, that it was done." She gave me the paper and on it were written a number of answers, none of which made any sense. On one question regarding the coefficient of friction she wrote, "My life is blue, my life is glue. You! You! You have done this to me. I hate you—I hate you—I hate you." Rather than let her leave, I asked her what was wrong. She said she had studied for four nights without sleep, that she had taken No-Doz to remain awake, that she had been crying and scared. She then started talking gibberish to me and was shaking and crying hysterically. I took her out of the room and to the campus psychological center. They told me later that she had had a psychotic reaction induced by uncontrollable test anxiety. She was hospitalized for three days and left school shortly thereafter.

Disorders Associated with Academic Progress

The disorders associated with academic progress differ from those of academic mechanics in that, in the latter, some specific skill deficit or blockage stops the student from satisfactorily fulfilling course requirements, whereas in the former, problems of motivation, competition, self-concept, and other emotional reactions intrude upon the student's functioning. In academic-progress disorders, the student usually has study skills and can take exams, but the desire to study or to do well on exams may be missing. Some students with academic-progress disorders may require either short- or long-term help. Since DSM-II doesn't clearly describe most college disorders, especially those of academic progress, we will describe these disorders in terms that are familiar to us and may be familiar to you.

Freshman Adjustment Reaction. The student who has a freshman adjustment reaction may be characterized by depression, severe homesickness, anxiety, restlessness, and withdrawal from or clinging to others. It frequently occurs in the student who shortly before was looked up to as a senior in high school and suddenly finds himself or herself a lonely freshman at the bottom of the collegiate academic and social heap. Further, the student usually has left home, parents, good friends, and familiar surroundings to take up residence in an often cold, sometimes old, frequently bare-walled dormitory from which he or she is daily to make forays into the unknown and potentially unfeeling and hostile world of the college. Although these students were probably "smart" in high school, now they are surrounded by the many "smart" kids in college. Now they may compare themselves with others and begin to worry that they might fail their courses or be dismissed.

The freshman adjustment reaction usually occurs during the first academic period (be it a quarter, semester, or trimester) and ends when the student learns that he or she can survive being away from home. The student usually finds out that he or she can do passing academic work and can make friends at college. The arrival of the new freshman class the following fall usually signals the end of the adjustment reaction. The student finally senses that he or she is *somebody* who is established within a new social milieu.

PERSONAL EXPERIENCE: *Freshman Adjustment Reaction*

I remember my first week at college. My parents drove me to the campus. It was rainy and dark. I felt sort of scared 'cause I'd come from a small town. All my high-school teachers said I'd do great at college. I wasn't so sure. What if they were wrong? What if I was really just a "big fish in a little ocean"? Well, the day was rainy, the other students walked around aimlessly as did I. I remember the sick feeling I had when my parents drove off and left me. I was left to grow up. Even with all the fighting and hate that went on in our house over the previous two years, and even though I couldn't wait to get away, I was scared, sad, unbelievably lonely. My roommate didn't seem very nice—he drank a lot, I guess 'cause he finally felt free also. I tried to talk to him, but he saw me as a "country" kid and he was from the "city," too sophisticated for me.

During the first week I went to the library every night to study. I didn't want to fall behind on anything. The guys in the dorm made fun of me. I went home the first weekend. There I felt secure, but I had to come back. I brought back clean clothes, some sandwiches, and some cookies my mother made. That night I went to the library as usual, but when I returned, my roommate and one of his sophisticated friends were in my room. I noticed the empty cookie bag on my bed. I didn't know why, but that really put me away. I thought, "My mother made those for me and they, who I don't like and who don't like me, enjoyed them and not me," and I started to scream at them and told them to get out. When they left I began to cry uncontrollably. My roommate went and got the dorm counselor who helped me then and for the rest of the quarter. I still feel a little sick when I look back on that first year in college.

Career Crisis. Beyond the period of the freshman adjustment reaction and somewhere during the second year of college, students typically are required to choose a major area of concentration and to begin developing some specific occupational goal. It is at this juncture that many students suffer severe depression and anxiety as a result of what we call a career crisis. Career crises don't occur in all students, for some are happy in their chosen direction. However, the number of such fortunate students is surprisingly small. It appears that the majority of students change their major (Nowicki & Duke, 1978). Of those who do experience career crises, there seem to be two major groups. The first type of career crisis occurs in the student who wants desperately to pursue a specific goal—say, dentistry—but who, owing to poor grades, has little chance of gaining admission to professional school. The other sort of career-crisis students differ from the first type in that they are typically doing well academically, but may be in the wrong program. Frequently, students in the wrong program have succumbed to family or social pressures to "follow in Dad's footsteps" or to be a doctor or a lawyer to please someone. These students' crises then usually revolve about two facts: first, they don't want to spend the rest of their lives doing something they don't like or want to do; and second, they may not be able to tell their parents that they don't want to spend their lives doing something they don't like or want to do.

The results of either type of career crisis can be anxiety, depression, worry, argumentativeness, and self-doubt. Many times, parents only find out that their child's career choice is a problem as a result of talking with deans or counselors who have tried to help the student through the crisis.

Senior Anticipatory Adulthood Reaction. Although usually respected by the college junior, sophomore, and freshman, the college senior is not without special stresses. In what we have termed the *senior anticipatory adulthood reaction,* the college senior who has enjoyed the "protection" of college for four years and who has yet to face the full-time responsibilities of career, productivity, and adulthood begins to experience anxiety and depression. Although not a frequent disorder, when seen, this pattern is typified by sadness about leaving the sanctuary of academic life, by fear of failure, constriction, and loss of youthful status. Of course, there are those who resolve these problems by going on to graduate school, thereby putting off adulthood for several more years; but if the student remains basically unprepared to assume adult responsibilities, the reaction can take place after graduate school as well.

Competition Reactions. Unlike the first three college-student reactions, which are tied to various crucial time periods in the undergraduate's development, the competition reaction cuts across age groups. Generally, competition may vary in importance from college to college and from department to department within a college. Some students thrive on competition, and others can be hurt badly by it. The competition reactions we have observed are often maladaptive responses to competition characterized by patterns such as suspiciousness, withdrawal from friends and fellow students, apathy toward studies, and a questioning of the academic process. The student suffering from competition reaction often has been exposed to a kind of other student whom we call the *Competicus premedicus, Competicus predentus,* or *Competicus pregradschoolus* (all of these are varieties of *Competicus preprofessionalus*). Of course, these are the preprofessional students who are striving to enter medical, dental, and graduate schools.

With the number of spaces in professional schools very limited, and the number of applicants growing larger, the chance of gaining admission to professional training seems slimmer than ever. As a result, although there was a time when only the specific aptitude test taken in the third or fourth year of college was seen as crucial in gaining admission, now *every* test and *every* evaluation can be seen as crucial. Even a weekly biology lab quiz can take on immense importance. Some students won't lend their notebooks to others who may have missed a lecture because of illness; there have been instances in which pointers marking structures to be identified on biology lab quizzes have been deliberately moved. "Why tell somebody else something you know? If it's on the test and you know it and he doesn't, you'll get a higher grade!"

Although not so widespread as many students would have us believe, "cut-throat" college competition does exist and does damage a number of students. Unfortunately, we in college counseling centers only see the students who are hurt or have given up in the face of extreme competition. We wish that we could also try to help the competitors, for somewhere they have lost something as well—seeing only our goals often blinds us to those who are standing beside us.

EXPLANATIONS

The task of explaining the sources of specific disorders among college students is not an easy one. As you have seen from our descriptions, the majority of the disturbances seem to be related to specific levels of college, career decisions, or preexisting psychiatric patterns. However, it is clear that the college student is living through a time of life often fraught with tensions, upheavals, and turmoil. The characteristics of this period may contribute to the vulnerability of many college students to the types of disorders we have described. As was true of adolescence, college age is often a time of growth, of confusion, and of specific developmental tasks. Or is it? We will look at two opposing views. First is the view that the college student is in a protracted or extended adolescence. A second theory is that college-age people are in a stage of life different and separable from adolescence—a stage of life called *youth*.

College Age as Protracted Adolescence

The concept that problems of people between 18 and 30 are the result of an extended adolescence is based upon the belief that some people leave adolescence chronologically before they are ready psychologically. In other words, many people of college age haven't completely resolved adolescent confusion, haven't established social, sexual, or personal identity, are still battling parents for freedom, and the like. The result of these incomplete adolescent tasks can be that difficulties are carried over into the college years (Ryle, 1969).

Entering college may be seen as a major transitional step toward adulthood, a step in which the authority of parents may be replaced in the student's mind by the less frequently used, yet nevertheless present, power of the college administration. Some people, therefore, view student unrest and rebellion as a continuation and displacement of incomplete adolescent rebellion. Problems among college students can then be seen as reflecting a lack of adequate role development in adolescence. According to the protracted-adolescence theory, when problems arise for the college student, the symptoms will "generally take the form of a re-enactment in the present situation of those conflicts not resolved in earlier stages" (Ryle, 1969, p. 27). College age, then, may be a continuation of adolescence—a late adolescence, if you will. Those remaining out of the mainstream of adulthood, those who don't begin careers immediately after high school, those whom we call "college students" are—according to the protracted-adolescence theory—destined to continue their adolescence long after their peers have made the transition to adult productivity and adjustment.

College Age as the Separate Life Stage of "Youth"

Many people are not comfortable with the concept of a 22-year-old still being in a protracted adolescence. One such person is Kenneth Keniston (1970, 1975), who has noted that, although many college-age people are indeed "victims of stretched adolescence, many others are less impelled by juvenile grandiosity than by a rather accurate analysis of the perils of injustices of the world in which they live" (1975, p. 304). For Keniston, modern society is markedly different from the one in which Hall (1904) first noted the emergence of adolescence as a separate stage of life. With the increased emphasis on advanced education, there is a delay of entry into adulthood for an increasingly large number of young people. Keniston notes that, whereas in 1900 there were only 238,000 college students, in the 1980s an estimated 10 million people will be enrolled in U.S. colleges. It may be difficult to say that these 10 million will all be protracted adolescents, and it probably will be impossible to say that all of their problems are due to unresolved adolescent rebellion, sexual confusion, and the like. According to Keniston, social change seems to have produced a new developmental period, a period he has named *youth*.

Like adolescence, youth is a transitional stage (not an end point) that occurs between the end of adolescence and the beginning of adulthood. Not all people will be involved in youth so clearly as the college student, who apparently delays entry into adulthood by enrolling for advanced education. Young people who begin work immediately after high school may "play the role" of the adult by day yet return to a countercultural "youthful" life-style by night and on weekends. According to Keniston, the presence of ten major themes determines youth, not necessarily college-student status alone.

Keniston outlines the following defining characteristics of youth:

1. *Tension between self and society.* Whereas the adolescent typically is struggling to define who he or she is, the youth usually *knows* and often recognizes great disparity between his or her self and the larger society.
2. *Pervasive ambivalence.* Ambivalence may be felt toward *self* and *society.* Rejection of the adolescent self may result in efforts at transformation of the self through meditation, drugs, religion, and the like. Ambivalence also occurs between the autonomous self and the socially involved self.
3. *The wary probe.* Serious forays into the adult world characterize youth. Adolescent probes or experimental youthful probes can lead to permanent commitment. Self-probes begin as well— "What are my strengths, weaknesses, vulnerabilities?"
4. *Alternating estrangement and omnipotentiality.* Feelings of isolation, absurdity, or unreality in an interpersonal social and phenomenological world may occur. "Who am I?" "Why am I here?" Also common are feelings of omnipotentiality—of total freedom, of being able to change or do anything, of being able to change others' lives completely, to do the socially impossible.
5. *Refusal of socialization.* In youth, earlier socializations may be criticized and questioned; the conformity of adolescence may be rejected. Attempts may be made to probe new social rules and to resist "capitulating."
6. *Emergence of youth-specific identities.* Youthful identities usually don't pass so quickly as those of adolescence or become so rigid as those of the adult. The identities may last from a few months to as many as ten years and include attachment to groups such as hippies, radicals, Moon children, and the like. Some youth-specific identities may be maintained as foundations for later life, but most seem to be abandoned.
7. *Valuing of movement and change.* Youth *requires* change; staying in one place physically or psychologically for too long often results in tension and imbalance. There are needs to move the self (that is, to grow); needs to move others (for example, attempts at political change); and needs to move through the world (to travel with great restlessness). Stasis seems to produce terror.
8. *Halting of movement may be seen as "death."* The greatest fear of youth probably is being unable to change, to "lose one's essential vitality." In some cases, suicide may be preferable to loss of movement potential or failure to effect desired changes.
9. *Adults may be viewed as "static" nonbeings.* Youths often see growing up as a cessation of living. The slower developmental changes of adulthood may be seen as complete stoppage; growing up may be a feared and avoided event.

10. *Emergence of youthful counterculture.* In hopes of staving off adulthood, solidarity with other youths is often established. Specific groups and entire youth cultures may develop so that deliberate distance from the existing social order can be maintained.

Keniston notes that youths tend to view adulthood as marked by "stasis, decline, foreclosure and death." However, he also indicates that youth may anticipate adulthood eagerly, because in adulthood there usually are financial security, career productivity, and so forth. Youth is thus a confusing time, a time that, according to Keniston, is a psychological stage not rigidly equated with any specific age range. It is a time of radicalism, of social action, a time when the themes of adolescent development may be outgrown but the commitment to adulthood not yet made.

Having known college students for many years, we believe in Keniston's conceptualization. It seems to be an accurate description of the majority of college students. Indeed, many of the problems we described earlier in this chapter can be understood in terms of Keniston's ten themes. For example, the existential crisis may be related to the sense of estrangement described in theme 4; the career crises are most likely affected by the pervasive ambivalence in theme 2, and so on. We encourage you to look at yourselves within the framework of Keniston's "youth" stage. What about it? Are you a protracted adolescent? Or do you consider yourself in a very different stage of development from people in high school?

TREATMENTS

In this section, we will first describe the general differences between therapy with college students and therapy with other people. We will then describe and give examples of individual therapy, group therapy, behavioral therapy, and community approaches with college students.

General Characteristics

Although most forms of traditional psychotherapy, group therapy, and behavioral therapy (all to be discussed in more detail in Section VIII) may be applicable to the college student, there are a number of differences between the college population and the general population that are worthy of mention. Treating the college student can be very different from treating the working person of the same age or the bulk of the rest of society. Not only are most college students in a specialized, highly structured and scheduled environment, but, as a group, they tend to be more intelligent, more critical, more ready to change, and more difficult to impress with fancy titles and terms. Based upon these and other special qualities of the college student, Whittington (1963) has noted a number of general characteristics of college-student therapy. First of all, change usually is more rapid among college students: the average number of therapy sessions is about five (Nowicki & Duke, 1978; Whittington, 1963), whereas for other groups the number is typically much higher. Further, rather than awaiting the establishment of trust and rapport, college students tend to be more open and self-disclosing earlier in therapy. Third, college students, with their youth, vitality, and frequent charm, can be quite attractive to young graduate-student therapists (and even professors!) and therefore often present special problems in treatment.

In addition to rapid change, greater openness, and possible attractiveness, college students tend to experience more extreme reactions to their therapists than people in the general population. Whereas a middle-aged client will generally feel somewhat positive or somewhat negative toward his or her therapist, college students have been known to experience deep love for the therapist and the very next day to absolutely hate the helper. Another difference is that therapy with college students may be especially difficult owing to the campus skepticism that often surrounds "shrinks" and to the fact that some college-student clients may know a great deal about psychology, psychiatry, and personality theory. A last difference is that there are often times in the college student's life when situational variables such as finals, midterms, papers, and the like may interfere with the smooth progress of therapy. This effect of scheduling upon psychotherapy can be critically felt when therapy must terminate prematurely due to the end of the school year, spring vacation, and the like. Therapists working with other sectors of the population rarely have to "say good-bye for the summer."

In addition to the points made by Whittington, the availability of psychological help to the college student is an important facet of college life. Most people in the 18–30 age group don't have access to such facilities as college counseling centers and campus mental-health centers. At these centers, college students usually can find immediate and competent help with any of the problems we described earlier. However, many centers don't offer treatment for psychotic disturbances, although they do help severely disturbed students get to places that can help them. Typical counseling centers may offer vocational guidance, group therapy, individual therapy, abilities testing, intellectual testing, and the like. Center staffs usually are composed of professionally trained psychotherapists and advanced students in the helping professions. Of course, the quality and variety of care will vary from campus to campus, and the main type of treatment offered will differ. We will now describe some of the types of treatment that may be found in a typical college counseling center.

Individual Therapy

Individual therapy with the college student usually involves a one-to-one relationship between a troubled student and a therapist. Meeting once or twice a week for a relatively brief period (10–20 weeks), the therapist and student-client attempt to use their relationship to ease the problems for which the student first came for help. The theoretical perspective of the therapist can vary widely, but currently popular modes of treatment (all of which are described more fully in Chapters 22 and 23) seem to be Gestalt therapy, reality therapy, and other approaches that fall under the general rubric of the humanistic-existential methods. Therapy with college students isn't always easy, as is demonstrated in the following excerpt from the fourth meeting with an individual-therapy client at a college counseling center:

> *Therapist:* OK, so how do you feel about that?
>
> *Client:* I don't like it! I mean, she tells me that she loves me and then turns around and goes out with Bob. Sheeit!
>
> *Therapist:* So you are very angry about what she did?
>
> *Client:* Wait a minute, Fred, do you think I'm dumb or something? You sit there "reflecting my feelings"! Christ, I know about Carl Rogers. "So you are very angry about what she did." Now I'm supposed to say, "Yes, I am" and go on from there and think that you empathize with me and care about me and unconditionally accept me.
>
> *Therapist:* What's this all about?
>
> *Client:* You tell me that you sincerely care about me. I have trouble believing it. I mean, you're a graduate student. You *have* to see me for a course. If I don't get better you fail or something. I don't believe you care about me—my case, maybe—but not me.
>
> *Therapist:* You're really angry at me and I don't really know why. I wish you'd put aside all this stuff about Rogers and cases and all and tell me what your feelings are toward me.
>
> *Client:* Fred, you're only four years older than I am. How can you help me? You're a student also. You're hung up on exams, courses, profs. How the hell can you help me?
>
> *Therapist:* I can if you let me try. I can if you stop seeing me as a student, as a young person, as a grade-grubber. I'm me, Fred—relate to me and not all the things I am or could be. I think you relate to other people in the same way you're doing to me now. You jump at their motives and don't look at them. Now you started the conversation with a gripe about Janet; how is your reaction to me similar to the reactions you had to Janet's going out with Bob?

As you can see from this excerpt, individual therapy with college students can be very challenging. You saw how the student seemed to find it difficult to relate to the graduate-student therapist because he (the client) felt too much like him. However, on the other side of the coin, the college student may see a fully trained professional who is also a professor. In that situation, the student often can't relate to a therapist who may be seen as distant, powerful, and not a helping person. The large number of mixed roles on the college campus can produce problems in helping the college student in individual therapy.

Group Therapy

Group therapy, a second major type of treatment offered in college counseling centers, differs from individual treatment in that several students meet with a therapist simultaneously. As was the case in individual treatment, a variety of groups based on different theoretical approaches usually is available to the student. Assignment to specific groups is made on the basis of preliminary interviews and evaluation of the student's particular problems. Groups usually meet once a week for an hour and a half and may extend anywhere from 10 to 20 weeks or more. Cotherapists frequently lead college-student groups, with one therapist perhaps being more advanced in his or her training than the other.

With regard to the special nature of college-student therapy groups, there are several things of note. For example, many college students have been in groups before and may bring some positive and negative expectations with them to their therapy groups; these expectations can be either helpful or destructive. In addition, many college students know about group therapy and may resist standard group techniques that are effective with most other people. One result of this resistance can be hostile, open challenges to the competence of the leader. A third characteristic of college-student groups is that they are often marked by frequent early termination (also called "quitting"), and by frequent additions of new members as the academic year progresses. Further, the fact that students, especially on small campuses, frequently see each other between group sessions can make it difficult to keep all group business confidential. Sometimes conflicts begun and not resolved in a group session will be resolved between sessions, cutting off the majority of members from being involved in important group interactions (Brandes & Gardner, 1973). Some of the special characteristics of college-student groups may be seen in the following excerpt from a group held in a college counseling center:

Jim: I really like the way this group is run.
Therapist: Are you being sarcastic?
Jim: Of course.
Sue: You're always complaining. I think this is a good group.
Jim: Well, I've been in groups before and . . .
Art: There he goes, telling us how much better he is than we are— "I've been in groups before!"
Therapist: It seems that you use your being in groups before to keep yourself out of this one.

Jim: If it gets to be good I'll expend my energy and take part. Right now I'm just watching.

Bob: Goddammit, Jim, you pompous ass, I get so mad at you. You sit there and watch us. Who the hell do you think you are?

Art: Ditto. You really have a lot of nerve. We sit here and expose ourselves. You sit smugly by.

Therapist: What does the group think we can do about Jim's feeling toward us?

Art: Ask him to leave.

Sue: But he's here for a reason. Maybe Jim can't admit he wants help.

Therapist: Jim?

Jim: I'm just listening.

Therapist: Let's let Jim listen for a while. When he feels he can share his real feelings with us we'll be ready to hear them. Bob, what's been going on with you?

Behavioral Therapy

In addition to individual and group "talk" therapies, behavioral therapy is frequently used in the college counseling center. The application of laboratory-derived principles of learning to the alteration of problem behavior, behavior therapy differs from traditional individual and group therapies in its focus on behavior as opposed to feelings. By using systematic variation of reinforcement, punishment, and extinction, behavior therapists can increase or decrease the frequencies of many desirable or undesirable behaviors (see Chapter 22). Although a number of college-student problems are existential and therefore not easily treated by behavior therapy, some "habit" problems, such as test anxiety, may be altered by behavioral methods.

Many college counseling centers offer several approaches to the behavioral treatment of test anxiety. Kotska and Galassi (1974) have described two such behavioral approaches. In *systematic desensitization*, groups of eight to ten students usually meet weekly. Through the repeated association of physical relaxation with thoughts of taking exams, these subjects can learn to face tests much more calmly. *Covert reinforcement* (Cautela, 1970a), a second approach, involves the students' imagining that they are without anxiety during test situations and, following these thoughts, "rewarding" themselves by imagining an especially pleasurable scene (natural, gastronomic, or sexual). Kotska and Galassi reported that both of these techniques were useful in reducing test anxiety.

In addition to desensitization and covert reinforcement, extinction of fear and establishment of an expectation of success in exams are used in the treatment of severe test anxiety, as illustrated by the following case history.

The client was a fifth-year graduate student in history who had attempted three times to take and pass his Ph.D. qualifying exams. Each time, he had failed even to finish the timed test owing to his inability to be satisfied with any one particular answer. As a result of his dissatisfaction, he spent most of the exam time rewriting one or two questions and worrying about possible imperfections. He was told that he would be required to *complete* and pass the next exam he was given; if he didn't, he would be dropped from the Ph.D. program.

Treatment involved specific training in relaxation so that he could control his tension during exams. Next, a series of ten (count them—ten) Ph.D. qualifying exams was prepared with the help of the more than cooperative history-department faculty. Each week for ten weeks, this student came to the psychological center and took a three-hour Ph.D. qualifying exam. During the exam, the therapist monitored his behavior, requiring the student to divide the test into time units and not to allow himself to work on an item for more than the allotted time. In this way, his finishing the exam was guaranteed, and he did so by the end of the fifth week. In addition, he learned to outline the answers to each question more efficiently before writing the full essay; using this method, he found he was quite satisfied with his work.

One week after the tenth practice exam, he took the "eleventh" exam. He passed quite easily and reported no difficulty with tension, problems in timing, or inability to be satisfied with an answer. He had learned through his practice exams that he could easily schedule himself and finish, and that he could complete the essays satisfactorily (*not* perfectly) within the time allotted to him.

Behavioral techniques such as these are being more and more widely used with college students. Numerous specific blockages, from fear of blood in a premedical student to fear of rats in a psychology graduate student, may be relieved rapidly by behavioral therapy.

Community Approaches

The treatment approaches we have discussed thus far focus on the problems of the individual alone or of the individual with a small group of peers. Community approaches, however, focus on the college community itself as the client. Moreover, the individual, group, and behavioral treatment approaches primarily evolve from a basic therapeutic position of passivity toward the student. That is, the therapist usually waits in his or her office for the troubled student to come to the counseling center, where attempts are made to "fix" the trouble. In contrast, the basic position of the advocates of community approaches is more active intervention. In community approaches, workers go out to offer help where the students are, on the students' home ground, and, it is hoped, at the time when students need it. Although many psychologists who espouse a community-intervention approach to the solution of mental-health problems are in college settings, surprisingly few adequate community programs are found on campuses. It may be, as Brigante (1965) pointed out, that many members of the academic community have a negative view of community efforts, so that cooperation may be difficult to achieve.

There have been a number of attempts to find community sources of student problems and to identify student problems soon enough to make early intervention possible (Webster & Harris, 1958; A. Wolff, 1969). One exemplary college community-intervention program has been developed at the University of Florida (Barger, 1963; Barger, Larson, & Hall, 1965). The first phase of this intervention program involved a number of studies to ascertain the sources of stress and strain, as well as the sources of relief, present in the college environment. For example, it was found that particular courses produced a high degree of stress around the time of midterm exams and that procedures such as athletic events, athletic participation, and concerts tended to relieve some of the stresses these difficult courses produced.

In the second stage of the Florida intervention program, students who were most likely to have problems were identified. To accomplish this, tests were administered to all incoming freshmen. On the basis of these test results, plus the information gleaned from previous studies concerning which students are likely to develop psychological problems in college, students who might need help were identified. Through private correspondence, these students were offered psychological counseling. In addition, psychologists worked with residence-hall counselors and faculty members to make them aware of the signs of potential problems in the students with whom they came in contact. The interventionists offered students a variety of treatments ranging from crisis hospitalization to chemotherapy. True to the active stance these and other community interventionists usually take, all services were offered on a no-wait basis.

In addition to programs initiated by professionals on college campuses, some community-treatment interventions have been initiated by students themselves. Most of these student-initiated interventions involve the development of hotlines or peer-counseling programs. In these projects, students meet the needs of fellow students who want someone to listen to them when they are troubled. Especially prevalent during the late sixties, the number of student-initiated programs seems to have decreased, perhaps because, in response to the needs of students, professionals now usually provide such crisis counseling.

Although the number of student-initiated interventions has decreased in recent years, the use by mental-health professionals of undergraduate and graduate students as helping agents has increased. Usually in such programs, students are asked to volunteer. These student volunteers are then trained in telephone counseling and role-playing. Meetings are scheduled to discuss the kinds of problems being called in (see Table 20-2) and the methods for dealing with them. Telephone hotlines are usually manned at times such as late afternoons, evenings, and weekends, when

Table 20-2. *Problems presented by telephone callers to Campus Crisis Center at Southern Colorado State College over three quarters*

Problem Area	Number of Calls	Percentage
Dating	66	29
Family	40	19
Loneliness	28	12
Pregnancy	22	9
Classes	21	9
Finances	8	3
Marriage	7	3
Drugs	6	2
Alcohol	5	2
Other[a]	28	12
Total	231	100

[a]Such as obesity, insomnia, selective service, employment, religion, housing.

From "Anatomy of a Campus Crisis Center," by B. J. Tucker, D. Megenity, and L. Virgil, *Personnel and Guidance Journal*, 1970, *48*(5), 343–348. Copyright 1970 by the American Personnel and Guidance Association. Reprinted by permission.

other helping agencies are often closed. It is difficult to evaluate such programs formally, but hotline facilities have been very helpful on campuses. Besides helping the troubled student, these programs give the student volunteers positive experiences within the community.

Other programs have been more radical in their intervention than the addition of a hotline agency. For example, at Kansas State University, students with a poor chance of completing their college programs were identified and offered the opportunity to live in a halfway house with a number of students who were likely to finish their programs without difficulty (Sinnett, Weisner, & Freiser, 1967). The residents of this halfway house were offered easy access to counseling help from project directors, and within the house there were a number of planned and some unplanned group activities that focused on increasing effective communication. The use of this therapeutic community appeared to be effective at least in reducing the dropout rate of those who participated as compared with those who did not.

Such community approaches may hold much promise for dealing with problems on college campuses. If the college environment can be changed to make it less stressful and more reinforcing, much will have been done to reduce the occurrence of disordered behavior in college students.

CONCLUDING COMMENTS

This chapter provides evidence that there are specific problems associated with the college experience. These problems must be faced by college counselors, deans, and faculty, whose responsibility it is to make the college experience a positive one. These people should realize that the "mental health" of an elite group of young men and women is in their hands, and they should exert all efforts to reduce the possibilities of psychological stress. The temporary or permanent loss of any of these young people because of psychological problems may reduce their potential to contribute to society as a whole and to themselves as individuals. We have described some procedures used to help students grapple with the difficulties of the college situation, but we believe more should be done. More college counseling services need to work with the administration to reduce stress in college dormitories, classes, and elsewhere. College problems will occur, but the sooner they are faced, the sooner they will be resolved. College students are among our brightest citizens, and we expect much from them. They deserve and will probably make good use of any help and support we can give them. We hope that, with reduced stresses and more available help, more college students will be able to realize their potential.

CHAPTER SUMMARY CHART

This chapter has dealt with the group of people to which most of our readers belong. Our discussion of the disorders among college students included:

Descriptions	Explanations	Treatments
Disorders associated with nonacademic concerns:	College as extended adolescence	Treating college students differs from treating others
Identity crisis	College age as a separate stage of life called youth	Individual therapy
Suicide		Group therapy
Apathy reaction		Behavioral methods
Disorders of academic mechanics:		Community approaches
Study disabilities		
"Mental blocks"		
Test anxiety		
Disorders of academic progress:		
Freshman adjustment reaction		
Career crisis		
Senior adulthood reaction		
Competition reactions		

CHAPTER 21
THE ELDERLY

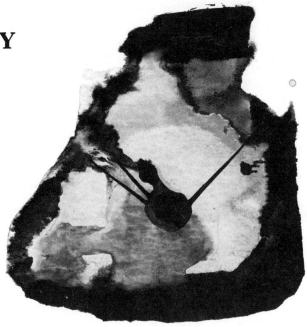

Most of our readers can probably identify easily with college students, but the elderly are often an unfamiliar and frightening group of people. Many young people view the old with feelings ranging from the neutral to the negative. The elderly are perhaps our largest group of alienated people. Simply living a great number of years places one automatically into this special group, with its own unique set of problems and disorders. The difficulties of the elderly need to be highlighted here because their numbers are increasing very rapidly. The number of Americans over the age of 65 has increased from 3.1 million in 1900 to an estimated 25 million in 1980 (Goldfarb, 1974). Further, since about one out of every three elderly people has some diagnosable mental disturbance, about half of all mental-hospital beds are occupied by patients 65 or older (Juel-Nielson, 1975).

In this chapter, psychological disorders among the elderly will be divided into the functionally and the organically based. Following descriptions of these two categories, we will describe several theories regarding unsuccessful and successful adjustment to later life. Last, we will describe some of the kinds of therapeutic efforts made in recent years by geriatric psychologists and psychiatrists in their attempts to treat people who, far too often, have been considered hopeless and untreatable.

DESCRIPTIONS

The disorders of the elderly may be categorized as either functional or organic. In the functional disorders, psychological stresses of aging and adjustments to limitations on daily life may be considered the primary sources of observed symptomatology. In the organic disorders, physical damage or natural deterioration is considered to be the primary cause of behavioral change.

Functional Disorders

Functional disorders among the aged can include all of the disturbances found among people of any age. However, given the greater incidence of such disturbances among the old, we must consider the special circumstances leading to the increased susceptibility of the elderly to psy-

The experience of increasing isolation and loneliness is a major problem of the aged in our society. (Photo by George Lazar.)

chological aberrations. In recent years, the study of the aging process has developed into a specific subdiscipline of psychology and psychiatry (Birren, 1964; Eisdorfer & Lawton, 1973; Howells, 1975; Verwoerdt, 1976). The knowledge gleaned from geriatric psychology and psychiatry has contributed greatly to more accurate perception of the elderly and their experience of being different. For example, Fozard and Thomas (1975) have reached several conclusions regarding the psychological characteristics of the elderly. Many of these conclusions can serve as guides to "normally occurring deviations" among the old. Among them are:

1. Mental abilities will deteriorate as a person passes 50, particularly to the extent that tasks are speeded.
2. Personality is remarkably stable over the adult years.
3. People tend to appear more rigid in thinking with age.
4. Older people are more likely to be introverted, controlled, less flexible, less energetic, lower in need to achieve and to socialize.
5. There is no such thing as *the* "old personality"; different people age in different ways.
6. Adaptation to current environment is usually fine; ability to adapt to new environments is impaired.
7. *Age is not the crucial variable in aging.*
8. The interdependence between a person and the environment increases with age.

When "normally occurring deviations" such as these result in significant emotional and personal stress, more severe disturbance can occur. Although all types of functional disorders are possible, the most frequent types of psychological disorders are the paranoid, depressive, and confusional states. Symptoms can range from mild to severe enough to warrant hospitalization. A listing of the types of symptoms typically seen among the elderly is given in Table 21-1.

Table 21-1. *Some symptoms observed in elderly disturbed people (based on Verwoerdt, 1976, and Kimmel, 1974)*

Mood levels	may range from feeling "blue" or "down" to incapacitating depression
Appetite	may range from poor to "none at all"
Sleep	may range from increased desire to sleep or be in bed to a refusal to leave bed day or night
Energy levels	may range from increased fatigue to either extreme slowing or hyperactivity
Self-confidence	may range from weakened self-confidence to complete helplessness
Bodily concerns	may range from increased fear of illness and death to delusions of bodily change
Weight loss	may range from none to 20 pounds or more

Paranoid Persecutory States. Among the most frequent psychological disorders in the elderly are the *paranoid persecutory states*. When severe, the paranoid pattern may be classified as psychotic and called *paraphrenia*, or paranoid psychosis of old age. Paraphrenic people typically have few intellectual difficulties, but their thinking usually is characterized by delusions and hallucinations; they may also be passive or lack control over their actions (Weinberg, 1975). Persecutory ideas regarding the motives of family, friends, and hospital staff often play a large part in paraphrenic thought processes. The possibility of such persecutory ideas beginning and, once begun, sustaining themselves may be increased in the elderly because of normal losses in hearing and vision that tend to decrease the ability to monitor reliably what others are doing or saying.

Depressive States. Whereas the major symptom continuum in paraphrenia is suspiciousness, in the depressive states, feelings can range from the relatively mild symptoms of neurotic depression to the severity of symptoms such as nihilistic ideas and incapacitating sadness found in severe depression. Generally, the more severe the depression, the greater the possibility of suicide among the old. For example, Batchelor (1957) noted that the percentage of successful suicides increases with advancing age. In addition, just as younger men are usually more successful than younger women in completing suicide attempts, the ratio of men to women who end their own lives rises to a high of 12 to 1 by age 85. Many depressive suicides can be related to the stress created by the loss of a spouse. For example, Bunch (1972) reports that, during the four years following the death of a spouse, the likelihood of death by suicide is greater in the elderly than death from all other causes. If there is one key contributor to the psychological functioning of the elderly, it seems to be loss—loss of loved ones, status, abilities, security, and so forth.

Confusional States. Besides suspiciousness and depression, a third frequent psychological difficulty encountered in the elderly is the *confusional states* (Kral, 1975; M. Roth, 1955). Typically occurring in the absence of permanent organic damage, the confusional state usually follows an experience of acute stress, such as physical injury or death of a loved one. Symptoms of confusional states may include clouding of consciousness, lowered level of awareness of self and environment, and disorientation in time and place. As in the brain syndromes (Chapter 16), short-term memory may also be impaired. In mild cases, the confusional state usually remits in a few days or weeks, as the person copes successfully to reduce the precipitating stressors. In many ways, the confusional states resemble the delirium associated with acute brain syndrome.

Organic Disorders

Unlike the functional disorders we have described, the organic disorders *seem to be* related primarily to physical deterioration of the brain and nervous systems. The reason for our emphasis on the words *seem to be* will become clear as we describe these disorders, for the amount of actual brain deterioration may not be related to the severity of observed behavioral symptoms of many aged people. With this in mind, let us look at the two major forms of organic brain disorders associated with aging, *senile dementia* and *arteriosclerotic dementia*. Remember that *any* of the other brain syndromes (except the presenile dementias) can also occur in this age group.

Senile Dementia. Among its symptoms, senile dementia includes all of the characteristics of permanent mental deterioration described in Chapter 16. However, the irreversible mental deterioration in senile dementia is due primarily to insidious atrophy of the brain and nervous system as part of the aging process. Kolb (1973) notes that, at age 75, the brain may be only 55% of the size it was in young adulthood; this means there may be significantly fewer brain cells available to carry on effective mental function. In addition to the mental deterioration accompanying senile dementia are the physical signs of old age: wrinkled skin, failing vision and hearing, loss of weight, flaccid muscles, slowed gait, and tremulous hands and legs. The combination of physical signs of aging with the mental symptoms of deterioration most frequently form the basis for the diagnosis of senile dementia.

In each subtype of senile dementia, there is some specific characteristic in addition to general senility that demarcates the particular pattern. For example, *paranoid senile dementia* is characterized by delusions of persecution. In the *presbyophrenic type*, the patients seem to attempt to compensate for lack of memory with fantasies or fabricated stories (Korsakoff's syndrome). The presbyophrenic is generally cheery and talkative and doesn't seem aware of substituting fantasy for real memory. Senile dementia may also be of the *depressive* or *confused* types. It seems that the specific subtype of senile dementia that appears depends more upon the premorbid personality of the person than on any other single factor.

Arteriosclerotic Dementia. Commonly referred to as "hardening of the arteries," cerebral arteriosclerosis is known to be a common adjunct of the aging process. Unlike senile dementia, which is characterized by slow onset, arteriosclerotic dementia usually occurs quickly, often over a few weeks' time. Symptoms may include loss of awareness, restlessness, and hallucinations. Often, these symptoms abate after a short time, leaving the person intellectually impaired and progressively deteriorating. As time goes by, the signs of dementia and chronic disorder may begin to appear and the ceaseless progress of the disease makes itself known. Personality, emotional stability, problem-solving ability, and judgment can be adversely affected. Psychotic and other less severe mental symptoms also often accompany the course of arteriosclerotic dementia.

Although patterns of disordered behavior seen in many elderly people have often been associated with arteriosclerosis, recent opinion and evidence suggest that the relationship may not be so strong as previously thought. For example, Goldfarb (1974) states that "arteriosclerosis is *infrequently* the cause of psychotic disorders in the elderly." Geriatric psychiatrists and researchers (Ernst, Beran, Badash, Kosovsky, & Kleinhauz, 1977; Ernst & Badash, 1977) also have noted that some data based on autopsies have shown that arteriosclerosis isn't always found in people who were diagnosed as having arteriosclerotic dementia. Moreover, these same researchers also found that arteriosclerosis is often found in people who never showed symptoms supposedly associated with such damage. The data suggest that those who assume that most of the psychological disorders of the aged are physically based may be doing a great disservice to the elderly. This disservice may be reflected in the very high prevalence rates of mental disturbance and the relative lack of treatment for such disturbances in this age group.

EXPLANATIONS

The task of explaining the development of behavioral disorders in elderly people hasn't been an easy one. Explanation may have been confounded by the fact that many symptoms of disturbance among the aged can be caused by both physical and psychological factors. Thus, most theories dealing with the effects of aging usually talk about adaptation *given* physical deterioration as a natural component of aging. In this way, psychological reactions *to* deterioration may be considered and understood. The theories of the effects of aging are the foundation of the relatively new science known as *gerontology* (Tibbetts, 1960). In general, to the gerontological theorist, abnormality is the absence of successful adjustment to aging, the lack of what various theorists consider to be the crucial health-maintaining components of later life. We will describe several gerontological theories, each of which is characterized by a slightly different focus in its explanations of the development of disordered behavior among the old. However, the theories seem most applicable to the functional disorders of later life; the truly organic disorders are similar in effect and character to the chronic brain syndromes described in Chapter 16 and will not be considered further here.

Disengagement Theory

The basis of disengagement theory (Cumming, 1964; Cumming & Henry, 1961) is that, due to the mortality of man and the relative perma-

As this 70-year-old Vista worker shows, disengagement from society is not a necessary part of growing old. (Photo courtesy of Vista.)

nence of society, there comes a time when society must disengage itself from specific members who are approaching the end of their contributions to society. Usually there are rules, such as mandatory retirement ages and the like, that allow society to disengage itself effectively from its working members. Likewise, at some point in later life, individuals may also choose to disengage from society. Older people manifesting signs of increasing disengagement from society typically cease attending meetings of organizations, reduce visits to friends, stop going to movies, and the like.

The result of disengagement from society is frequently an increase in preoccupation with the self and withdrawal into a more and more limited lifespace. The withdrawal often leads to fewer social interactions, decreasing feelings of self-worth, and difficulties in adjustment. However, Atchley (1972) notes that not all disengagement produces problems. If society *and* the individual agree on the time of disengagement, good postdisengagement adjustment can be expected. If, however, society isn't ready to let go (forced engagement), or the person isn't ready to retire (forced disengagement), problems of psychological adjustment are more probable.

An example of the effects of forced disengagement may be seen in the following personal experience.

PERSONAL EXPERIENCE: *Forced Disengagement*

I worked for ——— for over 40 years. Never had more than one week out sick the whole time. But when I turned 65, I . . . and my friend Dan . . . had to retire—we had to. . . . No ifs, ands, or buts—company rules. I had no financial worries, I was actually pretty excited at the thought of doing whatever I wanted whenever I wanted—no whistle, no fighting the traffic in ——— each morning. Mary and I made plans for a trip to Mexico. I always wanted to go there. . . .

After we got back from the trip, it hit me. God, I was restless. I couldn't sit at home. I had to get out. I decided to get a part-time job. No dice—"Too old"—"Sorry, we need a younger man"—"You're retired, enjoy it!" Crap! Enjoy it. It drove me nuts. As I look back on it, that was the worst few days I ever spent. I felt like crying, like hitting somebody. The company didn't help; they said my pension was all they owed me. I started having trouble sleeping. I couldn't eat, lost weight (for a while my wife didn't mind that because I lost a lot of my beer belly). I felt real bad. . . .

This part-time job is a godsend. I pump gas a few hours a day. I keep active. I talk to people. I don't care about the money, but I feel like I'm back in the world!

Activity Theory

Whereas disengagement theory emphasizes a certain time for middle-age activities to end, *activity theory* (Havighurst, 1963) generally asserts that behavioral norms and requirements for old age *are the same* as for middle age and that sound adjustment to aging may be measured in terms of how much of middle-age activity is maintained or lost in old age. To activity theorists, older people may be said to be poorly adjusted if they manifest significant amounts of behavior other than that appropriate to middle age, such as gainful employment, social interaction, travel, and the like. Absence of these kinds of patterns can indicate old age and deterioration, and is usually accompanied by depression or other symptoms.

For many elderly people and their families, activity theory serves as a guide to late-life adjustment. Many of you probably have seen old people who try to maintain their more youthful, middle-aged appearances through clothing, cosmetic surgery, and the like. According to activity theory, their attempts to "hold on" may be motivated by the social "requirement" to remain middle-aged. Of course, we often react to such efforts of the elderly with derision and lack of understanding and feel that they should "act their age." However, when they *do* act their age, we often ignore them completely.

Continuity Theory

Instead of engagement with society or activity, *continuity theory* (Neugarten, 1964; Rosow, 1963) proposes that successful coping with aging is reflected in the ability of the elderly person to maintain continuity from adulthood to old age in habits, relationships, activities, and the like. For example, if a person has led an extremely sedentary life, onset of physical slowing and loss of energy may cause little stress. On the other hand, in a person with a history of high levels of physical activity, loss of energy represents a discontinuity that could lead to poor adjustment and depression. Continuity theory can explain, therefore, why the same life occurrence can have such varying effects on different people. The theory also accounts nicely for the fact that no two people age in exactly the same way.

One continuity theorist (Rosow, 1963) proposes that certain crucial areas of change occur in the later years and that two specific factors determine how people adjust to these changes. The types of changes noted by Rosow include new occupations, changing relationships with others, role conflicts, and the like. The first factor that determines how well a person adjusts to change is *continuity versus discontinuity;* that is, is the changed situation continuous with (not necessarily identical to) the old? A second factor deals with the *subjective feeling of loss or gain* resulting from the changes. For example, if a person hates work, retirement probably will be a gain because it reduces negative stimulation. However, if a person's life is built around work, then retirement may be a traumatic event. Different histories can lead two people to react quite differently to the change of occupational status. The ability to explain individual differences in reaction to a similar event makes continuity theory very useful.

Isolation Theory

Unlike the three theories of the effects of aging we have already described, *isolation theory* attempts to describe the specific mechanism by which the deleterious effects of aging may occur. In brief, isolation theory holds that the elderly person experiences isolation as a result of factors such as disengagement, discontinuity, illness, death of friends, disinterest of family, and so forth. Typically the person may be isolated from the sources of stimulation to which he or she was accustomed throughout adult life. As a result, psychological changes associated with sensory deprivation may begin to appear. These changes include loss of interest in surroundings, increased focus on internal physical and mental processes, loss of ability to concentrate, increased anxiety, and restlessness (Freedman, Grunebaum, & Greenblatt, 1961; Zuckerman, Albright, Marks, & Miller, 1962).

Experimentally induced sensory deprivation can produce psychiatric symptoms in people of all ages, and isolation theorists propose that naturally occurring isolation is the source of deprivation in the old. For example, loss of hearing and vision can increase the chances of developing paranoid ideas. You probably know how unnerving it can be to think that someone is saying something important that you wish to hear and yet cannot. Hearing deficits often cause the elderly to feel isolated and frightened, and when questions such as "What did you say?" are met with "Oh, never mind, it's not important," fears and suspicions may be strengthened. So powerful can be the effects of isolation that some geriatric psychiatrists (Ernst & Badash, 1977) have concluded: "Isolation is the major cause of psychiatric disturbances in the aged. The frequency of organically based disturbances is small compared to those caused by loss of contact with the world and by stimulus deprivation" (p. 14). As you will see in the following section, those who support the isolation theory have a unique way of dealing with maladjustment among the elderly.

TREATMENTS

Treatment techniques for psychological disturbances among old people are primarily based upon the theoretical conceptualizations we have just outlined. However, the range of therapies is limited for several reasons. First, psychotherapy for the elderly was long thought to be a chancy affair, so few methods were developed over the years. Further, most theoretical and therapeutic research has been directed at other age groups, because psychotherapy seemed to many to be a more useful procedure for the young than for the old. Finally, many people (and that includes some psychotherapists) are afraid of old people (Bunze, 1972) and avoid being with or working with them; given a choice between a young person and an elderly one, many therapists, consciously or unconsciously, would probably choose to work with the younger. The relative scarcity of professional gerontologists and geriatric psychologists and psychiatrists attests to the avoidance of treatment of the aged.

Why Aren't More Old People Treated?

Before describing the specific therapies available for the elderly, we would like to consider why, until recently, few people 65 or older ever received treatment for psychological disturbances. Blau and Berezin (1975) have addressed themselves to this problem and have generated ten basic reasons why professionals may avoid treating this age group:

1. *Stereotype of rigidity:* All old people are set in their ways. "You can't teach an old dog new tricks."
2. *Stereotype of homogeneity:* All old people are alike. If you can't treat one you can't treat any.
3. *Stereotype of untreatability:* Disorders of aging are organic. They are insidious and progressive and nothing can be done about them—Why try?

4. *"Wastebasketing syndrome"*: All emotional symptoms of old age *are due to old age.* Depression in an old person is due to aging; in a young person it is due to something treatable.
5. *"Family rejection myth"*: The rejection of the old person by his or her family is the cause of the problems if they are psychological. Blame them. Don't think that other mental disturbances are possible.
6. *Gerontophobia:* I don't feel comfortable with old people.
7. *Therapists have a need to fully cure people:* The chances of fully curing an old person are much smaller than a younger one.
8. *Nothing will help:* Why bother. Their brains are deteriorating.
9. *Relatives and friends avoid help:* Relatives of old people do not seek help for them. If a young person is depressed, the family takes him to a therapist; if an old person is depressed, the family says, "What can you do; he's getting old."
10. *Denial on the part of children:* Children of the aged deny the need for help for their parents because it signals a change of life style for them.

The ten "excuses" we have just delineated are beginning to be seen for what they are—excuses—and the treatment of the aged is becoming a significant part of the overall services of the mental-health movement. There are several therapeutic approaches that show promise of being effective.

Group Therapy

Group therapy appears to be a basic mode of psychological treatment for the aged. One reason is that there aren't enough geriatric workers available to provide individual treatment. In addition, being in a group of one's peers seems to benefit an elderly person more than being forced to work individually with a younger therapist. Further, the sense of belonging found in a group often re-creates and replaces the sense of family that many institutionalized old people have lost.

The variety of group methods used in the treatment of the elderly has been reviewed by W. Klein, Lesham, and Furman (1965). Although the types of groups possible seem to be limited only by need and imagination, we will describe a few specific examples for you.

Socialization and discussion groups. In these groups, practicality is the major focus. Practical problems of money, retirement, children, and religion are discussed.

Remotivation groups. For severely withdrawn patients, remotivation groups involve a high staff-patient ratio (1:2 or 1:1). Nonthreatening interventions are used to "reawaken" the interests of members.

Predischarge groups. For people recovering from physical ailments and for other long-term patients, such groups deal with the anxiety of leaving the hospital, taking buses, going to the store, and so on.

Foster-grandparent programs show that there is no mandatory retirement age for love. (Photo by Joan Kelley courtesy of Vista.)

Conjoint and family therapy groups. Patients and their family members meet regularly to discuss problems of living together.

Patient-government groups. Patients govern their wards through a democratic process, giving them an increased sense of self-worth and a humanistic atmosphere.

Grooming and homemaker groups. Primarily for females, these groups rekindle interest in good appearance and domestic arts.

Inspirational groups. For religious people, groups with spiritual content use religious bonds and feelings to reawaken a verve for life. *Foster-grandparent groups.* Patients gain self-value by serving as foster grandparents for hospitalized children or for community children in need of companionship.

The list of possible groups for the elderly seems endless. We wouldn't go so far as to classify all of the groups we mentioned above as formal "group therapy" as we describe it in Chapter 23. However, since these people are seen in groups and *are* helped, *group therapy* may be an appropriate name for these approaches to the problems of the aged.

Sensory Stimulation

Whereas many of the types of groups for the elderly are based more on the "nuts and bolts" needs of living, sensory-stimulation therapy is based upon the idea that, if sensory deprivation can be counteracted, the

Physical activities can help overcome withdrawal and stimulate communication among people. (Photo by Joseph Czarnecki.)

symptoms of disturbance caused by that deprivation will disappear. Early evidence for this point of view was reported by Heron (1964), who studied psychological symptoms in people hospitalized for physical illnesses. Among those who experienced onset of symptoms due to sensory deprivation, no treatment other than sensory stimulation could effectively alter the behavioral patterns of anxiety, suspiciousness, and loss of concentration that resulted from the deprivation.

The formal application of sensory stimulation to the aged in an attempt to counteract the effects of isolation was proposed by Leona Richman (1969), an occupational therapist specializing in work with geriatric patients. Richman believes that the symptoms of schizophrenia and paranoia in the elderly are produced by sensory deprivation. To overcome the passive acceptance of sensory loss that may be manifest in old people who don't adjust well, Richman has designed a program of sensory stimulation designed to offset the symptoms she sees as caused by deprivation and to bring the elderly person back into the world.

Stimulation includes group exercises to induce awareness of body parts, touching of objects, smelling of odors, attending to varying sounds, and concentrated "looking." Many of Richman's techniques seem to have been adopted from those developed by Maria Montessori (1964) in her work with children. The results of stimulation therapy are often rapid and dramatic. Ernst and Badash (1977) report that, among a group of women treated with this technique, level of awareness and ability increased from a low rating of 3 to a high rating of 8 on a scale of 10 over a six-week treatment period. An example of a sensory-stimulation group may help you to envision eight or ten 65- to 90-year-old people "turning on" to themselves once again:

> *Dr. E.:* OK, Ora, what day is today?
> *Ora:* I don't know.
> *Sara:* It's Tuesday.
> *Dr. E.:* Right. What day of the month is it?
> *Mary:* The 28th.
> *Dr. E.:* No.
> *Jennie:* The 27th.
> *Dr. E.:* That's correct. Today is Tuesday, the 27th of—what?
> *Mary:* October!
> *Dr. E.:* Correct. Today is Tuesday the 27th of October, 1976. OK. I have a ball here and we're going to toss it around as I direct. First, I throw the ball to Ora. (He does so.)
> *Ora:* Now what?
> *Dr. E.:* Ora throws the ball to Jennie.
> *Ora:* Where is Jennie?
> *Jennie:* Here!
> *Ora:* OK. I throw the ball to Jennie. (She does so.)

> *Dr. E.:* OK. Jennie throws the ball to Ida. (Jennie does so.) Good!
> Now Ida throws the ball to Dr. E.
> *Ida:* Who is Dr. E.?
> *Ora:* He is!
> *Ida:* I'm sorry, I didn't remember your name. Here. (Throws the
> ball.)

For a time, the group tosses the ball until Dr. E. is sure that each knows the name of the others clearly and can relate through the ball-tossing.

> *Dr. E.:* Now. Everyone put your arms out in front of you like this
> (palms up). Now turn them the other way (palms down).

For a few moments the group exercises together.

> *Dr. E.:* Now we'll have some cookies and soft drinks. Ora, pass the
> plate to Ida. (Ora does so with ease.) Ida, pass it to Mary (and so
> on).

In this phase, Dr. E. is reaffirming the awareness of names.

> *Dr. E.:* How do the cookies taste?
> *Ida:* Good.
> *Mary:* Yes, good.
> *Dr. E.:* Have you ever made cookies like this, Jennie?
> *Jennie:* Yes.
> *Dr. E.:* Tell us about them. How did you make them?
> *Jennie:* Sugar, butter, eggs.
> *Dr. E.:* Then what?

The group continues, with each woman sharing a favorite recipe, describing from memory the details of its preparation. Dr. E. asks each member for an opinion and, if he sees a member slipping off into isolation, he calls her back:

> *Dr. E.:* Ida, what do you think of that recipe?
> *Ida:* What? What recipe?
> *Dr. E.:* Tell us what your favorite recipe is, Ida.
> *Ida:* OK.

In a personal observation of a sensory-stimulation group of a number of old people, one of us was impressed at the change in the patients within 30 minutes. Each woman was helped into the room and to her seat by staff at the beginning of the session, but at the end they all stood up with great energy and left the room unaided, talking and joking. Unfortunately, the results were temporary. A few days after the therapist had visited, many of the women were back in their withdrawn states again. It seems, therefore, that stimulation therapy may not effect permanent change. However, if it is regularly provided, many elderly people may be able to maintain a higher level of energy and awareness than was previously thought possible.

Other Techniques

In addition to the general group techniques and the sensory-stimulation methods we have already described, there are several techniques useful in helping the elderly person. Among these is *reality orientation*, as developed by Folsom (1968). In reality orientation, which is often a part of daily hospital activities, patients may be retaught basic information such as spelling, arithmetic, and the like. In an effort to keep the elderly person oriented, frequent reminders of date, year, and personal identity are also introduced.

A second technique used with the aged is *music therapy*, in which patients can be stimulated to remember and to interact by the emotional effects of music. Some of its proponents (Boxberger & Cotter, 1968) have reported that music therapy with the elderly results in less aggressive, more appropriate behavior, fewer severe symptoms, and improvement in self-care and personal appearance.

Reality and music therapy often are included in *therapeutic communities* for old people (L. Gottesman, 1967). In most hospital settings, old people are expected not to get well and to remain dependent on the staff; but, in the therapeutic community, it is expected—if not demanded—that patients try to learn ways to get out of the hospital and to be completely on their own. By being in an environment where they work for pay, live in homelike wards, and take care of most of their own affairs, patients in a therapeutic community can be helped to learn that they need not "check out" of society just because they are old.

CONCLUDING COMMENTS

After reading a chapter describing the disorders related to old age, you may be tempted to become melancholy about your future, or perhaps not to think about getting old at all. Probably neither reaction is best. Problems associated with any developmental period need to be faced realistically. We seem to have made the arbitrary decision to classify those over 65 as old, elderly, golden agers, senior citizens, or "over the hill." However, although older people suffer from a variety of psychological and physiological stresses, only 5% of Americans over 65 are institutionalized in such settings as mental hospitals, homes for the aged, and the like (Kalish, 1975). That leaves the vast majority of older people, like most of the rest of us, dealing with the stresses and strains of daily life. However, special psychological stresses like those caused by fixed incomes, loss of some abilities, and the deaths of friends and relatives need to be dealt with openly and fairly. Many older people don't want more than their fair share, but rather the same support, help, and guidance given to people dealing with life stresses—regardless of their age.

CHAPTER SUMMARY CHART

In this chapter, we described disorders of the elderly:

Descriptions	Explanations	Treatments
Functional disorders: 　Paranoid persecutory 　　states 　Depressive states 　Confusional states Organic disorders: 　Senile dementia 　Arteriosclerotic 　　dementia	Disengagement theory Activity theory Continuity theory Isolation theory	Why aren't old people 　treated? Group therapies with 　the elderly Sensory-stimulation 　therapy Reality orientation, 　music therapy, 　therapeutic 　communities

SECTION VIII
TREATMENTS FOR THOSE WHO ARE DIFFERENT

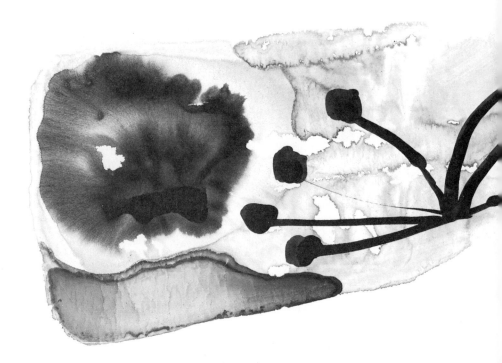

Chapter 22
The Individual Psychotherapies
Chapter 23
Group and Family Therapy
Chapter 24
Biological Therapies
Chapter 25
Community Approaches

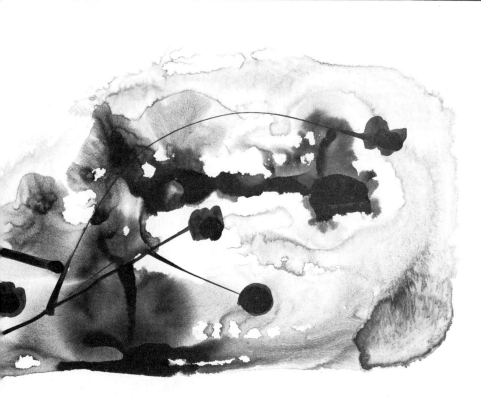

At this point in your study of abnormal psychology, we expect that you have an understanding of the vast array of behaviors that are potential targets for alteration or treatment. As you have seen, no one theory can explain everything; no one category of behavior is seen in all abnormal individuals. Likewise, you will learn in this section that no one form of psychological treatment is effective in all situations.

With the potential usefulness of all types of therapy in mind, we will now turn to the description of the variety of therapeutic procedures available. In Chapter 22, we will emphasize the individual psychotherapies, as exemplified primarily by psychoanalysis, humanistic-existentialist therapy, and behavior therapy. In Chapter 23, group and family therapy will be emphasized, with analytic, encounter, T-, and self-help groups described, as well as family-therapy methods. Chapter 24 changes the focus from psychological to physical treatment, including drug therapy, electrical shock, psychosurgery, and biofeedback. The final chapter presents the sweeping approaches of community psychology to the problems of disordered behavior. In the community approach, the emphasis is on prevention and, where possible, bringing treatment to the people.

Although all of the therapeutic approaches we will describe have probably been used to treat many of the disorders we have described in the text, some work better in specific cases than others. For example, the individual therapies seem to work well with people who exhibit neuroses (Chapter 10), psychophysiological disorders (Chapter 11), personality disturbances (Chapter 12), and most other forms of mild disturbance. The group approaches, on the other hand, often seem more beneficial in cases of special-age-group problems (Chapters 18–21) and among addicted people (Chapter 13). The physical therapies appear most helpful in treating the severe functional disorders (Chapters 7–9) and the problems associated with brain dysfunction (Chapter 16). It is possible to suggest *generally* that one type of therapy may be better than another in a particular case, but remember that each person and his or her problems are unique and that therapeutic decisions aren't made mechanically. Therapists have a wide range of available treatment techniques; and, in addition to diagnosis, factors such as interpersonal style, history of treatment, availability of therapists, and the like may play an important role in therapeutic decisions.

CHAPTER 22
THE
INDIVIDUAL
PSYCHOTHERAPIES

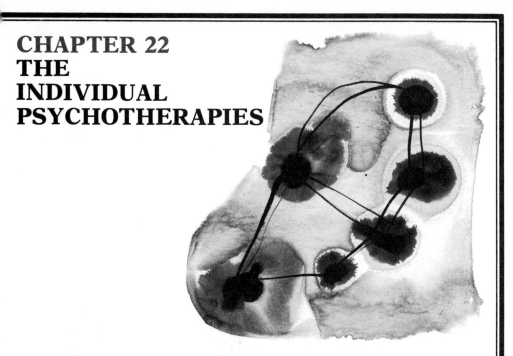

Individual psychotherapy may be defined as the coming together of two people, one a professional helper and the other someone in difficulty, for the purpose of engaging in interpersonal interaction directed at reducing the difficulties of the help seeker. This rather broad definition may be applied to all of the forms of individual psychotherapy. In each, there is an "expert" who has some theoretical frame of reference that he or she applies to understand and alter the client's personality and problems.

Over the years, we have found that psychotherapy has been a most intriguing area for our students. The many questions they ask may be grouped into five topics: What's it like to be in psychotherapy? Does psychotherapy work? How does psychotherapy work? Who can do psychotherapy? and What different types of psychotherapy are there? In the first section of this chapter we will provide some answers for the first four questions. In the remainder of the chapter we will begin to answer the fifth question by describing a selection of specific types of individual therapies. We have chosen to present many, but certainly not all (see Harper, 1959, 1975) individual therapies and have roughly categorized them into four groups: psychoanalytically based therapies, humanistic-existential thera-

551

pies, behavioral therapies, and other therapies. In Chapters 23, 24, and 25 we will continue to answer the fifth question with our coverage of group, physical, and community treatment.

GENERAL OVERVIEW

Before describing specific types of therapies, we would like to discuss some general characteristics of efforts to help people who are different.

What's It Like to Be in Psychotherapy?

The personal experience of psychotherapy may be studied from both informal and formal perspectives. The informal perspective is represented here by a personal experience obtained from a college student in individual psychotherapy.

The personal relationship between therapist and client is a crucial aspect of many forms of psychotherapy. (Photo by T. Farkas, courtesy of the World Health Organization.)

PERSONAL EXPERIENCE: *Being in Psychotherapy*

At the beginning of therapy I felt apprehensive and excited about starting. I was unsure of what the therapist would think of me and my chances for changing and becoming happier. The excitement increased, and I felt very optimistic about being committed to changing. However, my enthusiasm diminished as I saw that change was hard and would be slow in coming. It seemed as if there was so much to tell my therapist about my past so that he would understand me and not make any snap decisions, but my present life problems were also demanding attention. I had to rely on his judgment, knowing his understanding of me would be incomplete. My confidence in what was going on in therapy would vary from week to week. At times, I felt the therapist was not particularly attentive or concerned and that he was marking time with me and just trying to earn some money. At other times, I felt exhilarated and very confident of myself and what we were doing together. The continuity from one session to the next was often absent, and then I would feel as if therapy were just a crisis-oriented maintenance exercise. Nevertheless, most of the time I felt I really needed his attention and suggestions for my current crisis. We are now making some gradual headway in developing my understanding of what forces motivate me that I'm not aware of. Then I will have a reasonable chance, I hope, of being able to change those things about myself that hold me back.

Although the informal perspective on the experience of psychotherapy can be informative, it is difficult to know whether a single experience reflects what goes on with others. Howard and Orlinsky (1972; Orlinsky & Howard, 1975) studied the experience of a number of people in psychotherapy. Using a standardized report form, these investigators compiled data for 60 subjects in psychotherapy. In all, 890 therapy sessions with 17 different therapists were analyzed. The summary of these findings is presented in Table 22-1. The results suggest that many of the same feelings described in the personal experience just recounted are shared by others. Orlinsky and Howard note: "To the extent that these findings are representative, [Table 22-1] gives an idea of what most likely happens in the ordinary therapy session as it occurs in everyday practice" (p. 72).

Does Psychotherapy Work?

It is possible to identify common characteristics of psychotherapy sessions scientifically, but whether these characteristics are of any value in helping people who are different is a separate question. This issue has been addressed in investigations called *therapy-outcome studies*. There has been much controversy surrounding the possibility that psychotherapy may do little more

Table 22-1. *Typical therapeutic experiences*

Patient wants to:	"Get a better understanding of my feelings and behavior."
	"Get help in talking about what is really troubling me."
	"Work out a problem that I have."
	"Work together with my therapist on a person-to-person basis."
	"Get advice on how to deal with my life and with other people."
Patient talks about:	"Feelings and attitudes toward myself."
	"Social activities and relationships, friends and acquaintances."
	"Relationship with spouse, boyfriend, or girlfriend."
Patient feels:	"Anxious."
	"Tense."
Patient relates by:	Leading.
	Being interdependent.
	Being friendly.
	Being animated or feeling.
Therapist tries to:	"Increase my patient's insight and self-understanding."
	"Move my patient closer to experiencing her real feelings, what she really is."
	"Engage my patient in an honest person-to-person relationship, work together authentically."
Therapist feels:	"Interested."
	"Calm."
	"Involved."
	"Alert."
	"Confident."
	"Sympathetic."
Therapist relates by:	Reciprocating.
	Being interdependent.
	Being friendly.
	Being feeling.
Patient gets:	"A sense of having an honest person-to-person relationship with my therapist, of working together."
	"Help in being able to talk about what was troubling to me and really important."
	"Better insight and self-understanding."

Reprinted by permission of the publisher from David E. Orlinsky and Kenneth I. Howard, *Varieties of Psychotherapeutic Experience* (New York: Teachers College Press, Copyright © 1975 by Teachers College, Columbia University), p. 73.

good than no treatment at all. Early fuel for the fire of this controversy was provided by the interpretation of outcome studies by British psychologist Hans Eysenck (1952, 1965). Using records of the discharge rates of those in the New York State hospital system and those who were waiting to receive psychotherapy, Eysenck claimed that up to 72% of neurotic people improved without the benefit of psychotherapy. He concluded that these people improved because of *spontaneous remission,* or just getting better on their own.

Since the people who received no treatment seemed to improve at the same rate as those who were involved in psychotherapy, he asked whether there was a need for psychotherapy at all.

Needless to say, Eysenck evoked quite a response from the psychotherapeutic community. Numerous criticisms have been leveled at his conclusions. One major criticism has to do with his "no-treatment" groups. Did these people really receive no treatment? It seems safe to say that these distressed people on a waiting list didn't stop seeking relief from their discomfort. Chances are that they talked with friends, perhaps with other professionals such as ministers, teachers, and the like, or perhaps even with other therapists. Merely being placed on a waiting list doesn't mean that a person is going to stay and wait passively to improve. Some people do seem to improve spontaneously (Kiesler, 1966; Saslow & Peters, 1956; Subotnik, 1972), but they usually are diagnosed as psychotically or neurotically depressed (Kiesler, 1973).

Eysenck's interpretation has also been challenged because of his criteria for success. For example, is being discharged from a large state mental hospital equivalent to termination of a successful psychotherapeutic interaction? In some instances, state hospitals believe their obligation is met and patients have been successfully treated when they have been given drugs and "stabilized." Even the rate of spontaneous remission of 72% cited by Eysenck has been seriously questioned. Bergin (1971) has noted that, in long-term (up to 20 years) follow-up studies of untreated people, spontaneous remission occurs only about 30% of the time. The 30% figure is significantly lower than the improvement rate reported in a review of recent therapy-outcome studies (Bergin & Suinn, 1975). Eysenck's original interpretation has been refuted on many fronts.

How Does Psychotherapy Work?

Whereas outcome studies are directed at determining *whether* psychotherapy works, *process studies* are directed at determining *how* it works. Process researchers attempt to isolate the factors in the psychotherapeutic experience that may be responsible for bringing about the positive changes documented in outcome studies. Some factors may be general enough to span most types of therapy; others may be specific to certain approaches. Before we describe the process factors specific to individual theories and techniques, we will describe general factors that seem to cut across therapies.

The Placebo Effect and the Barnum Effect.   The first general factor proposed to account for the general effects of psychotherapeutic approaches comes from the fact that people tend to place faith in members of the healing professions. This faith allows for what are called *placebo effects* in psychotherapy (A. Shapiro, 1971). Placebo effects occur when a person is led to expect benefit from a therapeutic procedure or chemical substance that actually is neutral in its effects. For example, for some patients, physicians may prescribe pills that are no more than candy. Nevertheless, in some patients, these pills seem to have significant impact in eliminating discomfort or problems. In psychotherapy, the placebo effect may occur when "new" approaches are first used (A. Shapiro, 1971). If improvement is due to a placebo effect, then the positive effects usually will diminish as time passes and the placebo effect weakens.

Named because of its similarity to the promotional ability of P. T. Barnum, in the Barnum effect, the therapist actively "talks up" a mode of treatment to such a degree that the client's faith in the therapy magnifies the placebo effect. However, if faith in and acceptance of the therapy diminish, so can the effectiveness of the therapy.

Despite their possible beneficial characteristics, the placebo and Barnum effects can interfere with attempts to get a clear answer to the question of how psychotherapy works. For example, therapists could believe that their specific techniques are helpful when, in fact, it is not the techniques but the placebo or Barnum effect that produces change. Further, specific techniques may be helpful, but their actual potency may be distorted by variations in the placebo and Barnum effects.

Therapist Variables. The personal characteristics of the therapist may have a significant impact on the therapeutic process. These characteristics can be viewed from both experiential and scientific perspectives.

Experientially, most therapists would agree that all therapists cannot work with all clients, and that some therapists do especially well with certain types of clients. In the following statement from an experienced therapist we can see some of the therapist characteristics important to the process of psychotherapy.

PERSONAL EXPERIENCE: *Being a Therapist*

Having been a therapist for about 11 years now, I find myself loving what I do more and more. I've learned many things over the years. For one thing, I know that I'm not cut out to see married couples—I just don't feel comfortable with them, and I'm not sure that I can really help them. On the other hand, I *know* I can do individual therapy as well as any of my colleagues. I feel right in a one-to-one situation—I feel good. I've been able to train myself to shut out everything but my client during the therapy session. Sometimes that's hard, especially when I'm worried about some personal problem myself. But, to be a good therapist, I've got to be able to concentrate every ounce of my energy on the relationship with my client. I find therapy to be a draining experience; when I've had a good session (and, to tell the truth, I do have bad ones now and then), I feel almost shot for the rest of the day. I can't really handle more than three intense hours like that in any one day—some therapists can; I can't.

I've been able to help many people during my career, and I feel good about having touched the lives of my clients in some positive way. And my clients have touched my life as well. Each relationship has changed my life in some way, most times for the better, a few times for the worse. Being a therapist is an intense experience, one that is hard to describe in words. I can say, however, that it is an emotional, deeply human endeavor with which I continue to be enthralled.

Informal observations of differences among therapists have been documented by a variety of formal, scientific efforts. Some research has focused on the effects on the progress of therapy sessions of daily variations in the therapist's mood (Gurman, 1972, 1973; Orlinsky & Howard, 1967, 1975). Other efforts have been directed primarily at identifying more long-standing personality characteristics of effective therapists and at attempts to "match" therapists with the kinds of clients they would be most likely to help (Carson & Heine, 1962). For instance, on the basis of the therapist's vocational interest, Whitehorn and Betz (1954, 1960) isolated two basic types of therapists: A-type therapists, who tended to score high on interest scales for law, journalism, and advertising, and B-type therapists, who scored high on scales for mathematics and science teaching, personnel directing, printing, and the like. These A and B therapists differed in the manner in which they related to their clients. Generally, A-type therapists seemed to be better able to gain the confidence of clients, to understand the meaning of behavior better, to help clients to develop within their relationship, and to be more active and personally involved in the therapeutic process. B-type therapists seemed to prefer dealing in biographical material, to set strategic goals, to seek insight into problems, and to be more instructional yet remain basically passive. Research results suggest that A and B therapists differ in their effectiveness depending on the type of client. In an early study, McNair, Callahan, and Lorr (1962) reported that B-type therapists were more effective in dealing with people with neurotic problems, whereas A-type therapists were more effective in helping people with schizophrenic disorders. Although these results haven't been consistently supported by research, King and Blaney (1977) have noted that professionals unknowingly tend to refer schizophrenics to A-type therapists and neurotics to B-type therapists. The A-B therapist dimension represents one focus on therapist factors associated with effective psychotherapy and may be considered to span the variety of specific therapy techniques.

Client Variables.   Client characteristics can also affect success in psychotherapy. Bordin (1974) concluded that differences among clients served by therapists were more responsible for differences in success rates than the specific therapies used.

Informally, a number of therapists believe that the so-called YAVIS person may be the best candidate for successful psychotherapy. The letters Y-A-V-I-S stand for young, aggressive or anxious, verbal, intelligent, and successful. Based upon an extensive review of the psychotherapy literature, Strupp (1962) has summarized these and other characteristics of the successful therapy client:

> Patients considered good prognostic risks are described as young, attractive, well-educated, members of the upper middle class, possessing a high degree of ego strength, some anxiety which impels them to seek help, no seriously disabling neurotic symptoms, relative absence of deep characterological distortions and strong secondary gains, a willingness to talk about their difficulties, an ability to communicate well, some skill in the social-vocational area, and a value system relatively congruent with that of the therapist. Such patients also tend to remain in therapy, profit from it, and evoke the therapist's best efforts. By superficial criteria, such patients may not appear very sick; however, neither our culture nor our psychological tests are very sensitive to unhappiness, silent suffering, and despair [p. 62].

In addition to Strupp's observations, researchers have examined specific characteristics of clients. In one review of research on the role of client factors in the therapy process, Bordin (1974) has noted that successful clients generally stay in therapy longer, are dissatisfied with their level of functioning, experience emotional pain, have hope that they can be relieved of emotional pain, and can allow themselves to become temporarily dependent on the therapeutic relationship.

The Therapeutic Relationship. Therapist and client factors merge to form the therapeutic-relationship factor that is often the key to successful psychotherapy. For example, Beier (1966) concludes that the openness and genuineness of the relationship are the most important determinants of successful therapy. Similarly, communication analysts (Kiesler, Bernstein, & Anchins, in press) propose that, within the relationship, the clarity of communication, the types of messages sent, and the feelings evoked in the therapist should be the primary focuses of the search for effective, therapeutic process factors.

The importance of the relationship between therapist and client is underlined in the following statement by an experienced clinician and trainer of psychotherapists:

> The therapist offers himself by sharing with the patient something of his subjective experiencing of the vicissitudes of their relationship as this unfolds and develops in the course of their continued contact together. What is often most impressive to the

therapist is the relative failure of the patient to communicate with him forthrightly and genuinely in favor of holding himself back by maladaptive accommodations which prevent the emergence of a clear, uncluttered, full-bodied, three-dimensional human interaction. An intimate relationship is gradually but tortuously and unevenly built up by the steadfastness and openness of the therapist. And a sense of trust and security is awakened in the patient which ultimately generalizes to other human beings and brings about the successful resolution of treatment. What is therapeutic about psychotherapy is the opportunity afforded a distressed human being to re-enter the human arena by means of a non-punitive, non-demanding and increasingly satisfying relationship with his therapist. What the patient learns about himself is beside the point. What he experiences is the essential point [Frank, 1967, p. 1].[1]

Who Can Do Psychotherapy?

Up to this point, we have attempted to show what it's like to be in psychotherapy and the factors related to effective psychotherapy experiences. With this basic background of information, it now seems appropriate to look at *who does* the psychotherapy.

Psychotherapists are specially trained in the application of the psychotherapies to be described in the remainder of the book. Many people erroneously equate *psychotherapist* with *psychiatrist*. In truth, there are a number of professional groups trained in the practice of psychotherapy. Most of the treatment methods to be presented aren't the sole province of any one profession.

Psychiatrists. Psychiatrists are physicians who specialize in treating the mentally disturbed. In addition to college and medical school, psychiatry requires three to five years of professional psychiatric residency. Because of their medical training, psychiatrists are the only mental-health professionals permitted to prescribe drugs or administer shock therapy. *Psychoanalysts* most often are psychiatrists who take additional training in Freudian therapy techniques. Not all psychiatrists are psychoanalysts, but almost all psychoanalysts are psychiatrists.

Clinical Psychologists. Clinical psychology is the applied subdiscipline of psychology. In contrast to psychiatrists, who have M.D.'s, clinical psychologists hold the Ph.D. or Psy.D. (Doctor of Psychology) degree, which requires four to six years in graduate school and a year of additional training in a clinical internship. Clinical psychologists are the only mental-health professionals specially trained in developing, administering, and interpreting psychological tests. Psychologists are trained in a wide variety

---

[1]From *Training in Psychotherapy*, by I. Frank. Reprinted by permission of the author.

of therapeutic approaches, from the psychoanalytic to the humanistic or the behavioral. The clinical psychologist holding a research degree (the Ph.D.) is also trained in research methodology and statistical analysis. Psychologists must have licenses or certification in most states.

Psychiatric Social Workers. Although clinical psychology is primarily a post–World War II phenomenon, psychiatric social work has been a profession since the early 1900s. Fully trained social workers hold M.S.W. (Master of Social Work) degrees and belong to and are approved by a national organization called ACSW (Academy of Certified Social Workers). Social workers can provide psychotherapy to individuals and groups. They often work in the homes or working environments of disturbed people.

Psychiatric Nurses. In contrast to social workers, who traditionally work in the community, psychiatric nurses usually complete a postgraduate program in psychiatric nursing within a medical setting. Often in more direct contact with patients than any other professional, psychiatric nurses may administer medications (under physicians' guidance) and provide physical care as well as individual and group psychotherapy.

Pastoral Counselors. In addition to psychiatrists, psychologists, social workers, and nurses, psychotherapy can be provided by pastoral counselors—clergy who are specially trained in working with those who have behavioral and emotional disturbances. Pastoral counselors often serve internships in mental hospitals or other special mental-health facilities.

PSYCHOANALYTIC THERAPIES

By now, you probably can judge for yourself that psychotherapy is a very complex endeavor that can be viewed from a number of perspectives. In the remainder of this chapter and in the chapters to follow, we attempt to answer the fifth question we posed earlier: what different types of psychotherapy are there? Probably the first formalized type of psychotherapy was developed by Sigmund Freud. Psychotherapy performed strictly according to the methods outlined by Freud is given the special name *psychoanalysis*. Other modes of therapy—for example, the analytic therapy of Carl Jung—have evolved through modifications of psychoanalytic theory.

Psychoanalysis

To its practitioners, psychoanalysis may be more than a form of individual psychotherapy; it is often a philosophy of life. In what may be a slightly more than modest statement, Fine (1973) has said, "Psychoanalysis represents, in the social sciences, the greatest intellectual revolution of the 20th Century. It has given mankind a new research tool through the concept of the unconscious and allied factors; it has classified the possibilities of happiness that exist in philosophies that have been prevalent in previous centuries; and it has provided a solid basis for the investigation of man in all his psychological and social functioning" (p. 7).

In psychoanalysis, the patient (*analysand*) usually attends up to five sessions of 45 to 60 minutes each week. Initially, the analyst and the analysand may speak face to face, but, after a period of time, the patient usually is directed to lie on a couch facing away from the therapist, who typically sits off to the side, out of the patient's vision. At this point, the fundamental rule of *free association* is applied: the patient is asked to report, without censoring or inhibiting, all feelings, ideas, associations, and thoughts that come to mind. The therapist listens intently and makes infrequent comments and interpretations, as seen in this excerpt from a psychoanalytic session:

> *Therapist:* We can begin.
> *Client:* Last night I thought about not coming back today. I felt you were really bored with what I was saying. You never say anything to me, and I feel sometimes like I'm wasting my time and money. (Pause.) You see I wait for an answer and I don't get one! I really get mad when you do that.
> *Therapist:* Like when you were a child and you wanted your father to listen to you and to take care of your troubles?
> *Client:* (Pause.) Yes—sort of—that made me think of my father. I remember a time when we were at a lake for the summer. I was on the boat dock feeding bread to the fish and he came out and sat down beside me. He looked at me with such great love in his eyes. I feel like crying just thinking about it. He would do that when I didn't ask for it. But when I cried for help from him, he would say, "Try to do it yourself." Why? Why?
> *Therapist:* And I ask you to do it yourself, too. And I don't even look at you with love in my eyes.
> *Client:* I feel alone—like a child. . . . You're right. I do wonder if you really care about me. Do you? (Pause.) You won't answer me. So, DAMMIT, I get so angry at you, but I did at him too. I miss him.

Upon entering a relationship with a psychoanalyst, the analysand usually must agree always to come on time, to pay the fees (even if a session is missed, no matter what the reason), and to follow the guidelines for therapy. The therapeutic goals are to try to make conscious and harmless what is unconscious and harmful. To do this, the analyst focuses on *resistances* that the client places in the path of therapy. Examples of *direct resistance* would be refusal to pay, to talk, to lie on the couch, and so on.

Memories of parent/child relationships frequently are the focus of psychoanalytic sessions. (Photo by Joseph Czarnecki.)

Indirect resistances include such things as unreasonable demands for social involvement with the therapist, excess emotionality during the hour, and refusing to respond to interpretations.

If resistances are dealt with adequately and the analyst's rules of therapy are followed, the client usually acquires a series of *insights*. Insights are new and healthier ways of looking at one's life and feelings and represent the "core of the analytic growth process" (Fine, 1973, p. 21). For example, a particularly hostile client may discover that the reason he hates work so much is that he unconsciously perceives his boss as being like his father whom he feared and hated. Usually the client also will misperceive the therapist, a process called *transference*. In transference, the client projects thoughts and feelings about important others from the past onto the analyst. Upon recognizing this, the therapist makes efforts to resolve the transference and to institute *reality-testing* in the client.

Psychoanalysis may continue anywhere from one to ten years, often at great expense and sacrifice on the part of clients and their families. At the conclusion of successful treatment, a new philosophy of life often is observed, and a healthier, happier individual may emerge. However, psychoanalysis isn't for everyone and may be available only to a narrow stratum of our society. Nevertheless, the impact of psychoanalysis on forms of individual psychotherapy that developed later must not be underestimated or ignored.

Analytical Psychotherapy

Analytical psychotherapy is a form of individual and group treatment that has developed primarily out of the theories of Carl Jung. Although a disciple of Freud's, Jung didn't completely agree with Freud's theory. Out of his independent thought, he developed therapeutic techniques different from classical psychoanalysis. Analytical psychotherapy has been defined as "an attempt to create by means of a symbolic approach, a relationship between consciousness and unconsciousness" (Whitmont & Kaufman, 1973). In other words, the goal of analytical therapy is to get the conscious person in touch with the unconscious. To effect this, the symbolic communication of the meaning of *dreams* and *fantasies* is frequently the focus of therapy. According to Jung, the process of analytical therapy is one of increasing self-knowledge and reconstructing the personality (Jung, 1954/1964). The means by which these goals are met may vary widely from therapist to therapist, but the focus on dreams is common to the majority of analytical practitioners.

An Example of Dream Analysis

The dream: I am quite alone at the beginning of a long tunnel. I feel afraid to enter the tunnel, yet I hear footsteps coming closer behind me. I run into the tunnel—I run and run until I come to its end, at which I see a hill. It is green. I climb it and look down upon a swimming pool—the pool is empty. There is a child crying near the pool. I pick up the child and its face turns to that of a monster. I throw him into the pool and run away.

An interpretation: The client fears marriage. This is known from conscious history. The tunnel represents sex, and the footsteps are the encouragement of her family to get married because she is getting old. The hill at the end of the tunnel equals the swollen abdomen of pregnancy; the empty pool equals fear of lost sexuality following childbirth; the child is the client, and her hate for the child and sex and marriage is expressed in her hurling the child into the pool.

Analytical therapy typically begins with a face-to-face discussion of the client's conscious state. Life history and past influences may be combed in search of clues to the person's attitudes, values, and behavioral patterns. Following this focus on conscious information, the effort to establish contact with the unconscious may begin. Dreams may be described by the client, after which therapist and client together try to understand their symbolic communication value.

In dream interpretation, the analytical therapist attempts to understand the dream as a metaphorical play or drama. The three parts of a dream are the *exposition*, the *crisis*, and the *solution*. In the exposition, the mood of the dream is established and the conflicts identified; in the crisis, the conflicts become salient and are faced; in the solution, either something is done about the crisis or the dreamer awakes suddenly. By interpreting dreams, the analytical therapist directs the client toward greater psychological health by establishing better contact between conscious and unconscious functioning.

HUMANISTIC AND EXISTENTIAL THERAPIES

The humanistic and existential techniques differ from the analytic approaches in their basic view of people. Unlike Freudian theory, which assumes that people are driven by negative instincts and desires that need to be controlled, the humanists and existentialists generally believe that people are basically good and free. To the analyst, a behavior disorder most often means that the negative components of the personality have broken past the defenses against them and emerged; to the humanist-existentialist, behavioral problems indicate that inherent goodness and psychological health probably have been blocked from appearing by internal or external forces. Therefore, for the humanist-existentialist theorist, psychotherapy typically involves the construction of situations and relationships in which positive growth can occur unhampered. We will now consider several techniques that focus on removing the inhibition of the innate drive toward goodness rather than on replacing inhibition of negative drives toward instinctual satisfaction.

Client-Centered Therapy

Client-centered therapy is a humanistic mode of treatment developed by Carl Rogers (1942). As you remember from Chapter 4, Rogers's concept of behavior disorder was that it usually represented a stifling of the *self-actualizing process* inherent in each of us. Due to faulty life experiences, Rogers believed, people came to evaluate themselves incorrectly; that is, they seemed to adopt negative, nonaccepting attitudes about themselves which in turn made them anxious and unhappy.

Rogers devised client-centered psychotherapy to undo the faulty evaluations and their effects. The therapy relationship and the atmosphere produced by the therapist are the critical mechanisms of change. The therapist must be warm and responsive and produce a receptive climate in which the client can feel free to express anything he or she wishes to. The therapist produces the receptive climate through the process of empathy, congruence, and unconditional positive regard. By *empathy,* Rogers means the ability of the therapist to understand the world as the client sees it. *Congruence* describes the high level of therapist genuineness; that is, rather than planning the next statement or topic, the therapist responds primarily only to the moment-to-moment feelings of the client. By *unconditional positive regard,* Rogers means the therapist's complete, total, nonjudgmental acceptance of the client and all of his or her thoughts and feelings (Corey, 1977).

In such a therapeutic atmosphere, clients are faced with a therapist who won't guide them in any way. The therapist's behavior is based upon the belief that a warm, accepting atmosphere will soon allow the client's own self-actualizing tendency to reemerge and again guide healthy development.

As is shown in the following example of a client-centered-therapy interaction, this type of therapy sounds simple but is in fact difficult to perform effectively. Note that the therapist reflects feelings to the client, doing nothing more than stating for the client how the therapist perceives the client's feelings. The direction of the conversation rests with the client.

Client: I really feel bad today . . . just terrible.

Therapist: You're feeling pretty bad.

Client: Yeah, I'm angry and that's made me feel bad, especially when I can't do anything about it. I just have to live with it and shut up.

Therapist: You're very angry and feel like there's nothing you can safely do with your feelings.

Client: Uh-huh. I mean . . . if I yell at my wife she gets hurt. If I don't say anything to her I feel tense.

Therapist: You're between a rock and a hard place—no matter what you do, you'll wind up feeling bad.

Client: I mean she chews ice all day and all night. I feel stupid saying this. It's petty, I know. But when I sit there and try to concentrate I hear all these slurping and crunching noises. I can't stand it . . . and I yell. She feels hurt—I feel bad—like I shouldn't have said anything.

Therapist: So when you finally say something you feel bad afterward.

Client: Yeah, I can't say anything to her without getting mad and saying more than I should. And then I cause more trouble than it's worth.

Existential Therapy

Existential psychotherapy differs from Rogers's approach in the specifics of its basic philosophy. Existential therapy holds that the present is more important than the past in determining action and feelings. The *here-and-now* is important, and the *then-and-there* must not be allowed to dictate fully one's behavior. Existential therapy has some of its roots in the philosophies of Kierkegaard, Heidegger, and Sartre, but it took shape as a type of individual therapy with the *Daseinsanalyse* of Binswanger (1962, 1963), Boss (1963), and May (1967).

Rollo May is considered to be the founder of existential therapy in the United States. He believes in personal responsibility for one's own life and direct meeting of challenge. In the face of the psychoanalysts' belief in *psychic determinism* (all that we do is determined by past experience), May holds steadfastly to the concept of free will. He views behavior disorders as the result of "unlived possibilities" and "untimely deadness." Like Rogers, May believes in an innate growth potential that can direct the individual to a free and happy existence.

In existential psychotherapy, authenticity, encounter, and experiencing are sought (Gendlin, 1973). *Authenticity* refers to the ability to remain in touch with present, past, and future existence, but to live in the present and be open to it. An awareness of one's *encounters* with oneself and the world is also crucial. Existentialists feel that healthy people feel all interactions with the inner and outer world "exactly as they are." Gendlin describes this component of existential therapy as rarely being amenable to verbal description, but as something to be "bodily felt" and expressed.

Existential therapy is a very difficult technique to describe, because of the vagueness of many of its concepts. Generally, however, we can say that the focus of such therapy is on feelings more than thought, on freedom more than determinism, on goodness rather than evil, and on direct confrontation of problems rather than on passive hope that they will eventually disappear with treatment.

Gestalt Therapy

Gestalt therapy, as developed and described by Fritz Perls (1969a, 1969b; Perls, Hefferline, & Goodman, 1958) is among the most widely used and accepted of the humanistic-existential therapies. Based upon ideas quite similar to those of May, Perls's therapy is an ahistoric, here-and-now attempt to confront and resolve painful internal polarizations. Polarizations may be between good and evil, love and hate, mother and child, and so forth. The term *Gestalt* may be thought of as referring to Perls's focus upon one's *entire* experience as a source of self-understanding and growth.

For the Gestalt therapist, unhappy people aren't totally aware of all the elements of their here-and-now experiences. The client is responding, not to the total Gestalt of his or her life, but rather to a limited and often distorted portion of it. Awareness may be divided into two types. *Intelligent awareness* is an experience of oneself at an intellectual here-and-now level, such that we "know" why we hurt if we put a match to a finger or stub a toe. *Psychophysical awareness* is more subtle and often is ignored; for example, it may involve suddenly noticing that one's forehead is tense and wrinkled. Awareness is a complex phenomenon, as Kempler's (1973) description of it will demonstrate:

> We are not a happening; we are happening. At the moment we are aware and can describe what we are, we are not that at all. We are in transit, a point on a continuum, and awareness is at best capable only of immediate hindsight. To describe with awareness and seeming clarity what we are is at best a description of what we just were. What we are is describing. The experience of awareness is not precisely the same as the experience itself. Experience has no awareness. It is followed by awareness [p. 259].

In contrast to many forms of psychotherapy that focus primarily on verbal interaction, Gestalt therapy emphasizes the importance of nonverbal communication. (Photo by George Lazar.)

The goal of the Gestalt therapist is to coordinate intelligent awareness with psychophysical awareness so that the entire experience of a person is congruent. Saying that you are happy, yet acting as if you are miserable, is incongruent; an awareness of your "body language" can help you to experience yourself as you really are. The Gestalt therapist works toward awareness and acceptance of psychophysical experience. Intelligent awareness can be faked and consciously controlled for social or other reasons; the same isn't completely true of psychophysical expression. The manner in which total awareness can be reached and genuine self-experiencing and interpersonal communication reestablished is demonstrated in the following Gestalt-therapy transcript:

Client: You know, I wanted to talk today about my mother. She always was a problem for me as long as I remember. She used to . . .

Therapist: Tell me how you feel about your mother now.

Client: Now? I haven't seen her in a week so I'm not too angry. When I was with her . . .

Therapist: Right now, at this moment how do you feel about her?

Client: I guess I'm not too angry with her right now. When I think of some of our arguments I get a little angry.

Therapist: You say you are not angry, yet look at your hands; they are clenched into fists.

Client: Yes?

Therapist: Relax them—open them up. How do they feel?

Client: I feel like I want to close them again—they don't feel comfortable being open.

Therapist: So acting as if you aren't angry doesn't make the anger go away. Just opening your fists doesn't make them not tense.

Client: You mean I *am* angry at her even now?

Therapist: I don't really know what you are when you tell me. Let's try something. You make believe that the tightness in your fists is in that empty chair next to you. Talk to the tightness and tell it what you feel about it. I know that's hard to do, but go ahead.

Client: OK. (Pause.) OK, tightness, I don't like you. I wish you weren't there. I wish I could relax. I wish I could be free of you, but you won't go away. You even hold onto me when I am not aware of being angry. Why?

Therapist: OK, now say to the tightness, "I won't let you go because I like you!"

Client: What . . . but I don't!

Therapist: Say it, please, and try to mean it.

Client: I won't let you go because I like you.

Therapist: Again.

Client: I won't let you go because I like you. You mean I might actively want to be angry? To be mad at my mother? But why?

Therapist: How else can you relate to her? Unless you were angry you might have nothing to do with her. You would feel lost. You would have no one.

Reality Therapy

Whereas Gestalt therapy emphasizes the unification of feeling and psychophysical awareness, reality therapy focuses on the correction of inappropriate assumed responsibilities. Developed by William Glasser (1965), reality therapy is based upon the idea that the foremost need of people is to love and be loved. Glasser also contends that we must be able to feel competent and valuable to ourselves and others.

In reality therapy, clients usually are encouraged to talk about any topic and to experience at any level as long as they deal with and face responsibility. *Responsibility* is defined as the ability to fulfill one's needs in a way that doesn't deprive others of their ability to fulfill their needs. Problems are seen as manifestations of an individual's inability to separate *true responsibilities* from inappropriate *assumed responsibilities.* True responsibilities are those things for which a person realistically can be responsible, such as taking care of his or her health. Inappropriate responsibilities are those which have been adopted by or foisted upon people, such as making sure other people are happy.

The reality therapist strives to free clients of believing that they are responsible for things for which they aren't realistically responsible. Further, the therapist helps the client to set realistic goals for life and to find realistic ways to reach these goals. Glasser and Zunin (1973) state: "Through accepting responsibility for one's own behavior and acting maturely to constructively change their behavior individuals find they are no longer lonely, symptoms begin to resolve and they are more likely to gain maturity, respect, and love" (p. 345).

BEHAVIORAL THERAPIES

The humanistic and Freudian therapies developed from the work of clinicians interacting with their clients. Behavioral therapy, however, grew primarily from laboratory studies of learning in animals and humans. Behavior therapy—or behavior modification, as it is often called—is a mode of individual treatment of psychological disturbances in which basic rules of learning discovered and tested in the laboratory are applied to the solution of human problems. Many proponents of behavior modification hold that, owing to its basis in experimental psychology, this mode of treatment is more scientifically sound and testable than the psychoanalytic and humanistic therapies.

We have divided the behavioral therapies into two groups on the basis of the goal of the therapy. Some therapeutic efforts aim at *increasing* the frequency of certain behaviors. For example, we might wish a shy person to socialize more or a person who fears and avoids flying to be able to fly. Other therapy goals may involve *reducing* the frequency of specific behaviors; examples would be the reduction of eating, smoking, or drinking behaviors in those who overindulge in these activities. The majority of behavioral therapies can be seen as directed at either increasing or decreasing behavioral frequencies.

Increasing Frequency of Behaviors

The behavior therapies that seek to increase behaviors are directed at people who either don't know how to emit desired behaviors or can't emit desired behaviors because of fear. Depending upon the type of basic problem involved, the behavior therapist may choose different ways of increasing behavioral frequency.

Systematic Desensitization. First developed by Joseph Wolpe (1958), systematic desensitization is based upon the belief that it is possible systematically to institute conditions under which learned fears can be overcome. Early in his thinking, Wolpe realized that certain pairs of behaviors or feelings were *reciprocally inhibitory*; that is, if one member of the pair were present, its reciprocal could not be. Reciprocally inhibitory pairs include relaxation–tension and sexual arousal–tension. However, the reciprocal response that has been found most effective in inhibiting anxiety is muscle relaxation as learned by methods similar to that of *progressive relaxation* developed by Jacobson (1938). Wolpe reasoned that, if he could replace tension (anxiety) with one of its reciprocals as a response to any given stimulus, he could "cure" neurosis. A glance at Figure 22-1 may help explain: using Wolpe's methods, the neurotic stimulus-response pair (S-R) is weakened and replaced by a new, more adaptive pair. The specific way in which the old S-R pair is weakened and replaced is called *systematic desensitization*. In this method, the client is helped not to fear situations or objects, thereby increasing the probability of desired behavior.

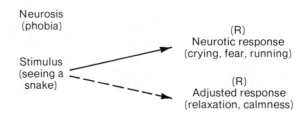

Figure 22-1. *The mechanism through which systematic desensitization operates to replace a maladaptive S-R pair with a more adaptive response*

In the systematic-desensitization procedure, progressive relaxation is taught to the client first. When the relaxation response is under the client's control, it can then be associated with feared situations. Based upon a principle much like that of "little steps for little feet," Wolpe devised a *hierarchy* of anxiety ranging from the least threatening kind of imagined event to the most threatening. Figure 22-2 is a diagram of one such hierarchy; note that items at the bottom produce little tension—the S-R bond between the feared event and anxiety is weak. Weaker S-R bonds usually are easier to replace than stronger ones, so Wolpe begins at the bottom and doesn't move up the hierarchy until the client can easily imagine the specific fear situation and feel relaxed. In time, the hierarchy is traversed, and, at its completion, the individual usually is able to respond to all items on the list with little difficulty.

Systematic desensitization has been used to treat a wide variety of disturbed behavior. Irrational fears of objects and situations, social withdrawal, sexual problems, school fears, test anxiety—all have been found amenable to systematic desensitization. As one of the earliest forms of behavior therapy, it has given impetus to the development of most of the others we will describe. It represents a clear application of experimental psychology to the reduction of human suffering and is often seen as a bridge between some of the diverse subdisciplines of psychology.

Implosion and Flooding.   Sharing the same goal as systematic desensitization, *implosion* is a method, first described by Stampfl (Stampfl & Levis, 1967), in which an approach essentially opposite to systematic desensitization is taken. Whereas Wolpe feels that a slow build-up of resistance to the anxiety response is most appropriate, Stampfl believes that, once people experience the worst of their fears and see that they are still all right, the fear will be reduced. Thus, Stampfl forces his clients to face their fears, to think the unthinkable; Stampfl starts at the very top of the hierarchy, Wolpe at the bottom.

Implosion refers to an *imaginary* trip to the top of the anxiety hierarchy, but a complementary technique, *flooding*, includes the frequent, actual facing or handling of feared objects or situations (Ullmann & Krasner,

Most fear
(Strong S → R Anxiety)

Least fear
(Weak S → R Anxiety)

1. A cockroach is walking on your body.
2. A cockroach is one inch from your big toe.
3. A cockroach is three inches from your big toe.
4. A cockroach is one foot away.
5. A cockroach is two feet away.
6. A cockroach is five feet away.
7. A cockroach is outside the doorway, and you see it.
8. A cockroach is nowhere in sight, but you sense it.
9. There are no cockroaches in sight.

Figure 22-2. *Example of a fear hierarchy for fear of cockroaches*

1975). In both approaches, the therapist is very active, attempting to produce fear in the client and to drive the client into intense anxiety experiences, from which he or she will emerge, in reality, unscathed. From this experience, clients can learn that their fears are groundless and that they probably imagine things to be much worse than they really are. An example of an implosive-therapy interaction follows:

> *Therapist:* Imagine that you are in a room—the room is dark—you are alone. Suddenly you begin to hear a faint scratching sound at the base of the closed door. You look and see several small shadows in the light coming through beneath the door. Then, you can see some forms coming under the door into the darkness; there are hundreds of small forms—you can see tiny legs and wings and antennae. You know at once what they are—large, brown and black cockroaches with spiny wings and legs—coming toward you. You can't see them, but you know they are there and they are coming closer—closer. Suddenly you feel something on your big toe—a faint wisp of feeling—an antenna—the leader of the pack has found you! You are afraid—you are panicking—your heart is pounding.
>
> *Client:* Please . . .
>
> *Therapist:* No—face the fear—feel it! The roach has now gotten onto your toe and is crawling up your foot—others follow it—on your other foot as well. Hundreds of tiny feet are crawling on you now—coming up your legs. You try to brush them off but they stick to your hand—they are on your fingers—you are panicked. Here they come! They are on your hair—on your face—a cockroach is in your nose! Crawling on your eyes and into your ears and mouth. You are covered with them! They're choking out your air! Creepy, crawly, dirty, filthy cockroaches!

Think about how you, as a client, would react to implosive therapy or, for that matter, flooding—in which you would actually handle cockroaches! According to its proponents, the approach works well, although it is very controversial.

Assertion Training. Systematic desensitization and implosion may be indicated when some external object or situation is feared, but when desired behaviors are prevented by personal timidity or interpersonal hesitancy, assertion training may be used. In assertion training, people who have difficulty in insisting upon their legitimate rights can be taught to express themselves without fear. Often, neurotic and socially withdrawn individuals are nonassertive because they fear "stepping on toes" or incurring the real or imagined wrath of others. For example, nonassertive people probably couldn't say anything if someone broke into a theater line ahead of them; they might quietly fume and ruminate about what they *should* have said.

The absence of assertive behavior may be due to several things. First, people may not even know *how* to assert themselves; this is a problem based on lack of learning. A further possibility is that people know how to be assertive but misinterpret their assertion as hostility. People may be so fearful of a hostile or unmanageable response from others that they keep their gripes to themselves. Regardless of the source of the nonassertiveness, the result usually is the same—a frightened, withdrawn, often neurotic and miserable person who may internally seethe with unleashed feelings.

In assertion training, the socially fearful person is first assessed to determine the degree of nonassertiveness. For example, Wolpe (1973) presents five basic questions to his clients. Each represents a situation with which a comfortably assertive person usually can cope:

1. What do you do if after having bought an article in a shop you walk out and find your change is a dollar short?
2. Suppose that, arriving home after buying an article on the way, you find it slightly damaged. What will you do?
3. What do you do if someone pushes in front of you in a line?
4. At a shop, while you wait for the clerk to finish with the customers ahead of you, another customer arrives and also waits. What do you do if the clerk then directs his attention to the new customer before he serves you?
5. You order a steak rare and it arrives well done. What do you do? [p. 84].

Once the degree of nonassertiveness is estimated, the behavior therapist typically presents clients with a series of tasks in which they must try to defend their rights. Individuals are asked to rehearse assertiveness in the safety of the therapist's office and to experience themselves as capable of assertion, not fearful and avoiding of it. The specific manner in which clients attain confidence varies widely, but, as a basic method, we will describe the original idea of Salter (1949). Salter believed that six modes of behavior had to be increased or instituted in nonassertive people. First there is *feeling talk*, in which clients begin to describe their feelings in everyday conversations—for example, "I like this sandwich. I'm glad we ate here," as opposed to "This is a pretty good place to eat." Next, Salter insists upon *facial talk*, where feelings are communicated by facial gestures and expressions as well as words. To communicate properly in *contradict and attack*, clients are taught that, if they disagree with someone, they must not pretend to agree, but must disagree *with* appropriate feeling. In addition, clients are told to use the word *I* more frequently in order to involve them more. Salter also believes clients should *express agreement when praised*, and reasonable amounts of self-praise are encouraged. The last mode is *improvisation*, in which clients learn that they must respond spontaneously to situations and not ruminate and avoid expression of feelings.

Salter's advice and much practice can help the nonassertive person to experience great satisfaction and increased self-confidence. Perhaps the greatest insight during the process of obtaining this self-confidence is the realization that *to be assertive is not necessarily to be hostile.* Many of us have grown up believing that demanding one's rights is a hostile act; as a result, when we finally do ask for our share, we may ask angrily. The response to this anger is usually anger in others, followed by discomfort and anxiety. Table 22-2 is a continuum that depicts behavior ranging from passive to hostile. The goal of the assertion therapist is to move the passive person from the extreme left side of the dimension to somewhere in the middle. Many people could benefit from moving from the extreme right toward the middle, but such people rarely are as miserable as the nonassertive person and usually don't seek help.

Operant Conditioning. The methods of increasing behavioral frequency we have described so far are mainly verbal and nonmanipulative. However, by using rewards and punishments in operant conditioning, behavior therapists can apply their knowledge of animal-learning principles to human problems. In Chapter 4, we described the way in which reinforcement can be manipulated to increase or decrease behavioral frequencies. The same principles may be applied in the therapeutic use of reinforcement.

An example of the application of positive reinforcement is provided by Bachrach, Erwin, and Mohr (1965), who treated a woman with anorexia nervosa (Chapter 11). In order to increase the frequency of eating behavior, the initially 47-pound client was placed on a reinforcement schedule in which she ate her meals with a therapist each day. During the meals, the therapist would speak to her only if she made some movement toward eating. After any meal in which she even touched her food, she would receive some TV time or a chance to listen to music. As time went on, she was required to eat more and more of her meal in order to receive her positive reinforcement. She had to finish her meal to be able to watch TV or listen to the radio. The therapist reported that, after two months, the client had

Table 22-2. *The range of passive-assertive-aggressive responses to violation of legitimate rights: a steak, ordered medium, is brought to you well done.*

Passive	Assertive	Aggressive
Passive acceptance, quiet misery, rumination, internal anger, automatic agreement.	Healthy disagreement, state one's own rights, anger, disappointment. Appropriately expressed feelings.	Automatic disagreement, the other's rights don't matter. Anger, blaming, belligerent attitude.
"It's fine this way, thank you."	"I ordered the steak medium and it's well done. Please bring me a different one."	"You can take this steak and shove it."

gained 14 pounds and become an outpatient and that, after 18 months, she weighed a stable 88 pounds and was living at home.

As seen in this case, it is possible to control the frequency of desired behaviors by manipulating reinforcers. The application of such operant techniques has been helpful in altering specific behavior patterns and in making hospitalized patients more manageable and treatable. Operant methods have been especially successful in the treatment of retarded people (Chapter 17) and children (Chapter 18).

Decreasing Frequency of Behaviors

The second major group of behavior therapies are directed primarily at reducing the frequency of undesirable behaviors. When such behaviors occur too frequently, individuals may not have adequate means of controlling themselves, may not wish to control themselves, or may not be aware of various situations in which behavioral excess is or is not acceptable.

The types of behavioral excesses toward which frequency-reduction methods may be directed include alcohol consumption, drug use, overeating, deviant sexual behavior, petty theft, and hallucinations. In each type of excess, some physical or social damage usually accrues to the individual with continued emission of the behavior.

Aversive Conditioning. Aversive conditioning, or aversive therapy, refers to the use of noxious or painful stimuli in a systematic program designed to reduce the frequency of undesirable behavior. Aversive conditioning represents a clinical application of procedures such as avoidance and escape learning, in which electric shock or drugs that induce nausea are used to reduce undesirable behavior.

The use of electric shock in the treatment of a compulsive gambler will serve as one example. Barker and Miller (1973) reported the successful treatment of a man who had been "addicted" to slot machines for 12 years. During treatment, the client was wired to a 70-volt shock source and instructed to begin gambling as usual. During a series of three-hour sessions, he received at least 150 shocks per session on a random basis. Sometimes he was shocked for putting tokens in the machine, other times for picking up his winnings. After six hours in front of the machine, he stopped gambling; this was followed by another six hours at the machine with no gambling and no shocks. He reported no desire to gamble and reportedly did not do so for 18 months after the aversive therapy.

Instead of electric shock, nausea-inducing drugs such as apomorphine may be used to produce aversion. These drugs are administered in such a way as to lend their aversive properties to once pleasant behaviors, thereby rendering these behaviors aversive. One behavior often treated this way is excess use of alcohol.

In aversive therapy for alcoholics, the client may be given a nausea-inducing drug a few minutes before the conditioning procedure. Prior to the onset of the nausea, a glass of an alcoholic beverage is given to the individual, who is instructed to drink it down. Then, a second drink is offered; with proper timing, nausea begins at about the time the second drink is tasted. The result is the association of alcohol in the mouth and stomach and a slightly "high" sensation with the feeling of nausea. As the client regurgitates, his vomit is filled with the beverage ingested in his first drink. An avoidance of alcohol is thus built up through classical conditioning. Initial reports (Lemere & Voegtlin, 1950) indicated about a 40% chance of long-term success with drug-induced aversion therapy for alcoholics. Aversive therapy may be successful, but the procedure is lengthy and often offensive to even a tough-minded therapist. More important, some of those with whom electrical or drug-induced aversion is used soon develop a *discrimination;* that is, the aversion response may be present *only* if wires are connected or drugs are ingested. Outside the experimental setting, the person once again may drink freely.

Covert Sensitization. Although it is a form of aversive therapy, covert sensitization deserves separate consideration because it seems to avoid many of the problems of shock and drug-based treatment. Rather than use unwieldy equipment, covert sensitization, as developed by Cautela (1967), uses the client's own imagination to reduce behavioral frequency.

The basic procedure of covert sensitization was described in our discussion of its use in the treatment of alcohol abuse (Chapter 13). Using scenes composed by the therapist, clients are led to associate their undesirable behavior with nausea, vomiting, fear, and a whole host of other aversive stimuli. Since the associations are in the imagination, they aren't dependent upon the presence of shock devices or drugs. As a result, generalization of aversion to real-life settings is more easily accomplished.

Once covert sensitization has successfully reduced the frequency of undesirable behavior, it is often necessary to strengthen desirable activity patterns. To do this, Cautela (1970a) has devised the method of *covert reinforcement.* In covert reinforcement, clients are instructed to reward themselves with "thoughts of pleasant things" (for example, sitting by a mountain stream or lying in a cool breeze at the beach) each time they have successfully avoided target behaviors such as overeating or drinking. By the way, covert reinforcement can be a good way to reward yourself for studying. After 50 minutes of concentration, sit back and allow yourself to think of something really nice to do for 10 minutes. You may find your study time and efficiency are improved.

Thought-Stopping. So far, we have spoken primarily of behavioral techniques directed at actions or anxiety. Thought-stopping, however, is directed at disturbed or disturbing *thoughts.* Often, the major problem to be treated isn't excessive behavior, but uncontrollable ideas (obsessions) or mental perceptions (hallucinations). Thought-stopping may be used for these difficulties.

Wolpe (1973) credits the development of thought-stopping to J. G. Taylor in 1955. The procedure usually begins with the client's being asked to close his or her eyes and to think deliberately the offending thought or to await the onset of a hallucinatory experience. When the thoughts occur, the client signals the therapist in some prearranged way (the lifting of a finger, for example). The therapist then shouts "STOP!" and asks the client to note that the offending thoughts are gone. The client is then told that, by saying *stop* to himself, he too can halt the thoughts. What seems to happen in thought-stopping is that saying "stop" repeatedly becomes aversive, and almost *any* behavior followed by an aversive stimulus—even if self-imposed—tends to occur less frequently.

Negative Practice. Our final example of methods directed at reducing behavioral frequency, *negative practice*, is based upon the laboratory-established phenomenon called *satiation*. Simply conceptualized, satiation refers to the repetition of a particular behavior until the individual tires of emitting it. Negative practice, in which undesirable behaviors are temporarily encouraged rather than discouraged, is a clinical application of satiation.

Negative practice may be exemplified by a treatment program reported by Ayllon and Michael (1959) for an institutionalized psychotic woman who had the undesirable habit of hoarding as many as 30 soiled towels in her room. The researchers decided to give her all the towels she wanted. At first she eagerly took towel after towel to her room. Then, as the number of towels grew to 600 or more, she began to stop taking new ones. She soon seemed to tire of so many towels and the clutter they produced and *asked* that they be removed. She had been allowed to emit the undesirable response as often as she liked, soon tired of it, and the behavior reduced in frequency.

OTHER INDIVIDUAL THERAPIES

The therapies that don't fit easily into the psychoanalytic, humanistic-existential, or behavioral categories include new approaches and less well-known techniques. An introduction to some of these methods will help to emphasize the broad range of ways to help those who are different.

Primal Therapy

Primal therapy, developed by Arthur Janov (1970), is based on the theory that all people have basic or primal needs, which include being fed, being kept warm, being stimulated and held, having privacy, and being allowed to develop inherent potential. When any of these needs is denied at an early age, a *primal pain* can occur, which remains in the person and produces tension long into adulthood. For Janov, neurosis usually is the result of primal pain; even if reality must be sacrificed, abnormal behavior is emitted because of an incessant need to overcome primal pain.

In primal therapy, buried primal pains may be uncovered and relieved. A unique aspect of the process is that some clients may see the therapist continuously each day, all day, for the first three weeks of treatment. Often the therapist sees no one else during this period. The client usually is isolated in a hotel for the entire time. Using physical techniques such as superficial breathing, lying on the floor like an infant, and running about nude, the client soon may be able to remember and reexperience early primal pain. Janov reports that a common phenomenon occurs among his clients: when they reach back to the source of their neurosis and begin to feel it, their memory is punctuated by a loud, spine-chilling cry. Janov calls this the *primal scream* and contends that it represents the choked-off cry of the infant whose primal needs were denied.

Although each person's specific pains differ, we will present an example of a primal-therapy interaction to give you the flavor of this approach:

Client: I can see the house we lived in, but it doesn't look the same—it doesn't feel the same.

Therapist: Lie on the floor on your back, hold your legs up and flail your arms and legs around like you did when you were a baby. How do things look from there?

Client: Wow . . . everything looks bigger. I feel like I'm looking up at monstrous things. Your face looks different from down here—it looks mean—the feeling is kind of scary. I can't get up easily from way down here.

Therapist: Close your eyes and imagine yourself in your house as a baby.

Client: (Pause.) I'm on the floor, just like this. My mother is at the kitchen table peeling potatoes for supper. I feel alone . . . I feel cold . . . I want my mommy . . . I start to cry (client makes crying noises) . . . she says something I don't understand, but it sounds soft and nice. But I still want her to hold me . . . to make me warm. . . . (Client is getting visibly agitated.) Mommy! Mommy! Please come and get me! (There is fear in his voice now.) I hear her again, she's yelling at me now. She's not coming—wait, yes she is—she's coming—I can see her teeth gritted—she's hitting me! (Client cries hysterically—moaning and choking—primal scream—client lies exhausted, almost motionless, on the floor.)

Kaiserian Psychotherapy

Focusing more on interpersonal communication than on early pain, Kaiserian therapy was developed by Helmuth Kaiser (Fierman, 1965), who believed that basic problems in adjustment stemmed primarily from two sources. First is the *illusion of fusion,* the false belief that one person can get so close to another as to fuse with that person. Kaiser believed that the illusion occurs because of our desire not to face our essential aloneness when under stress. A second source of emotional problems is *duplicity,* or lack of genuineness. According to Kaiser, duplicitous communication can occur in the voice, facial expression, posture, emotional tone, and so forth. An everyday example of such communication might be the father who says to his son "Yes, I'd like to play ball," when he wouldn't. Although his words say one thing, his voice seems to say the opposite. Kaiser contended that the process of therapy was to point out similar discrepancies in communication. A woman who acts seductively, yet says she is afraid of men coming near her, must learn that *she* is probably responsible for many of the unwelcome advances. The young woman who claims she can never get ahead because her boss picks on her must learn that *her* behavior probably contributes to her boss's attitude.

Kaiserian psychotherapy frequently is characterized by direct confrontation of character style, by minimal therapist-induced structure, and by a goal of genuine, nonduplicitous interaction between client and therapist. Although the method, exemplified below, isn't widely used, some of its proponents (Fierman, 1965; Frank, 1967) feel that Kaiser's ideas may be relevant to many other therapeutic approaches.

> *Client:* So I said to him, I said, "Why don't you ever think of me? All you think about are the children."
>
> *Therapist:* And what did he say?
>
> *Client:* He told me I was crazy. He said that no matter what he did for me it wasn't enough. That makes me so mad.
>
> *Therapist:* What are you saying to me right now?
>
> *Client:* What do you mean?
>
> *Therapist:* Are you asking me for some support in your problem with your husband?
>
> *Client:* That makes me angry at you! What do you think I came here for?
>
> *Therapist:* I'm starting to feel a little like your husband must feel. I feel on the defensive—I feel like if I don't deliver something to you that you will be very angry.
>
> *Client:* And?
>
> *Therapist:* Don't you see, Mary, you are saying with your words, "I'm tough" and "I demand attention that will satisy my needs," but with your behavior you're saying, "Nothing can

satisfy me because I know, deep down, that you don't really mean what you say."

Client: You mean I'm telling you to help me but I'm also saying don't help me? I don't understand.

Therapist: You are saying, "Like me as much as I want *without* my having to ask you." But no one can do that, so you ask—because you ask—you don't believe the liking is really felt, and then you feel rejected and angry. You are demanding openly and indirectly, Mary, and I think it causes you trouble—with me, with your husband, with lots of people.

Client: I just want to be cared for . . . no one really cares. (Begins to weep.)

Therapist: I care, but not because you demand it—but because I want to.

Rational-Emotive Therapy

Rational-emotive therapy focuses on irrational beliefs as the core of behavioral disorders. Developed by Albert Ellis (1973), rational-emotive therapy assumes that emotional disturbance stems, not from what people experience, but from how they *perceive* what happens to them. Ellis proposes that, when a highly emotional response, *C*, follows a significant activity event, *A*, *A* doesn't actively cause *C*. Rather, *B*, the individual's perception-belief about *A*, causes *C*. Thus, *A* may be a dirty carpet in the living room and *C* may be crying. Dirty carpets don't cause crying, but the irrational belief (*B*) that one must be a perfect housekeeper or face unbearable shame and embarrassment can cause crying.

Since irrational beliefs are seen as being at the core of emotional problems, the goal of the therapist is to rid the client of irrational beliefs so that the client is free to have a logical existence filled with appropriate emotion. Ellis believes that people are born with the potential to lead such a logical existence and that faulty learning and attitudes produce people with tendencies to irrational thought, wishful thinking, and intolerance of self (Corey, 1977).

Rational-emotive therapists seem to be anything but unconditionally accepting in Rogers's sense. They wish to stop the client's irrational thoughts in any way they can. Thus, it isn't uncommon for loud and abusive language to be used by the therapist in hopes of establishing three basic and required insights (Ellis, 1973). The first insight is the realization that self-defeating behavior is related to understandable causes and perceptions of events in which the person is involved. In the second insight, clients learn that *they made themselves disturbed* in the past and that they continue to be disturbed because of their own irrational perceptions of life events. The third insight is that, since they got themselves into the problems, with hard work and practice, they can get out of them as well.

Armed with this theory and a firm belief in his philosophy of life, Ellis often cajoles, teases, encourages, and even curses his clients. He doesn't seem to relent until his points are accepted and his clients begin to realize what they're doing to themselves. He seeks out their particular type of irrational thinking (see Table 22-3) and then exerts immense effort to alter the misperceptions. The following is an example of rational-emotive therapy. Needless to say, Ellis is very controversial, but frequently very successful as well.

Client: I need to do a better job at work. I'm afraid they'll fire me.
Therapist: Who'll fire you?
Client: The boss. He'll find out that I'm not doing a good job and he'll fire me.
Therapist: Who says you're not doing a good job?
Client: Nobody really . . . but *I* know I'm not, and if the boss finds out . . .
Therapist: How long have you had the job?
Client: Fourteen years—I started just after college.
Therapist: You've had the job for 14 years and haven't been fired yet? How do you explain that?
Client: I've been careful. Whenever the boss comes around, I'm sure that everything is just right in my section and that the work is getting done.

Table 22-3. *Ellis's listing of 11 basic irrational thoughts*

1. It is essential that one be loved by virtually everyone in his community.
2. One must be perfectly competent, adequate, and achieving to consider oneself worthwhile.
3. Some people are bad, wicked or villainous and therefore should be blamed and punished.
4. It is a terrible catastrophe when things are not as one wants them to be.
5. Unhappiness is caused by outside circumstances and the individual has no control over it.
6. Dangerous or fearsome things are causes for great concern and their possibility must be continually dwelt upon.
7. It is easier to avoid certain difficulties and self-responsibilities than to face them.
8. One should be dependent on others and must have someone stronger on whom to rely.
9. Past experiences and events are the determiners of present behavior and cannot be eradicated.
10. One should be quite upset over other people's problems.
11. There is always a right and perfect solution to every problem, and it must be found or the result will be catastrophic.

Therapist: And you've done this for 14 years?

Client: Yes. He's never caught me not doing a good job, but I'm always afraid he'll find out that I really don't always know exactly what to do.

Therapist: What's so terrible about that?

Client: I'm supposed to know! I'm a supervisor.

Therapist: Oh, a supervisor who doesn't always know just what to do. What a terrible thing!

Client: It is terrible—I'm supposed to know.

Therapist: And you don't! So what does that make you—a turd?

Client: Well, no, but . . .

Therapist: So you're not the best f—king supervisor in the world—you're mediocre. What's so terrible about being mediocre?

Client: I shouldn't be mediocre—the boss thinks I know what I'm doing. I'm afraid . . .

Therapist: Who says you shouldn't be mediocre? What if you really *are* mediocre? Should you be upset?

Client: You mean it's OK to be mediocre?

Therapist: If that's what you really are—a mediocre manager—why be upset? You are what you are!

CONCLUDING COMMENTS

Given the wide array of over 130 different forms of individual psychotherapy (Parloff, 1976a), it is often difficult to answer the question, which therapy is best? A better question probably would be, which therapy or therapist will be best *for me?* There are some therapists with whom a given person can work well and others with whom he or she will make little progress. Parloff has noted that seeking a therapist can be like shopping, and that a prospective client should "select carefully from among an array of qualified therapists (not thera*pies*) the one whose style of relating is acceptable to him—and preferably from a school of thought whose philosophy, values, and goals are most congenial to his own" (p. 20).

Having chosen a therapist, what can today's therapy clients expect from the experience? Earlier in this century, they probably could expect relief of symptoms, but many modern therapies include the added goal of "positive psychological growth" beyond the level of basic adjustment. Expansion of awareness and a search for self-actualization can be goals of modern psychotherapy just as often as relief of such problems as anxiety and depression.

CHAPTER SUMMARY CHART

In this chapter on individual therapy, we first discussed some general questions about psychotherapy:

Does psychotherapy work?
 	
Eysenck: No
Other psychotherapists:
    Yes
Outcome studies
	How does psychotherapy work?
	
	Process studies
	Placebo effect,
	    Barnum effect
	Therapist variables
	Client variables
	Relationship factors

Who does psychotherapy?
 	
Psychiatrists
Clinical psychologists
Psychiatric social
    workers
Psychiatric nurses
Pastoral counselors
	What's it like to be in psychotherapy?
	
	Personal experiences of a
	    client and a therapist

We then reviewed a selection of major types of individual psychotherapies:

Psychoanalytic therapies Psychoanalysis Psychoanalytic therapy	*Humanistic-existential therapies* Client-centered therapy Existential therapy Gestalt therapy Reality therapy

Behavioral therapies
 	
Increasing behavioral
    frequency:
Systematic
    desensitization
Implosion and
    flooding
Assertion training
	Other individual therapies
	
	Primal therapy
	Kaiserian therapy
	Rational-emotive
	    therapy

SECTION VIII:
TREATMENTS FOR
THOSE WHO ARE
DIFFERENT

Behavioral therapies
(continued)

Operant
conditioning
Decreasing behavioral
frequency:
Aversive conditioning
Covert sensitization
Thought-stopping
Negative practice

CHAPTER 23
GROUP AND
FAMILY
THERAPY

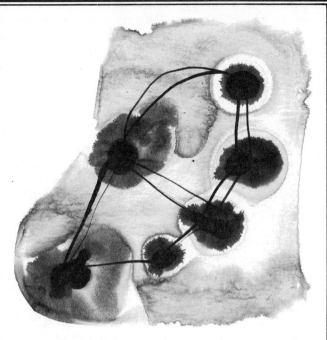

Group therapy differs from the individual therapies in several ways. The most obvious difference is that group therapy involves one, or sometimes two, therapists and seven to ten clients. Further, group therapy provides clients with an atmosphere in which they can relate to other "different" people and learn how they are coping. Third, being in a group can produce interactions, feelings, and difficulties that may be completely ignored or missed in a one-to-one treatment situation. Many people believe that clients are seen in groups so that a therapist can treat ten in one hour rather than one, but group therapy is *not* "diluted" individual treatment. Rather, group therapy is a unique mode of helping disturbed people, a technique that has acquired a distinct place in the treatment of those who are different.

GENERAL OVERVIEW

As is true of the individual therapies, there is no one "group therapy"; rather, there is a variety of group techniques, each within a different theoretical framework and with different specific content. The differences among the approaches will be clearer after we describe each technique; however, we will first mention the similarities among the group therapies. Therapy groups are composed of members and one or more leaders. Typically, the members are interviewed by the leaders before they join a group and are usually assigned to groups on the basis of their problem, the type of people already in the group, and the varying desires of the leaders, who may want their groups to have certain compositions. Some therapists prefer *homogeneous groups*, composed of people having similar characteristics such as age, sex, marital status, and type of problem. Other leaders may choose *heterogeneous groups*, whose composition may be decided on a first-come, first-served basis or on the basis of some "mixture" of member characteristics desired by the therapist. Groups usually meet for anywhere from an hour to an hour and a half (except for marathon groups, to be described later) and begin and end promptly. Members usually sit in a circle, in comfortable chairs or on the floor. As a rule, groups meet regularly, at the same time and place, and may continue meeting from a few weeks to, in some cases, several years. Instead of relating only to a therapist, a group-therapy client must react to a number of people. The therapeutic use of this interaction is believed to be the definitive mechanism of change (Nichols & Zax, 1977).

Among the best introductions to the characteristics of group therapy is that provided by Irwin Yalom (1970). Yalom discusses the basic procedures and fundamentals of group therapy, but he also includes an invaluable discussion of *why* group therapy works. Yalom notes that, as *curative factors*, group therapies depend upon varying amounts of ten basic group phenomena:

> *Imparting of information.* Groups provide didactic instructions about adjustment and disturbance; some groups offer advice, suggestions, and guidance.
> *Instillation of hope.* Being in a group with others who are showing progress helps instill and maintain hope for one's own chances of recovery.
> *Universality.* Group members may learn that they aren't the only ones with problems and that their own problems may not be unique. Great relief can be obtained from this realization.
> *Altruism.* In the course of group therapy, members typically help one another through support, reassurance, and the like. Helping others can make members feel valuable and enable them to accept help more easily themselves.
> *Corrective recapitulation of the primary family group.* Groups are like families, with leaders being like parents and members being similar to siblings. Experiencing a healthy "family" can help correct early damage done by maladjusted family life.
> *Development of socializing techniques.* Social learning occurs in groups, in which members learn new ways of relating to other

Group therapy provides for experiences in social interaction that are not possible in individual psychotherapy. (Photo courtesy of the authors.)

people and can practice these new social skills in a warm, accepting atmosphere before trying them out in the "real" world.

Imitation of adaptive behavior. Group therapists can serve as models of better adjustment and often provide members with temporary new behaviors while they develop patterns comfortable to them.

Interpersonal learning. One of the two most important curative factors, interpersonal learning, describes the acquisition of corrective emotional experience in groups. Members exist in a social microcosm where their problems may be magnified, assessed, and corrected among understanding and accepting others.

Group cohesiveness. The other most important curative factor, group cohesiveness, is the therapy analogue of a relationship or intimacy. Members of a cohesive group often value their group above themselves: they may weep when one member is sad and rejoice if one of them achieves some progress. The sense of belonging seems to be of crucial therapeutic importance.

Catharsis. Group members can experience relief after releasing long-pent-up feelings of sadness, anger, joy, and so on. Ventilating feelings among those to whom one is close can be curative.

Each of the specific types of group therapy or group techniques described in this chapter includes some or all of Yalom's curative factors. Our descriptions of these group approaches to being different will be arranged into four major categories. We first will describe the early efforts in group therapy; next we will consider more recent approaches, some of which are designed for abnormal people and others for normal individuals. Third, we will present self-help groups, in which people with similar problems band together in an effort to aid one another, without professional therapists. Last, we will describe family therapy, a form of therapy for special groups in which nature, and not the group therapist, is responsible for group composition.

EARLY GROUP THERAPIES

Writers on group therapy (Ruitenbeek, 1969; Shaffer & Galensky, 1974) generally agree that the earliest use of group techniques was by the physician Joseph H. Pratt in his treatment of tuberculosis patients (Pratt, 1906). Pratt found that meeting regularly with a "class" of patients who couldn't afford inpatient care had dramatic effects upon the mood and life functions of these individuals. Within the field of psychiatry, Alfred Adler is generally credited with the development of formal group therapy (Dreikurs, 1959). In the 1920s, Adler and his psychoanalytic followers devised an approach known as *collective therapy*, in which several clients were seen simultaneously for psychoanalytically oriented treatment. First use of the term *group psychotherapy* is credited to Jacob Moreno in 1932 (Shaffer & Galensky, 1974); Moreno later became most widely known as the developer of psychodrama, a group technique to be discussed shortly. It seems that, when the psychoanalytic world accepted it, group therapy began to spread rapidly. In the section on the early forms of group therapy, we have selected two approaches to describe—psychoanalytic group therapy and psychodrama.

Psychoanalytic Groups

In 1921, Freud published an article entitled "Group Psychology and the Analysis of the Ego," in which he emphasized the importance of the leader in group formation and function. He likened a group to what he termed "the primal horde," a basic group of early people in which the leader usually was responsible for group survival, yet was envied and often hated because of his authority. Similar group reactions to a therapist are often considered by analytic therapists to be the result of transference and can represent important therapeutic material.

Psychoanalytic group therapy doesn't involve a half-dozen people lying on couches formed into a circle! Rather, the technique derives its name from the facts that a healthy balance of id, ego, and superego is typically the primary goal and that methods such as free association, regression, insight, transference, removal of defense mechanisms, and the like may all be involved in group interactions. To encourage transference and to produce anxiety sufficient to require the appearance of defenses, analytic group therapists may be quite passive and withdraw from the group. They sometimes interpret and correct, but may not say anything during an entire group session. The group's need to depend upon the therapist for guidance ("transference onto the father") and anger at him or her for not helping them to interact easily often result in the following kinds of interactions:

Jack: OK, we've been sitting here for 20 minutes and so far we've talked about Burt's dental office, my boat, Carol's troubles in law school, and Wendy's bad foot. This is ridiculous—this is group therapy, isn't it? Dr. D., what should we talk about?

Dr. D.:   You feel pretty lost, all of you, and especially Jack. Why should I be the one to help? Does someone always need to help? Am I like your father? Should I hold your hands?

Burt: Jack, he's right! Why don't we just do what we think is right? I guess if it's wrong, he'll tell us.

Wendy: No, he won't tell us anything—he never has before. Sometimes I wonder why I keep coming here. It's a waste of money and time.

Burt: Yeah, what are we getting for our $15 a week? Dr. D., why should we keep coming?

Dr. D.:   You're all very angry with me. But I'll bet you feel other things as well. Carol, you're being quiet in all this.

Carol: Oh, Dr. D., I feel terrible that they're talking to you like this. I mean . . . they shouldn't yell at you.

Dr. D.:   Why?

Carol: You must feel terrible when they do. We sit here and do nothing and blame you.

Dr. D.:   Do you feel terrible when people scream at you?

Carol: My God, I can't stand it—it makes me sick and scared.

Dr. D.:   Tell us more.

Carol: I've always felt that way. I get scared if *I* yell at someone and I try to avoid situations where people might get mad at me and yell.

In this transcript, you can see that the leader, although not directly involved, seemed to be the focus of the discussion. Were the excerpt to continue, we might expect the leader to ask Carol to think back to her childhood and her early experiences with screaming. Also, her modes of defending against her fear might be further explored. The group members probably would share in the discussion and compare Carol's feelings and attitudes with their own. The therapist would indirectly guide the group in an effort to analyze resistances, resolve transferences (in the therapist as well as other group members), and work through individual and group blockages.

Psychodrama

Rather than allowing people to interact freely, as they usually do in traditional groups, *psychodrama* involves a structured, theaterlike technique in treatment. Developed by Jacob Moreno in the 1920s and 1930s, psychodrama is a therapeutic approach in which, by actually acting out problems, individuals can be helped to gain new insights and to experience blocked and threatening feelings.

Typically, psychodrama is carried out informally in special "theaters" set up in small auditoriums. The stage is usually composed of three circles of decreasing size placed one on top of the other so that there are three levels of stage height. The "cast" usually consists of the director (chief therapist), client-protagonist, and people who will play important figures in the client-protagonist's life or, at times, the client at various times in his or her life. Once the cast is assembled, the therapist directs them in some warm-up experiences, such as describing a feeling or even telling jokes. Once the group is "loose," the drama begins.

The therapist asks the protagonist (client) to step to the stage. If the problem on which they will focus has been predetermined, the therapist will normally ask the protagonist to describe it to the group. The therapist then may help the client to set the stage so the actual life stress can be re-created, acted out, worked through, or resolved in the safety of the "theater."

Specific techniques developed by Moreno foreshadowed many of the "innovations" later introduced by the modern group therapists. For example, during the psychodrama, Moreno would often assign a *role reversal*, in which the protagonist might switch roles with his or her "father" and experience a life situation from a different perspective. Such reversals are among the basic techniques of the Gestalt approach (described in Chapter 22). Other methods developed by Moreno include *soliloquy*, in which protagonists speak of their uncensored thoughts and feelings to the "audience"; the *mirror technique*, in which protagonists, with feedback from the audience, learn to see themselves as others do, and the *magic shop*, in which protagonists are given the opportunity to "buy" some desired new personal characteristic at the cost of temporarily sacrificing a desirable characteristic they already possess. Although it is difficult to communicate the actual experience of psychodrama, we hope the following transcript will help:

> *Protagonist:*   OK, I'm at my office and I can't talk with my boss without choking on my words and sounding like a fool. This is how it would look. (He rearranges the furniture, and so on.)
> *Therapist:*   Put the boss's chair on the top level of the stage—you put him there in your feelings anyway, it seems.
> *Protagonist:*   Yes, that's true.
> *Therapist:*   Who else is needed? Someone to play the boss? A secretary? OK, John and Mary go up and sit where Jim places you.

OK, how about a couple of alter egos for Jim—to say things he can't say right now. Bill, Burt, would you please play those roles? (All characters go to the stage, and the plot is devised.)

Protagonist: OK. The boss last week told me to stay late and get some things out. I had a date, but stayed anyway. I was very angry and upset and wanted to tell him, but I didn't know what to do.

Therapist: OK, play it out.

"Boss": Jim, will you stay and finish this after work?

Protagonist: No. No, that's not how he would say it. He'd say "Jim, this has to be done today, before you leave, even if you need to stay over, get it done."

The drama will proceed, with the protagonist describing the characters to the cast so that they may play more realistic roles.

Boss: What do you mean you have a date—that you won't stay?

Protagonist: I'm sorry, Mr. _____, I know you need it done, but had you asked me earlier I could have finished it today. I'd be glad to stay overtime if you give me a few days' notice so I can be sure not to have any early-evening appointments. But today I just can't stay. I hope you understand.

Audience: (Applause.)

LATER INNOVATIONS IN GROUP TECHNIQUES

To be sure, many recent group methods have grown out of the therapy or theory of the first half of this century, but they are often different in form and focus from those we have already described. One major difference is that many of the more recent group techniques don't seem to be directed at people who are different. Rather, a large number of modern approaches may be termed *human-development groups* rather than psychotherapy groups (Shaffer & Galensky, 1974). As a rule, human-growth groups aren't specifically designed to help only people with psychological maladjustments but are also for relatively normal people who are seeking awareness and emotional experiences frequently unavailable in daily life. In this section, we describe both psychotherapy groups and human-growth groups.

Psychotherapy Groups

Psychotherapy groups of recent vintage generally reflect a shift in focus from the early emphasis on people as bubbling cauldrons of forbidden needs and wishes to the belief in the basic goodness of people. In modern

Nontraditional group therapy can take many forms. (Photos by Joseph Czarnecki.)

therapy groups, this shift in emphasis usually has resulted in more active and involved therapists and shorter duration of treatment; people typically learn to relate better, to practice new modes of behavior in the safety of their groups, to take responsibility for their own progress, and to allow themselves to express their "inherent" potential. These goals may be achieved in a variety of ways.

Behavior-Modification Groups. Given the success of behavior modification and the large number of people who could benefit from it, it was probably inevitable that group behavioral approaches would develop. However, behavioral group therapy seems more like "individual therapy in groups" than any other type of group we will describe. Frequently, people may be placed in behavioral groups more for the sake of multiple treatment than for the special characteristics of intervention that a group setting provides.

Behavioral-therapy groups may be roughly categorized as being of three types (Shaffer & Galensky, 1974). The *systematic-desensitization group* usually involves people with similar fears who are brought together for multiple individual treatment. Fishman and Newes (1971) describe such a group, in which a standardized anxiety hierarchy (see Chapter 22) is designed for the group as a whole. Relaxation may be learned in a group setting, and a fixed time schedule for progressing up the fear hierarchy may be applied. Fishman and Newes reported that their desensitization group lasted five to six sessions with good results. Whereas Fishman and Newes's group included little interaction among group members, McManus (1971) reports that the encouragement of group relationships was an important part of his desensitization groups. In McManus's treatment of a group of college students experiencing test anxiety, he found that mutual support and group reinforcement were helpful adjuncts to movement through the anxiety hierarchy.

In *behavioral-practice groups*, individuals are afforded the opportunity to learn and rehearse social, interpersonal skills with which they have had problems. One widely used and successful type of practice group is the assertion-training group, as described by Fensterham (1972). The assertion-training group usually includes eight or ten people who experience difficulty in asking for what is due them and in protecting their rights. In assertion group therapy, a number of supportive others as well as a therapist are typically available to aid in the firm establishment of assertive behavior patterns. Assertion-training groups often last for 15 to 20 sessions of 90 minutes to two hours.

In *specific-behavioral-control groups*, rather than general characteristics such as assertiveness, easily measured and clearly observable behaviors are the common target. Most frequent among the specific targeted behaviors are probably excessive smoking or eating. As in the other types of behavioral groups, mutual support and encouragement from other group members is important, but specific therapeutic techniques often disallow or counteract group interaction. An example of the often strict direction of specific-behavioral-control groups comes from the work of Marrone, Merksamer, and Salzberg (1970), who applied a group method to the treatment of smoking. Using a technique called *stimulus satiation*, Marrone and his colleagues kept clients in group meetings for up to 20 hours out of a 40-hour period. During group sessions, clients were allowed to interact freely *as long as they were smoking continuously*. A one-dollar fine was levied against people not holding a cigarette or inhaling at least once every few minutes. Most clients were nauseated by the smoky air and constant smoking, and more than half of them stopped smoking even before the conclusion of the group sessions. Marrone et al. reported that 60% of their clients weren't smoking four months after treatment.

The three categories of behavioral group therapy vary in content and specific method, but all share a focus on overt behavior, the delineation of clear goals, the scientific assessment of outcome, and a sound basis in laboratory psychology. To many other group therapists, behavioral group therapy isn't true "group therapy" but a form of "wholesale" individual treatment.

Bioenergetic Group Therapy. Unlike behavior-therapy groups, which focus on specific behaviors primarily through language and structured experiences, *bioenergetic groups* treat psychological problems by involving the mind *and* body in the therapeutic process (Lowen, 1969). Clients in a bioenergetic group are often minimally clad—men in swim trunks, and women in leotards—so that the body is "available for expression." Physical contact among group members is usually encouraged, and therapist-directed breathing and movement are often crucial to group sessions. Bioenergetic theory holds that, by including the body in the therapy process, this approach obviates the split between the physical experience of emotion and mental interpretation of emotions and unlocks human experiential phenomena. In essence, the *total* person, rather than a part, is the object of therapeutic efforts.

Bioenergetic theory probably sparked recent interest in body language (Lowen, 1969)—communication based upon body position, facial expression, and the like which is supposedly out of the immediate, conscious control of communicators. In bioenergetic therapy, body language is often interpreted and focused upon to the exclusion of more willful, and often less genuine and trustworthy, verbal communication. An example of the emphasis on body language in bioenergetic therapy follows:

Therapist: Let's all try to loosen up now. I'd like each of you to bend forward, feet about 12 inches apart, toes in, knees slightly bent, and breathe as I do. (Group follows these and other exercise instructions.) Anybody feeling anything?

Mr. J.: Yes, my legs are shaking.

Miss L.: Mine, too. (Rest of group agrees, except for Mrs. D.)

Therapist: Mrs. D., you say your legs are not shaking—that's interesting. Most of our bodies respond to these exercises with *some* vibration in their legs. What do you think is going on with you?

Mrs. D.: I don't really know.

Mr. M.: Maybe you're too tense—you didn't let go.

Therapist: You seem very tight, Mrs. D. Can you even allow your body to do as it needs to?

Mrs. D.: I wasn't aware that I was tight.

Therapist: What would happen if you let your legs completely relax right now. I mean if you let them go limp?

Mrs. D.: I guess I'd fall down.

Therapist: Precisely. And if you let yourself as a person relax, you would fall down as a person, wouldn't you? You'd be weak, a passive blob on the floor. Does that scare you?

Mrs. D.: Of course it does, but I didn't try to stop my legs from relaxing while we did the exercise.

Therapist: Mrs. D., we really can't know what we're doing to our bodies until we see how our body language compares with other peoples', and compared with others in the group, you're tight as hell!

As seen in this excerpt, the therapist in a bioenergetic group may be very active and focus on physical as well as verbal communication. The bioenergetic therapist uses information concerning the participant's physical behavior to treat the "total" person.

Marathon Group Therapy. As opposed to the usual hour-and-a-half or two-hour session of most group approaches, marathon therapy sessions may last anywhere from four hours to four days—or longer. Groups usually meet in large rooms and remain together for the entire time. If a participant is sleepy, he or she just dozes off. Food and soft drinks are freely available.

One philosophy behind the marathon group is that, over a long period of time, it is impossible for anyone to "slip by" and not get involved in the group. As time passes, group pressures usually increase and fatigue may cause a dropping of defenses and an opening-up of personal thoughts and feelings. Bach (1966) has stated that the therapeutic effect of the marathon is its helping members to move from hiding behind façades and avoiding others to the more desirable states of *transparent self* and *psychological intimacy.* The process by which members move to these desirable states usually is guided by the "ground rules" in Table 23-1. A note of warning on marathon groups: they look easy to run and fun to do, but because their major impact is to wear down a person's psychological strength quickly, they can be very damaging if not led by skilled, trained therapists.

Table 23-1. *The ten marathon commandments*

1. Stay together in the same place and don't leave until the prearranged time.
2. Creature comforts are self-regulated and must be taken care of without disrupting the continuity of the group.
3. The group leader follows all rules of members except he or she may rest *away* from the group for up to four hours. Group continues in the leader's absence.
4. All forms of physical assault and threat of real violence are forbidden.
5. Group "techniques" such as role-playing, psychodrama, and so on are to be avoided.
6. Encountering others is a four-phase experience: (1) individual behaviors are reacted to; (2) reactions are fed back; (3) counterreactions to feedback are expressed; (4) all the group participates.
7. "Show me now . . . do not tell me when" is the basic theme of the marathon. Stay in the here-and-now.
8. "As you are in the group, so you are in the world." Members learn about themselves and try new ways of relating.
9. Members' changes and improvements will be noticed and reinforced by the group.
10. Information gained in the group session is absolutely confidential.

From "The Marathon Group: Intense Practice of Intimate Interaction," by G. Bach, *Psychological Reports*, 1966, *18*, 995–1002. Reprinted by permission of the author and publisher.

Human-Growth Groups

Human-growth groups differ from the innovative psychotherapy groups already discussed in that they are designed primarily for normal individuals and involve attempts at increasing the quality of emotional experience, expanding self-awareness, and improving interpersonal sensitivity. In the proper hands, growth groups can be valuable and helpful to almost everyone; in amateur or not fully trained hands, growth groups have been known to produce severe psychological damage, often precipitating psychotic episodes.

T-Groups. Among the earliest of the human-growth groups were the sensitivity-training or T-groups (*T* stands for training). A T-group may be defined as "an intensive effort at interpersonal self-study and an attempt to *learn* from this raw experience of member participation in a group how to improve interpersonal skills and to understand the phenomena of group dynamics" (Shaffer & Galensky, 1974, p. 189). Currently administered by the National Training Laboratory, T-groups are specialized experiences in which a skilled leader, called a trainer, directs a group of people through a series of exercises designed to increase their interpersonal and intrapersonal awareness and sensitivity.

Alteration in sensitivity levels may be achieved in T-groups through several key growth factors. Among these factors are a focus on the here-and-now, group support and trust, increased self-disclosure, and, most important, feedback. In the T-group, feedback is often structured and directed

Table 23-2. *Typical T-group exercises*

Blind milling. Participants stand and, with eyes closed, mill around the room for several minutes. No one speaks, but all try to experience the group through the senses of touch and smell.

Eyeball to eyeball. Without speaking or moving, members pair off and stare into each other's eyes for one or two minutes.

Strength bombardment. Each group member, in turn, is told something nice about himself or herself by every other group member. Also, each member may be asked to say good things about himself or herself for one minute.

Metaphorical description. Each member moves around the group and stops at each other member. Staring at the other member, the speaker describes the other in metaphorical terms such as "mashed banana" or "scary gorilla."

Trusting the group. Each person, in turn, stands in the center of a circle formed by other members. With eyes closed, they allow themselves to fall—members of the group catch them. It may be difficult for some people to trust the group to break their fall.

Breaking in. The group forms a tight circle with shoulders together and arms interlocked. One member is outside the group circle and must physically break in and become a part of it. Those in the circle may try to keep the intruder out. A reverse of the procedure occurs when someone is trapped *inside* the circle and must fight to get out.

Who am I. In turn, each member must complete the phrase "I am . . ." in as many ways as possible for a period up to one minute. It sounds easy, but it's quite hard.

so that all members are assured of gaining previously unknown information about themselves. Exercises such as *metaphorical descriptions* and *strength bombardment*, as described in Table 23-2, are often used to structure feedback. These and other group exercises are not ends in themselves but are ways of physically experiencing psychological states (alienation, for example) or of generating strong feelings in the group. After each exercise, the group usually sits down with the trainer and describes feelings experienced during the exercise. It is in the feedback about the exercises, and not the exercises themselves, that benefit most frequently may be gained.

The T-group experience may be as varied as the leader wishes. However, T-group researchers have observed that a general pattern is usually followed in most T-groups. Bennis (1964) has provided a description of the phases of a T-group from beginning to end.[1]

Major Phase I: Dependence

Sub-phase Ia: Dependence-Flight. The group tries to find a common goal and a means to reach it. Group both demands help from leaders *and* rejects or flees from help.

Sub-phase Ib: Counterdependence-Flight. Members actively seek to avoid the leader. Part of group wants structure, part does

[1]From "Patterns and Vicissitudes in T-Group Development," by W. Bennis. In L. Bradford, J. Gibbs, and K. Bennes (Eds.), *T-Group Therapy and Laboratory Method.* Copyright 1964 by John Wiley & Sons, Inc. Used by permission.

not. Whole group is angry with leader and feels he is unwilling to help or unable to help.

Sub-phase Ic: Resolution-Catharsis. Feelings toward trainer surface and group attacks him. This brings about recognition of attitudes toward authority and signals beginning of group's self-examination. Fighting is over.

Major Phase II: Interdependence

Sub-phase IIa: Enchantment-Flight. Group focuses on positive feelings for one another. Group soon tires of this and wishes to "flee" or move to something else.

Sub-phase IIb: Disenchantment-Flight. Group divides in two on issue of desired degree of personal involvement. Some want to really open up, others are fearful of doing so and withdraw from total group.

Sub-phase IIc: Consensual Validation. With awareness of the group ending, all members begin to talk about feelings during group session and each learns that many of his feelings were similar to other members'. A sense of validation and unity emerges.

T-groups have had wide application among business executives, people in the helping professions, community groups, and the like. They can be very effective when directed by a skilled trainer. However, T-group instructions are also available to the public on cassette tapes, and many people have tried this type of "growth experience." It is our feeling that such groups can be dangerous, because if something goes awry, no skilled person is available to maintain order or recognize and deal with problems.

Encounter Groups. Deriving much of their early impetus from the T-groups, but much less structured than their precursors, encounter groups represent a variety of theoretical and empirical approaches to human growth. Encounter groups may be defined as intensive group experiences designed to place people in closer contact with themselves, with others, and with the world of nature and pure physical sensation (Shaffer & Galensky, 1974). With their general emphasis on feeling and sensation, as opposed to thinking and reflection, encounter groups have been characterized (Back, 1972) as reflecting part of the social changes of the 1960s, which saw many people move away from interpersonal alienation and isolation and toward humanness and interpersonal sharing and intimacy.

Although there are several distinct types of encounter techniques, we have chosen to focus on one of the best developed and most influential—the *open-encounter* method developed by William Schutz at the Esalen Institute at Big Sur, California (Schutz, 1967, 1971, 1973). Theoretically, Schutz believes people have three basic interpersonal requirements that must be recognized and fulfilled in the encounter group. These requirements are *inclusion* (to be accepted and to feel worthwhile), *control* of one's world, and *affection*. Schutz sees encounter as a method of dealing with the *whole* person as he or she expresses these three basic needs.

In the encounter group itself, little structure is usually provided beyond the ground rules listed in Table 23-3. Typically, the leader encourages each member to share good and bad feelings with the group and may use group "exercises" to achieve *unfreezing* (release of inhibitions). An example of an interaction from an encounter session follows:

> *Leader:* I want each of you to close your eyes and to walk around the room. When you bump into someone, stop and explore that person's face with your hands, try to get to know the person without the sense of sight and hearing. Smell him, touch him, experience his physical being. (Group does this, silently, for ten minutes.) Now let's sit down in a circle on the floor. What feelings do you have about what we did?
>
> *Jim:* I felt a little tense doing that.
>
> *Leader:* Where were you tense?
>
> *Jim:* In my face—my face got tight when other people touched me.
>
> *Leader:* So they really got to feel your face as it is—you presented a tension-filled "you" even at the physical level.
>
> *Gordon:* Jim does that all the time.
>
> *Leader:* What do you mean?
>
> *Gordon:* I mean I never really feel I know Jim after we talk here; he seems to be hiding behind something.
>
> *Leader:* Gordon, Jim—move out into the center of the circle and sit facing each other. (Rest of group remains in outside circle.) Now, Gordon, get Jim to show you his true self.

Table 23-3. *Some ground rules of encounter groups*

1. Be honest with everyone, including yourself.
2. Concentrate on feelings.
3. Don't drink coffee or eat during a meeting; these are undesirable diversions that dissipate much of the energy a group has generated.
4. Whenever there is an opportunity to express something physically rather than verbally, do it physically.
5. Fight when it feels right.
6. Take off your clothes when it feels right.
7. Take responsibility for yourself and for what you get or fail to get from the group experience. Take responsibility for your statements, body messages, choices.
8. Speak for yourself; say "I feel" instead of "People feel" or "It's natural to feel."
9. If something is happening that you don't like, take responsibility for doing something about it.
10. If you're saying something about yourself that you've said before, stop, and say something else.
11. Do whatever you're most afraid of doing.

Adapted from *Elements of Encounter*, by W. C. Schutz. Copyright © 1973 by Joy Press, Big Sur, California. Used by permission of the author.

Gordon: How?

Leader: You'll find a way.

Gordon: Jim, who are you?

Jim: I'm me, I guess, but I'm nervous now.

Gordon: Can you relax enough to let me see you?

Jim: I'm trying—believe me.

Leader: You're tight as a drum, Jim. Lie down on your back and relax.

Gordon: You look scared.

Jim: I am—this is uncomfortable for me.

Gordon: Me, too. Do you think I like having trouble getting to know you?

Leader: Gordon, take Jim's hand in yours and squeeze it tightly and say something you feel.

Gordon (takes hand): Don't be afraid, Jim, I won't hurt you no matter who you are.

Jim: I feel scared of you. I want to pull my hand away . . .

In this example of an encounter session, you can see how the leader can use physical factors to focus on psychological problems and encourage the participants to encounter their blockages. Encounter groups can be very emotional experiences; crying, screaming, and arguing may be expected and encouraged. Few people leave such groups unchanged. In the same way that certified T-group leaders are approved by the National Training Laboratory, there are approved encounter-group leaders trained by Esalen Institute or any of more than 50 similar growth centers throughout the United States.

PEER SELF-HELP GROUPS

By definition, self-help groups neither seek nor want the guidance of a trained leader. Yet most of the curative factors cited by Yalom may be at work in self-help groups, so they seem worthy of representation in this text. Although numerous types of self-help groups exist, we will mention only well-established efforts directed at the alteration of disordered behavior and/or the improvement of normal functioning.

Alcoholics Anonymous

Alcoholics Anonymous is the prototype of self-help groups. Begun in 1935 by an alcoholic physician, Alcoholics Anonymous (AA) is believed by many professionals to be basic to rehabilitation of the alcoholic. We described AA in more detail in Chapter 13 and won't repeat ourselves here; rather, we will provide an example of an AA interaction to familiarize you with the happenings at AA meetings from a group-therapy perspective. AA groups can be either open to all or closed (just for members). At each meeting, a member is chosen to be in charge of the group; he or she isn't necessarily the leader, but more a starter and guide:

> *Tom:*   Well, let's begin.
>
> *Fred (comes up from audience):*   My name is Fred and I'm an alcoholic. I took my white chip two weeks ago and I'm going through hell. Sometimes I want to say "who cares" and go get a drink. Other times I want to make it this time, for good. Over the past year I've lost my job—a damn good one—I lost my car because I couldn't make payments. I've gone pretty far down. I'm ready to kick the booze, but I'm scared.
>
> *Tom:*   Anybody else here ever feel scared?
>
> *Group:*   (All agree "yes," "of course," and so on.)
>
> *Tom:*   You know, Fred, I think we all know what you're going through. We've all been there. It's a nightmare. You have a sponsor here, Fred, don't you?
>
> *Fred:*   Yes—Bill W.
>
> *Tom:*   Bill? Are you out there?
>
> *Bill:*   Yeah. Fred, I know what you're going through. You remember you called me the other night? I was worried—you sounded like you were going to pack it up. I think our talk helped. Didn't it?
>
> *Fred:*   If you hadn't talked to me I'd be in the "tank" today.

Mutual support and sharing of experience seem to be crucial to the success of AA. Signs of progress are the acceptance of poker chips (white for a pledge to stop drinking, red for six months' sobriety, and blue for one year) and the announcement to the group of abstinence. Statements to the group as a whole are typically preceded by, "My name is_____ and I'm an alcoholic"; this practice reflects the anonymity of the group and the belief that the first step toward recovery is the admission that one has lost control over drinking. In addition to group meetings for alcoholics themselves, AA chapters also provide groups for families of alcoholics (Alanon) and children with alcoholic parents (Alateen and Alatot).

Synanon

Synanon was developed in 1958 by Charles Dederich to deal with problems of drug addiction (Brecher, 1972). The group meeting, which usually involves 10 to 15 people, is called a *synanon* and, with few exceptions, is led by an ex-addict called the *synanist*. The primary mode of interaction is *attack therapy*, a procedure in which verbal ridicule, overstatement, and extreme candor may be directed at forcing the participants to deal with their psychological and interpersonal problems.

Strong confrontation is an integral part of the synanon. (Photo by Robert Foothorap.)

Attack therapy normally evokes intense emotions during the synanon. Catharsis, feedback, and gaining of new information seem to be the primary curative factors at work. Membership in the group may change frequently, so numerous new points of view are usually available. No drugs of any kind (except tobacco) are allowed any Synanon members; use of a drug as simple as aspirin may elicit rage and fury from other members. As for the success of this seemingly extreme form of self-help, Yablonsky (1973) reports that Synanon seems to resolve a variety of frustrations, feelings of loneliness, alienation, and human conflict. Just as AA seems effective in treating the alcoholic, the Synanon group experience seems to be effective in rehabilitating the drug addict.

A brief example of a Synanon session will demonstrate the powerful interactions that can characterize this method:

Ben: I can't stand the way people treat me because I was a junkie.
Bob: Do you think you don't deserve it?
Ben: I'm trying to stay clean.

Bob: Listen to this! He's "trying to stay clean." Do you think you're cleaner now just because you stopped chipping on weekends? You still are the same piece of shit who used the stuff in the first place! You can't get along with people so you chipped horse.

Ben: Look who's talking . . .

Bob: Look, you can have at me when you need to, but don't get me off of you by turning on me.

Gus: Yeah, Ben, you feel so bad because people treat you like a freak. Well, you *are* a freak—we all are. You think they should come up and say, "Ben, I hear you're an ex-junkie. Congratulations! I'd like you to marry my daughter!" No, they tell their daughter to stay the hell away from you. You're poison to the rest of the world.

Ben: Who needs them!

Gus: You do, shithead. Without them, all you have is us, and we're all ex-addicts. You need to be able to get out and relate to them as well as us. If not, you're dead, man. You'll be back on junk before you know what's happened to you!

FAMILY THERAPIES

Family therapy differs from the other forms of therapy with groups of people in several important ways. One difference is that the family therapist can't select members for the group—nature has already done the selection. Further, whereas nonfamily groups are temporarily organized for the duration of treatment, the family group is together permanently. In addition, although in group therapy, participants can look at one another objectively if necessary, in the family group, each participant usually is emotionally involved with the others. The last and perhaps most important difference is that, in family therapy, the group persists and must function *between* sessions; conflicts that arise in the therapist's presence may be continued in his or her absence. This aspect of the family group can also have positive effects, in that insights gained in the therapy session needn't wait a week before they are again experienced; new ways of seeing things may be implemented and reinforced immediately and continuously.

Because of its special nature, family therapy isn't easily understood within the framework of traditional group-therapy theory. Over the years, a number of therapy systems have developed that are specifically applicable to the basic family unit. Early theorists in family therapy, such as Ackerman (1963), Bell (1975), Bowen (1971), and others, pioneered the belief that individuals' symptoms reflect problems in the family. Generally, their philosophy was that emotionally unhealthy family systems produced emotionally unhealthy individuals. The goal of family therapy, therefore, was primarily to restructure family life so that normal functioning would once again be possible for the family as well as its individual members. This is an important deviation from traditional group therapy, in which the primary goal typically is symptom relief for each of the individual members and not for the group as a continuing unit.

In this section, we will first review two major systems, the conjoint family therapy of Virginia Satir and the structural family analysis of Salvador Minuchin. We will then conclude with a brief description of several variations on family techniques.

Satir's Conjoint Family Therapy

Conjoint family therapy (Satir, 1964) is a popular method in which family members are seen together rather than individually. The method grew from Virginia Satir's belief that individual problems arise from faulty communication within a family unit. When faulty communication and harmful rigid rules are part of a family system, one or more members of the family may eventually exhibit "symptoms." For Satir and for other family therapists, symptoms don't mean that an individual family member is disturbed; they mean that the *family system is disturbed*.

For Satir, the major source of family-system disturbance is *how* messages are sent, not necessarily the content of the messages. Thus, a mother who tells her children she loves them dearly, yet communicates disdain with her tone of voice and facial expression, may be contributing to an unhealthy family system. Growing up in such an unhealthy system can result in tension, unhappiness, and, sooner or later, behavior that may be identified as "deviant." Seeing the family as a "factory which makes people" (Hays, 1975), Satir lays most of the responsibility for "imperfect" people on the "manufacturers"—the family system.

Family disturbances don't occur randomly, according to Satir. In fact, there are ten identifiable points when families may face crises to which they must react and adjust. If flexibility isn't built into a family system, communication can break down, and problems may appear. The ten potentially critical events are: the birth of the first child, speech in the first child, first child's going to school, first child's becoming a teenager, first child's leaving the home, first child's marrying, the wife's menopause, the husband's climacteric, the birth of the first grandchild, and the death of one of the spouses. The majority of families can cope effectively with these crises; the families that can't may need help.

Inability to cope with family crises can manifest itself in many types of faulty communication. Satir describes four basic types of "hurtful" communicators in disturbed families. The *placator* tries to smooth over everything; he or she will prefer to feel bad so others won't be upset or angry. A second faulty communicator, the *blamer*, is just the opposite of the placator and protects himself or herself from psychological damage by assigning responsibility and guilt for troubles to other family members. The *computer* is an intellectualizing person who typically expresses little or no feeling and tends to describe perceptions of family events in cold, clinical terms. Last, Satir describes the *distractor,* who indulges in purposeless communication (such as shown in schizophrenic behavior) in an effort not to deal with family stresses.

In conjoint family therapy, Satir attempts to uncover such faulty communication patterns and to help the family see how the patterns block them from healthy interaction. To Satir, such healthy communication in the family is the sine qua non of adjustment. Her goals in therapy are the establishment of communication that is direct, clear, specific, and honest; the increase of feelings of self-worth among family members; and the development of rules that are flexible, humane, appropriate, and subject to change (Hays, 1975). The following example of Satir's approach to families will give you a feeling for what is done:

Therapist: How are things this week?

Mom: Jimmy is still at it. He just doesn't seem to want to change things. We're all trying, but he isn't.

Jimmy: I am too!

Mom: I don't think so; what was it you did on Thursday? You and your friend . . .

Therapist: Let's look at what's happening now. Mom, you are being a blamer and telling Jimmy that it's his fault that the family isn't making progress. Jimmy doesn't like this and is getting mad and defensive. How about it, the rest of you, does this go on a lot?

Dad: I guess it does. Marjorie [Mom] had a mother who did that same thing—always finding fault—always blaming people for being human. I think that blaming is at the root of the trouble.

Therapist: But, aren't you blaming right now? Aren't you saying that the problems are Marjorie's fault? Or if not Marjorie's, her mother's?

Dad: I . . . I guess I am.

Bob: Dad blames as much as Mom. Jeez, if you knock over a glass of Coke, he yells as if you could have prevented it or something.

Dad: Now, Bob . . .

Therapist: Uh-oh, it looks like Dad is going to pull some strong-arm tactics. He sounds like he's going to try to stop Bob but without sounding angry and authoritarian. How does that make you feel, Bob?

Bob: I don't know. He always does that. It makes me mad, to be truthful.

Therapist: Is being truthful something you have to excuse yourself for? That's one of the problems in the family.

In the example, note that Satirian therapy may be very active; unlike the often passive traditional group or early family therapists, Satirian family therapists often are more open about their attitudes and opinions. Such an open therapeutic person affords the family a model for genuine communication that, it is hoped, they will be able to adopt.

Structural Family Therapy

Like Satir's approach, structural family therapy, developed by Salvador Minuchin (1974), focuses on the organization and structure of family interaction and communication as the targets of therapeutic efforts. For Minuchin, however, a family is a system structured around the *support, regulation, nurturance,* and *socialization* of its members. If the family is structured in such a way that these functions can't be fulfilled, one or more of the family members may manifest "symptoms" or signs of trouble. The treatment for these "symptoms" may not be therapy for the individual (or *identified client*), but help for the system of which he or she is a part.

To understand the families he treats, Minuchin has developed a system to analyze communication patterns and structures of families and their interactions. The system allows the structural family therapist to record and, if necessary, rearrange family communication patterns. According to Minuchin, families are made up of individuals who must first of all be separated by *clear boundaries.* That is, each person must feel special and independent of the others, yet must be able to communicate freely with them. If separateness isn't felt, as when two children are treated and perceived by parents as totally alike, a *diffuse boundary* may exist. When no communication is possible between two family members, a *rigid boundary* exists. Both diffuse and rigid boundaries are considered undesirable elements in a family structure.

In addition to the boundaries between individuals, there are required subsystems. Most important are the *executive subsystem* and the *sibling subsystem* (see Figure 23-1). In the healthy family, the executive subsystem is composed of mother and father; in many disturbed families, one of the children may be elevated to the subsystem because of age or ability. To Minuchin, such a situation is unhealthy because children should be in the sibling subsystem, which is subordinate to the executive subsystem. Put more simply, when your brother acts like your father and has no right to because "he's a kid, too," it makes you angry and can cause trouble in your family. When boundaries and subsystems are normal and adaptive, the family system usually functions well. However, the structure can change over time in response to temporary crises such as Satir describes. Also, when boundaries aren't clear and subsystems aren't separate, problems can occur in the family.

For Minuchin, family therapy involves an active restructuring of families through conjoint family meetings, spouse meetings, children meetings, and every possible freely chosen type of family interaction. Using

A Healthy Family Structure

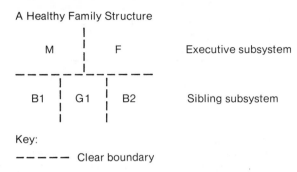

Key:

– – – – – Clear boundary

Figure 23-1. *Structural family analysis.* Adapted from *Families and Family Therapy*, by S. Minuchin. Copyright © 1974 by Harvard University Press. Used by permission of the President and Fellows of Harvard College.

warmth, cajoling, and active involvement, Minuchin aims toward a healthy family structure, one that can work efficiently and develop new structures when necessary. It is the opinion of some family experts (Nichols, 1976) that Minuchin's approach is one of the most effective methods of family treatment yet developed. An example of structural family analysis will help to familiarize you with this method:

Therapist: OK, what's going on this week?

Mother: All right—you're ready? This week, Bobby just did terribly in school. He won't do his work; his teacher calls us up. Jim [father] won't do a thing about it!

Father: You know I'd like to. How can I? I've got to work, you know. You have more time than I do.

Mother: But I've got the baby to take care of. I can't just leave him. He hasn't felt well this week, you know. The colic has been bad.

Therapist: You're both pretty angry about this. How do you feel about all this, Bobby?

Bobby: I don't like all the noise.

Mother: We wouldn't fight if you did better in school. Why don't you do your work, for heaven's sakes!

Therapist: So Bobby makes you fight? It's his doing?

Father: I could help him with his homework, but I don't have time.

In this situation, the parents are fighting and making Bobby the focus of *their* battle. The family members are separated by inappropriate boundaries, as depicted in Figure 23-2.

Therapist: You know, I think this is a problem between Mom and Dad. Bobby, you go out and play in the waiting room. (The baby isn't in this session.) OK, now, Mom and Dad, what's the problem between the two of you?

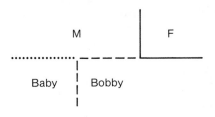

Key:

•••••••••• Diffuse boundary (individuality is lost)
———— Rigid boundary (little or no interaction with, or effect on, family)
— — — — Clear boundary (normal individuation and communication)

Figure 23-2. *The structure of the unhealthy family described in the text*

Here, the therapist forces the parents to face conflict and isolates them from the sibling subsystem.

> *Mother:* Well, he leaves me all day and when he gets home and there's trouble with Bobby, he yells at me! Like it's my fault! He does nothing and I have to do everything. Then when something goes wrong, I'm to blame. I'm sick of this! (Starts crying.)
>
> *Therapist:* So, Dad, look at this!
>
> *Father:* I'd like to help. I don't have time.
>
> *Therapist:* If you really wanted to help, you could make the time. I think you are afraid to be a parent.
>
> *Mother:* I don't think that's entirely true. He does work hard.

In this exchange, the therapist gets the parents together by engaging them in conflict with him. As you can see from this transcript, family patterns are changeable. By manipulating group communication and by following some clinical hunches, the therapist attempts to help the family move toward a basically healthy and flexible structure. Having a clear structural goal in mind seems to help structural family therapists to see where they are going and to know when they have gotten there. This characteristic makes Minuchin's approach especially attractive to clinicians and researchers alike.

Other Systems

Satir's and Minuchin's methods aren't the only forms of family treatment, but it is impossible to review all of the other variations. We will therefore present only four additional approaches. All are similar in that the focus of treatment for a given individual's problems is on the family system of which he or she is a part. The systems differ in their definitions of the basic family unit or in their perceptions of the pathological aspects of family life.

Triadic-Based Family Therapy. Developed by Gerald Zuk (1972), triadic-based family therapy sees the basic malfunction in disordered families in problematic triads of family members. Zuk believes that pathogenic relationships most often involve three people; for example, both parents may give the "symptom-carrier" (supposed problem person) the silent treatment. Zuk sees such "taking sides" and forming of coalitions as being at the core of later psychological problems.

In triadic-based family therapy, the therapist serves as a "go-between." Rather than being passive and nonjudgmental, the therapist actively intervenes and forces the breakdown of family coalitions. Some of Zuk's critics (Beels & Ferber, 1972) believe that his active, direct approach can be unhealthy in that he seems to use the manipulation of his own power as a curative agent. However, Zuk has been successful in his treatment of families. Whether this success is due to Zuk's personality and his own dynamics as a therapist or to his theoretical notions hasn't yet been determined.

Multiple-Impact Therapy. Perhaps even more active in its intervention than triadic-based family therapy is *multiple-impact family therapy* as developed by Robert MacGregor (1971). In multiple-impact therapy (MIT), a varied group of professionals (psychiatrists, psychologists, social workers, psychiatric nurses, and so on) works intensively and simultaneously with a disturbed family, conjointly *and* individually.

MIT usually begins with a conference among the family and all of the treatment staff. At this meeting, probing questions are often asked and the reactions of the family to stress are assessed. Following this united assessment, each family member is seen individually by one or more members of the MIT team. Conferences, therapy, group meetings, and the like may then continue for two to two and a half days. After a final staff meeting in which all therapists provide their perceptions and opinions, the family and staff meet for a last time. At the meeting, recommendations are made, feedback is provided, and the family is sent on its way, usually not to be seen again for two to six months. In their review of MIT, Beels and Ferber (1972) concluded that the intensive therapeutic effort is quite striking to see and experience and that its positive effects seem to be durable.

Social-Network Therapy. The therapy approaches we have described so far focus primarily on the immediate family members, but social-network therapy uses "that group of persons who maintain an ongoing significance in each others' lives by fulfilling specific human needs" (Speck & Attneave, 1972). It isn't unusual for distant relatives, friends, and neighbors—as well as the immediate family—to be involved in therapeutic meetings.

The therapists, called *network interveners,* meet with the social network (sometimes numbering about 40 people!) in the disturbed family's home or a large hall. Using large-group techniques such as encounter-group exercises, the network interveners attempt to produce a cohesive, supportive group of people called a *tribe*. Over several weeks, six sessions with the tribe lasting four hours each are usually held. From these sessions and the open experiences guided by the therapists, a new social network may emerge. This new network is believed to be more healthy, genuine, and comfortable for *all* its members, and especially for the family originally seeking treatment. The very logistics of social-network therapy boggle the senses, but its proponents believe it is effective.

Multiple-Family Therapy. Multiple-family therapy (MFT) involves a large group composed of four or five hospitalized patients and their families (Laqueur, 1972). In MFT there are essentially several "individuals," each being a family unit. The therapy involves intervention with each family and among the families as well. As is true of separate individuals in traditional group therapy, in MFT, separate families can support and model upon one another in their struggle to become more stable.

In multiple-family therapy, little or no attempt usually is made to compose homogeneous groups; families are readily mixed, and educational and economic factors are often irrelevant. Families may be given the freedom to drop out of the group after the first or second session and need talk only when they feel comfortable. Once several sessions have passed and the group has stabilized, treatment normally continues for 12 to 18 months. During this time, families can learn that they aren't alone in their conflicts or in their inability to resolve difficult problems. They can observe and imitate different, and often better, marital relationships, parent-child relationships, and sibling relationships. Through this type of experience, many once disturbed families can find new ways to relate and can experiment with these new ways in the safety of a cohesive, trusting group.

CONCLUDING COMMENTS

We have chosen to present group therapy and family therapy in the same chapter, but some professionals would disagree with this decision because they perceive these two forms of treatment as quite different. For example, Bloch (1976) and Reiss (1976) have noted that group therapy usually focuses on the problems of individuals within a group, whereas family therapy typically emphasizes the group or system itself and not the individuals within it. This seemingly small difference often has been magnified to the extent that, as Roman (1976) has noted, "the two approaches have been seen as antithetical to each other conceptually and methodologically" (p. 281). However, Roman also points out that, in many ways, the "old established" group-therapy community may be hesitant to accept fully the family-therapy "newcomers" in much the same way that many traditional "talk" therapists tended to resist accepting the behavior modifiers in the 1950s and 1960s.

In addition to possible resistance to new ideas, Parloff (1976b) believes that both group and family therapists may be at odds because of what he calls a narcissistic attitude in both camps. Parloff has noted that some of the problems appear to be caused by an inappropriate emphasis on mediating goals as opposed to ultimate goals. Specifically, if mediating goals are considered more important, group and family approaches probably will be seen as dissimilar in their focus upon individuals in the former and systems in the latter. However, if ultimate goals are more salient, group and family techniques may be considered merely separate methods of helping people who are different. From the perspective of ultimate goals, therefore, group therapy and family therapy may not be irreconcilably distinct. Our inclusion of both of these methods in a single chapter reflects our agreement with Parloff's conclusions.

CHAPTER SUMMARY CHART

We began our discussion of the group-treatment techniques with a look at the basic characteristics of these approaches:

Curative factors

Imparting of information
Universality
Altruism
Corrective family
Socialization practice
Imitation of adaptive behavior
Interpersonal learning
Group cohesiveness
Catharsis

We then looked at the specific types of group therapy:

Early group therapies	*Recent group techniques*	*Peer self-help groups*
Psychoanalytic groups	Psychotherapy groups	Alcoholics Anonymous
Psychodrama	Behavior-modification groups	Synanon
	Bioenergetic groups	
	Marathon groups	
	Human-growth groups	
	T-groups	
	Encounter groups	

Finally, we described the therapies especially developed for groups we call *families:*

Conjoint family therapy (Satir)	*Structural family therapy (Minuchin)*	*Other systems*
Disturbed family system, not disturbed individuals	Boundaries: diffuse, clear, rigid	Triadic-based therapy
Placator, blamer, computer, distractor	Executive and sibling subsystems	Multiple-impact therapy
	Restructuring equals treatment	Social-network therapy
		Multiple-family therapy

CHAPTER 24
THE PHYSICAL
THERAPIES

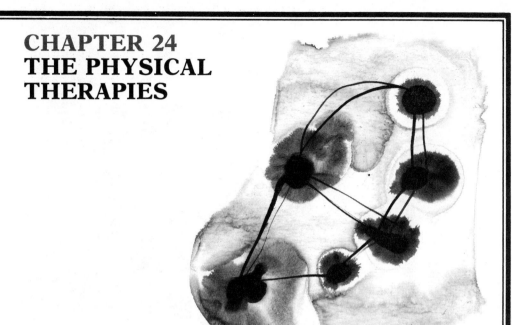

The physical therapies center upon physical treatments or manipulations for their effects. Although the "talk" therapies may be used for almost all forms of disturbance, they seem to be most effective with milder patterns of disorder such as the neuroses. By contrast, the physical therapies often are more effective in dealing with severe disturbances such as the psychoses. Physical treatments such as chemical therapy, electroconvulsive therapy, psychosurgery, and biofeedback usually are used together with nonphysical treatment procedures and can play a significant role in a total approach to helping people who are different.

CHEMICAL THERAPY

Although herbs and organic derivatives have been used in medicine for a long time, the massive clinical use of chemicals to control mental symptoms has been with us for less than three decades. In fact, it wasn't until the early 1950s that tranquilizers were widely introduced as a treatment for the mentally disturbed. Generally, the use of these drugs has been

Although the advent of physical therapies has led to more humane treatment, there still are places in the world where mental patients are treated poorly. (Left photo by R. S. Murthy, right photo by Eric Schwals. Both courtesy of the World Health Organization.)

associated with a decreasing inpatient population (Bloom, 1977). With the advent of the drug therapies, patients who might have been kept in restraints or locked up in closed wards often were able to leave institutions and to function satisfactorily at home with a daily dosage of medication. So long a major drain on mental-health resources, the institutional management of mental patients was eased markedly. Even patients who remained in the hospital often became easier to work with through drug therapies. For example, in a large hospital where one of us served his clinical internship, only 2 of 32 wards were locked, and most patients were free to walk the grounds of the hospital. This was a dramatic change from ten years before, when there were 14 locked wards and limited freedom. However, it must be remembered that in general drugs do not *cure*, but rather *control*, symptoms of disordered behavior in much the same manner that antihistamines merely control symptoms of colds.

Psychoactive chemicals aren't all alike in their effects. Some of these chemicals calm us, whereas others can give us an emotional lift. And, in addition to their therapeutic effects, they can have adverse side effects (see box). Surveys of our past classes in abnormal psychology (on about 1600 students) indicated that half had taken either major or minor tran-

CHAPTER 24:
THE
PHYSICAL
THERAPIES

What's It Like to Take Psychoactive Medications?

Sinequan: "It makes me drowsy . . . I go to sleep, and my dreams are different. I don't dream too well."
"I stopped dreaming."
Haldol: "You go from highs to lows; depending on how much you take, you can go through the floor. A little like amphetamines. When I went off it, I had a tremendous anxiety reaction. It was very scary . . . terrible withdrawal reactions."
Stelazine: "I feel groggy, fuzzy-headed. My mouth is very dry."
"When I went off it, I found myself talking a blue streak, getting very aggressive and domineering in a conversation." (This probably represents the return of symptoms.)
Thorazine: "I have respiratory problems with it, and my doctor changed to something else. It was terrible. I couldn't stay out in the sun at all. I'd get roasted. It slows you down, especially thinking."
"It made my mouth so dry that at one job I was interviewing for they thought I had a speech impediment, and they wouldn't hire me. I get hyper without it, though."
Mellaril: "I felt lowered, and I had more anxiety problems. In fact I even started to get a little paranoid."
"I get groggy, dry-mouth . . . but it relaxes me. If I go off it, I start sweating and get tense and light-headed."

---

quilizers at some time in their lives. Psychoactive drugs may be categorized on the basis of their effects: the *antipsychotics*, the *antidepressants*, the *antimanics*, and the *minor tranquilizers* and *hypnotics* (Goodman & Gilman, 1970).

The Antipsychotic Drugs (Major Tranquilizers)

The major tranquilizers used to treat psychotic symptoms are chemicals that can reduce schizophrenic behavior such as hallucinations as well as alleviate severe anxiety and agitation. Usually the classification of the major tranquilizers is based not so much upon their antipsychotic action as on their chemical source. Among the earliest of the tranquilizers to be used were the phenothiazines.

The Phenothiazine Derivatives. According to one reviewer (Jarvik, 1970), the widely prescribed phenothiazines were taken by about one out of every four Americans in the decade 1955 to 1965. The most common derivative of the group, chlorpromazine (Thorazine), has been the most frequently used medication for treating the broad range of the schizophrenias. However, the phenothiazines aren't a new "miracle" drug. In fact, they were first synthesized in 1883, and as late as 1934 they were used primarily as antiworm medicine and even as an insecticide! In 1953, a French psychiatrist, Courvoisier, reported a large number of psychological and physical effects of the drug. Delay, Deniker, and Harl (1952, cited in Jarvik, 1970) have been credited with the first use of phenothiazines (in the form of chlorpromazine) in the treatment of mental disorders. Soon after their reports of success, the drug was introduced in the United States, and its use expanded quickly. It was not uncommon for a severely disturbed schizophrenic to be placed on a daily dosage of up to 5000 milligrams of chlorpromazine. This is 200 times the usual recommended dosage for treating nausea in nonpsychotic individuals (*Physicians' Desk Reference*, 1977). The 5000-milligram dose would probably produce a coma or even death in a normal person, but in many schizophrenic patients it produces calmness and manageability. The great tolerance for high doses in schizophrenics led one psychiatric wit (Yager, 1974) to suggest that "schizophrenia is nothing more than a Thorazine deficiency!"

The clinical effects of chlorpromazine and the other phenothiazines are described as follows: "They exert a quieting effect on excited or hyperactive patients. Combativeness disappears and relaxation and cooperativeness become prominent. Clouding of consciousness does not occur" (Jarvik, 1970, p. 167). As with many major tranquilizers, there may be negative side-effects, such as dryness of the mouth, nasal stuffiness, slight constipation, and Parkinsonism (muscular shaking). These side-effects can usually be controlled by simultaneous administration of other medications. The trade names of the phenothiazine derivatives are listed in Table 24-1.

The Butyrophenones.   Like the phenothiazines, the butyrophenones were first developed in Europe (Jarvik, 1970). Exemplified by haloperidol, the butyrophenones seem to be just as effective as the phenothiazines in controlling psychoses and can often be used in their stead. Although there are a limited number of butyrophenones in use (see Table 24-1), they seem to be the chemicals of choice in some rare disorders. In Gilles de la Tourette's syndrome, for example, they have been reported to reduce involuntary tics, obscene verbalizations, and explosiveness.

The Rauwolfia Alkaloids.   The natural source of the rauwolfia alkaloids is the Indian shrub *Rauwolfia serpentina.* Not so widely used as the phenothiazines, the first use of the rauwolfia alkaloids in the treatment of mental disturbances was reported in an Indian medical journal as early as 1931 (Jarvik, 1970). Again, however, it wasn't until the 1950s that these major tranquilizers were used widely in the United States as antipsychotic agents. Their trade names are listed in Table 24-1.

Other Major Tranquilizers.   Thiothixene (Navane) and molindone (Moban) (Ayd, 1975) are relatively new major tranquilizers. Similar to the

Table 24-1. *The major tranquilizers, the antidepressants, and the antimanic drugs*

Grouping	Generic Names	Trade Names
The Major Tranquilizers		
Phenothiazine derivatives	chlorpromazine	Thorazine, Largactil, Mezaphen
	promazine	Sparine
	trifluopromazine	Vespirin
	fluphenazine	Permatil, Prolixin
	perphenazine	Trilafon
	prochlorperazine	Compazine
	trifluoperazine	Stelazine
	thioridazine	Mellaril
Butyrophenones	haloperidol	Haldol
Rauwolfia alkaloids	Rauwolfia serpentina	Raudixin
	reserpine	Rauloydin, Serfin, Serpasil, Sandril
	rescinnamine	Moderil
	deserpidine	Harmonyl
Thioxanthenes	thiothixene	Navane
	chlorprothixene	Taractan
Dihydroindolones	molindone	Moban
The Antidepressants		
Tricyclics	imipramine	Tofranil
	desmethylimipramine	Norpramin, Pertofran
	amitryptyline	Elavil
	nortryptyline	Aventyl
Monoamine oxidase inhibitors	isocarboxazid	Marplan
	nialamide	Niamid
	tranylcypromine	Parnate
The Antimanic Drugs		
Lithium salts	lithium carbonate	Eskalith, Lithane

phenothiazines in their effects, these drugs are often tried when the phenothiazines haven't had satisfactory effects. Molindone is especially fast acting, usually reaching its peak blood level within an hour of administration. Thiothixene seems to have greater mood-elevating and sedative effects than the other major tranquilizers and is therefore more widely used in affective psychosis and agitated depressions (Ayd, 1975).

The Antidepressant Drugs

When depression is the major symptom, rather than agitation, hallucination, or social withdrawal, antidepressant chemical agents may be used. The antidepressant drugs can elevate the mood of severely depressed people. Like the antipsychotic drugs, the first effective antidepressants were first used widely in the 1950s. The imipramine-type drugs and the monoamine oxidase (MAO) inhibitors can have remarkable effects upon depressive symptoms and, if time permits, are reasonable alternatives to electroconvulsive therapy. We say "if time permits," because it can take some of these drugs three to ten days to produce their mood-elevating effect.

The Imipramine-Type Antidepressants (Tricyclics). Imipramine, the first of the tricyclics to be isolated for use with depression (Cole & Davis, 1975), was first tested as an antipsychotic. Quite by accident, its developer found that imipramine had excellent antidepressant qualities. When it was given to tubercular patients to help them breathe better, the staff noticed a positive change in the mood of the ward. Although there are currently a number of similar antidepressant medications (see Table 24-1 for trade names), we will limit our discussion to one of the most commonly used drugs, imipramine (Tofranil). In normal people (Cole & Davis, 1975), Tofranil typically produces only a slight sedative effect, but in severely depressed psychotics, it can yield a striking reduction of depression within three to ten days. About seven out of ten patients given Tofranil show significant mood elevation, compared with only four out of ten patients treated with a placebo (sugar pill). Unfortunately, like a number of psychoactive medications, Tofranil can have several significant adverse side-effects, such as dryness of the mouth, palpitations, dizziness, nausea, and constipation. Dry mouth is among the most common side-effects of psychiatric drug use and causes the people taking these drugs to experience parched corners of the mouth and cracking speech. Tofranil seems to affect the presence of neural transmitters at the nerve synapse. All the tricyclic antidepressants may inhibit the reuptake of norepinephrine and thus increase the ease of nerve transmission, especially in the brain (Cole & Davis, 1975).

The MAO Inhibitors. Increasing the availability of neurotransmitters in a different way from imipramine, the monoamine oxidase (MAO) inhibitors reduce the breakdown of the neurotransmitter serotonin. Like the other transmitter substances, serotonin is necessary for the efficient functioning of the nervous system. By keeping the levels of serotonin from being depleted, antidepressants like the MAO inhibitors may increase the ease of neural transmission (Remmen, Cohen, Ditman, & Frantz, 1962). The MAO inhibitors frequently produce the usual side-effect of dry mouth, as well as the often disconcerting symptoms of delayed ejaculation or impotence in males. One note of caution: MAO inhibitors must not be taken at the same time as imipramine-type drugs, for the combination can produce a sometimes fatal reaction. Some of the MAO inhibitors are no longer available because of the danger involved in their uncontrolled use.

Antimanic Drugs—The Lithium Salts

Antidepressants have been used for some time to lift people's moods, but only in 1970 was any reasonably effective chemical treatment for the manic aspects of affective psychoses made available. The discovery of lithium as a treatment for mania was due to yet another "accident" in psychochemotherapy. Its potential usefulness was first noted in 1949 by the Australian psychiatrist Cade, who reported that lithium markedly calmed excitable manic patients (Fieve, 1975). In the United States, the drug was first used as a salt substitute for patients with heart trouble. However, lithium use wasn't controlled, and overuse led to severe toxic reactions and death in some heart patients. As a result, lithium was withdrawn from use for 20 years. However, in 1970, lithium was approved for use in the treatment of manic patients by the Food and Drug Administration. As a rule, lithium carbonate must be administered under careful medical supervision. Frequent blood tests are necessary so that the physician can monitor the levels of the substance in the body (Fieve, 1975). When administered appropriately, lithium therapy has resulted in marked reduction of manic symptoms within five to ten days. In addition, unlike the other psychoactive drugs, lithium seems to have relatively few side-effects when used properly. Further, lithium carbonate can be used as a prophylactic medication; that is, to prevent future episodes, patients who have had manic attacks in the past can sometimes be maintained on daily doses of the drug.

The Minor Tranquilizers and Hypnotics— Drugs for Anxiety

Unlike the "major" drugs we have discussed, the minor tranquilizers and hypnotics usually are used, not to treat severe psychotic symptoms, but rather to combat mild tension and anxiety and the sleeplessness and irritability that may accompany such states. This group of medications has been called the most widely prescribed pharmaceutical in the United States. Cole and Davis (1975) report that 80 million prescriptions were written for minor tranquilizers in one year! Just about everyone has taken a minor tranquilizer at one time or another or knows someone who has. A survey of our students indicated that more than half had taken some minor tranquilizing medication. Not prescribed exclusively by psychiatrists, these mild drugs compose the majority of the psychoactive drugs prescribed by other medical specialists (primarily internists). The names of the minor tranquilizers are well known: Librium (chlordiazepoxide), Valium (diazepam), and Miltown (meprobamate) are among the most commonly used. We will specifically consider three general groups of mild tranquilizing drugs: meprobamate, benzodiazepine compounds, and hypnotics.

Meprobamate. Developed in 1954 (Cole & Davis, 1975), meprobamate typically makes a person feel more relaxed, less anxious and tense, and slightly sleepy. When the chemical is taken in large doses over a long period of time and then is stopped, a severe withdrawal syndrome— including convulsions, shaking, hallucinations, anxiety, and tremors—can result. Heavy use of meprobamate can produce physical dependence, loss of consciousness, shock, depression of breathing, and, in rare instances, death.

Benzodiazepine Compounds. More recently developed than meprobamate, the benzodiazepine compounds (chlordiazepoxide, diazepam, and oxazepam) also can be effective in reducing mild to moderate anxiety, producing skeletal muscle relaxation, and combating alcoholism.

Like meprobamate users, heavy users of these drugs can develop a physical dependence. Withdrawal from the prolonged heavy use of benzodiazepine can result in convulsions, depression, agitation, inability to sleep, and loss of appetite (Jarvik, 1970). Side-effects of normal use of the benzodiazepines may be increase in appetite, skin rash, nausea, headache, impairment of sexual function, and light-headedness. Jarvik states: "These drugs are extremely popular with both physicians and patients and apparently are used with some success in mild anxiety states, all varieties of neurosis, tension states associated with organic conditions and also concurrently with other drugs or treatments in depressions and psychoses" (p. 180). Valium, probably the most popular of these drugs, is perhaps the most widely prescribed medication in the United States (Brantley, 1975).

The Hypnotics. At times, the minor tranquilizers won't reduce tension sufficiently to allow sleep in stressed people. As a result, another class of medications whose function it is to induce sleep may be used. These sleep-inducing chemicals are termed the *hypnotics* or *sedatives*. Although meprobamate and the benzodiazepine-type drugs may be used for inducing sleep, the more commonly used drugs are barbiturates (Cole & Davis, 1975) such as barbital (first introduced in 1903), phenobarbital, pentobarbital, and amobarbital. Over 2500 barbiturates have been synthesized, of which 50 or more are used as medications. Their usefulness and importance seem to stem from the fact that sleeping difficulties are frequently a part of a large array of behavioral disorders. Difficulty in getting to sleep and maintaining normal sleep can be closely linked to depressions of both the exogenous and endogenous types (see Chapter 8), as well as to mania, schizophrenia, and neuroses. Sedatives can also be beneficial in the treatment of situationally induced sleep disturbances (such as those occurring prior to surgery).

Because they are so easy to get, the minor tranquilizers and the hypnotics are probably the most widely abused of the legitimate psychiatric drugs. It is likely that few homes don't have at least one of these drugs in their medicine cabinet. If younger children see their parents take "calmatives" as if they were candy, they may quickly learn that popping a pill can be the easiest way to get through a stressful day or a bad night.

Many students ask how psychiatrists see the role of medication in their practice and in the control of mental disturbances. In response to this question, we present a personal experience from a psychiatrist of what it's like to prescribe drugs in the treatment of abnormal behavior.

PERSONAL EXPERIENCE: *Prescribing Drugs for People Who Are Different*

About 95% of my patients are taking some form of medication. The most common among the ones I use are the antipsychotics and the antidepressants. A few of my patients are on minor tranquilizers, but we [psychiatrists] don't prescribe as many of these as the other specialists. They often give them haphazardly, which is disturbing; they are not cure-alls. Deciding on the proper medication for a patient is most often a matter of trial and error. We begin with the dosage recommended by the drug company and then raise or lower the amount according to the patient's response. With the antipsychotics [major tranquilizers] the effect is quite rapid and we can decide more quickly, but the antidepressants take about seven to ten days to take effect, so *titration* [alteration of dose until a suitable level is found] takes longer. Even within a given class of drugs, we find that one may work and another may not. Therefore, we may try a phenothiazine for a time and, if the response isn't satisfactory, we'll try Haldol or something. Recently, many of us began using combinations of medications. For example, the level of antidepressants in the bloodstream can be elevated with no increase in antidepressant dosage by the simultaneous administration of certain other drugs. The drug companies have provided us with such compounds as Triavil, which are combinations of antipsychotics and antidepressants. Some psychiatrists use these, but others prefer to develop their own combinations.

The advent of the antidepressant has made electroconvulsive therapy [ECT] less likely, but ECT is still the treatment of choice in acute depression with suicidal dangers present. Shock can lift a depression within a day or so, whereas it takes the antidepressants up to two weeks sometimes. Obviously, if a person is suicidal we can't wait that long. . . . I would hope that students realize the psychiatric medications do not *cure* mental disorders; they ameliorate symptoms so that psychotherapy and other forms of nonbiological treatments can be more effectively utilized. There are cases, however, where some form of medication may be required on a lifelong basis; this is especially true in some forms of severe depressive illness where the threat of suicide is great when the person is not medicated. Since neuroleptics [psychoactive drugs] arrived on the scene, psychiatry has advanced dramatically; its future rests, I feel, in the development of more sophisticated drugs and the combined use of these in psychotherapeutic approaches to mental illness.

ELECTROCONVULSIVE THERAPY (ECT)

In addition to chemical treatments, modern physical therapies include a selection of other physical manipulations. For example, as the psychiatrist we have just heard from indicates, electroconvulsive therapy, or shock therapy, must often be used in lieu of chemotherapy. Many people misunderstand shock therapy and fear it. Many may imagine a sinister, darkened room with a mass of wires and electrodes into which a helpless patient is dragged and subjected to "electrified" tortures. Indeed, many people are very concerned about family members and friends who have had ECT, and students often ask whether any danger is involved. As you will see, ECT seems to be a relatively safe and highly effective procedure, especially in treating depressions.

ECT owes its beginnings to a Hungarian physician, Von Meduna, who noticed that patients in his mental hospital often would lose their psychotic symptoms whenever they experienced a spontaneous convulsion such as that which occurs in epilepsy. He also knew that schizophrenia and epilepsy rarely occurred simultaneously in the same individual. Von Meduna began to experiment with various means to induce convulsions in mental patients who hadn't responded to other forms of treatment. He first experimented with intramuscular injection of camphor oil, and, although some patients experienced convulsions, most just became very sick. He then arrived at a synthetic camphor preparation, Metrazol, which produced a convulsion in the majority of patients within 30 seconds. Chemicals such as Metrazol, and later insulin, weren't widely used because they sometimes produced a variety of undesirable side-effects, including convulsions often severe enough to produce death. To induce a convulsion safely, Cerlitti and Bini (1938) developed electrically induced convulsions. These researchers named their technique *electroshock*, a term that is still used.

In one form of ECT procedure (which is usually under the supervision of a psychiatrist), electrodes are attached to both temples and a current of 70 to 130 volts is passed for anywhere from 0.1 to 0.5 seconds (Kalinowsky, 1975a). A problem with the early method of electroshock was that the seizure produced by this current often resulted in a rapid contraction of all skeletal muscles that frequently caused broken bones and other severe injuries. Bennett introduced the idea of administering *curare* (a powerful muscle relaxant) to paralyze the muscles prior to the shock. With this alteration, only the central nervous system experienced the convulsion, but the therapeutic results didn't seem to change.

Modern ECT usually causes surprisingly few complications and can be used safely even in some patients with heart disease. Kalinowsky (1975a) reports that the fatality rate for 100,000 treatments over an eight-year period was 0.002. As a recognized expert in this area, Kalinowsky believes that ECT is safe and doesn't deserve the sinister reputation it still has in many professional and nonprofessional circles. However, patients may per-

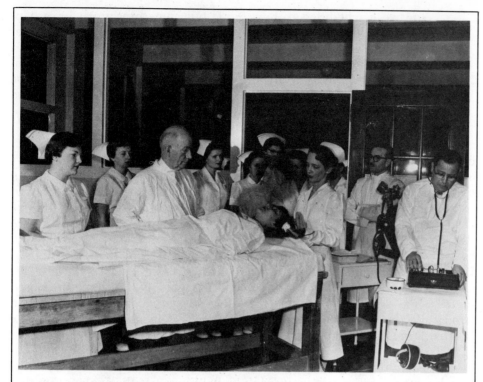

Under proper medical supervision, electroconvulsive therapy is often the treatment of choice for psychotic depression. (Photo by Wide World Photos.)

ceive ECT with fear and dread, as shown in the following account of what it's like to receive shock treatment:

> Strapped to a stretcher, you are wheeled into the ECT room. The electroshock machine is in clear view. It is a solemn occasion; there is little talk. The nurse, the attendant, and the anesthetist go about their preparation methodically. Your psychiatrist enters. He seems quite matter-of-fact, businesslike—perhaps a bit rushed. "Everything is going to be just fine. I have given hundreds of these treatments. No one has ever died." You flinch inside. Why did he say that? But there is no time to dwell on it. They are ready. The electrodes are in place. The long clear plastic tube running from the bottle above ends with a needle in your vein. An injection is given. Suddenly—terrifyingly—you can no longer breathe; and then . . . You awaken in your hospital bed. There is a soreness in your legs and a bruise on your arm you can't explain. You are confused to find it so difficult to recover memories. Finally, you stop struggling in the realization that you have no memory for what has transpired.

You were scheduled to have ECT, but something must have happened. Perhaps it was postponed. But the nurse keeps coming over to you and asking, "How are you feeling?" You think to yourself: "It must have been given"; but you can't remember. Confused and uncomfortable, you begin the dread return to the ECT room. You have forgotten, but something about it remains. You are frightened [Taylor, 1975].[1]

Although Von Meduna first believed that convulsions would be helpful in alleviating symptoms of schizophrenia, research has shown that ECT is most consistently effective in psychotic depression. Electroshock is known to be able to reduce some severe depressions after one to four treatments and is actually preferred over antidepressant medications in about 10% of cases (Brantley, 1975). Since antidepressant medication can take up to ten days to take effect, in cases where suicide is feared, the physician may not have the luxury of waiting for a chemical approach to work. In these instances, ECT is often the treatment of choice because it can quickly alleviate the depression and the accompanying suicidal thoughts. ECT is sometimes used to treat the schizophrenias, but usually only in acute episodes with a strong affective (emotional) component. However, in those instances, there is often a greater possibility of relapse within a short time after cessation of ECT.

Why does shock therapy work? We asked several psychiatrists, who very honestly told us that they didn't know! Some use the explanation that people *learn not to show their symptoms* because of the pain involved in ECT. However, this explanation doesn't seem adequate. First of all, the present-day use of muscle relaxants and premedication usually prevents the patient from experiencing much stress or pain. Second, one of the typical side-effects of the shock therapy is that the person's memory of the treatment may be completely erased.

Freudian theorists have proposed that the effectiveness of shock is derived from the guilty patient wishing for punishment. However, again, the lack of memory of the treatment itself argues against such an explanation. From another perspective, it has been suggested that ECT may change brain biochemistry, especially the amounts of neural transmitters at brain synapses. For example, Kety (1975a) reports that electroshock actually may increase the availability of certain neurotransmitters in the same way as the antidepressant drugs. Furlong (1972) claims that a "mythology" surrounds the use of ECT. He contends that the lack of any sound explanation for its basic effectiveness often reinforces the tendency of those opposed to the use of ECT to evaluate its performance upon hearsay. However, if we look at the statistics, we must conclude that ECT, when used appropriately,

[1]From "Electroconvulsive Treatment (ECT): The Control of Therapeutic Power," by R. Taylor, *Exchange*, May-June, 1975. Reprinted by permission of the California State Department of Health.

can be an effective form of therapy. Because of this, it probably will continue to be a mainstay of treatment.

PSYCHOSURGERY

Although retaining ECT in the physical-treatment repertoire seems to be appropriate and accepted by most mental-health professionals, the recent increase in the use of psychosurgery has been more equivocally received. In Ken Kesey's novel, *One Flew over the Cuckoo's Nest* (1962), an affable nonpsychotic criminal is placed in a mental hospital for observation. After a series of difficult experiences, he tries to kill the head nurse. The final result is that he is given a lobotomy to control his violent behavior. His good friend kills him rather than let him live out his life with his personality so apparently deadened. Lobotomy is an example of the form of treatment known as psychosurgery.

Psychosurgery is the term applied to a group of surgical treatments in which various parts of a patient's brain may be destroyed or made inoperative in an attempt to alter behavioral or emotional aberrations. Although there are numerous historical examples of accidental psychosurgery, it was not until 1888 that a Swiss psychiatrist, Burckhardt, reported on the purposeful destruction of part of the cerebral cortex of mental patients (Kalinowsky, 1975b). However, Burckhardt's "discovery" soon was forgotten, and it wasn't until 1936 that a Portuguese physician, Moniz, proposed frontal-lobe surgery as a possible treatment for schizophrenia. The operation, called a *bilateral prefrontal lobotomy* (also a *leucotomy*), involved surgically opening the skull and destroying various tissues connecting the frontal lobes with the rest of the brain. With time, the trend shifted toward smaller, less drastic brain operations, such as the *transorbital lobotomy* (Freeman & Watts, 1950). In such an operation, the central nerve tracts are severed by introducing an instrument through the eye sockets above the eyes. No surgical incision or skull opening is necessary.

Unlike ECT, psychosurgery doesn't appear to be the treatment of choice for any particular disorder, but it has sometimes been used in intractable psychoses. With the advent of the psychoactive drugs, the use of psychosurgery decreased dramatically. However, over 40,000 patients were operated on before the 1950s. The major psychological reaction patients had to such surgery seems to be an insensitivity to problems that were previously of serious concern. For example, if a man had hallucinations, postsurgically he might not be frightened by them; if he were paranoid and heard voices, they might no longer bother him. However, after surgery, patients also often required lengthy rehabilitation programs to overcome the effects of the treatment. Psychosurgery rarely is performed today, except in cases of what are called "completely intractable" emotional illness.

In other words, for patients who are very dangerous to themselves and others, for whom nothing else works, surgery may be considered. Psychosurgery is a drastic step because its effects are irreversible.

Modern psychosurgery does differ somewhat from the lobotomies we described above. Rather than drastically and inaccurately "scrambling" brain areas, modern psychosurgery is often done by carefully implanting electrodes into specific sites through which electrical impulses are passed selectively, destroying predetermined areas (Valenstein, 1973). The areas most commonly destroyed are in the limbic system, which is known to be related to the integration and control of emotional behavior (see Chapter 6). In the *cingulectomy*, for example, a part of the limbic system, the *cingulate gyrus*, is destroyed. Holden (1973) has reviewed research in which cingulectomy has been used successfully in people with intractable pain or with psychiatric disorders such as manic-depressive psychosis, anorexia nervosa, and severe disabling anxiety. A second modern form of psychosurgery is the *amygdalectomy*, in which the amygdala is destroyed electrically in an attempt to control violent behavior (Mark & Ervin, 1970; Snodgrass, 1973). Mark and Ervin have reported that amygdalectomy may be used successfully in treating children and adults who manifest evidence that some central-nervous-system defect is causing violent antisocial behavior. In a *thalamotomy*, the thalamus is destroyed in the hope of modifying aggressiveness in adults and hyperactivity in children. Initially a treatment for the shaking in Parkinson's disease, the thalamotomy has been used in children as young as 6 (Chorover, 1974), with the frequent result of making the patient calmer and more easily handled. Critics of such surgery (Bregin, 1973; Holden, 1973) have noted that, in many cases, the decision to perform psychosurgery may be made without extremely careful diagnosis of brain involvement and assured exhaustion of all reversible methods. Psychosurgery does often work as expected, but who can confidently agree to such an irreversible procedure when a future advance may make chemical or psychological treatment possible?

BIOFEEDBACK

Biofeedback techniques are particularly useful in the treatment of neurotic anxiety, psychophysiological disorders, and other patterns associated with stress. Biofeedback methods have been defined as "procedures in which an external sensor is used to provide a person with an indication of the state of a specific bodily process such as heart rate, blood pressure, skin temperature and the like" (Schwartz & Beatty, 1977, p. 1). Typically, biofeedback is used in combination with some sort of learned method for gaining control of processes once thought to be involuntary. Among these learned methods are hypnosis, transcendental meditation, Hatha Yoga, other systems of relaxation, and specialized self-control instructions. Although biofeedback has been applied to a variety of special problems such as epilepsy, stuttering, and asthma, and is the subject of lively research literature (Barber, Dicara, Kamiya, Miller, Shapiro, & Stoyva, 1976; Miller & Dworkin, 1977), we will limit our discussion to some examples of its most common uses in the treatment of anxiety and psychophysiological disturbances.

An example of biofeedback treatment of anxiety is the work of Coursey (1975), who used feedback information about muscle tension to help his subjects relax. Connected to a device called an electromyograph (EMG), Coursey's subjects received continuous feedback about the amount of tension in their foreheads (frontalis muscle). Coursey demonstrated that, with EMG feedback, subjects were able to reduce anxiety faster and better than with simple verbal relaxation instructions similar to those for systematic desensitization described in Chapter 22.

Just as the relaxation of the frontalis muscle can be related to reduced tension, it can also be used in the biofeedback treatment of severe stress-related headaches. For example, Miller (1976) describes research in which 75% of patients with muscle-tension headaches and migraine headaches (see Chapter 11) benefited from biofeedback from frontalis muscles and skin temperature.

Other stress-related symptoms more serious than headaches, such as high blood pressure and cardiac arrhythmias, can result in severe incapacity or premature death. Miller reports that biofeedback techniques have been used to teach voluntary control of blood pressure and heart rhythm. Whereas results of attempts to control blood pressure have often been discouraging, biofeedback treatment for cardiac arrhythmias has been called "the most convincing therapeutic application of biofeedback training to date" (Miller, p. 245). In one example of learning to control arrhythmias (Weiss & Engel, 1971), subjects were first taught to speed up and slow down their heart rates in response to feedback in the form of signal lights. Once convinced that they could control their heart rates, subjects were taught to maintain their heart rates within a narrow range. After a period of training, most subjects were able immediately to be aware of a spontaneous arrhythmia and to suppress it almost instantly.

Needless to say, the skill to control possible dangerous cardiac problems may be an extremely valuable contribution of biofeedback techniques. We don't yet know the limits of biofeedback, but as research progresses it seems clear that it will play an increasingly important role in the treatment of people who are different.

CONCLUDING COMMENTS

For many, the physical therapies we have described represent psychiatry's *finally* getting to the point where it can "cure" mental disturbances by direct medical influence. It has been said that up to 80% of depressed patients may be helped chemically (Wolff, 1976) and that there are "several million Americans who need lithium therapy" (Fieve, 1976). However, there are voices of caution as well. For example, Zwerdling (1973) has suggested that drug companies actually may be "inventing" patterns of disorders for which their medications seem to be the best treatment. Further, there seems to be some concern that physical treatments such as psychosurgery and chemotherapy often may be used indiscriminately. In this regard, Restak (1973) has noted that one "lobotomy zealot calculated he had personally performed over 4000 operations, using a gold-plated ice pick" (p. 57). Psychosurgery isn't the only physical treatment with potential for excessive use. For example, it has been estimated that over 250 million prescriptions for psychoactive drugs are written yearly, with only 15% of those taking such drugs reporting that they received them from a psychiatrist (Gillenkirk, 1973).

There seems to be little doubt that physical treatments for mental disorders can be helpful and, in many cases, perhaps the best possible therapeutic regimen. However, there can be significant dangers in the uncontrolled use of such treatments, especially by medical professionals not specifically trained in their administration. We believe that physical treatments, carefully monitored and applied, eventually may emerge as one of the major approaches to treating the psychoses. However, the idea that they eventually will be applicable to the majority of mental disorders has yet to gain significant support.

CHAPTER SUMMARY CHART

In this chapter, we presented the physical approaches to the treatment of being different. We first discussed psychochemotherapy:

Antipsychotics	*Antidepressants*
Reduce psychotic symptoms such as agitation, hallucinations, and severe anxiety Phenothiazine derivatives Butyrophenones Rauwolfia alkaloids Thiothixene Molindone	Reduce depression by altering levels of available neurotransmitters Imipramines (tricyclics) MAO inhibitors
Antimanic drugs	*Minor tranquilizers and hypnotics*
Newest of the drugs; must be carefully monitored.	Very widely used and addictive in large amounts

Antimanic drugs
(continued)

Lithium carbonate

Minor tranquilizers
and hypnotics
(continued)

Meprobamate
Benzodiazepines
Barbiturates

We then described some aspects of electroconvulsive therapy, psychosurgery, and biofeedback:

Electroconvulsive therapy
(ECT)

Von Meduna
Electroshock
The convulsion, not
the electricity, is most
important.
Experts feel it is safe.
Reduces severe
depression and
suicide threat faster
than drugs
Why it works isn't yet
known.

Psychosurgery

First done by
Burckhardt
A drastic remedy
Bilateral prefrontal
lobotomy
Transorbital lobotomy
Used in "intractable"
cases only

Biofeedback

Learning to control
"involuntary"
processes
Can reduce anxiety,
relieve headaches,
aid in control
of cardiac
arrhythmias
Much is still
unknown.

CHAPTER 25
COMMUNITY
APPROACHES

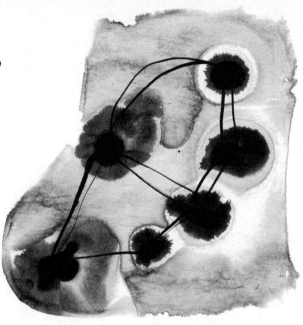

Although individual, group, and physical therapies most frequently are administered by professionals in offices or hospitals, professionals recently have been leaving such traditional sites and offering their help right in the community. Both inside and outside the field of mental health, people have grappled with issues and considered radically new approaches to helping those who are different. The field of mental health has widened tremendously. Programs involving parents, homemakers, and innumerable lay people as therapists have combined efforts with other mental-health programs. In cities, small towns, and rural areas, attempts have been made to change entire social systems so that they will help to develop psychologically well-adjusted people. Problems of disordered behavior, which previously may have been swept under the rug, now more often are being met head-on in community-psychology movements. Although we will use the phrase community *psychology* in this chapter, the term includes all mental-health professionals—psychiatrists, public-health officials, and social workers—who hold beliefs consistent with the community approach to treatment for those who are different.

In addition to mental-health professionals, community psychology necessarily involves people from many different walks of life. Despite some

630

lingering prejudice and ignorance, today's general population is probably history's most enlightened regarding disordered behavior. Some mental patients now live in people's homes, experiencing normal behavior instead of being left to stagnate in the back wards of some huge institution. The number of patients in mental hospitals has decreased steadily over the past 20 years, and although there are other reasons for this decrease (such as the psychoactive drugs), the community-psychology movement has contributed significantly to this decrease. Yet this is only a beginning. Like the start of a marathon race, community psychology began with a great deal of enthusiasm and optimism; and, as in the marathon, many of those not used to experiencing frustration and difficulties have dropped out along the way. The community approach seems to be much more realistic than when it began, and it seems to hold much promise for the alleviation of psychological problems.

Since the community approach to psychological problems is complex, we first present an overview and history. Next we will cover the factors that either encourage or inhibit the community approach to disordered behavior. Further, to give you an idea of what the community approach is, we will describe a community-psychology theory and a sample of some community programs. Finally, we will evaluate the status of the community approach and reflect on its future.

HISTORICAL PERSPECTIVE

The community-psychology movement emphasizes the environment as the chief source of psychological difficulties and environmental manipulation as the main approach to alleviating these difficulties. As we indicated in Chapter 3, over the years, people have seen the source of their difficulties in nature, in devils, and more recently in "being sick." In most of these instances, the individual is primarily a passive victim of the disorder. Further, people who treat disordered behavior have also been generally passive, in that they usually wait for the patient to seek help before intervening. This passive stance is inconsistent with the approach of most community workers, who intervene actively.

The definition of community psychology we will work with was offered by Zax and Specter (1974):

> Community psychology is regarded as an approach to human behavior problems that emphasizes contributions made to their development by environmental forces as well as the potential contributions to be made toward their alleviation by the use of these forces [p. 3].

Community approaches to the treatment of disordered behavior share some of the credit for reducing the number of patients in mental hospitals. (Photo by Joseph Czarnecki.)

This definition has several implications. It suggests a shift away from an intrapsychic approach to disordered behavior. It also implies involvement with a wide variety of behavior problems, not just the extreme ones that characterized the study of abnormal behavior until the 20th century. Finally, it includes the use of environmental intervention to deal with disordered behavior.

The recent history of the community-treatment movement as defined by Zax and Specter probably begins with the call in 1953 for a public examination of the state mental hospitals. Two years later, the Joint Commission on Mental Illness and Health was authorized by the U. S. Congress to undertake such an examination. Many of the results of the commission's six-year study were dismaying. On the basis of its survey, the commission concluded that institutional care was hopelessly custodial—little real treatment was offered to patients. It was asserted that patients in these institutions should have the right to receive treatment and that steps should be taken to ensure that treatment takes place. In addition, the commission recommended that there be a fulltime mental-health clinic available for every 50,000 people. The main emphasis of the commission's report was on getting better care for extremely disturbed patients in the state mental hospitals. However, the federal government subsequently emphasized other elements of the report as well—specifically, prevention and treatment services for those who are mildly disturbed. In 1963, President Kennedy proposed the Community Mental Health Centers Act:

> We must seek out the causes of mental illness and of mental retardation and eradicate them. . . . For prevention is far more desirable for all concerned. It is far more economical and it is far more likely to be successful. Prevention will require both selected specific programs directed especially at known causes, and the general strengthening of our fundamental community, social welfare, and educational programs which can do much to eliminate or correct the harsh environmental conditions which often are associated with mental retardation and mental illness.

The aim of Kennedy's program was to provide accessible comprehensive services for all mental-health needs and to aid in the *prevention* of disordered behavior. To accomplish these goals, for every 100,000 people, a *community mental-health center* was to provide inpatient care, outpatient care, partial hospitalization (including day care), 24-hour emergency service, and consultation to other agencies in the community. With the Community Mental Health Center Act, the federal government got into the business of dealing with disordered behavior as it never had before. Many mental-health workers saw in this act the potential for creating a network of community-based centers that would make possible realistic prevention programs.

It was in this optimistic and exciting atmosphere that, in May 1965, a group of psychologists met at Swampscott, Massachusetts, to consider the role of the psychologist in community approaches. They published a statement strongly advocating that community psychologists be "change agents, social-systems analysts, consultants in community affairs, and students of the whole man in relation to all his environments" (Bennett, 1965, p. 833).

MOTIVATING FORCES

Federal encouragement gave early impetus to treating people outside traditional settings, and several other forces played significant roles in the continuing development of community approaches (Bloom, 1977; Iscoe & Spielberger, 1970; Zax & Specter, 1974).

Dissatisfaction with Traditional Approaches

George Albee (1959), a former president of the American Psychological Association, believes that traditional psychotherapy alone probably couldn't meet all of society's psychological needs. One reason for this may be that the traditional mental-health services of psychotherapy and hospitalization are rarely distributed equitably. For example, in their survey of New Haven, Connecticut, Hollingshead and Redlich (1958) found that patients from the lower classes were likely to be seen in a public agency rather than in private practice, and were more likely to receive physical or drug treatment than verbal therapy. Since it is known that more disordered behavior seems to be found in the lower social classes (Dohrenwend & Dohrenwend, 1974), it is dismaying to find that it is just this group that receives a smaller share of traditional treatment. These disheartening findings have led some mental-health workers to conclude that traditional approaches, even if effective, may not always be supplied to those who need them most. The community-psychology approach is committed to reaching all classes of people fairly.

The Overwhelming Need for Mental-Health Services

Even if traditional therapy were clearly effective for all sorts of mental illness, the immense need for psychological care probably never could be met by traditional means alone. Epidemiological studies of a rural community (Leighton, 1959) and of a city (Srole et al., 1962) suggest that about one out of every four individuals has psychological difficulties that could require professional help. In the United States, that translates into about 60 million people! If even a small portion of those who need help were to ask for it, mental-health services would be quickly overwhelmed. Community psychology is one response to this need to deal with the psychological problems of vast numbers of people.

The Shortage of Trained Mental-Health Personnel

There may not be enough trained personnel to provide traditional psychological services to all who need them. One analysis of this problem was prepared by Albee (1968). Albee had concluded in 1959 that there *always* had been more demand for mental-health professionals in public agencies than there were professionals and that these demands seemed to be increasing. In 1959, only one-fourth of the positions budgeted for physicians and psychologists in state and county hospitals were filled. Further, although increasing numbers of psychologists and psychiatrists were being trained, many of them were going into college teaching or private practice rather than into large treatment facilities. Similar shortages in personnel were also found in psychiatric social work and psychiatric nursing. Albee was pessimistic in 1959, and his reexamination of the state of mental-health manpower in 1967 left him just as dismayed.

More recently, Bloom (1977) has pointed out that a relative lack of available positions and a shortage of mental-health professionals can exist at the same time. In other words, what may seem like an adequate or even abundant supply of professionals in terms of actual positions may, in reality, be a shortage. For example, only a small proportion of the proposed 1500 community mental-health centers are in operation. Thus, there may be too few funded positions rather than too many professionals. If the funds were made available, the supply of mental-health professionals would soon be exhausted.

Additionally, Bloom notes that mental-health professionals aren't evenly distributed across geographical locations. More than half of all psychiatrists in the U.S., for instance, are located in the five states of New York, California, Pennsylvania, Massachusetts, and Illinois. Even more startling is the fact that "one-third of all persons under 18 years of age live in rural areas that are served by only 3% of America's mental-health facilities" (Bloom, 1977, p. 222). Thus, it seems that mental-health manpower using traditional approaches is woefully small and inadequate to deal with the large number of people in need. Again, the need for a community approach seems obvious.

Emphasis on Prevention Rather than Treatment

The preference to *prevent* rather than treat is a distinguishing characteristic of community psychology. If disorders can be prevented, shortages of treatment personnel may become irrelevant, needs for services will be reduced, and the question of the effectiveness of traditional therapy versus drugs versus hospitalization becomes moot. Of course, prevention of abnormal behavior isn't a new idea. In the early 1900s, Adolf Meyer proposed that mental-health workers become involved in *aftercare* (preparing patients to reenter the community after hospitalization) and *prevention*. Although Meyer held a prestigious position within the mental-health field, he apparently failed to interest many others in prevention. It wasn't that others disagreed with him; they just seemed to ignore him.

In the 1940s, the next significant rallying point for prevention advocates emerged as a result of the Coconut Grove fire, a terrible disaster in which many people lost their lives needlessly because of panic. Lindemann (1944) studied the reaction of bereavement in those who lost loved ones in the fire. He was able to identify a positive, predictable grief process through which a person could be helped. With this helping, called *intervention*, many disruptive and negative reactions to loss could be shortened, and many people could return more quickly to effective functioning. Lindemann also noted that "helpers" didn't have to be mental-health professionals.

The knowledge that people under stress could be helped before diagnosable psychological disturbances emerged suggested that "mental illness" could be prevented. From the early ideas and findings of Meyer,

Lindemann, and others, new ideas and prevention programs soon developed.

INHIBITING FORCES

In addition to the forces motivating the development of community psychology, numerous factors have tended to inhibit this approach. Zax and Specter (1974) have identified several sources of opposition to community approaches.

Insufficient Knowledge to Establish Preventive Programs

Most professionals and lay people aren't opposed to the goals of preventive approaches, but many see them as impossible. Some members of the 1955 Joint Commission were among those who believed that we lack the knowledge to plan successful prevention programs. These dissenters pointed to mental-health professionals' lack of political expertise and the fact that we aren't always sure we can help one person, let alone an entire community. Objections based on lack of knowledge are reflected in the following statement concerning the future of community psychiatry:

> Here, I am most skeptical concerning the adequacy of our knowledge to develop significant techniques for treating social collectivities or for developing techniques on the community level that will really result in a reduction of mental disturbances in the community. It seems that such expectancies are likely to remove the psychiatrists still further from the bona fide cases of mental illness that develop within the community context [Dunham, 1965, p. 311].

Community psychology's response to such criticism has usually been that, although it is true that we don't have *full* knowledge of the antecedents of behavior disorders, intervention based on fragmentary knowledge is probably better than no intervention at all. In epidemiology, there are instances of successful prevention of diseases such as cholera and typhoid without full knowledge of their antecedents. Furthermore, in the absence of active, aware, and planned intervention by trained community professionals, we may end up with uncritical, unconscientious, and perhaps even damaging intervention by others.

The Need Is Too Great—The Cost Is Too High

Even if it were conceded that community psychologists have sufficient knowledge of prevention, there are those who would still object because of the size of the community-treatment task and its potentially prohibitive costs. Many people fear that a truly effective program of prevention would require the complete renovation of our society. It might be too expensive to run and have little guarantee of payoff.

Those who favor a community approach point out that a task's complexity shouldn't discourage attempts to solve it. The cost of such attempts may be high, but community psychologists believe that these costs should be placed in proper perspective. Cowen (1967) points out that the cost of traditional treatment of mental disorders within our institutional system can be tremendous. For example, residential treatment for one emotionally disturbed person can cost between $15,000 and $20,000 per year, and the cost of lifetime care for one permanently hospitalized individual may exceed a quarter of a million dollars. From the financial perspective, the costs of innovative community approaches to preventing emotional disturbance seem very small in comparison. Community workers point out that theirs isn't a "soft-headed" approach to mental-health problems; it is sound in terms of dollars and cents.

Preventive Programs Invade Personal Privacy

Community approaches have also been criticized as being an unwarranted invasion of personal privacy. Further, there is the fear that those in positions of power might use the excuse of "deviant behavior" to squelch criticism and opposition to a political system.

As a rule, advocates of the community approach are aware of the potential for abuse of new social programs. However, they point out that other "invasions of privacy," such as inoculations for dread diseases and fluoridation of water have been accepted by most people because they were deemed necessary by respected professionals. Most community advocates are aware that infringements of individual rights and the relinquishing of individual control are often resisted by Americans; if community approaches continue, it will most likely be because the majority sees some merit in these programs. Professionals may institute programs, but the public still has the power to avoid them and thereby end them.

Social Need for Winners and Losers

Another force inhibiting community approaches is the belief that those who work hard and persevere will be successful and happy. Known as the "Protestant Ethic," this idea has been reinforced by what Rome (1969) calls the values of "Frontier Psychology," or admiration of the strong individualist who battles social controls and nature. From this perspective, failure or illness can be evidence that a person is deficient in some incorrectable way.

The community-psychology response to "Frontier Psychology" is simply that the frontier is gone. Although many would like to adopt such a simplistic way of looking at the world, there are any number of good reasons why people have difficulties, the least of which is that they are "weak."

Prevention Results in Poorer Treatment for the Impoverished

A very different objection to community approaches is posed by those who feel that the disadvantaged and poor may actually suffer from community-psychology programs. For example, Halleck (1969) pointed out that community attempts to bring better care to more people may actually increase inequities in our mental-health system. He feared that community approaches wouldn't include intensive psychotherapy for the lower classes, who might only receive some combination of environmental manipulation, drugs, and brief psychotherapy. Halleck believed a better approach to solving manpower problems would be to train more therapists to do intensive psychotherapy.

Threat to the Roles of Mental-Health Professionals

The final force inhibiting community psychology comes from mental-health professionals themselves. Community advocates point out that many mental-health professionals may be loath to give up techniques with which they are familiar. Further, some therapists don't want to lose the respect they gain from the patients they treat and the community in which they work; they may prefer not to attempt unknown procedures with people who may be neither bright nor well motivated and who may represent greater possibilities of therapeutic failure. Indeed, the resistance among many professionals to giving up the comfortable surroundings of the private office to venture into unknown areas can be formidable.

A THEORY OF PREVENTION AND COMMUNITY INTERVENTION

In spite of the objections inhibiting its growth, the motivating forces behind community psychology have led to its becoming a major component in national and worldwide efforts to help people who are different. What distinguishes true community-psychology efforts from haphazard attempts at social intervention is the use of a guiding theory. For many community workers, the most influential theorist in community psychology is probably Gerald Caplan.

Caplan (1974) identifies three different types of prevention, each of which falls within the domain of the community worker. *Primary prevention* refers to the alteration of circumstances that might promote disordered behavior. Reducing crowding and violence in inner cities is an example of primary prevention, since it is known that people living under crowded conditions tend to experience more psychopathology.

Whereas primary prevention focuses on stopping a disorder from ever occurring, *secondary prevention* seeks primarily to reduce the rate or severity of an already existing disorder. Early detection and successful treatment of disorders are implicit in any program of secondary prevention. Therefore, accurate, quick assessment processes close to "where the action is" are necessary so workers can evaluate a person's potential for developing a specific disorder or can determine the stage of an existing disorder. Thus, remedial procedures can begin early.

Tertiary prevention focuses on shortening the period of disability and minimizing damage resulting from disordered behavior. Traditional forms of treatment such as psychotherapy, rehabilitation, and hospitalization are examples of tertiary prevention.

Efforts to apply the three types of prevention at the community level require programs based upon a sound theory relating people to society. Caplan's theory is a developmental one in which he assumes that people go through specific stages from birth to death and that certain "supplies" are needed for successful completion of each stage. These "supplies" are *physical* (such as food, shelter, and exercise), *psychosocial* (cognitive and emotional satisfactions received through interaction with others), and *sociocultural* (fulfilling the expectations of others concerning one's roles and activities in society). Caplan assumes that crises inevitably occur during development and separates predictable *developmental crises* from unpredictable *accidental crises*. In the former, there typically is stress involved in passing from one developmental stage to the next. For example, a child moving into adolescence may experience stress that must be resolved before the youngster can deal adequately with the problems of young adulthood. Caplan's emphasis on developmental crises is similar to that found in the theories of Anna Freud, Sullivan, and Erikson.

In contrast to the commonly occurring developmental crises, *accidental crises* usually involve sudden losses of "supplies," such as the loss of a parent or spouse. The way in which early accidental crises are resolved can affect the person's ability to meet the demands of future crises and stresses. Caplan views a crisis as an opportunity: it includes the possibility for people to become stronger as well as a danger that they might become weaker in dealing with future stresses. According to Caplan, too many crises and limited ability to deal with them can result in the emergence of disordered behavior.

Caplan believes that there are two ways to prevent disordered behavior: *social action* and *interpersonal action*. Social action refers to improving the environment in which people live and interact. In Caplan's terms, social action means ensuring that the environment yields an adequate amount of "supplies." To accomplish this, community mental-health professionals often must get involved in legislative and political activities. This involvement is required to guarantee the availability of physical supplies (for example, creating work opportunities that allow families to stay together), psychosocial supplies (perhaps reducing the isolation of certain groups such as the aged), and sociocultural supplies (such as providing ties to society at large). Social action also means providing ways to deal with both predictable and unpredictable crises. For example, there are groups of people called "populations at risk" who are in a potentially stressful situation and whose members may be in need of help to resolve their crises in a positive fashion. Pregnant women, beginning college students, and retiring workers all qualify as populations at risk. Such groups deserve special attention, both to prepare the individuals who must face impending stressful situations and to train caregivers, such as doctors, nurses, and counselors, who will be interacting with them.

Interpersonal action usually means face-to-face interaction between a mental-health professional and an individual or group. Since professionals can see only a few members of a community, they usually must choose those with whom they interact in a way that maximizes the benefits to the community as a whole. By selecting those who are in positions to supply the needs of many members of a community (such as prison wardens, political leaders, or others in positions of authority), the mental-health worker can have maximum impact. For example, helping a teacher to be more effective often can do much more to increase conditions for growth in school children than an effort to help each child individually. Caplan emphasizes the importance of educating community leaders about the mental-health needs of their community and of having mental-health professionals stationed in the community. Support given by community psychologists to other health personnel involved in the well-being of the community can be invaluable in organizing a positive and sustained response to the psychological needs of the community.

PROBLEMS AND SOLUTIONS

The concept of community psychology and a theory such as Caplan's aren't developed for abstract purposes. They are to be applied in an effort to help people who are different. In this section we will present a selection of community-psychology programs described by Zax and Specter (1974) designed to solve some of the major problems faced by community mental-health professionals.

Overcoming Shortages of Trained Helpers

Earlier in this chapter we mentioned that one of the prime factors motivating community approaches to abnormality was the shortage of helpers. Programs aimed at solving this problem are exemplified by those in which homemakers and college students become therapists.

Homemakers as Helpers. One approach to solving the shortage of "people power" in the mental-health field has been to involve homemakers whose children have grown or who are ready for second careers. In 1958,

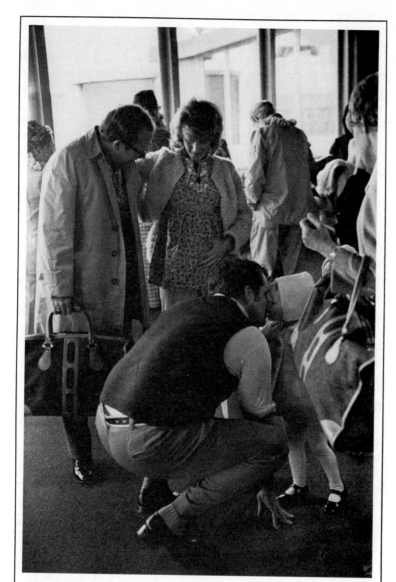

Families of pregnant women, as well as pregnant women themselves, constitute a "population at risk." (Photo by David Powers.)

Rioch (1967) began a program to train homemakers as helpers and set the goal of having her trainees able to perform the whole gamut of mental-health workers' activities. To prepare these women to deal with troubled adolescents, Rioch created a two-year training program. From a group of 50 volunteers, 8 homemakers were chosen. They were described as intelligent, psychologically stable, and relating well to others. All were college graduates, and half had been in psychotherapy for two or more years. Training consisted mainly of practical work and supervision instituted early in the program. In other words, the homemakers obtained practical experience in working with people before any academic work was introduced. Evaluations of the clinical work of these trainees by outside psychotherapists were typically favorable. Although Rioch's trainees were rated significantly poorer therapists than advanced psychiatric residents, they were rated significantly better than freshman medical students and hospital volunteers and no different from first-year psychiatric residents.

College Students as Helpers. A second source of potentially effective mental-health workers is college students. Poser (1966) compared the effects of group psychotherapy carried out by college undergraduates to that carried out by experienced professional therapists. The patients were chronically ill schizophrenics who had been hospitalized for at least three years. What the groups actually did was left up to the discretion of the group leaders. At the end of five months, the groups led by trained professionals were found to be poorer on three and no different on three other measures of improvement than the groups led by college students. Thus, it appeared that untrained therapists dealing with this type of patient in certain instances could do as well as—or even better than—trained workers. Poser hypothesized that the improvements brought about by college students may have been due to their greater enthusiasm. In similar research, Rappaport, Chinsky, and Cowen (1971) support the conclusions that effective group therapy sometimes can be carried out by relatively untrained leaders.

Besides being used as leaders of group-psychotherapy sessions, college students have successfully taken part in college-student–mental-patient companion programs (Holzberg & Knapp, 1965; Kreitzer, 1969; Reinherz, 1964). In an early companion program (Umbarger, Dalsimer, Morrison, & Breggin, 1962), college students were asked to volunteer for work at one of two large mental hospitals in the Boston area. Little screening of the volunteers was done, for the organizers believed that the students would screen themselves as the program continued. Of the approximately 500 students who volunteered, a little fewer than half made ten or more visits to patients. The student volunteers were simply instructed to "be with" the patients and weren't prepared or helped in any significant way. They were given a specific day to visit and were assigned to a person who organized the visits to fit into the hospital routine. However, it didn't take long for the students to impose their own structure on the program in the form of various projects calculated to contribute to growth in the patients with whom they worked. For example, some students organized a campaign to "beautify" the hospital surroundings by painting walls and trying to make the hospital environment more stimulating and pleasant. Anyone who has worked in a large hospital can appreciate what these kinds of changes in environment can mean to patient and staff morale.

Today, college-companion programs are widespread. Some have been described in professional journals (Holzberg & Knapp, 1965; W. Klein & Zax, 1965), and more have been reported in community newspapers. In general, it appears that the inclusion of college students has had a positive effect on a number of mental-health programs. We know from conversations with people across the country that successful use of college students in mental-health programs isn't an isolated event. Untrained, but willing to give of themselves, college students have become a valuable source of manpower in dealing with disordered persons. The benefits of these programs aren't limited to mental-health clients, either. For example, investigators have shown that students involved in such programs have become more tolerant and accepting of others as a result of their experiences (Holzberg, Gewirtz, & Ebner, 1964; Holzberg, Knapp, & Turner, 1967). An account of one experience as a companion may give you some insights into what these kinds of programs can mean to the students involved in them.

PERSONAL EXPERIENCE: *A College-Student Companion*

10-6 The adventure begins

My first exposure to the patients today was an experience I'm sure I'll never forget. We were at community meeting this morning knowing essentially nothing about the job we had or what would be expected of us. Bobby opened the meeting up for general discussion and there was a little griping about the TV not working right and there never being enough coffee. Then a lady looked up and said, "Bobby how come leather craft is always at 1:00? I'm in alcohol groups and so I never get to go." Another patient looked up and said in a very matter-of-fact tone of voice, "That sure is a shame, honey! I guess it's because you're an alcoholic nut instead of a regular nut."

Barbara and I looked at each other in disbelief. I guess we just weren't prepared for such a blunt, frank, or open confrontation of the problems of the patients by the patients. I found myself chuckling along with the older staff and the patients. I think I'm going to like this place. That introduction to patient contact and life on the unit certainly relaxed me at a moment when my nerves weren't at their calmest.

After community meeting we headed back up toward the nurses' station to see what to do next. At the door of the nurses' station I was confronted by a woman in her mid-50s. She looked exactly like the stereotype crazy, complete with glazed eyes, uncombed hair, unsteady gait. She was wearing three shirts and two pairs of pants. She caught me by the hands and said, "You're Roy Clark and I'm Granny Fannie and I'm ready to boogie!" She dropped my hands and began to dance around in front of the nurses' station. Gloria finally took hold of Fannie's hands and brought her over to where I was standing and told her that indeed I was not Roy Clark. "Her name is Linda and she works here." Fannie pleasantly agreed to this and walked happily off down the hallway.

I turned those words over in my mind and all of a sudden it hit me like a ton of bricks. Finally, after eight months, not only do I have a job, but it's a job in my field. I have my foot in that door. This job will probably be interesting, exciting, scary, funny, depressing, encouraging, and a lot of hard work. I say let me at it!

10-11

Arrived at work this morning and went to report, where we were told an absolutely astounding story. Last Saturday evening a patient was admitted to the unit. At some point this woman became agitated and combative. As procedure dictates, the staff called the emergency room in the general hospital for assistance in restraining her. For some reason, and no one is quite sure why, an off-duty police sergeant came with the emergency medical technicians to assist in restraining her. This police officer was off duty, out of uniform, and had his gun stuck in the back of his pants. The unit has a rule (for obvious reasons) that any time a police officer comes onto the unit he must have his gun locked up. This officer came along to "help." This patient was very agitated and kicked the cop in the shins. He reacted to this by hitting her in the face hard enough to raise a welt on her face. She then spat in his face whereupon he grabbed a pillow and put it in her face. Needless to say, the staff members were very upset. Pat went to call the nursing supervisor to fill out the incident report. After the patient was restrained, the police officer demanded to leave the unit. Lottie and Karen asked him to wait until the nursing supervisor arrived. He responded with, "If you don't unlock the goddamned door I'm gonna blow the hinges off." He pulled his gun out of his pants, so Karen quickly unlocked the door and allowed him to leave. Evidently he realized that he had messed up bad. The next thing anybody knew there were police everywhere with warrants for the arrest of Karen and Lottie for obstructing a police officer. They were actually charged off to jail. That crazy cop was meanwhile telling the papers we tried to lock him up. He said, "I just wasn't ready for the rubber hose squad."

No one knows for sure what is going to happen yet, but the feeling is that the charges are going to be dropped and the record is going to be expunged, but that is still small comfort to Karen and Lottie.

This whole thing has raised serious questions in my mind about what the hell people really think about a psychiatric hospital. The thing that really bothers me is that I can't think of any way we can show people that we don't use "rubber hoses." Maybe I want to solve all the problems of the world, a little too much, a little too soon.

11-3

Fannie went home today, and I am still sort of questioning what exactly happened with her. She wandered around for days talking crazy and never sleeping. Finally her doctor decided to do ECTs on her. The ECTs helped. Fannie didn't act crazy anymore and she quit wearing three shirts at a time, but to my knowledge and as far as the chart goes she never really dealt with the death of her son. I have to wonder what exactly we did for her besides just make the behavior we didn't like go away.

12-24

Today there were six staff members here and three patients on the unit. All the other patients have gone home for Christmas. My heart goes out to those still here. All three of them tell of either family problems or physical trouble. One is an extremely somatic woman with a voice that sort of reminds me of fingernails on a blackboard. Ever since she came here her daughter has snuck in and out with things for her at times when she knew she wouldn't be allowed to see her. On the one hand, I can understand the daughter's desire to get away from her mother's complaints that are nonstop, but on the other hand, the patient is her mother and I know I couldn't leave my mother alone in the hospital over Christmas if there was an order written that she could come home.

2-19

We have a new patient here. He's been at the center for three days now and all he's done is pace the halls and try to find a way to get off the unit. He refuses to talk to anyone. Today he got away on the elevator and walked seven miles to his home. His mother brought him back and he agreed to stay, "but only because my mom said I couldn't come home to live until I'm discharged." About 7:00 tonight I smelled something that resembled pot in the day room. When I walked in, Don tried to walk out. I stopped him and told him to give me whatever it was he was smoking. He handed me a hand-rolled cigarette—not tobacco, not pot, but tea—Lipton tea! I came down on him pretty hard about it and told him I thought he needed to decide why he was here and begin to play by our rules if he wanted to get out. I left and sat at the back desk to let visitors in. About 15 minutes later Don approached me, sat down, and told me all about the fact that he had been hospitalized a total of seven times since 1973. He stopped and started and laughed inappropriately at the hard-to-talk-about parts (like his mother moved out and left him with his two younger brothers in an apartment to go live with her boyfriend).

We talked for the entire hour, me mostly just sitting back and listening to the story of this 19-year-old kid who is convinced he's crazy and that that's all he'll ever be. His thinking is confused and unrealistic. He used drugs and sees no reason to stop. "They help me get somewhere where no one tells me I'm bad, or if they do I don't care." I don't know how to respond to that. I only know I feel myself wanting to touch this kid. He is moving me more than any patient I've dealt with yet. At 8:30 I have to go back up front, and I try to and for now our conversation stops. He says, "How come you're different? How come you let me sit here and tell you everything when I never could do that in any of those other hospitals before?" I don't know what to say to him. I haven't done anything—he has. He took the chance and right now I don't know who's happier about it, me or him. I am on top of the world. For the first time in three months I really feel like I accomplished something tonight. I really feel like I made a difference.

2-20

Don went home today. He's still talking more than when he came in, but he really doesn't look too much better. He is supposed to be in the day program but I doubt that will last long. Good-bye, Don. I really wish I could honestly believe that this time was the last time you had to be hospitalized.

2-25

Don is back. He didn't take his cogentin and had a reaction to his prolixin. All he said was, "I didn't like it out there. That was the only way that I knew for sure that they'd let me back in."

Someone, somewhere—either the doctor, the therapist, the inpatient staff, the family, or Don—*has* to try harder.

Prevention Programs

Another way to meet needs for manpower and treatment is to focus on preventing disorders from occurring or from developing to the point where extensive intervention is needed.

Primary Prevention through Planned Communities. Primary-prevention programs often are directed at producing social conditions that minimize personal crises and stress. Such programs may be exemplified by the development of communities that have been carefully planned to avoid the "unhealthy" components of many freely developing population centers. Although many people claim to know what is wrong with the communities

Primary prevention assumes that by improving environments we can reduce the occurrence of disordered behavior. (Photo by Marc Rutt-ner.)

we now have, only a few have attempted to use this information systemati-cally to try to build better communities from scratch.

One recent attempt at developing a new community based on a psychological theory is Twin Oaks, established in Virginia in 1967. Twin Oaks is loosely based on principles described by Skinner in his utopian novel *Walden II*. The psychological principles of reward and punishment offered by Skinner were followed within Twin Oaks as long as they appeared to be workable. Although attempts were made to equalize income, members weren't required to give up their financial resources upon entering the community. The goal of the founders of Twin Oaks was to have members do what they ought because that is what they want to do, but it seems they are a long way from realizing this goal. For example, criticism of others' behavior now often takes place in private, after the apparent failure of various schemes to handle criticisms publicly. The crisis of dealing with the first new generation of children hasn't yet occurred, but since this has been a most important turning point for past utopian communities, it may be the hardest test for Twin Oaks.

A similar opportunity to plan a community presented itself in the late 1960s with a new town called Columbia, Maryland. The city was to contain 100,000 people, and it presented an extraordinary opportunity for social planning. Panels of experts from all fields were convened. A health and welfare committee was given the responsibility for planning the community so that its physical structure might be maximally beneficial to the "health" of its members. This task was immensely complex. Struggles among members of the committee often centered about political and ethical considerations, but there was agreement on certain issues. For example, it was agreed that comprehensive mental- and physical-health facilities should be close at hand. It was also decided that it would be very difficult for members of Columbia to have a sense of community in a city of 100,000, so smaller social units of around 10,000 to 15,000 were planned for. It was within these smaller social units that planning for shopping areas and the like took place. The planners also decided on having a downtown area with high-rise structures and to mix social classes within social units. One major goal of the social scientists was to reduce sources of stress within the social unit. Therefore, some care was given to welfare planning and to several types of prevention programs, such as parent education, adult education, and access to counseling. Further, the planners sought to make recreational, occupational, and vocational opportunities available for all age groups. It will be a while before we know how successful the social scientists were in planning Columbia. Our guess is that they will fail in some areas and succeed in others, but will learn from the failures much that can be applied more successfully to other communities.

Secondary Prevention. Whereas primary-prevention programs focus on avoiding the development of disorders, secondary-prevention programs usually require that a "population at risk" be identified and that attempts be made to reduce the incidence or prevalence of disordered behavior within that population. Secondary-prevention efforts typically are directed at people who have a strong chance of eventually being diagnosed as being different. An example of secondary prevention was the Residential Youth Center (RYC) program (Goldenberg, 1971). The purpose of RYC was to create a residential setting in which personal growth of inner-city adolescents and their families could take place. The program differed in a number of ways from the more traditional juvenile-home programs: it was based in the neighborhood where the youngsters lived, nonprofessionals living in the area usually were used as staff members, and goals and decisions affecting the program were arrived at cooperatively by staff and residents. The organization of RYC was unusual in that its structure was horizontal, with all members, staff and clients alike, sharing jobs ranging from administration to cooking. Staff members were chosen primarily on the basis of their knowledge of inner-city life, their experience in working with adolescents, and their willingness to voice dissatisfaction when necessary. Those chosen as staff members came from a wide variety of occupational backgrounds, ranging from mechanics to professional singers. The youngsters selected for the program were chosen from a group of adolescents who had been "given up on" by other agencies. They all had made poor progress in school and had police records. The RYC worked with 20 such boys and their families at any one time. During the day, the boys were expected to work outside the center; RYC staff took this opportunity to meet with the boys' families. In addition to relating to the boys personally, staff members worked directly on the environment surrounding the youngsters by setting up special days and programs for families and for the entire community. Boys and their families had free access to the RYC center at any time of the night or day. The staff worked very hard to get these youngsters environmental support for new positive behavior.

Goldenberg reported that, in comparison to a control group, RYC youngsters showed better records of employment and less feeling of alienation, and had fewer run-ins with the law. Studies are now under way to test the long-term effects of such a program; if proved to be successful, its implications for intervention are numerous.

Tertiary Prevention. Tertiary prevention involves procedures to soften the effects of a disorder that has already appeared. The college-companion programs discussed earlier are examples of tertiary prevention. Other tertiary-prevention programs also may use innovative methods to help mental patients recover in the quickest and most effective fashion.

Maxwell Jones (1953, 1968) is among those most responsible for introducing tertiary-prevention programs into mental hospitals. Called a *therapeutic community*, Jones's program dealt primarily with patients who had significant difficulties with their social environment. He assigned patients to semiskilled jobs and had them meet daily with staff for either a one-hour gripe session or a work-related learning session. One morning each week ordinarily was reserved for psychodrama. Jones's most significant innovation was perhaps increased personal contact between patients and staff, and among staff members themselves. Titles were kept to a minimum, and first names were used for everyone. The nursing staff, only a few of whom had formal nurses' training, had three main responsibilities: to mediate quarrels among patients, to socialize with patients, and to help patients become involved with the community. The doctor gave up the usual doctor role. He wore no white coat and carried no stethoscope. His main role was that of a facilitator of social growth and interaction.

Evaluation of the therapeutic-community program was generally favorable. Especially in view of the fact that many of the participants were initially the most difficult in the hospital, they did quite well. As a result of Jones's success, a number of similar programs were begun in England and in the United States (Sanders, 1967). Today it is the rare mental hospital that has no tertiary-prevention program such as the therapeutic community. These programs usually are characterized by informal arrangements between staff and patients, significant patient control over social and community life, and transition steps between the hospital and the community.

CONCLUDING COMMENTS

What does the future hold for community approaches? The forecast for the community mental-health centers is unclear. Although evaluated as successful by the federal government, few of these centers have become financially self-sufficient, either with state help or through insurance payments. What may occur is a battle between the federal and state governments, with each wanting the other to pick up the financial responsibility for continued or new programs. We believe the battle between federal and state governments may lead to a slowdown in the construction of new centers in the near future. However, there is at present much support for national health insurance. Should national health insurance become a reality, it might spur a new round of building of comprehensive health-care facilities. It is apparent that the actions of the federal government are crucial in determining the number and scope of community programs, and those who support community approaches have stepped up lobbying efforts in Washington, as have those who oppose them.

With regard to training community psychologists, the picture is a bit clearer, although it too is intimately affected by what happens in Washington, D.C. We believe that the trend toward training community interventionists who are familiar with the wide variety of people who are troubled will continue. The need for flexibility in dealing with community problems remains essential. However, with the continual feedback regarding the adequacy of certain training experiences, programs should become both more circumscribed and more specialized. We see a trend on many fronts in the use of "nonprofessionals" to deal with disordered behavior. Lay volunteers, college students, and homemakers have all been invaluable in stemming the tide of disordered behavior, and their use should increase in the future. These "nonprofessional" workers can help meet the vast manpower needs of mental-health treatment, as well as help themselves to more interesting and fulfilling lives. For example, in inner cities or rural settings, the "nonprofessional" often contributes an effective manner of dealing with disordered behavior that cannot be obtained from formal training programs. The woman who works as a school cook but is known and trusted by adolescents, the inner-city youth living on the edge of crime who knows the thinking and values of his peers, and the public-health nurse who visits every home in his or her district are some examples of invaluable community workers. Although some professionals may not like the idea of nonprofessionals dealing with those who are different, these community helpers are here to stay.

The future of community approaches is uncertain. Great strides in dealing with disordered behavior have been made, but there is a long way to go. Progress is by no means assured, but mental-health problems are of sufficient magnitude, and enough people are involved, that we are confident the future will bring new approaches and new successes in community efforts to deal with the problems of being different.

CHAPTER SUMMARY CHART

In this chapter we discussed community psychology, the newest approach to the treatment of those who are different:

Motivating forces	*Inhibiting forces*
Dissatisfaction with traditional treatment Overwhelming need for services Shortage of trained personnel Belief in prevention	Lack of knowledge about prevention The need is too great—the cost too high Prevention invades personal privacy Social need for winners and losers Poor people lose out with prevention programs Threat to roles of professionals

Caplan's theory of prevention	*Problems and solutions*

Primary, secondary, and tertiary prevention
Physical, psychosocial, and sociocultural supplies
Developmental and accidental crises
	Overcoming shortages in trained helpers:
	    Homemakers
	    College students
	Prevention programs:
	    Planned communities
	    Identifying high risks
	    Therapeutic inpatient communities

GLOSSARY

Abreaction: The reliving or reexperiencing of feelings about past events; catharsis.

Academic-mechanics disorders: Patterns in college students in which specific academic skills, such as the ability to take tests, are either lacking or impaired.

Acetylcholine: A catecholamine serving as a neurotransmitter at many sites throughout the nervous system.

Acquisition: The learning of a response in classical or operant conditioning.

Acute brain syndrome: A pattern of symptoms, including delirium, occurring as a result of some sudden trauma, intoxication, or the like.

Acute versus chronic schizophrenia: A dimensional representation of schizophrenia ranging from that with sudden onset (acute) to that associated with long-term symptomatology (chronic).

Addiction: A physiological dependence on a drug characterized by increased bodily tolerance and withdrawal symptoms.

Adolescent crisis: An adjustment reaction of adolescence that can range from normal turmoil to severe disturbance.

Affect: A term referring to the expression of emotions in general, as in "flat affect."

Affective disorders: A group of psychotic disorders characterized by severe disturbance of mood.

Affective personality: A personality disorder in which the primary personality style is marked by alternating and recurring episodes of depression and elation.

Affective psychosis: *See* Affective disorders.

Agitated depression: Feelings of sadness and dejection accompanied by an inability to stop moving about or talking rapidly.

Alcoholics Anonymous: A self-help organization begun by recovered alcoholics to aid in the rehabilitation of other alcoholics through group meetings and mutual support.

Alcoholism: Dependence on alcohol with increased bodily tolerance and the presence of withdrawal symptoms.

Ambivalence: Often a primary sign of schizophrenia, this term describes the mixture of positive and negative feelings about a given thing, person, or situation.

Amnesia: Disruption of memory processes associated with dissociative reactions, organic brain syndromes, or hypnosis.

Amphetamines: A group of drugs that function as central-nervous-system stimulants.

653

Anal stage: Freudian psychosexual stage in which satisfactions center about the retention or passage of feces.

Anhedonia: A defect in the capacity to feel pleasure.

Anomie: Emil Durkheim's term for the feelings surrounding social isolation and alienation.

Anorexia nervosa: A psychophysiological disorder characterized by a prolonged inability to eat or retain food.

Antidepressant drugs: A group of chemicals, including tricyclics and monoamine oxidase inhibitors, that can relieve the symptoms of depression.

Antimanic drugs: A group of drugs, the most effective of which is lithium carbonate, that can reduce the symptoms of manic disorders.

Antipsychotic drugs: A group of chemicals known to reduce (not cure) many symptoms of severe psychosis.

Anxiety: An unrealistic and irrational fear of some thing or situation.

Anxiety-blissfulness psychosis: An atypical cycloid psychosis in which behaviors range from anxiety to blissfulness.

Anxiety neurosis: A neurosis distinguished by the subjective experience of panic or overconcern as the primary symptom.

Apathy reaction: A pattern seen in college students in which malaise and boredom seem to overpower the motivation to study.

Apraxia: An inability to perform a specific motor act.

Arteriosclerosis: A disorder affecting blood flow in the blood vessels which is believed to be involved in the onset of some cases of senile dementia.

Assertion training: A behavioral therapy technique in which people learn through behavioral rehearsal to defend their rights and assert themselves appropriately.

Asthenic personality: A personality disorder in which the primary personality style is marked by fatigue and lack of energy to carry on normal daily activities.

Asthma: A respiratory disorder characterized by difficulty in breathing sometimes brought about by stress.

Atypical cycloid psychosis: A group of rare psychoses in which behavior ranges from one extreme of a dimension to another.

Autism: A self-centered involvement with one's own feelings and thoughts, often to the exclusion of the rest of the world.

Autonomic conversion reaction: A nonorganic hysterical reaction resulting in impairment of some autonomic process.

Autonomic nervous system: That part of the nervous system which controls "involuntary" processes like breathing, perspiration, digestion, and the like.

Autoscopic experiences: Disorders in which people perceive themselves as being projected outside their own bodies.

Aversive conditioning: A behavioral-therapy technique in which behavioral frequency is decreased by associating an undesirable behavior with an aversive consequence.

Avoidance learning: A form of operant learning in which an organism learns to avoid aversive experiences and situations.

Axon: A fiber emanating from the cell body of a neuron that is primarily involved in carrying impulses to other cells.

Barbiturates: Addictive sedatives that function as central-nervous-system depressants.

Barnum effect: A magnification of the placebo effect in psychotherapy through the "selling" of a technique by a therapist.

Basedow's disease: A condition caused by a hyperactive thyroid gland and marked by irritability and anxiety.

Bedlam: The colloquial name for St. Mary's of Bethlehem, a mental hospital noted for its inhumane treatment of inmates.

Behavioral psychotherapy: Psychotherapy derived from laboratory principles of learning and behavior change; also known as behavior modification or behavior therapy.

Behavior modification: See Behavioral psychotherapy.

Behavior-modification groups: Group application of behavioral methods such as systematic desensitization or covert sensitization.

Bestiality: Sexual activity between humans and animals.

Biochemical theory of schizophrenia: A general belief that schizophrenia is caused by some biochemical aberration in the body.

Bioenergetic group therapy: Group treatment of psychological problems through involvement of the mind *and* body in the therapy process.

Biofeedback: Presentation of physiological responses as a means of training an individual to gain conscious control over those responses.

Biogenic: Physically based or caused.

Blunting of affect: A muffling of the intensity of expressed feelings often seen in schizophrenic people.

Calamitous death: An often degrading premature or unexpected death, usually due to violence.

Campus crisis center: A location on many college campuses where, on a 24-hour basis, immediate help is available for emotional problems.

Cannula: A small tube implanted in a specific site in the brain through which chemicals under study may be passed.

Capgras' syndrome: A condition marked by the belief that familiar objects and persons are actually frauds or impostors.

Catatonia: A psychotic behavior pattern usually marked by mutism, waxy flexibility, automatic obedience, and withdrawal, but sometimes indicated by severe agitation and hyperactivity.

Catecholamine hypothesis: The belief that deviations in certain neurotransmitters play a role in the development of the affective disorders.

Catecholamines: A group of biochemicals, some of which (acetylcholine and norepinephrine, for example) are involved in neural transmission.

Catharsis: Discharge of pent-up feelings; believed to be of therapeutic value.

Central nervous system: Neural system composed of the brain and spinal cord.

Ceruloplasmin: A blue plasma protein once thought to be a toxic factor in schizophrenia.

Childhood depression: Depressive patterns in children through age 12.

Chronic brain syndrome: A pattern of symptoms, including dementia, usually occurring as the result of some form of progressive brain disease.

Circumscribed delusions: Unfounded beliefs that are limited in scope to a specific thing, person, or situation.

Classical conditioning: The association of a neutral stimulus (conditioned stimulus) with an unconditioned stimulus such that the neutral stimulus comes to bring about a conditioned response; also known as *respondent learning.*

Client-centered therapy: A form of psychotherapy developed by Carl Rogers that emphasizes providing an atmosphere in which clients' innate self-actualizing tendencies can produce positive growth.

Clinical psychologist: A person holding a Ph.D. in applied or clinical psychology who is specially trained in diagnostic testing, psychotherapy, and research methodology.

Cocaine: A pain-reducing stimulant obtained from the leaves of the coca plant.

Cognitive dysfunctions: Thinking disorders.

Colitis: A sometimes psychophysiologically based disorder in which intense abdominal pain, bleeding stools, and irritation of the colon are common symptoms.

Community psychology: An approach to mental disturbances that focuses on prevention at the societal level rather than on treatment at the individual level.

Compulsive neurosis: A neurotic disorder characterized by compulsions to repeat specific acts in order to allay anxiety.

Concordance rate: The percentage of twin pairs in which both members manifest the same disturbance under study.

Conditioned emotional reaction: A learned fear of a once neutral and usually harmless situation.

Conditioned response (CR): In classical conditioning, the response elicited by the conditioned stimulus.

Conditioned stimulus (CS): In classical conditioning, the originally neutral stimulus which, through association with an unconditioned stimulus, comes to elicit a conditioned response.

Confusional psychosis: An atypical cycloid psychosis in which behavior ranges from excited confusion to inhibited confusion.

Conjoint family therapy: A method of therapy developed by Virginia Satir in which an entire family is seen in an attempt to help one of its members.

Conscience: That part of the superego composed of thoughts and behaviors to be avoided; a listing of "don't's."

Conscious: According to Freud, those needs, wishes, thoughts, memories, and motives of which a person is aware at any given time.

Continuous reinforcement: A schedule of reinforcement in which rewards are administered every time a response is emitted.

Conversion hysteria: Also known as conversion reaction, a form of neurosis characterized by the appearance of physical symptoms or malfunctions without actual physical bases.

Coprolalia: The use of obscene and lewd language, often in an impulsive and uncontrolled way.

Covert reinforcement: A method used in behavior therapy in which a person strengthens desirable behavior by imagining a pleasant event or situation as a reward.

Covert sensitization: A behavioral-therapy technique in which, in the imagination, undesirable behaviors or thoughts are reduced in frequency by association with aversive thoughts and images.

Cretinism: A condition caused by hypoactivity of the thyroid gland, marked by inhibited growth, bodily distortion, and retarded intellectual development.

Crisis-intervention theory: The belief that people are most responsive to helping efforts when in a state of crisis, as when contemplating suicide or under other great stress.

Cycloid psychosis: See Atypical cycloid psychosis.

Defense mechanism: A general name for a variety of methods through which a person protects the integrity of the ego.

Delirious mania: A degree of manic excitement so severe that the individual becomes delirious and loses touch with the environment.

Delirium: A set of symptoms usually caused by reversible and temporary cessation of brain function; symptoms may vary but include clouding, bewilderment, hallucinations, and fear.

Delirium tremens: Hallucinations, delusions, and other symptoms often accompanying withdrawal from alcohol addiction.

Delusion: A belief or attitude system not shared by the majority of others and seemingly not based upon realistic assessment of events.

Dementia: A progressive loss of brain function usually associated with chronic and irreversible brain disease.

Dementia praecox: A little-used term for schizophrenia meaning "early madness."

Demographic variables: Characteristics of people, such as age, sex, marital status, and the like, that often are related statistically to differential incidence or prevalence of disorders.

Dendrites: Fibers emanating from a neuron cell body that are primarily involved in receiving impulses from other neurons.

Denial: A defense mechanism that involves denying specific aspects of the internal or external environment.

Depression: A type of disorder, of either neurotic or psychotic degree, characterized by sadness, apathy, and self-deprecation.

Depressive neurosis: A neurotic disorder marked by excessive sadness usually precipitated by some specific environmental event.

Depressive stupor: A degree of depression so severe that the person does not move, talk, or show many signs of responsivity.

Dereism: A tendency toward fantasies and hallucinations.

Detachment level: The degree to which an immigrant group has been assimilated (or not) into a new culture.

Diathesis-stress theory: The belief that schizophrenia and several other disturbances are the result of the interaction between some inherited predisposition and some adverse environmental circumstances.

Direct analysis: A form of psychotherapy developed by John Rosen that is especially effective with psychotic people.

Displacement: A defense mechanism characterized by a shift of feelings from an original thing, person, or situation to some less threatening thing, person, or situation.

Dizygotic twins: Fraternal twins having different genetic makeup.

Dopamine hypothesis: The belief that excessive amounts of the neurotransmitter dopamine may be involved in the development of schizophrenia.

Dopamine-norepinephrine-imbalance hypothesis: The belief that excesses in dopamine and shortages in norepinephrine may contribute to the development of schizophrenia.

Double-bind communication: A type of communication in which the tone of the message and the verbal content of the message contradict or negate each other.

Down's syndrome: A type of mental retardation caused by an extra chromosome, once termed *mongolism* because of the characteristic epicanthan fold about the eyes.

Drug abuse: Use of any drug in a manner for which it was not prescribed or developed.

DSM-II: The second edition of the *Diagnostic and Statistical Manual of Mental Disorders* published by the American Psychiatric Association.

DSM-III: The revised edition of DSM-II, scheduled for adoption in the 1980s.

Dysfunction: A malfunction of a behavioral system; a disorder or disturbance.

Dyspnea: A feeling of difficulty in getting sufficient air; difficulty in breathing.

Dyspraxia: An inability to perform a specific motor act adequately.

Dyssocial personality: A pattern of personality developed in and approved by a subculture but often rejected or condemned by the dominant culture.

Echolalia: A symptom characterized by mimicking of the verbalizations of others.

Echopraxia: A symptom characterized by mimicking of the behaviors of others.

Educable mentally retarded: Retarded people with IQs ranging from 50 to 75 who can be expected to achieve from a third- to a sixth-grade educational level.

Ego: According to Freud, that part of the psychic triumvirate which mediates between id and superego requirements and the limits of reality.

Ego boundary: A psychoanalytic term referring to the limits set by the ego between the self and the rest of the world.

Ego disintegration: The loss of the ability of the ego to mediate between the demands of the id and superego and the outside world; personality breakdown.

Ego ideal: That part of the superego which is composed of positive goals; a listing of "do's."

Electra phase: See Oedipal/Electra phase.

Electroconvulsive therapy (ECT): Electrical induction of convulsive seizures that can be effective in the treatment of depression.

Electroencephalogram (EEG): A recording of the electrical activity of the brain.

Emotive imagery: A therapeutic technique for children in which fears are countered with images of special relationships with heroes, valued objects, and the like.

Encopresis: Weak or absent control over bowel movements in older children and adults.

Encounter group: A form of group therapy emphasizing personal growth and improved interpersonal communications through direct confrontation and reduction of defenses.

Endocrine system: The group of glands that secrete behavior-affecting chemical substances (hormones) directly into the bloodstream.

Endogenous depression: Depression seemingly caused by internal processes of a chronic nature.

Enuresis: Weak or absent control over urination in older children and adults; bedwetting.

Epilepsy: A chronic brain disorder characterized by some form of seizure, often accompanied by loss of consciousness.

Eros: According to Freud, the innate life instinct.

Essential hypertension: High blood pressure with no discernible physical basis.

Etiology: Causative factors in a disease or disturbance.

Eugenics: The application of genetics to the alteration of a species.

Exhibitionism: Arousal related to the display of one's sexual organs in public.

Existential anxiety: According to Søren Kierkegaard, a universal experience occurring when a person faces responsibility for his or her own fate.

Existential therapy: A form of psychotherapy emphasizing a person's need to live within the "now" and to exercise free choice in life.

Exogenous depression: Depression seemingly caused by some external stressful life event.

Exorcism: A method through which those believed to be possessed by demons are released through prayer, incantation, and sometimes physical abuse.

Expectancies: Beliefs in the chance of occurrence of certain events based upon previous experiences in similar situations.

Experimental neurosis: An abnormal behavior pattern produced in animals by specific classical- or operant-conditioning procedures.

Explosive personality: A personality disorder in which the primary style is marked by dangerous episodic outbursts of physical aggression.

Extinction: Reduction of the frequency of a response due to lack of reinforcement (operant conditioning) or to repeated presentation of a conditioned stimulus in the absence of an unconditioned stimulus (classical conditioning).

Family therapy: A method of treatment in which the family rather than one individual in the family is the target of therapeutic efforts.

Fetishism: Sexual attraction to an inanimate object or specific body part.

Final common pathway theory of affective disorders: The belief that symptoms of affective disorders may be the final pathway for a variety of disturbances based on social, psychological, biological, or genetic factors.

Final common pathway theory of schizophrenia: The belief that schizophrenic behavior may be the end result of not one but a variety of problems, be they social, psychological, biological, or genetic.

Fixations: According to Freud, an abnormal degree of psychological energy invested at some psychosexual stage.

Flooding: A method of behavioral therapy in which a person is made to confront anxiety-arousing stimuli until irrational fear is extinguished.

Folie à deux: A shared psychosis in which two or more people have the same delusional belief systems.

Free association: A basic procedure in psychoanalysis in which the individual is asked to say, without censoring, all of the things that come to mind.

Freshman adjustment reaction: Depression, severe homesickness, anxiety, and restlessness sometimes seen in college students during their freshman year.

Frottage: Sexual arousal through rubbing against another person.

Fugue state: A hysterical dissociative reaction marked by amnesia and running away, often resulting in the beginning of an entire new life elsewhere.

Functional disorders: Disorders without organic or physical basis.

Ganglion: A group of neurons clumped together.

Ganser's syndrome: A disorder characterized by "passing beside the point," in which the person just misses the correct answers to questions. It is often mistaken for conscious malingering.

General paresis: A chronic brain syndrome occurring in some cases of untreated syphilis.

Genital stage: Freudian psychosexual stage, considered to be the height of development and marked by mature heterosexual relationships.

Gestalt therapy: A method of psychotherapy developed by Frederick Perls that emphasizes the "here and now" in attempts to break down the deleterious effects of the past.

Gilles de la Tourette's syndrome: A behavior pattern characterized by uncontrollable, bizarre facial movements and often obscene verbal utterances.

Grand mal: A major form of epileptic seizure often accompanied by loss of consciousness.

Group therapy: A treatment technique involving one or two therapists meeting regularly with a group of people (usually seven to ten).

Hallucination: Perception of a stimulus when there is no actual source for such a stimulus.

Hebephrenic schizophrenia: A subtype of schizophrenia marked by extreme disorganization of personality, bizarre mannerisms, and flighty behavior and speech.

Heritability: The statistical chance that a given relative of a proband will inherit a specific disorder.

Higher-order conditioning: In classical conditioning, the establishment of a new conditioned stimulus through association with an established conditioned stimulus.

Homeostasis: A physiological and psychological process whereby an organism in a state of need or tension tends to be motivated to return to a state of neutrality or balance.

Huntington's chorea: A genetically based chronic brain syndrome of unknown origin.

Hyperactive: More active than normal.

Hyperventilation: Rapid breathing often accompanying anxiety; if uncontrolled by breathing into a paper bag over the mouth and nose, can result in passing out.

Hypoactive: Less active than normal.

Hypochondriacal neurosis: A neurotic disorder characterized by a preoccupation and overconcern with imagined physical illness.

Hypomania: The mildest form of manic psychosis.

Hysteria: A disorder, known even to the ancient Greeks and Romans, in which physical symptoms occur with no apparent physical cause (now known as conversion hysteria or conversion reaction).

Hysterical neurosis: A neurotic disorder characterized by impaired functioning of some bodily system (conversion hysteria) or altered state of consciousness (dissociative reaction).

Hysterical personality: A personality disorder in which the primary style is marked by emotional instability, excess excitability, overreactivity, and a tendency to overdramatize.

Id: In Freudian theory, the part of the psychic triumvirate in which instincts and psychic energy lie.

Identity crisis: According to Erik Erikson, the stressful emergence of identity during adolescence.

Implosive therapy: A behavioral therapy technique in which anxiety-arousing stimuli are presented intensively (in the imagination or in fact) and individuals are encouraged to experience and eventually extinguish the anxiety.

Incest: Sexual activity between close relatives.

Incidence rates: The number of new cases of a particular syndrome per a given number of people over a set period of time.

Individual psychotherapy: Psychotherapy in which one therapist meets with one client on a regular basis.

Indoleamine hypothesis: The belief that variations in certain biochemicals called indoleamines may play a role in the development of the affective disorders.

Infantile autism: A childhood psychosis marked by extreme withdrawal, unresponsiveness to social stimuli, and absence of ability to relate to others.

Insight: The experience of self-understanding that often occurs in psychotherapy.

Instrumental behavior: Behavior emitted in order to obtain a specific desired result.

Insulin coma therapy: A type of "shock treatment" in which seizures and coma are produced chemically through the administration of insulin, rather than electrically as in electroconvulsive therapy.

Intrapsychic censor: According to Freud, a mental process by which threatening ideas and feelings are repressed.

Involutional melancholia: A depressive psychosis appearing in older people and having no clear environmental precipitator.

Involutional paraphrenia: Paranoid psychosis of old age.

Kaiserian psychotherapy: A treatment method developed by Helmuth Kaiser that focuses upon communication and relationship patterns in disturbed people.

Korsakoff's syndrome: Pseudomemory in which a person reminisces about events that never happened and fills in memory gaps with fantasies.

Latency stage: Freudian psychosexual stage characterized by sexual dormancy prior to the onset of puberty.

Latent schizophrenia: A psychotic condition in which a person functions at a very minimal level owing to an as yet undeveloped psychosis.

Learned helplessness: An attitude resulting from repeated experiences of inescapable aversive stimulation; thought to play a role in the development of depression.

Learning disability: A discrepancy between achievement level and general abilities caused by a specific expressive, associative, or receptive deficit.

Libido: According to Freud, the collective sexual instincts.

Limbic system: A section of the brain below the cortex that is involved in regulating emotional reactions.

Lithium carbonate: A drug used in the control and treatment of manic psychosis.

Lobotomy: A surgical technique in which the neural pathways between the frontal lobes and thalamus are severed.

Locus of control of reinforcement: The degree to which people perceive what happens to them to be the result of their own behavior (internal control) or uncontrollable factors such as fate or powerful others (external control).

Logorrhea: An endless stream of verbalization often seen as a symptom in psychosis.

Lycanthropy: The belief, widespread in the Middle Ages, that one is a wolf.

Lysergic acid diethylamide (LSD): A drug that produces hallucinations, delusions, and other schizophreniclike symptoms.

Mainstreaming: Placement of mentally retarded or other "different" children in classrooms with normal children.

Major tranquilizers: A group of antipsychotic and antianxiety agents, including phenothiazine derivatives, butyrophenones, and the like.

Mania: An affective psychosis marked by extreme elation and euphoria, grandiose thoughts, and excess activity.

Manic-depressive psychosis: A severe psychological disturbance marked by either excess depression, excess mania, or a cycling between both moods.

Marathon group therapy: A method of treatment in which group meetings last 24 hours or more. The resultant fatigue and weakening of defenses often allow for greater ease of insight and openness to change.

Marital schism: A family situation thought by some to be conducive to schizophrenia in children; for example, the family may bicker constantly.

Marital skew: A family situation thought by some to be conducive to schizophrenia in children; the family's energies are inordinately focused on one of its members, but to outsiders the family appears harmonious.

Masochism: Sexual arousal related to being subjected to pain.

Mental retardation: Subaverage intellectual functioning combined with deficits in adaptive behavior; may be mild, moderate, severe, or profound.

Mental-status examination: An evaluation of the psychological condition of an individual, usually involving assessment of orientation in time, place, person, and circumstance and of perceptual abilities.

Mescaline: A psychedelic chemical that produces hallucinations, delusions, and other perceptual-cognitive distortions.

Methadone: An addictive synthetic narcotic that has been widely used as a substitute for heroin.

Migraine headache: Intense psychophysiologically based headaches due to dilation of arteries in the brain.

Milieu therapy: A method of treatment in which the total environment of a disturbed individual is controlled and therapeutic.

Minnesota Multiphasic Personality Inventory (MMPI): True-false questionnaire composed of 566 items used in the diagnosis of mental disturbance.

Minor tranquilizer: Any of a variety of drugs used to reduce mild to moderate anxiety, agitation, and tension.

Monoamine oxidase (MAO) inhibitors: A class of drugs especially useful in the treatment of certain depressions.

Monozygotic twins: Identical twins having the same genetic makeup.

Moral anxiety: Psychoanalytic term for the ego's fear of punishment for violating the constraints of the superego.

Motility psychosis: An atypical cycloid psychosis in which behavior ranges from hyperkinetic to akinetic.

Motor conversion reactions: Hysterical reactions resulting in a nonorganic impairment of some motor process.

Multiple-family therapy: Treatment in a large group composed of several entire families.

Multiple-impact therapy: Method of treatment in which an entire set of professionals works with a disturbed family during an intensive, limited period of time.

Multiple personality: A rare dissociative hysterical reaction in which a person has a number of distinct personalities.

Muscle-contraction headache: A common headache due to nervous tension, fatigue, and the like.

Mutism: Absence of speech secondary to physical or psychological disturbance.

Myocardial infarction: Medical term for heart attack.

Nature-nurture controversy: The theoretical and experimental "battle" over whether heredity or environment is more important in the development of personality and abnormal behavior.

Necrophilia: Sexual attraction toward dead bodies.

Negative practice: A behavioral-therapy technique in which behavioral frequency is reduced by requiring a person to emit undesirable behaviors to such a degree that he or she wishes to stop them due to the build-up of an aversion to their expression.

Neologisms: "New words" sometimes created by psychotic people.

Neurasthenic neurosis: A neurotic disorder characterized by chronic fatigue and weakness.

Neuron: The primary cell of which the brain and nervous system are composed.

Neurosis: See Psychoneurosis.

Neurotic anxiety: Fear of dangers or threats that aren't based on reality.

Neurotransmitters: Chemical substances located near synapses that are involved in the chemical transmission of impulses from one neuron to another.

Norepinephrine: Also known as noradrenaline, this biochemical is important as a neurotransmitter; when present in abnormal amounts, it also seems to be related to the presence of certain forms of psychotic symptoms.

Norms: Standards against which the performance of one person on a test may be compared with the performance of others.

Observational learning: Learning of new behaviors by observing others responding and receiving some form of consequence.

Obsessive-compulsive personality: A personality disorder in which the primary style is marked by excessive concern with sameness and rigid thoughts and behavior.

Obsessive neurosis: A neurotic disorder characterized by the intrusion of persistent and uncontrollable thoughts.

Oedipal/Electra phase: Stage of psychosexual development at which a child is sexually attracted to the parent of the opposite sex.

Operant conditioning: A basic learning procedure in which a person or animal learns to respond in specific ways in order to obtain a specific reinforcement.

Opiates: A class of highly addictive narcotics obtained from the poppy plant.

Oral stage: The Freudian psychosexual stage in which satisfactions are centered about the mouth.

Outcome studies: Investigations of psychotherapy focusing on different rates of success or improvement in different forms of treatment.

Paranoia: A psychotic disorder characterized by a well-developed and wide-ranging delusional system.

Paranoid conditions: A group of disorders of varying severity having in common the presence of delusional systems.

Paranoid eroticism: A condition in which, due to a delusional belief, a person feels some important other secretly is in love with him or her.

Paranoid litigious state: A condition in which, due to a delusional system, a person continuously brings legal actions against others.

Paranoid personality: A personality disorder in which the primary interpersonal style is marked by rigidity, suspiciousness, jealousy, envy, and a tendency to blame others.

Paranoid pseudocommunity: A term proposed by Norman Cameron to describe the extensive delusional systems in which the paranoid person may live.

Paranoid psychosis: A severe disturbance marked primarily by delusional beliefs of various kinds.

Paranoid state: A circumscribed and transient condition marked by a specific delusional belief.

Paraphrenia: Paranoid psychosis in old age.

Parasympathetic nervous system: That part of the autonomic nervous system concerned with the production and conservation of energy.

Partial reinforcement: In operant conditioning, a schedule of reinforcement in which rewards are not given every time a response is emitted; one result is increased resistance to extinction.

Pastoral counselors: Clergymen who, in addition to their religious training, have been trained in certain forms of counseling and psychotherapy.

Pedophilia: Sexual attraction toward young children.

Peripheral nervous system: All neural systems outside the brain and spinal cord.

Permissive-amine hypothesis: The belief that reduced serotonin levels may permit other biochemicals to vary unchecked, thereby producing affective psychotic patterns of behavior.

Personality: A collection of behaviors and response patterns that may be seen as characterizing a specific individual.

Personality disorders: Patterns of disturbance characterized by a tendency to depend upon one specific style of responding to a wide variety of different situations.

Petit mal: A mild form of epileptic seizure in which a person loses touch with the environment for a short time but doesn't usually have a convulsive seizure.

Phallic stage: Freudian psychosexual stage in which satisfaction centers in the genital area.

Phenothiazine derivatives: A group of psychoactive drugs especially effective as antipsychotic agents.

Phenylketonuria (PKU): A metabolic disorder that causes severe mental retardation unless controlled by a restricted diet.

Phobia: Neurotic fear associated with a specific thing, person, or situation.

Pica: A symptom involving the eating of inedible materials such as dirt, plaster, and the like.

Pituitary gland: The "master" endocrine gland which controls growth as well as the function of other endocrine glands.

Placebo effect: The belief that a neutral therapeutic method will be beneficial.

Play therapy: A therapeutic technique for children that uses play rather than straight verbal interaction as the major mode of communication.

Postpartum depression: Depression in the mother following the birth of a child.

Postvention: Therapeutic intervention efforts aimed at helping those who survive the suicide or murder of a loved one.

Preconscious: According to Freud, those needs, wishes, thoughts, memories, and motives which, although not in awareness at a given moment, can be brought into awareness quite easily.

Presenile dementia: Chronic loss of brain function due to presenile conditions such as Alzheimer's disease or Pick's disease.

Prevalence rate: The total number of cases of a type of disorder in existence at any one time.

Primal therapy: A method of therapy devised by Arthur Janov that focuses on release of primal pains experienced in early childhood and infancy.

Primary affective disorders: Affective disorders occurring in the absence of any other syndromes.

Primary deviance: The violation of rules, laws, or mores of a group.

Primary drives: Innate motivations for behavior that require satisfaction for survival and that don't weaken if unsatisfied—for example, hunger and thirst.

Primary prevention: Altering of circumstances that might promote disordered behavior.

Primary-process thought: According to Freud, the psychoticlike thinking characteristic of the id.

Primary reinforcer: Stimuli that almost always increase the probability of responses that they follow.

Proband: In genetic studies, the person about whom hereditary information is sought.

Process schizophrenia: A type of schizophrenia characterized by slow insidious onset, poor prognosis for recovery, and previous history of maladjustment.

Process studies: Investigations of psychotherapy focusing on the characteristics of the therapeutic interaction that appear to be responsible for positive change.

Projection: A defense mechanism in which an individual attributes his or her impulses or motives to someone else.

Projective tests: Tests such as the Rorschach Inkblot Test and TAT in which people's responses to unstructured stimuli are used to understand personality and diagnose disorder.

Propfhebephrenic psychosis: A psychotic behavior pattern superimposed upon or concomitant with mental retardation.

Pseudocyesis: False pregnancy, a hysterical reaction with symptoms that closely resemble actual pregnancy.

Pseudoneurotic schizophrenia: A special type of schizophrenia, the symptoms of which often lead to a misdiagnosis of neurosis.

Psyche: A term used by Freud to refer in general to the mental apparatus.

Psychedelic drugs: Drugs that are capable of producing visual hallucinations and other psychoticlike experiences.

Psychiatric nurse: A registered nurse specially trained in the care of psychologically disturbed hospital patients.

Psychiatric social worker: A social worker specially trained in dealing with psychiatric problems of individuals and their families.

Psychiatrist: A physician specializing in the diagnosis, treatment, and management of people who are different.

Psychic triumvirate: According to Freud, the three-part governing system of the personality: the id, ego, and superego.

Psychoanalysis: A special form of psychotherapy devised by Sigmund Freud. The term should not be used interchangeably with *psychotherapy.*

Psychoanalyst: A practitioner of psychoanalysis.

Psychochemotherapy: The use of chemicals in the treatment of psychological disturbances.

Psychodrama: A method of group treatment devised by Jacob Moreno in which individuals act out their conflicts and problems with the help of "actors" who are other members of the group.

Psychogenetics: The study of the inheritance of emotional and behavioral characteristics.

Psychogenic: Psychologically produced or caused.

Psychological autopsy: An attempt to understand the psychosocial components of a calamitous death.

Psychomotor epilepsy: A kind of epileptic seizure in which consciousness is disturbed and automatic involuntary behavior may occur in the absence of convulsions.

Psychoneurosis: Also known as *neurosis.* A mild to moderately severe disturbance characterized by anxiety or self-defeating attempts to deal with anxiety.

Psychopath (sociopath): A person with a chronic personality or character disturbance marked by lack of interpersonal responsibility, needs for immediate need fulfillment, lack of conscience, and few apparent signs of psychological disorder.

Psychophysiological disorders: Patterns of psychological disturbance in which actual physical symptoms occur as a result of psychological factors. Not to be confused with conversion reactions, in which there is typically no real physical damage.

Psychosexual development: In Freudian theory, the process of passing through five basic stages with varying loci of need satisfaction: oral, anal, phallic, latency, and genital stages.

Psychosis: A severe form of psychological disturbance typically characterized by loss of touch with reality and personality disintegration.

Psychosocial stages: Stages of development of the personality from the perspective of Erik Erikson; also known as the "eight stages of man."

Psychosurgery: Surgical manipulation of neural pathways to change behavior.

Psychotherapy: A form of primarily verbal treatment for psychological disorders. There is a wide variety of types of psychotherapy.

Psychotic depressive reaction: A severe depression brought about by some highly stressful environmental event such as the death of a loved one.

Psychotic mannerisms: Stereotypic behaviors associated with many types of psychoses; they include gestures, facial grimacing, repetitive body movements, and the like.

Psychotomimetic drugs: Drugs that produce psychic and behavioral changes similar to psychosis.

Rational-emotive therapy: A method of therapy devised by Albert Ellis that focuses on identifying irrational beliefs and altering cognitive styles.

Reaction formation: A defense mechanism characterized by behaving in ways directly opposite of one's true desires.

Reactive mania: An episode of manic excitement typically in response to the removal of some chronic emotional stress.

Reactive schizophrenia: A type of schizophrenia characterized by abrupt onset, good prognosis for recovery, and little history of severe maladjustment.

Realistic anxiety: Fear of dangers and threats that are based on reality.

Reality therapy: A method of therapy devised by William Glasser that focuses on individual needs for love and acceptance of responsibility.

Regression: According to Freud, the psychological return to some previous stage of psychosexual development. It often occurs in the face of severe stress.

Reinforcement schedule: A schedule according to which reinforcements are administered in classical and operant conditioning, either continuous or partial.

Reinforcer: A stimulus that increases the probability of occurrence of a response that it follows.

Remission: The disappearance of symptoms and the return to normality.

Repression: A defense mechanism that involves the unconscious forgetting of threatening thoughts or memories.

Residual rules: Unwritten rules that aren't noticed until they are broken, such as standing too close to someone when conversing.

Resistance: In psychoanalysis, an unconscious process that blocks an individual from gaining insight into conflicts and unconscious motives.

Respondent learning: See Classical conditioning.

Rorschach Inkblot Test: A series of ten unstructured inkblots used to elicit responses that can help in psychological diagnosis.

Rumination syndrome: An infant's bringing up of food without vomiting or retching; if uncontrolled it can lead to failure to thrive and death.

Sadism: Sexual arousal related to inflicting pain on another.

Schemas: Ways of conceptualizing the world or of organizing perceptions.

Schizoaffective schizophrenia: A subclassification of schizophrenia marked by symptoms of both mania and schizophrenia.

Schizoid personality: A personality disorder in which the primary style is marked by withdrawal from others, shyness, reticence to interact, and "eccentric" behavior.

Schizophrenia: A form of psychosis involving disturbed thought processes and a variety of specific emotional and behavioral symptoms.

Schizophrenia spectrum: A conceptualization of schizophrenic disorders such that they are seen as composing a range of patterns from some forms of mild neuroses and character disorders all the way to severe schizophrenic psychosis.

Schizophreniform psychosis: Psychotic disorder that is schizophrenic*like* but actually may not be true schizophrenia.

Schizophrenogenic environment: An environment that may produce schizophrenia in those genetically predisposed to the disorder.

Schizotaxia: An inherited predisposition to schizophrenia, according to Paul Meehl.

Secondary affective disorders: Affective disorders occurring simultaneously with other disorders.

Secondary deviance: Being labeled as deviant for breaking the rules of a group and then becoming someone who fits the label applied by the group, such as "criminal" or "mental patient."

Secondary drives: Motives to emit certain behaviors developed out of associations with primary drives—for example, a need to work or to be married.

Secondary prevention: Efforts to reduce the rate or severity of existing disorders.

Secondary-process thought: According to Freud, the rational thinking that is characteristic of the ego.

Secondary reinforcers: Stimuli that aren't innately rewarding but that acquire reinforcing properties owing to their association with primary reinforcers.

Security operations: Defense mechanisms within the theoretical framework of Harry Stack Sullivan.

Self-actualizing tendency: According to Carl Rogers, an innate tendency toward positive self-growth.

Self-labeling: The decision that something is deviant about oneself and the resultant changes in self-concept and behavior that may ensue.

Senile dementia: A mental disturbance most likely caused by degeneration of nerve and brain tissue with advancing age.

Senior anticipatory adulthood reaction: Anxiety sometimes seen in students leaving the "protection" of college and entering the "real world."

Sensory conversion reaction: Hysterical reaction resulting in impairment of some sensory process.

Sensory-stimulation therapy: A treatment for the elderly in which symptoms of senility are countered by increased activity.

Serotonin: A neurotransmitter substance believed to be involved in some way in the development of certain psychotic disorders.

Sexual dysfunction: Impairment or disturbance in the functioning of the sexual organ systems.

Sexual-orientation disturbance: Term now applied to sexual and emotional attraction to members of the same sex.

Simple schizophrenia: A subclassification of schizophrenia marked by increasing loss of interest in and withdrawal from the environment but not typically involving the specific symptoms of the other subclassifications.

Social-network therapy: Therapy with a "tribe" of up to 40 people composing the "network" of relatives and friends surrounding a disturbed family or individual.

Social theory of schizophrenia: The belief that schizophrenia is produced primarily by social factors.

Societal-reaction theory: The belief that the reaction of society to the deviant behavior of its members has much to do with the establishment of abnormal behavior patterns.

Socioenvironmental theory: The belief that abnormality is caused by stresses brought about by significant life events.

Sociopath: See Psychopath.

Soma: The cell body of a neuron.

Somnambulism: A hysterical dissociative reaction that occurs in a sleeplike state; sleepwalking.

Spontaneous recovery: In conditioning, the increase in strength of an extinguished response following a period of time.

Spontaneous remission: The disappearance of symptoms without *formal* treatment.

Stimulus generalization: A learning phenomenon in which an individual responds to stimuli similar to those with which original learning took place even though no actual learning experience has been had with the similar stimulus.

Structural family therapy: A method of family therapy devised by Salvador Minuchin that emphasizes the need for certain types of healthy family structures and communications boundaries.

Successive approximation: A method used in conditioning in which small steps toward the final behavior are reinforced in an effort to shape the final pattern of responding.

Suicide-prevention center: Crisis-intervention program typically involving paraprofessional volunteers who answer hotline phones and meet with emergency walk-ins.

Superego: According to Freud, that part of the psychic triumvirate which includes internalized cultural and parental values and mores.

Symbiotic psychosis: Extreme parent-child interdependency such that separation may result in severe psychotic disturbance in either one or both individuals.

Symbolism: The representation of one object, person, or situation by some often unrelated object, person, or situation.

Sympathetic chain: The interconnections among the ganglia of the sympathetic nervous system.

Sympathetic nervous system: That part of the autonomic nervous system activated in emergency or stress situations.

Symptom: A specific behavior or characteristic typically associated with a specific disorder.

Synanon: A self-help organization begun by former drug addicts to help rehabilitate active drug addicts through residential treatment and group encounters.

Synapse: The minute space between the fibers of adjoining neurons through which neurotransmitters travel during nerve transmission.

Syndromes: A cluster of symptoms usually appearing together.

Systematic desensitization: A behavioral therapy method in which counterconditioning is used to treat anxiety, phobias, and the like.

Tarantism: The dancing mania of the Middle Ages thought to be caused by the bite of a spider.

Tertiary prevention: Efforts to shorten or minimize the impact of disorders after they have appeared.

Test reliability: The degree to which a test measures the same thing from one time to another.

Test validity: The degree to which a test measures what it purports to measure.

T-groups: Training (T) groups in which members learn about human interactions within a semistructured framework.

Thematic Apperception Test (TAT): A series of pictures about which people tell stories that can be used in the diagnosis of mental disturbance and the study of personality.

Therapeutic community: A setting in which disturbed people live and are cared for in a total and constant therapeutic atmosphere.

Thought-stopping: A behavioral-therapy technique in which obsessive thoughts or hallucinations may be stopped by repeated verbalizations of the word *stop.*

Token economy: A method of treating groups of people in which desired behaviors are emitted in return for tokens, which may then be used to "buy" privileges.

Trainable mentally retarded: Retarded people with IQs ranging from 25 to 49 who cannot achieve useful academic skills but can learn basic self-care skills.

Tranquilizers: Psychoactive drugs that relax and pacify, usually without interrupting consciousness.

Transference: In psychoanalysis, the projection onto the therapist of feelings and early attitudes toward parents and other significant figures in one's life.

Transmethylation hypothesis: The belief that, through some metabolic defect, certain normal body chemicals are turned into schizophrenia-producing LSD-like chemicals in the brain.

Transsexualism: The belief that one's biological sex is incongruent with one's true gender. Such people may undergo surgery to change their physical sexual characteristics.

Transvestism: Sexual arousal related to dressing in the clothing of the opposite sex.

Trephinization: Ancient "treatment" for the mentally disturbed in which a hole was chipped in the skull so that evil spirits could escape.

Triadic-based family therapy: A method of treatment devised by Gerald Zuk that focuses on disordered triads within families.

Trichotillomania: Hair-pulling behavior.

Tricyclic drugs: A class of antidepressant medications.

Ulcer: A painful sore on a mucous membrane, such as in the mouth or stomach.

Unconditioned response (UCR): In classical conditioning, a response that occurs spontaneously to an unconditioned stimulus (UCS).

Unconditioned stimulus (UCS): In classical conditioning, a stimulus that, without special teaching of the trainee, is capable of producing a specific response (UCR).

Unconscious: According to Freud, those needs, wishes, thoughts, memories, and motives which motivate much behavior but of which one is not aware and cannot easily become aware.

Unipolar versus bipolar affective disorders: A dimension of affective disorders ranging from those in which only depression *or* mania occurs (unipolar) to those in which both occur (bipolar).

Verbigeration: A symptom of schizophrenia in which repetitions of often long series of verbalizations emanate from a person over an extended period of time.

Viral hypothesis of schizophrenia: The belief that some type of schizophrenia may be caused by some prenatal or postnatal viral infection.

Voyeurism: Sexual arousal related to watching others undress or engage in sexual activity; Peeping Tomism.

Waxy flexibility: A symptom of stuporous catatonic schizophrenia in which a person's body or limbs will remain in positions in which they are placed for a period of time.

Wechsler intelligence scales: A series of intelligence tests for varying age groups developed by David Wechsler. The series includes the Wechsler Adult Intelligence Scale (WAIS), the Wechsler Intelligence Scale for Children—Revised Form (WISC-R), and the Wechsler Preschool and Primary Scale of Intelligence (WPPSI).

REFERENCES

Abraham, K. *Selected papers of Karl Abraham* (3rd ed.). London: Hogarth Press, 1948.

Ackerman, N. Family diagnosis and therapy. In J. Masserman (Ed.), *Current psychiatric therapies* (Vol. 3). New York: Grune & Stratton, 1963.

Agras, S., Sylvester, D., & Oliveau, B. The epidemiology of common fears and phobias. Unpublished manuscript, 1969. (Cited in G. C. Davidson & J. M. Neale, *Abnormal Psychology*. New York: John Wiley, 1974).

Akerfeldt, S. Oxidation of N, N-dimethyl-P-phenylenediamine by serum from patients with mental disease. *Science*, 1951, *125*, 117.

Akiskal, H., & McKinney, W. Depressive disorders: Toward a unified hypothesis. *Science*, 1973, *182*, 20–30.

Akiskal, H., & McKinney, W. Overview of recent research in depression. *Archives of General Psychiatry*, 1975, *32*, 285–305.

Alanen, A. A review of psychoanalytic theories of childhood psychoses. In J. Howells (Ed.), *Perspectives in child psychiatry*. Edinburgh: Oliver & Boyd, 1965.

Albee, G. *Mental health manpower trends*. New York: Basic Books, 1959.

Albee, G. Models, myths and manpower. *Mental Hygiene*, 1968, *52*, 168–180.

Alexander, F. The neurotic character. *International Journal of Psychoanalysis*, 1930, *2*, 299–311.

Alexander, F. The influence of psychological factors upon gastrointestinal disturbances. *Psychoanalytic Quarterly*, 1934, *3*, 501–539.

Alexander, F. *Psychosomatic medicine*. London: Allen & Unwin, 1952.

Alexander, G. Tension can be licked. *Los Angeles Times*, July 6, 1975, pp. 1; 5.

Allport, G. W. *Personality: A psychological interpretation*. New York: Holt, Rinehart & Winston, 1937.

American Psychiatric Association. *Diagnostic and statistical manual of mental disorders* (2nd ed.) (DSM-II). Washington, D.C.: American Psychiatric Association, 1968.

American Psychiatric Association. *Diagnostic and statistical manual of mental disorders* (3rd ed.) (DSM-III, Draft). Washington D.C.: American Psychiatric Association, April 15, 1977.

Anastasi, A. *Psychological testing*. New York: Macmillan, 1976.

Andy, O. Quoted in S. Wellborn, New ways to heal disturbed minds. *U.S. News & World Report*, February 16, 1976, p. 57.

Arieti, S. *Interpretation of schizophrenia*. New York: Brunner/Mazel, 1955.

Arieti, S. Schizophrenic cognition. In P. Hoch & J. Zubin (Eds.), *Psychopathology of schizophrenia*. New York: Grune & Stratton, 1966.

Arieti, S. *The intrapsychic self.* New York: Basic Books, 1967.

Arieti, S., & Meth, J. Rare, unclassifiable, collective and exotic psychiatric syndromes. In S. Arieti (Ed.), *American handbook of psychiatry.* New York: Basic Books, 1959.

Arthurs, R., & Cahoon, E. A clinical and electroencephalographic study of psychopathic personality. *American Journal of Psychiatry,* 1964, *120,* 875–877.

Ascher, A. Psychodynamic considerations in Gilles de la Tourette's syndrome. *American Journal of Psychiatry,* 1948, *105,* 267.

Atchley, R. *Social forces in later life.* Belmont, Calif.: Wadsworth, 1972.

Axline, V. *Play therapy.* Cambridge, Mass.: Riverside Press, 1947.

Axline, V. The eight basic principles. In M. Haworth (Ed.), *Child psychotherapy.* New York: Basic Books, 1964.

Ayd, F. *Rational psychopharmacotherapy and the right to treatment.* Baltimore: Ayd Medical Communication, 1975.

Ayllon, T., & Azrin, N. *The token economy: A motivational system for therapy and rehabilitation.* New York: Appleton-Century-Crofts, 1968.

Ayllon, T., & Michael, J. The psychiatric nurse as a behavioral engineer. *Behaviour Research and Therapy,* 1959, *2,* 323–334.

Babigian, H. Schizophrenia: Epidemiology. In A. Freedman, H. Kaplan, & B. Sadock (Eds.), *Comprehensive textbook of psychiatry/II.* Baltimore: Williams & Wilkins, 1975.

Bach, G. The marathon group: Intense practice of intimate interaction. *Psychological Reports,* 1966, *18,* 995–1002.

Bachrach, A., Erwin, W., & Mohr, J. The control of eating behavior in an anorexic by operant conditioning techniques. In L. Ullmann and L. Krasner (Eds.), *Case studies in behavior modification.* New York: Holt, Rinehart & Winston, 1965.

Back, K. *Beyond words: The study of sensitivity training and the encounter movement.* New York: Russell Sage Foundation, 1972.

Bandura, A. *Principles of behavior modification.* New York: Holt, Rinehart & Winston, 1969.

Bandura, A. *Social learning theory.* Englewood Cliffs, N.J.: Prentice Hall, 1977.

Barbellion, W. N. P. (Introduction by H. G. Wells). *The journal of a disappointed man.* New York: George H. Doran, 1919.

Barber, T., Dicara, L., Kamiya, J., Miller, N., Shapiro, D., & Stoyva, J. *Biofeedback and self control: 1975/1976.* Chicago: Aldine, 1976.

Barger, B. The University of Florida mental health program. In B. Barger and E. Hall (Eds.), *Higher education and mental health.* Gainesville: University of Florida, 1963.

Barger, B., Larson, E. A., & Hall, E. Preventive action in college mental health. *Journal of the American College Health Association,* 1965, *15,* 80–93.

Barker, J., & Miller, M. Recent developments and some future trends in the applications of aversive conditioning. Unpublished manuscript. (Cited in J. Wolpe, *The practice of behavior therapy.* New York: Pergamon, 1973.)

Barker, M. Impressions of a "normal" news reporter who gained admission to a mental hospital for five days. *Washington Post,* July 16, 1972, p. 19.

Bastiaans, J. The place of personality traits in specific syndromes: Cause or effect? In J. Wisdom & J. Wolff (Eds.), *The role of psychosomatic disorder in adult life.* London: Pergamon, 1965.

Batchelor, I. Suicide and old age. In E. Shneidman and N. Farberow (Eds.), *Clues to suicide.* New York: McGraw-Hill, 1957.

Bateson, G., Jackson, D., Haley, J., & Weakland, J. Toward a theory of schizophrenia. *Behavioral Science,* 1956, *1,* 251.

Bauer, M. *Health characteristics of low income persons* (DHEW Publication No. HSM 73-1500). Washington, D.C.: National Center for Health Statistics, 1972.

Beach, F. *Hormones and behavior.* New York: Hoeber, 1948.

Beck, A. *Depression.* New York: Harper & Row, 1967.

Beck, S. J., Beck, A. G., Levitt, E. E., & Molish, H. B. *Rorschach's test* (Vol. 1, *Basic Processes*, 3rd ed.). New York: Grune & Stratton, 1961.

Becker, H. *Outsiders*. New York: Free Press, 1963.

Becker, W. Consequences of different kinds of parental disciplines. In M. Hoffman & L. Hoffman (Eds.), *Review of child development research*. Lafayette, Ind.: Society for Research in Child Development, 1964.

Beels, C., & Ferber, A. What family therapists do. In A. Ferber, M. Mendelsohn, & A. Napier (Eds.), *The book of family therapy*. New York: Science House, 1972.

Beers, C. W. *A mind that found itself*. Garden City, N.Y.: Doubleday, 1931.

Beier, E. *The silent language of psychotherapy*. Chicago: Aldine, 1966.

Bell, J. *Family therapy*. New York: Aronson, 1975.

Belmont, J. Medical-behavioral research in retardation. In N. Ellis (Ed.), *International review of research in mental retardation* (Vol. 5). New York: Grune & Stratton, 1971.

Benda, C. *Mongolism and cretinism*. New York: Grune & Stratton, 1946.

Bender, L. A visual motor gestalt test and its clinical use. *American Orthopsychiatry Association Research Monographs*, 1938, *3*.

Bender, L. Schizophrenia in childhood: Its recognition, description and treatment. *American Journal of Orthopsychiatry*, 1956, *26*, 499.

Bender, L. Diagnostic and therapeutic aspects of childhood schizophrenia. In P. Bowan (Ed.), *Mental retardation*. New York: Grune & Stratton, 1960.

Bender, L. The nature of childhood psychosis. In J. Howells (Ed.), *Modern perspectives in international child psychiatry*. New York: Brunner/Mazel, 1971.

Bennett, C. Community psychology: Impressions of the Boston conference on the education of psychologists for community mental health. *American Psychologist*, 1965, *20*, 832–835.

Bennis, W. Patterns and vicissitudes in T-group development. In L. Bradford, J. Gibbs, & K. Bennes (Eds.), *T-group theory and laboratory method*. New York: Wiley, 1964.

Benson, H., Shapiro, D., Tursky, B., & Schwartz, G. Decreased systolic blood pressure through operant conditioning techniques in patients with essential hypertension. *Science*, 1971, *173*, 740–742.

Benton, A. *Revised visual retention test: Manual*. New York: Psychological Corporation, 1974.

Berg, I. The clinical interview and the case record. In I. Berg & L. Pennington (Eds.), *An introduction to clinical psychology*. New York: Ronald Press, 1966.

Bergin, A. The evaluation of therapeutic outcomes. In A. Bergin & S. Garfield (Eds.), *Handbook of psychotherapy and behavior change*. New York: Wiley, 1971.

Bergin, A., & Suinn, R. Individual psychotherapy and behavior therapy. In *Annual review of psychology*, Vol. 16. Palo Alto: Annual Reviews Press, 1975.

Berkovitz, I. *Adolescents grow in groups*. New York: Brunner/Mazel, 1972.

Berman, J., & Ford, R. Intelligence quotients and intelligence loss in patients with phenylketonuria and some variant states. *Journal of Pediatrics*, 1970, *77*, 764–770.

Bettelheim, B. *The empty fortress*. New York: Free Press, 1967.

Bibring, E. The mechanisms of depression. In P. Greenacre (Ed.), *Affective disorders*. New York: International Universities Press, 1953.

Bieber, I., Dain, H., Dince, P., Drellich, M., Grand, H., Gundlach, R., Kremer, M., Rifkin, A., Wilbur, C., & Bieber, T. *Homosexuality: A psychoanalytical study*. New York: Random House, 1962.

Binet, A., & Simon, T. Methodes nouvelles pour le diagnostic du niveau intellectuel des anormaux. *Année psychologique*, 1905, *11*, 191–244.

Binswanger, L. *Grundformen und Erkenntnis menschlichen Daseins*. Munich: Rinehardt, 1962.

Binswanger, L. *Being-in-the-world*. New York: Basic Books, 1963.

Birren, J. *The psychology of aging.* Englewood Cliffs, N.J.: Prentice-Hall, 1964.

Blaine, G., & McArthur, C. (Eds.). *Emotional problems of the student.* New York: Appleton-Century-Crofts, 1971.

Blanchard, E., & Young, L. Clinical applications of biofeedback training. *Archives of General Psychiatry,* 1974, *30,* 573–589.

Blau, D., & Berezin, M. Neurosis and character disorders. In J. Howells (Ed.), *Modern perspectives on the psychology of aging.* New York: Brunner/Mazel, 1975.

Bleuler, E. Primary and secondary symptoms in schizophrenia. *Zeitschrift fur generalische neurologische Psychiatrie,* 1930, *124,* 607.

Bliss, E., & Branch, C. *Anorexia nervosa,* New York: Harper & Row, Hoeber Medical Division, 1960.

Bliven, N. Who gets what? *New Yorker,* 1972, *49,* 158.

Bloch, D. Family therapy and group therapy. *International Journal of Group Psychotherapy,* 1976, *26,* 289–300.

Bloom, B. *Community mental health: A general introduction.* Monterey, Calif.: Brooks/Cole, 1977.

Blos, P. Psychological counseling of college students. *American Journal of Ortho-psychiatry,* 1946, *16,* 571–580.

Bolles, R. *Theory of motivation* (2nd ed.). New York: Harper & Row, 1975.

Bordin, E. *Research strategies in psychotherapy.* New York: Wiley, 1974.

Boss, M. *Psychoanalysis and daseinanalysis.* New York: Basic Books, 1963.

Bowen, M. Family therapy and family group therapy. In H. Kaplan & B. Sadock (Eds.), *Comprehensive group psychotherapy.* Baltimore: Williams & Wilkins, 1971.

Boxberger, R., & Cotter, V. Music therapy for geriatric patients. In F. Gaston (Ed.), *Music in therapy.* New York: Macmillan, 1968.

Bradley, C., & Bowen, M. Behavior characteristics of schizophrenic children. *Psychiatric Quarterly,* 1941, *15,* 298–315.

Brady, J. V. Ulcers in executive monkeys. *Scientific American,* 1958, *199,* 95.

Braginsky, B., & Braginsky, D. Schizophrenic patients in the psychiatric interview: An experimental study of their effectiveness at manipulation. *Journal of Consulting Psychology,* 1967, *31,* 543–547.

Braginsky, B., & Braginsky, D. *Methods of madness: The mental hospital as a last resort.* New York: Holt, Rinehart & Winston, 1969.

Brandes, N., & Gardner, M. *Group therapy for the adolescent.* New York: Jason Aronson, 1973.

Brantley, M. Personal communication, 1975.

Brecher, E. *Licit and illicit drugs.* Boston: Little, Brown, 1972.

Breese, G., Smith, R., Mueller, R., Howard, J., Prange, A., Lipton, M., Young, L., McKinney, J., & Lewis, J. Induction of adrenal catecholamine synthesizing enzymes following mother-infant separation. *Nature,* 1973, *246,* 94.

Bregin, P. Psychosurgery. *Journal of the American Medical Association,* 1973, *226,* 1121.

Brener, J. Learned control of cardiovascular processes: Feedback mechanisms and therapeutic applications. In K. S. Calhoun, H. E. Adams, & K. M. Mitchell (Eds.), *Innovative treatment methods in psychophysiology.* New York: Wiley, 1974.

Brigante, T. Opportunities for community mental health training within a residential college campus context. *Community Mental Health Journal,* 1965, *1,* 55–61.

Brosin, H. Acute and chronic brain syndromes. In A. Freedman & H. Kaplan (Eds.), *Comprehensive textbook of psychiatry.* Baltimore: Williams & Wilkins, 1967.

Brown, H. *Brain and behavior.* London: Oxford University Press, 1976.

Bruun, R., & Shapiro, A. Differential diagnosis of Gilles de la Tourette's syndrome. *Journal of Nervous and Mental Diseases,* 1972, *155,* 328.

Bunch, J. Recent bereavement and suicide. *Journal of Psychosomatic Research*, 1972, *163*, 361.

Bunze, J. Note on the history of a concept—gerontophobia. *Gerontologist*, 1972, *2*, 150.

Bureau of Narcotics and Dangerous Drugs. *Drugs of abuse* (Document 0-459-616). Washington, D.C.: U. S. Government Printing Office, 1972.

Buros, O. (Ed.). *Seventh mental measurements yearbook*. Highland Park, N.J.: Gryphon Press, 1972.

Buros, O. *Tests in print II*. Highland Park, N.J.: Gryphon Press, 1974.

Burton, T. Education for trainables: An impossible dream? *Mental Retardation*, 1974, *12*, 45–46.

Busch, A., & Johnson, W. Lysergic acid diethylamide (LSD-25) as an aid in psychotherapy. *Diseases of the Nervous System*, 1950, *11*, 204.

Cameron, N. The paranoid pseudocommunity. *American Journal of Sociology*, 1943, *32*, 32.

Cameron, N. *The psychology of behavior disorders*. Boston: Houghton Mifflin, 1947.

Cameron, N. *Personality development and psychopathology*. Boston: Houghton Mifflin, 1963.

Cannon, W. *Bodily changes in pain, hunger, fear, and rage*. New York: Appleton-Century-Crofts, 1929.

Cantwell, D. Psychiatric illness in the families of hyperactive children. *Archives of General Psychiatry*, 1972, *27*, 414–418.

Caplan, G. *Principles of preventive psychiatry*. New York: Basic Books, 1964.

Caplan, G. *Support systems and community mental health*. New York: Behavioral Publications, 1974.

Carlsson, A., & Lindqvist, M. Effect of chlorpromazine or haloperidol on formation of 3-methoxy-tyramine and normetanephrine in mouse brain. *Acta Pharmacologica Toxicologica*, 1973, *20*, 140.

Carson, R. *Interaction concepts of personality*. Chicago: Aldine, 1969.

Carson, R., & Heine, R. Similarity and success in therapeutic dyads. *Journal of Consulting Psychology*, 1962, *26*, 38–43.

Cashman, J. *The LSD story*. Greenwich, Conn.: Fawcett Publications, 1966.

Cassell, J. Planning for public health: The case for prevention. Conference on education of nurses for public health, 1973. Cited by N. Robinson & H. Robinson, *The mentally retarded child*. New York: McGraw-Hill, 1976.

Cautela, J. Covert sensitization. *Psychological Reports*, 1967, *20*, 459.

Cautela, J. Personal communication, 1968.

Cautela, J. Covert reinforcement. *Behavior Therapy*, 1970, *1*, 33–50. (a)

Cautela, J. Treatment of alcoholism by covert sensitization. *Psychotherapy: Theory, Research, and Practice*, 1970, *7*, 86–90. (b)

Cavan, R. *Suicide*. Chicago: University of Chicago Press, 1926.

Cerlitti, V., & Bini, L. L'elettroshock. *Archiva Generale Neurologia Psichiatria Psicoanalysia*, 1938, *19*, 266.

Chess, S., Korn, S., & Fernandez, P. *Psychiatric disorders of children with rubella*. New York: Brunner/Mazel, 1971.

Chorover, S. The pacification of the brain. *Psychology Today*, May 1974, pp. 59–60; 63–64; 66; 69.

Clark, D. Rumination in a failure-to-thrive infant. *Maternal-Child Nursing Journal*, 1975, *4*, 9–22.

Clark, M. Troubled children: The quest for help. *Newsweek*, April 8, 1974, pp. 52–53, 56, 58.

Cleckley, H. *The mask of sanity* (5th ed.). St. Louis: Mosby, 1976.

Cohen, M., Baker, G., Cohen, R., Fromm-Reichmann, F., & Weigart, F. An intensive study of twelve cases of manic-depressive psychosis. *Psychiatry*, 1954, *17*, 103–137.

Cohen, R. Manic depressive illness. In A. Freedman, H. Kaplan, & B. Sadock (Eds.), *Comprehensive textbook of psychiatry/ II*. Baltimore: Williams & Wilkins, 1975.

Cohen, S. LSD and the anguish of dying. *Harper's Magazine*, 1965, *231*, 69–78.

Cole, J., & Davis, J. Antipsychotic drugs; antidepressant drugs; minor tranquilizers, sedatives, and hypnotics. In A. Freedman, H. Kaplan, & B. Sadock (Eds.), *Comprehensive textbook of psychiatry/II*. Baltimore: Williams & Wilkins, 1975.

Coleman, J. *Abnormal psychology and modern life* (4th ed.). Glenview, Ill.: Scott Foresman, 1974.

Coleman, J. *Abnormal psychology and modern life* (5th ed.). Glenview, Ill.: Scott Foresman, 1976.

Collaborative study of children treated for PKU (Preliminary Report no. 8). Presented to the Eleventh General Medical Conference, Stateline, Nevada, 1975.

Cools, A. R. An integrated theory of the aetiology of schizophrenia. In H. Van Praag (Ed.), *On the origins of schizophrenia*. Amsterdam: De Erven Bohn, 1975.

Coppen, A. Indoleamines and affective disorders. *Journal of Psychiatric Research*, 1972, *9*, 163.

Corey, G. *Theory and practice of counseling and psychotherapy*. Monterey, Calif.: Brooks/Cole, 1977.

Coursey, R. Electromyograph feedback as a relaxation technique. *Journal of Consulting and Clinical Psychology*, 1975, *43*, 825–834.

Cowen, E. Emergent approaches to mental health problems: An overview and directions for future work. In E. Cowen, E. Gardner, & M. Zax (Eds.), *Emergent approaches to mental health problems*. New York: Appleton-Century-Crofts, 1967.

Cowie, V. The genetical aspects of neurosis in child psychiatry. In J. Howells (Ed.), *Perspectives in child psychiatry*. Edinburgh: Oliver & Boyd, 1965.

Craft, M., Stephanson, G., & Granger, C. A controlled trial of authoritarian and self-governing regimes with adolescent psychopaths. *American Journal of Orthopsychiatry*, 1964, *34*, 543–554.

Craig, L., & Senter, R. Student thoughts about suicide. *Psychological Record*, 1972, *22*, 355–358.

Creak, M., Cameron, K., Cowie, V., Ini, S., MacKeith, R., Mitchell, G., O'Gorman, G., Orford, F., Rogers, W., Shapiro, A., Stove, F., Stroh, G., & Yudkin, S. Schizophrenia syndrome in childhood. *British Journal of Medicine*, 1961, *2*, 889–890.

Cronbach, L. *Essentials of psychological testing* (4th ed.). New York: Harper & Row, 1976.

Crowe, R. An adoption study of antisocial personality. *Archives of General Psychiatry*, 1974, *31*, 785–791.

Cumming, E. New thoughts on the theory of disengagement. In R. Kastenbaum (Ed.), *New thoughts on old age*. New York: Springer, 1964.

Cumming, E., & Henry, W. *Growing old: The process of disengagement*. New York: Basic Books, 1961.

Dalen, P. *Season of birth in schizophrenia and other mental disorders*. Goteborg: University of Goteborg, 1974.

Davies, D. Normal drinking in recovered alcohol addicts. *Quarterly Journal of Studies on Alcohol*, 1962, *23*, 94–104.

Davies, M. Blood pressure and personality. *Journal of Psychosomatic Research*, 1970, *14*, 89–104.

Dederick, C. (Cited in E. Brecher [Ed.], *Licit and illicit drugs*. Boston: Little, Brown, 1972, p. 81.)

Deleon, G., & Mandell, W. A comparison of conditioning and psychotherapy in the treatment of enuresis. *Journal of Clinical Psychology*, 1966, *22*, 320–330.

Delgado, R., & Mannino, F. Some observations on trichotillomania in children. *Journal of the American Academy of Child Psychiatry,* 1969, *8,* 229–246.

Deutsch, A. *The mentally ill in America.* Garden City, N.Y.: Doubleday, 1937.

Dingemanse, E., & Freud, J. Identification of catatonine. *Acta Brevia Neerlandica Physiologica Pharmacologica Microbiologica,* 1933, *3,* 49.

Dohrenwend, B. Social status and stressful life events. *Journal of Personality and Social Psychology,* 1973, *28,* 228–235.

Dohrenwend, B. Sociocultural and socio-psychological factors in the genesis of mental disorders. *Journal of Health and Social Behavior,* 1975, *16,* 365–392.

Dohrenwend, B. Clues to the role of socioenvironmental factors. *Schizophrenia Bulletin,* 1976, *2,* 440–444.

Dohrenwend, B., & Dohrenwend, B. Social and cultural influences on psychopathology. In *Annual review of psychology,* Vol. 25. Palo Alto: Annual Reviews Press, 1974.

Dole, V., & Nyswander, M. A medical treatment for diacetylmorphine (heroin) addiction: A clinical trial with methadone hydrochloride. *Journal of the American Medical Association,* 1965, *193,* 646.

Dole, V., & Nyswander, M. The use of methadone for narcotic blockade. *British Journal of Addiction,* 1968, *63,* 55.

Dollard, J., & Miller, N. *Personality and psychotherapy.* New York: McGraw-Hill, 1950.

Dorpat, T. Suicide in murderers. *Psychiatry Digest,* 1966, *27,* 51–55.

Dreikurs, R. Early experiments in group psychotherapy. *American Journal of Psychotherapy,* 1959, *13,* 882–891.

Duke, M., & Mullens, M. Preferred interpersonal distance as a function of locus of control orientation in chronic schizophrenics, non-schizophrenic patients, and normals. *Journal of Consulting and Clinical Psychology,* 1973, *41,* 230–234.

Duncan, G., Frazier, S., Litin, E., Johnson, A., & Barron, A. Etiological factors in first degree murder. *The Journal of the American Medical Association,* 1958, *168,* 1755–1758.

Dunham, H. Community psychiatry: The newest therapeutic bandwagon. *Archives of General Psychiatry,* 1965, *12,* 303–313.

Dunn, L. Special education for the mildly retarded—Is much of it justified? *Exceptional Children,* 1968, *35,* 5–24.

Dunn, L. Children with moderate and severe general learning disabilities. In L. Dunn (Ed.), *Exceptional children in schools* (2nd ed.). New York: Holt, Rinehart & Winston, 1973.

Durkheim, E. *Suicide.* New York: Free Press, 1951.

Eckstein, G. *The body has a head.* New York: Harper & Row, 1970.

Edwards, D. *Sexual behaviors of college students.* Unpublished manuscript, Emory University, 1977.

Eisdorfer, C., & Lawton, M. (Eds.). *The psychology of adult development and aging.* Washington, D.C.: American Psychological Association, 1973.

Eisenberg, L. Normal child development. In A. Freedman & H. Kaplan (Eds.), *Comprehensive textbook of psychiatry.* Baltimore: Williams & Wilkins, 1967.

Ellis, A. Rational-emotive psychotherapy. In R. Corsini (Ed.), *Current psychotherapies.* Itasca, Ill.: Peacock, 1973.

Engel, D., & Helfand, I. *Stuttering is a family affair.* Pamphlet published by Cleveland Speech and Hearing Center. Cleveland, Ohio, 1964.

Engel, G. Psychophysical gastrointestinal disorders. In A. Freedman, H. Kaplan, & B. Sadock (Eds.), *Comprehensive textbook of psychiatry/II.* Balitmore: Williams & Wilkins, 1975.

Engel, G., & Romano, J. Delirium: A syndrome of cerebral insufficiency. *Journal of Chronic Diseases,* 1959, *9,* 260–277.

Erikson, E. *Childhood and society.* New York: Norton, 1950.

Erikson, E. *Childhood and society* (2nd ed.). New York: Norton, 1963.

Erikson, E. *Identity, youth and crisis.* New York: Norton, 1968.

Erikson, E. Introduction. In G. Blaine & C. McArthur (Eds.), *Emotional problems of the student* (2nd ed.). New York: Appleton-Century-Crofts, 1971.

Eriksson, K. Genetic selection for voluntary alcohol consumption in the albino rat. *Science,* 1968, *159,* 734–741.

Ernst, P., & Badash, D. Sensory stimulation in the elderly. *Annals of Israeli Psychiatry,* 1977, *15,* 12–15.

Ernst, P., Beran, B., Badash, D., Kosovsky, R., & Kleinhauz, M. Treatment of the aged mentally ill: Further unmasking of the effects of a diagnosis of chronic brain syndrome. *Journal of the American Geriatric Society,* 1977, *10,* 466–469.

Ervin, F. Brain disorders associated with epilepsy. In A. Freedman & H. Kaplan (Eds.), *Comprehensive textbook of psychiatry.* Baltimore: Williams & Wilkins, 1967.

Evans, R. Childhood parental relationships of homosexual men. *Journal of Consulting and Clinical Psychology,* 1969, *33,* 129–135.

Evarts, A. Dementia praecox in the colored race. *Psychoanalytical Review,* 1913, *1,* 338–403.

Eysenck, H. The effects of psychotherapy: An evaluation. *Journal of Consulting Psychology,* 1952, *16,* 319–324.

Eysenck, H. *The dynamics of anxiety and hysteria.* New York: Praeger, 1957.

Eysenck, H. The effects of psychotherapy. *International Journal of Psychiatry,* 1965, *1,* 97–178.

Faris, R., & Dunham, H. *Mental disorders in urban areas.* Chicago: University of Chicago Press, 1939.

Federal Bureau of Investigation, U.S. Department of Justice. *Uniform crime reports.* Washington D.C.: U.S. Government Printing Office, 1975.

Federal Register, Vol. 41, No. 23, Monday, November 29, 1976. Public Law 94–142, Section 5(B).

Feldman, M., & MacCulloch, M. The application of anticipatory avoidance learning to the treatment of homosexuality. I: Theory, technique and preliminary results. *Behaviour Research and Therapy,* 1965, *2,* 165–183.

Fensterham, H. Behavior therapy: Assertive training in groups. In C. Sager & H. Kaplan (Eds.), *Progress in group and family therapy.* New York: Brunner/Mazel, 1972.

Ferster, C. Classification of behavior pathology. In L. Krasner & L. Ullmann (Eds.), *Research in behavior modification.* New York: Holt, Rinehart & Winston, 1965.

Fierman, L. *Effective psychotherapy.* New York: Free Press, 1965.

Fieve, R. Lithium therapy. In A. Freedman, H. Kaplan, & B. Sadock (Eds.), *Comprehensive textbook of psychiatry/II.* Baltimore: Williams & Wilkins, 1975.

Fieve, R. *Moodswing: The third revolution in psychiatry.* (Cited in A. Wolff, Medicine for melancholy, *Saturday Review,* February 1976, 34–35.)

Fine, R. Psychoanalysis. In R. Corsini (Ed.), *Current psychotherapies.* Itasca, Ill.: Peacock, 1973.

Fischer, J. Negroes and whites and rates of mental illness: Reconsideration of a myth. *Psychiatry,* 1969, *32,* 428–446.

Fischer, M. Genetic and environmental factors in schizophrenia. *Acta Psychiatrica Scandinavicus,* 1973, Suppl. 238.

Fish, B., Wile, R., Shapiro, T., & Halpern, F. The prediction of schizophrenia in infancy. In P. Hoch & J. Zubin (Eds.), *The psychopathology of schizophrenia.* New York: Grune & Stratton, 1966.

Fishman, S., & Newes, N. Standard desensitization method in group treatment. *Journal of Counseling Psychology*, 1971, *18*, 520–527.

Folsom, J. Reality orientation for the elderly mental patient. *Journal of Geriatric Psychiatry*, 1968, *1*, 291–307.

Ford, C., & Beach, F. *Patterns of sexual behavior*. New York: Harper & Row, 1952.

Ford, H. Involutional melancholia. In A. Freedman, H. Kaplan, & B. Sadock (Eds.), *Comprehensive textbook of psychiatry/II*. Baltimore: Williams & Wilkins, 1975.

Fozard, J., & Thomas, J. Psychology of aging. In J. Howells (Ed.), *Modern perspectives on the psychology of aging*. New York: Brunner/Mazel, 1975.

Frank, I. Training in psychotherapy. Unpublished manuscript, 1967.

Frazier, S. The psychotherapy of headache. In A. Freedman (Ed.), *Research and clinical studies in headaches: An international review*. Baltimore: Williams & Wilkins, 1969.

Freedman, A., Kaplan, H., & Sadock, B. (Eds.). *Comprehensive textbook of psychiatry/II*. Baltimore: Williams & Wilkins, 1975.

Freedman, S., Grunebaum, H., & Greenblatt, M. Perceptual and cognitive changes in sensory deprivation. In P. Solomon (Ed.), *Sensory deprivation: A symposium*. Cambridge, Mass.: Harvard University Press, 1961, 58–71.

Freeman, W., & Watts, J. *Psychosurgery*. Springfield, Ill.: Charles Thomas, 1950.

French, T., & Alexander, F. *Psychogenic factors in bronchial asthma*. Washington, D.C.: National Research Council, 1941.

Freud, A. *The ego and mechanisms of defense*. New York: International Universities Press, 1946.

Freud, A. Adolescence. In *Psychoanalytic study of the child* (Vol. XIII). New York: International Universities Press, 1958.

Freud, J., & Dingemanse, E. Uber katatonin, einen giftigen Stoff im Lipoid Ekstrakt von Harm, Gewirbsflussigkeiten und Organen. *Biochemische Zeitschrift*, 1932, *255*, 464.

Freud, S. The Schreber case. *Collected papers of Sigmund Freud* (Vol. 3). London: Hogarth Press, 1925.

Freud, S. *Civilization and its discontents*. New York: J. Cope & H. Smith, 1930.

Freud, S. *The problem of anxiety*. New York: Norton, 1936.

Freud, S. *Group psychology and the analysis of the ego*. New York: Bari & Liveright, 1940. (Originally published, 1921.)

Freud, S. Three essays on the theory of sexuality. In J. Strachey (Ed.), *Standard edition of the complete works of Sigmund Freud* (Vol. 7). London: Hogarth Press, 1953. (Originally published, 1930.)

Freud, S. Mourning and melancholia. In J. Strachey (Ed.), *Standard edition of the complete works of Sigmund Freud* (Vol. 14). London: Hogarth Press, 1957.

Friedman, C., & Friedman, A. Sex concordance in psychogenic disorders: Psychosomatic disorders in mothers and schizophrenia in daughters. *Archives of General Psychiatry*, 1972, *27*, 611–617.

Friedman, M., & Rosenman, R. Association of specific overt behavior pattern with blood and cardiovacular findings: Blood cholesterol level, clotting time, incidence of arcus semilis and clinical coronary artery disease. *Journal of the American Medical Association*, 1959, *169*, 1286.

Furlong, F. The mythology of electroconvulsive therapy. *Comprehensive Psychiatry*, 1972, *13*, 235.

Gagnon, J., & Davison, G. Asylums, the token economy, and the metrics of mental health. *Behavior Therapy*, 1976, *7*, 528–534.

Gallatin, J. *Adolescence and individuality*. New York: Harper & Row, 1975.

Gardner, W. Use of behavior therapy with the severely retarded. In F. Menolascino (Ed.), *Psychiatric approaches to mental retardation*. New York: Basic Books, 1970.

Garmezy, N. Children at risk: The search for the antecedents of schizophrenia. Part II: Ongoing research programs, issues and intervention. *Schizophrenia Bulletin*, 1974, *1*, 55–125.

Garmezy, N., & Streitman, S. Children at risk: The search for the antecedents of schizophrenia. Part I: Conceptual models and research methods. *Schizophrenia Bulletin*, 1974, *1*, 14–50.

Gebhard, P., Gagnon, J., Pomeroy, W., & Christenson, C. *Sex offenders*. New York: Harper & Row, 1965.

Gendlin, E. Experiential psychotherapy. In R. Corsini (Ed.), *Current psychotherapies*. Itasca, Ill.: Peacock, 1973.

Gentry, W., Harburg, E., & Havenstein, L. Effects of anger expression-inhibition and guilt on elevated diastolic blood pressure in high-low stress and black-white females. Proceedings of the 81st Annual Convention of the American Psychological Association, Montreal, Canada, 1973.

Gerard, J. Shifting attitudes toward criminal responsibility. *Medical World News: Psychiatry*, 1973, *14*, 39–40.

Gersten, J., Langner, J., Eisenberg, J., & Orzek, L. Child behavior and life events. In B. Dohrenwend & B. Dohrenwend (Eds.), *Stressful life events: Their nature and effects*. New York: Wiley, 1974.

Gillenkirk, J. Psychodrugs. *The Washingtonian*, October 1973, 92.

Ginott, H. *Between parent and child*. New York: Macmillan, 1964.

Glasser, W. *Reality therapy*. New York: Harper & Row, 1965.

Glasser, W., & Zunin, L. Reality therapy. In R. Corsini (Ed.), *Current psychotherapies*. Itasca, Ill.: Peacock, 1973.

Glatt, M. *A guide to addiction and its treatment*. New York: Wiley, 1974.

Goble, F. *The third force*. New York: Grossman, 1970.

Goddard, H. *Heredity and feeblemindedness*. Cold Springs Harbor, N.Y.: Eugenics Record Office, Bulletin No. 1, 1911.

Goddard, H. *Feeblemindedness—Its causes and consequences*. New York: Macmillan, 1914.

Goddard, H. *The Kallikak family*. New York: Macmillan, 1919.

Goldenberg, I. *Build me a mountain: Youth, poverty, and the creation of new settings*. Cambridge, Mass.: MIT Press, 1971.

Goldfarb, A. The evaluation of geriatric patients following treatment. In P. Hoch & J. Zubin (Eds.), *Evaluation of psychiatric treatment*. New York: Grune & Stratton, 1967.

Goldfarb, A. *Aging and organic brain syndrome*. Fort Washington, Pa.: McNeill Labs, 1974.

Goldfried, M., & Davison, G. *Clinical behavior therapy*. New York: Holt, Rinehart & Winston, 1976.

Goldman, H., Goldman, J., Kaufman, I., & Liebman, O. Later effects of early dietary protein intake on low birth weight infants. *Journal of Pediatrics*, 1974, *85*, 764–769.

Goodman, L., & Gilman, A. (Eds.). *The pharmacological basis of therapeutics* (4th ed.). London: Collier-Macmillan, 1970.

Gottesman, I., & Shields, J. A critical review of recent adoption, twin, and family studies of schizophrenia: Behavioral genetic perspectives. *Schizophrenia Bulletin*, 1976, *3*, 360–400.

Gottesman, L. The response of long-hospitalized aged psychotic patients to milieu treatment. *Gerontologist*, 1967, *7*, 47–48.

Gough, H. A sociological theory of psychopathy. *American Journal of Sociology*, 1948, *53*, 359–366.

Gove, W. Societal reaction as an explanation of mental illness: An evaluation. *American Sociological Review*, 1970, *35*, 873–884.

Gove, W., & Howell, P. Individual resources and mental hospitalization: A comparison and evaluation of the societal reaction and psychiatric perspectives. *American Sociological Review*, 1974, *39*, 86–100.

Graham, E., Ernhart, C., Craft, M., & Berman, P. Brain injury in the preschool child: Some developmental considerations. *Psychological Monographs*, 1963, 77, 573–574.

Graham, P., Rutter, M., Yule, N., & Pless, I. Childhood asthma: A psychosomatic disorder? Some epidemiological considerations. *British Journal of Preventative Social Medicine*, 1967, *21*, 78.

Greenacre, P. Conscience in the psychopath. *American Journal of Orthopsychiatry*, 1945, *15*, 495–509.

Greer, S. Study of parental loss in neurotics and psychopaths. *Archives of General Psychiatry*, 1964, *11*, 177–180.

Grier, W., & Cobbs, P. *Black rage*. New York: Basic Books, 1968.

Grossman, H. (Ed.). *Manual of terminology and classification in mental retardation* (1973 revision). Washington, D.C.: American Association on Mental Deficiency, 1973.

Grossman, S. Eating or drinking elicited by direct adrenergic or cholinergic stimulation of the hypothalamus. *Science*, 1960, *132*, 301–302.

Group for the Advancement of Psychiatry. *Psychopathological disorders in childhood: Theoretical considerations and a proposed classification*. New York: Group for the Advancement of Psychiatry, June 1966.

Guardo, C. *The adolescent as individual*. New York: Harper & Row, 1975.

Gurman, A. Therapist's mood pattern and therapeutic facilitativeness. *Journal of Counseling Psychology*, 1972, *19*, 169–170.

Gurman, A. Effects of therapist and patient mood on the therapeutic functioning of high and low facilitative therapists. *Journal of Consulting and Clinical Psychology*, 1973, *40*, 48–58.

Guttmacher, M. *The mind of a murderer*. New York: Farrar, Straus & Giroux, 1960.

Guttmacher, M. The normal and the sociopathic murderer. In M. Wolfgang (Ed), *Studies in homicide*. New York: Harper & Row, 1964.

Hahn, W. Psychophysiological reactivity of asthmatic children. *Psychosomatic Medicine*, 1967, *29*, 526.

Haim, A. *Adolescent suicide*. Paris: Tavistock Publications, 1974.

Haley, J. *Strategies of psychotherapy*. New York: Grune & Stratton, 1959.

Hall, C. Emotional behavior in the rat. I: Defecation and urination as measures of individual differences in emotionality. *Journal of Comparative Psychology*, 1934, *18*, 385.

Hall, G. *Adolescence*. New York: Appleton, 1904.

Halleck, S. Community psychiatry: Some troubling questions. In L. Roberts, S. Halleck, & M. Loeb (Eds.), *Community psychiatry*. Garden City, N.Y.: Doubleday, 1969.

Hare, E., Price, J., & Slater, E. Mental disorders and season of birth. *British Journal of Psychiatry*, 1974, *124*, 81–86.

Hare, R. Detection threshold for electric shock in psychopaths. *Journal of Abnormal Psychology*, 1968, *73*, 268–272. (a)

Hare, R. Psychotherapy, autonomic functioning and the orienting response. *Journal of Abnormal Psychology Monograph Supplement*, 1968, *73*, No. 3, Pt. 2, 1–24. (b)

Hare, R. *Psychopathy*. New York: Wiley, 1970.

Harper, R. *Psychoanalysis and psychotherapy–36 systems*. Englewood Cliffs, N.J.: Prentice-Hall, 1959.

Harper, R. *The new psychotherapies*. Englewood Cliffs, N.J.: Prentice-Hall, 1975.

Harwood, T. Cocaine. *Drug Enforcement*, Spring, 1974, pp. 20–24.

Hathaway, S., & McKinley, J. *Minnesota multiphasic personality inventory: Revised manual*. Minneapolis: University of Minnesota Press, 1942.

Havighurst, R. Successful aging. In R. Williams, C. Tibbitts, & W. Donahue (Eds.), *Process of aging.* New York: Atherton, 1963.

Hays, M. Conjoint family therapy. In H. Gazda (Ed.), *Basic approaches to group psychotherapy and group counseling* (2nd ed.). Springfield, Ill.: Charles Thomas, 1975.

Hearst, E. The classical-instrumental distinction: Reflexes, voluntary behavior and categories of associative learning. In W. Estes (Ed.), *Handbook of learning and cognitive processes* (Vol. 2). Hillsdale, N.J.: Erlbaum, 1975.

Heath, R. (Ed.). *Studies in schizophrenia.* Cambridge, Mass.: Harvard University Press, 1954.

Heath, R., & Mickle, W. Evaluation of seven years experience with depth electrode studies in human patients. In E. Ramey & D. O'Doherty (Eds.), *Electrical studies of the unanesthetized brain.* New York: Paul Hoeber, 1960.

Heilbrun, A. *Aversive maternal control: A theory of schizophrenia.* New York: Wiley, 1974.

Hellman, L., & Pritchard, J. *Williams obstetrics* (14th ed.). New York: Appleton-Century-Crofts, 1971.

Henderson, D. Incest. In A. Freedman, H. Kaplan, & B. Sadock (Eds.). *Comprehensive textbook of psychiatry/II.* Baltimore: Williams & Wilkins, 1975.

Henry, A., & Short, J. *Suicide and homicide: Some economic, sociological and psychological aspects of aggression.* New York: Free Press, 1954.

Henryk-Gutt, R., & Rees, W. Psychological aspects of migraine. *Journal of Psychosomatic Research,* 1973, *17,* 141–153.

Hentoff, N. *A doctor among the addicts.* Chicago: Rand-McNally, 1969.

Heron, W. Cognitive and physiological effects of perceptual isolation. (Cited in M. Zuckerman & N. Cohen, Sources of reports of visual and auditory sensations in perceptual isolation experiments, *Psychological Bulletin,* 1964, *62,* 1–20.)

Hertzberg, H., & McClelland, D. Paranoia. *Harper's Magazine,* June 1974, pp. 51–54; 59–60.

Heston, L. Psychiatric disorders in foster home reared children of schizophrenic mothers. *British Journal of Psychiatry,* 1966, *112,* 819–825.

Hippocrates. *The genuine works of Hippocrates* (Vol. 2) (F. Adams, trans.). London: Sydenham Society, 1848.

Hoch, P., & Polatin, D. Pseudoneurotic forms of schizophrenia. *Psychiatric Quarterly,* 1949, *23,* 248.

Hoffer, A., & Osmond, H. Schizophrenia: An autonomic disease. *Journal of Nervous and Mental Diseases,* 1958, *122,* 448.

Hoffer, A., & Osmond, H. The adrenochrome model and schizophrenia. *Journal of Nervous and Mental Diseases,* 1955, *128,* 18.

Hoffer, A., Payza, A., Szara, S., & Axelrod, J. The presence of adrenochrome in the blood. *American Journal of Psychiatry,* 1960, *116,* 664.

Hokanson, J., & Burgess, M. The effects of three types of aggression on vascular processes. *Journal of Abnormal Psychology,* 1962, *65,* 446–449.

Hokanson, J., DeGood, D., Forrest, M., & Brittain, T. Availability of avoidance behaviors for modulating vascular-stress responses. *Journal of Personality and Social Psychology,* 1971, *19,* 60–68.

Holden, C. Psychosurgery: Legitimate therapy or laundered lobotomy? *Science,* 1973, *179,* 1109–1112.

Hollingshead, A., & Redlich, F. *Social class and mental illness: A community study.* New York: Wiley, 1958.

Holmes, T., & Rahe, R. The social readjustment rating scale. *Journal of Psychosomatic Medicine,* 1967, *11,* 213–218.

Holzberg, J., Gewirtz, H., & Ebner, E. Changes in moral judgment and self acceptance in college students as a function of companionship with hospitalized mental patients. *Journal of Consulting Psychology,* 1964, *28,* 299–303.

Holzberg, J., & Knapp, R. The social interaction of college students and chronically ill mental patients. *American Journal of Orthopsychiatry*, 1965, *35*, 487–492.

Holzberg, J., Knapp, R., & Turner, J. College students as companions to the mentally ill. In E. Cowen, E. Gardner, & M. Zax (Eds.), *Emergent approaches to mental health problems*. New York: Appleton-Century-Crofts, 1967.

Holzman, P., Proctor, L., & Hughes, D. Eyetracking patterns in schizophrenics. *Science*, 1973, *181*, 179–181.

Holzman, P., Proctor, L., Levy, D., Yasillo, N., Meltzer, R., & Hurt, S. Eyetracking dysfunctions in schizophrenic patients and their relatives. *Archives of General Psychiatry*, 1974, *31*, 143–151.

Howard, K., & Orlinsky, D. Psychotherapeutic practices. In *Annual review of psychology* (Vol. 23). Palo Alto: Annual Reviews Press, 1972.

Howells, J. (Ed.). *Modern perspectives on the psychology of aging*. New York: Brunner/Mazel, 1975.

Humphreys, L. *Tearoom trade: Impersonal sex in public places*. Chicago: Aldine, 1970.

Innes, I., & Nickerson, M. Drugs acting on postganglionic adrenergic nerve endings and structures innervated by them. In L. Goodman & A. Gilman (Eds.), *The pharmacological basis of therapeutics* (4th ed.). London: Collier-Macmillan, 1970.

Isaacs, W., Thomas, J., & Goldiamond, I. Application of operant conditioning to reinstate verbal behavior in psychotics. *Journal of Speech and Hearing Disorders*, 1960, *25*, 8–12.

Iscoe, I., & Spielberger, C. D. *Community psychology: Perspectives in training and research*. New York: Appleton-Century-Crofts, 1970.

Jacobson, E. *Progressive relaxation*. Chicago: University of Chicago Press, 1938.

Jacobson, E. Contributions to the metapsychology of cyclothymic depression. In P. Greenacre (Ed.), *Affective disorders*. New York: International Universities Press, 1953.

Janet, P. *Psychological healing: A historical and clinical study*. (E. and C. Paul, Trans.). London: George Allen and Unwin, 1925.

Janov, A. *The primal scream*. New York: Putnam, 1970.

Jarvik, M. Drugs used in the treatment of psychiatric disorders. In L. Goodman & A. Gilman (Eds.), *The pharmacological basis of therapeutics* (4th ed.). London: Collier-Macmillan, 1970.

Jarvis, E. *Insanity and idiocy in Massachusetts: Report of the Cambridge Commission on Lunacy, 1855*. Cambridge, Mass.: Harvard University Press, 1971.

Jellinek, E. *The disease concept of alcoholism*. New Haven: Hillhouse Press, 1960.

Jenkins, R. The varieties of children's behavioral problems and family dynamics. *American Journal of Psychiatry*, 1968, *124*, 134–139.

Jenkins, R. The runaway reaction. *American Journal of Psychiatry*, 1971, *128*, 168–173.

Johnson, D., & Myklebust, H. *Learning disabilities: Educational principles and practices*. New York: Grune and Stratton, 1967.

Johnson, W. *Stuttering in children and adults*. Minneapolis: University of Minnesota, 1955.

Joint Commission on Mental Illness and Health. *Action for Mental Health*. New York: Basic Books, 1961.

Jones, K., Smith, D., Streissguth, A., & Myrianthopoulos, N. Outcome in offspring of chronic alcoholic women. *Lancet*, 1974, *i*, 1076–1078.

Jones, M. *The therapeutic community*. New York: Basic Books. 1953.

Jones, M. *Beyond the therapeutic community*. New Haven: Yale University Press, 1968.

Josselyn, I. The ego in adolescence. *American Journal of Orthopsychiatry*, 1954, *24*, 223–237.

Juel-Nielson, N. Epidemiology. In J. Howells (Ed.), *Modern perspectives on the psychology of aging*. New York: Brunner/Mazel, 1975.

Jung, C. *The development of personality.* In *Collected works* (Vol. 17). Bollingen Series (Vol. 20). Princeton: Princeton University Press, 1964. (Originally published, 1954.)

Kalinowsky, L. The convulsive therapies. In A. Freedman, H. Kaplan, & B. Sadock (Eds.), *Comprehensive textbook of psychiatry/II.* Baltimore: Williams & Wilkins, 1975. (a)

Kalinowsky, L. Psychosurgery. In A. Freedman, H. Kaplan, & B. Sadock (Eds.), *Comprehensive textbook of psychiatry/II.* Baltimore: Williams & Wilkins, 1975. (b)

Kalish, R. *Late adulthood: Perspectives on human development.* Monterey, Calif., Brooks/Cole, 1975.

Kallmann, F. *The genetics of schizophrenia.* New York: J. J. Augustin, 1938.

Kallmann, F. The genetic theory of schizophrenia. *American Journal of Psychiatry,* 1946, *103,* 309.

Kallmann, F. The genetics of psychoses. *American Journal of Human Genetics,* 1950, *2,* 385.

Kallmann, F. Comparative twin study in the genetic aspects of male homosexuality. *Journal of Nervous and Mental Disease,* 1952, *115,* 283–298.

Kallmann, F. *Heredity in health and mental disorder.* New York: Norton, 1953.

Kanner, L. Autistic disturbances of affective contact. *New Child,* 1943, *2,* 217–250.

Kanner, L. Early infantile autism. *American Journal of Orthopsychiatry,* 1948, *19,* 416–426.

Kanner, L. *Child psychiatry* (4th ed.). Springfield, Ill.: Charles Thomas, 1972.

Kanner, L. *Childhood psychoses: Initial studies and new insights.* Washington, D.C.: Winston, 1973.

Kantor, R., Wallner, J., & Winder, C. Process and reactive schizophrenics. *Journal of Consulting Psychology,* 1953, *17,* 157–162.

Kaplan, B. *The inner world of mental illness.* New York: Harper & Row, 1964.

Kaplan, H. S. *The new sex therapy.* New York: Brunner/Mazel, 1974.

Kaplan, H. S. *The illustrated manual of sex therapy.* New York: Quadrangle, 1975.

Karpman, B. The structure of neuroses. *Archives of Criminal Psychodynamics,* 1961, *4,* 599–646.

Kazdin, A., & Bootzin, R. The token economy: An evaluative review. *Journal of Applied Behavioral Analysis,* 1972, *5,* 343–372.

Keith, S., Gunderson, J., Reifman, A., Buchsbaum, S., & Mosher, L. Special report: Schizophrenia. *Schizophrenia Bulletin,* 1976, *2,* 510–565.

Kelly, E., & Zeller, B. Asthma and the psychiatrist. *Journal of Psychosomatic Research,* 1969, *13,* 377–395.

Kempler, W. Gestalt therapy. In R. Corsini (Ed.), *Current psychotherapies.* Itasca, Ill.: Peacock, 1973.

Kendall, R. Relationship between aggression and depression. *Archives of General Psychiatry,* 1970, *22,* 308–317.

Keniston, K. *Youth and dissent.* New York: Harcourt, Brace & Jovanovich, 1970.

Keniston, K. Youth as a stage of life. In C. Guardo (Ed.), *The adolescent as individual.* New York: Harper & Row, 1975.

Kennedy, W. School phobia: Rapid treatment of 50 cases. *Journal of Abnormal Psychology,* 1965, *70,* 285–287.

Kesey, K. *One flew over the cuckoo's nest.* New York: Viking, 1962.

Kessler, J. *Psychopathology of childhood.* Englewood Cliffs, N.J.: Prentice-Hall, 1966.

Kety, S. Biochemical hypotheses and studies. In L. Bellak & L. Loeb (Eds.), *The schizophrenic syndrome.* New York: Grune & Stratton, 1969.

Kety, S. Biochemistry of the major psychoses. In A. Freedman, H. Kaplan, & B. Sadock (Eds.), *Comprehensive textbook of psychiatry/II.* Baltimore: Williams & Wilkins, 1975. (a)

Kety, S. Mental illness and the biological and adoptive families of adopted individuals who have become schizophrenic. In H. M. Von Praag (Ed.), *On the origin of schizophrenic psychoses.* Amsterdam: De Erven Bohn, 1975. (b)

Kety, S., Rosenthal, D., Wender, P., & Schulsinger, F. The types and prevalence of mental illness in the biological families of adopted schizophrenics. In D. Rosenthal & S. Kety (Eds.), *The transmission of schizophrenia.* London: Pergamon, 1968.

Kety, S., Rosenthal, D., Wender, P., & Schulsinger, F. Studies based on a total sample of adopted individuals and their relatives. *Schizophrenia Bulletin,* 1976, *2,* 413–428.

Kety, S., Rosenthal, D., Wender, P., Schulsinger, F., & Jacobsen, B. Mental illness in the biological and adoptive families of adopted individuals who have become schizophrenic. In R. Fieve, D. Rosenthal, & H. Brill (Eds.), *Genetic research in psychiatry.* Baltimore: Johns Hopkins Press, 1975.

Kierkegaard, S. *A Kierkegaard anthology* (R. Bretall, Ed.). Princeton: Princeton University Press, 1946.

Kiesler, D. Some myths of psychotherapy and the search for a paradigm. *Psychological Bulletin,* 1966, *65,* 110–136.

Kiesler, D. *The process of psychotherapy.* Chicago: Aldine, 1973.

Kiesler, D., Bernstein, R., & Anchins, J. *Interpersonal communication: Relationship and the behavior therapies* (in press).

Kilch, L., & Garside, R. The independence of neurotic depression and endogenous depression. *British Journal of Psychiatry,* 1963, *109,* 451–463.

Kimmel, D. *Adulthood and aging.* New York: Wiley, 1974.

King, D., & Blaney, P. Effectiveness of A & B therapists with schizophrenics and neurotics: A referral study. *Journal of Consulting and Clinical Psychology,* 1977, *45,* 407–411.

Kingsley, L. *A comparative study of certain personality characteristics of psychopathic and non-psychopathic offenders.* Unpublished doctoral dissertation, New York University, 1956. (Cited in R. Hare, *Psychopathy.* New York: Wiley, 1970.)

Kinsey, A., Pomeroy, W., & Martin, C. *Sexual behavior in the human male.* Philadelphia: Saunders, 1948.

Kinsey, A., Pomeroy, W., Martin, C., & Gebhard, P. *Sexual behavior in the human female.* Philadelphia: Saunders, 1953.

Kirk, S. *Educating exceptional children.* Boston: Houghton Mifflin, 1972.

Kittrie, N. *The right to be different.* Baltimore: Johns Hopkins Press, 1971.

Klee, G. An ecological analysis of diagnosed mental illness in Baltimore. In R. Monroe (Ed.), *Psychiatric epidemiology and mental health planning.* Washington, D.C.: American Psychiatric Association, 1967.

Klein, M. The psychoanalytic play technique. *American Journal of Orthopsychiatry,* 1955, *25,* 223–238.

Klein, W., Lesham, E., & Furman, S. *Promoting mental health of older people through group methods.* New York: Manhattan Society for Mental Health, 1965.

Klein, W., & Zax, M. The use of a hospital volunteer program in the teaching of abnormal psychology. *Journal of Social Psychology,* 1965, *65,* 155–165.

Kleinmuntz, B. *Personality measurement: An introduction.* New York: Dorsey Press, 1967.

Klempel, H. False recognition—A pattern of the Capgras syndrome. *Psychiatric Clinics,* 1973, *6,* 17.

Klerman, G. Overview of depression. In A. Freedman, H. Kaplan, & B. Sadock (Eds.), *Comprehensive textbook of psychiatry/II.* Baltimore: Williams & Wilkins, 1975.

Klopfer, B., Ainsworth, M., Klopfer, W., & Holt, R. *Developments in the Rorschach technique* (Vol. 1: *Technique and theory*). Yonkers, N.Y.: World Book, 1954.

Knapp, P., Mushatt, C., Nemetz, S., Constantine, H., & Friedman, S. The context of reported asthma during psychoanalysis. *Psychomatic Medicine*, 1970, *32*, 167.

Kohn, M. Class, family, and schizophrenia: A reformulation. *Social Forces*, 1972, *50*, 295–304.

Kolb, L. C. Psychiatric aspects of the treatment of migraine. *Neurology*, 1963, *13*, 34.

Kolb, L. C. *Modern clinical psychiatry* (8th ed.). Philadelphia: Saunders, 1973.

Kolb, L. S. Therapy of homosexuality. In J. Masserman (Ed.), *Current psychiatric therapies*. New York: Grune & Stratton, 1963.

Kopp, S. The character structure of sex offenders. *American Journal of Psychotherapy*, 1962, *16*, 64–70.

Koppitz, E. *The Bender Gestalt test for young children: Research and application.* New York: Grune & Stratton, 1975.

Kotses, H., Glaus, K., Crawford, P., Edwards, J., & Scherr, M. Operant reduction of frontalis EMG activity in the treatment of asthma in children. *Journal of Psychosomatic Research*, 1976, *20*, 453–459.

Kotska, M., & Galassi, J. Group desensitization versus covert positive reinforcement in the reduction of test anxiety. *Journal of Counseling Psychology*, 1974, *21*, 464–468.

Kraepelin, E. *Lehrbuch der psychiatrie* (5th ed.). Leipzig: Barth, 1896.

Kral, V. Confusional states. In J. Howells (Ed.), *Modern perspectives on the psychology of aging.* New York: Brunner/Mazel, 1975.

Krasner, L., & Ullmann, L. *Research in behavior modification.* New York: Holt, 1965.

Kreitzer, S. College students in a behavior therapy program with hospitalized emotionally disturbed children. In B. Guerney, Jr. (Ed.), *Psychotherapeutic agents: New roles for non-professionals, parents, and teachers.* New York: Holt, Rinehart & Winston, 1969.

Kringlen, E. Heredity and social factors in schizophrenic twins: An epidemiological clinical study. In J. Romano (Ed.), *The origins of schizophrenia.* Amsterdam: Excerpta Medica, 1967.

Kringlen, E. Twins—Still our best method. *Schizophrenia Bulletin*, 1976, *2*, 429–433.

Kübler-Ross, E. *On death and dying.* New York: Macmillan, 1969.

Kübler-Ross, E. *Death: The final stage of growth.* Englewood Cliffs, N.J.: Prentice-Hall, 1975.

Lacey, J. I., & Lacey, B. C. Verification and extension of the principle of autonomic response stereotype. *American Journal of Psychology*, 1958, *71*, 56–73.

Lamberti, J. W., Blackman, N., & Weiss, M. A. The sudden murderer. *The Journal of Social Therapy*, 1958, *41*, 2–14.

Laqueur, H. Mechanisms of change in multiple family therapy. In C. Sager & H. Kaplan (Eds.), *Progress in group and family therapy.* New York: Brunner/Mazel, 1972.

Laufer, M., & Gair, D. Childhood schizophrenia. In L. Bellak & L. Loeb (Eds.), *The schizophrenic syndrome.* New York: Grune & Stratton, 1969.

Laughlin, H. T. *The neurosis in clinical practice.* Philadelphia: W. B. Saunders, 1956.

Lazarus, A. *Behavior therapy and beyond.* New York: McGraw-Hill, 1971.

Lazarus, A., & Abramovitz, A. The use of "emotive imagery" in the treatment of childhood phobia. *Journal of Mental Science*, 1962, *108*, 191–195.

Lehmann, H. Schizophrenia: Clinical features. In A. Freedman, H. Kaplan, & B. Sadock (Eds.), *Comprehensive textbook of psychiatry/II.* Baltimore: Williams and Wilkins, 1975. (a)

Lehmann, H. Unusual psychiatric disorders and atypical psychoses. In A. Freedman, H. Kaplan, & B. Sadock (Eds.), *Comprehensive textbook of psychiatry/II.* Baltimore: Williams and Wilkins, 1975. (b)

Leighton, A. H. *My name is legion* (Vol.1 of Sterling County Studies in Psychiatric and Sociocultural Environment). New York: Basic Books, 1959.

Leland, H., Shellhaas, M., Nihira, K., & Foster, R. Adaptive behavior: A new dimension in the classification of the mentally retarded. *Mental Retardation Abstracts*, 1967, *4*, 359–387.

Leland, H., & Smith, D. *Play therapy with mentally subnormal children.* New York: Grune & Stratton, 1965.

Leland, H., & Smith, D. Psychotherapeutic considerations with mentally retarded and developmentally disabled children. In I. Katz (Ed.), *Mental health services for the mentally retarded.* Springfield, Ill.: Charles Thomas, 1972.

Lemere, F., & Voegtlin, W. An evaluation of the aversive treatment of alcoholism. *Quarterly Journal of Alcoholic Studies*, 1950, *11*, 199.

Levy, L. *Conceptions of personality.* New York: Random House, 1970.

Lewinsohn, P., & Atwood, G. Depression: A chemical research approach. *Psychotherapy: Theory, Research and Practice*, 1969, *6*, 166–171.

Liberman, R. *A guide to behavioral analysis and therapy.* New York: Pergamon, 1972.

Lidz, T., Cornelison, A., Fleck, S., & Terry, D. The intrafamilial environment of the schizophrenic patient. *Archives of Neurological Psychiatry*, 1958, *74*, 305.

Liebert, R., Neale, J., & Davidson, E. *The early window: Effects of television on children and youth.* New York: Pergamon, 1973.

Lindemann, E. Symptomatology and management of acute grief. *American Journal of Psychiatry*, 1944, *101*, 141–148.

Lipowski, Z. Psychophysiological cardiovascular disorders. In A. Freedman, H. Kaplan, & B. Sadock (Eds.), *Comprehensive textbook of psychiatry/II.* Baltimore: Williams & Wilkins, 1975.

Litman, R. When patients commit suicide. *American Journal of Psychotherapy*, 1965, *19*, 570.

Litman, R. Sigmund Freud on suicide. In E. Shneidman (Ed.), *Essays in self destruction.* New York: Science House, 1967.

Loraine, J., Ismael, A., Adamopoulos, P., & Dove, G. Endocrine function in male and female homosexuals. *British Medical Journal*, 1970, *4*, 406.

Lorr, M., Klett, C., & McNair, D. *Syndromes of psychosis.* New York: Pergamon, 1963.

Lovaas, I. Behavior therapy approach in treating childhood schizophrenia. In J. Hill (Ed.), *Minnesota symposium on child development.* Minneapolis: University of Minnesota Press, 1967.

Lovaas, I., & Koegel, R. Behavior therapy with autistic children. In C. Thoreson (Ed.), *Behavior modification and education.* Chicago: University of Chicago Press, 1973.

Lowen, A. Bioenergetic group therapy. In H. Ruitenbeek (Ed.), *Group therapy today.* New York: Atherton, 1969.

Lukianowicz, N. Autoscopic phenomona. *Archives of Neurology and Psychiatry*, 1958, *80*, 199.

Lukianowicz, N. Incest. *British Journal of Psychiatry*, 1972, *120*, 301.

Lykken, D. A study of anxiety in the sociopathic personality. *Journal of Abnormal and Social Psychology*, 1957, *55*, 6–10.

Maas, J., Fawcett, J., & Dekirmenjian, W. Catecholamine metabolism, depressive illness, and drug response. *Archives of General Psychiatry*, 1972, *26*, 252–262.

MacGregor, R. Multiple impact psychotherapy with families. In J. Howells (Ed.), *Theory and practice of family psychotherapy.* New York: Brunner/Mazel, 1971.

MacKinnon, J. Production of gastric ulcer in the unrestrained rat. *Physiology and Behavior*, 1973, *10*, 825–827.

MacLennen, B., & Felsenfeld, N. *Group psychotherapy and counseling with adolescents.* New York: Columbia University Press, 1968.

MacMillan, D., Jones, R., & Meyers, C. Mainstreaming the mentally retarded: Some questions, cautions, and guidelines. *Mental Retardation*, 1976, *14*, 3–10.

Mahler, M. *On child psychosis and schizophrenia: Autistic and symbiotic infantile psychosis (Psychoanalytic study of the child*, Vol. 7). New York: International Universities Press, 1952.

Mahoney, M. *Cognition and behavior modification.* Cambridge, Mass.: Ballinger, 1974.

Maltzberg, B. Mental disease among native and foreign born Negroes in New York State. *Journal of Negro Education*, 1956, *25*, 175–181.

Maltzberg, B. Mental disease among Negroes. *Mental Hygiene*, 1959, *43*, 457–459.

Margolese, M. Homosexuality: A new endocrine correlate. *Hormones and Behavior*, 1970, *1*, 151.

Mark, V., & Ervin, E. *Violence and the brain.* New York: Harper & Row, 1973.

Marks, I., & Lader, M. Anxiety states (anxiety neurosis): A review. *Journal of Nervous and Mental Disease*, 1973, *156*, 3–18.

Markush, R., & Favero, R. Epidemiologic assessment of stressful life events. In B. Dohrenwend & B. Dohrenwend (Eds.), *Stressful life events: Their nature and effects.* New York: Wiley, 1974.

Marrone, R., Merksamer, M., & Salzberg, P. A short duration group treatment of smoking behavior by stimulus satiation. *Behavior Research and Therapy*, 1970, *8*, 347–352.

Maser, J., & Seligman, M. *Psychopathology: Experimental methods.* San Francisco: Freeman, 1977.

Maslow, A. *Motivation and personality.* New York: Harper & Row, 1954.

Maslow, A. *Toward a psychology of being* (2nd ed.). New York: Van Nostrand, 1968.

Maslow, A. *The farther reaches of human nature.* New York: Viking, 1971.

Masters, W., & Johnson, V. *Human sexual inadequacy.* Boston: Little, Brown, 1970.

Matarazzo, J. *Wechsler's measurement and appraisal of adult intelligence.* Baltimore: Williams & Wilkins, 1972.

Matte-Blanco, I. A study of schizophrenic thinking. *International Congress of Psychiatry—Congress Report*, 1959, *1*, 254.

May, R. *Psychology and the human dilemma.* Princeton: Van Nostrand, 1967.

McCall, R. Neurotic disorders. Unpublished manuscript, Marquette University, 1963.

McCandless, B. Personal communication, 1975.

McCord, W., & McCord, J. *The psychopath: An essay on the criminal mind.* New York: Van Nostrand Reinhold, 1964.

McGhee, A., & Chapman, L. Disorders of attention in early schizophrenia. *British Journal of Medical Psychology*, 1961, *34*, 103–116.

McManus, M. Group desensitization of test anxiety. *Behavior Research and Therapy*, 1971, *9*, 55–56.

McNair, D., Callahan, D., & Lorr, M. Therapist type and patient response to psychotherapy. *Journal of Consulting Psychology*, 1962, *26*, 425–429.

Mednick, S. A learning theory approach to schizophrenia. *Psychological Bulletin*, 1958, *55*, 316–327.

Meehl, P. Schizotaxia, schizotypy and schizophrenia. *American Psychologist*, 1962, *17*, 827–838.

Meltzer, H. Neuromuscular dysfunction in schizophrenics. *Schizophrenia Bulletin*, 1976, *2*, 106–135.

Meltzer, H., & Stahl, S. The dopamine hypothesis of schizophrenia: A review. *Schizophrenia Bulletin*, 1976, *2*, 19–76.

Mendels, J. *Concepts of depression.* New York: Wiley, 1970.

Menninger, K. *Man against himself.* New York: Harcourt, Brace, 1938.

Menninger, K. *The human mind* (3rd ed.). New York: Knopf, 1945.

Mesibov, G. Implications of the normalization principle for psychotic children. *Journal of Autism and Childhood Schizophrenia*, 1976, *6*, 360–364.

Meyers, J., Lindenthal, J., & Pepper, M. Life events and psychiatric impairment. *Journal of Nervous and Mental Disease*, 1971, *152*, 149–157.

Meyers, J., Lindenthal, J., & Pepper, M. Life events and psychiatric symptomatology. In D. Ricks, A. Thomas, & M. Roff (Eds.), *Life history research in psychopathology* (Vol. 3). Minneapolis: University of Minnesota Press, 1974.

Meyers, J., Lindenthal, J., & Pepper, M. Life events, social integration, and psychiatric symptomatology. *Journal of Health and Social Behavior*, 1975, *16*, 421–429.

Milkovich, L., & Vandenberg, B. Effects of prenatal meprobamate and chlordiazepoxide hydrochloride on human embryonic and fetal development. *New England Journal of Medicine*, 1974, *291*, 1268–1271.

Millby, J. A review of token economy treatment programs for psychiatric inpatients. *Hospital and Community Psychiatry*, 1975, *26*, 651–658.

Miller, N. Biofeedback: Evaluation of a new technic. *New England Journal of Medicine*, 1974, *240*, 684–685.

Miller, N. Clinical applications of biofeedback. In T. Barber, L. Dicara, J. Kamiya, N. Miller, D. Shapiro, & J. Stoyva (Eds.), *Biofeedback and self-control: 1975/1976*. Chicago: Aldine, 1976.

Miller, N., & Dworkin, B. Critical issues in therapeutic applications of biofeedback. In G. Schwartz & J. Beatty (Eds.), *Biofeedback: Theory and research*. New York: Academic Press, 1977.

Milt, H. Serious mental illness in children. *Public Affairs*, 1963, No. 352.

Minuchin, S. *Families and family therapy*. Cambridge, Mass.: Harvard University Press, 1974.

Mischel, W. Theory and research on the antecedents of self-imposed delay of reward. In B. Maher (Ed.), *Progress in experimental personality research* (Vol. 3). New York: Academic Press, 1966.

Mitchell, K., & Mitchell, D. An exploratory treatment application of programmed behavior therapy techniques. *Behavior Research and Therapy*, 1973, *72*, 137–151.

Monks, J., & Heath, C. A classification of academic, social and personal problems for use in a college student health department. *Student Medicine*, 1954, *2*, 44–62.

Montessori, M. *The Montessori method*. New York: Schocken, 1964.

Mora, G. Historical and theoretical trends in psychiatry. In A. Freedman, H. Kaplan, & B. Sadock (Eds.), *Comprehensive textbook of psychiatry/II*. Baltimore: Williams & Wilkins, 1975.

Morphew, J., & Sim, M. Gilles de la Tourette's syndrome: A clinical and psychological study. *British Journal of Medical Psychology*, 1969, *42*, 293.

Morrison, J., & Stewart, M. The psychiatric status of the legal families of adopted hyperactive children. *Archives of General Psychiatry*, 1973, *28*, 888–891.

Mosher, L., & Feinsilver, D. *Special report: Schizophrenia*. Washington, D.C.: U.S. Government Printing Office, 1971.

Moustakas, C. *Psychotherapy in children*. New York: Harper & Row, 1959.

Mowrer, O., & Mowrer, W. Enuresis: A method for its study and treatment. *American Journal of Orthopsychiatry*, 1938, *8*, 436–459.

Murdock, B. *The other children*. New York: Harper & Row, 1975.

Murray, H. *Explorations in personality*. New York: Oxford University Press, 1938.

Muuss, R. *Theories of adolescence*. New York: Random House, 1962.

Muuss, R. *Adolescent behavior and society*. New York: Random House, 1971.

National Alcoholic Beverage Control Association. *It's best to know . . . about alcohol*. Ontario: Alcoholism and Drug Addiction Research Foundation of Ontario.

National Commission on Marihuana and Drug Use. *Drug use in America: Problem in perspective*. Washington, D.C.: U.S. Government Printing Office, 1973.

National Institute of Mental Health. *Mental illness and its treatment* (DHEW Publication No. HSM 72-9030). Washington, D.C.: DHEW, 1971.

National Institute of Mental Health. *Schizophrenia: Is there an answer?* (rev. ed., DHEW Publication No. 73-9086). Washington, D.C.: DHEW, 1974.

National Institute of Mental Health. *Learning about depressive illness* (DHEW Publication No. ADM 76-288). Washington, D.C.: DHEW, 1975.

National Institute on Alcohol Abuse and Alcoholism. *Occupational alcoholism: Some problems and solutions.* Rockville, Md.: Author, 1972.

Nemiah, J. Obsessive compulsive neurosis. In A. Freedman, H. Kaplan, & B. Sadock (Eds.), *Comprehensive textbook of psychiatry/II.* Baltimore: Williams & Wilkins, 1975. (a)

Nemiah, J. Phobic neurosis. In A. Freedman, H. Kaplan, & B. Sadock (Eds.), *Comprehensive textbook of psychiatry/II.* Baltimore: Williams & Wilkins, 1975. (b)

Nemiah, J. Depressive neurosis. In A. Freedman, H. Kaplan, & B. Sadock (Eds.), *Comprehensive textbook of psychiatry/II.* Baltimore: Williams & Wilkins, 1975. (c)

Neugarten, B. *Personality in middle and later life.* New York: Atherton, 1964.

Nichols, M. Personal communication, 1976.

Nichols, M., & Zax, M. *Catharsis in psychotherapy.* New York: Gardner, 1977.

Nihira, K., Foster, R., Shellhaas, M., & Leland, H. *Adaptive behavior scales: Manual.* Washington, D.C.: American Association on Mental Deficiency, 1969.

Niswander, K., & Gordon, M. *Women and their pregnancies* (Vol. 1). Philadelphia: Saunders, 1972.

Nowicki, S., & Duke, M. An examination of counseling variables within a social learning framework. *Journal of Counseling Psychology,* 1978, *25,* 1–7.

Nowicki, S., & Hopper, A. Correlates of locus of control in an alcoholic population. *Journal of Consulting and Clinical Psychology,* 1974, *42,* 735–736.

Nowicki, S., & Strickland, B. A locus of control scale for children. *Journal of Consulting and Clinical Psychology,* 1973, *40,* 148–155.

Nowlis, H. *Drugs on the college campus.* Detroit: National Association of Student Personnel Administrators, 1967.

Office of Mental Retardation Coordination. *Mental retardation sourcebook* (DHEW Publication No. OS-73-81). Washington, D.C.: DHEW, 1972.

Oltman, J., & Friedman, S. Parental deprivation in psychiatric conditions. *Diseases of the Nervous System,* 1967, *28,* 298–303.

Orlinsky, D., & Howard, K. The good therapy hour. *Archives of General Psychiatry,* 1967, *16,* 621–632.

Orlinsky, D., & Howard, K. *Varieties of psychotherapeutic experience.* New York: Teachers College Press, 1975.

Orton, S. *Reading, writing and speech disorders in children.* New York: Norton, 1937.

Osmond, H. A review of the clinical effects of psychotomimetic drugs. In D. Solomon (Ed.), *LSD—The consciousness expanding drug.* New York: Putnam, 1966.

Osmond, H., & Smythies, J. Schizophrenia: A new approach. *Journal of Mental Science,* 1952, *98,* 304–315.

Palmer, S. Psychological frustration: A comparison of murderers and their brothers. In M. Wolfgang (Ed.), *Studies in homicide.* New York: Harper & Row, 1964.

Papez, J. A proposed mechanism of emotion. *AMA Archives of Neurology and Psychiatry,* 1937, *38,* 725–744.

Parloff, M. Shopping for the right therapy. *Saturday Review,* February 21, 1976, pp. 14–16, 18–20. (a)

Parloff, M. Narcissism of small differences—And some big ones. *International Journal of Group Psychotherapy,* 1976, *26,* 311–319. (b)

Parrill-Burnstein, M. Personal communication, 1978.

Pasamanick, B. Some misconceptions concerning differences in the racial prevalence of mental disease. *American Journal of Orthopsychiatry*, 1963, *33*, 72–86.

Pascal, G., & Suttell, B. *The Bender Gestalt Test: Identification and validity for adults.* New York: Grune & Stratton, 1951.

Patterson, C. *Theories of counseling and psychotherapy.* New York: Harper & Row, 1973.

Patterson, R. *Maintaining effective token economies.* Springfield, Ill.: Charles Thomas, 1975.

Pavlov, I. *Conditioned reflexes.* New York: Oxford University Press, 1927.

Payne, R. An object classification test as a measure of overinclusive thinking in schizophrenic patients. *British Journal of Social Psychology*, 1962, *7*, 213–221.

Payne, R. The measurement and significance of overinclusive thinking and retardation in schizophrenic patients. In P. Hoch & J. Zubin (Eds.), *Psychopathology of schizophrenia.* New York: Grune & Stratton, 1966.

Peck, M., & Seiden, R. Youth suicide. *exChange* (California State Department of Health), May 1975, pp. 17–20.

Penn, H., Racy, J., Lapham, L., Mandel, M., & Sandt, J. Catatonic behavior, viral encephalopathy and death: The problem of fatal catatonia. *Archives of General Psychiatry*, 1972, *27*, 758–761.

Perlin, S., & Schmidt, C. Psychiatry. In S. Perlin (Ed.), *A handbook of suicide.* New York: Oxford, 1975.

Perls, F. *Gestalt therapy verbatim.* Lafayette, Calif.: Real People Press, 1969. (a)

Perls, F. *In and out the garbage pail.* Lafayette, Calif.: Real People Press, 1969. (b)

Perls, F., Hefferline, R., & Goodman, P. *Gestalt therapy.* New York: Julian, 1958.

Perris, C. A study of bipolar (manic-depressive) and unipolar recurrent depressive psychosis. *Acta Psychiatrica Scandinavicus (Suppl.)*, 1966, *194*, 1.

Peshkin, M. Intractable asthma of childhood. *International Archives of Allergy*, 1959, *15*, 91.

Phillip, R., Wilde, G., & Day, J. Suggestion and relaxation in asthmatics. *Journal of Psychosomatic Research*, 1971, *16*, 193–204.

Physicians' Desk Reference (31st ed.). Oradell, N.J.: Medical Economics, 1977.

Planansky, K., & Johnston, H. The incidence of and relationship of homosexual and paranoid features in schizophrenics. *Journal of Mental Science*, 1962, *108*, 604.

Popham, R., & Schmidt, W. Some factors affecting the likelihood of moderate drinking by treated alcoholics. *Journal of Studies in Alcohol*, 1976, *37*, 868–883.

Poser, E. G. The effect of therapist training on group therapeutic outcome. *Journal of Consulting Psychology*, 1966, *30*, 283–289.

Potter, H. Schizophrenia in children. *American Journal of Psychiatry*, 1933, *12*, 1253–1268.

Prange, A., Wilson, I., & Lynn, C. L-tryptophan in mania: Contributions to a permissive amine hypothesis of affective disorders. *Archives of General Psychiatry*, 1974, *30*, 56–62.

Pratt, J. *The "home sanitorium" treatment of consumption.* Paper presented to the Johns Hopkins Medical Society, January 1906.

Premack, D. Toward empirical laws of behavior. I: Positive reinforcement. *Psychological Review*, 1959, *66*, 219–233.

Premack, D. Reinforcement theory. In D. Levine (Ed.), *Nebraska symposium on motivation* (Vol. 13). Lincoln: University of Nebraska Press, 1965.

Prince, M. *The dissociation of personality.* New York: Longmans, 1906.

Prostitutes: The new breed. *Newsweek*, July 12, 1971, p. 78.

Quay, H. Psychopathic personality as pathological stimulation seeking. *American Journal of Psychiatry*, 1965, *122*, 180–183.

Quay, H., & Werry, J. *Psychopathological disorders of childhood.* New York: Wiley, 1972.

Rachman, S., Marks, I., & Hodgson, R. The treatment of obsessive-compulsive neurotics by modelling and flooding in vivo. *Behavior Research and Therapy,* 1973, *11,* 463–471.

Ramsey, J. Guide to recognizing and handling mental illness. *Family Circle,* October 1974, 163–170.

Rappaport, J., Chinsky, J., & Cowen, J. *Innovations in helping chronic patients.* New York: Academic Press, 1971.

Rees, L. The significance of parental attitudes in childhood asthma. *Journal of Psychosomatic Research,* 1964, *7,* 253–262.

Reinherz, H. The therapeutic use of student volunteers. *Children,* 1964, *2,* 137–142.

Reiser, D. Psychosis of infancy and early childhood as manifested by children with atypical development. *New England Journal of Medicine,* 1963, *269,* 790–798; 844–850.

Reiss, B. Family therapy as seen by a group therapist. *International Journal of Group Psychotherapy,* 1976, *26,* 301–310.

Remmen, E., Cohen, S., Ditman, K., & Frantz, J. *Psychochemotherapy.* Los Angeles: Western Medical Publications, 1962.

Restak, R. The promise and peril of psychosurgery. *Saturday Review/World,* September 25, 1973, 54–57.

Richman, L. Sensory training for geriatric patients. *Journal of Occupational Therapy,* 1969, *23,* 254–257.

Rimland, B. *Infantile autism.* New York: Appleton-Century-Crofts, 1964.

Rimland, B. Psychogenesis versus biogenesis: The issues and the evidence. In S. Plog & R. Edgerton (Eds.), *Changing perspectives in mental illness.* New York: Holt, Rinehart & Winston, 1969.

Rioch, M. Pilot projects in training mental health counselors. In E. Cowen, E. Gardner, & M. Zax (Eds.), *Emergent approaches to mental health problems.* New York: Appleton-Century-Crofts, 1967.

Robins, E., Muñoz, R., Martin, S., & Gentry, K. Primary and secondary affective disorders. In J. Zubin & F. Freyhan (Eds.), *Disorders of mood.* Baltimore: Johns Hopkins Press, 1972.

Robins, E., Smith, K., & Lowe, I. Neuropharmacology. In *Transactions of the Josiah Macy, Jr., Foundation* (4th Conference), 1957. New York: Josiah Macy, Jr. Foundation.

Robins, L. *Deviant children grow up.* Baltimore: Williams & Wilkins, 1966.

Robinson, N., & Robinson, H. *The mentally retarded child.* New York: McGraw-Hill, 1976.

Rodgers, D. Factors underlying differences in alcohol preference among inbred strains of mice. *Psychosomatic Medicine,* 1966, *28,* 498–513.

Rogers, C. *Counseling and psychotherapy.* Boston: Houghton Mifflin, 1942.

Rogers, C. A theory of therapy, personality, and interpersonal relationships as developed in a client-centered framework. In S. Koch (Ed.), *Psychology: A study of science* (Vol. 3). New York: McGraw-Hill, 1959.

Roman, M. Family therapy and group therapy—Similarities and differences. *International Journal of Group Psychotherapy,* 1976, *26,* 281–288.

Rome, H. Barriers to the establishment of comprehensive community mental health centers. In L. Roberts, S. Halleck, & M. Loeb (Eds.), *Community psychiatry.* Garden City, N.Y.: Doubleday, 1969.

Rorschach, H. *Psychodiagnostics* (P. Lemkau and B. Kronenberg, Trans.). Berne: Huber Verlag, 1942.

Rosen, J. *Direct analysis.* New York: Grune & Stratton, 1953.

Rosenbaum, M. Group therapy with adolescents. In B. Wolman (Ed.), *Manual of child psychopathology.* New York: McGraw-Hill, 1972.

Rosengarten, H., & Friedhoff, A. A review of recent studies of the biosynthesis and excretion of hallucinogens formed by the methylation of neurotransmitters or related substances. *Schizophrenia Bulletin*, 1976, *2*, 90–105.

Rosenhan, D. On being sane in insane places. *Science*, 1973, *179*, 250–253.

Rosenthal, D. *Genetics of schizophrenia*. New York: McGraw-Hill, 1971.

Rosenthal, D., & Kety, S. *The transmission of schizophrenia*. London: Pergamon, 1968.

Rosenthal, D., Wender, P., Kety, S., Welner, J., & Schulsinger, F. The adopted away offspring of schizophrenics. *American Journal of Psychiatry*, 1971, *128*, 307–311.

Rosow, I. Adjustment of the normal aged: Concept and measurement. In R. Williams, C. Tibbitts, & W. Donahue (Eds.), *Process of aging*. New York: Atherton, 1963.

Ross, A. *Psychological disorders of children: A behavioral approach to theory, research and therapy*. New York: McGraw-Hill, 1974.

Roth, M. The natural history of mental disorders in old age. *Journal of Mental Science*, 1955, *101*, 281–301.

Roth, S., & Bootzin, R. R. Effects of experimentally induced expectancies of external control: An investigation of learned helplessness. *Journal of Personality and Social Psychology*, 1974, *29*, 253–264.

Rotter, J. Generalized expectancies for internal versus external control of reinforcements. *Psychological Monographs*, 1966, *80* (1, Whole No. 609).

Ruitenbeek, H. *Group therapy today*. New York: Atherton, 1969.

Rutter, M. Concepts of autism: A review of research. *Journal of Child Psychology and Psychiatry*, 1968, *9*, 1–25.

Ryle, A. *Student casualties*. London: Penguin, 1969.

Saenger, G. *Factors influencing the institutionalization of mentally-retarded individuals in New York City*. Albany: Interdepartmental Health Resources Board, 1960.

Saghir, M. T., & Robins, E. Homosexuality. I: Sexual behavior of the female homosexual. *Archives of General Psychiatry*, 1969, *20*, 192–201. (a)

Saghir, M. T., & Robins, E. Homosexuality. II: Sexual behavior of the male homosexual. *Archives of General Psychiatry*, 1969, *20*, 219–229. (b)

Sainsbury, P., & Barraclough, B. Differences between suicide rates. *Nature*, 1968, *220*, 1252.

Salter, A. *Conditioned reflex therapy*. New York: Creative Age Press, 1949.

Samuels, H. Quoted in Hernsinger, S., Legal-heroin debate. *Christian Science Monitor*, July 13, 1971, p. 11.

Sanders, R. New manpower for mental hospital service. In E. L. Cowen, E. A. Gardner, & M. Zax (Eds.), *Emergent approaches to mental health problems*. New York: Appleton-Century-Crofts, 1967.

Sankar, D., Cates, N., Broer, P., & Sankar, B. Biochemical parameters in childhood schizophrenia (autism) and growth. *Recent Advances in Biological Psychiatry*, 1963, *5*, 76.

Sartorius, N., Shapiro, R., & Jablensky, A. The international pilot study of schizophrenia. *Schizophrenia Bulletin*, 1974, *1*, 21–34.

Saslow, G., & Peters, A. A follow-up study of "interested" patients with various behavior disorders. *Psychiatric Quarterly*, 1956, *30*, 283–302.

Satir, V. *Conjoint family therapy*. Palo Alto: Science and Behavior Books, 1964.

Sawrey, W. Conditioned responses to fear in relationship to ulceration. *Journal of Comparative and Physiological Psychology*, 1961, *54*, 347–348.

Schacht, T., & Nathan, P. But is it good for psychologists? Appraisal and status of DSM-III. *American Psychologist*, 1977, *32*, 1017–1025.

Schaefer, H. H. A cultural delusion of alcoholics. *Psychological Reports*, 1971, *29*, 587–589.

Scheff, T. *Being mentally ill.* Chicago: Aldine, 1966.

Scheff, T. (Ed.). *Labelling madness.* Englewood Cliffs, N.J.: Prentice-Hall, 1975.

Scheflen, H. *Psychotherapy of schizophrenia: Direct analysis.* Springfield, Ill.: Charles Thomas, 1961.

Schildkraut, J. *Neuropsychopharmacology of the affective disorders.* Boston: Little, Brown, 1970.

Schildre, P. The attitude of murderers toward death. *Abnormal and Social Psychology,* 1936, *31,* 348.

Schlesinger, K. Genetic and biochemical correlates of alcohol preference in mice. *American Journal of Psychiatry,* 1966, *122,* 767–773.

Schneider, K. Primare und sekundare Symptome bei Schizophrenie. *Fortschrift fur Neurologische Psychiatrie,* 1957, *25,* 487.

Schreiber, F. *Sybil.* New York: Warner, 1974.

Schulsinger, F. Psychopathy, heredity and environment. *International Journal of Mental Health,* 1972, *1,* 190–206.

Schutz, W. *Joy.* New York: Grove Press, 1967.

Schutz, W. *Here comes everybody.* New York: Harper & Row, 1971.

Schutz, W. Encounter. In R. Corsini (Ed.), *Current psychotherapies.* Itasca, Ill.: Peacock, 1973.

Schwartz, G., & Beatty, J. (Eds.). *Biofeedback: Theory and research.* New York: Academic Press, 1977.

Screams, slaps and love. *Life Magazine,* 1965, *58,* 90–101.

Seiden, R. H. Campus tragedy: A study of student suicide. *Journal of Abnormal Psychology,* 1966, *71,* 389–399.

Seidensticker, J. F., & Tzagournis, M. Anorexia nervosa: Clinical features and long term follow-up. *Journal of Chronic Diseases,* 1968, *21,* 361.

Seligman, M. *Helplessness.* San Francisco: Freeman, 1975.

Selinsky, H. Psychological study of the migraine syndrome. *Bulletin of the New York Academy of Medicine,* 1939, *155,* 897.

Shaffer, T., & Galensky, M. *Models of group therapy and sensitivity training.* Englewood Cliffs, N.J.: Prentice-Hall, 1974.

Shakow, D. Segmental set. *Archives of General Psychiatry,* 1962, *6,* 1–17.

Shakow, D. Some observations on the psychology (and some fewer on the biology) of schizophrenia. *Journal of Nervous and Mental Diseases,* 1971, *153,* 300.

Shapiro, A. Placebo effects in medicine, psychotherapy, and psychoanalysis. In A. Bergin and S. Garfield (Eds.), *Handbook of psychotherapy and behavior change.* New York: Wiley, 1971.

Shapiro, A., Shapiro, E., & Wayne, H. Treatment of Tourette's syndrome. *Archives of General Psychiatry,* 1973, *28,* 92.

Shapiro, D. *Neurotic styles.* New York: Basic Books, 1965.

Shaw, D., Camps, F., & Eccleston, F. 5-Hydroxytryptamine in the hindbrain of depressive suicides. *British Journal of Psychiatry,* 1967, *113,* 1407–1411.

Shepard, T. Teratogenicity from drugs: An increasing problem. In *Disease-a-Month.* Chicago: Yearbook Medical Publishers, June 1974.

Sherman, A. Reactions to music of autistic (schizophrenic) children. *American Journal of Psychology,* 1953, *109,* 823–831.

Shields, J. Heredity and psychological abnormality. In H. Eysenck (Ed.), *Handbook of abnormal psychology* (2nd ed.). New York: Robert Knapp, 1973.

Shields, J., Heston, L., & Gottesman, I. Schizophrenia and the schizoid: The problem for genetic analyses. In R. Fieve, D. Rosenthal, & H. Brill (Eds.), *Genetic research in psychiatry.* Baltimore: Johns Hopkins Press, 1975.

Shields, J., & Slater, E. Heredity and psychological abnormality. In H. Eysenck (Ed.), *Handbook of abnormal psychology.* New York: Basic Books, 1961.

Shields, M. Looking for Mrs. Sizemore. *Atlanta Journal Constitution Magazine,* August 14, 1977, pp. 7–8; 22.

Shneidman, E. S. Suicide, lethality, and the psychological autopsy. In E. J. Shneidman & M. Ortega (Eds.), *Aspects of depression.* Boston: Little, Brown, 1969.

Shneidman, E. S. Prevention, intervention and postvention. *Annals of Internal Medicine,* 1971, *75,* 453.

Shneidman, E. S. *Deaths of man.* New York: Quadrangle, 1973.

Shneidman, E. S. Suicide. In A. Freedman, H. Kaplan, & B. Sadock (Eds.), *Comprehensive textbook of psychiatry/II.* Baltimore: Williams and Wilkins, 1975.

Shneidman, E. S., & Farberow, N. L. *Some facts about suicide.* Washington, D.C.: U.S. Government Printing Office, 1961.

Shoemaker, K. (Regional Director, Addiction Treatment Program, State of Georgia). Personal communication, 1975.

Shopper, M. Interview: The challenge of adolescence, by Don Crinklaw. *Marriage and Family Living,* July 1976, pp. 5–9.

Sigerist, H. E. *Civilization and disease.* Ithaca: Cornell University Press, 1943.

Simmons, J. *Deviants.* Berkeley: Glendessary, 1969.

Sinnett, E. R., Weisner, E. F., & Freiser, W. S. Dormitory half-way house. *Rehabilitation Record,* 1967, *8,* 34–37.

Sizemore, C., & Pittillo, E. *"I'm Eve."* New York: Doubleday, 1977.

Skibbe, A. *My experience as a student in a college crisis counseling center.* Unpublished manuscript, Emory University, 1973.

Skinner, B. F. *The behavior of organisms.* New York: Appleton, 1938.

Skinner, B. F. *Cumulative record.* New York: Appleton, 1959.

Slater, E., & Cowie, V. *The genetics of mental disorders.* London: Oxford University Press, 1971.

Snodgrass, V. Medical news. *Journal of the American Medical Association,* 1973, *225,* 1035–1046.

Snyder, S., Banerjee, S., Yamamura, H., & Greenberg, D. Drugs, neurotransmitters, and schizophrenia. *Science,* 1974, *184,* 1243–1253.

Snyder, S. H. Biology. In S. Perlin (Ed.), *A handbook for the study of suicide.* New York: Oxford University Press, 1975.

Sobell, M., & Sobell, L. Alternative to abstinence: Time to acknowledge reality. *Addictions* (Toronto), 1974, *21,* 2–29.

Solomon, R., Turner, L., & Lessac, M. Some effects of delay of punishment on resistance to temptation in dogs. *Journal of Personality and Social Psychology,* 1968, *8,* 233–238.

Solomon, R., & Wynne, L. Traumatic avoidance learning: The principles of anxiety conservation and partial irreversibility. *Psychological Review,* 1954, *61,* 353–385.

Speck R., & Attneave, C. Social network intervention. In C. Sager & H. Kaplan (Eds.), *Progress in group and family therapy.* New York: Brunner/Mazel, 1972.

Spielberger, C. D. Theory and research on anxiety. In C. D. Spielberger (Ed.), *Anxiety and behavior.* New York: Academic Press, 1966.

Spitzer, R., Sheehy, M., & Endicott, J. DSM-III: Guiding principles. In V. Rakoff (Ed.), *Psychiatric diagnoses.* New York: Brunner/Mazel, 1977.

Spitzer, R., & Wilson, P. Nosology and the official psychiatric nomenclature. In A. Freedman, H. Kaplan, & B. Sadock (Eds.), *Comprehensive textbook of psychiatry/II.* Baltimore: Williams and Wilkins, 1975.

Srole, L., Langner, T., Michael, S., Opler, M., & Rennie, T. *Mental health in the metropolis.* New York: McGraw-Hill, 1962.

Srole, L., Langner, T., Michael, S., Opler, M., & Rennie, T. *Mental health in the metropolis* (rev. ed.). New York: Harper & Row, 1975.

Stampfl, T., & Levis, D. Essentials of implosive therapy: A learning theory based psychodynamic behavioral therapy. *Journal of Abnormal Psychology,* 1967, *72,* 496.

Staton, T. *Dynamics of adolescent adjustment.* New York: Macmillan, 1963.

Stauder, K. Lethal catatonia. *Archives fur Psychiatrische und Nervenkrankheiten,* 1934, *102,* 614.

Stenzel, E. *Suicide and attempted suicide.* London: Penguin, 1964.

Stephan, C., Stephano, S., & Talkington, L. Use of modeling in survival skill training with educable mentally retarded. *The Training School Bulletin,* 1973, *70,* 63–68.

Stevenson, G. Drug addiction in British Columbia: A research survey, 1956. (Cited in E. Brecher, *Licit and illicit drugs.* Boston: Little, Brown, 1972.)

Stoller, R. Parental influences in male transsexualism. In R. Green & J. Money (Eds.), *Transsexualism and sex reassignment.* Baltimore: Johns Hopkins Press, 1969.

Storr, A. *Sexual deviation.* Baltimore: Penguin, 1964.

Stromgren, E. Genetic factors in the origin of schizophrenia. In H. Van Praag (Ed.), *On the origins of schizophrenia.* Amsterdam: De Erven Bohn, 1975.

Strupp, H. Psychotherapy. In *Annual review of psychotherapy* (Vol. 13). Palo Alto: Annual Reviews Press, 1962.

Subotnik, L. Spontaneous remission: Fact or artifact? *Psychological Bulletin,* 1972, *77,* 32–49.

Sullivan, H. *The interpersonal theory of psychiatry.* New York: Norton, 1953.

Sullivan, H. *Clinical studies in psychiatry.* New York: Norton, 1956.

Sundberg, N. D. The practice of psychological testing in clinical services in the United States. *American Psychologist,* 1961, *16,* 79–83.

Szara, S., Axelrod, J., & Perline, S. Is adrenochrome present in the blood? *American Journal of Psychiatry,* 1958, *115,* 162.

Szasz, T. *The myth of mental illness: Foundation of a theory of personal conduct.* New York: Harper & Row, 1961.

Szasz, T. The ethics of suicide. *Antioch Review,* 1971, *7,* 31.

Szurek, S. Psychotic episodes and psychotic maldevelopment. *American Journal of Orthopsychiatry,* 1956, *26,* 519–543.

Talbott, D. (Director, Georgian Clinic for the Treatment of Alcohol). Personal communication, 1974.

Talkington, L., Hall, S., & Altman, R. Use of peer-modeling procedure with severely retarded subjects as a basic communication response skill. *Training School Bulletin,* 1973, *69,* 145–149.

Tamarin, G. Observations on asthma and psoriasis patients: Brief remarks on the clinical aspects of psychosomatic diseases. *Zeitschrift Psychosomatic Medicine,* 1963, *9,* 26.

Taylor, J. Personal communication to J. Wolpe. In J. Wolpe, *The practice of behavior therapy.* New York: Pergamon, 1969.

Taylor, R. Electroconvulsive treatment (ECT): The control of therapeutic power. *exChange,* May/June 1975, 32–37.

Terman, L. M. *The measurement of intelligence.* Boston: Houghton Mifflin, 1916.

Terman, L. M., & Merrill, M. A. *Measuring intelligence.* Boston: Houghton Mifflin, 1937.

Terman, L. M., & Merrill, M. A. *Stanford-Binet intelligence scale: Manual for the third revision, Form L-M.* Boston: Houghton Mifflin, 1960.

Thigpen, C. H., & Cleckley, H. *The three faces of Eve.* Kingsport, Tenn.: Kingsport Press, 1954.

Thorndike, E. *The psychology of learning.* New York: Teachers College, 1913.

Thorndike, E. L. *Stanford-Binet intelligence scale—Form L-M, 1972 norms table.* Boston: Houghton Mifflin, 1973.

Thorpe, D. E., Schmidt, E., Brown, P. T., & Castell, D. Aversion-relief therapy: A new method for general application. *Behaviour Research and Therapy,* 1964, *2,* 71–82.

Thurber, J. The unicorn in the garden. *Fables for our time.* New York: Harper & Row, 1940.

Tibbitts, C. *Handbook of social gerontology*. Chicago: University of Chicago Press, 1960.

Torrey, E., & Peterson, M. The viral hypothesis of schizophrenia. *Schizophrenia Bulletin*, 1976, *2*, 136–146.

Toynbee, A. *A man's concern with death*. New York: McGraw-Hill, 1968.

Travis, L. *Speech pathology*. New York: Appleton-Century-Crofts, 1931.

Tryon, R. Genetic differences in maze learning ability in rats. *Proceedings of the Association for Research in Nervous and Mental Disease*, Pt. 1, 1940, 111.

Tucker, B. J., Megenity, D., & Virgil, L. Anatomy of a campus crisis center. *Personnel and Guidance Journal*, 1970, *48*, 343–348.

Tustin, F. *Autism and childhood psychosis*. London: Hogarth Press, 1972.

Ullmann, L., & Krasner, L. (Eds.). *Case studies in behavior modification*. New York: Holt, 1965.

Ullmann, L., & Krasner, L. *A psychological approach to abnormal behavior*. Englewood Cliffs, N.J.: Prentice-Hall, 1969.

Ullmann, L., & Krasner, L. *A psychological approach to abnormal behavior* (2nd ed.). Englewood Cliffs, N.J.: Prentice-Hall, 1975.

Umbarger, C. C., Dalsimer, J. S., Morrison, A. P., & Breggin, P. R. *College students in a mental hospital*. New York: Grune & Stratton, 1962.

United States Department of Health, Education and Welfare. Mental Health Statistical Report 138, August 1977. Publication No. (ADM) 77-158.

Usdin, E., & Bunney, W. *Pre- and post-synaptic receptors*. New York: Marcel Dekker, 1975.

Usdin, E., & Snyder, S. (Eds.). *Frontiers in catecholamine research*. New York: Pergamon, 1973.

Valenstein, F. *Brain control*. New York: Wiley, 1973.

Van der Valk, J. M. Comparison of the social setting and behavior of patients with bronchial asthma, coronary occlusions, and healthy subjects. *Fortschrift Psychosomatic Medicine*, 1960, *1*, 284.

Van Praag, H. (Ed.). *On the origins of schizophrenia*. Amsterdam: De Erven Bohn, 1975.

Van Praag, H., Korf, J., & Schut, D. Cerebral mono-amines and depression: An investigation with the probenecid techniques. *Archives of General Psychiatry*, 1973, *28*, 827–831.

Van Putten, G. Milieu therapy: Contraindication? *Archives of General Psychiatry*, 1973, *130*, 52.

Van Riper, C. *Speech therapy: A book of readings*. Englewood Cliffs, N.J.: Prentice-Hall, 1953.

Venables, P., & Wing, J. Level of arousal and the subclassification of schizophrenia. *Archives of General Psychiatry*, 1962, 7, 114–119.

Verwoerdt, A. *Clinical geropsychiatry*. Baltimore: Williams & Wilkins, 1976.

Vogt, D. Literacy among youths 12–17 years (DHEW Publication No. HRA 74-1613). Washington, D.C.: U.S. Government Printing Office, 1973.

Von Brauschitsch, W., & Kirk, W. Childhood schizophrenia and social class. *American Journal of Othopsychiatry*, 1967, *37*, 400.

Wald, E., MacKinnon, J., & Desiderto, O. Production of gastric ulcers in the unrestrained rat. *Journal of Physiology and Behavior*, 1973, *10*, 825–827.

Wallace, S. *After suicide*. New York: Wiley, 1973.

Walters, P. A. Student apathy. In G. B. Blaine, Jr., & C. C. McArthur (Eds.), *Emotional problems of the student* (2nd ed.). New York: Appleton-Century-Crofts, 1971.

Waltzer, H. The psychotic family: Folie à douze. *Journal of Nervous and Mental Disease*, 1963, *137*, 63.

Ward, A. Early infantile autism: Diagnosis, etiology and treatment. *Psychological Bulletin*, 1970, *73*, 350–362.

Watson, J. B., & Rayner, R. Conditioned emotional reactions. *Journal of Experimental Psychology*, 1920, *3*, 1–14.

Webster, T., & Harris, H. Modified group psychotherapy: An experiment in group psychodynamics for college freshmen. *Group Psychotherapy*, 1958, *11*, 283–298.

Wechsler, D. *Manual for the Wechsler Adult Intelligence Scale.* New York: Psychological Corporation, 1955.

Wechsler, D. *Manual: Wechsler Preschool and Primary Scale.* New York: Psychological Corporation, 1967.

Wechsler, D. *Manual: Wechsler Intelligence Scale for Children* (rev. ed.). New York: Psychological Corporation, 1974.

Weinberg, J. Psychopathology. In J. Howells (Ed.), *Modern perspectives on the psychology of aging.* New York: Brunner/Mazel, 1975.

Weinberg, S. *Incest behavior.* New York: Citadel, 1955.

Weiner, H., Thaler, M., Reiser, M. F., & Mirsky, I. A. Etiology of duodenal ulcer. I: Relation of specific psychological characteristics to rate of gastric secretion. *Psychosomatic Medicine*, 1957, *19*, 1–10.

Weiner, I. The effectiveness of a suicide prevention program. *Mental Hygiene*, 1969, *53*, 357–363.

Weisman, A. D. Thanatology. In A. Freedman, H. Kaplan, & B. Sadock (Eds.), *Comprehensive textbook of psychiatry/II.* Baltimore: Williams and Wilkins, 1975.

Weisman, A. D., & Kastenbaum, R. *The psychological autopsy.* New York: Behavioral Publications, 1968.

Weiss, T., & Engel, B. Operant conditioning of heart rate in patients with premature ventricular contraction. *Psychosomatic Medicine*, 1971, *33*, 301–321.

Welch, A., & Welch, B. Isolation, reactivity and aggression. In B. Elefthesious & J. Scott (Eds.), *The physiology of aggression and defeat.* New York: Plenum, 1971.

West, D. J. *Murder followed by suicide.* London: Heinemann, 1965.

White, R. *Lives in progress.* New York: Dryden Press, 1952.

White, R. W. *The abnormal personality.* New York: Ronald Press, 1964.

White, R. W., & Watt, J. *Experience and environment: Major influences on the development of the young child* (Vol. 1). Englewood Cliffs, N.J.: Prentice-Hall, 1973.

Whitehorn, J., & Betz, B. A study of psychotherapeutic relationships between physicians and schizophrenic patients. *American Journal of Psychiatry*, 1954, *111*, 321–331.

Whitehorn, J., & Betz, B. Further studies of the doctor as a crucial variable in the outcome of treatment of schizophrenic patients. *American Journal of Psychiatry*, 1960, *117*, 215–223.

Whitmont, E., & Kaufman, Y. Analytical psychotherapy. In R. Corsini (Ed.), *Current psychotherapies.* Itasca, Ill.: Peacock, 1973.

Whittington, H. *Psychiatry on the college campus.* New York: International Universities Press, 1963.

Wikler, A. Dynamics of drug dependence: Implications of a conditioning theory for research and treatment. In S. Fisher & A. Freedman (Eds.), *Opiate addiction: Origins and treatment.* Washington, D.C.: Winston, 1973.

Williams, A. H. The psychopathology of sexual murderers. In I. Rosen (Ed.), *The pathology and treatment of sexual deviation.* London: Oxford University Press, 1964.

Wilson, M. A proposed diagnostic classification for adolescent psychiatric cases. In S. Feinstein, P. Giovacchini, & A. Miller (Eds.), *Adolescent psychiatry.* New York: Basic Books, 1971.

Winick, C. A content analysis of drug related network entertainment prime time programs, 1970–1972. In National Commission on Marihuana and Drug Use, *Drug use in America: Problem in perspective.* Washington, D.C.: U.S. Government Printing Office, 1973.

Winick, M., & Rosso, P. Effects of malnutrition on brain development. *Biology of Brain Dysfunction*, 1973, *1*, 301–317.

Winokur, G., Clayton, P., & Reich, T. *Manic-depressive illness.* St. Louis: Mosby, 1969.

Wise, D., & Stein, L. Dopamine-B-hydroxylase deficits in the brains of schizophrenics. *Science*, 1973, *181*, 344–351.

Wohlberg, G., & Kornetsky, C. Sustained attention in remitted schizophrenics. *Archives of General Psychiatry*, 1973, *28*, 533–537.

Wolf, S., & Wolff, H. *Human gastric function.* New York: Oxford University Press, 1947.

Wolff, A. *Community mental health on campus: Evaluating group discussions led by dormitory advisors and graduate students.* Unpublished doctoral dissertation, University of Rochester, 1969.

Wolff, A. Medicine for melancholy. *Saturday Review*, February 21, 1976, 34–35.

Wolfgang, M. *Studies in homicide.* New York: Harper & Row, 1964.

Wolman, B. Schizophrenia in childhood. In B. Wolman (Ed.), *Manual of child psychopathology.* New York: McGraw-Hill, 1972.

Wolpe, J. *Psychotherapy by reciprocal inhibition.* Stanford: Stanford University Press, 1958.

Wolpe, J. *The practice of behavior therapy* (2nd ed.). New York: Pergamon, 1973.

Woltman, A. Play therapy and related techniques. In D. Brower & L. Abt (Eds.), *Progress in clinical psychology* (Vol. 3). New York: Grune & Stratton, 1959.

Wood, A. Crime and aggression in changing Ceylon. *Transactions of the American Philosophical Society*, 1961, *51*, 8.

Woodworth, R. S. *Personal data sheet.* Chicago: Stoelting, 1920.

Woolley, D. *The biochemical bases of psychoses.* New York: Wiley, 1962.

Woolley, D., & Shaw, E. A biochemical and pharmacological suggestion about certain mental disorders. *Science*, 1954, *119*, 587.

World Health Organization. *The prevention of suicide.* Geneva: Author, 1968.

World Health Organization. *Homicide rates in United Nations countries.* Geneva: Author, 1970.

World Health Organization. *Suicide.* Geneva: Author, 1975.

Yablonsky, L. Synanon. In R. Jurjevich (Ed.), *Direct psychotherapy* (Vol. 2). Coral Gables: University of Miami Press, 1973.

Yager, J. (Director of Psychiatry, U.S. Army Hospital, Fort Ord, Calif.). Personal communication, 1974.

Yalom, I. *Theory and practice of group psychotherapy.* New York: Basic Books, 1970.

Yates, A. The application of learning theory to the treatment of tics. *Journal of Abnormal and Social Psychology*, 1958, *56*, 175–182.

Zahn, T. Psychophysiological concomitants of task performance in schizophrenia. In M. Kietzman, S. Sutton, & J. Zubin (Eds.), *Experimental approaches to psychopathology.* New York: Academic Press, 1975.

Zax, M., & Specter, G. *An introduction to community psychology.* New York: Wiley, 1974.

Zilboorg, G., & Henry, G. *A history of medical psychology.* New York: Norton, 1941.

Zubin, J., Eron, L., & Schumer, F. *An experimental approach to projective techniques.* New York: Wiley, 1965.

Zuckerman, M., Albright, R., Marks, C., & Miller, G. Stress and hallucinatory effects of perceptual isolation and confinement. *Psychological Monographs*, 1962, *76* (Whole No. 549).

Zuk, G. *Family therapy: A triadic based approach.* New York: Behavioral Publications, 1972.

Zung, W. A self rating depression scale. *Archives of General Psychiatry*, 1965, *12*, 63.

Zwerdling, D. Pills, profits and people's problems. *Progressive*, October 1973, 44–47.

NAME INDEX

Abraham, K., 206, 208
Abramovitz, A., 482
Ackerman, N., 603
Adamopoulos, P., 372
Adler, A., 85, 588
Agras, S., 244
Ainsworth, M., 37
Akerfeldt, S., 139
Akiskal, H., 214–215
Alanen, A., 463
Albee, G., 634
Albright, R., 539
Alexander, F., 248, 273, 286, 289–290
Alexander, G., 294
Allport, G., 31
Altman, R., 447
Anastasi, A., 33, 35, 36, 43, 47, 49
Anchins, J., 558
Andy, O., 430
Arieti, S., 158, 170, 232, 309
Arthurs, R., 311
Ascher, A., 229
Atchley, R., 537
Atteneave, C., 609
Atwood, G., 210
Axelrod, J., 140
Axline, V., 480
Ayd, F., 616–617
Ayllon, T., 187, 481, 577
Azrin, N., 187, 481

Babigian, H., 153
Bach, G., 595
Bachrach, A., 574
Back, K., 598
Badash, D., 536, 540, 544

Baker, G., 208–209
Bandura, A., 100–101, 405, 447
Banerjee, S., 180
Barbellion, W., 258
Barber, T., 627
Barger, B., 528
Barker, J., 575
Barker, M., 28–29
Barnum, P., 556
Barraclough, B., 385
Barron, A., 404
Bastiaans, J., 276
Batchelor, I., 534
Bateson, G., 173
Bauer, M., 440
Beach, F., 368, 375
Beatty, J., 626
Beck, A., 36, 209
Beck, S., 36
Becker, H., 106
Becker, W., 98
Beels, C., 609
Beers, C., 67–68
Beier, E., 558
Bell, J., 603
Belmont, J., 436
Benda, C., 436
Bender, L., 47, 457, 465
Bennes, K., 597
Bennett, C., 633
Bennis, W., 597
Benson, H., 283
Benton, A., 48
Beran, D., 536
Berezin, M., 540
Berg, I., 43
Bergin, A., 555
Berkovitz, I., 499
Berlin, I., 157

Berman, J., 437
Berman, P., 439
Bernstein, R., 558
Bettelheim, B., 464
Betz, B., 557
Bibring, E., 207
Bieber, I., 373–375
Bieber, T., 373–375
Binet, A., 47
Bini, L., 622
Binswanger, L., 90–91, 566
Birren, J., 533
Blackman, N., 404
Blaine, G., 506–507
Blanchard, E., 268
Blaney, P., 557
Blau, D., 540
Bleuler, E., 154, 176
Bliss, E., 254
Bliven, N., 190
Bloch, D., 610
Bloom, B., 614, 633, 635
Blos, P., 506
Bolles, R., 100
Bootzin, R., 187
Boozer, R., 211
Bordin, E., 557–558
Boss, M., 566
Bowen, M., 457, 603
Boxberger, R., 546
Bradford, L., 597
Bradley, C., 457
Brady, J., 286
Braginsky, B., 27–28
Braginsky, D., 27–28
Braid, J., 60, 74
Branch, C., 254
Brandes, N., 525
Brantley, M., 620, 624

Brecher, E., 332, 337, 340, 343, 601
Breese, G., 183
Breggin, P., 642
Bregin, P., 626
Brener, J., 284
Breuer, J., 63, 74
Brigante, T., 523
Brittain, T., 282
Broer, P., 466
Brosin, H., 420
Brown, H., 131–136, 138
Brown, P., 268
Bruun, R., 229
Buchsbaum, S., 174
Bunch, J., 534
Bunney, W., 180
Bunze, J., 540
Burckhardt, H., 625
Burgess, M., 282
Buros, O., 49
Burton, T., 444
Busch, A., 343

Cade, W., 619
Cahoon, E., 311
Callahan, D., 557
Cameron, K., 457
Cameron, N., 194, 197, 226–228, 257
Camps, F., 213
Cannon, W., 132
Cantwell, D., 311
Caplan, G., 396, 638–640
Carlsson, A., 180
Carson, R., 314–315, 557
Cashman, J., 341
Cassell, J., 440
Castell, D., 268
Cates, N., 466
Cautela, J., 330–331, 366–367, 562, 576
Cavan, R., 382
Cerlitti, V., 622
Chapman, L., 171
Charcot, J., 60–63, 74
Chess, S., 438
Chinsky, J., 642
Chorover, S., 626
Christenson, C., 359–360
Cicero, 52
Clark, D., 468
Clark, M., 486
Clayton, P., 201, 203
Cleckley, H., 248, 307, 310, 314
Cobbs, P., 283
Cohen, M., 208–209
Cohen, R., 192–193, 208–209
Cohen, S., 343, 618

Cole, J., 618–620
Coleman, J., 153, 198
Constantine, H., 289
Cools, A., 183
Coppen, A., 213
Corey, G., 565, 580
Cornelison, A., 173
Cotter, V., 546
Coursey, R., 627
Cowen, E., 637
Cowen, J., 642
Cowie, V., 177, 311, 457, 464–465
Craft, M., 314, 439
Craig, L., 511
Crawford, P., 291
Creak, M., 457
Cronbach, L., 49
Crowe, R., 311
Cumming, E., 536

Dain, H., 373–375
Dalen, P., 179
Dalsimer, J., 642
Davidson, E., 400
Davies, D., 331
Davies, M., 282
Davis, J., 618–620
Davison, G., 187, 268
Day, J., 290–291
Dederick, C., 601
DeGood, D., 282
Dekirmenjian, W., 213
Delay, F., 616
Deleon, G., 470
Delgado, R., 472
Deniker, M., 616
Desiderto, O., 285
Deutsch, A., 66
Dicara, L., 627
Dince, P., 373–375
Dingemanse, E., 139
Ditman, K., 618
Dix, D., 59, 66
Dohrenwend, B. and B., 115, 123, 174–175, 177, 634
Dole, V., 337
Dollard, J., 265
Dorpat, T., 407, 409
Dove, G., 373
Dreikurs, R., 588
Drellich, M., 373–375
Duke, M., 115, 506–508, 512, 518, 523
Duncan, G., 404
Dunham, H., 126, 636
Dunn, L., 444
Durkheim, E., 390
Dworkin, B., 627

Ebner, E., 643
Eccleston, F., 213
Eckstein, G., 133
Edwards, D., 353, 355, 365–366
Edwards, J., 291
Eisdorfer, C., 533
Eisenberg, J., 175
Eisenberg, L., 463
Ellis, A., 580–581
Endicott, J., 23
Engel, B., 627
Engel, D., 473
Engel, G., 287, 420
Erikson, E., 85, 87, 106, 226, 495, 497, 498, 501–503, 507–508, 639
Eriksson, K., 327
Ernhart, C., 439
Ernst, P., 536, 540, 544
Eron, L., 38
Ervin, E., 626
Ervin, F., 425
Erwin, W., 574
Esquirol, J., 57
Evans, M., 425
Evans, R., 374
Evarts, A., 126
Evsenck, H., 263, 554–555

Farberow, N., 386–387
Faris, R., 126
Favero, R., 175
Fawcett, J., 213
Feinsilver, D., 153
Feldman, M., 376
Felsenfeld, N., 499
Fensterham, H., 593
Ferber, A., 609
Fernandez, P., 438
Ferster, C., 210, 464
Fierman, L., 579
Fieve, R., 619, 628
Fine, R., 560, 562
Fischer, J., 126–127
Fischer, M., 175
Fish, B., 465
Fishman, S., 593
Fleck, S., 173
Folling, E., 437
Folsom, J., 546
Ford, C., 368
Ford, R., 437
Forrest, M., 282
Foster, R., 434
Fournier, A., 58
Fozard, J., 533
Frank, I., 559, 579
Franklin, B., 60
Frantz, J., 618
Frazier, S., 291, 404

NAME
INDEX

Freedman, S., 539
Freeman, W., 625
Freiser, W., 529
French, T., 290
Freud, A., 493–495, 501, 639
Freud, J., 139
Freud, S., 19, 63, 68, 74–77,
    79–86, 88, 92, 102, 169, 170,
    207–208, 225–226, 233,
    246, 261–262, 326, 373–
    375, 388–389, 404, 409,
    560, 563, 588
Friedhoff, A., 181–182
Friedman, A., 174
Friedman, C., 174
Friedman, M., 279
Friedman, S., 289, 312
Fromm-Reichmann, F.,
    208–209
Furlong, F., 624
Furman, S., 541

Gagnon, J., 187, 359, 360
Gair, D., 457
Galassi, J., 526
Galen, 52, 57
Galensky, M., 588, 591, 593,
    596, 598
Gallatin, J., 495
Gardner, M., 525
Gardner, W., 447
Garmezy, N., 177
Garside, R., 259
Gebhard, P., 353, 359, 360,
    369
Gendlin, E., 566
Gentry, K., 204
Gentry, W., 283
Gerard, J., 16
Gersten, J., 175
Gewirtz, H., 643
Gibbs, J., 597
Gillenkirk, J., 628
Gilman, A., 615
Ginott, H., 480
Glasser, W., 569
Glatt, M., 324–325, 339–341,
    344–346
Glaus, K., 291
Goddard, H., 140–143
Goldenberg, I., 648–649
Goldfarb, A., 418, 457, 531,
    536
Goldfried, M., 268
Goldiamond, I., 187
Goldman, H., 439
Goldman, J., 439
Goodman, L., 615
Goodman, P., 566
Gordon, M., 439
Gottesman, I., 175, 177

Gottesman, L., 546
Gough, H., 312
Gove, W., 107, 122, 125
Graham, E., 439
Graham, P., 289
Grand, H., 373–375
Granger, C., 314
Greenacre, P., 311
Greenberg, D., 180
Greenblatt, M., 539
Greer, S., 312
Grier, W., 283
Griesinger, W., 57
Grossman, H., 432–434, 440
Grossman, S., 147
Grunebaum, H., 539
Guardo, C., 495
Gunderson, J., 174
Gundlach, R., 373–375
Gurman, A., 557
Guttmacher, M., 401, 404–
    405, 407

Hahn, W., 290
Haim, A., 491
Haley, J., 173
Hall, C., 143
Hall, E., 528
Hall, G., 488, 492, 520
Hall, S., 447
Halleck, S., 638
Halpern, F., 465
Harburg, E., 283
Hare, E., 179
Hare, R., 310–312, 314
Harl, S., 616
Harper, R., 551
Harris, H., 528
Harwood, T., 339
Haslam, J., 57
Hathaway, S., 34
Havenstein, L., 283
Havighurst, R., 538
Hays, M., 604–605
Hearst, E., 96
Heath, C., 506
Heath, R., 139–140
Hefferline, R., 566
Heidegger, M., 566
Heilbrun, A., 174
Heine, R., 557
Helfand, I., 473
Hellman, L., 438
Henderson, D., 358
Henry, A., 390–391
Henry, G., 51, 54, 56–57, 59
Henry, W., 536
Henryk-Gutt, R., 293
Hentoff, N., 337
Heron, W., 544
Hertzberg, H., 233

Heston, L., 175–176
Hippocrates, 52, 56, 245
Hoch, P., 164
Hodgson, R., 268
Hoffer, A., 140
Hoffmann, A., 341–342
Hokanson, J., 282–283
Holden, C., 626
Hollingshead, A., 120, 122,
    634
Holmes, T., 174
Holt, R., 37
Holzberg, J., 642–643
Holzman, P., 172
Hopper, A., 115
Horney, K., 85
Howard, J., 183
Howard, K., 553, 557
Howell, P., 122, 125
Howells, J., 533
Hughes, D., 172
Hume, D., 384
Humphreys, L., 372
Hurt, S., 172

Ini, S., 457
Innes, I., 340
Isaacs, W., 187
Iscoe, I., 633
Ismael, A., 372

Jablensky, A., 154–155
Jackson, D., 173
Jacobson, E., 207, 570
Janet, P., 61–63, 74, 246, 258
Janov, A., 577–578
Jarvik, M., 615–616, 620
Jarvis, E., 120
Jellinek, E., 321–322
Jenkins, R., 489
Johnson, A., 404
Johnson, D., 477
Johnson, V., 351–354
Johnson, W., 343, 473
Johnston, H., 226
Jones, K., 438
Jones, M., 409, 649
Jones, R., 445–446
Josselyn, I., 504
Juel-Nielson, N., 423, 531
Jung, C., 85, 423, 560, 563

Kaiser, H., 579
Kalinowsky, L., 217, 622, 625
Kalish, R., 546
Kallmann, F., 144–146, 175,
    372
Kamiya, J., 627
Kanner, L., 457–459, 463,
    467–469, 471, 474
Kantor, R., 164–165

Kaplan, B., 242
Kaplan, H., 354, 376
Karpman, B., 309
Kastenbaum, R., 398
Kaufman, I., 439
Kaufman, Y., 563
Kazdin, A., 187
Keith, S., 174
Kelly, E., 290
Kempler, W., 567
Kendall, R., 207
Keniston, K., 520–522
Kennedy, J., 633
Kennedy, W., 475
Kesey, K., 625
Kessler, J., 473
Kety, S., 145, 147, 166, 168,
    175–177, 180, 213–214, 624
Kierkegaard, S., 91, 566
Kiesler, D., 555, 558
Kilch, L., 259
Kimmel, D., 533
King, D., 557
Kingsley, L., 310
Kinsey, A., 353, 368, 369
Kirk, S., 444
Kirk, W., 457
Kittrie, N., 15–16
Klee, G., 126
Klein, M., 479
Klein, W., 541, 643
Kleinhauz, M., 536
Kleinmuntz, B., 31–32, 37,
    40, 42, 44
Klempel, H., 232
Klerman, G., 190
Klett, C., 166–167
Klopfer, B., 36
Klopfer, W., 37
Knapp, P., 289
Knapp, R., 642–643
Koegel, R., 484
Kohn, M., 115, 122, 175
Kolb, L. C., 228, 292, 325, 418,
    420–423, 535
Kolb, L. S., 372
Kopp, S., 365
Koppitz, E., 48
Korf, J., 213
Korn, S., 438
Kornetsky, C., 172
Korsakoff, S., 326, 535
Kosovsky, R., 536
Kotses, H., 291
Kotska, M., 526
Kraepelin, E., 59, 203, 463
Krafft-Ebing, R., 58
Kral, V., 534
Krasner, L., 19, 111–113, 174,
    263, 376, 571
Kreitzer, S., 642

Kremer, M., 373–375
Kringlen, E., 145, 175
Kübler-Ross, E., 381, 410

Lacey, B., 273
Lacey, J., 273
Lader, M., 241–242
Lamberti, J., 404
Langner, J., 175
Langner, T., 121–124, 126
Lapham, L., 179
Laqueur, H., 610
Larsen, E., 528
Laufer, M., 457
Laughlin, H., 253
Lawton, M., 533
Lazarus, A., 210, 482
Lehmann, H., 153–154, 157,
    169, 230
Leighton, A., 121, 126, 634
Leland, H., 434, 446
Lemere, F., 576
Lesham, E., 541
Lessac, M., 311
Levis, D., 571
Levitt, E., 36
Levy, D., 172
Levy, L., 85
Lewinsohn, P., 210
Lewis, J., 183
Liberman, R., 187
Lidz, T., 173
Liebert, R., 400
Liebman, O., 439
Lindemann, E., 396, 635–636
Lindenthal, J., 115, 118–119,
    198
Lindqvist, M., 180
Lipowski, Z., 278–281
Lipton, M., 183
Litin, E., 404
Litman, R., 388, 395, 397
Loraine, J., 372
Lorr, M., 166–167, 557
Lovaas, I., 484, 486
Lowe, J., 140
Lowen, A., 594
Lukianowicz, N., 231, 358
Lykken, D., 310
Lynn, C., 213

Maas, J., 213
MacArthur, C., 506–507
MacCulloch, M., 376
MacGregor, R., 609
MacKeith, R., 457
MacKinnon, J., 285
MacLennen, B., 499
MacMillan, D., 445–446
Mahler, M., 462
Mahoney, M., 367

Maltzberg, B., 126
Mandel, M., 179
Mandell, W., 470
Mannino, F., 472
Margolese, M., 373
Mark, V., 626
Marks, C., 539
Marks, I., 241–242, 268
Markush, R., 175
Marrone, R., 594
Martin, C., 353, 368–369
Martin, S., 204
Maser, J., 211
Maslow, A., 90–91
Masters, W., 351–354
Matarazzo, J., 47
Matte-Blanco, I., 158
May, R., 566
McCall, R., 258, 269–270
McCandless, B., 469
McClelland, D., 233
McCord, J., 310, 314
McCord, W., 310, 314
McGhee, A., 171
McKinley, J., 35
McKinney, J., 183
McKinney, W., 214–215
McManus, M., 593
McNair, D., 166–167, 557
Mednick, S., 159, 170–171
Meehl, P., 146, 147
Megenity, D., 529
Meltzer, H., 178–180
Meltzer, R., 172
Mendels, J., 192, 205–206,
    216
Menninger, K., 169, 260, 389
Merksamer, M., 594
Merrill, M., 47
Mesibov, G., 445
Mesmer, A., 60–62, 74
Meth, J., 232
Meyer, A., 635
Meyers, C., 445–446
Meyers, J., 115, 118–119, 198
Michael, J., 577
Michael, S., 121–124, 126
Mickle, W., 139
Milkovich, L., 438
Millby, J., 187
Miller, G., 539
Miller, M., 575
Miller, N., 265, 627
Milt, H., 456
Minuchin, S., 606–608
Mirsky, I., 285
Mischel, W., 312
Mitchell, D., 293
Mitchell, G., 457
Mitchell, K., 293
Mohr, J., 574

Molish, H., 36
Monks, J., 506
Montessori, M., 544
Moore, J., 58
Morel, B., 57
Moreno, J., 588–590
Morphew, J., 229
Morrison, A., 642
Morrison, J., 311
Mosher, L., 153, 174
Moustakas, C., 481
Mowrer, O., 470
Mowrer, W., 470
Mueller, R., 183
Mullens, M., 115
Munoz, R., 204
Murdock, B., 437
Murray, H., 38
Mushatt, C., 289
Muuss, R., 492
Myklebust, H., 477
Myrianthopoulos, N., 438

Nathan, P., 23
Neale, J., 400
Nemetz, S., 289
Nemiah, J., 255, 258, 269
Neugarten, B., 539
Neuringer, C., 394
Newes, N., 593
Nichols, M., 62, 586
Nickerson, M., 340
Nihira, K., 434
Niswander, K., 439
Noguchi, H., 58
Nowicki, S., 115, 506–508,
    512, 518, 523
Nowlis, H., 340
Noyes, A., 425
Nyswander, M., 337

Odegaard, S., 177
O'Gorman, G., 457
Oliveau, B., 244
Oltman, J., 312
Opler, M., 121–124, 126
Orford, F., 457
Orlinsky, D., 553, 557
Orton, S., 473
Orzek, L., 175
Osmond, H., 140, 181, 341

Palmer, S., 404
Papez, J., 134
Parloff, M., 582, 611
Parrill–Burnstein, M., 477
Pasamanick, B., 127
Pascal, G., 48
Patterson, R., 187
Pavlov, I., 92–96
Payne, R., 158, 172

Payza, A., 140
Peck, M., 385
Pemberton, J., 338
Penn, H., 179
Pepper, M., 115, 118–119, 198
Perlin, S., 389
Perline, S., 140
Perls, F., 566
Perris, C., 204
Peshkin, M., 291
Peters, A., 555
Peterson, M., 179
Phillip, R., 290–291
Pinel, P., 64–65
Pittillo, E., 248–249
Planansky, K., 226
Pless, I., 289
Polatin, D., 164
Pomeroy, W., 353, 359–360,
    368–369
Popham, R., 332
Poser, E., 642
Potter, H., 457
Prange, A., 183, 213
Pratt, J., 588
Premack, D., 98
Price, J., 179
Prince, M., 248
Pritchard, J., 438
Proctor, L., 172

Quay, H., 311, 458
Quince, T., 332

Rachman, S., 268
Racy, J., 179
Rahe, R., 174
Ramsey, J., 7
Rappaport, J., 642
Rayner, R., 94, 264, 267
Redlich, F., 120, 122, 634
Rees, L., 290
Rees, W., 293
Reich, T., 201, 203
Reifman, A., 174
Reinherz, H., 642
Reiser, D., 463
Reiser, M., 285
Reiss, B., 610
Remmen, E., 618
Rennie, T., 121–124, 126
Restak, R., 628
Richman, L., 544
Rifkin, A., 373–375
Rimland, B., 459–460, 465
Rioch, M., 641–642
Robins, E., 140, 204, 369
Robins, L., 312–313
Robinson, H., 432, 436–437,
    439, 443, 445, 447

Robinson, N., 432, 436–437,
    439, 443, 445, 447
Rodgers, D., 327
Rogers, C., 41, 88–90, 102,
    564–566, 580
Rogers, W., 457
Roman, M., 610
Romano, J., 420
Rome, H., 637
Rorschach, H., 36
Rosen, J., 186
Rosenbaum, M., 499
Rosengarten, H., 181–182
Rosenhan, D., 25–26, 28
Rosenman, R., 279
Rosenthal, D., 145, 147, 166,
    168, 175, 177
Rosow, I., 539
Ross, A., 474, 476
Rosso, P., 438
Roth, M., 534
Roth, S., 211
Rotter, J., 115
Rousseau, J., 384
Ruitenbeek, H., 588
Rutter, M., 289, 463, 465
Ryle, A., 503, 510, 515, 520

Saenger, G., 448
Saghir, M., 369
Sainsbury, P., 385
Salter, A., 573
Salzberg, P., 594
Samuels, H., 338
Sanders, R., 650
Sandt, J., 179
Sankar, B., 466
Sankar, D., 466
Sartorius, N., 154–155
Sartre, J., 566
Saslow, G., 555
Satir, V., 604–606, 608
Sawrey, W., 285
Schacht, T., 23
Schaefer, H., 332
Scheff, T., 106–109, 111–112
Scheflen, H., 186
Scherr, M., 291
Schildkraut, J., 212
Schildre, P., 403
Schlesinger, K., 327
Schmidt, C., 389
Schmidt, E., 268
Schmidt, W., 332
Schneider, K., 154
Schreiber, F., 248
Schulsinger, F., 166, 168, 175,
    311
Schumer, F., 38
Schut, D., 312
Schutz, W., 598–599

Schwartz, G., 283, 626
Seiden, R., 385, 511–512
Seidensticker, J., 254
Seligman, M., 211–212, 286
Selinsky, H., 292
Senter, R., 511
Shaffer, T., 588, 591, 593, 596, 598
Shakow, D., 159, 171
Shapiro, A., 229, 457, 555
Shapiro, D., 283, 300, 627
Shapiro, E., 229
Shapiro, R., 154–155
Shapiro, T., 465
Shaw, D., 213
Shaw, E., 181–182
Sheehy, M., 23
Shellhaas, M., 434
Shepard, T., 438
Sherman, A., 459
Shields, J., 145–146, 175, 177
Shields, M., 250
Shneidman, E., 384, 386–387, 392, 394–395, 398
Shoemaker, K., 327
Shopper, M., 500
Short, J., 390–391
Sigerist, H., 55
Sim, M., 229
Simmons, J., 128
Simon, N., 80
Simon, T., 47
Singer, M., 174
Sinnett, E., 529
Sizemore, C., 248–250
Skibbe, A., 511
Skinner, B., 96–97, 263
Slater, E., 146, 175, 177, 179, 311
Smith, D., 438, 446
Smith, K., 140
Smith, R., 183
Smythies, J., 181
Snodgrass, V., 626
Snyder, S., 180
Snyder, S. H., 391–392
Sobell, L., 332
Sobell, M., 332
Solomon, R., 99–100, 311
Speck, R., 609
Specter, G., 631–633, 636, 640
Spielberger, C., 263, 633
Spitzer, R., 20, 23
Srole, L., 121-124, 126, 634
Stahl, S., 180
Stampfl, T., 571
Staton, T., 497–498
Stauder, K., 161
Stein, L., 180
Stenzel, E., 510

Stephan, C., 447
Stephano, S., 447
Stephanson, G., 314
Stevenson, G., 337
Stewart, M., 311
Storr, A., 355, 365–366
Stove, F., 457
Stoyva, J., 627
Streissguth, A., 438
Streitman, S., 177
Strickland, B., 115
Stroh, G., 457
Stromgren, E., 176
Strupp, H., 558
Subotnik, L., 555
Suinn, R., 555
Sullivan, H., 85–87, 106, 228, 314, 494–495, 501, 639
Sundberg, N., 36
Suttell, B., 48
Sylvester, D., 244
Szara, S., 140
Szasz, T., 23, 269, 382
Szurek, S., 464

Talbott, D., 324–325
Talkington, L., 447
Tamarin, G., 289
Taylor, J., 577
Taylor, R., 624
Terman, L., 47
Terry, D., 173
Thaler, M., 285
Thigpen, C., 248
Thomas, J., 187, 533
Thorndike, E., 95
Thorndike, E. L., 47
Thorpe, D., 268
Thurber, J., 104–106
Tibbitts, C., 536
Torrey, E., 179
Toynbee, A., 395
Travis, L., 473
Tucker, B., 529
Turner, J., 643
Turner, L., 311
Tursky, B., 283
Tustin, F., 460
Tzagournis, M., 254

Ullmann, L., 19, 111–112, 174, 263, 376, 571
Umbarger, C., 642
Usdin, E., 180

Valenstein, F., 626
Vandenberg, B., 438
Van der Valk, J., 289
Van Praag, H., 167, 213
Van Putten, G., 184
Van Riper, C., 473

Venables, P., 159
Verwoerdt, A., 533
Vigil, L., 529
Voegtlin, W., 576
Vogt, D., 440
Von Brauschitsch, W., 457
Von Meduna, N., 622

Wald, E., 285
Wallace, S., 398
Wallner, J., 164–165
Walters, P., 512
Waltzer, H., 231
Ward, A., 463
Watson, J., 94, 264, 267
Watt, J., 442
Watts, J., 625
Wayne, H., 229
Weakland, J., 173
Webster, T., 528
Wechsler, D., 47–48
Weigart, F., 208–209
Weinberg, J., 534
Weinberg, S., 358
Weiner, H., 285
Weiner, I., 397
Weisman, A., 382, 398
Weisner, E., 529
Weiss, M., 404
Weiss, T., 627
Welch, A., 183
Welch, B., 183
Welner, J., 175
Wender, P., 166, 168, 175
Werry, J., 458
West, D., 407
Weyer, J., 64
White, R., 262, 442, 508
Whitehorn, J., 557
Whitmont, E., 563
Whittington, H., 523
Wikler, A., 346
Wilbur, C., 373–375
Wilde, G., 290–291
Wile, R., 465
Williams, A., 409
Wilson, J., 213
Wilson, M., 491–492, 501
Wilson, P., 20
Winder, C., 164–165
Wing, J., 159
Winick, C., 347
Winick, M., 438
Winokur, G., 201, 203
Wise, D., 180
Wohlberg, G., 172
Wolf, S., 286
Wolff, A., 528, 627
Wolff, H., 286
Wolfgang, M., 399, 403, 406
Wolman, B., 457

NAME
INDEX

Wolpe, J., 267, 570–571, 573, 577
Woltman, A., 479
Wood, A., 409
Woolley, D., 181–182
Wynne, L., 99–100, 174

Yablonsky, L., 602
Yager, J., 616
Yalom, I., 586

Yamamura, H., 180
Yasillo, N., 172
Yates, A., 471
Young, L., 183, 268
Yudkin, S., 457
Yule, N., 289

Zahn, T., 171
Zax, M., 62, 586, 631–633, 636, 640, 643

Zeller, B., 290
Zilboorg, G., 51, 54, 56–57
Zubin, J., 38
Zuckerman, M., 539
Zuk, G., 609
Zung, W., 195–196
Zunin, L., 569
Zwerdling, D., 628

SUBJECT INDEX

Abnormal behavior:
  classification of (*see also* DSM-I, DSM-II, DSM-III), 19–23
  conceptual approaches, 11–19
  diagnosis of, 19–28
  as "different," 9
  early classification of, 59
Abnormal psychology:
  components of (figure), 8
  conceptualization of, 7–10
Abreaction, 63, 74
A-B therapists, 557
Acetylcholine, 133, 147
Acquisition, 93
A.C.S.W. (*see* Psychiatric social worker)
Acute brain syndrome, 420, 422
Acute depression, 197
Acute mania, 192, 194, 195
Acute schizophrenia, 164, 166, 170–171, 182, 185
Addiction, physiological, 318 (*see also* Alcoholism, Drug abuse)
Addison's disease, 137
Adolescence:
  as delay of adulthood, 497
  disorders of, 488–492
  Erikson's stages of development in, 495–496
  group-delinquency reaction in, 490
  group therapy in, 499–500
  guidelines for therapy in, 498–499
  identity crisis in, 495
  individual therapy in, 497–498
  normal abnormality, 493
  reeducational counseling in, 497
  situational counseling in, 497
  suicide in, 491
  theories of, 492–497
  treatment of disorders in, 497–501
Adolescent crisis, 491–492
Adolescent psychotherapy, 497

Adoption studies of schizophrenia, 175–177
Adrenal corticoids, 137
Adrenal glands, 137
Adrenaline, 136
Adrenochrome, 140
Affective personality, 301
Affective psychoses (*see also* Depression, Mania):
  alternative classifications of, 204, 206
  description, 190, 191–192
  DSM-II, 192–204
  treatment, 215–217
Aging, theories of, 536–540
Agitated depression, 195
Agitation, 617
Agoraphobia, 245
Ailurophobia, 245
Al-Anon, 330, 601
Ala-Tot, 330, 601
Alcoholic paranoia, 326
Alcoholics Anonymous (AA), 328–330, 600–601
Alcoholism:
  aversive conditioning, 576
  behavioral therapy, 330–331
  consequences, 325
  degrees of, 321–323
  demographic data, 321
  drugs in treatment of, 620
  explanations of, 326–327
  genetic factors, 327
  withdrawal, 324–325
Alzheimer's disease, 423
Ambivalence, 146
American Association on Mental Deficiency, 432–434
American Law Institute, Model Penal Code of, definition of insanity, 16
American Psychiatric Association, 9, 20, 270, 273, 300, 368

SUBJECT
INDEX

Amnesia:
  and alcoholism, 326
  and electroconvulsive therapy, 217
  and hysteria, 63, 246
Amobarbital, 620
Amphetamines, 339–340
Amygdala, 626
Amygdalectomy, 626
Anal phase, 80
Analysand, 561
Anesthesia, tactual, 356
Anhedonia, 146
Animal magnetism, 60
Anna O., case of, 63
Anorexia nervosa, 254
Anoxia, 439
Antidepressants, 147–148, 212–213, 216–217, 617–618
Antimanic drugs, 618–619
Antipsychotic drugs, 180, 185, 615–617
Antisocial behavior, treatment for, 626
Antisocial personality (see also Psychopathy), 307
Anxiety:
  conflict theory, 265–266
  description, 239–240
  existential, 91–92
  free-floating, 242
  learning view of, 263–265
  neuroses, 237–238, 260–261
  panic reaction, 242
  paranoia, 228
  physiological symptoms (table), 274
  psychoanalytic view, 261–263
  Rogers' view, 90
  in schizophrenia, 170
  and sexual arousal, 254
  Sullivan's view, 85–87
  treatment:
    behavior modification, 267–268, 570–572
    biofeedback, 268, 626–627
    drug therapy, 267
    psychotherapy, 267
Anxiety attack, 242
Anxiety-blissfulness psychosis, 232–233
Anxiety neurosis, 241–243
Apathy reaction, 508
Apraxia, 471
Arteriosclerosis (see Coronary heart disease)
Arteriosclerotic dementia, 535
Asceticism, 493
Assertion training, 572–574
Assessment techniques (see also Personality assessment):
  for brain damage, 47–49
  for intelligence, 47
  for personality, 31–46
Astasia-abasia, 252
Asthenic personality, 205, 303–304
Asthma, 288–291
Atypical cycloid psychoses, 232–233

Authenticity, 566
Autism (see Early infantile autism)
Autistic communication, 85
Autonomic nervous system, 134–136, 253
Autoscopic experience, 231
Aversive conditioning, 575–576
  and alcoholism, 330
  and homosexuality, 375–376
Avoidance learning: 100, 264
Awareness:
  intelligent, 567
  psychophysical, 567
Axon, 131–133

Barbital, 620
Barbiturates, 269, 620
Barnum effect, 555–556
Basedow's disease, 137
Behavior therapy:
  and alcoholism, 330–331
  and autism, 484, 486
  for college students, 526–527
  emotive imagery in, 482–484
  for groups, 593–594
  for mentally retarded persons, 447
  and migraine headache, 293
  and neuroses, 267–268
  and schizophrenia, 187
  and sexual deviations, 366–367
  and token reinforcement systems, 481–482
Behavioral theories (see Learning views; Learning theories)
Bender Visual Motor Gestalt Test, 47, 49 (figure), 419
Benton Visual Retention Test, 48, 49 (figure), 419
Benzedrine, 339
Benzodiazepine compounds, 619–628
Bestiality, 359
Bilateral prefrontal lobotomy, 625
Bilirubin, 439
Biochemical factors:
  in alcoholism, 327
  in childhood psychosis, 466
  in depression, 212–214
  in schizophrenia, 147, 178–182
Bioenergetic groups, 594–595
Biofeedback:
  and anxiety disorders, 268, 627
  description, 626–627
  and hypertension, 283–284
  and migraine headaches, 293
  and psychophysiological disorders, 627
Black Rage, 283
Body language, 568
Brain damage, assessment of, 47–49
Brain syndromes:
  acute versus chronic (table), 421
  deficits, 418–420
  family counseling, 429
  infection, 423

Brain syndromes (continued)
  toxic factors, 423
  tumor, 427
  vitamin deficiency, 427
Brain waves:
  and asthma, 289–290
  and psychopathy, 311
Brawner rule, 16
Butyrophenones, 185, 616

Cannabis sativa, 343
Cannula, 147
Capgras' syndrome, 232
Cardial arrythmias, 627
Cardiovascular disorders:
  coronary heart disease, 277–281
  essential hypertension, 281–284
Castration anxiety, 81
Cataplexy, 426
Catatonia, 232
Catatonic schizophrenia, 161
Catecholamines:
  in depression, 212–214, 392
  description, 216–217
  in schizophrenia, 183
Catharsis, 74, 587
Central nervous system, 131, 133–134
Cerebral insufficiency, 422 (see also Brain syndromes)
Ceruloplasmin, 139
Chemical therapy (see Drug therapy)
Childhood disorders:
  behavioral treatment, 480–485
  eating, 467–468
  elimination, 468–470
  learning, 474–478
  play therapy, 479–481
  psychoses, 456–463
  school phobia, 475–476
  sleep, 466, 467
  speech, 472–474
  thumbsucking, 471–472
  tics, 470–471
Childhood psychoses:
  behavioral treatment, 484–486
  description, 456–457
  genetic factors, 464–465
  learning view, 464
  psychoanalytic theory, 463–464
Childhood schizophrenia:
  biological factors, 465–466
  description, 457–458
  GAP diagnostic criteria, 457–458
Chlordiazepoxide, 619–620
Chlorpromazine (Thorazine), 185, 227, 615–616
Chromosomal aberrations in mental retardation, 435–436
Chronic brain syndrome, 421, 423–427
Chronic schizophrenia, 166, 171, 182
Chum relationship, 494
Cingulate gyrus, 626

Cingulectomy, 626
Cirrhosis of liver, 321
Clang association, 162
Classical conditioning, 92–96, 100, 171, 576
Client-centered therapy, 186, 564–565
Clinical psychologist, 559–560
Cocaine, 338–339
Codeine, 333
Cognitive deficits:
  brain damage, 418–420
  schizophrenia, 157–159
Cognitive theories of depression and mania, 209
Colectomy, 288
Colitis, 287–288
College students:
  apathy reaction in, 508
  behavior therapy, 526–527
  as being in stage of life called "youth," 520–522
  career crisis, 517–518
  classification of disorders, 506–507
  community approach to problems, 527–529
  competition reaction in, 518–519
  conceptualization of stage of life, 519–522
  disorders of, 504–519
  disorders of academic mechanics, 513–516
  disorders associated with academic progress, 516–519
  disorders of nonacademic personal concerns, 507–513
  frequency of disorders in, 503
  freshman adjustment reaction, 516
  greatest problems, 507
  group therapy, 525–526
  identity crisis, 508
  individual therapy, 525
  protracted adolescence, 519–520
  senior anticipatory adulthood reaction, 518
  study disabilities, 514–515
  suicide, 508
  suicide prevention, 511
  treatment for disorders, 522–529
  view of insanity, 504–505
Coma, in brain syndrome, 422
Communication deficits in schizophrenia, 173, 186
Community Mental Health Center Act, 633
Community psychology:
  on college campuses, 527–529
  growth-promoting forces, 634–637
  history of movement, 631–633
  inhibiting factors, 636–638
  paraprofessionals, 640–643, 650–651
  preventive programs, 646–650
Compulsive neuroses, 255–258
Concordance, 144
Concordance rate, 175–177
Concussion, 422
Conditioned emotional response, 95
Conditioned response, 93
Conditioned stimulus, 93

Confessions of an Opium Eater, 332
Conflict theory of anxiety, 265–266
Confusional psychosis, 232
Confusional states in the elderly, 534
Congruence, 565
Conjoint family therapy, 604–606
Conscious, definition, 75
Consciousness, levels of, 76
Consensual validation, 86
Conversion hysteria, 248–255
Convulsions, 619
Coprolalia, 229
Coprophagy, 468
Coronary heart disease, 277–281
Covert reinforcement, 576
Covert sensitization:
    and alcoholism, 330–331
    description, 576
    and sexual deviations, 367
Creatine phosphokinase (CPK), 178
Cretinism, 136–137
Cross-tolerance in opiates, 337
Crowding, 127
Curare, 622
Cushing's disease, 137

Daseinsanalyse, 566
Death instinct, 388
Death, stages of, 381, 410
Defense mechanisms (*see also* Ego):
    definition, 78
    in neuroses, 240, 261
    types (table), 79
Delirious mania, 192, 195
Delirium:
    in acute brain syndrome, 420, 422
    drug-induced, 423
Delirium tremens, 325
Delusions:
    contagious, 230–231
    in depression, 197, 200
    in mania, 194–195
    in paranoia, 220–225, 233
    in schizophrenia (table), 158
Dementia, 421
Dementia praecox, 59
Dendrites, 131–133
Denial, in alcoholism, 328
Dependence, psychological, 318 (*see also* Drug
    abuse)
Depression:
    adaptive aspects, 190–191
    biochemical factors, 212–214
    biopsychological model, 214–215
    drug treatment, 617–618
    electroconvulsive therapy, 622–623
    explanations of:
        cognitive, 209
        learned helplessness, 210–212
        neural transmission, 212–214
        reduced reinforcement, 208–210

Depression (*continued*)
    involutional melancholia, 200
    neurotic versus psychotic (table), 259
    postpartum, 201–208
    psychoanalytic view, 207–208
    rating scale for, 196
    and suicide, 388
Depressive disorder, DSM-III criteria (table), 24
Depressive neurosis, 258–259
Depressive psychosis, 195–197
Depressive stupor, 197
Dereism, 146
Detachment level, 123–124
Developmental subtasks (Erikson), 295–296
Deviance:
    society's role in producing, 106–107
    sociological view, 128
Diabetes, 327
Diagnosis of abnormal behavior, hazards of,
    23–28
Diagnostic and Statistical Manual of Mental
    Disorders (*see* DSM-I; DSM-II; DSM-III)
Diathesis-stress theory, 146–147
    of suicide, 177
Diazepam, 619–620
Direct analysis, 186–187
Discordance, 144
Discrimination learning, 94, 576
Disease model, 18
Displacement, 82
Dissociation neuroses, 246–248
District of Columbia Court of Appeals, 16
Dizygotic twins, 144–145
Dopamine:
    chemical structure, 181
    in schizophrenia, 180, 183–184
Dopamine-B-hydroxylase, 180
Dopamine-norepinephrine-imbalance
        hypothesis of schizophrenia, 180
Double-bind hypothesis of schizophrenia, 173
Down's syndrome, 436
Dream analysis, 563
Dreams, 563–564
Drive reduction, 97–98, 265
Drug abuse:
    alcohol, 320–332
    amphetamines, 339–340
    barbiturates, 340–341
    cocaine, 338–339
    marijuana, 343–344
    opiates, 332–338
    psychedelics, 341–343
Drugs:
    generic and trade names (table), 617
    side effects of, 616, 618, 619
Drug therapy:
    antidepressants, 216–217, 617–618
    antimanic drugs, 618–619
    antipsychotic drugs, 615–617
    for anxiety, 619–621
    dangers, 269

Drug therapy (*continued*)
  for depression, 216–217
  effects on hospitalization, 613–614
  for migraine headache, 293
  for mania, 213, 217
  for paranoid conditions, 227–228
  for neuroses, 269
  for schizophrenia, 185–186
Drug use:
  degrees of, 318–319
  genetic factors, 345
  summary of symptoms (figure), 334–335
  trifactorial-interactional theory, 344–346
DSM-I, 20
DSM-II, 20–22, 23, 488, 491
  affective psychoses, 203–204
  categories (table), 21
  drug use, 318
  manic-depressive illness (table), 24, 192–204
  paranoia, 220
  personality disorders, 300–304
  problems with, 20–22
  psychophysiological disorders, 273
  schizophrenia, 164, 166, 167
  socialization disturbances, 307
  unclassified types, 229
DSM-III, 20, 22–23, 28
  concept of neurosis, 270
  multiaxial (table), 22
  depressive disorder (table), 24
  schizophrenia, 164
Dual-process theory, 99
Duplicitous communication, 579
Durham rule, 15, 16
Dyspnea, 288
Dyspraxia, 471
Dyssocial personality, 307

Early infantile autism:
  behavioral treatment, 484, 486
  contrasted with childhood schizophrenia
    (table), 460
  description, 458–462
  learning view, 464
  psychoanalytic theory, 463–464
  special abilities, 459
Eating disturbances, 468
Echolalia, 160
Echopraxia, 156
ECT (*see* Electroconvulsive therapy)
EEG (*see* Electroencephalogram)
Ego, 75, 77–78
Ego analysis, 207
Ego boundaries, schizophrenia, 155
Ego ideal, 77
Ego psychology (*see* Neo-Freudianism)
Ejaculatory disturbances, 352, 353
Elderly persons:
  arteriosclerotic dementia in, 535
  common symptoms of disturbance, 533

Elderly persons (*continued*)
  confused states, 534
  depressive states, 534
  disorders among, 532–536
  functional disorders, 532–534
  group therapy, 541–542
  music therapy, 546
  normally occurring deviations, 533
  organic disorders, 534–536
  paranoid persecutory states, 534
  reality orientation, 546
  reasons for avoidance of treatment, 540
  sensory stimulation therapy, 546
  therapeutic communities, 546
  treatments for disorders, 540–546
Electra complex, 81–82, 374
Electroconvulsive therapy (ECT):
  depression, 217
  description, 622–625
Electroencephalogram (EEG), and asthma,
  289–290
Electromyograph, 627
Electroshock therapy (*see* Electroconvulsive
  therapy)
Elimination disturbances, 468–470
EMG (*see* Electromyograph)
Emotional disorders (*see* Mania; Depression)
Encephalitis, 440
Encopresis, 468
Encounter groups, 598–600
Endocrine glands, 137
Endocrine system, 136–138
  functions (table), 138
Enuresis, 467, 470
Epidemiological investigation, 121
Epilepsy, 424–426, 622
Epinephrine, 136
Erectile dysfunction (*see* Impotence)
Ergotamine tartrate, 293
Erythroxylon coca, 338
Esalen Institute, 598, 600
Essential hypertension, 281–284
Eugenics, 141
Eve, case of, 248–250
Exhibitionism, 360–362
Existential anxiety, 92
Existential theories of behavior, 90–92
Existential therapy, 564–569
Exorcism, 52
Experiential view of abnormality, 16–18
Experimental neurosis, 96
Explosive personality, 304
Extinction, 93

Family therapies, 604–610
Fear hierarchy, 571
Fecal retention, 468–469
Federal Bureau of Investigation, 401
Fetishism, 356
Fixations, 80
Flashbacks with LSD use, 343

Flicker threshold, 205
Flooding, 268, 571
Folie à deux, 230–231
Food and Drug Administration, 619
Forensic psychiatry, 16
Free association, 74, 561
Free-floating anxiety, 242
Frigidity, 353
Frontalis muscle, 627
Frottage, 360
Fugue states in hysteria, 246–247
Functional disorder:
    definition, 22
    in the elderly, 532–534
    problems in living, 25

Gamblers Anonymous, 330
Ganglia, 134–135
Ganser's syndrome, 229–230
GAP (see Group for the Advancement of Psychiatry)
Gastric ulcer, 284–286
Gastrointestinal disorders, 284–288
Generalization of anxiety, 264
General paresis, 57–59, 424
Genetic factors:
    in affective psychoses, 145
    in alcoholism, 137
    in childhood psychoses, 464–465
    in depression, 213–214
    in drug abuse, 345
    in emotionality, 143
    in feeblemindedness, 142–143
    in mental retardation, 435–437
    in psychopathy, 311
    in schizophrenia, 144–147, 175–177
Genital stage, 82
Gerontology, 536
Gestalt therapy, 566–569
Gilles de la Tourette's syndrome, 229, 616
Grand mal seizures, 425–426
Grandma's rule, 98
Group for the Advancement of Psychiatry (GAP), on childhood disorders, 20, 455–456
Group therapy:
    with adolescents, 499–500
    Alcoholics Anonymous, 600–601
    behavior modification, 593–594
    bioenergetic, 594
    with college students, 525–526
    curative factors, 586–587
    description, 585, 586
    with the elderly, 541
    encounter, 598–600
    marathon, 595–596
    psychoanalytic, 588–589
    psychodrama, 590–591
    Synanon, 601–603
    T-groups, 596–598

Habituation, 267, 364
Hair-pulling, 472
Haldol (see Haloperidol)
Hallucinations:
    and alcohol withdrawal, 324–325
    and mania, 194–195
    and schizophrenia, 157, 170
Haloperidol, 180, 229, 616
Hashish, 344
Headaches, 290–293, 627
Head-banging, 472
Heart attack (see Coronary heart disease)
Hebephrenic schizophrenia, 162, 204
Hematophobia, 245
Heritability, 144
Heroin, 333, 336, 337, 338
High blood pressure (essential hypertension), 281–284
Higher-order conditioning (figure), 94
High-risk studies of schizophrenia, 177
Homeostasis, 76
Homosexuality:
    aversive conditioning, 375–376
    cross-cultural studies, 368–369
    description, 368
    DSM-II, 368
    explanations, 372–374
    genetic factors, 372
    male versus female, 369
    paranoia, 225–226
    psychopathology, 375
Hormones, 136
Hospitalization, 216, 227
Humanistic theory of personality:
    and neurosis, 90
    and psychosis, 90
Humanistic therapies, 564–565
Huntington's chorea, 427
Hydraulic model, 84
Hyperactivity and psychopathy, 311
Hyperesthesia, 251, 252
Hypertension (see Essential hypertension)
Hyperventilation, 288
Hypnosis, 62–63, 74
Hypnotic drugs, 619
Hypochondriasis, 260
Hypomania, 192–193, 194
Hysteria:
    early approaches, 60–63
    history, 245–246
    psychoanalytic view, 74
    treatment, historical, 54
Hysterical aphonia, 253
Hysterical neurosis:
    conversion type, 248–254
    description, 245–246
    dissociative type, 246–248
Hysterical personality, 246, 302–303

Id, 76–78, 82, 169
Identity crisis, 87, 495, 508

Ileostomy, 288
Illusion of fusion, 579
Imipramine (Tofranil), 269, 617–618
Implosion, 571
Impotence, 351–353, 354–355
Incest, 357–358
Incidence, 118–119
Individual therapy:
　with adolescents, 497–498
　behavioral therapies, 569–577
　with college students, 523–525
　general overview, 552–560
　humanistic-existential therapy, 564–569
　psychoanalytic therapies, 560–564
Indoleamines in depression and mania, 213–216
Infantile psychosis, 463
Infection:
　and meningitis in brain pathology, 423
　and mental retardation, 438
　and syphilis in brain pathology, 424
Insanity, legal definition, 15–16
Intellectual deficits (see Cognitive deficits; Mental retardation)
Intellectualization, 493
Intelligence tests, 47
Interpersonal theory (Sullivan), 85–87
Interviewing, 41–43, 46
Intractable abnormality, 625–626
Introjection, 77
Involutional melancholia, 200
Involutional paraphrenia, 225

Jacksonian seizure, 426
Joint Commission of Mental Illness and Health, 68

Kaiserian therapy, 579–580
Kallikak family, 140–143
Kernicterus, 439
Korsakoff's psychosis, 326

Labeling, 107, 109, 113, 128
　and violation of expectations, 112–114
Labeling theory (see Societal-reaction theory)
"La belle indifference," 250
La Bicetre, 65
Latency phase, 82
Latent prevalence, 120–121
Latent schizophrenia, 163–164
Law of effect, 97
Lead poisoning, 423
Learned helplessness model of depression, 210–212
Learning disabilities, 476–478
Learning disturbances in children, 474–478
Learning theory:
　and abnormal behavior, 19
　and alcoholism, 327
　and anxiety neuroses, 263–265
　of behavior, 92–101

Learning theory (continued)
　of childhood psychoses, 464
　and depression, 209–210
　and homosexuality, 374
　and murder, 404
　and neurosis, 100
　and phobias, 98–100
　and schizophrenia, 174, 187
　and suicide, 389–390
Legal view of abnormality, 14
Lesbianism (see Homosexuality)
Leucotomy, 625
Libido, 76
Librium, 340
Life events, 115–120
　and likelihood of pathology (table), 119
　types of (table), 117–118
Limbic system, 134, 626
Lithium carbonate, 213, 217, 619
Lithium salts, 618–619
Little Albert, 264
Lobotomy, 625
Locus of control of reinforcement, 115
Logorrhea, 192
LSD (lysergic acid diethylamide), 180, 182, 341, 343
Lycanthropy, 55

Mainstreaming, 444
Malleus Maleficarum, 54, 251
Mania, 56, 191–195, 208–210, 212–214
Manic-depressive psychosis, 59, 206–209
　in childhood, 203
　circular type, 197–198
　depressive type, 195–197
　description, 192
　DSM-II guidelines (table), 24
　familial aspects, 192
　manic type, 192–195
Marathon groups, 595–596
Marijuana, 343–344
Marital schism, 173
Marital skew, 173
Mask of Sanity, 307
Masochism, 363
Masturbation, 472
Melancholia, 56 (see also Depression)
Memory impairment and brain damage, 418–419
Memory loss (see Amnesia)
Meningitis, 440
Mental hospitals:
　atmosphere, 27–28
　history and nature, 64–68
　reform, 67–68
Mental retardation:
　behavior therapy and, 447
　definition, 432–434
　environmental causes, 437–440
　genetic factors, 435–437
　levels of, 434–435

Mental Retardation (*continued*)
  mainstreaming, 444–445
  residential treatment for, 447–449
  sociocultural factors, 440–442
  special education, 442–444
  symptoms, 432
Meprobamate, 269, 619–620 (*see also* Miltown)
Mescaline, 180, 181, 341
Metabolic problems, 140
Methadone, for heroin addiction, 337
Methamphetamine (methedrine), 340
Methedrine, 340
Metrazol, 622
Migraine headaches:
  behavior methods of treatment for, 293
  drug therapy, 293
  psychogenic factors, 292–293
  symptoms, 291–292
Milieu therapy:
  and alcoholism, 330
  and psychopathy, 314
  and schizophrenia, 184–185
Miltown, 340 (*see also* Meprobamate)
Minnesota Multiphasic Personality Inventory
  (MMPI), 34–35
M'Naughton rules, 15
Modeling, 101
Models:
  definition, 11
  descriptive versus explanatory, 11, 18
Models of abnormality:
  behavioral, 19
  cultural-situational, 13–14
  "disease," 18–19
  experiential, 16–18
  legal, 14–16
  statistical, 11–13
Molindone, 616–617
Monamine-oxidase (MAO) inhibitors, 212, 618
Mongolism, 436
Monozygotic twins, 144–146, 179
Moral-treatment programs, 66–67
Morphine, 333, 337
Motility psychosis, 232
Motor disturbances:
  cycloid psychoses, 232
  hysteria, 252–253
Mourning and Melancholia, 207
M.S.W. (*see* Psychiatric social worker)
Mucous colitis, 287
Multiple personality, 247–250
Murder:
  descriptive statistics, 400–401
  followed by suicide, 407
  and frustration, 404
  insanity, 401
  legal definition, 400
  modeling theory, 405
  psychoanalytic theory, 404–405, 409
  sociocultural factors, 403–404
Murder-suicide syndrome, 407–410

Muscle relaxation, 628
Music therapy, 546
Mutism, 160, 473–474
Myocaridal infarction, 277

Narcolepsy, 426
Narcotics, 332–338
National Commission on Marihuana and Drug
  Abuse, 317, 318
National Committee for Mental Hygiene, 67
National Institute of Alchohol Abuse and Al-
  coholism, 321–323
National Institute of Mental Health (NIMH), 7,
  188, 217
Necrophilia, 359
Need hierarchy (Maslow), 90, 91 (figure)
Negative practice, 577
Neoanalysis, 208–209
Neo-Freudianism, 85–88
Neo-Freudian theory of anxiety neurosis, 262–
  263
Neologisms, 160, 183
Neoplasm (*see* Tumor)
Nervous system, 131–136
  (table), 131
  and schizophrenia, 178
Neurasthenia, in DSM-II, 259
Neurohumoral transmission theory, 133
Neurons, 131–132, 147
  (figure), 132
Neuroses:
  as diagnostic category, 269–270
  experimental, 96
  explanations:
    conflict theory, 265–267
    learning, 263–265
    neo-Freudian, 262–263
    psychoanalytic, 84–85, 261–262
  Rogers' view, 90
  as self-defeating, 240
  and social class, 120
  Sullivan's view, 87
  treatment:
    behavior modification, 767-769
    biofeedback, 268
    drug therapy, 268–269, 570
    psychotherapy, 268
  types:
    anxiety, 241–243
    compulsive, 255–258
    depressive, 258–259
    hysterical, 245–254
    obsessive, 255
    phobias, 243–245
Neurotics Anonymous, 330
Neurotransmitters:
  in depression, 212–214
  effects on eating and drinking, 147
  implantation of, 147
  neutral stimulus, 93
  and psychopathology, 133, 180, 624

Night terrors, 467
Nightmares, 467
Nonassertiveness, 573
Norepinephrine:
  chemical structure, 181
  and depression, 212–214
  and psychopathology, 133, 147
  and schizophrenia, 180, 183–184
Norms, 33

Obscene communications, 363
Observation:
  controlled sampling, 44–45
  direct, 43–44
  naturalistic, 44, 46
Observational learning, 100–101
  of phobias, 101
Obsessive-compulsive personality, 206, 303
Obsessive neurosis, 255
Odd Couple, The, 80
Oedipal phase, 80–81
Oedipal stage and homosexuality, 373
Operant conditioning:
  in depression, 209–210
  description, 96–100
  as therapy, 574–575
Opium, 332–333, 337
Oral stage, 80, 169, 206–207
Organic brain syndrome (*see* Brain syndromes)
Organic disorders, definition, 21
Orgasmic dysfunction, 351–353
Oxazepam, 620

Panic reaction, 242
Paranoia:
  as adaptive, 233
  and alcoholism, 326
  and amphetamines, 340
  and niacin deficiency, 417
Paranoid conditions:
  description, 220–221
  developmental factors, 226
  psychoanalytic view, 225–226
  treatments, 227–229
Paranoid eroticism, 225
Paranoid litigious state, 224–225
Paranoid persecutory states, 534
Paranoid personality, 300–301
Paranoid pseudocommunity, 226–227
Paranoid schizophrenia, 162–163, 223, 227
Paranoid state, 223–224
Paraprofessionals, 640–643, 650–651
Parasympathetic nervous system, 131, 134–136
Parkinsonism, 626
Parkinson's disease, 179, 427
Pastoral counselor, 560
Pedophilia, 359
Pellagra, 427
Penis envy, 82
Pentobarbital, 620
Pepsin, 285

Perception deficits in schizophrenia, 157
Peripheral nervous system, 131, 134–136
Personality assessment, 31–46
  by interviewing, 40–43
  by observation, 43–45
  psychological tests, 32–40
Personality development:
  interpersonal style, 314–315
  interpersonal theory, 85–87
  tension reduction modes, 305
Personality disorders, 301–304
Petit mal seizures, 426
Peyote (mescaline), 341
Phallic stage, 80
Phenobarbital, 620
Phenomenological theories (*see* Existential theories)
Phenothiazine, 185, 227
Phenothiazine derivatives, 615–617
Phenylalanine, 437
Phenylketonuria (PKU), 436–437
Phobias:
  description and prevalence, 244
  learning view of, 95, 99–101
  types, 244–245
  (table), 245
Phoenix House, 338
Phrenitis, 56
Physical therapies for abnormality, 613–629
  biofeedback, 626–627
  drug therapies, 613–621
  electroconvulsive therapy, 622–625
  psychosurgery, 625–626
Pica, 468
Pick's disease, 424
Pituitary gland, 136
Placebo effect, 555–556
Planned communities, 646–647
Play therapy:
  description, 479
  nondirective, 480–481
  psychoanalytic, 479–480
  relationship, 481
  with retarded children, 446
Pleasure principle, 76
Postpartum depression, 201–202
Preaddictive personality, 345
Preadolescence, 494
Preconscious, definition, 75–76
Pre-discharge groups, 541
Premature birth, 439
Premature ejaculation, 351–352, 354–355
Prevalence, 118–119
Prevention of mental illness, 638–639, 646–650
Primal pain, 578
Primal scream, 578
Primal therapy, 577–578
Primary deviance, 106
Primary drives, 263
Primary personality, 247–248, 249, 250
Primary prevention, 638, 646–648

Primary-process thought, 169, 170
Primary versus secondary process thought, 77
Principle of prepotency, 98
Proband, 144
Process schizophrenia, 164–165
Progressive relaxation, 570
Projective techniques, 35–40, 46
Propfhebephrenic psychosis, 463
Pseudocyesis, 253–254
Pseudo-memory in alcoholism, 326
Pseudoneurotic schizophrenia, 164
Psilocybin, 181, 341
Psychasthenia, 63
Psyche, 76
Psychedelic drugs, 341–343
Psychiatric nurse, 560
Psychiatric social worker, 560
Psychiatrist, 559, 620–621
Psychic determinism, 566
Psychic triumvirate, 76
Psychoactive drugs, 613, 621, 628 (see also Drug therapy)
Psychoanalysis, 186, 560–563
Psychoanalytic Review, 126
Psychoanalytic theory:
    and alcoholism, 326–327
    and anxiety neurosis, 261–262
    and asthma, 289
    of behavior, 75–85
    and childhood psychoses, 463–464
    and depression and mania, 206–207, 208
    history of, 74–75
    and homosexuality, 373
    and murder, 404–405, 409
    and neurosis, 84–85
    and paranoid conditions, 225–226
    psychic triumvirate in, 76–79
    of psychosexual development, 79–82
    and psychosis, 82–83
    and schizophrenia, 169–170
    and suicide, 388–389, 409
Psychoanalytic therapies:
    analytical psychotherapy, 563–564
    psychoanalysis, 560–563
Psychochemotherapy (see Drug therapy)
Psychodrama, 590–591
Psychogenetics, 143
Psychological tests (see Assessment techniques;
    Personality assessment)
Psycholytic agent, LSD as, 343
Psychoneuroses (see Neuroses)
Psychopathy:
    authoritarian milieu therapy, 314
    classifications of, 309
    cortical underarousal, 310–311
    description, 307, 309–311
    explanations:
        biological, 311
        family characteristics (table), 311–312
        psychoanalytic, 311
    genetic factors, 311

Psychopathy (continued)
    hyperactivity, 311
    underarousal, 310–311
Psychophysiological disorders:
    cardiovascular, 277–284
    description, 272, 275–276
    in DSM-II, 273, 277
    gastrointestinal, 284–288
    headaches, 291–293
    respiratory, 288–291
    target organ systems, 273
    treatment with biofeedback, 626–627
Psychosexual development, 79–82, 206
Psychosexual stages, 80–82
Psychosis (see also Affective psychoses; Child-
        hood psychosis; Paranoid psychoses;
        Schizophrenia):
    drug treatment, 620
    psychoanalytic view, 82, 83
    Rogers' view, 90
    social class and, 120
    sociological view, 115
    Sullivan's view, 87
Psychosocial stages, Erikson's (table), 87
Psychosurgery, 625–628
Psychotherapists, choice of, 582
Psychotherapy (see also Group psychotherapy;
        Individual psychotherapy):
    analytical, 563–564
    client variables, 557–558
    outcome studies of, 553–555
    placebo and Barnum effects, 555–556
    process studies of, 555–559
    therapeutic relationships, 558–559
    therapist variables, 556–557
    schizophrenia, 186–187
    YAVIS pattern in, 558
Psychotic depressive reaction, 24, 198, 200
Psychotomimetic drugs, 341–343

Rape, 364–365
Rational-emotive therapy, 580–581
Rauwolfia alkaloids, 616
Reaction formation, 78–79
Reactive depression, 200–201, 210
Reactive mania, 204
Reactive schizophrenia, 164–165
Reality principle, 77
Reality testing, 562
Reality therapy, 569
Reciprocal inhibition, 267, 482, 570
Regression:
    description, 83–84
    in schizophrenia, 169–170
Reinforcement:
    definition, 97
    effects on behavior, 98, 99 (figure)
Reinforcement schedules, types (table), 97, 98
Reinforcement theory (see Learning theory)

Relaxation training:
  and asthma, 290–291
  and migraine headache, 293
Reliability, 33
Remotivation groups, 541
Repression, 76
Residential Youth Center, 648–649
Residual deviance, 108–109
Residual rules, 108
Respiratory disorders:
  asthma, 288–291
  dyspnea, 288
  hyperventilation, 288
Respondent conditioning (see Classical conditioning)
Restitutional symptoms, 170
Retarded ejaculation, 353
Robinson v. California, 336
Role identity in adolescence, 491
Rorschach inkblot test, 36–38
Rubella and mental retardation, 438
Rumination syndrome, 468

Sadism, 363, 364
Sadomasochism, 363
St. Mary's of Bethlehem, 64
Salem witch trials, 55
Satiation, 577
Schema, 209
Schizo-affective schizophrenia, 164
Schizoid personality, 302
Schizophrenia:
  adoption studies, 145, 175–177
  affective dysfunctions, 159–160
  alternative classifications of, 164, 166–167
  arousal problems, 170–171
  behavioral dysfunctions, 155–157
  biochemical factors, 140, 178–182
  childhood, 457–458; 465–466
  cognitive dysfunctions, 157–159
  communication deficits, 173
  core characteristics, 154, 155 (table)
  definition, 153
  diagnostic subtypes, 161–164
  dopamine hypothesis, 180
  drug therapy, 615–617
  explanations:
    attentional-interference, 171–173
    diathesis-stress, 177
    double-bind hypothesis, 173
    learning, 174
    psychoanalytic, 169–170
    social-stress, 174–175
  family pathology, 173–174
  genetic factors (table), 176
  high-risk studies, 177
  neuromuscular dysfunction, 178–179
  perceptual dysfunctions, 157

Schizophrenia (continued)
  prevalence, 153
  regression in, 169–170
  sociocultural factors, 174–175, 177
  spectrum classification, 166–167, 168 (table), 175
  speech problems, 160–161, 170
  Sullivan's view of, 87
  symptom-cluster approach, 166, 167 (table)
  symptoms, 24
  thought disturbances, 158–159, 162
  transmethylation hypothesis, 180–182
  treatment, 184–187, 615–617, 622–623
  twin studies, 144–147, 175–176
  viral hypothesis, 179
Schizophrenia spectrum, 166–167, 176
Schizophreniform psychoses, 176
Schizophrenogenic mother, 146
Schizotaxia, 146, 177
Schizotypic personality, 146
School phobia, 475–476
Scoptophilia, 362
Secondary deviance, 106
Secondary drives, 263
Secondary gain, 251–252, 260
Secondary personality, 247–248
Secondary prevention, 638–639, 648–649
Security operations, 86–87
Sedatives, 620
Seizures, epileptic, 425–426
Self–actualization, 88
Self-esteem, and depression, 207
Self-report inventories, 34–35, 45–46
Senile dementia, subtypes, 535
Sensory stimulation therapy, 543–546
Serial compulsions, 256–257
Serotonin:
  and depression, 213–214
  and mania, 213–214
  and schizophrenia, 181–184
Sexual deviations, 357–365
Sexual dysfunctions, 351–355
Shaping, 96
Simple depression, 195
Simple schizophrenia, 163
Skinner box, 96
Sleep disturbances, 466, 467
  drug treatment, 620
Sleepwalking, 247
Social class:
  and diagnosed mental illness (table), 120
  and labeling, 109
  and likelihood of pathology, 121–123
  and locus of control, 115
  and murder, 403–404
  and schizophrenia, 175
  and severity of symptoms (table), 122
Social isolation, 127
Socialization disturbances, 307–311
Socialization groups, 541
Societal-reaction theory, 106–111

Sociocultural factors (*see also* Social class; Sociological factors and rates of abnormal behavior):
 in coronary heart disease, 280
 in depression, 192, 198
 in drug use, 345
 in mania, 192, 198
 in mental retardation, 440–442
 in murder, 403–404
 in schizophrenia, 175
Socioenvironmental theory, 114–118
Sociological factors and rates of abnormal behavior:
 age, 125
 marital status (table), 124–125
 national origin (table), 123–124
 race, 125–127
 religion (table), 123
 social class, 120–123
Sociopathy, 298
Sociopsychological theory, 111–114
Soma, 131–132
Somnambulism, 247
Sophomore slump, 512
Speech disorders, 473–474
Speech problems:
 in adolescence, 489–491
 in schizophrenia, 160–161, 170
Spontaneous recovery, 93
Spontaneous remission, 192, 554
Stereotyped behavior, 156
Stimulus generalization, 93–94, 95 (figure), 170–171
Stress (*see also* Diathesis-stress theory):
 in depression, 198
 and pathology, 115
 and psychophysiological disorders, 272–273
 and schizophrenia, 146, 183
Structural family therapy, 606–608
Studies in Hysteria, 74
Study disabilities, 515
Stuttering, 473–474
Successive approximation, 96
Suicide:
 adolescent, 491, 510–511
 assessing lethality, 392–394
 crisis centers, 397
 depression, 195, 258–259, 388
 descriptive statistics, 385
 explanations:
  biological, 391–392
  social-learning, 389–390
  societal-integration, 390
  psychoanalytic, 388–389, 409
 historical views, 383–384
 postvention, 398
 predictive clues, 386
 prevention, 395–397
Suicide Act, 384
Suicidology, 383
Superego, 77–78, 82

Superstition, 257
Sybil, case of, 248
Symbiotic psychosis, 462
Symbolism, 154
Sympathetic nervous system, 133, 134–135, 136
Synanon, 339–340, 601–603
Synapse, 131–133, 180
Syntonic personality, 205
Syphilis, 58, 424
Systematic desensitization, 570–571, 593

Tarantism, 55
Taraxein, 139–140
Terminal illness (stages of death), 381, 410
Tertiary prevention, 639, 649–650
Test anxiety, 515–516
Tetrahydrocannabinol (THC), 341
T-groups, 596–598
Thalamotomy, 626
Thalamus, 626
Thalidomide, 438
Thanatology, 410
Thanatos, 388
Thematic Apperception Test (TAT), 38–40
Therapeutic community, 184, 546
Thioridazine (Mellaril), 227
Thiothixene (Navane), 616–617
Thioxanthenes, 185
Thorazine, 615–616
Thought disorder:
 and depression, 209
 and mania, 209
 and schizophrenia, 158, 162
Thought stopping, 576
Thumbsucking, 471–472
Thyroid gland, 136, 137
Tics, 470–471
Titration, 216
Token economy:
 systems, 481–482
 in treatment of schizophrenia, 187
Tower of Vienna, 64
Toxicity:
 and alcohol, 325
 and etiology of schizophrenia, 139
Tranquilizers, 148
 major, 227–228
 minor, 340–341
Transference, 562
Transmethylation hypothesis of schizophrenia, 180–182
Transorbital lobotomy, 625
Transsexualism, 357
Transvestism, 357
Tremors, 619
Trephines, 52
Treponema pallidum, 424
Trichotillomania, 472
Tricyclic antidepressants (*see* Imipramine type)
Triskaidecaphobia, 245